Second Canadian Edition

JOHN D. CARL
Rose State College

MARC BÉLANGER
Vanier College

PEARSON

Toronto

Editor-in-Chief: Michelle Sartor
Acquisitions Editor: Matthew Christian
Senior Marketing Manager: Lisa Gillis
Program Manager: Söğüt Y. Güleç
Project Manager: Andrea Falkenberg
Supervising Developmental Editor: John Polanszky
Developmental Editor: Katherine Goodes
Production Services: Cenveo® Publisher Services
Permissions Project Manager: Daniela Glass
Photo Permissions Research: Jen Simmons/PreMediaGlobal
Text Permissions Research: Jill Dougan/Electronic Publishing Services
Art Director: Zena Denchik
Cover Designer: Suzanne Behnke
Cover Image: wong yu liang, Shutterstock, Inc.

Credits and acknowledgments for material borrowed from other sources and reproduced, with permission, in this textbook appear on the appropriate page within the text.

7 17

Library and Archives Canada Cataloguing in Publication

Carl, John D., author

Think sociology / John D. Carl, Marc Bélanger. — Second Canadian edition.
Includes bibliographical references and index.

ISBN 978-0-205-92993-1 (pbk.)

1. Sociology. 2. Sociology—Research. 3. Sociology—Methodology. I. Bélanger, Marc, 1967–, author II. Title.

HM585.C365 2014 301 C2013-906846-5

ISBN 978-0-205-92993-1

BRIEF CONTENTS

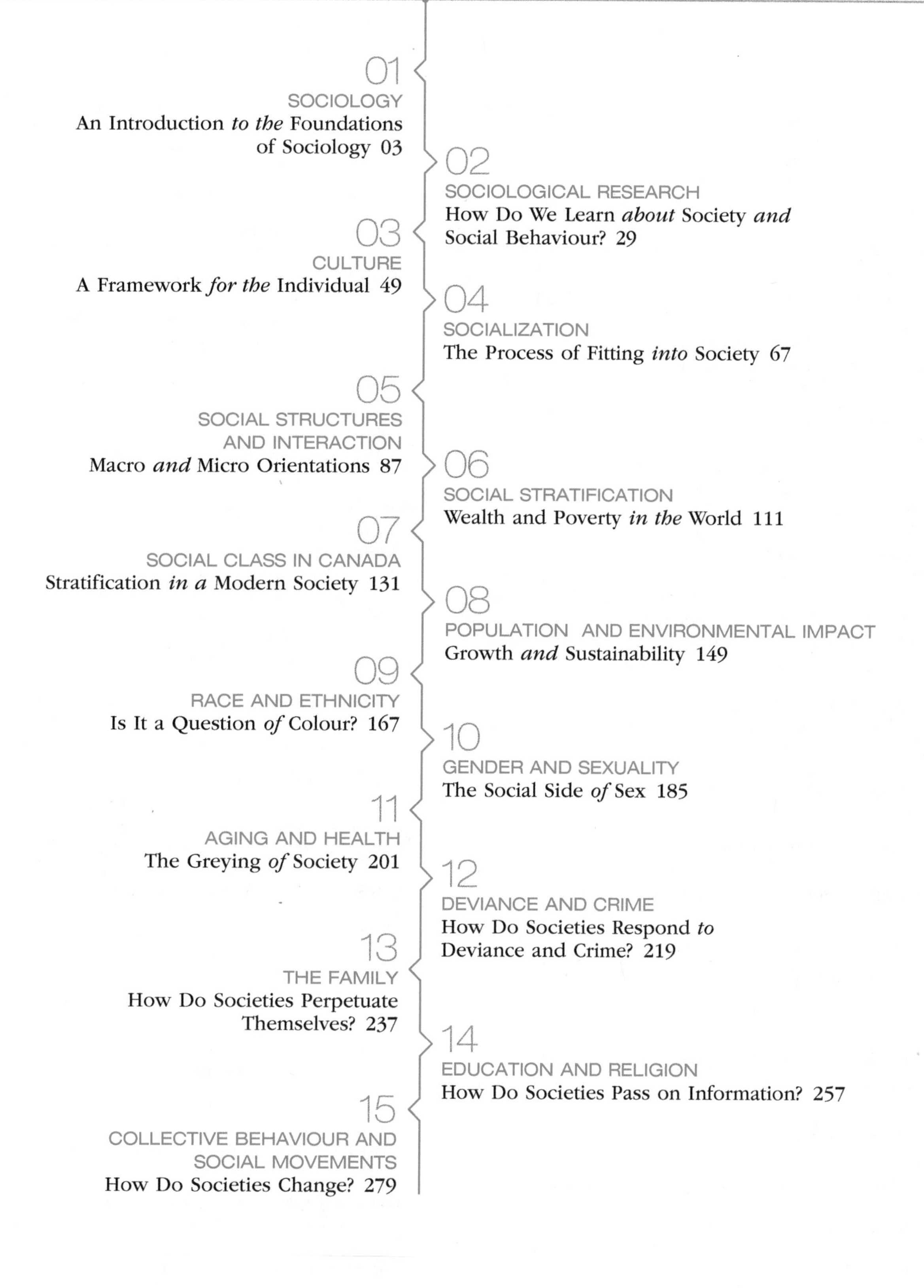

CONTENTS

05 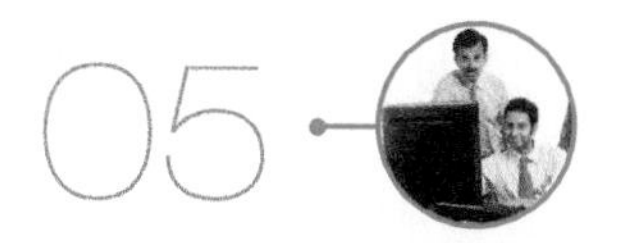

SOCIAL STRUCTURES AND INTERACTION

06 

SOCIAL STRATIFICATION

07 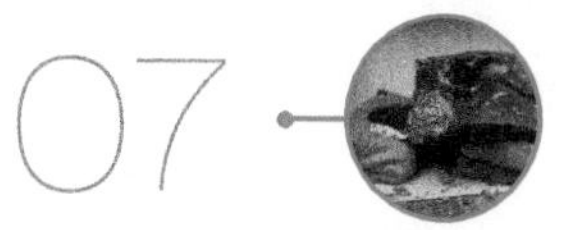

SOCIAL CLASS IN CANADA

08 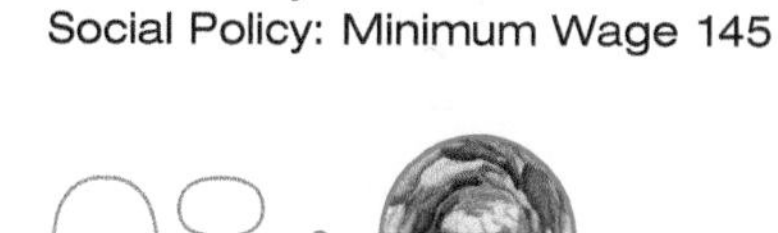

POPULATION AND ENVIRONMENTAL IMPACT

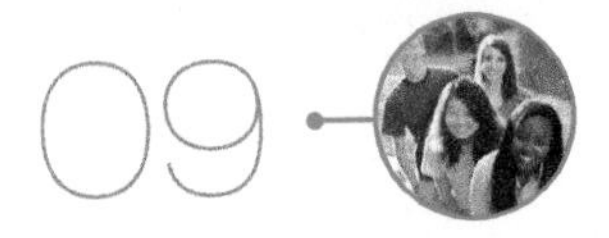

PREFACE

Think Sociology, Second Canadian Edition, is part of the popular THINK series of textbooks and follows the distinctive format of that series. It is a good basic introduction to sociology, and while it provides a firm theoretical grounding, it also includes many practical and applied examples. This makes it appealing to students who might want to pursue further study in the field of sociology. It is also suitable for students who are interested in finding employment in any domain that involves working with groups of people.

The first Canadian edition of this book was well received, and we appreciate the feedback and suggestions from the many reviewers, instructors, and especially students who have used this text. Many of their suggestions have been incorporated into this second edition. While the concise writing style and brevity of the chapters are appealing to both instructors and students, one of the recurring requests was for more content. In the second edition, this has been addressed. More concepts have been included in a number of topics, and the theoretical discussions have been expanded to include more applied examples. Overall, the goal was to make this edition more "sociological" while still maintaining the succinct presentation.

As with the first edition, we have not attempted to write an exhaustive explanation of the field of sociology. Rather, we present a brief and interesting introduction to the subject and show students that it is relevant to everything they do in social settings. One advantage of a new edition is the chance to benefit from the feedback of those who have used the text. In addition to updating the statistics and presenting more recent research, we have made the following improvements:

- An entirely new chapter (Chapter 8), titled "Population and Environmental Impact," has been added. This chapter focuses on the Canadian context and also includes a global perspective on these important topics.
- Many students and teachers have expressed much appreciation for the feature called "Wrap Your Mind around the Theory," popularly referred to as the "Theory Wheels." We have kept them, but in many cases we have significantly revised them to reflect the content changes in the chapters.
- The box titled "From Classroom to Community" has been deleted from each chapter in order to allow space for greater topic coverage and additional examples within the chapters.
- In Chapter 1, the all-important theory chapter, we have revised and expanded the four major perspectives. Since these are the foundation of sociology, we have given particular attention to making the different theoretical perspectives clear and easy to understand.
- Chapter 2, "Sociological Research," has been reorganized in order to make this challenging topic easier to understand.
- The first edition chapters titled "Social Structure and Interaction" and "Groups and Societies" have been combined, and some of their material has been distributed to other chapters.
- Chapter 10 has a new title: "Gender and Sexuality." This reflects the addition of the important topics of sexuality and sexual orientation, which were absent in the first edition.
- Chapter 12 also has a new title: "Deviance and Crime." The discussion of deviance is broader, and crime is described as a particular kind of deviance.
- Chapter 13 has been retitled "The Family" instead of "Marriage and Family." This is an acknowledgment of the increasing diversity of family forms in Canada. These new family forms have been presented in greater detail, and information on mate selection has also been added. The theoretical section of this chapter has been significantly revised.
- In Chapter 15, "Collective Behaviour and Social Movements," a section on the theories of collective behaviour has been added.

While it is essential that an introductory text present the primary theories, concepts, and issues of the field, it is also important that the text challenges students to explore these topics as well. In sociology, we want students to learn and to practise using their sociological imagination. Hopefully, it is apparent that the main orientation of *Think Sociology* is practical and that it invites students to realize that the theoretical perspectives and concepts of sociology can help them better understand and appreciate their social lives.

THINKING TOOLS

Within this text are the following tools to help students succeed:

- **Theory Wheels** visually connect chapter topics to four theoretical perspectives—functionalism, conflict theory, feminist theory, and symbolic interactionism—and help students see how these theories apply to everyday life.

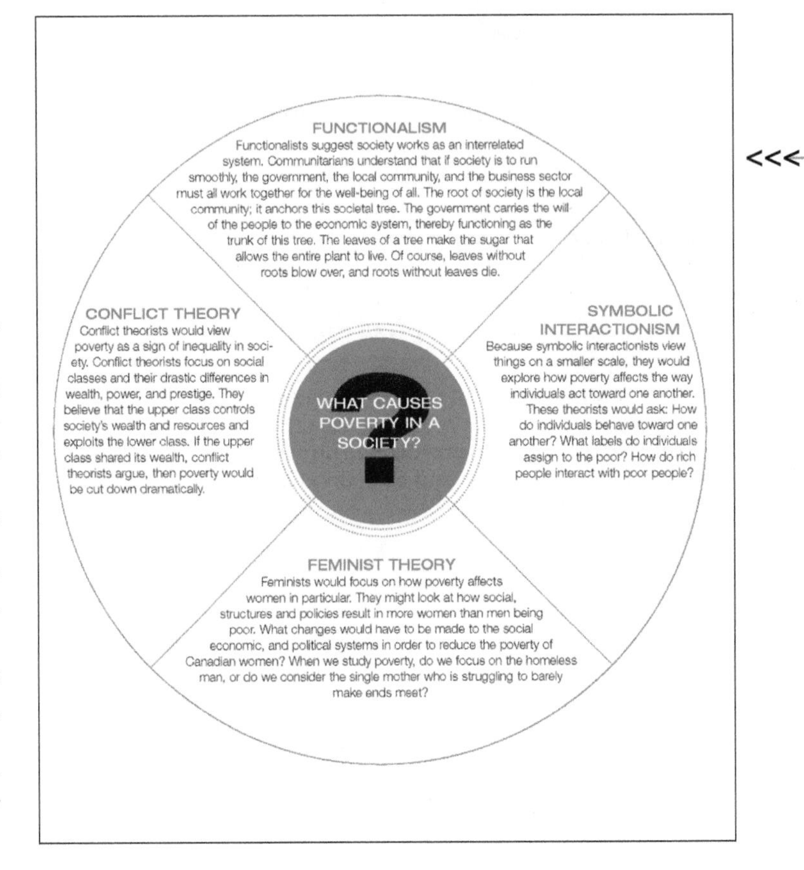

FUNCTIONALISM
Functionalists suggest society works as an interrelated system. Communitarians understand that if society is to run smoothly, the government, the local community, and the business sector must all work together for the well-being of all. The root of society is the local community; it anchors this societal tree. The government carries the will of the people to the economic system, thereby functioning as the trunk of this tree. The leaves of a tree make the sugar that allows the entire plant to live. Of course, leaves without roots blow over, and roots without leaves die.
CONFLICT THEORY
Conflict theorists would view poverty as a sign of inequality in society. Conflict theorists focus on social classes and their drastic differences in wealth, power, and prestige. They believe that the upper class controls society's wealth and resources and exploits the lower class. If the upper class shared its wealth, conflict theorists argue, then poverty would be cut down dramatically.
WHAT CAUSES POVERTY IN A SOCIETY?
SYMBOLIC INTERACTIONISM
Because symbolic interactionists view things on a smaller scale, they would explore how poverty affects the way individuals act toward one another. These theorists would ask: How do individuals behave toward one another? What labels do individuals assign to the poor? How do rich people interact with poor people?
FEMINIST THEORY
Feminists would focus on how poverty affects women in particular. They might look at how social, structures and policies result in more women than men being poor. What changes would have to be made to the social economic, and political systems in order to reduce the poverty of Canadian women? When we study poverty, do we focus on the homeless man, or do we consider the single mother who is struggling to barely make ends meet?

- Concept maps illustrate relationships among topics in each chapter and show students how these topics connect to form the overall picture.
- Think Sociology boxes present sociological findings on provocative topics, demonstrating how research can help students better understand the everyday world.
- Go Global boxes provide insights into topics and issues from countries around the world, allowing students to draw comparisons between Canada and international communities.
- Where to Start Your Research Paper sections at the end of each chapter feature trustworthy internet sources that can serve as a starting point for students researching an essay.
- A tear-out Study Card at the end of the text highlights key terms and points for every chapter and can make studying on-the-go easy.
- The Think Spot is an open-access website at **www.thinkspot.ca** that helps students review the material with chapter-by-chapter quizzes.

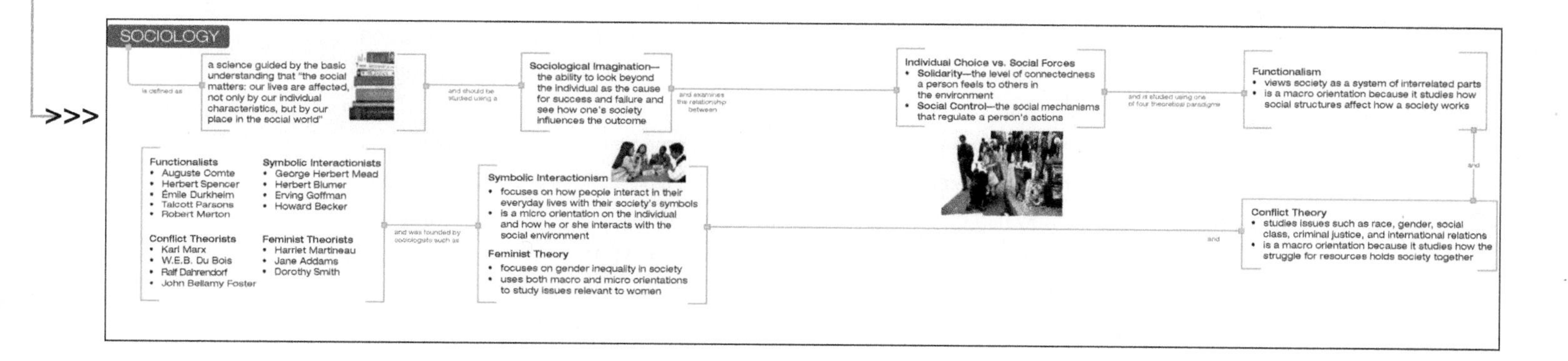

ACKNOWLEDGMENTS

Thank you to Matthew Christian, acquisitions editor at Pearson Canada, who promoted my proposal for a second Canadian edition until it was accepted. Since that time, I have had the pleasure of working with many wonderful, inspired, and dedicated people. Thank you to Lisa Gillis, the marketing manager for the project. Katherine Goodes has been amazing as developmental editor; she managed to coordinate a very complicated project and made everything run smoothly. Andrea Falkenberg was the project manager at Pearson Canada who ensured that this book got produced. Many talented people at Cenveo helped in the production of this book. Heidi Allgair was the production editor, and she did an amazing job of keeping countless edits and revisions in order. Her dedication to this project has been admirable. Kitty Wilson was a fantastic copy editor. Suzanne DeWorken was an incredible and thorough proofreader; many small (and not so small) details have been corrected, thanks to her sharp eye.

Thank you to the many educators who provided helpful feedback for this new edition, including:

Tara Gauld, Confederation College
Cindy Gervais, Fleming College
Thomas Groulx, St. Clair College
Wendi Hadd, John Abbott College
Marc Leger, Algonquin College
Karen Moreau, Niagara College
Greg Nepean, University of Guelph

Thank you especially to all my colleagues at Vanier College. You inspire me with your ideas and your dedication to teaching, and it is a joy to work alongside so many talented people.

My parents continue to teach me, by their words and by their actions, that with hard work and perseverance, anything is possible.

Christine, you have helped me in so many ways. You encourage me, you challenge me, and you make me feel special.

I have had many wonderful teachers, but one especially stands out. Donald Von Eschen was my thesis adviser many years ago. He showed me what good teaching and good sociology are all about.

Thank you to all the wonderful, curious, and brilliant students I have had over the years. Your genuine interest has inspired me to explain the wonders of sociology more clearly. This book is for you.

Finally, to my wonderful children, Tommy and Katerina, you are my constant inspiration. I am so proud to watch you both growing up and making your own way in the world. It has been a very difficult time for all of us, but you have patiently allowed me the time to work on this project.

Marc Bélanger

ABOUT THE AUTHORS

JOHN CARL'S interest in sociology grew from his interests and job experiences after college, which included working in hospitals, schools, churches, and prisons. John reflects, "In these many diverse encounters, I continued to notice how often the structures of society frequently did not support the change so desperately sought after by the individual. I began to reflect on my sociology courses from my undergraduate work and decided to return to graduate school to study sociology."

At the University of Oklahoma, he became passionate about the study of criminology and stratification, and he completed his Ph.D. while teaching full time at Rose State College. John says, "I found that every part of my life, to this point, fit perfectly with the study of sociology. It is a diverse and exciting field that helps each of us understand our world."

Today, teaching remains his primary focus. John Carl has excelled in the classroom, winning awards for his teaching and working to build and improve the sociology program at Rose State College. "I teach the introductory class every semester because I believe it is the most important course in any department. It is where students get the foundation they need for their continued study of sociology. In these classes, my goal is simple: to teach students to think sociologically so that they can consider any new event in the light of that thought."

When asked why he wrote *THINK Sociology*, the answer was simple: "This book is truly a labour of love for me. I wanted to write a book that is filled with examples used in the classroom and written in a language that students can understand without compromising the core concepts of sociology."

John lives in Oklahoma with his family: wife, Keven, and daughters, Sara and Caroline. In his free time, John plays golf, gardens, throws pottery, and plays his guitar. He continues to move from the classroom to community by being active in non-profit leadership in his home community and providing training to non-profit boards so they may better achieve their goals. John suggests, "It is all part of sociology, not only to understand the world in which we live, but to take that understanding from the classroom and use it to improve the community."

MARC BÉLANGER'S natural curiosity about why people do the things they do and a passion for anything academic led to his study of sociology. Marc holds a B.A. and an M.A. from McGill University in Montreal, and he is currently working on a master's in education from the Université de Sherbrooke. In the 10 years that he has been at Vanier College, Marc has taught the introductory sociology course many times.

"When I first saw John Carl's book, like many, I was attracted by the visual format. After a closer reading, I also appreciated that there was a lot of good sociology in it. It has been an honour and a pleasure to work on the Canadian edition of *THINK Sociology*."

Marc lives in Montreal with his wonderful children, Tommy and Katerina.

The authors welcome your comments and suggestions about this *THINK Sociology* text at jcthinksociology@gmail.com and belangem@vaniercollege.qc.ca.

To Keven: Thanks for everything you do.
I love you.

—J. D. C.

In memory of Denise Papadatos-Bélanger,
1965–2011

A wonderful wife and mother.

—M. B.

SOCIOLOGY

Monkey Business/Fotolia

WHAT IS SOCIOLOGY?
WHAT ARE THE FOUR MAJOR SOCIOLOGICAL PERSPECTIVES?
WHY IS COMMUNITY LEARNING IMPORTANT?

"Although historically, poverty has been thought of as a matter to be dealt with privately, through charity or the family, during important decades in Canada, principally between the 1950s and the 1980s, protection from poverty was also regarded as a critical subject matter for legislation and redistributive measures. Lately, however, governments have been allowing poverty to disappear from the social policy agenda, apparently content to permit poverty and extreme disparities in income and wealth to flourish . . .

"The idea that all human beings are equal in worth is the foundation of the rule of law and of democracy, positing that every person is entitled to be treated with equal concern and respect by governments and to have an equal voice in political decision making. The poverty and economic inequality of some, disproportionately of those who are already disadvantaged because of their female sex, non-white race, or disability, stands in marked contrast to these commitments to equality. . . ."[1]

An Introduction *to the* Foundations of Sociology

CHAPTER 01

It is shameful that in a country like Canada, there are people who are poor. In *Poverty: Rights, Social Citizenship, and Legal Activism*, the contributing authors take an interdisciplinary perspective on poverty in Canada. Rather than simply ask why a particular individual is poor, they examine the structural causes of poverty—how society and its distribution of resources are the primary causes of poverty.

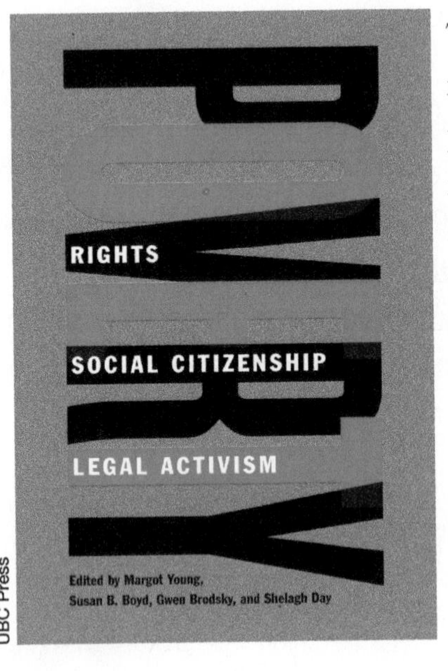

UBC Press

The poor are often viewed as nameless, faceless, voiceless people loitering on street corners or huddled away in decrepit apartments. It's easy for us to turn a blind eye to the problem of poverty if we don't feel a personal connection to the man panhandling on the sidewalk or the woman standing in line at the soup kitchen with her children.

Nobody chooses to be poor, but sometimes circumstances turn against people. Poverty can be seen anywhere, even on a college campus, as I found out one semester: One day, I saw a student looking through the large garbage bin behind the cafeteria. He found a sandwich, still in its wrapper. As I watched, he quickly opened the wrapper and wolfed down the sandwich. I later learned that this student lived with his mother, who was a drug addict. Often, there was no money for food, and he was forced to rummage in the garbage if he wanted something to eat. Of course, none of this was planned, and most people would agree that it is not his fault. I was left to wonder why in a country as prosperous as Canada there are still young people who live like this.

SOCIOLOGY

is

a science guided by the understanding that our lives are affected not only by our individual characteristics but by powerful social forces and our place in the social world

and should be studied using the

sociological imagination, which is the ability to understand how social forces influence the lives of individuals.

Moreno Novello/Fotolia

Society is studied from different perspectives:

Symbolic Interactionism

- focuses on how individual people interact with others in their everyday lives
- studies how the use of symbols influences how people communicate and follows a micro approach because it is concerned with the individual's role in creating society

and

Feminist Theory

- views society as being based on a patriarchal ideology that benefits men and discriminates against women
- uses both macro and micro approaches and focuses on gender inequality

get the topic: WHAT IS SOCIOLOGY?

Sociology Defined

Most sociologists would agree that **sociology** is a science guided by the basic understanding that our lives are affected not only by our individual characteristics but by powerful social forces and our place in the social world. Sociology is a science because it uses a method based on the collection and analysis of empirical evidence—things that we can observe. Sociologists look at society and at social behavior. **Society** refers to a group of people who live in a defined territory and who share social structures and who interact with each other.

SOCIOLOGY is a science guided by the understanding that our lives are affected not only by our individual characteristics but by powerful social forces and our place in the social world.

SOCIETY refers to a group of people who live in a defined territory and who share social structures and who interact with each other.

MAKE CONNECTIONS

The Sociology of Driving

Driving is a familiar and poignant example of social forces in action. Think about it. You hop into a 1-ton metal box on wheels and send it hurtling down the pavement at 100km/h! And thousands of others are doing the same thing at the same time! Yet, for the most part, this seemingly bizarre behaviour occurs smoothly and without mishap. Why? Because driving, like all our other public behaviour, is governed by social rules that we have learned and follow without thinking. You have learned to drive on the right side of the road (and to stay there), to stop on red and go on green, to keep a certain distance between your car and other cars (and pedestrians). And the vast majority of others sharing the road with you are all doing the same thing and behaving in the same way. As a society, we can undertake this dangerous and potentially destructive activity (driving) because there is a certain order and predictability to our behaviour. Each time you drive, you make an unspoken agreement to follow the rules of the road and act in a certain way, and all the other drivers sharing the road with you have made this same agreement. Society as a whole functions in much the same way. We have all made agreements to act in a certain way so that our behaviour is conventional and predictable. This allows us to work together and accomplish feats that would not be possible without a governing structure of rules that guide and motivate us.

We can have a science of sociology because human social behaviour is regular. Most of us do follow the rules (most of the time). Sociologists study the nature of these rules that govern our behaviour and the means by which each and every one of us learn and internalize these rules. Sociologists want to understand the social forces that act upon us.

>>> **CLASS DISCUSSION** When you walked into your classroom, how did you know where to sit? When you go to see a movie, why do you stand in line to buy a ticket? When you are with your friends, how do you act? Think about and discuss other activities that are governed by social rules.

Micro—a small-scale perspective that focuses on individuals and small groups
Macro—a large-scale perspective that focuses on the social structure

There are four major sociological theories:

Functionalism

- defines society as a system of interrelated parts
- is a macro orientation because it focuses on larger social structures rather than individuals

and

Conflict Theory

- views society as an unequal system that brings about conflict and change
- focuses on macro issues and is concerned with inequality as it relates to wealth and power

and

Developing a Sociological Imagination

My son recently lost his job at Zellers. He wasn't fired for being lazy, or for stealing merchandise, or for being late. He was laid off because all the Zellers stores in Canada were bought by the larger American department store chain Target. This was an economic decision made at a level far beyond my son's control. But because of that decision, he lost his job. And he was really disappointed.

The American sociologist C. Wright Mills (1916–1962) asserted that people must understand how outside forces contribute to their own individual situations. In other words, Mills wanted us to develop a **sociological imagination**—the ability to understand how social forces influence the lives of individuals.[2] At the same time, we also need to understand how individuals can create and change the societies they live in. Developing a sociological imagination helps us understand our place in a complex world. We must grasp both the history and the biography of a situation to generate this imagination. Mills argued that most of us see problems through biography; that is, we focus on our private troubles.[3] This **micro**, or small-scale, perspective focuses our

"The sociological imagination enables us to grasp history and biography and the relations between the two within society. That is its task and its promise." (Mills, *The Sociological Imagination*, 1959, p. 6)

attention on the individual. For my son who lost his job at Zellers, this was a private problem. Without a job, he had no money, and he was unable to buy things he needed. In order to fix this private trouble, he had to find another job. However, we must also understand how history and social structure affect the individual. By including this **macro**, or large-scale, perspective we can understand how the social structure also influences individuals.

Peter Berger (1929–), another sociologist, has described the sociological perspective as "seeing the general in the particular."[4] Although each individual is unique, sociologists look for patterns in the behavior of individuals. Sociology looks at what many people are doing. We can study a few individuals in order to understand the characteristics of social behaviour and to see social trends. Berger also invited us to "see the

>>> **The fact that Target bought all the Zellers stores and closed some of them was a decision made at the level of corporations. The result was that many people, including my son, lost their jobs.** Each one of those people faced his or her own private troubles. But to fully understand the situation, we also need to see that each one lost his or her job as a result of wider social forces.

Igor kisselev/Alamy

Michael Neelon/Alamy

Suicide might be seen as an individual decision, but there are many social factors that seem to influence suicide rates. We cannot use these factors to specifically predict who will and will not kill themselves, but we can understand that one's environment influences the rate of suicide in a society. Other factors, such as one's family makeup and the relative size of a group of people born during the same time period, also play a role.[5]

SOCIOLOGICAL IMAGINATION is the ability to understand how social forces influence the lives of individuals.

MICRO is a small-scale perspective.

MACRO is a large-scale perspective.

DEBUNKING is the practice of looking beyond the surface or obvious explanation and seeking out deeper explanations.

strange in the familiar."[6] He used the term **debunking** to describe the practice of looking beyond the surface or obvious explanation and seeking out deeper explanations. Sociology challenges us to question the assumptions we have about societies, especially our own.

Émile Durkheim's Theory on Suicide

A famous study that is often used to illustrate the sociological perspective was conducted by Émile Durkheim, one of the first sociologists.[7] Durkheim studied suicide, but instead of looking for the reasons a particular individual commits suicide, he looked at the social facts. He examined and compared suicide rates in various regions of Europe. What he found was that the regions varied in their suicide rates. He then looked for social factors in those areas that might explain the difference in rates. One of the factors that he found that had an association was religion: Areas that were primarily Catholic had lower suicide rates than those that were Protestant. Durkheim then asked what is it about the Catholic religion that might explain why Catholics are less likely than Protestants to kill themselves. His explanation was that the Catholic religion encourages a greater degree of social interaction relative to the more individualistic character of the Protestant religions. Catholics overall felt a greater sense of connectedness to those around them. Another factor that Durkheim found to be associated was marital status; married people were less likely to commit suicide than single people. Again, the degree of social connectedness seemed to be a common feature.

The important and sociological conclusion of Durkheim's study was that suicide—a seemingly individual act—was in fact more or less likely to occur depending on the social characteristics of that individual. While each individual act of suicide is unique, each individual is influenced by their wider social context, and this makes a person more or less likely, even as an individual, to commit suicide.

INDIVIDUAL CHOICE AND SOCIAL FORCES

Sociologists recognize that social factors often influence our personal choices. They provide a context in which we make decisions. Again, consider the act of suicide. Most people believe that this is entirely an individual choice, and ultimately it is. However, certain trends arise in the data on suicides which indicate that some people are at increased risk of taking their own lives.

A person's sex, age, and the province where he or she lives all predict the likelihood of suicide. According to Statistics Canada:

- Studies have found males to be at least four times more likely than females to commit suicide. Males are also more likely to die in their first attempt.
- For both males and females, the suicide rate is highest among those aged 30 to 59.
- Historically, suicide rates in Canada have tended to increase from east to west. However, since 1993, Quebec has had the highest rate of all the provinces.[8]

It is important to note that these factors do not cause individuals to commit suicide *per se*; however, they do indicate groups that are at increased risk of killing themselves. When sociologists examine an issue, such as suicide, poverty, or any other social event, they use their sociological imagination to help consider how social factors influence an individual's choice. How do sociologists use the sociological imagination to study the larger world? Let's examine four important theoretical perspectives and the sociologists who helped develop them.

THINK SOCIOLOGICALLY

Homelessness—Individual Choice vs. Social Factors

Have you ever heard someone argue that people choose to be poor? You might have even made the argument yourself. We may ask: do people become poor because they dropped out of school, or because they are lazy or unmotivated, or because they adopt deviant lifestyles, or because they live in bad situations? Alternatively, we may ask: do people become poor as a result of public policies that create unjust and inequitable distribution of economic and social resources? By now, you must be starting to realize that society has a powerful influence on each of us. If we want to address the issue of poverty in Canada, we have to realize that there are social causes of poverty. Until we realize this, any solutions that we propose will only touch the surface but will not get to the root causes.

>>> **ACTIVITY** Visit a homeless shelter in your community. Talk to the people there and find out how social factors contributed to their situation. How did they arrive at the shelter? What was their life like before? Write a paragraph describing one of the people you met and analyzing the factors that led to that person's homelessness.

think sociologically: WHAT ARE THE FOUR MAJOR SOCIOLOGICAL PERSPECTIVES?

Before I ever knew anything about sociology, I had a worldview. Being born in Canada to a middle-class family, my parents' teachings shaped my point of view. So did my friends, my schools, and the media. Had I been born in China, Chad, or Chile, I would likely think differently about the world. How do you view the world? What personal beliefs or ideas do you value most? It might be difficult to respond to these questions, but I bet you have some pretty definitive answers. When sociologists look at society or social behaviour, they do so from a particular perspective. In Canada, most sociologists view the world through four major perspectives—functionalism, conflict theory, symbolic interactionism, and feminist theory. Each perspective has developed its own theories—descriptions or explanations of how things work.

Functionalism is a theoretical perspective that defines society as a system of interrelated parts. This perspective is a macro approach to sociological study because it focuses on larger social structures rather than individuals. When you think about functionalism, it may be helpful to think about the human body. The body has different parts, and each part has a function in keeping the body running. Society is similar in many ways. It is made up of social institutions—ways of organizing social behaviour. Some examples of social institutions are the government, schools, and the family. Each institution exists because it fulfills some function in society.

Conflict theory is a theoretical perspective that views society as various groups that are in a constant struggle over scarce resources. This constant struggle inevitably results in inequality. Much like functionalism, conflict theory is also a macro approach, as this theory is concerned with various groups battling for power. Inequality of wealth and power in society is often the focus of modern conflict theory. For example, conflict theorists might examine how the chasm between the rich and the poor affects people's opportunities in our society. It's no surprise that children who come from privileged backgrounds can afford to receive the best educations, participate in organized sports, and take music lessons. Children from poorer families may not get these same opportunities, and this lack of opportunity puts them at a disadvantage.

Symbolic interactionism is a theoretical perspective that focuses on how individual interactions between people influence them and how these interactions can impact society. Symbolic interactionism is primarily a micro approach to sociology because it is concerned with the individual's role in creating society. The use of "symbols," such as words, gestures, body language, and facial expressions, enables people to communicate. Our actions communicate meaning. For example, if you're having a "bad day," what does that mean? One student once told me he had a bad day every time it rained. If that is the case, could such a definition of reality influence how you behave toward others on your job or in the classroom? How might his "bad day" influence the "days" of others? Interactionists constantly seek to understand how small interactions influence the larger society.

Feminist theory has made two important contributions to sociology. First, on a theoretical level, feminist theory contends that most societies are **patriarchal**; that is, they are controlled by and benefit men. The feminist perspective emphasizes the social inequality between men and women. If we are to have true social equality, we must first acknowl-

sumnersgraphicsinc/Fotolia

>>> Poverty is a social issue, even in a prosperous country like Canada. Why do you think that there are poor people in Canada? **How would each of the sociological perspectives look at the issue of poverty?**

edge that our social structures create and perpetuate gender inequality. Feminist researchers often use both macro and micro approaches. At the macro level, feminists examine the gendered institutions of the social structure. On the micro level, many feminist researchers choose to study individuals and small groups by using more qualitative methods, such as interviews and focus groups. The second contribution of feminist theory is in the topics that are studied. Many feminists study issues such as lone-parenthood, domestic violence, or prostitution that have a greater impact on women.

As you have seen, sociologists approach their study of society from either a macro or micro perspective. The macro approach examines larger social groups and institutions and their effects on individuals. The micro approach focuses on small groups and the interactions between individuals. Both seek to understand the process by which people influence society and society affects them.

Sociologists use the different perspectives to analyze similar issues, such as why poverty exists or how children learn about the social world. However, the questions they ask as they analyze these issues differ. The chart below illustrates how functionalists, conflict theorists, symbolic interactionists, and feminists approach the study of society.

Sociologists use these questions to help them build theories about the world. So, is one school of thought better than the others? Not necessarily. In fact, most sociologists have worldviews that are rather eclectic or diverse. They may use each perspective to illuminate different issues or use all four to look comprehensively at a single issue. If you consider Dennis Raphael's work, for example, you'll see that he uses bits and pieces of each perspective to understand poverty. Raphael finds that a society's structures create poverty (functionalism), and people with wealth and power control those structures and are generally abusive to the poorest of the poor (conflict theory). Those who experience poverty often create in themselves self-fulfilling prophecies that help them remain mired in their plight (symbolic interactionism). In Canada, women are more likely than men to be poor. Even if they are working, women are more likely to have a part-time job and to earn less (feminist theory). Raphael uses each of these ideas to create a complete view of why poverty exists in our society.

FUNCTIONALISM is a theoretical perspective that sees society as a system of interrelated parts.

CONFLICT THEORY is a theoretical perspective that views society as various groups that are in a constant struggle over scarce resources.

SYMBOLIC INTERACTIONISM is a theoretical perspective that focuses on how people interact with others in their everyday lives.

FEMINIST THEORY is a theoretical perspective that focuses on gender inequalities which are built into the social structure.

PATRIARCHAL refers to a social system that benefits men.

Now that you have a general understanding of each perspective and know what kinds of questions it asks, let's take a closer look at each one.

The Functionalist Perspective

Functionalism, also called structural functionalism, is a macro perspective that focuses on the structure of society and how each part fulfills a function in the system. The main parts of the system are social institutions. Social institutions such as the family, economy, educational system, and political system are critical for society to function properly. According to functionalists, society is relatively stable, and social institutions provide different functions which help maintain this stability. Understanding how social institutions work in a society is of great interest to functionalists. Since institutions are interrelated, each has an impact on the others.

Functionalism suggests that a society's values and norms provide the foundation for the rules and laws that it creates. These norms regulate the relationships among social institutions. Therefore, general agreement on these norms must occur for a society to achieve balance.

On the next few pages, we'll investigate some early functionalists and you can see who these ideas come from. Early theorists like Herbert Spencer and Émile Durkheim contributed to the growth and development of the functionalist perspective.

COMPARING THE THEORETICAL PERSPECTIVES

	Functionalism	Conflict Theory	Symbolic Interactionism	Feminist Theory
Level of Analysis	Macro	Macro	Micro	Macro and Micro
Core Questions	• What keeps society functioning smoothly? • What are the parts of society, and how do they relate to each other? • What are the intended and unintended outcomes of an event?	• How are wealth and power distributed in society? • How do people with wealth and power keep them? • How are society's resources and opportunities divided?	• How do people interact with each other? • How does social interaction influence, create, and sustain human relationships? • Do people change their behaviour from one setting to another, and if so, why?	• How does society advantage men and disadvantage women? • What social issues are important to women? • How can social structures be changed to benefit men and women equally?

SOCIAL LAWS are statements of fact that are unchanging under given conditions and can be used as ground rules for any kind of society.

SOCIAL STATICS are the existing structural elements of society.

SOCIAL DYNAMICS are changes in the structural elements of society.

SOCIAL DARWINISM is a notion which suggests that strong societies survive and weak ones become extinct.

FUNCTIONS are social factors that affect people in a society.

MANIFEST FUNCTIONS are factors that lead to an expected consequence or outcome.

LATENT FUNCTIONS are factors that lead to unforeseen or unexpected consequences.

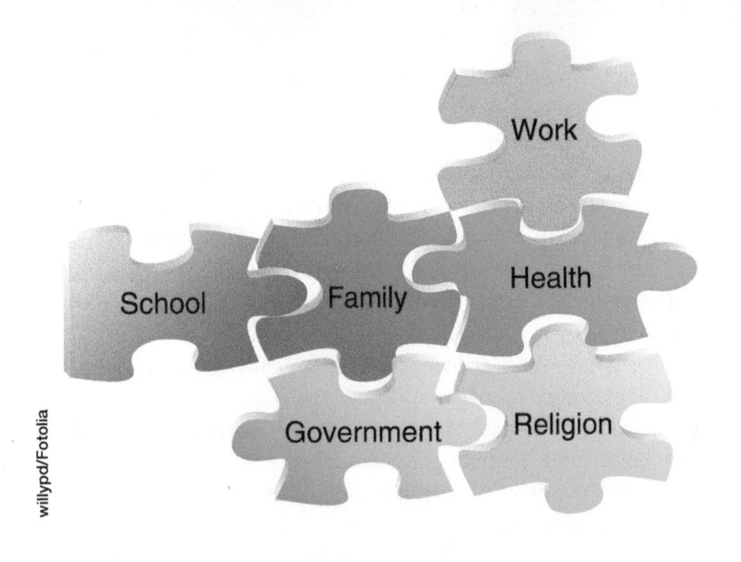

willypd/Fotolia

^ Functionalists see society as being made up of different social institutions. **Each institution fulfills a social function and is connected to other social institutions.**

AUGUSTE COMTE

The functionalist perspective owes much to Comte (1798–1857), and he also coined the term *sociologie* that gave the discipline its name.[9]

Comte felt that sociology should strive to discover **social laws**—statements of fact that are unchanging under given conditions and can be used as ground rules for any study of society. In order to discover these laws, Comte proposed that we study **social statics**, or the existing structural elements of society, and **social dynamics**, or the change in those elements. He believed that by discovering the interplay between structures and dynamics we could develop social laws that would help improve society. His basic ideas are the groundwork on which functionalism is based.

HERBERT SPENCER

Herbert Spencer (1820–1903) was a British intellectual whose ideas furthered the development of functionalism. Spencer's study of sociology was informed by Charles Darwin's theory of natural selection. Darwin argued that natural selection—a process resulting in the reproduction of organisms best adapted to their environment—makes evolution occur. Spencer viewed society as an organism, and as such, it can evolve, thrive, or die. For him, some societies are "more fit" than others because they adapt better to changes in the environment. From Spencer, you can see a type of thinking often called **social Darwinism**—a notion which suggests that strong societies survive and weak ones become extinct.[10] Do you think some societies are superior to others? Would you suggest that Canada reached its success due to its own merit? If so, you think a bit like a social Darwinist.

ÉMILE DURKHEIM

Like Spencer, French sociologist Émile Durkheim (1858–1917) also viewed society as an organism. You should recognize Durkheim's name from our discussion of suicide earlier in the chapter. Durkheim was one of the first true sociologists, in that he used data to test theories. His work provides the basis for much of functionalist thought.

Durkheim's work suggested that solidarity is a vital component that holds society together. Solidarity integrates—or holds together—a society because people see themselves as unified. Durkheim pointed out that the type of society influences the type of solidarity. You will read more about this in Chapter 5.

Durkheim's ideas about solidarity are just the tip of the iceberg, though. A number of thinkers drew inspiration from Durkheim and expanded his ideas into what is known as functionalist thought. One of these thinkers was Talcott Parsons.

TALCOTT PARSONS

Talcott Parsons (1902–1979) was a giant in the field of sociology. Parsons was interested in creating grand theories that attempted to explain every aspect of the human experience and how social systems interconnect. For Parsons, society is much like a bicycle wheel, made up of independent yet interdependent parts. When properly balanced, each independent spoke connected to the hub keeps the wheel spinning. But if just one spoke on a wheel breaks, the entire wheel will eventually fall out of balance. Similarly, society is an interrelated system, and if one part fails to work, the whole system suffers.[11]

Parsons also commented on the inertia of social systems, meaning that they tend to remain at rest if they are at rest, and they tend to stay in motion if they are already in motion. For example, when you go bowling, you must take a bowling ball and use your own force to make it roll down the lane. Once the ball starts rolling, it tends to keep rolling until the pins and the end of the lane stop it. Although the friction from the floor may slow it down, some other force must stop it. Parsons pointed out that the social world acts the same way. Thus, in order to change a society, some great force must impact the system, or it will remain unchanged. This is because societies naturally will find a balance. Thus change is unlikely and often disruptive. Of course, once the process of change starts, the system will continue on that path until some counter-reaction occurs due to social inertia.[12]

ROBERT MERTON

Robert K. Merton (1910–2003) was a contemporary of Parsons. One of Merton's greatest theoretical contributions to functionalism was his understanding that social institutions have both intended and unintended **functions**. Merton identified two types: **manifest functions**, or factors that lead to an expected consequence or outcome, and **latent functions**, or factors that lead to an unforeseen or unexpected consequence.[13] Merton suggested that when looking at any social event, soci-

Ralph R. Echtina/Shutterstock

<<< Mennonite farm communities in Ontario have mechanical solidarity because everyone lives in much the same way, does the same things, and shares the same values.

ologists should ask the question, "What are the functions of this event?" By doing this, we'll do a complete analysis because we'll consider both manifest and latent functions. For example, many families sit down to eat dinner together. The manifest function of this activity is to provide food, because we all need to eat. However, there is also a latent function that comes from eating together. It provides an opportunity for the family members to exchange information and to develop a greater sense of togetherness. For Merton, one cannot complete a functional analysis without considering both manifest and latent functions.[14]

CRITICISMS OF FUNCTIONALISM

In the mid twentieth century, functionalism was the dominant theoretical approach. However, its dominance has waned in recent years. Critics of functionalism sometimes claim that this perspective focuses too much on what keeps society stable and balanced, and that it is not very good at explaining how societies change.

Functionalists are also accused of supporting the status quo, even when it may be harmful to do so. If you think about certain social problems such as poverty, is this something that should be addressed slowly or quickly? The lack of affordable housing in society remains a problem.

THE FUNCTIONALISTS—AT A GLANCE

BOURGEOISIE refers to members of the capitalist class who own the means of production.

PETITE BOURGEOISIE refers to the class of people who have their own businesses but do not employ others.

PROLETARIAT refers to members of the working class who sell their labour for wages.

FALSE CONSCIOUSNESS is a person's lack of understanding of his or her position in society.

CLASS CONSCIOUSNESS is an understanding of one's position in the class system.

Although Raphael argues that there are many causes of poverty in Canada, he points out that a lack of a decent wage drives much of the poverty in Canada. In this way, he criticizes the functional argument that the current situation is fair. Thus, is Canada really a land of opportunity for everyone?

As you consider poverty or other societal issues, ask yourself For whom is the system functional? Whom does the system benefit? Functionalists might argue that society works for the greatest number of people. Change will arise when problems become "big enough." However, critics would argue that this belief results in many minorities being ignored. Who speaks for the poor? What choice did my son have about the loss of his job at Zellers? The functionalist perspective often fails to recognize how inequalities in social class, race, and gender cause an imbalance in our society.

The conflict theory perspective arose as a response to some of functionalism's weaknesses. Conflict theorists want to analyze how these social inequalities affect society as a whole.

The Conflict Perspective

Conflict theory is a theoretical perspective that views society as a collection of social groups that are in a constant struggle for scarce resources. So, what is scarce? Two main concerns for conflict theorists are economic wealth and power. Conflict theorists acknowledge that we live in an unequal society. Why? It could be because there is not enough "stuff" to go around, or it could be because those with the "stuff" don't want to let go of it. In either case, conflict theory suggests that we're all struggling for more "stuff," whether that "stuff" is power in a marriage or wealth in the world.

Conflict theorists, like functional theorists, tend to focus on macro issues, viewing how society's structures contribute to the conflict. Modern conflict theorists often look at the inequality of the capitalist economic system. Such a system breeds inequality, as it rewards some at the expense of others. Once you have power, you want to keep it. For this reason, the wealthy elites are more likely to create advantages for themselves, even if their actions put others at a disadvantage.

In general, the essence of conflict theory suggests that a pyramid structure of power and wealth exists in society. The elite at the top of the pyramid determine the rules for those below them. Under such a system, laws, institutions, and traditions support their authority. When Raphael discusses the lack of adequate wages and the blame we all deserve because we permit poverty to exist, he is in essence suggesting that those of us who are not poor are, in part, responsible for those who are because we allow the system to ignore these people.

Many theorists who use the conflict perspective might examine macro conflicts between different groups of society, different countries, or different social classes. The study of inequality in sociology always involves a consideration of conflict theory. Thus, you can see this perspective applied to social class, race, gender, marriage, religion, population, environment, and a host of other social phenomena. If you believe that discrimination, ageism, sexism, racism, and classism occur in society because some people have the power to inflict their desires on others, then you think like a conflict theorist.

KARL MARX

Karl Marx (1818–1883) was a German theorist, social activist, and writer who analyzed the effects of capitalism—an economic system in which private individuals own businesses and control the economy.

Marx suggested that in a capitalist system, the **bourgeoisie**, or capitalist class, own most of the wealth because they control the means of production. Means of production include the machines, buildings, land, and materials used in producing goods and services. Labour power is bought and sold for wages by the owners of the means of production. Since increasing profit is their first goal, owners pay workers as little as possible. Raphael, too, notices this when he describes poor women who actually have some form of employment but don't make enough money to afford decent housing. Employers generally pay these women as little as possible, and the women have no way to fight the system.

The **petite bourgeoisie** have their own businesses but do not employ others. A private electrician who has his own company but works alone is a member of the petite bourgeoisie.

Marx called the workers in a capitalist system the **proletariat**, or working class, who do not own the means of production and who sell their labour for wages. The proletariat live in an unending cycle in which they work for low pay and then use those wages to survive. According to Marx, workers will never get ahead if they do not share in the wealth they create.

Why don't workers do something to change their fate? Marx suggested that it is because people have a **false consciousness**, or a lack of understanding of their position in society. The workers feel that they are alone in their plight. Marx proposed that the workers must develop **class consciousness**, or an understanding of their social position in the system. Marx suggested that most workers do not truly understand how capitalism enslaves them. They think if they work hard, they'll get by and perhaps thrive.

Marx believed that once workers recognized their positions, they would unite to end the tyranny. He proposed an overthrow of the private ownership of capitalism and instead suggested socialism. In such a system, the government controls the economic system, ensuring that all people share in the profits generated by their own labour.[15]

Sociologists' opinions on Marxist theory vary. While some may hope for a type of class consciousness to arise and replace our current system, others think Marx oversimplified class struggle. His simple system of social class is difficult to apply to a complex postindustrial capitalist society, and even if you try, where would you draw the line between owners and workers?

What is undeniable is that Marx's ideas inspired many others to look at society critically. While the functionalist perspective focuses on social stability, the conflict perspective often considers that there are alternatives to how society may be organized.

Let's next look at the work of three other conflict theorists—Du Bois, Dahrendorf, and Foster—to study how social inequalities affect a society.

W.E.B. DU BOIS

W.E.B. Du Bois (1868–1963) was an African American conflict theorist who agreed with a great deal of Marx's thinking. After attending Fisk

University, Du Bois moved on to Harvard, where he would eventually complete both his undergraduate and graduate work. His writings are vast, but he is often credited for initiating the study of race in America. He was particularly interested in issues of racial inequality in the United States.[16]

In his book *The Philadelphia Negro*, Du Bois showed that poverty among African Americans in the United States primarily results from prejudice and discrimination.[17] In the book, he reviewed the history of African Americans in Philadelphia and connected that history to the problems his contemporaries were facing. Implying that slavery and capitalism led to African Americans' problems, Du Bois pointed out that history was influential over the present. He also noted that African Americans of his time had to live in two worlds, a white one and a black one. In one world, they were second-class citizens, while in the other they were equals. This idea, which Du Bois termed "double consciousness," created tension and conflict for African Americans. He felt that with greater assimilation into the mainstream culture, African Americans would eventually lead better-quality lives.[18]

When Du Bois saw extreme poverty, oppressive governments, and many wars in Africa, he realized that colonizing Europeans had caused many of these problems. Colonialism was a primary way for European powers to generate wealth for capitalists while doing little to improve the lives of the African poor. Du Bois increasingly believed that the greed of the United States and western Europe was the cause of war and poverty throughout the world. To counter this, promoting economic justice and equality helps the world be at peace.[19]

In many respects, Du Bois was one of the first and perhaps most influential sociologist to study race. He was a social activist, and he became more interested in working to improve life on the African continent and less interested in life in the United States. Du Bois eventually came to believe that African Americans would never be equal to whites because the white population would not allow it. For this reason, he left the United States and spent his remaining years in Africa.

RALF DAHRENDORF

Ralf Dahrendorf (1929–2009) served as commissioner for the European Economic Community, as a German foreign minister, and as director of the London School of Economics. Among sociologists, he is most known for his critique of classical Marxist theory. In his book *Class and Class Conflict in Industrial Society*, Dahrendorf argued that Marx's two-class system (*proletariat* and *bourgeoisie*) was no longer relevant to describe twentieth-century society, which he described as "post-capitalist." Instead of focusing only on property ownership as the definitive social distinction, Dahrendorf recognized that other social factors divide people into groups. While still deeply inspired by the Marxist view of social interaction as being essentially based on conflict and struggle for power, Dahrendorf opened the door for subsequent sociologists to explore other arenas of social conflict.[20]

CYCLE OF WEALTH IN A CAPITALIST SYSTEM

JOHN BELLAMY FOSTER

John Bellamy Foster (1953–), a contemporary professor of sociology, often writes using a conflict perspective. His work is primarily concerned with the negative effects of capitalism on society and the planet as whole. In his article "The End of Rational Capitalism," he points out that purely capitalist economies, or economies in which markets are totally free, are disappearing throughout the world. In free-market capitalism, businesses seek short-term rewards by working to expand markets. They do not care about long-term consequences. As a result, Foster argues that businesses' pursuit of wealth has created environmental and global problems, including extreme global poverty and inequality.

Foster argues that markets cannot "solve problems" because there are no profits to be had from such an endeavour. Often, people suggest that the United States is the wealthiest country in the world because it has worked harder and used the capitalist system to give opportunity and incentive to people. Foster reminds us that such a perspective ignores important parts of history, namely the period after World War II when most of the "industrialized world" was destroyed (except the United States), and the expansion of the U.S. economy was largely related to building up these devastated countries. This had very little to do with the superiority of the American capitalist system. Developments such as the fall of the USSR and the privatization of the Chinese economy seem to indicate that capitalism has won—and, thus, is "superior" to socialism.

Wavebreakmedia Micro/Fotolia

The studies of W.E.B Du Bois revealed inequality in the U.S. democratic system. What about in Canada? **Is the Canadian system fair for each person in the photograph?**

However, totally free-market capitalism will result in the destruction of the environment and the exploitation of workers throughout the world.[21] The long and short of it, according to Foster, is that capitalism cannot continue to expand because we are reaching a stagnant point.

CRITICISMS OF CONFLICT THEORY

While functionalists are accused of being too conservative, critics of conflict theory often say that it is too radical. A simple reading of conflict theory can seem to make the notion of conflict seem like a "bad" thing. However, in practice, a lot of conflict is actually institutionalized in society. When issues are debated in the House of Commons, Members of Parliament may represent conflicting viewpoints, but this conflict may result in a more equitable solution for all.

Because one of the important principles of the conflict perspective is to look at society with a critical eye, many supporters of the conflict perspective are also social activists, usually in support of groups, like the poor, who lack social power and influence. For this reason, conflict theorists are accused of being biased and lacking in scientific objectivity. They counter this accusation by stating that observing social arrangements that are unfair, but doing nothing to change them, is immoral.

After examining the works of functionalists and conflict theorists, you're probably thinking in a macro manner. Whether you're using functionalism or conflict theory, you are thinking like many sociologists. Yet sociologists can also take a more micro view. If you believe that the way to understand the social world is through the individual, you might find symbolic interactionism appealing.

The Symbolic Interactionist Perspective

Unlike the macro perspectives that focus on social institutions and large social groups, symbolic interactionism focuses on the way people interact with each other to create the social world in which they live. Communication is central to all human interactions. Symbolic interactionists believe that communication is possible because of symbols. Symbols are things that represent ideas or objects. The symbols we use are arbitrary, meaning that they vary from culture to culture.

Of course, words are not the only symbols. Consider the photograph on page 16 of flags from countries around the world. The flag that probably has meaning for you is the Canadian flag. However, people from China, Brazil, Belgium, and the United Kingdom probably feel the same way about their flags as you do about yours. These symbols represent entire nations, and yet you cannot identify many of them, and they probably don't hold much interest to you. This is because the

Do you know what LOL means? **As long as you are with other people who speak the same language, you can interact.**

THE CONFLICT THEORISTS—AT A GLANCE

importance of a symbol is rooted in the culture from which it comes. Just as languages vary between people, so, too, do their symbol systems.

Interactionists argue that individuals have the power to co-create the world, to make it what they want it to be. People develop standards and norms through a process of interacting with others. This way, we learn what is "normal" and acceptable behaviour. Widespread social acceptance of a behaviour is the main criterion in declaring it to be normal, and we quickly learn that different situations allow for different behaviours. For example, kissing your boyfriend or girlfriend on the lips is a perfectly acceptable behaviour. However, trying to kiss a co-worker on the lips could result in your being charged with sexual harassment.

Context and setting affect our understanding of a social event. You probably behave differently in your sociology class than you would if you were at a friend's house. Social order results when the members of society share common definitions of what is appropriate.

Disputes arise when we do not share the same definitions. For example, if your roommate eats your food without asking your permission, you might interpret that behaviour as disrespectful and rude. However, he might feel that his behaviour shows that the two of you are friends and share everything with one another. This principle has come to be known as the **Thomas theorem**, which states that:

> "If men define situations as real., they are real in their consequences."[22]

If you believe that your roommate was being rude, you will probably change how you behave toward him. It doesn't matter what his real intentions were; you will react based on what you believe they were.

THOMAS THEOREM states that situations that are defined as real are real in their consequences.

Symbolic interactionism is the most micro of sociological approaches, as it often studies the activities of individuals and then draws connections to larger society from these. Studies of relationships, deviance, and even social movements can all use a symbolic interactionist approach.

In many ways, symbolic interactionism blends sociology and psychology. Let's take a look at the work of its founder, George Herbert Mead.

GEORGE HERBERT MEAD

George Herbert Mead (1863–1931) was an American sociologist from the University of Chicago. Mead's former students were so committed to him that after his death in 1931, they combined his articles, notes, and lectures into the book *Mind, Self, and Society*. This book introduced a new theory called "symbolic interactionism."[23]

In *Mind, Self, and Society*, Mead suggested that the root of society is the symbols that teach us to understand the world. We then use these symbols to develop a sense of self, or identity. It is this identity that we then take into the world, and we interact with other identities to create society. Thus, the initial building blocks of society are our minds, the place we interpret symbols.

How do you learn to interpret symbols? Mead suggested that you do this through the micro interactions you have every day. You have

romantiche/Fotolia

<<< This is a collection of flags from many countries. Which of these do you recognize? **Do any of these flags have meaning to you?**

probably learned that in a classroom, you should raise your hand if you have something to say. When the teacher calls your name, or points to you, then it is your turn to speak. Mead argues that all these various symbols enter our minds, where their meaning is interpreted and we are told how to react. Mead suggests that this process is never-ending; therefore, we have a fluid sense of who we are. Our selves can change, and they do change based on how we interpret the symbols thrown our way.

In this way, your self develops. **Self** is your identity. It's what makes you who you are and separates you from others. According to Mead, you couldn't have a self without symbols or without someone to pass those symbols on to you. In other words, you learn who you are through others.

In high school, did you ever feel embarrassed by your parents? Do you feel the same level of embarrassment today? The answer to both questions is probably yes and no. When I ask this in class, most of my students report that they don't find their parents nearly as embarrassing as they used to. Why does this occur? It is because when you were younger, you didn't have a well-developed sense of self, yet you were trying to develop your identity. You were anxious, taking your cues from others as to what was "cool" or acceptable. You worried that your parents' actions might reflect upon you. As you grew older, you experienced thousands of interactions that helped teach you who you are. Therefore, the older you get, the less embarrassing your parents seem. You know yourself much better now.

Mead proposed that symbols build society. Symbols have meaning, and meaning directs our lives. The symbols a society uses help us understand the people in that society. In Canada, we have accepted that we need the word homeless to discuss people who cannot afford housing. Symbols help us define a situation and determine what we should do about it. For example, if someone told you about a homeless person, you might feel sympathy and want to help him—but if the person talked about a "filthy, lazy bum" you might not feel the same desire to help.

HERBERT BLUMER

Herbert Blumer (1900–1987) was a disciple of George Herbert Mead and former chair of the sociology department at the University of California–Berkeley. He established three basic premises that define the symbolic interactionist perspective:

1. Human beings behave toward things on the basis of the meanings they ascribe to those things.
2. The meanings of such things are derived from, or arise out of, the social interaction that one has with others and society.
3. These meanings are handled in and modified through an interpretive process used by the person in dealing with the things he or she encounters.[24]

What does Blumer mean? First, we all react to situations and people based on how we perceive them. Have you ever noticed that you can "dis" your mom, but if someone else does, you get defensive? This is because you ascribe meaning to the act of dissing—that it's okay for someone in the family, but when outsiders join in, you move to defend the group.

How did your feelings emerge? They probably developed from the many years in which your mother cared for you. While she may drive you crazy sometimes, she once fed you, tucked you in at night, and nurtured you when you were sick. In other words, the social interactions you had with her support the meaning you ascribe to who can and cannot dis her.

Blumer proposed that the primary focus of the interactionist approach involves studying individual interactions with symbols. This micro focus places great importance on the idea that symbols have great power to affect society as a whole. The way we talk about something creates the way we deal with it. Consider this example: In the 1950s, many whites spoke using racial slurs. Today, such language is socially unacceptable. Has this change eliminated racism? Certainly not, but the level of racism in Canada has certainly declined. Are these two factors connected? Blumer would suggest that they are. Words convey meaning, and meaning creates reality. Eliminating racist language moves society closer to eliminating racism.

Normally, people interpret the words and actions of those around them and determine their behaviour based on this interpretation. This results in rational behaviour, meaning that we tailor our responses to

SELF refers to a person's identity and what makes that person different from others.

DRAMATURGY is a theory of interaction in which all social life is like acting.

the setting after we've interpreted the reactions. However, in a group setting, our behaviours are somewhat different. Blumer suggests that, generally, in a group setting we react without the same degree of thought we use in an individual decision. At some point, people stop thinking rationally and act in ways that they might not consider acceptable in a different setting. Last hockey season, our hometown team was losing an important game. A man in the stands became extremely agitated; four-letter words poured from his mouth like water over Niagara Falls. The stands were filled with men, women, and children, and I'm sure this man would never have behaved this way at a business meeting. So why did this happen? Blumer would suggest that it was the result of collective excitement, an intense emotional behaviour that makes it hard for individuals to think and act rationally. In such a setting, people "lose their heads" and react emotionally, not rationally. In this way, you can see that individual interactions can create social realities. I was thankful at that game that I had not taken my children, but someone in the crowd eventually did tell the man to watch his mouth because there were children around. Initially, the foul-mouthed man seemed angry to be scolded in public, but he quickly cooled down as he noticed that a number of people around him were watching his behaviour closely. How do we react when others are watching? Sociologist Erving Goffman developed a theory about this.

Goffman's primary insight is that we are constantly trying to manage the impressions that others have of us. Impression management is the action we use to control what others think of us. When the angry man at the hockey game calmed down, it was probably because he was a season ticket-holder and he knew that we'd all see him again next week. He didn't want to come off as the "jerk who cusses."

ERVING GOFFMAN

Canadian sociologist Erving Goffman (1922–1982) developed a theory he called **dramaturgy**, a theory of interaction in which all social life is like acting.[25] Goffman used this theory to compare daily social interactions to the gestures of actors on a stage. He said that people are constantly "acting" in order to convince people of the character that they wish to portray to the outside world. This is not to say that people are always faking it, but rather that people are concerned about what the rest of the world will think of them, and they adjust their social interactions accordingly.

Frequently, we alter our behaviour without much deliberate thought. For example, if you're on a first date, do you behave differently than you do with an old friend? Usually, on a first date you dress differently, talk differently, and eat more carefully. You may be nervous, but you will also, without thinking about it, change your behaviour. Why? Because you are taking extra care to make a good first impression, even if it means not being completely yourself. Goffman points out that managing impressions involves a complex series of actions and reactions. As a person gets older and has more practice in socializing, he or she may be better equipped to gauge the reactions that his or her actions will receive.[27] Chapter 4 provides more detail on dramaturgy.

HOWARD BECKER

Howard S. Becker (1928–), a sociologist from Chicago, suggests that human action is related to the labels attached to it. In his book *Outsiders: Studies in the Sociology of Deviance*, Becker suggested that a label is attached to a certain behaviour by a group with powerful social status. If the behavior is labeled as negative, it is called deviance. He suggests that deviance is rooted in the reactions and responses of others to an individual's acts.[28]

The label of deviant—or conformist, for that matter—is applied when people see our behaviour and react to it. This sets up a self-fulfilling prophecy for behaviour as people seek an identity that will match up to the expectations that others hold of them. Becker applied these ideas to the study of deviant behaviour, but the idea of labelling theory applies to all identity issues, including gender, sexual orientation, and personal identity.

Consider the example of a 5-year-old girl who has been labelled a "good girl." The theory would suggest that somewhere along the line, she did what others expected of her and that these people had power over her. Her parents asked her to take a bath, and she did. She received a positive reward, "she's a good girl," and through repeated events throughout her life, she developed that sense of self whereby she never does anything remotely dangerous or out of line—and always takes a bath. However, if this "good girl" becomes a "terrible teen" and her parents label her as a delinquent, she might stop bathing and start smoking. Becker would suggest that the label we ascribe to people has a major influence on their behaviour.

GO GLOBAL

Homeless Labels around the World

Assigning negative labels to the homeless isn't unique to Canada; it occurs in countries all over the world. In Finland during the 1980s, homelessness became associated with alcoholism. People related the two ideas so closely that the government in Finland had to step in to prevent such negative stereotyping. In China and India, people connect homelessness with a lack of governmental registration, which means that the homeless aren't seen as true citizens. In Peru, children living on the street are called *piranitas*, or little piranhas, which implies that they are dangerous and likely to resort to criminal behaviour. People in Bangladesh equate homelessness with having a lack of morals.[26]

Criminal, alcoholic, immoral—these are only a handful of labels that exist for the homeless around the world. As we noted above, negative labels make it even more difficult for poor individuals to rise above their situation. If people who are poor are given an opportunity and adequate support, they can be just as successful and stable as any other members of society.

THE SYMBOLIC INTERACTIONISTS—AT A GLANCE

CRITICISMS OF SYMBOLIC INTERACTIONISM

Critics of symbolic interactionism suggest that this perspective ignores the powerful effects of the social structure, focusing too much on the power of the individual to co-create his or her world. If, for example, you're a prisoner in jail, it doesn't matter whether you reject the prisoner label or not. If you try to leave, you'll be stopped.

Of course, we are all born into a culture and social setting; we don't create them as we go along. As a result, your parents, neighbourhood, and nation of birth all influence how you see things. Had you been born in a different time or in a different culture, you might have believed totally different things.

The Feminist Perspective

Feminist theory, or the study of how gender affects the experiences and opportunities of men and women, often takes a conflict-oriented point of view. Women throughout the world are still subordinate to men. In some countries, this might mean women cannot choose their husbands, while in this country it may be more linked to employment opportunities afforded to women. You'd be hard-pressed to find women CEOs in the very biggest companies: Women lead only 19 of the top 500 companies in Canada.[29] Feminists suggest that this occurs because men want to maintain their positions of power in society and strive to keep women out. Do you see the conflict perspective here?

LIBERAL VS. RADICAL FEMINISM

Although there are many different kinds of feminism, and there is no universal agreement about the titles of the different types, we will address two types here: liberal feminism and radical feminism.

Liberal feminists tend to be in line with their historical roots, suggesting that women's equality is the primary motivation for the movement. If you believe that women should receive the same pay for the same work; have equal opportunities in education, the workplace, and political office; and be free from domestic violence, then you are a liberal feminist. This group is the larger group because most people agree that women should not be discriminated against based on their gender. As a result, they support the idea that women should be free to pursue their own interests and achieve equality.

Radical feminists agree with the liberal agenda but generally carry the ideas further. They might focus on capitalism and the ways that men use their historical advantage over money to maintain control over women. Radicals see that patriarchy is firmly rooted in society. Some suggest that only an overthrow of capitalism can result in equality for women.

ANDROCENTRIC BIAS is a focus on men that influences sociology in terms of how social research is done and which issues and topics are studied.

Others suggest that women should avoid "traditional activities" such as childbearing, which often lead women to subordinate their own goals for their husbands and families.

The feminist perspective brings attention to the **androcentric bias** both in the wider society and in the traditional practice of sociology. The androcentric bias influences sociology in two ways. First, it assumes that the social research done on males is applicable to both males and females. Second, it focuses on issues and topics that are of greater concern to males than to females. For example, traditional sociological studies on crime have often focused on males as the perpetrators of crimes; the findings are then generalized to all criminals, both male and female. Conversely, the feminist perspective is more likely to focus on the female victims when studying crime. While all feminists are primarily concerned with gender inequalities, many have also drawn attention to other areas of inequality—especially race and ethnicity, social class, and sexual orientation. If you believe that society is often unfair because there are many advantages for males and many injustices for females, then you are thinking like a feminist theorist.

HARRIET MARTINEAU

Harriet Martineau (1802–1876), like Karl Marx, came from a bourgeois family and received the benefits and status that came with such a class distinction. However, she hoped that capitalism and industrialization would bring greater justice and opportunity. Martineau, one of the first female sociologists, did not just examine the inequalities in the economic system: She also focused on the inequality between the sexes.

In the book *Society in America*, Martineau analyzed the impact of slavery, the position of women in society, and the social customs within U.S. political and economic systems.[30] She pointed out how these systems favour men who hold the power in society.

Martineau's studies noted hypocrisy and favouritism in the United States. For example, only white men could vote, despite the nation's democratic ideals. Enslaved people and women did not have equal opportunities for political, economic, and educational involvement. Martineau pointed out that some people did not have the same opportunities as others. She not only paved the way for other female sociologists but also expanded people's thinking about the world, enlightening what would become the conflict perspective.[31]

JANE ADDAMS

Laura Jane Addams (1860–1935) was born in Cedarville, Illinois. Addams's father, a businessperson and politician who worked to elect President Abraham Lincoln and strongly opposed slavery, raised her. Jane earned a bachelor of arts degree from Rockford Women's Seminary in 1882 and then travelled to Europe, where she saw things that changed her life.

In London's Toynbee Hall, Addams witnessed the settlement house movement.[32] The settlement house movement supported the idea that poverty results from ignorance and structural barriers, not from failings in the morality of the person. The settlement house workers actually lived and worked in the slums. Jane and a friend, Ellen Gates Starr, decided to create a settlement house in Chicago. In 1889, they opened Hull-House, with these three principles:

1. Workers would live in the slums to better understand the problems there.
2. Every person has dignity and worth, regardless of race/ethnicity, gender, or social class.
3. Dedication, education, and service can overcome ignorance, disease, and other problems often associated with poverty.

Offering services ranging from medical to educational, Addams also used her position at Hull-House to write articles and books on a variety of topics, like the rights of women and the poor. In many ways, Hull-House became a laboratory for the application of sociological principles. In 1931, Jane Addams won the Nobel Peace Prize for her lifetime of service and dedication to peace.[33]

Through her teaching, writing, and action, Jane Addams embodied the best of sociology principles. Along with Albion Small, she helped found the American Sociological Association and often guest lectured in sociology classes at the University of Chicago. In order to understand the poor, Addams felt that she must live among them. Once she comprehended a situation, she wrote about it to inform others. These theories impacted her work at Hull-House. These are the steps you will take in learning to think like a sociologist.

DOROTHY SMITH

Dorothy Smith (1926–) is one of the most influential and well-known Canadian sociologists. Like many other sociologists, Smith understands that culture is socially constructed. But Smith recognizes that this also includes the practice of sociology, which, in its tradition, reflects a very male perspective. In *The Conceptual Practices of Power: A Feminist Sociology of Knowledge*, Smith critiqued traditional sociology for adopting an "objectifying discourse."[34] When sociologists use census data and labour statistics to describe and understand social behaviour, they are ignoring the lived experiences of individuals. By overlooking these experiences, most (male) sociologists perpetuate an ideology that justifies the existing social structure. Smith called this type of writing the "father tongue." It is a symbol of a patriarchal system that downplays the importance of individual experience and prefers to pursue objective knowledge—a typically male approach.

Smith argued that the work of a sociologist should be to recognize the everyday experiences of ordinary people, including women, workers, and other marginalized groups. We should develop a sociology that is relevant for all members of society and which explains the social world, including our subjective experiences of it.[35]

CRITICISMS OF FEMINIST THEORY

You have seen that some of the earliest sociologists, such as Harriet Martineau and Jane Addams, were women. Nevertheless, sociology has primarily been practised by men. The feminist perspective brought a new theoretical focus to sociology, one that recognized the patriarchal nature of society and the inequality that exists between men and women. Some have criticized feminist theory for placing too much emphasis on the impact of gender on social relations. While it is true that 100 years ago most social institutions were explicitly biased against women, this is not necessarily the case today. Gender inequalities still exist, but there has been incredible improvement in the social, political, and economic position of women in Canadian society. It is probably due to the work of feminist sociologists that the social structure has changed.

THE FEMINIST THEORISTS—AT A GLANCE
THE GRANGER COLLECTION, NEW YORK

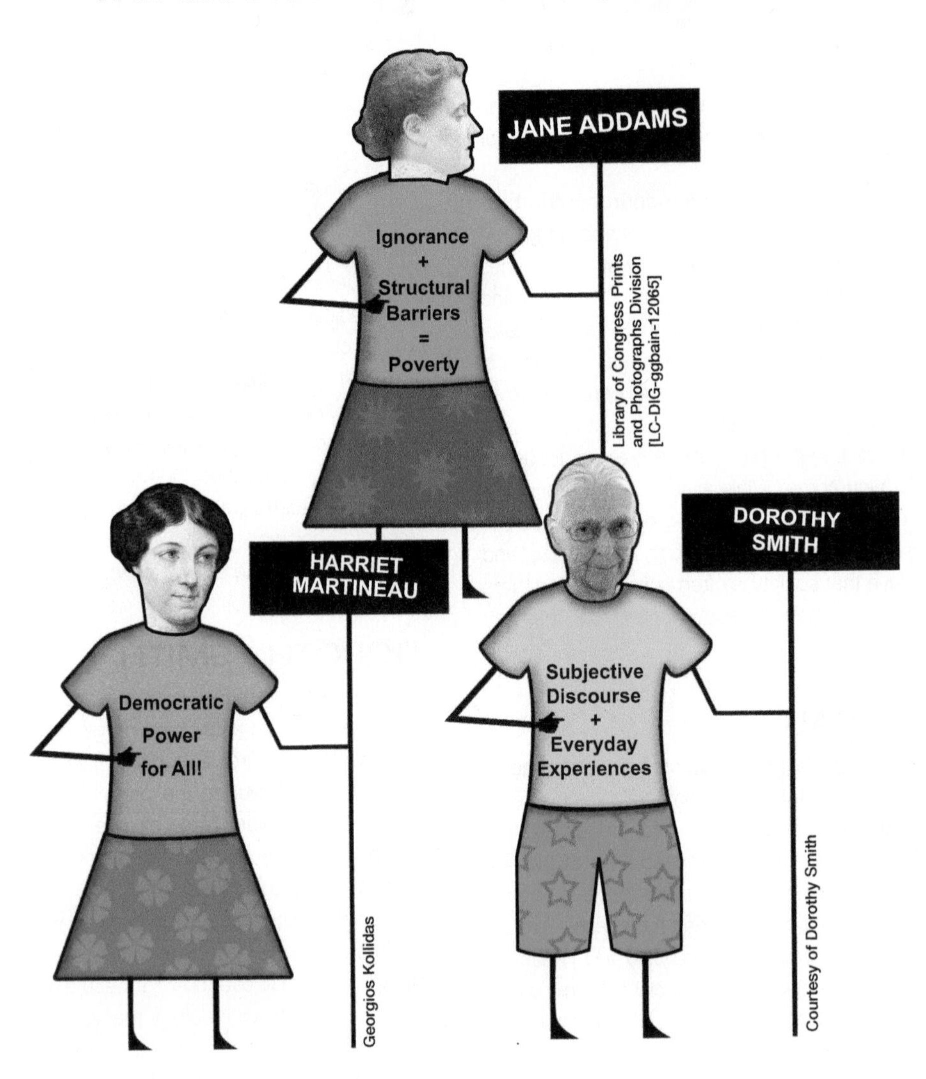

The feminist perspective has also challenged the principle of objectivity in studying social behaviour. The quest for objectivity, it is argued, is a particularly male view. Feminists are more likely to try to understand the subjective meaning and individual experiences of the people and groups they are studying. However, this has resulted in the accusation that feminist research methods lack scientific validity.

The Four Perspectives—How Are They Interrelated?

In the sports arena, we tend to associate phenomenal players with the teams on which they play. Such a player's name and the team name become synonymous. Sidney Crosby and the Pittsburgh Penguins. Michael Jordan and the Chicago Bulls. Derek Jeter and the New York Yankees. You get the idea. The same is true of sociologists: We associate the theorist with the perspective that he or she favoured or had a hand in developing. For example, Marx is a symbol of conflict theory, whereas Durkheim and functionalism go hand in hand. However, sometimes it can be tricky to confine sociologists to such a tight box because they might use parts of each perspective in their analyses. In fact, I know of no colleague of mine who is a "purist" in anything. That's because no single perspective perfectly fits every situation. To get a complete picture, many sociologists use all four perspectives. In this way, the four perspectives are interrelated and work together to help us figure out why society is the way it is.

Think about sociologist Robert Merton and his concept of latent and manifest consequences. He takes a functionalist stance but adds to it the notion that intended and unintended results can arise. Thus, we should ask, for whom is this functional? Can you see a bit of conflict theory here?

Becker's labelling theory can be linked to conflict theory because the labelling tradition suggests that those with power determine what is and is not labelled as deviant or criminal. In other words, the power of the label influences the outcome for the individual, but people with the ability to get what they want put the label on all of us. Like a conflict theorist, Becker acknowledges that a system of inequality exists within our society. Consider this question: Why are cigarettes legal, while marijuana is illegal? Labelling theorists would argue that this is because people with power smoke cigarettes, but not pot. If powerful people ever started smoking pot, the practice would probably become legal.

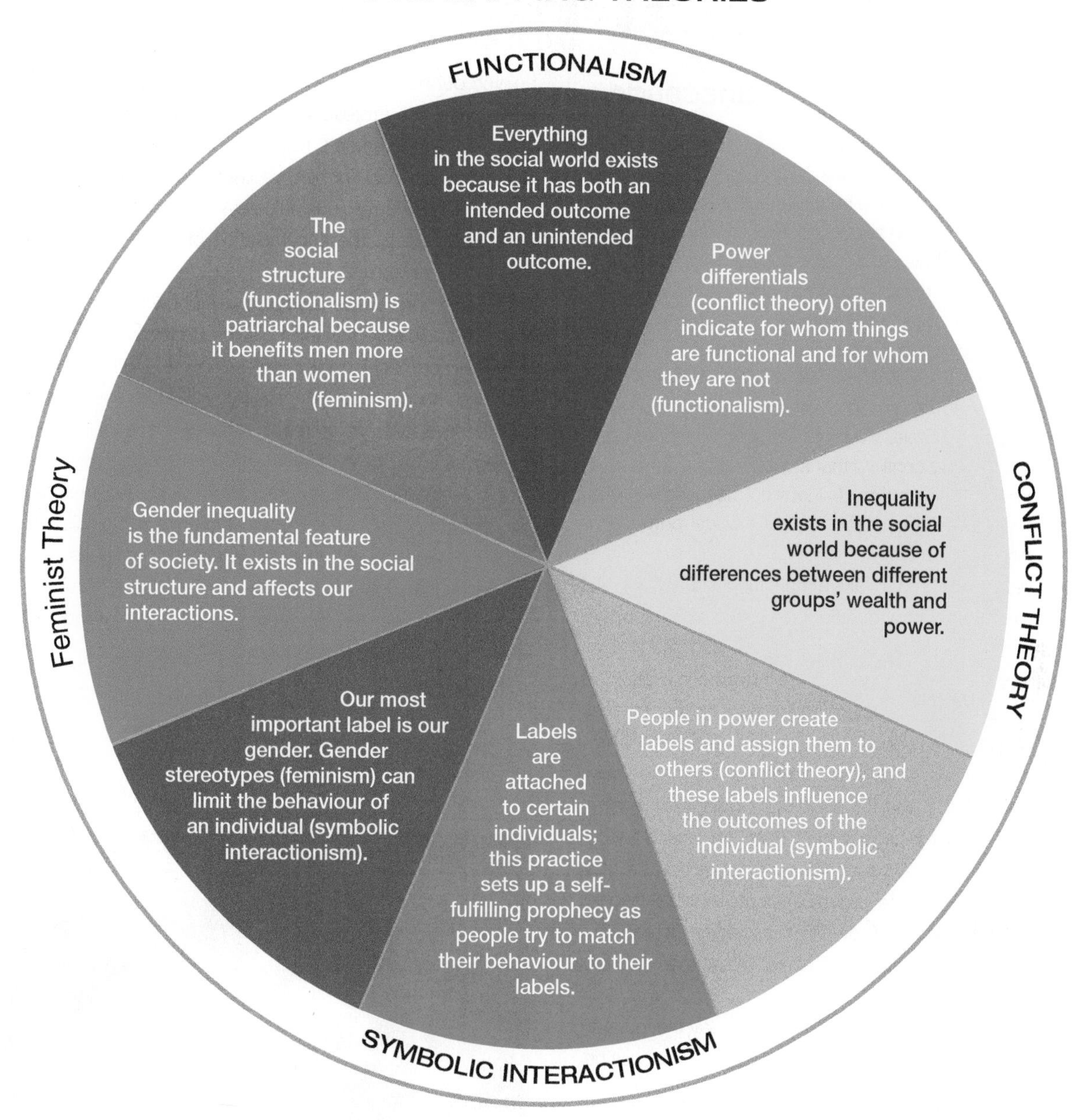

OVERLAPPING THEORIES
FUNCTIONALISM
CONFLICT THEORY
SYMBOLIC INTERACTIONISM
Feminist Theory
Everything in the social world exists because it has both an intended outcome and an unintended outcome.
Power differentials (conflict theory) often indicate for whom things are functional and for whom they are not (functionalism).
Inequality exists in the social world because of differences between different groups' wealth and power.
People in power create labels and assign them to others (conflict theory), and these labels influence the outcomes of the individual (symbolic interactionism).
Labels are attached to certain individuals; this practice sets up a self-fulfilling prophecy as people try to match their behaviour to their labels.
Our most important label is our gender. Gender stereotypes (feminism) can limit the behaviour of an individual (symbolic interactionism).
Gender inequality is the fundamental feature of society. It exists in the social structure and affects our interactions.
The social structure (functionalism) is patriarchal because it benefits men more than women (feminism).

We've seen how conflict theory overlaps with both functionalism and symbolic interactionism, but does functionalism ever overlap with symbolic interactionism? When Émile Durkheim suggests that values unify people, he sounds a bit like George Herbert Mead. The solidarity of a society for Durkheim is related to what it values, and he acknowledges that values change as societies become more modern.

We've said that feminism takes both macro and micro approaches. When feminists argue that the social structure is patriarchal, they are overlapping with many of the assumptions of the functionalists. You have seen that functionalists study social institutions such as the family or the educational system. Feminists draw attention to the fact that many of these social institutions have gender bias because they provide more benefits to men. When feminists focus on the subjective meaning of gender stereotypes, they are sharing a worldview with the symbolic interactionists. Our gender is an important part of who we are. You probably act differently around someone, depending on whether they are male or female.

The point for you as a student of sociology is to be aware that just because a sociologist is classified as a functionalist, conflict theorist, symbolic interactionist, or feminist doesn't mean that he or she won't use other points of view in making an analysis of the world. In fact, at times, a theorist's point of view can be so eclectic that he or she can't be pinned down to a single category. This sentiment is especially true of sociologist Max Weber.

APPLYING SOCIOLOGICAL THEORIES

Now it's time to think like a sociologist. Thinking like a sociologist means that you understand the topic, and you examine it from one or more of the four sociological theories covered in this section. Consider the problem of poverty in a society. How might a functionalist view poverty? How might a conflict theorist view it? A symbolic interactionist? A feminist?

THINK SOCIOLOGICALLY

Max Weber—Theorist Who Transcends Categorization

To some sociologists, Max Weber (1864–1920) was the German counterpart of Émile Durkheim because he wrote about a great variety of topics, used data in his analysis, and laid the foundations for high-quality sociological research. In his work, students often see a variety of ideas that seem to blend different schools of thought. Yet he wrote at a time before many of these "schools" were clearly defined or established.

Because Weber wrote partly as a response to some of Karl Marx's ideas, many consider him a conflict theorist. Weber accepted that social classes influence our social situation; however, he felt that Marx's social class system was too simple. He proposed that all people have economic, political, and cultural conflicts that are related to their relative social position. As a result, being an owner does not necessarily make you important in society. Wealth is important, but political power and social standing are also important.

In other ways, Weber appeared to take a more functional approach, particularly when he discussed how bureaucracies function in society. Bureaucracies are formal organizations that are organized into a hierarchy of smaller departments. You might think of a large corporation or a government agency as a bureaucracy. Weber proposed that rational and ideal bureaucracies naturally occur because we need them. They provide clear lines of authority, divide tasks so that workers can specialize, and clearly define rules and expectations. Under such a type of leadership, societies and large organizations function smoothly and improve the function of society. Although Weber was well aware that few perfect bureaucracies exist, he argued that responsible leadership will tend toward the ideal because Western society is increasingly focused on achieving goals, and a rational bureaucracy is an efficient system for achieving those goals.[36]

Others have suggested that Weber's ideas seem to lay the foundation for the symbolic interactionist school of thought. Why? Because he pointed out how values influence our goals and affect our behaviours. In his book *The Protestant Ethic and the Spirit of Capitalism*[37], Weber clearly linked a person's religious values to the societal creation of a capitalist economy. For him, capitalism arose in the Western world primarily because a religious value system that he called "the Protestant ethic" emphasizes the accumulation of wealth as a marker of God's favour on a person.

Furthermore, Weber also discussed how values are important to the study of sociology. For example, he understood that sociologists are at risk of approaching their profession with personal values that might influence the outcome of their study. Weber stressed that sociology should strive to be value-free. In other words, sociologists should study society as it is, not as they would like it to be. They should put aside their biases when analyzing a topic. He implied that personal values may impact social research, and therefore sociologists must strive to put such values aside when they make their analyses.

So, where does your professor put Weber? The more you read about social theorists, the more you will find that most of them blend ideas from all schools of thought.

>>> Is Max Weber (pronounced VAY-bur) a conflict theorist? A functionalist? A symbolic interactionist? Or is he all three? **Sociologists everywhere disagree on how to classify Weber. That's because his views are so varied that he almost defies categorization.**

Everett Collection Inc/Alamy

WRAP YOUR MIND AROUND THE THEORY

Darrin Henry/Fotolia

Functionalists look at how **social institutions such as the economy and the government may contribute to poverty.**

Conflict theory sees the **inequality of wealth in a society is aleading cause of poverty.**

Pearson Education

FUNCTIONALISM

Functionalists suggest that society works as an interrelated system. If we want to understand the causes of poverty, we need to look at the entire social structure. Different social institutions may contribute to poverty. Changes in the economy may result in many people either losing their jobs or working for low wages. This can cause them to become poor. If the education system fails to give people the knowledge and skills necessary to get high-paying jobs, more people will be poor. If the government makes changes to the social support system such as employment insurance (EI), more people will be at risk of experiencing poverty.

CONFLICT THEORY

Conflict theorists view poverty as a result of inequality in society. Conflict theorists focus on social classes and the differences in wealth, power, and prestige. They believe that the upper class controls society's wealth and resources and exploits the lower class. If the upper class shared its wealth, conflict theorists argue, then poverty would be cut down dramatically. Some conflict theorists take a wider view of inequality. They would look at inequalities not just between social classes but between different social groups. They would look at how individuals in some social groups, such as certain ethnicities, are more likely to be poor.

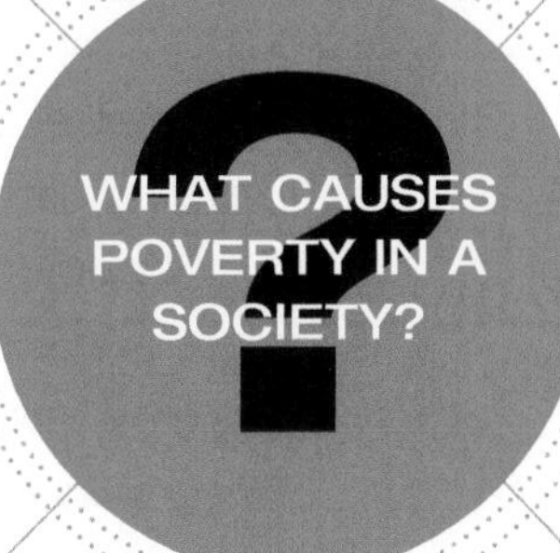

WHAT CAUSES POVERTY IN A SOCIETY?

SYMBOLIC INTERACTIONISM

Symbolic interactionists examine what it means to be poor. They look at how we define poverty and what it means to be poor from the perspective of those who are labelled as poor. They ask: What labels do we assign to the poor? This perspective also looks at how poverty affects the way individuals act toward one another. They ask: How do people behave toward poor individuals?

FEMINIST THEORY

Feminists focus on how poverty affects women in particular. They might look at how social structures and policies result in more women than men being poor. What changes would have to be made to the social, economic, and political systems in order to reduce the poverty of Canadian women? When we study poverty, do we focus on the homeless man, or do we consider the single mother who is struggling to barely make ends meet?

Joseph Vacanti/Shutterstock

Ed Kashi/VII/Corbis

Symbolic interactionists look at **how people act toward those who are poor.**

Feminist theory focuses on the **inequality of women as a cause of their poverty.**

discover sociology in action: WHY IS COMMUNITY LEARNING IMPORTANT?

"Homeless people are just a bunch of drug addicts, aren't they?"

I wasn't surprised when Theo, one of my first-year sociology students, made this comment during a lecture. However, I was disappointed because I knew that many people around the world share this view. After a lively debate on the subject, I realized I hadn't changed Theo's mind, so I challenged him to volunteer at a local homeless shelter.

Day after day, Theo worked with the families at the shelter—feeding, clothing, and talking with them. While at the shelter, he met a homeless mother who had been the victim of domestic violence.

"When I looked into that mother's face and the faces of her children, I realized how narrow my viewpoint had been," Theo remarked to me later. "How did I ever think you could label an entire group of people?"

At the end of Theo's volunteer period, he wrote a paper for class, revealing how much he had learned about the homeless. He even decided to continue working at the shelter. Volunteering made him feel like he was making a difference in the lives of the people he encountered, and he knew they were making a difference in his. Theo's experiences helped him realize that the people at the shelter were just like him. The only difference was that they had fallen on some bad luck.

ACTIVITIES

1. What community learning opportunities are available in your area? Surf the Web to find local shelters, food banks, or other organizations in your community. Choose an organization and volunteer there. Write about your experience.
2. Research your local and provincial governments. Who are the important government officials? What roles do they play in the government? What policies and issues do they support?
3. Poverty is just one of many issues that plague today's society. What other social issues do you think are important to address and why? How would you try to solve these problems?

Getting Involved in Sociology—Community Learning

Theo's story shows how moving out of the classroom and into the community helps people gain new perspective. They can get out of their individual boxes and view the world as a sociologist would.

It's easy for people to believe that social problems are so widespread that there is nothing we can do about them. Often, we feel so out of touch with the world around us that we do not vote, we do not know our neighbours, and we cannot name our town council members. Community learning, however, can help you see things with fresh eyes. Working in the community expands your understanding of sociology and your world. When you actually take a minute to view the world from someone else's perspective, you'll find it hard to just sit around and do nothing.

CHAPTER

01

WHAT IS SOCIOLOGY? 5

a science guided by the basic understanding that our lives are affected not only by our individual characteristics but also by powerful social forces and our place in the social world

WHAT ARE THE FOUR MAJOR SOCIOLOGICAL PERSPECTIVES? 8

functionalism: sees society as a system of interrelated parts; a macro orientation because it focuses on larger social structures rather than individuals

conflict theory: views society as various groups that are in a constant struggle over scarce resources; focuses on macro issues and is concerned with inequality and how it brings about conflict and change

symbolic interactionism: focuses on how individual people interact with others in their everyday lives; studies how the use of symbols influences how people communicate; uses a micro approach because it is concerned with the individual's role in creating society

feminist theory: views society as being based on a patriarchal ideology that benefits men and discriminates against women; focuses on issues that are relevant to women; uses both macro and micro approaches; is concerned with gender inequality

WHY IS COMMUNITY LEARNING IMPORTANT ? 24

provides you with a fresh perspective and expands your understanding of sociology and your world

get the topic: WHAT IS SOCIOLOGY?

Theories

FUNCTIONALISM 9

- focuses on society as a system of connected parts working together to keep society intact
- it is important to consider the manifest and latent functions of any issue or institution
- society is fairly stable

CONFLICT THEORY 12

- focuses on social classes and groups and the differences in wealth, power, and prestige
- powerful groups control society's wealth and resources and exploits the weaker groups
- groups that have power are likely to create advantages for themselves

SYMBOLIC INTERACTIONISM 14

- focuses on the way people interact with each other to create the social world
- communication is central to all human interactions and is possible because of symbols
- disputes arise when people do not share the same definitions of symbols

FEMINIST THEORY 18

- focuses on gender inequality in society
- social structures are patriarchal, meaning that they benefit men more than women
- traditional sociology has ignored issues that are important to women

Key Terms

sociology is a science guided by the understanding that our lives are affected not only by our individual characteristics but by powerful social forces and our place in the social world. *5*

society refers to a group of people who live in a defined territory and who share social structures and who interact with each other. *5*

sociological imagination is the ability to understand how social forces influence the lives of individuals. *7*

micro is a small-scale perspective. *7*

macro is a large-scale perspective. *7*

debunking is the practice of looking beyond the surface or obvious explanation and seeking out deeper explanations. *7*

functionalism is a theoretical perspective that sees society as a system of interrelated parts. *9*

conflict theory is a theoretical perspective that views society as various groups that are in a constant struggle over scarce resources. *9*

symbolic interactionism is a theoretical perspective that focuses on how people interact with others in their everyday lives. *9*

feminist theory is a theoretical perspective that focuses on gender inequalities which are built into the social structure. *9*

patriarchal refers to a social system that benefits men. *9*

social laws are statements of fact that are unchanging under given conditions and can be used as ground rules for any kind of society. *10*

social statics are the existing structural elements of society. *10*

social dynamics are changes in the structural elements of society. *10*

social Darwinism is a notion which suggests that strong societies survive and weak ones become extinct. *10*

functions are social factors that affect people in a society. *10*

manifest functions are factors that lead to an expected consequence or outcome. *10*

latent functions are factors that lead to unforeseen or unexpected consequences. *10*

bourgeoisie refers to members of the capitalist class who own the means of production. *12*

petite bourgeoisie refers to the class of people who have their own businesses but do not employ others. *12*

proletariat refers to members of the working class who sell their labour for wages. *12*

false consciousness is a person's lack of understanding of his or her position in society. *12*

class consciousness is an understanding of one's position in the class system. *12*

Thomas theorem states that situations that are defined as real are real in their consequences. *15*

self refers to a person's identity and what makes that person different from others. *17*

dramaturgy is a theory of interaction in which all social life is like acting. *17*

androcentric bias is a focus on men that influences sociology in terms of how social research is done and which issues and topics are studied. *19*

Sample Test Questions

These multiple-choice questions are similar to those found in the test bank that accompanies this textbook.

1. What is the sociological imagination?
   - **a.** The ability to understand how social forces influence the lives of individuals.
   - **b.** The belief that sociology is the best explanation of human behaviour.
   - **c.** How sociologists wish society could be.
   - **d.** A term that non-sociologists use to insult sociologists.
2. Which of the following questions might a symbolic interactionist ask about the social world?
   - **a.** Why does inequality exist in society?
   - **b.** Why do women typically earn less than men?
   - **c.** How do social institutions keep society running smoothly?
   - **d.** How does a particular social setting affect a person's behaviour?
3. Erving Goffman's theory of dramaturgy suggests that
   - **a.** people behave similarly in a variety of situations.
   - **b.** people change their behaviour to fit the setting they are in.
   - **c.** people's behaviour has little to do with others' perceptions of them.
   - **d.** people's behaviour is not affected by the behaviour of others around them.
4. Who does a patriarchal social structure benefit?
   - **a.** The poor
   - **b.** The rich
   - **c.** Men
   - **d.** Mothers
5. All of the following are macro orientations except
   - **a.** functionalism.
   - **b.** conflict theory.
   - **c.** social Darwinism.
   - **d.** symbolic interactionism.

ANSWERS: 1. a; 2. d; 3. b; 4. c; 5. d

ESSAY

1. The four sociological perspectives often overlap with one another. Choose a sociologist discussed in the chapter. Discuss how his or her ideas connect to at least two different sociological perspectives.
2. Why is it important for a sociologist to use the sociological imagination? What consequences might arise if a sociologist failed to use this way of thinking?
3. How might a conflict theorist study poverty?
4. Why is suicide a compelling sociological issue?
5. Describe possible manifest and latent functions of a law that would legalize drugs.

WHERE TO START YOUR RESEARCH PAPER

To learn more about sociology as a scientific discipline, go to www.csa-scs.ca.

To find useful information about the famous figures of sociology, go to http://media.pfeiffer.edu/lridener/dss/.

To find an in-depth sociology dictionary, go to www.webref.org/sociology/sociology.htm and http://bitbucket.athabascau.ca.

For more information about sociology departments in Canada, go to www.mcmaster.ca/socscidocs/w3virtsoclib/cansoc.htm and www.sociolog.com/canada/links.html.

To find a guide for sociological internet sources, go to www.socioweb.com.

For more information about the study of symbolic interactionism, go to http://uregina.ca/~gingrich/f100.htm.

To find an online journal of sociology, go to http://en.wikipedia.org/wiki/List_of_journals_in_sociology.

To find an excellent source for different information on sociology, go to www.trinity.edu/~mkearl/theory.html.

For more information about feminist sociology, go to http://uregina.ca/~gingrich/o28f99.htm and www.sociosite.net/topics/women.php.

Remember to check www.thethinkspot.ca for additional information, downloadable flashcards, and other helpful resources.

SOCIOLOGICAL RESEARCH

STR/AFP/Getty Images/Newscom

WHAT ARE RESEARCH METHODS?
HOW DO SOCIOLOGISTS USE RESEARCH METHODS?
HOW IS RESEARCH INVOLVED IN SOCIAL POLICY?

"Most social scientists who have worked 'in the field' are aware of the impact that they might have and take this into account when they come to analyze their data. To what extent does the involvement enhance or diminish our 'scientific' study of religion? ...

"First of all, just being there can make a difference. When I began studying the Unification Church [often called the Moonies*] in the early 1970s, it was a relatively closed community with strong boundaries distinguishing 'them' from 'us.' To have someone living in the community who was not part of 'us' threatened and weakened the boundary and, thus, the beliefs and actions associated with a strong-group situation (Douglas 1970). The very fact that a normally impermeable boundary *can* be permeated by an outsider affects the group and its members in a number of concrete ways. For example, one girl left, not because I advised her to do so but, she said, because my anomalous existence as someone who could live both within and without led her to realize that she did not have to make the stark choice between *either* a godly *or* a satanic lifestyle; there could be a middle way which would allow her to pursue an alternative way of serving God without having to deny all that was good about her Unification experience.

"At the same time, it is possible that others stayed in the movement, at least for slightly longer than they might otherwise have done, because of the existence of a 'professional stranger' (Barker 1987). My presence meant there was someone who would neither report back to the leadership, nor go to the media, but on whom they could off-load their anxieties and frustrations.

"Asking questions (in formal interviews, general discussions, or through questionnaires) that no one else has previously asked can lead to an unexpected 'raising of consciousness.' . . . Sometimes, I was told, the result was a deeper understanding of the theology, but on other occasions the consequence was a growing irritation or suspicion of the leadership. . . .

"As my research into NRMs [new religious movements] progressed, I found myself affecting the situation more consciously. First, I was being asked to mediate between members of movements and their parents, who also formed part of my data. . . .

"Once the results of my research became public it became increasingly obvious that they would not go unchallenged. . . . To the astonishment and/or amusement of anyone who knew me, I found myself being labelled a Moonie, a Scientologist, a fundamentalist Christian, or a cult lover—or, by the more benign, an innocent who was being deceived by the movements. *What* I said was rarely questioned."[1]

* "Moonies" is slang for the followers of Sun Myung Moon, founder of the Unification Church.

How Do We Learn *about* Society *and* Social Behaviour?

CHAPTER 02

In a chapter of *Cults and New Religious Movements: A Reader,* British sociologist Eileen Barker explains how doing research into a new religious movement or cult can leave a scientist "bruised and confused."[2]

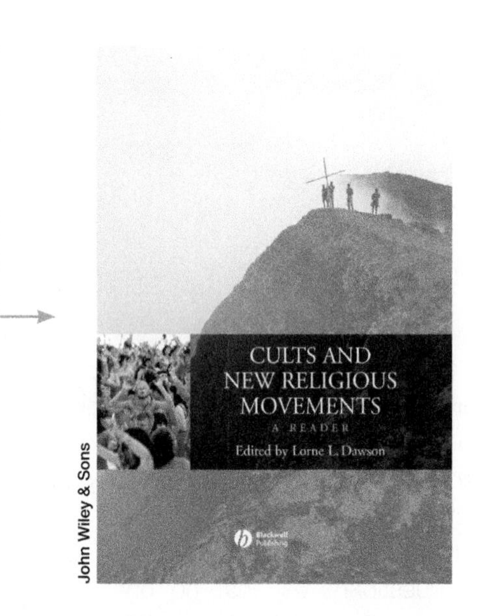
CULTS AND
NEW RELIGIOUS
MOVEMENTS
A READER
Edited by Lorne L. Dawson
John Wiley & Sons

"Cults," or new religious movements (NRMs), are found around the world. In 1980s Canada, for example, Roch Thériault, who called himself Moses, set up a cult commune with his followers near Burnt River, Ontario. One of his eight wives called him a psychopath after he cut off one of her arms. After pleading guilty to second-degree murder in the death of another of his wives, who was disembowelled with a kitchen knife during a cult ritual, he was sentenced to life in prison.[3]

Sociologists study all kinds of social groups. University of Waterloo sociologist Lorne Dawson wrote in *Cults and New Religious Movements* that cults emerged as a social problem in Western societies in the late twentieth century, which helps explain why they started coming under scrutiny after that.[4]

In studying controversial groups like cults, it is especially important that the social researcher be objective and scientific in his or her study. In our ongoing quest to help you think like a sociologist, this chapter will equip you with a precise understanding of the various research methods that we use.

get the topic: WHAT ARE RESEARCH METHODS?

Hearing jargon like *sociological research* and *statistical analysis* may trigger horrid visions of crunching numbers and memorizing formulas for hours on end. However, practising the actual nitty-gritty of research methods is very different from that. While it's true that research requires dealing with data and measurements, it also allows you to delve into the behaviours of your society. **Research methods** are the scientific procedures that sociologists use to conduct research and collect data about a particular topic. So, to fully understand what sociology *is*, you have to be aware of what a sociologist *does*. And that means learning to think and act like a sociologist.

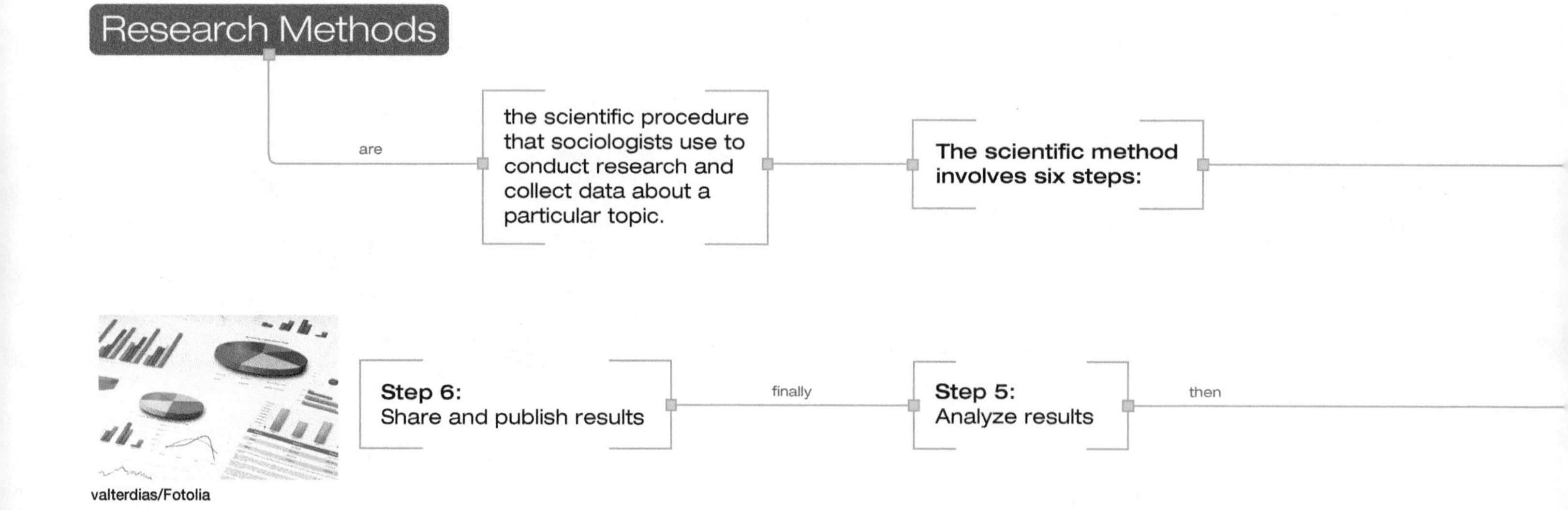
Research Methods
are
the scientific procedure that sociologists use to conduct research and collect data about a particular topic.
The scientific method involves six steps:
Step 6:
Share and publish results
finally
Step 5:
Analyze results
then
valterdias/Fotolia

Objectivity

An important concern for most sociologists is objectivity, the foundation for all sociological research. For sociologists, **objectivity** is the ability to conduct research without allowing personal biases or prejudices to influence them. They must put their own opinions and preconceived notions aside to study human behaviour objectively. Being objective may seem simple, but it can be very difficult in practice. We all have our own opinions and prejudices, which can skew an objective point of view. I happen to think that reading this textbook is important in learning sociology. However, if I were studying what kinds of things lead to students successfully learning sociology, I might focus on reading the textbook and neglect to look at other factors. My bias might influence my results.

Whether you're studying how students learn sociology or researching religious communities in your area, it's important to be objective. We can objectively observe what people do, but to fully understand their motives, we need what Max Weber called ***verstehen***—understanding the meaning of action from the actor's point of view.[5] Weber argued that sociologists should try to understand and explain a person's behaviour by listening to what that person says about his or her behaviour. He used the term *value-free sociology* to describe this approach.

Odua Images/Fotolia

RESEARCH METHODS are the scientific procedures that sociologists use to conduct research and collect data about a particular topic.

OBJECTIVITY is the ability to conduct research without allowing personal biases or prejudices to influence findings.

VERSTEHEN means understanding the meaning of action from the actor's point of view.

LITERATURE REVIEW is a study of relevant academic articles and information.

Scientific Method: What Are the Six Steps of Social Research?

Doing sociological research follows the same procedures as any other type of scientific research. After all, sociology is the scientific study of society. By following a logical and organized series of steps, sociologists ensure accurate results. In this section of the chapter, we will review the six steps of the scientific method. The first step is to decide what topic you want to find out more about.

1 **Decide on a Topic** The first step of the scientific method involves determining what you want to study. In order to take this step, researchers think of a question they want answered. Sociologists select topics on the basis of importance, personal interest, or the availability of prior research and data. Don't kid yourself: This can be the most difficult part of the process. The best research is often that which is focused on a clear and precise research question. You may, for example, be interested in the relationship between level of education and income. This is the topic you want to study.

2 **Review the Literature** After you select a topic, you need to perform a **literature review**, which is a study of relevant academic articles and information. This is essentially an organized effort to research your topic.

<<< Max Weber's idea of *verstehen* suggests that **sociologists try to understand the meaning of action from the actor's point of view.**

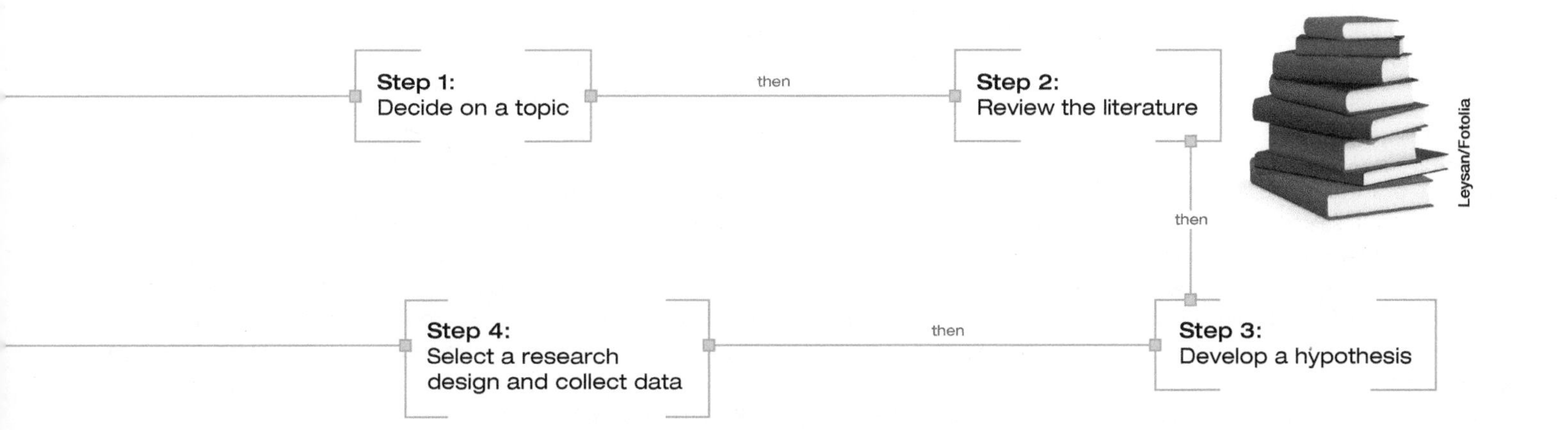
Step 1:
Decide on a topic
then
Step 2:
Review the literature
then
Step 3:
Develop a hypothesis
then
Step 4:
Select a research design and collect data

Leysan/Fotolia

Leysan/Fotolia

^^^ Literature reviews let you know what other researchers think about **a particular topic and what they have discovered through their research.**

For example, if you were examining the relationship between education and income, you might review scholarly articles written by others who have examined the same idea. Perhaps there is a theory that links level of education with income. Seeing how others researched this issue will help you improve on their work and avoid making any of the same mistakes they made.

3 **Develop a Hypothesis** After you have completed the initial research of your topic, it is time to formulate a hypothesis. It's important not to confuse a hypothesis with a theory. As you saw in Chapter 1, a theory is a comprehensive and systematic explanation of events that lead to testable predictions. These testable predictions are the basis for what we call a hypothesis.[6] Every year that I teach about research methods, I ask the class to tell me what a hypothesis is. I always get the same definition: A hypothesis is an educated guess. Well, not really. A **hypothesis** is a statement about how two or more variables relate. A hypothesis is used to test a theory. For example, you might make a hypothesis that people who have more education earn higher incomes. This hypothesis is a way for you to test the theory that income results not just from effort but from other social characteristics.

Variables

A **variable** is a characteristic or trait that can be measured. In stating a hypothesis, a researcher describes a relationship between variables. In the example above, the two variables are (1) level of education and (2) income. It is important to distinguish between the two types of variables in the relationship. **Independent variables** are variables that are presumed to cause changes in the dependent variables. **Dependent variables** are presumed to be changed or caused by the independent variables. Let's say you want to know if there's a connection between education and income. In this case, education occurs first and is the independent variable, and income depends on the level of education and is the dependent variable.

HYPOTHESIS is a statement about how variables relate.

VARIABLE is a characteristic or trait that can be measured.

INDEPENDENT VARIABLES are variables that are deliberately manipulated in an experiment.

DEPENDENT VARIABLES are the response to the manipulated variable.

CONTROL VARIABLES are variables that are kept constant to accurately test the impact of an independent variable.

CONCEPTS are abstract ideas that refer to objects, ideas, or behaviours.

OPERATIONALIZING is turning abstract ideas into something measurable.

RELIABLE means you get consistent results each time you measure.

VALIDITY means that you're actually measuring what you set out to measure.

Social situations are complicated. There are many things that determine someone's income. To determine the effect of education on income, though, you need to control for these variables. **Control variables** are variables that are kept constant to accurately test the impact of an independent variable. These variables must be controlled because they might influence the results, which would lead the researcher to a false conclusion. If you compare the incomes of people with different levels of education, you have to make sure that all other factors are controlled. From your review of the literature, you may have read that sex, age, and social class all have effects on income, so you would want to make sure that the people you study are the same on all these other factors. Control variables ensure that you are testing *only* the independent variable.

You now need to measure these variables in order to understand the relationship between them.

CONCEPTS AND OPERATIONALIZING VARIABLES

So how are you supposed to measure these variables, anyway? You might notice that the two variables above are not very specific. Does level of education refer only to academic learning? What about people who learn skills on the job? What is income exactly? Is it money that you earn from a job? Do you include inheritances, interest from investments, or lottery winnings as part of income? In order to create a testable hypothesis, you need to be a bit more specific. Right now, "level of education" and "income" are just **concepts**, or abstract ideas that refer to objects, ideas, or behaviours. Turning these abstract ideas into something measurable is called **operationalizing** the variables. If you operationalize "level of education" into "years spent in school," you now have a variable that's measurable. Likewise, you can change the abstract idea of "income" into a more measurable "money earned through employment." The measures that you use need to be both reliable and valid. For a measure to be **reliable**, you must get consistent results each time. Asking people about their income may not be as reliable as looking at their pay cheque. **Validity** means that you're actually measuring the thing you set out to measure in the first place. You wouldn't want to look at the kind of car that someone drives in order to measure his or her income. Once you have a hypothesis and variables that you can measure, you can move on to designing a research strategy.

Cause and Correlation

All the social sciences typically work with models that are probabilistic—they state what is likely to happen. You saw in Chapter 1 that Durkheim identified several social characteristics that are associated with higher suicide rates. This does not mean that an individual with one or more of these characteristics *will* commit suicide, only that the person is *more likely* to commit suicide.

A **causal relationship** is a relationship in which a condition or variable leads to a certain consequence. To understand causal relationships, you need to recognize the difference between causation and correlation. Causation is the relationship between cause and effect. Consider this with the example we have been using: People who have higher levels of education generally have higher incomes than people with lower levels of education. We know that many jobs that pay well also require advanced degrees. If someone has an advanced degree, then this can be the cause of their high income.

Correlations, unlike causes, are simply an indication that when one factor changes, so does another. In Durkheim's study (described in Chapter 1), he identified several factors, such as religion, sex, and marital status, that are correlated with a higher likelihood of committing suicide. However, none of these factors *cause* someone to commit suicide.

There are three types of correlations—positive, negative, and spurious. A **positive correlation** involves two variables moving in the same direction. In other words, you can find a positive correlation when variables increase or decrease together. Take the relationship between one's level of education and income. It has been observed that people with higher levels of education earn higher incomes.[7] This is a positive correlation because both variables trend in the same direction. A second type of relationship between variables is called a **negative correlation**, which occurs when the variables move in opposite directions. So, if you notice your grades go down as the number of hours you spend on Facebook increase, this is a negative correlation. The third type is a spurious correlation. *Spurious* means not genuine or authentic, so a **spurious correlation** occurs when two variables appear to be related but actually both may have an underlying cause. Several studies have found a positive correlation between height and income.[8] However, if we look a bit deeper, this is a spurious relationship, and there is another variable, sex, which is influencing both height and income together. Men are generally taller than women, and they also generally earn more. So it is not being taller that causes higher income, but being male makes it more likely that you will be taller and also makes it more likely that you will earn a higher income. This illustrates that researchers should always be wary of spurious correlations.

4 **Select a Research Design and Collect Data** When most people think about "doing research," this is the step that they tend to focus on. A **research design** refers to the process used to collect data. This involves deciding what kind of study you want to do and choosing a method for collecting data. Sociologists typically conduct three kinds of studies.

COMPARATIVE, CROSS-SECTIONAL, AND LONGITUDINAL STUDIES

Comparative studies use data from different sources in order to compare them against each other. International comparisons often use data from different countries and put them side by side. You should be aware, though, that comparative data across cultures might have methodological problems. For example, definitions of drug offences can differ greatly between countries, resulting in very different statistics.

The majority of available data in sociology are the result of **cross-sectional studies**. Like a camera capturing a singular moment, a cross-sectional study looks at an event at a single point in time. Researchers may use a variety of cross-sectional studies to try to track trends in society. However, these may not always include data gathered from the same people. To learn how specific people change over time with the changes in society, researchers conduct longitudinal studies.

Longitudinal studies include data from observations over time using a specific group of people called a **cohort**. These types of studies allow the researcher to provide measures of the same group over a period of time. The period of time can be extensive, and researchers frequently take multiple measures over a period of years. Although gathering this longitudinal information can be expensive and time-consuming, this information is useful in illustrating trends and showing how segments of society change.

Quantitative and Qualitative Data

Sociologists conduct research in order to collect data. Data are pieces of information. If you were asked to identify your age in years, your income in dollars, or the number of text messages you send and receive each day, these would be examples of quantitative data. Simply put, the term **quantitative data** refers to data based on numbers. Quantitative data can be derived from people's responses to survey questions. For example, you might ask whether students prefer multiple-choice or short-answer tests. You can then calculate a proportion—say, 87 percent of students prefer multiple-choice tests.

Qualitative data may include words, pictures, photos, or any other type of information that comes to the researcher in a non-numeric

CAUSAL RELATIONSHIP is a relationship in which one condition or variable leads to a certain consequence.

CORRELATION is an indication that when one factor changes, so does another.

POSITIVE CORRELATION describes two variables that move in the same direction.

NEGATIVE CORRELATION describes two variables that move in opposite directions.

SPURIOUS CORRELATION occurs when two variables appear to be related but both may have an underlying cause.

RESEARCH DESIGN refers to the process used to collect data.

COMPARATIVE STUDIES use data from different sources in order to compare them against each other.

CROSS-SECTIONAL STUDIES look at an event at a single point in time.

LONGITUDINAL STUDIES include data from observations over time using a cohort.

COHORT is a specific group of people used in a study.

QUANTITATIVE DATA refer to data based on numbers.

QUALITATIVE DATA include words, pictures, photos, or any other type of information that comes to the researcher in a non-numeric form.

form. A researcher who interviews students in order to understand why they don't read their sociology textbook or how they feel before a test would be collecting qualitative data. Both quantitative and qualitative data require evaluation. The way in which the evaluation is measured is different, but both allow sociologists to better understand an issue.

The choice to use either qualitative or quantitative data pertains to all four theoretical perspectives, but some general trends appear. Functionalist and conflict theorists tend to address more structural issues, and so they often use quantitative measurements. Conversely, symbolic interactionists might prefer qualitative data because they deal with the words and meanings attached to events. Feminist theorists may use both approaches. There is no hard-and-fast rule that connects a particular theoretical perspective to a single research method. Both qualitative and quantitative data can be appropriate.

POPULATION is the entire group of people you wish to describe.

PARAMETER is a number that describes a population.

SAMPLE is a subset of the population.

STATISTIC is a number that describes a sample.

REPRESENTATIVE SAMPLE is a sample in which the relevant characteristics of the sample are the same as the characteristics of the population.

GENERALIZATION is the extent that what is learned from a sample can be applied to the population from which the sample is taken.

POPULATIONS

Researchers need to determine the specific **populations**, or target groups, from which they wish to gain information. A population is the entire group of people you wish to describe. Perhaps you're interested in discovering what students who drive to school think about the parking situation on campus. Ideally you'd ask every student who drives, but that could take a lot of time and money. A **parameter** is a number that describes a population. We rarely know its value (unless we measure the entire population).

SAMPLES

Because some populations are quite large, sociologists usually get their data from a **sample**, or subset, of the population. A **statistic** is a number that describes a sample. We use a statistic to estimate a parameter.

In sociology, the populations we study are usually groups of people. People are very interesting, but they are also very complex. There are different sexes, different ages, different ethnicities, and different religions. Some people live in the city, others in the country. Some are lawyers, others are nurses. They may be married, single, divorced, or widowed. When we do research, we don't know whether these different characteristics will have an impact on what we are studying, so we want to try to get a sample that is representative of the population. A **representative sample** is a sample in which the relevant characteristics of the sample are the same as the characteristics of the population.

The sample needs to look like the population so we can generalize the findings. **Generalization** is the extent that what is learned from a sample can be applied to the population from which the sample is taken. Would it be fair to say that people who join cults are representative of all Canadians with religious beliefs? Certainly not. If you were studying one particular cult, you would select a sample of members of that cult and generalize your findings to all members of that cult, but not to members of every religion. To do that, you would need a sample of members from different religious groups.

The best way to get a representative sample is to choose a **random sample** from the population. This ensures that each member of the population has the same chance of being selected. If the sample is large enough, it is very likely to be representative of the population. Taking a random sample is the best method for a social scientist to know that his or her sample looks like the population.

METHODS OF QUANTITATIVE ANALYSIS

Robert Kneschke/Fotolia

Many national surveys, therefore, rely on random samples and can, with as few as 1000 people, make predictions about what Canadians think about specific issues. Although sample size can affect the power of the predictions, after a certain point, the advantage of a bigger sample becomes almost irrelevant. Thus, samples are usually as small as possible.

Convenience Samples

Even though random samples are preferred, other types of samples are often used. Researchers may use a **convenience sample**, which is a nonrandom sample of people conveniently or easily available to the researcher. These samples are usually not representative. For example, if a student athlete is doing a study on the exercise habits of students at his college but only chooses the other guys on his basketball team, this would be a convenience sample. It is certainly not representative of all students at the college. Convenience samples often suffer from **bias**—that is, the likelihood that a nonrepresentative sample may lead to inaccurate results.

Imagine that you have been doing field research on a new religious movement, or cult. Your questioning reveals that 56 percent of them—24 of the 43 people who belong to this cult—were recruited while they were doing summer work in a small beach town. However, your findings would not imply that more than half of all people participating in cults around the world were recruited in beach towns. Why? Because what you have is a sample of convenience. Of course, nonrandom samples can be quite valuable because they help illustrate a problem, illuminate issues, and test theories, but one cannot generalize the findings from them to the larger population. Therefore, all people who join cults probably are not mirror images of the members in your study.

RANDOM SAMPLE is a sample chosen so that each member of the population has the same chance of being selected.

CONVENIENCE SAMPLE is a nonrandom sample of people conveniently or easily available to the researcher.

BIAS is the likelihood that a nonrepresentative sample may lead to inaccurate results.

SURVEY is an investigation of the opinions or behaviours of a group of people by asking them questions.

Collecting Data

Sociologists use a variety of methods to collect data.

SURVEY

A **survey** is an investigation of the opinions or behaviours of a group of people. This is done by asking them questions. In sociological research, surveys are the most commonly used method for obtaining quantitative data. Institutions ranging from government agencies to marketing teams rely on survey responses to determine how the general public feels about their policies or their products. Surveys include interviews and questionnaires. Because it would be nearly impossible to survey every single individual within a specific population, researchers need to be more focused. A big advantage of surveys is that they allow researchers to collect a lot of information from a large group at relatively low cost. However, respondents may not always answer truthfully. Surveys measure what people *say* they do, not what they *actually* do.

MAKE CONNECTIONS

Music and Suicide

In 1992, researchers wanted to study the relationship between country music and suicide. Researchers Steven Stack and Jim Gundlach found positive correlations between country music airplay and white male suicide rates in American metropolitan areas.[9] According to their research, common themes in country music created a subculture that essentially led men to suicide. The same researchers also explored the link between the strength of the heavy metal subculture (measured as the rate of subscriptions to the major magazine *Metal Edge*) and suicide rates in 50 states.[10] They found that states with a stronger heavy metal subculture had higher youth suicide rates. Another study explored the hypothesis that sad themes and low notes in national anthems were associated with high national suicide rates.[11] Indeed, the greater the proportion of low notes in national anthems, the higher the national suicide rates.

The sociological perspective would suggest that the impact of music on suicide is best understood in relationship to a subculture where the music reflects and reinforces the values, attitudes, and behaviours of its members. For example, members of a particular music-based subculture may be initially drawn to a music genre based on individual differences, but then social influences may intensify their commitment to the norms of the subculture.

If you were conducting sociological research on music and suicide, how would you conduct the study?

>>> **ACTIVITY** Pick three songs within a particular genre (e.g., hip-hop, rock, pop) and examine their lyrics. Do these songs express anything about the culture in which we live? If so, how do you think this affects people who listen to this type of music? Is there a spurious correlation?

lassedesignen/Fotolia

<<< **Could music have led** this man **to the edge?**

GO GLOBAL

Serious Pot Problems: North America versus Europe

In 2010, the latest figures placed North America as the number-one region in the world for cannabis herb seizures, at 48 percent of all seizures, with western and central Europe at only 2 percent.[12]

Based on just this information, you might assume that North America (including Canada) has the most serious marijuana problem in the world. But figures don't always tell the whole story: They can reflect different attitudes and different government policies.[13]

Some countries in Europe have very different drug policies than those in North America. The Dutch, for example, believe the best course of action with drugs is to implement a harm reduction approach, which focuses on minimizing risks typically associated with drug use instead of on total drug suppression.[14] In the Netherlands, a harm reduction approach includes increased drug treatment and needle exchange programs. Drug use is a public health problem, not a criminal one. Since Dutch authorities believe "soft" drugs, like cannabis, are ultimately harmless and simply associated with youthful indiscretion, marijuana is legalized in small amounts. Moreover, the predominant thinking regarding these soft drug users is that they are less likely to get mixed up with hard drugs, like cocaine or heroin. Therefore, the focus is less on incarceration and more on treatment and prevention.[15]

In North America, the issue of differing national policies raised its head when Canadian marijuana policy reform advocate Marc Emery ended up in an international tangle. For years Emery openly ran a business selling pot seeds out of Canada, until a Vancouver police raid was made, at the request of the U.S. Drug Enforcement Agency.[16] Emery was extradited to the United States and sentenced to five years in prison for shipping marijuana seeds across the border. The U.S. Attorney's office estimated that 75 percent of the seeds that Emery's company had sold over 10 years ended up in the United States.[17] Ontario lawyer Karen Selick suggested that the United States had targeted Emery and two of his employees because they had taken a "principled, public stand against the U.S. government's war on drugs."[18]

In Canada, marijuana was banned in 1923, but control laws have been described as "spottily enforced, with the west coast (British Columbia) being well known for its high quality cannabis and low levels of enforcement."[19] Many Canadian companies have openly sold pot seeds, using a legal loophole within the country's Controlled Drugs and Substances Act that calls "non-viable" seeds legal but fails to address the issue of "viable" seeds. One online news report noted that a seed is viable if it produces a cannabis plant containing the active ingredient THC and that viable marijuana seeds are only implied as illegal.[20]

Nevertheless, Canada and the United States have arrested hundreds of thousands of people for possession and use of marijuana over the years. In 2009, 97 666 drug offences were recorded in Canada alone, including 48 981 involving the possession of marijuana and 16 335 for the trafficking, production, or distribution of pot.[21] The kind of possession arrests made in North America may not have been made in the Netherlands, which reflects a methodological problem. The number of drug offences generally reflects the ideologies that countries have about drug policy enforcement and prevention.

PERCENTAGE OF WORLD MARIJUANA SEIZURES

North America 48%

BlueSkyImages/Fotolia

markrussellphoto/Fotolia

Source: Adapted from the *World Drug Report 2010* (pp. 8–9) and the associated document "Global and Regional Seizure Totals" for cannabis herb in 2008 (p. 1), United Nations Office on Drugs and Crime, both accessed through www.unodc.org/unodc/en/data-and-analysis/WDR-2010.html on September 24, 2010.

EXPERIMENTS

EXPERIMENT is a method in which researchers control variables in order to test causes and effects.

In an **experiment**, researchers control variables in order to test causes and effects. Sociological experiments may test people's interactions or other social causes of human behaviour. The advantage of experiments is that the researcher can control other factors and therefore try to isolate and measure how one factor causes another. The disadvantage is that experiments are conducted under artificial conditions. People probably act differently in a lab than they do when they are out in the real world going about their business. Read the "Think Sociologically" feature to learn about a series of experiments Stanley Milgram conducted in the 1960s.

Hawthorne Effect

The seminal Milgram experiment documented what happens when a subject is unaware that he or she is being experimented on. But what about people who are cognizant of the experiment? In the 1930s an electric company hired researchers to test worker productivity in its Hawthorne Works factory outside Chicago. After pretesting worker performance, researchers made the lighting brighter. They quickly noticed that brighter lights seemed to make people work harder. However, when they later turned down the lights, productivity increased once again. In fact, every step the researchers took helped boost the workers' productivity.

Why did every change, even ones that seemed likely to hinder productivity, have the same effect? Researchers believed it was because the subjects knew they were being studied. Thus, the term **Hawthorne effect** was coined for situations in which people behave differently because they know they are being studied.[22] Unlike the experiment at the Hawthorne factory, Milgram's experiment used subjects who did not know why they were being studied. When conducting experiments and studies, sociologists must make sure that the Hawthorne effect does not influence their findings. Remember that in the opening vignette, sociologist Eileen Barker observed that her presence among the Moonies did affect some of them. One member left the movement, and others began to question the leadership.

HAWTHORNE EFFECT occurs when people behave differently because they know they are being studied.

FIELD RESEARCH is research conducted in a natural setting.

PARTICIPANT OBSERVATION is a type of field research in which the researcher poses as a person who is normally in the environment.

FIELD RESEARCH

It would be difficult to study a society without actually mingling with the people you're observing. Therefore, researchers need to venture out and conduct studies in a natural setting. This **field research** takes sociologists out into the streets, or homes, or classrooms. Many believe that field research is the best method for observing what people really do in social situations. If done properly, field research can be objective and unbiased. Field research often requires a greater commitment of time from the researcher. Some people spend months and even years "in the field" observing a particular group. There are three common methods of field research—participant observation, case studies, and ethnography.

Participant Observation

In the excerpt from Eileen Barker's description of studying the Unification Church (page 29) she clearly was not pretending to be a Moonie herself, but if she had done so, she would have been making use of covert **participant observation**.

THINK SOCIOLOGICALLY

Milgram Obedience Study

Social psychologist Stanley Milgram created a series of experiments to test a subject's obedience to the orders of a perceived superior. In the experiment, two subjects entered a room where a man in a lab coat met them. This individual, called "the experimenter," took on the role of the authority figure. The subjects were told they were going to be part of a study to test the effects of punishment on learning. One of the subjects role-played the "teacher," while the other—who was secretly one of Milgram's assistants—was the "learner."

The subjects were then led into a room where the "learner" was strapped into a chair with electrodes attached to him. The experimenter assured both subjects that while pain would result, no permanent damage would occur.

The teacher was placed in front of an electroshock machine and separated from the learner, who could be heard but not seen. If the learner failed to recall a series of paired words, the teacher was supposed to administer an electric shock. With each error, the teacher was instructed to increase the voltage. In reality, the learner was only acting and never received a shock, unbeknownst to the teacher.

Throughout the experiment, some subjects would pause when they heard learners cry "ouch" or "I want to quit." The scripted responses also included groans, screams, and even silence. When teachers questioned whether they should continue to inflict pain on the learner, they were told, "Please go on" and/or "You must go on."

Milgram found that 65 percent of the teachers administered up to 450 volts, even when there was no reply and despite the fact that the dial on the machine for this voltage read "danger."

In the experiment, Milgram observed that subjects would shock others to unconsciousness and even death on the command of a stranger who represented authority. Thus, Milgram suggested that when faced with an authority figure, most people follow orders, even if those orders go against their better judgment.[23]

snapfoto105/Fotolia

If you were the teacher in Milgram's research, **what action would you have taken, based on the learner's response?**

CASE STUDIES are investigations of one person or event in detail.

ETHNOGRAPHY is a research method that aims to understand the social perspective and cultural values of a particular group by participating in or getting to know their activities in detail.

SECONDARY DATA ANALYSIS is the process of using and analyzing data that others have collected.

CONTENT ANALYSIS is a type of research in which the sociologist looks for common words or themes in newspapers, books, or structured interviews.

TRIANGULATION is the process of using multiple approaches to study a phenomenon.

Participant observation is a type of field research in which the researcher poses as a person who is normally in the environment. Research that deliberately misleads the public or other study participants is extremely controversial.[24] However, it does give researchers access to information that would otherwise be unavailable and decreases the chances of the Hawthorne effect occurring because subjects do not know they are being studied.

CASE STUDIES

Unlike participant observations, **case studies** investigate one person or event in detail. Such a study is able to illuminate a complex issue through the lens of an individual case. Isabelle, a feral child who had spent most of her six years in a dark room with minimal human contact, is an example of a case study.[25] This case study not only includes a history of both emotional and physical neglect but also provides a compelling tale about experts who worked to develop the child's potential. When Isabelle was discovered, she could communicate using only grunts and invented gestures. Remarkably, Isabelle was able to improve her social skills and fully integrate into mainstream society. Some critics believe case studies are subjective because it's tricky to generalize the findings of an individual case to fit a larger group.[26] For example, the findings in Isabelle's case don't fit *all* feral children because some might not be able to fully develop.

ETHNOGRAPHY

Ethnography is a research method that aims to understand the social perspective and cultural values of a particular group by participating in or getting to know their activities in detail.

In one well-known ethnographic line of study from the 1950s and 1960s, Morris Freilich focused on Mohawk men who were drawn to dangerous jobs—as so-called skywalkers—on high-rise construction sites in New York, away from their traditional homes. His research included field work in Kahnawake, the Mohawk reservation south of Montreal, and in Brooklyn, New York.[27] A bar turned out to be a good place for such field work. Freilich met with hostility when he took out his notebook there, so carried a book in his pocket and would disappear to the washroom every now and then to make notes.[28]

Mohawk are members of the Iroquois peoples. In the end, Freilich found that working in dangerous steel construction jobs was a way for Mohawk men to experience their traditional role as brave warriors in a modern world that no longer required them to go to war against non-Iroquois peoples.[29]

SECONDARY DATA ANALYSIS

Sociologists don't always have to collect new data. Instead, they sometimes use secondary data, or data that others have already collected and published. The process of using and analyzing data others have collected is known as **secondary data analysis**. A variety of data sources exist for sociologists to use. Not surprisingly, the World Wide Web contains many of these sources. Census data, crime statistics, journal entries, and transcripts of speeches are just a few of the examples of secondary data found on the Web. The advantage of using these data is that they are often free or inexpensive (compared to collecting data yourself). A disadvantage is that the data may not always be exactly what you need. Critically evaluating the information you find is key to successful academic research. When you write a research paper based on books that you find in your school library or articles that you find in a database of academic journals, you are conducting secondary research. Consider the following criteria when evaluating information:

One common type of secondary analysis is a **content analysis**—a type of research in which the sociologist looks for common words or themes in newspapers, books, or structured interviews.

TRIANGULATION

Triangulation is the process of using multiple approaches to study a phenomenon. Sociologists often use triangulation by using both quali-

USING TRIANGULATION

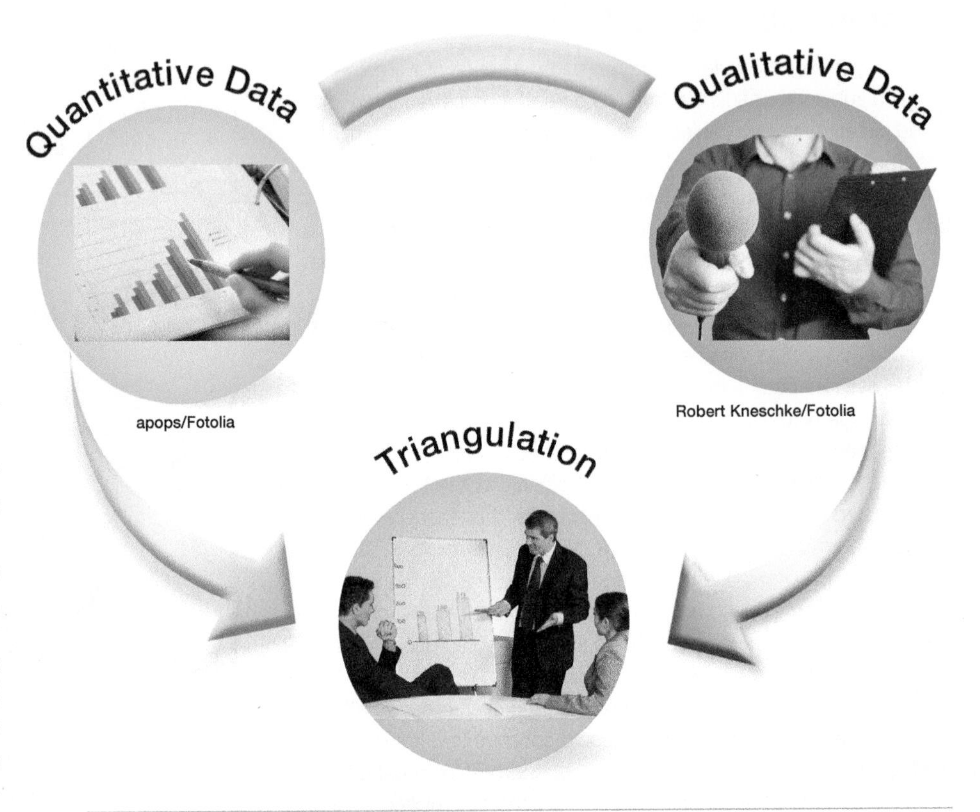

<<< **Here's how someone might use the process of triangulation to study an issue—a particular cult, for example.**

EVALUATING WEB SOURCES

Accuracy	Authority	Currency	Purpose	Relevance
The reliability of the information.	The source of the information.	The timeliness of the information.	The possible bias present in the information.	The depth and importance of the information.
• Is the information correct? • Can it be verified from other sources? • Is the information cited? • Are there spelling, grammatical, or typographical errors? • Has the information been refereed?	• Who is the author of the page? • What are the author's credentials? • What institution is the author affiliated with? • Is that producing institution reputable? • Is there an email address or other contact information? • .ca—Canadian-based website • .gov—U.S. government • .edu—U.S. educational institution • .org—Organizations or special interest groups, usually nonprofit • .com, .net, .biz—companies, pretty much everything else	• Is there a date of publication or last update? • When was the page created? • Do the links work? • Is the page maintained on a regular basis? • Is the information considered current for your topic/research?	• Is this information meant to teach? Inform? Persuade? Entertain? • Do the authors/sponsors make their intentions or purpose clear? • Is the information fact? Opinion? Propaganda? • What other websites are linked to this one? • Is there advertising on the site? What is being advertised? • Does the point of view appear to be objective and impartial? • Are there political, ideological, cultural, religious, institutional, or personal biases?	• Does the information relate to your topic or answer your question? • Who is the intended audience, and is the information at an appropriate level (not too basic or advanced) for your needs? • Does the site claim to be comprehensive? How does it meet those claims? • Have you looked at a variety of sources before determining that this is one you will use? • Why is this site preferable to other resource types or formats?

Source: The CRAAP Test. Reprinted with permission of Sarah Blakeslee.

tative and quantitative methods. For example, if you want to study the influence of hip-hop music on white, teenage, suburban culture, you might look at the quantitative data of hip-hop CD sales among white teens. Afterward, you would conduct in-depth qualitative interviews with the consumers who buy hip-hop CDs to gauge how the music influences their lives. When you follow this process, you're triangulating the issue, or studying it from multiple points of view. Triangulation allows you to better explain a social event because you use two or more methods to study it.[30]

If you relied on only one method, you might draw an inappropriate conclusion about a social issue because all the facts would not be not available.

Triangulation helps researchers use the strengths of one approach to compensate for the weaknesses in another.

5 **Analyze Results** The fifth step of the scientific method, analyzing results, often involves statistical analysis. Because sociological research can delve into very complex statistics, it's important that you learn a few basics that will help you confidently confront any statistics you encounter now or in the future.

CENTRAL TENDENCY is the middle of the distribution of a variable.

MEAN is an average.

MEDIAN refers to the midpoint in a distribution of numbers.

MODE refers to the most common value in a distribution.

MEASURES OF CENTRAL TENDENCY

You know how news outlets report on the national price of a litre of gasoline? Sometimes, the price you hear on the radio ends up being lower—or higher—than the one at the pump. This is because the reporters were only finding a measure of **central tendency**. To put it more simply, researchers look at the distribution of a variable and find the middle. There are three measures of central tendency: mean, median, and mode. Imagine that a student received the test scores listed below. How would you calculate the mean, median, and mode?

John's Test Scores

Test 1: 90

Test 2: 70

Test 3: 80

Test 4: 20

Test 5: 80

Mean

A **mean** is an average. You add up all the scores and then divide by the number of scores. John's mean score is 68. Does this average accurately measure his performance? He failed one exam but received a C or better on all other tests. It doesn't seem fair for one bad grade to leave John with a D average for the class. That's the problem with calculating mean scores. Extremely high or low scores (called *outliers*) can have dramatic impacts on statistical means.

$$90 + 70 + 80 + 20 + 80 = 340$$

$$340 \div 5 = 68$$

$$\text{Mean} = 68$$

Median

When you're cruising down the highway—after blowing your savings on that full tank of gas—you might notice that the northbound lanes are separated from southbound ones by a median. In statistical analysis, the **median** refers to the midpoint in a distribution of numbers. If you line up the numbers from lowest to highest, the median is the one in the middle. The median does not vary much when you have extremely high or extremely low values in the distribution. John's median score is 80.

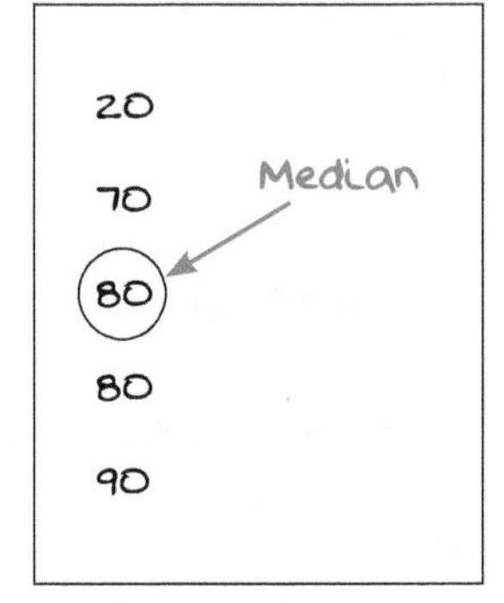

Mode

The **mode** refers to the most common value in a distribution. Extremely high or low scores do not impact this measure either. It's possible to have more than one mode in a distribution. In our simple example, 80 is the mode because it occurs twice. You will notice that the modal score in this example is the same as the median. Both give John a final grade of an A. Which measure of central tendency best shows John's performance?

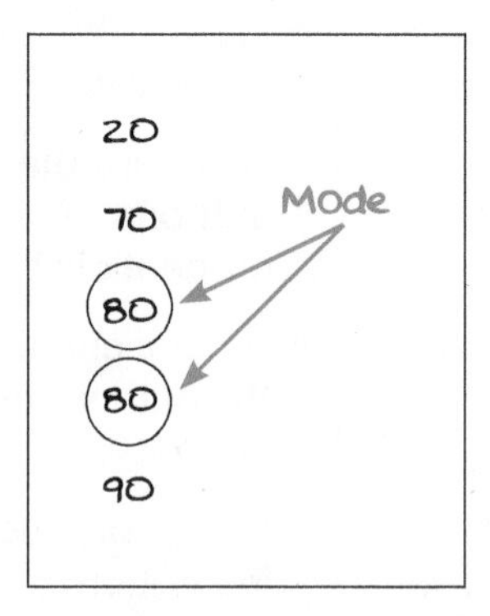

Most colleges have a policy of using averages to calculate grades. However, when I review grades at the end of the semester, I frequently take all three measures of central tendency into account. In most cases, the mean is close to the median and the mode. However, an extreme score can alter the mean score dramatically, as in John's case. If you have a low score on an exam, consider asking your professor to consider other measures of central tendency to calculate your performance. It might just raise your grade!

EVALUATING DATA

Evaluating and interpreting data are important parts of conducting research. What's the use of gathering data if you don't know what to do with them? It's vital to be able to make sense of the data you collect. The tables and graphs you will encounter during the research process may seem daunting at first. But it's really not as complicated as you might think, as long as you know what steps to take.

HOW TO READ A TABLE

The table on page 42 provides data on the proportion of people who intend to marry or remarry, by marital status and region of residence in Canada in 2011. What do the data in the table tell you?

If you struggled to make sense of the table, don't worry. You're not alone. Fortunately, the four simple steps that follow will help make reading this and other tables second nature to you:

1. Carefully read the title of the table. Ask yourself: What do I expect the table to show me?
2. Notice the structure of the table. This one is made up of columns and rows. Each column represents a specific category, such as Region or Marriage Intentions, and each row lists data from a geographic region.
3. Notice that the main columns are divided into subgroups such as Single and Common-law.
4. Read any text and notes provided below the table. This table has an important note. At the bottom of the table, you see the phrase "Percentages may not add to 100%. Totals include the 'don't know' and 'refused' categories, which are not shown in the table."
5. Notice that the source note indicates where the data come from.

RESEARCH METHODS: HOW DO THEY MEASURE UP?

Method	Description	Pros	Cons
Survey	**An investigation of the opinions or behaviours of a group of people by asking them questions**	• **A lot of information can be collected from a large group at relatively low cost**	• **Measures what people say they do, not what the actually do**
Experiments	**Control of variables in order to test causes and effects**	• **Gives researcher control over other factors** • **Good for showing cause and effect**	• **Conducted under artificial conditions**
Field research	**Research conducted in a natural setting**	• **Observes social behaviour in a natural environment**	• **Can be time-consuming**
Secondary data analysis	**Use and analysis of data that others have collected**	• **Inexpensive** • **Reduces time spent collecting data**	• **Data not collected for the purpose for which you are using it**

Now review the table again. Do the data make more sense this time?

6 **Share and Publish Results** Doing research is important; however, if we don't share what we learn with others, our work is meaningless. Sharing allows others to read and use your findings in their own research, which ultimately expands the base of knowledge.

Publishing requires an appropriate writing style. There are many accepted academic and publication styles, including ASA, APA, and MLA. Check out these links:

- For ASA, see www.asanet.org/students/Quick%20Style%20guide.pdf.
- For APA, see www.apastyle.org/learn/index.aspx.
- For basics on MLA, see the Canadian sources http://library.mcmaster.ca/guides/mla.pdf, www.mcgill.ca/files/library/mla.pdf, or http://library.concordia.ca/help/howto/mla.php.

Most sociology research follows the American Sociological Association style. In the ASA style guide, you'll find standards for using language and directions on how to cite sources appropriately. If you need a quick style guide, be sure to visit the ASA website, at www.asanet.org.

valterdias/Fotolia

ETHICS is a system of values or principles that guide one's behaviour.

Ethical Concerns

Have you ever been asked to do something that violated your personal beliefs or values? Of course you have. Sociologists struggle with this issue all the time. Sometimes, a sociologist's findings have the potential to hurt or embarrass the human subjects of a particular study. Deciding how to protect human subjects is a major concern for sociological researchers.

Ethics is a system of values or principles that guide one's behaviour. For some, it means following the law, and for others, it means trusting one's gut. In Canada, the three big federal research agencies—the Canadian Institutes of Health Research, the Natural Sciences and Engineering Research Council, and the Social Sciences and Humanities Research Council—have created a document known as the *Tri-Council Policy Statement: Ethical Conduct for Research Involving Humans*, or TCPS.[31] The TCPS identifies three core principles in research ethics[32]:

1 **Respect for Persons** recognizes the intrinsic value of human beings and the respect and consideration they are due.

2 **Concern for Welfare** means that researchers should aim to protect the welfare of participants, and in some circumstances to promote that welfare. To do so, researchers must ensure that participants are not exposed to unnecessary risks.

3 **Justice** refers to the obligation to treat people fairly and equitably.

The Canadian Sociological Association's (CSA's) multipoint Code of Ethics[33] reaches out into the following areas: (1) organizing and initiating research; (2) protecting people in the research environment; (3) informed consent—"As far as possible, research should be based on the freely given informed consent of those studied"; (4) covert research and deception—"Deception should not be used where another methodology would accomplish the research objectives"; (5) dissemination of findings—"Researchers have an obligation to disseminate results openly except those likely to endanger research participants or to violate their anonymity or confidentiality"; (6) relations

PROPORTION OF PEOPLE WHO INTEND TO MARRY OR REMARRY, BY MARITAL STATUS AND REGION OF RESIDENCE, CANADA, 2011

Region	Marriage Intentions (persons never married)			Remarriage Intentions (persons who have already been married)				Total Intentions
	Single	Common-law	Total	Common-law	Divorced	Widowed	Total	
Canada	Percentage							
Yes	62	39	56	24	10	2	10	44
No	20	38	24	50	66	89	71	37
Uncertain	17	22	18	25	23	8	18	18
Atlantic	Percentage							
Yes	62	56	61	34	10	n/a	10	46
No	22	25	23	36	68	89	71	37
Uncertain	15	17	16	32	22	10	18	16
Quebec	Percentage							
Yes	44	30	38	14	6	n/a	7	30
No	33	46	39	66	74	91	77	48
Uncertain	22	24	23	19	19	7	15	21
Ontario	Percentage							
Yes	69	44	65	27	11	1	10	51
No	16	30	18	43	61	88	70	31
Uncertain	14	23	16	29	26	8	18	16
Prairies	Percentage							
Yes	67	53	64	31	13	2	13	51
No	16	26	17	38	64	85	66	30
Uncertain	17	20	17	27	22	11	19	18
British Columbia	Percentage							
Yes	64	51	62	34	11		11	48
No	16	34	19	38	62	90	69	33
Uncertain	19	14	18	26	26	9	19	19

Note: Percentages may not add to 100%. Totals include the "don't know" and "refused" categories, which are not shown in the table.

Source: Statistics Canada, General Social Survey, 2011, retrieved from www.statcan.gc.ca/pub/89-650-x/2012001/tbl/tbl01-eng.htm. This does not constitute an endorsement by Statistics Canada of this product.

with colleagues and the discipline; (7) faculty appointments; (8) relations with students; (9) harassment and exploitative relations; and (10) relations with institutions.

RESEARCH ETHICS IN OPERATION

Consider for a moment the scope of the above-mentioned principles and guidelines for ethical behaviour. Do you think research practices can easily be labelled as either ethical or unethical? Do you think that Eileen Barker was using unethical practices in her Unification Church study? Or do you think she succeeded in respecting her subjects' dignity and worth?

The issues raised by sociological field investigations helped create the need for codes of research ethics in the first place and prompted federal governments to play a role in research ethics. Earlier, we mentioned the *Tri-Council Policy Statement: Ethical Conduct for Research Involving Humans* (TCPS); these days in Canada, researchers or institutions that receive funding from any of the main federal research funding agencies are obliged to use the TCPS as a condition of their funding.[34]

Nonetheless, sociologists do not all agree about the ways in which studies should be conducted. Some researchers who study deviant behaviours, for example, suggest that deception is essential in collecting accurate information. The issue of how to use deception is a critical question in field research. If you fully disclose what you are doing, how can you be sure the Hawthorne effect is not affecting your results? If you deceive, how can you protect the subjects' dignity and worth? This is why a debate on ethics rages on within the sociological research community today.

So the question is: How can you avoid ethical dilemmas? One way is to get your subjects' consent. Hand out an informed consent form before the study begins. Informed consent means that the research subjects understand the general purpose of the study and its main features. If the researcher is using deception, subjects deserve to know when they will find out the truth. Subjects must know that they can cease their participation at any time without risk to themselves.

Sociologists try to measure and record social behavior as accurately as possible while respecting the rights and dignity of the people they are studying.

Monkey Business/Fotolia

think sociologically: HOW DO SOCIOLOGISTS USE RESEARCH METHODS?

No single research method applies only to functionalism, conflict theory, symbolic interactionism, or feminist theory. But these theoretical frameworks do lend themselves to using types of data in different ways.

Research Methods and the Four Paradigms

Although our theoretical paradigm does not dictate the research method we use, it does affect how we interpret data. Conflict theorists and functionalists can look at the same data and come to different conclusions. Imagine that a conflict theorist and a functionalist studied data showing the rise of income inequality in a community. In other words, they studied the widening of the gap between the "haves" and the "have-nots" in the community. How might the two sociologists interpret the data? Remember, both functionalists and conflict theorists have a macro orientation, so they study how a certain issue affects the whole society and not individual people. However, functionalists examine how a certain issue functions in a society, whereas conflict theorists study how the unequal distribution of goods affects society.

Functionalists studying the data might suggest that income inequality serves the society well, as more rich people are able to start businesses and invest in long-term projects that will one day make society better for everyone. These businesses might one day be able to employ the poor members of the community and help them rise above their situation. Functionalists would not necessarily view income inequality as a negative phenomenon. Conflict theorists, meanwhile, might suggest that the same numbers show that the rich exploit the poor and that this exploitation is only getting worse. You can see how two researchers can look at the same data and come to different conclusions.

Because symbolic interactionists have a micro orientation, they might focus more on how the income inequality affected people at an individual level. These researchers might conduct interviews in order to learn more about wealthy individuals' perceptions of the poor and low-income individuals' perceptions of the rich. They might observe how being poor affects an individual's lifestyle—for example, how the lack of money affects the kind of clothes that a person wears or the place he or she lives. Like functionalists and conflict theorists, feminist theorists would also look at quantitative data on inequality, but they would focus on the inequality of women relative to men. They might also adopt a micro orientation that would examine how women in particular experience poverty. Here, too, you can see the same set of data can be interpreted differently, depending on the theoretical lens through which the data are viewed.

discover sociology in action: HOW IS RESEARCH INVOLVED IN SOCIAL POLICY?

The Canadian Sociological Association's Code of Ethics calls upon sociologists to "enter into dialogue with the communities we research."[35] Working on social policies and participating in community learning projects are just two of the ways sociologists can better the community.

Social Policy and Statistics

Social policies arise because people recognize a problem and take action to deal with it. Often the first step is to get more information about the problem, which involves analyzing statistics. When consuming statistical evidence, it's important that you:

- **Beware the Headline.** Sensationalism can lead to a newspaper headline like MURDER RATE WORST IN DECADES even when the actual rate is falling. The word *rate* is shorter than *numbers* and so might be easier to use in a headline, but it doesn't mean the same thing.
- **Check Term Definitions.** Each researcher makes decisions about how to measure certain constructs. Beware of any study that uses value-laden terms such as *conservative* or *liberal* without properly defining them. What you consider "liberal" might not be interpreted the same way by your neighbour or a community in another province.
- **Find Out Who Funded the Study.** Groups that fund research often have an interest in the outcome. You should always consider the possibility that stakeholders want to use research to support their positions. Remember, objectivity is the foundation of sociological research. Be on the lookout for groups or individuals that have ulterior motives.
- **Look for Spuriousness and Selection Effects.** When reading research, ask yourself: Could something else be causing this result? Has the researcher really looked at every possible angle?
- **Look for Agendas.** Agendas are often political in nature. Many times politicians quote statistics, but that doesn't mean they're true. Regardless of party affiliation, many politicians choose to manipulate statistics to make their claims appear stronger than they actually are.[36]

ACTIVITIES

1. Check out the online resources at your school's library. Which search engines does your school suggest are best for sociological research? Make a list. Then write a paragraph evaluating each one.
2. Conduct a class survey. Talk with your professor and create a 10-question survey to give to your classmates about something that interests you.
3. Have a class discussion about whether the end justifies the means in social research. Can a researcher truly hope to find out about a subculture without deception?

CHAPTER

get the topic: WHAT ARE RESEARCH METHODS?

Key Terms

research methods are the scientific procedures that sociologists use to conduct research and collect data about a particular topic. *31*

objectivity is the ability to conduct research without allowing personal biases or prejudices to influence findings. *31*

verstehen means understanding the meaning of action from the actor's point of view. *31*

literature review is a study of relevant academic articles and information. *31*

hypothesis is a statement about how variables relate. *32*

variable is a characteristic or trait that can be measured. *32*

independent variables are variables that are deliberately manipulated in an experiment. *32*

dependent variables are the response to the manipulated variable. *32*

control variables are variables that are kept constant to accurately test the impact of an independent variable. *32*

concepts are abstract ideas that refer to objects, ideas, or behaviours. *32*

operationalizing is turning abstract ideas into something measurable. *32*

reliable means you get consistent results each time you measure. *32*

validity means that you're actually measuring what you set out to measure. *32*

causal relationship is a relationship in which one condition or variable leads to a certain consequence. *33*

correlation is an indication that when one factor changes, so does another. *33*

positive correlation describes two variables that move in the same direction. *33*

negative correlation describes two variables that move in opposite directions. *33*

spurious correlation occurs when two variables appear to be related but both may have an underlying cause. *33*

research design refers to the process used to collect data. *33*

comparative studies use data from different sources in order to compare them against each other. *33*

cross-sectional studies look at an event at a single point in time.

longitudinal studies include data from observations over time using a cohort. *33*

cohort is a specific group of people used in a study. *33*

quantitative data refer to data based on numbers. *33*

qualitative data include words, pictures, photos, or any other type of information that comes to the researcher in a non-numeric form. *33*

population is the entire group of people you wish to describe. *34*

parameter is a number that describes a population. *34*

sample is a subset of a population. *34*

statistic is a number that describes a sample. *34*

representative sample is a sample in which the relevant characteristics of the sample are the same as the characteristics of the population. *34*

generalization is the extent that what is learned from a sample can be applied to the population from which the sample is taken. *34*

random sample is a sample chosen so that each member of the population has the same chance of being selected. *35*

convenience sample is a nonrandom sample of people conveniently or easily available to the researcher. *35*

bias is the likelihood that a nonrepresentative sample may lead to inaccurate results. *35*

survey is an investigation of the opinions or behaviours of a group of people by asking them questions. *35*

experiment is a method in which researchers control variables in order to test causes and effects. *36*

Hawthorne effect occurs when people behave differently because they know they are being studied. *37*

field research is research conducted in a natural setting. *37*

participant observation is a type of field research in which the researcher poses as a person who is normally in the environment. *37*

case studies are investigations of one person or event in detail. *38*

ethnography is a research method that aims to understand the social perspective and cultural values of a particular group by participating in or getting to know their activities in detail. *38*

secondary data analysis is the process of using and analyzing data that others have collected. *38*

content analysis is a type of research in which the sociologist looks for common words or themes in newspapers, books, or structured interviews. *38*

triangulation is the process of using multiple approaches to study a phenomenon. *38*

central tendency is the middle of the distribution of a variable. *40*

mean is an average. *40*

median refers to the midpoint in a distribution of numbers. *40*

mode refers to the most common value in a distribution. *40*

ethics is a system of values or principles that guide one's behaviour. *41*

Sample Test Questions

These multiple-choice questions are similar to those found in the test bank that accompanies this textbook.

1. "Children who participate in organized sports are less likely to suffer from obesity later in life." This statement is an example of a
   - **a.** Hawthorne effect.
   - **b.** positive correlation.
   - **c.** negative correlation.
   - **d.** case study.
2. Which of the following is the first research step?
   - **a.** Collect the data
   - **b.** Review the literature
   - **c.** Deciding on a topic
   - **d.** Developing a hypothesis
3. Which research method observes people in natural social situations?
   - **a.** Field research
   - **b.** Survey
   - **c.** Content analysis
   - **d.** Experiment
4. Which of the following is not a core principle in Canadian research ethics?
   - **a.** Justice
   - **b.** Concern for welfare of participants
   - **c.** Timeliness
   - **d.** Respect for persons
5. Which measure of central tendency is affected by extreme high or low scores?
   - **a.** Mean
   - **b.** Mode
   - **c.** Middle
   - **d.** Median

ANSWERS: 1. c; 2. c; 3. a; 4. c; 5. a

ESSAY

1. If you are doing a study on cults, what kinds of ethical issues should you consider?
2. What criteria should you keep in mind when evaluating Web sources?
3. Suppose you are conducting a study of how people of different racial and ethnic backgrounds feel about a particular political candidate. How might you collect quantitative data for this study? How might you collect qualitative data?
4. How did Morris Freilich approach his ethnographic study about Mohawk skywalkers?
5. Provide an example of a hypothesis. Next, explain how you would develop a research design to test that hypothesis.

WHERE TO START YOUR RESEARCH PAPER

The best source for Canadian Statistics is the Statistics Canada website: www.statcan.gc.ca/start-debut-eng.html.

Other good sources are

http://srds.ca/index.htm.

www.ipsos.ca/en/.

www.legermarketing.com/canada_en/home.asp.

http://ejournals.library.ualberta.ca/index.php/CJS/index.

For more on music and suicide:

http://onlinelibrary.wiley.com/doi/10.1111/j.1943-278X.2012.00120.x/full.

Remember to check www.thethinkspot.ca for additional information, downloadable flashcards, and other helpful resources.

Garry Black/Alamy

CULTURE

WHAT IS CULTURE?
HOW DO THE SOCIOLOGICAL PERSPECTIVES INTERPRET CULTURE?
HOW DOES SOCIAL POLICY INFLUENCE CULTURE?

"A Canadian is . . . always unsure of what it means to be Canadian. Maybe this is a strength. Maybe it is evidence of our tolerance and pluralism and of our enlightened postmodernism. Let a thousand identities bloom! Or maybe it just reveals our hollow core—a vacuity at the centre of our soul. Outside of Quebec, at least, we do not really know who we are or what we represent—other than that we have made ourselves remarkably comfortable in a cold land, and that we are good at hockey.

"A country with a clear identity and self-understanding would find it easier to develop a consensus around its *projet de société.* To the extent that Canadians do not have a clear identity, it hampers our larger social task of deciding what kind of society we want, and then getting on with building it.

"Still, we have created an extraordinary country, one that regularly ranks among the very best in terms of quality of life. People from around the world strive to come here to enjoy our economic opportunity, social tolerance, and political freedoms. Canadians today are among the most fortunate human beings to have ever lived. But sometimes it seems to have happened almost by accident—as if we have created this remarkable country more by luck and happenstance than by consensus and design."[1]

A Framework *for the* Individual

CHAPTER 03

In his book ***What Is a Canadian? Forty-Three Thought-Provoking Responses***, Irvin Studin has collected 43 essays from various Canadians in which they give various insights into culture in Canada.

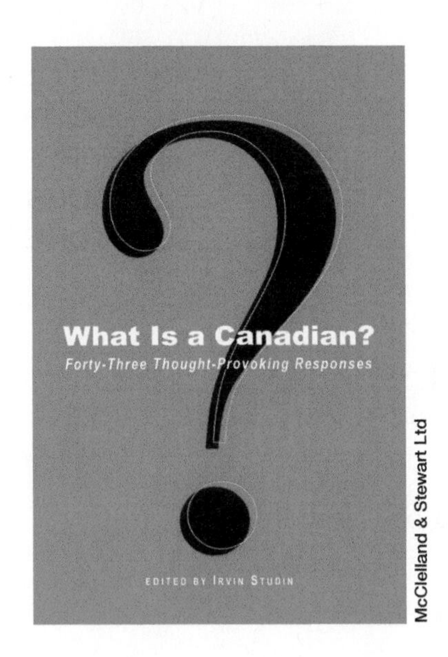
What Is a Canadian?
Forty-Three Thought-Provoking Responses
EDITED BY IRVIN STUDIN
McClelland & Stewart Ltd

I deliberately wrote "culture in Canada" instead of "Canadian culture." Canada is often described as a multicultural society, but does this mean that there is no unique "Canadian culture"? Keep this question in mind as you read through this chapter. See if your answer changes.

get the topic: WHAT IS CULTURE?

CULTURE is the symbols, values, norms, and material objects that societies create.

CULTURAL TRANSMISSION is culture passing from one generation to the next.

The languages we speak, the foods we eat, how we dress, and the way we do things may seem perfectly natural to us. If you want to think like a sociologist, you'll need to understand not only what **culture** is but also how culture affects our lives. We use culture in order to relate to the natural world and to each other.

Because we see the world through the lens of our culture, it's easy for us to take our own culture for granted, accepting it without much thought. In fact, we're often not even aware of the ways in which culture guides (or misguides) our thoughts and actions. The fact that you may speak only English, for example, is indicative of the culture in which you grew up. Had the French run the English out of Canada in the 1600s, we might all be saying "Salut!" instead of "How's it goin', eh?" The tangible and intangible aspects of culture have a significant impact on your daily life.

Cultural Transmission

Culture passes from one generation to the next. We call this phenomenon **cultural transmission**. Thanks to cultural transmission, you can use information others have learned to improve your own life. Cultural transmission also helps spread technology: Scientific studies of electricity

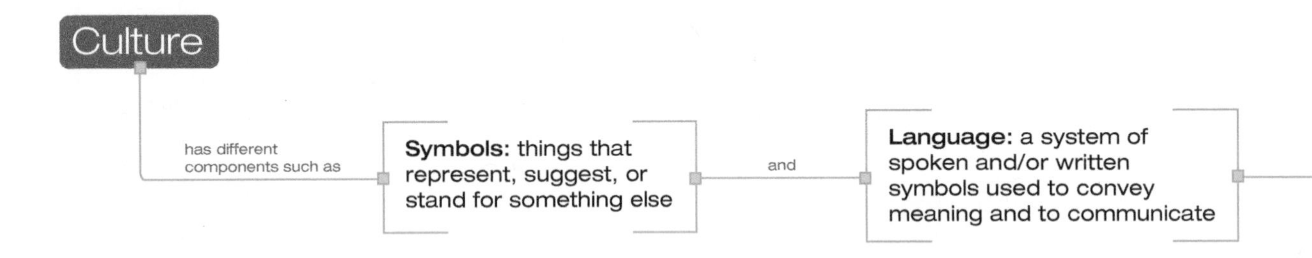
Culture
has different components such as
Symbols: things that represent, suggest, or stand for something else
and
Language: a system of spoken and/or written symbols used to convey meaning and to communicate

Invention: something that is deliberately changed or made to produce something new
Discovery: better understanding or observation of something that already exists
Diffusion: the transmission of an item or a method of doing things from one culture to another
Cultural lag: the time between when technological changes occure and when social and cultural changes occur

components of cultural change are

CHANGE AHEAD

Arcady/Fotolia

Ethnocentrism: using your own culture to judge another culture
Xenophobia: fear and hostility toward people from other cultures
Xenocentrism: perceiving other cultures as superior to your own
Cultural relativism: making a deliberate effort to appreciate other cultures without prejudice
Cultural shock: an emotional response to the differences between the cultures
Cultural imperialism: a situation in which powerful cultural industries dominate other cultures

and can lead to

and the development of microwave technology and the microchip made today's cell phones and computers possible.

Material Culture

One category of culture is **material culture**: the physical items that we use. The jewellery, art, tools, clothing, architecture, and machines a society creates are all examples of material culture. Of course, the natural resources available to a culture can influence that culture's creations. For example, while seven countries (Canada, the United States, Japan, Russia, Germany, France, and the United Kingdom) use more than 37 percent of the world's electricity and oil, these countries combined hold only about 12 percent of the world's population. What do these statistics tell you about material culture? On a tour of these countries, you'd be likely to stumble across plenty of cars, air conditioners, heaters, blow dryers, and a host of other modern conveniences. If you took a trip to Nigeria, though, you'd notice that a lack of access to energy also influences material culture. Nigeria is the eighth largest country in the world by population, yet it ranks 69th in the world's electricity use and 45th in the world's use of oil. Few people there own a car, and many live without regular access to electricity.[2]

Nonmaterial Culture

Not all elements of culture are tangible. **Nonmaterial culture** consists of the nonphysical products of society, such as values and beliefs. Traditions, language, music, the belief in gender equality, and valuing the democratic process are all examples of nonmaterial culture.

COMPONENTS OF CULTURE

Every human society has developed a culture based on certain fundamental components. The specific form of these components differs from culture to culture, and this is what produces the rich diversity of cultural practices that we see across the world's societies. However, all cultures have the same components—they all have material objects, they all use symbols and develop language, they all have values that tell people what is good and bad, and they all have norms that tell people how to behave.

SYMBOLS

What do you think of when you see the Canadian flag? To most of us, it's more than just a piece of cloth—it's a symbol. **Symbols** are things that represent, suggest, or stand for something else. They can be words, gestures, or objects, and they often represent abstract or complex concepts. For example, wedding rings represent a legal bond of marriage and an emotional bond of love between two people.

Symbols are an important part of culture because they allow us to communicate. Each culture determines the meaning of its own symbols and uses these symbols to share thoughts and concepts with others. If you know what Timbits and double-doubles are, then you recognize these symbols of Canadian culture. When the interpretation of symbols is shared, interaction usually occurs smoothly. Misunderstandings and other problems may occur when people interpret symbols differently.

In 2008, one of the recommendations of the Bouchard-Taylor Commission—which was set up to gather public input on the issue of "reasonable accommodation" in Quebec—was that the crucifix in the Quebec National Assembly should be removed because it was a symbol of one particular religious group, and the state should be neutral. However, Premier Jean Charest argued that the crucifix represents 350 years of history in Quebec, and he was not about to erase that important heritage.[3] Symbols are powerful things.

MATERIAL CULTURE consists of the physical items that we use.

NONMATERIAL CULTURE consists of the nonphysical products of society, such as values and beliefs.

SYMBOLS are things that represent, suggest, or stand for something else.

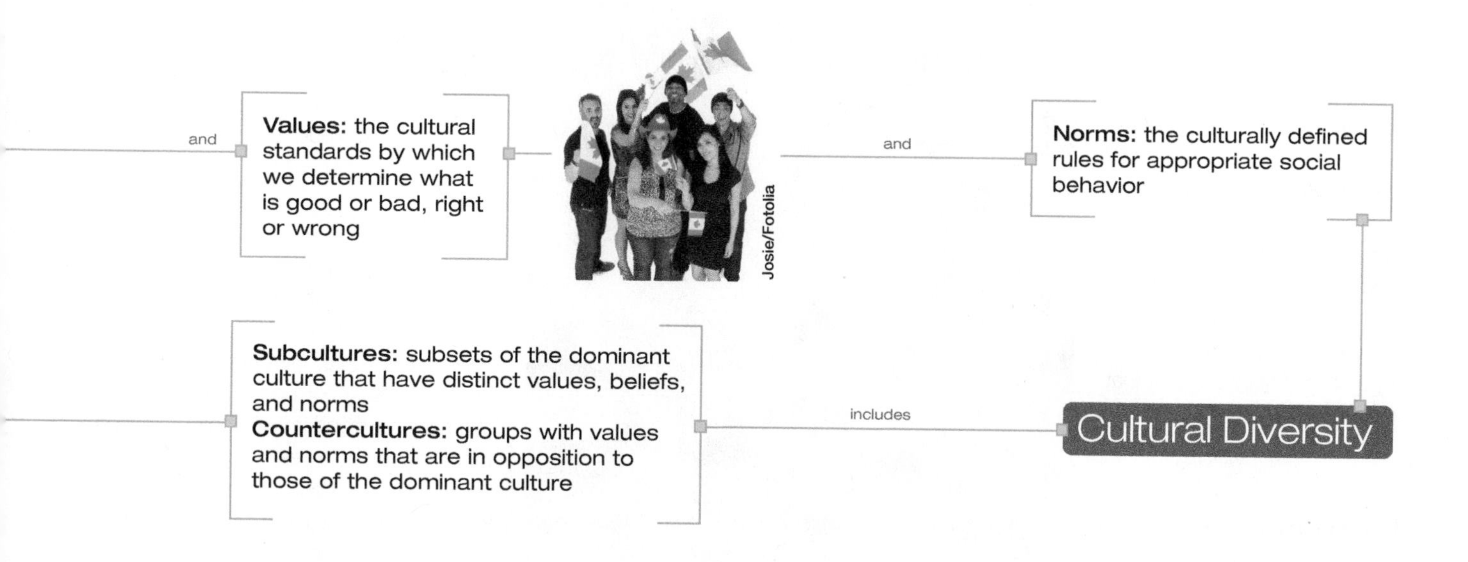
and
Values: the cultural standards by which we determine what is good or bad, right or wrong
Josie/Fotolia
and
Norms: the culturally defined rules for appropriate social behavior
Subcultures: subsets of the dominant culture that have distinct values, beliefs, and norms
Countercultures: groups with values and norms that are in opposition to those of the dominant culture
includes
Cultural Diversity

LANGUAGE is a system of spoken and/or written symbols used to convey meaning and to communicate.

THE SAPIR-WHORF HYPOTHESIS is a hypothesis that the structure of a language determines a native speaker's perception and categorization of experience.

GESTURES are symbols we make using our bodies, such as facial expressions, hand movements, eye contact, and other types of body language.

VALUES are a part of a society's nonmaterial culture that represent cultural standards by which we determine what is good or bad, right or wrong.

LANGUAGE

Language is a system of spoken and/or written symbols used to convey meaning and to communicate. Some languages exist only in the oral tradition, while other languages are expressed through both speech and writing systems, but all cultures use some form of language. The United Nations reports that currently there are more than 6000 different languages on the planet. Due to conquest, commerce, assimilation, and failure to write down some languages, about half of these are in danger of extinction.[4]

Two main factors determine the number of speakers of a language: population size and colonial history. China and India are the world's largest countries by population, a fact that single-handedly explains the large percentage of people who speak Mandarin Chinese and Hindi. The English language is widely spoken throughout the world, but this has little to do with Great Britain's population size. If you've ever heard the phrase, "The sun never sets on the British Empire," you know that the British Empire once ruled territory on every continent. As Great Britain colonized countries around the world from the 1700s to the early 1900s, English was introduced to these places.

Universal Grammar

The famous linguist Noam Chomsky suggests that human beings' ability to use language comes from common roots.[5] All languages contain what Chomsky calls a "universal grammar." This term refers not to particular language rules but to the way in which languages are constructed. Chomsky theorizes that, among other things, commonalities in sentence construction and word pronunciation connect languages throughout the world. Furthermore, he says, universal grammar begins in children at about the same age, regardless of culture. Chomsky's observations suggest that humans have an innate need for language.

RENAULT Philippe/hemis.fr/Hemis/Alamy

>>> The crucifix in the Quebec National Assembly is a powerful symbol.

Research by Coppola and Newport supports much of Chomsky's theory. In their study of deaf subjects who were isolated and knew no official sign language, Coppola and Newport found that these people's "home sign language" (i.e., language that they developed themselves) follows a predictable grammatical style.[6] For instance, the subject of a sentence generally appears at the beginning of the statement. Such findings point to an innate logic in the construction of language and support Chomsky's theory of universal grammar.

Language doesn't just advance our knowledge; it also brings us together by helping us create social consensus, or agreement. If you and I were to meet, we could use language to exchange ideas, debate, or decide on a course of action. Language is inherently social: It serves as a tool for sharing past memories, making future plans, and building and maintaining relationships.

The Sapir-Whorf Hypothesis

It's difficult to overstate the importance of language in our lives. In 1929, anthropologist Edward Sapir, after studying many different languages and the people who spoke them, suggested that language and thinking patterns are directly connected.[7] This idea was further developed by Benjamin Whorf, one of Sapir's students. It is now known as the **Sapir-Whorf hypothesis**. The Sapir-Whorf hypothesis proposes two key points:

1. The differences in the structure of language parallel differences in the thinking of the people who speak languages.
2. The structure of a language strongly influences the speaker's worldview.

Have you ever considered how much language actually influences our thinking? I was out shopping with my daughter one day because she wanted to find a pink shirt. I saw a shirt on the rack and held it up and asked, "What about this one?" She just stared at me and said "Dad, I said I need a *pink* shirt." I said, "Well, this one is pink," to which she answered, "No it's not. It's fuchsia." When she finally did find a pink shirt, I could *see* a difference between the pink shirt and the fuchsia shirt. However, my limited vocabulary meant that I *thought* that both shirts were a colour called pink. Ongoing research into the Sapir-Whorf hypothesis suggests that because language influences thinking, it also influences culture.

GESTURES

Although language is a primary component of nonmaterial culture, it's not the only one. Another symbol system that differs by culture is gesture. **Gestures** are symbols we make using our bodies, such as facial expressions, hand movements, eye contact, and other types of body language. A gesture's symbolic meaning can vary widely between cultures. I once interpreted a Pakistani student's lack of eye contact as distrust or boredom until I realized that in her culture, making eye contact with someone, particularly a male teacher, is considered rude.

>>> **Language influences how we perceive things,** which in turn influences our experience of the world. **Our experiences help us develop language, but our use of language also influences our experience.**[8]

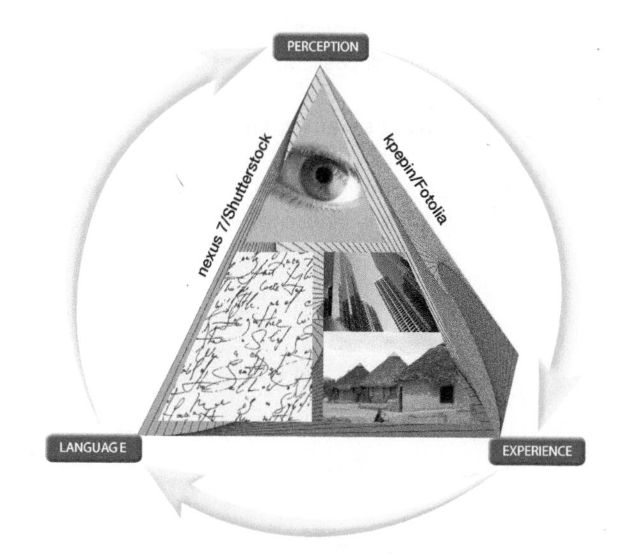

VALUES

Values are a part of a society's nonmaterial culture. They represent the cultural standards by which we determine what is good or bad, right or wrong. Values may be specific, such as children listening to their parents, or they may be more general, such as belief in democracy or gender equality. Because societies are capable of growth and change, it's possible for values to change over time.

IDEAL VS. REAL CULTURE

Is there a difference between culture as we'd like it to be and culture as it really is? Often, the answer is yes. Ideal culture represents the values to which a society aspires, and real culture represents a society's actual behaviours. Democracy, for example, has always been part of the ideal culture of Canada, but voter turnouts for the 2000, 2004, 2008, and 2012 federal elections indicate that only about 60 percent of the eligible population exercised their democratic right and turned out to vote.[9]

Canadian Values

On November 1, 1990, the federal government announced the creation of the *Citizens' Forum on Canada's Future.* The forum's task was to get Canadians talking and to listen to the people to find out what kind of country Canadians wanted for themselves and their children. The comments were collected in a variety of ways: a toll-free Idea Line so that Canadians could call from wherever they lived, group discussions held in communities all across the country, and special kits for individuals to use alone.

After analyzing and organizing the hundreds of thousands of comments, the forum commissioners identified seven major issues facing Canada:

- Canadian identity and values
- Quebec and Canadian unity
- Official languages
- Aboriginal issues
- Cultural diversity
- The Canadian economy
- Responsible leadership and participatory democracy

The forum commissioners also identified seven "Canadian values." Many Canadians spoke or wrote eloquently to the forum on the subject of the core values they saw as essential elements of Canadian society. The following list represents the core values that emerged very strongly from participants in all regions of Canada:

- **Belief in equality and fairness in a democratic society:** Canadians are fortunate to live in a country that allows democratic elections. This is important to Canadians. Canadians also value the principles of equality and fairness to all groups in society.
- **Belief in consultation and dialogue:** This forum was an example of consultation and dialogue. Given the number of people who participated, it is obvious that Canadians value the opportunity to talk with one another and to be consulted on important issues.
- **Importance of accommodation and tolerance:** Canada is a multicultural society. Many different groups wish to sustain their own culture, and even different regions of the country have different interests (this is most prominent in Quebec). Canadians said that, as a country, we should strive to be accommodating and tolerant of all groups and regions, as long as they also demonstrate their own acceptance of accommodation and tolerance as key values.
- **Support for diversity:** Diversity in Canada has a number of facets, including linguistic, regional, ethnic, and cultural differences. Canadians repeatedly emphasized that Canada's diversity is one of the most important things they value about this country.
- **Compassion and generosity:** Canada is known for its compassionate and generous character, as exemplified by our universal and

Mark Peterson/Corbis

<<< **This stop sign is a familiar part of material culture. The three languages (Cree, French, and English) are a part of the nonmaterial culture of the region.**

extensive social services, our health care system, our pensions, our willingness to welcome refugees, and our commitment to regional economic equalization.

- **Attachment to Canada's natural beauty:** While the North has long been part of Canadian myth and legend, participants indicated that Canada's unspoiled natural beauty is a matter of great importance to them and that it is threatened by inadequate attention to protecting our environment.

NORMS are culturally defined rules for appropriate social behavior.
SANCTION is a reward for following a norm or a punishment for violating it.

- **Our world image—Commitment to freedom, peace, and non-violent change:** In 1957, future Prime Minister Lester B. Pearson was awarded the Nobel Peace Prize for his role in defusing the Suez Crisis. Since then, Canada has been recognized as an international peacekeeper. This is a valued role that many Canadians believe we should maintain.[10]

ojka/Shutterstock

Norms and Sanctions

How can people uphold and enforce their values in everyday life? Social values give rise to norms. **Norms** are the culturally defined rules for appropriate social behavior. They help people know how to act in different social situations. Norms vary from culture to culture, so things that are considered norms in one culture may not be norms in another culture. For example, in Canada it is usually a norm to maintain eye contact when talking with someone. In other societies, such as in Pakistan, direct eye contact is considered rude. (Remember my student who wouldn't make eye contact with me.)

Norms are important because they help make social interactions more predictable. We expect people to follow the norms, and we use sanctions to encourage compliance. A **sanction** is a reward for following a norm or a punishment for violating it. If you do what you are supposed

<<< **While we often think of values as something that individuals hold, they are also part of a society's nonmaterial culture.**

GO GLOBAL

Canadian vs. American Values

In 1990, Seymour Martin Lipset wrote *Continental Divide: The Values and Institutions of the United States and Canada*, in which he contrasted and compared these two North American nations. For Lipset, one essential difference between the two cultures is how they achieved nationhood. The Americans won their independence after fighting a revolutionary war, whereas the Canadian provinces peacefully formed a confederation (a counter-revolution) while still maintaining ties to Britain. According to Lipset, this has influenced how each country developed its identity and values. And it is the difference in values that has influenced the development of each country's social structure and activities, both within their own borders and on the international stage.

Historically, Canadians have defined themselves as being "not American." This has been a central feature of the Canadian identity. But what of the different ideologies? Lipset examined Canadian and American literature for examples of ideology. He found that American literature was more likely to focus on themes of winning, opportunism, and confidence, while Canadian literature more often dealt with defeat and difficult circumstances. He quoted Margaret Atwood, who identified the defining symbol of the United States as "the Frontier," which represented something *new*. In Canada, the symbol is *survival* in a hostile wilderness.[11]

Lipset's research showed how different values and ideologies created important differences between the cultures of Canada and the United States, which are close neighbours, both geographically and culturally.

mema/Fotolia

^^^ **Although we have a lot in common with Americans, many Canadians identify themselves as "not American."**

ITAR-TASS Photo Agency/Alamy

It's customary for players and fans alike to remove their hat or helmet and sing the national anthem before sporting events. Why do so at an event that has nothing to do with politics, patriotism, or war?

to do, you get a positive sanction; if you break the rules, you earn a negative sanction.

Most sanctions are informal, like when your friend rolls her eyes at your terrible joke. However, if we violate a law, we receive a formal negative sanction. A speeding ticket is one example of a formal sanction. Sanctions, both positive and negative, can reinforce a culture's values by rewarding people who hold those values and punishing those who have opposing values.

FOLKWAYS

Folkways are informal types of norms that are not strictly enforced. They provide a framework for our everyday behaviour and are based on social expectations. Because they are less serious types of norms, the sanctions applied are less severe than for other types of norms. For example, if you see a person struggling with packages, you will hold the door for him or her. If you let the door slam on the person, you might be considered rude, but you won't go to jail. Folkways are often social customs that, when violated, call for minor, informal negative sanctions.

FOLKWAYS are informal types of norms that are not strictly enforced.

LAWS are formal norms that are enforced through social institutions.

MORES are norms that represent a community's most important values.

LAWS

Norms that society perceives as being more serious than folkways often get written into laws. **Laws** are formal norms that are enforced through social institutions. Breaking a law is called a crime and is subject to formal sanctions.

MORES

Although folkways are informal norms, mores (pronounced MORE-ayes) are more serious. **Mores** are norms that represent a community's most important values. For example, if you murder a person, you've violated one of society's mores. People who violate mores are given more serious sanctions.

Peter Wey/Fotolia

Canada's unspoiled natural beauty is a matter of great importance to many Canadians.

Cultural Diversity

Human societies have developed an incredible diversity in meeting their needs. This is why we see so many differences between cultures. But are there any common features of culture? You saw above that every culture has material and nonmaterial elements, as well as the shared components of symbols, values, and norms. The American anthropologist George Murdock identified more than 70 **cultural universals**. These are elements that are common to all human cultures worldwide.[12] Every culture has developed a way to deal with each of these elements; how

GO GLOBAL

Individualistic and Collectivistic Views

Individualism, while it may be a core Canadian value, is hardly universal across the globe; people in countries such as China are more apt to see things through the lens of collectivism.[13] In a collectivist culture, interdependence is valued over independence, group goals valued over individual wants and needs.

How do our individualist or collectivist views affect us in practical terms? For starters, let's consider how we respond to questions. Research has shown that people from more collectivist societies, such as China and Japan, are less likely to answer with extremes on surveys. On a survey that allowed participants to strongly agree, agree, disagree, and strongly disagree, Canadian and American students were more likely to choose "strongly agree" and "strongly disagree," whereas Chinese and Japanese participants tended to choose the less extreme responses.[14]

Important cultural differences like these can inform business situations. One study compared how Canadian and Chinese executives dealt with conflict situations. The researchers found that the Chinese executives preferred to avoid conflicts before they occurred, but when conflict did arise, they were more likely to use negative resolution strategies, such as ending negotiations. The authors suggested that because groups in collectivist cultures are harder to get into, stable and harmonious relationships are more important. In individualistic cultures, an individual can more easily leave the situation and join another group.[15]

nyul/Fotolia

TODD KOROL/Reuters/Corbis

Like all other social behavior, folkways are defined by those who use them. They also change over time. Shaking hands with someone you meet was a common folkway in Canada. After the H1N1 flu scare in 2010, many people abandoned the hand-shaking folkway and adopted the "elbow bump" as a safer alternative.

different cultures do so is incredibly varied. Some examples of cultural universals that Murdock identified are sports, bodily adornment, cooking, dancing, funeral rites, hair styles, marriage, music, toilet training, puberty customs, and sexual restrictions.

CULTURAL UNIVERSALS are elements that are common to all human cultures worldwide.

DOMINANT CULTURE is usually but not always practised by the majority and controls many of the social institutions.

SUBCULTURE is a subset of the dominant culture that has distinct values, beliefs, and norms.

SUBCULTURES AND COUNTERCULTURES

In most societies, there is a **dominant culture**, which is usually but not always practised by the majority and which controls many of the social institutions. However, some groups with common interests may form a subculture. A **subculture** is a subset of the dominant culture that has its own distinct values, beliefs, and norms. In complex societies, subcultures allow people to connect with other people who have similar interests. Churches, clubs, sports teams, and even online communities can become subcultures.

MAKE CONNECTIONS

The Subcultures of Facebook

Are you a member of a Facebook subculture? Considering that Facebook has more than 500 million active users worldwide, you probably are. Facebook, an online social networking site, helps connect people through mutual interests. When you use this site, your friends are always at your fingertips.

When you join Facebook, you create a profile that includes personal information, such as interests, beliefs, or hobbies. The more information you include, the larger your world can become because Facebook connects you to others in the system who have similar characteristics. For example, you can connect to people who have the same class schedule or who play the same sports. You're linked to people who have similar values: your subculture of friends.

Like any other culture or subculture, Facebook has norms and sanctions. Many Facebook users believe that the more friends you have, the more popular you are. One norm for interacting with friends on the site is to "poke" a person. The person you poke may poke you back or ignore your poke. An informal sanction might occur if your poke goes unanswered. Though non-traditional, Facebook creates a virtual community in which people interact with others who share norms and values.

>>> **ACTIVITY** Log on to a social networking site, like Facebook, and identify a subculture.

- **Make** a list of the values of that subculture.
- **What** are the norms of this subculture?

Ethnic subcultures are a good example. Many immigrant groups in Canada live in the same neighbourhood, practise their religion, speak their language, and maintain their norms of dress and food. Many subcultures are based on race, ethnicity, religion, sexual orientation, and recreational activities. Whenever a group of people perceive that their symbols, norms, and values are distinctive enough from those of the dominant culture, they see themselves, and are seen by others, as a subculture.

While subcultures are different from the dominant culture, they are usually able to peacefully and respectfully coexist within the dominant culture. However, sometimes a group becomes significantly distinct from the dominant culture and is identified as a **counterculture**. Theodore Roszak used this term to describe the movements of the 1960s that questioned traditional cultural values and conventional lifestyles.[16] The fundamental difference between a counterculture and a subculture is that a counterculture opposes or rejects the norms and values that unite the dominant culture, while a subculture finds ways of respecting the dominant culture and the fundamental values of the dominant society.[17]

When a subculture expresses values or beliefs that are in direct opposition to the dominant group's values, it becomes a counterculture.

COUNTERCULTURE is a group with values and norms that are in opposition to the dominant culture's values and norms.

ETHNOCENTRISM occurs when a person uses his or her own culture to judge another culture.

XENOPHOBIA refers to fear and hostility toward people who are from other countries or cultures.

XENOCENTRISM is perceiving other groups or societies as superior to your own.

CULTURAL RELATIVISM means making a deliberate effort to appreciate a group's ways of life without prejudice.

ETHNOCENTRISM AND CULTURAL RELATIVISM

When studying culture from a sociological perspective, you must not allow your personal biases to complicate your understanding. **Ethnocentrism** occurs when a person uses his or her own culture to judge another culture. Nearly all people in the world are ethnocentric, but ethnocentrism is potentially dangerous to sociologists because it can lead to incorrect assumptions about different cultures.[18]

In extreme forms, ethnocentrism may become xenophobia. **Xenophobia** refers to fear and hostility toward people who are from other countries or cultures. Despite being a multicultural society, Canada has experienced episodes of xenophobia. After Japan bombed Pearl Harbor in 1941, people in Canada began to fear Japanese Canadians and imprisoned many in internment camps.

Not all personal biases result in negative views of foreign cultures. Sometimes, we engage in **xenocentrism** when we perceive other groups or societies as superior to our own. When living in Mexico, I noticed that my host family watched very little television. Instead, the family spent more time talking to each other. I remember wishing that people in my own culture would follow suit and interact with one another more.

Thinking like a sociologist means striving to practise cultural relativism when studying other cultures. **Cultural relativism** is a deliberate effort to appreciate a group's ways of life in its own context, without prejudice. In some Islamic countries, for instance, women are not encouraged to seek education. Within the context of these countries, this practice is a reflection of the values of that culture. However, if women in Canada were not allowed to get an education, the practice would seem unfair because it would violate Canadian cultural values.

Some people, however, argue that there are universal human values that are standards by which we should evaluate cultures.[19] According to this argument, women in every culture should be educated, and any culture that does not allow this is inferior and exploitive of women.

Have you ever been to a foreign country and felt lost, anxious, and overwhelmed at how the culture differed from your own? If so, you

THINK SOCIOLOGICALLY

Technology and Cultural Change

The history of Napster illustrates another example of cultural lag.

Napster began in 1998, when Shawn Fanning, Napster's creator, was at Northeastern University in Boston. By combining existing technologies and computer programs, Fanning invented P2P (peer-to-peer) programming that allowed millions of users to share MP3 digital music files between their computers. According to some reports, Napster was the fastest-growing internet site to that point. In its first year online, Napster had 20 million users. At its peak, more than 3 million people exchanged more than 350 million songs in a one-hour period.

From the beginning, lawyers, musicians, and record company executives vilified Napster as a pirate that violated copyright laws. Many saw this as a smokescreen covering what the record companies really feared: losing control over the distribution and sale of their music. By making it possible to share and transfer copyrighted material, Napster raised the ire of the Recording Industry Association of America (RIAA), and on December 7, 1999, the industry filed a lawsuit against Napster. A few songwriters and artists, most notably Metallica and Dr. Dre, also filed lawsuits against Napster. An injunction was issued on March 5, 2001, ordering Napster to prevent the trading of copyrighted music on its network. In July 2001, Napster shut down its entire network in order to comply with the injunction.

After Napster's shutdown, several imitation sites, such as Gnutella, Kazaa, and Morpheus, kept P2P file sharing accessible. The debate on copyright infringement related to downloading music continues to this day. Of course, the greatest legacy is that we now take it for granted that we can download whatever song we want to listen to without ever leaving the comfort of our home.

The story of Napster shows how a new technology can threaten existing business conditions and challenge legislators to regulate a completely unique situation with outdated laws.[20]

Library of Congress Prints and Photographs Division Washington, D.C[LC-USZ62-34565]

<<< Propaganda posters popped up all over the nation after the Japanese bombed Pearl Harbor. **Thousands of Canadians of Japanese descent were forcibly sent to internment camps for the duration of the war.**

were probably experiencing culture shock. **Culture shock** occurs when a person encounters a culture foreign to his or her own and has an emotional response to the differences between the cultures. During my time in Sri Lanka, I was surprised to see live chickens being slaughtered at the market, right before my eyes. It took some time, but I eventually accepted this cultural difference.

Global Village

In the 1960s, the noted Canadian intellectual Marshall McLuhan popularized the term **global village**, which refers to the "shrinking" of the world through immediate electronic communications.[21] McLuhan's work suggests that time and space differences are rapidly becoming irrelevant as a result of technology. But is technology really bringing people closer together? Are we developing a global culture?

From a different perspective, some have described this process as **cultural imperialism**. This refers to a global situation in which powerful culture industries located almost exclusively in the West, in particular in the United States, dominate other local, national, and regional cultures.

CULTURAL CHANGE

Cultures are constantly changing because societies are constantly facing new social and technological challenges. One way that cultural change is encouraged is following an invention or innovation. **Invention** occurs when something is deliberately changed or made to produce something new. Think of how societies have had to adapt and create new norms, values, and symbols following the invention of cars, computers, and cell phones.

Sometimes new items or methods are not deliberately created but come about by discovery. **Discovery** occurs when we better understand or observe something that already exists. The discovery of penicillin by Sir Alexander Fleming has saved the lives of millions of people and dramatically influenced medicine.

CULTURE SHOCK occurs when a person encounters a culture foreign to his or her own and has an emotional response to the differences between the cultures.

GLOBAL VILLAGE refers to the "shrinking" of the world through immediate electronic communications.

CULTURAL IMPERIALISM refers to a global situation in which powerful culture industries located almost exclusively in the West, in particular in the United States, dominate other local, national, and regional cultures.

INVENTION occurs when something is deliberately changed or made to produce something new.

DISCOVERY occurs when we better understand or observe something that already exists.

DIFFUSION occurs when an item or a method of doing things is transmitted from one culture to another.

CULTURAL LAG occurs when social and cultural changes occur at a slower pace than technological changes.

Diffusion occurs when an item or a method of doing things is transmitted from one culture to another. In the past, this most often happened as a result of migrating populations. During the colonial era, cultural diffusion reflected a form of cultural imperialism. Today, the internet and information technology allow ideas and values to spread around the world instantly.

Cultural lag happens when social and cultural changes occur at a slower pace than technological changes.[22] This is often the case when new technology enters and changes a culture. In the late 1970s, scientists were concerned with the deforestation of poorer regions of the world. People used most of the felled lumber to heat stoves for cooking. To combat this problem, more energy-efficient cookstoves were developed. However, initial tests in Africa and Haiti showed that people were reluctant to use these cookstoves. After learning of the cookstoves' benefits, people's reluctance waned, and today more than 120 million cookstoves are used around the world.[23]

think sociologically: HOW DO THE SOCIOLOGICAL PERSPECTIVES INTERPRET CULTURE?

Now we will turn to the major theoretical perspectives on culture. The theoretical perspectives affect how sociologists view language, gestures, and values in a culture.

RE-APPROPRIATION is the process by which a group reclaims—re-appropriates—terms or objects that were previously used in a negative way toward that group.

Symbolic Interactionism—Culture as Interaction

Symbolic interactionists explore how small-group interactions create the elements of culture. From this perspective, culture is constantly created and re-created through these interactions. While the symbols, values, and norms of a society may be common to most members, the real meaning of these elements of culture lies in how individuals interpret and use them. This is where culture is created, and this is how culture changes.

A slur is a negative term that is used to deprecate members of certain groups, usually minority groups. **Re-appropriation** is the process by which those groups reclaim—re-appropriate—a slur. Re-appropriation usually starts within the community that experienced oppression under that word. Individuals who are part of the minority group can use the insulting term with each other as a means of poking fun at the social circles where the slur is seriously used. By creating a sense of solidarity and togetherness through the use of the slur, members signal to each other that they are not alone and that others like them share in their pain. In some cases, re-appropriation is so successful that the previously disparaging word loses its negative sense. For example, since the early 1970s, some derogatory terms referring to homosexuality have been re-appropriated.[24] For example, the word *gay*, previously an insult, is now preferred to *homosexual*.

Functionalism—The Functions of Culture

The functionalist perspective focuses on the social structure and how it influences society and social behavior. Functionalists would look at how culture serves an important function in helping societies meet their basic needs. They would also look at how culture, which consists of shared symbols, values, and norms, helps bind people together. The functionalist perspective is likely to look for cultural universals and emphasize how culture facilitates social stability and continuity.

Because culture is such a significant aspect of all societies, it may be functional to direct and support the diffusion of certain cultural values. Radio, television, and other media are powerful transmitters of culture. The Canadian government regulates these important services to ensure that they contribute to Canada's culture and economy and meet the social needs of Canadians.

In 1936, the Canadian government created the Canadian Radio Broadcasting Commission (CRBC). The CRBC regulated and controlled all radio broadcasting in Canada and provided a national broadcasting service. The CRBC regulated the number and location of radio stations, as well as the amount of time that was devoted to national and local programming. The CRBC was replaced by the Canadian Radio-television and Telecommunications Commission (CRTC) in 1968. Today, the CRTC supervises and regulates Canadian broadcasting and telecommunications. It reports to Parliament through the minister of Canadian Heritage.

In 1971, the CRTC introduced a regulation that 30 percent of the songs played on the radio must be Canadian; this was increased to 35 percent in 1998. Since 1968, 60 percent of television programming has had to be Canadian shows. These regulations are known as Cancon (Canadian content). The function of these policies has been to ensure that Canadian songs and shows are seen and heard, and therefore Canadian culture is preserved and promoted. Canadian content remains a controversial issue. Some say that it artificially protects Canadian productions, so artists are not challenged to produce top-quality work. Others claim that Cancon violates the right of consumers to make their own choices about what they want to listen to and watch.[25]

Conflict Theory—Cultural Conflict

Conflict theorists suggest that society is characterized by a struggle for scarce resources. The unequal distribution of wealth means that some groups win and others lose. The values and norms that are most prominent in any society probably reflect the interests of certain social groups or classes. The conflict perspective is more likely to focus on different

Residential schools operated in Canada from the late 1870s until the last school closed in 1996. The schools were meant to force the assimilation of young aboriginal people into European Canadian society.[26]

REUTERS/Andy Clark

cultural groups within a society, such as subcultures and countercultures, and how they interact with or oppose the dominant culture. They also focus on how these struggles lead to cultural change.

In the nineteenth century, the Canadian government developed a policy called "aggressive assimilation." Believing that aboriginal culture was inferior, the government thought the best chance for First Nations people to succeed was for them to learn English and adopt Christianity and Canadian customs. Ideally, these people would pass their adopted culture on to their children, and aboriginal traditions would be completely abolished in a few generations.

The government felt that children were easier to mould than adults, and it created boarding schools, or residential schools. The Department of Indian Affairs ran these schools, and attendance was mandatory. By 1931, the peak of the residential school system, there were 80 schools operating in Canada. In all, about 150,000 aboriginal, Inuit, and Métis children were removed from their communities and forced to attend the schools. The students were discouraged from speaking their native language or practising their traditions. If they were caught, they experienced severe punishment.

This system was an unqualified failure. When the students returned to their communities, they often found that they didn't fit in. They didn't have the skills to help their families, and they had become ashamed of their native heritage. Yet they also found it hard to function in an urban setting. In 1991, the government convened the Royal Commission on Aboriginal Peoples, and many people told the commission about their residential school experiences. In 2007, the federal government announced a $1.9-billion compensation package for those who had been forced to attend residential schools. Former residential school students were eligible for $10,000 for the first year or part of a year they attended school, plus $3000 for each subsequent year. As of April 15, 2010, $1.55 billion had been paid, representing 75,800 cases.[27]

Feminist Theory—Gender Inequality in Culture

The feminist perspective emphasizes the importance of gender in social institutions and social interactions. From the macro perspective, feminist theorists examine the gendered nature of many cultural norms and values. The culture that is most prominent in any society reflects the interests of males. This androcentric bias means that women may be culturally invisible or devalued. From the micro perspective, feminist theorists would focus on the interactions between individuals. They would look at the symbols that are used and the values that are expressed and ask whether these fairly represent women as well as men. The feminist perspective and the feminist movement, by drawing attention to the gender issues in culture, have in fact brought about a cultural change in how women are seen and in how they participate in many societies.

On a Sunday afternoon in late February, it is estimated that 22 million Canadians—nearly two-thirds of the population—watched as Sidney Crosby scored in overtime and the Canadian team won the gold medal in Men's Hockey at the 2010 Vancouver Olympics. Just three days earlier, one-third that number of people (7.5 million) watched the Canadian Women's Hockey team also win a gold medal.

Hockey is certainly an important part of Canadian culture. In fact, it is our national winter sport. But it seems like one version of the game—the men's version—is the one that really counts. Feminist theorists are likely to recognize this imbalance and to try to explain it. Although women playing hockey is not a twenty-first-century event, it is only in the past 20 to 30 years that women's hockey has really become recognized and somewhat respected. In *Higher Goals: Women's Ice Hockey and the Politics of Gender,* Nancy Théberge suggests that both structural and ideological changes were necessary before women's hockey could attain the popularity and legitimacy it has today. On the structural side, the absence of teams and coaches meant that there was little opportunity for females to play hockey. The most critical resource for hockey is ice time, and the male teams were always given preference. On the cultural side, an ideology that viewed hockey as a tough, masculine sport discouraged many females from crossing this powerful gender barrier.[28]

Women's hockey was first introduced as an Olympic event at the Nagano Winter Olympics in 1998. This has further legitimized and popularized women's hockey in many countries. However, as the significant difference in viewership between the two Olympic gold medal games illustrates, female hockey players still have a way to go before they are considered as exciting and respected as their male counterparts.

Helen Sessions/Alamy

>>> This is a familiar sight in communities across Canada. **Tim Hortons is one of Canada's most successful businesses in part because of its links to minor hockey in small towns across the country.**

WRAP YOUR MIND AROUND THE THEORY

The CRTC is an independent public authority in charge of regulating and supervising Canadian broadcasting and telecommunications.

FRED CHARTRAND, The Canadian Press/AP Images

FUNCTIONALISM

The functionalist perspective focuses on the social structure and how this influences society and social behavior. Functionalists look at how culture serves an important function in helping societies meet their basic needs. They also look at how culture, which consists of shared symbols, values, and norms, helps to bind people together. The functionalist perspective is likely to look for cultural universals and emphasize how culture facilitates social stability and continuity.

CONFLICT THEORY

Conflict theorists suggest that society is characterized by a struggle for scarce resources. The unequal distribution of wealth means that some groups win and others lose. The values and norms that are most prominent in any society reflect the interests of certain social groups or classes. The conflict perspective is likely to focus on different cultural groups within a society, such as subcultures and countercultures, and how these interact with or oppose the dominant culture. It also focuses on how these struggles lead to cultural change.

SYMBOLIC INTERACTIONISM

Symbolic interactionists explore how small-group interactions create the elements of culture. From this perspective, culture is constantly created and re-created through these interactions. While the symbols, values, and norms of a society may be common to most members, the real meaning of these elements of culture is how individuals interpret and use them. This is where culture is created, and this is how culture changes.

FEMINIST THEORY

The feminist perspective emphasizes the importance of gender in social institutions and social interactions. From the macro perspective, feminist theorists examine the gendered nature of many cultural norms and values. The culture that is most prominent in any society reflects the interests of males. This androcentric bias means that women may be culturally invisible or devalued. From the micro perspective, feminist theorists focus on the interactions between individuals. They look at the symbols that are used and the values that are expressed and ask whether these fairly represent women as well as men. The feminist perspective and the feminist movement, by drawing attention to the gender issues in culture, have in fact brought about a cultural change in how women are seen and in how they participate in many societies.

The term gay used be an insult, but the term has now been **re-appropriated.**

Mar Photographics/Alamy

Although still not as popular as men's hockey, women's hockey is becoming a significant part of Canadian culture.

Xinhua/Photoshot

discover sociology in action: HOW DOES SOCIAL POLICY INFLUENCE CULTURE?

Social Policy—Bill 101

It was August 27, 1977. In Quebec, and especially in Montreal, the rich and powerful English-speaking minority was the dominant group. Bilingualism meant that francophones had to learn to speak English. The thousands of immigrants who arrived each year seemed to more naturally and easily assimilate into English culture. Camille Laurin was a psychiatrist, politician, and member of the separatist *Parti Québécois.* That summer, he was the driving force behind the passing of Bill 101, the infamous language law. The *Charter of the French Language* proclaimed that every Quebec resident had the right to work, shop, study, be administered, treated, and judged in French, everywhere, all the time. Nearly overnight, the changes were apparent. Immigrants were obliged to send their children to school in French. The use of English on commercial signs was no longer allowed, although this was soon revised so that English could be used, as long as it was smaller and less obvious than the French. In all businesses, organizations, and government offices, French was the only language allowed to be used.

Camille Laurin understood the power of social policy in cultural change. He envisioned Bill 101 as much more than a mere language law. It was a bold attempt at altering the social order. As an ardent separatist, Laurin believed that this was a first step on the road to Quebec independence. More than thirty years later, we can see that Bill 101 has certainly resulted in a cultural shift in Quebec. French is now firmly established as the language of business and government. But there have been changes that neither Laurin nor anyone else could have anticipated. Montreal today boasts the highest proportion of people speaking three or more languages in all of North America. The forced integration of immigrant children in French schools has created a truly multicultural society, which is in stark contrast to the traditional, homogenous, and xenophobic Québécois culture, at once diluting it and enriching it. And rather than stimulating a drive to independence, the language law reassured many francophones that their culture was being protected. It was no longer necessary to leave Canada in order to protect Quebec's cultural integrity.[29]

ACTIVITIES

1. Research language laws in different Canadian provinces. Are any Canadian provinces officially bilingual?
2. Imagine that you moved to another country and were banned from speaking English. How might you feel? What would you do to adapt?
3. Visit an ESL (English as a second language) classroom in a school in your community. Ask the teacher about the importance of language in cultural transmission.

CHAPTER

get the topic: WHAT IS CULTURE?

Theories

SYMBOLIC INTERACTIONISM 60

- small-group interactions create the elements of culture
- the real meaning of the elements of culture is how individuals interpret and use them
- some derogatory terms referring to homosexuality, such as the word *gay*, have been re-appropriated

FUNCTIONALISM 60

- culture holds society together through shared values and norms
- looks at the interaction of social structures
- in Canada, the CRTC regulates radio and television to protect and promote Canadian culture

CONFLICT THEORY 60

- social groups struggle for resources
- culture reflects the values and norms of the dominant group
- the Canadian government used residential schools in order to abolish aboriginal culture

FEMINIST THEORY 61

- gender is an important feature in social institutions and social interactions
- the culture that is most prominent in any society reflects the interests of males
- social structures can restrict the access of women and girls to certain activities, such as hockey

Key Terms

culture is the symbols, values, norms, and material objects that societies create. *50*

cultural transmission is culture passing from one generation to the next. *50*

material culture consists of the physical items that we use. *51*

nonmaterial culture consists of the non-physical products of society, such as values and beliefs. *51*

symbols are things that represent, suggest, or stand for something else. *51*

language is a system of spoken and/or written symbols used to convey meaning and to communicate. *52*

The Sapir-Whorf hypothesis is a hypothesis that the structure of a language determines a native speaker's perception and categorization of experience. *52*

gestures are symbols we make using our bodies, such as facial expressions, hand movements, eye contact, and other types of body language. *52*

values are a part of a society's nonmaterial culture that represent cultural standards by which we determine what is good or bad, right or wrong. *52*

norms are culturally defined rules for appropriate social behavior. *54*

sanction is a reward for following a norm or a punishment for violating it. *54*

folkways are informal types of norms that are not strictly enforced. *55*

laws are formal norms that are enforced through social institutions. *55*

mores are norms that represent a community's most important values. *55*

cultural universals are elements that are common to all human cultures worldwide. *57*

dominant culture is usually but not always practised by the majority and controls many of the social institutions. *57*

subculture is a subset of the dominant culture that has distinct values, beliefs, and norms. *57*

counterculture is a group with values and norms that are in opposition to the dominant culture's values and norms. *58*

ethnocentrism occurs when a person uses his or her own culture to judge another culture. *58*

xenophobia refers to fear and hostility toward people who are from other countries or cultures. *58*

xenocentrism is perceiving other groups or societies as superior to your own. *58*

cultural relativism means making a deliberate effort to appreciate a group's ways of life without prejudice. *58*

culture shock occurs when a person encounters a culture foreign to his or her own and has an emotional response to the differences between the cultures. *59*

global village refers to the "shrinking" of the world through immediate electronic communications. *59*

cultural imperialism refers to a global situation in which powerful culture industries located almost exclusively in the West, in particular in the United States, dominate other local, national, and regional cultures. *59*

invention occurs when something is deliberately changed or made to produce something new. *59*

discovery occurs when we better understand or observe something that already exists. *59*

diffusion occurs when an item or a method of doing things is transmitted from one culture to another. *59*

cultural lag occurs when social and cultural changes occur at a slower pace than technological changes. *59*

re-appropriation is the process by which a group reclaims—re-appropriates—terms or objects that were previously used in a negative way toward that group. *60*

Sample Test Questions

These multiple-choice questions are similar to those found in the test bank that accompanies this textbook.

1. Which is an example of nonmaterial culture?
   - **a.** A piano
   - **b.** A book
   - **c.** A hamburger
   - **d.** The Canadian national anthem
2. Which of the following is not a component of culture?
   - **a.** Values
   - **b.** Ethnocentrism
   - **c.** Symbols
   - **d.** Norms
3. Using your own culture to judge other cultures is called
   - **a.** xenocentrism.
   - **b.** cultural relativism.
   - **c.** ethnocentrism.
   - **d.** culture shock.
4. A counterculture forms when
   - **a.** a subculture's values are opposed to the dominant group's values.
   - **b.** a subgroup is different from the dominant culture.
   - **c.** the dominant culture is different from the subculture.
   - **d.** the subculture adopts the values of the dominant culture.
5. In order for sociologists to practise cultural relativism when studying polygamists in Canada, they must consider
   - **a.** Canadian laws.
   - **b.** Canadian norms.
   - **c.** polygamist norms.
   - **d.** cultural universals.

ANSWERS: 1. d; 2. b; 3. c; 4. a; 5. c

ESSAY

1. What aspects of Bill 101 have been positive for Canadian culture?
2. How does culture influence sociological theory and study?
3. What are the different aspects of cultural change?
4. What are Canadian values?
5. What are the different aspects of cultural diversity?

WHERE TO START YOUR RESEARCH PAPER

Canadian Heritage is a federal department responsible for national policies and programs that promote Canadian content; foster cultural participation, active citizenship, and participation in Canada's civic life; and strengthen connections among Canadians.
www.pch.gc.ca/eng/1266037002102/1265993639778.

The purpose of the Popular Culture Association of Canada is to promote scholarly understanding of popular culture in Canada and elsewhere. www.canpop.ca/about.

Citizenship and Immigration Canada
www.cic.gc.ca/english/index-can.asp.

For more on Bill 101, see www2.publicationsduquebec.gouv.qc.ca/dynamicSearch/telecharge.php?type=2&file=/C_11/C11_A.html and www.thecanadianencyclopedia.com/articles/bill-101.

Remember to check www.thethinkspot.ca for additional information, downloadable flashcards, and other helpful resources.

SOCIALIZATION

Scott S. Warren/National Geographic Society/Corbis

WHAT IS SOCIALIZATION?
HOW DO THE FOUR THEORETICAL PERSPECTIVES VIEW SOCIALIZATION?
HOW DOES UNDERSTANDING SOCIALIZATION HELP US IMPROVE OUR SOCIETY?

"The Marines... draw their recruits from the most extravagantly individualistic civilian society in the world and turn them into elite combat soldiers in twelve weeks.

"It's easier if you catch them young. You can train older men to be soldiers; it's done in every major war. But you can never get them to believe that they like it, which is the major reason armies try to get their recruits before they are twenty.

"Young civilians who have volunteered and been accepted by the Marine Corps arrive at Parris Island, the Corps's East Coast facility for basic training, in a state of considerable excitement and apprehension. Most are aware that they are about to undergo an extraordinary and very difficult experience. . . .

"During a period of only seventy-two hours, in which they are allowed little sleep, the recruits lay aside their former lives in a series of hasty rituals (like being shaven to the scalp) whose symbolic significance is quite clear to them even though they are deliberately given no time for reflection, nor any hint that they might have the option of turning back from their commitment. . . .

"The first stage of any conversion process is the destruction of an individual's former beliefs and confidence, and his reduction to a position of helplessness and need. . . . The training, when it starts, seems impossibly demanding for most of the recruits—and then it gets harder week by week. . . . But it is all carefully calculated by the men who run the machine, who think and talk in terms of the stress they are placing on the recruits. . . . The aim is to keep the training arduous but just within reach of most of the recruits' capability to withstand. One of the most striking achievements of the drill instructors is to create and maintain the illusion that basic training is an extraordinary challenge, one that will set those who graduate apart from others, when in fact almost everyone can succeed."[1]

The Process of Fitting *into* Society

CHAPTER 04.

In this excerpt from *War: The New Edition,* Gwynne Dyer describes the arrival of new U.S. Marine Corps recruits at Parris Island, South Carolina.

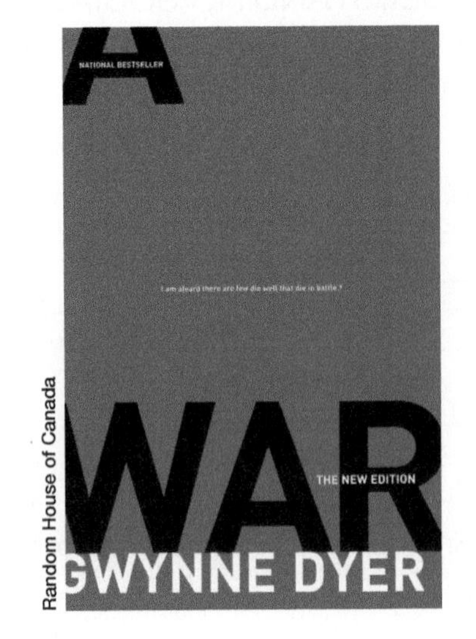

Random House of Canada

In 2002, I had the opportunity to visit Parris Island and to work there for one week. As someone who had studied sociology and was familiar with the terms *resocialization* and *total institution,* I was still deeply affected by what I saw, and the overall design and efficiency of the training that these young men and women were undergoing. Every day that I was there, I would think about the enormity of the transformation that was happening before my eyes. The Marine Corps has trained hundreds of thousands of recruits to do something that, for most of us, is the most terrible thing we could ever do—to kill another person.

get the topic: WHAT IS SOCIALIZATION?

SOCIALIZATION is the lifelong process by which the norms, values, and other aspects of a culture are learned and internalized by group members and provides the individual with the skills necessary for participating in society.

How did you learn the language you speak? What does a red light mean? There are many different clothing styles, so why are you wearing *those* clothes? From the minute you are born, you are being socialized into the world around you. At a baseball game I recently attended, a young man did not remove his hat during the national anthem. Offended, an older man reached over and snatched the hat off the young man's head. The two men's values, in terms of respect for their country, were miles apart. How did they learn these differing values? Through socialization, of course.

Socialization is the process by which the norms, values, and other aspects of a culture are learned and internalized by group members and provides the individual with the skills necessary for participating in society. It is a lifelong process of creating and maintaining group membership.

Socialization

is

the lifelong process by which the norms, values, and other aspects of a culture are learned and internalized by group members and provides the individual with the skills necessary for participating in society

and is categorized as

primary socialization: occurs during childhood
secondary socialization: continues throughout our lives

Tyler Olson/Fotolia

Agents of socialization
- family
- peers
- school
- media

Socialization is carried out by

Carol Gilligan
- males and females make moral decisions differently

Lawrence Kohlberg
- moral reasoning occurs on three levels

Socialization also gives us a social sense of identity; it lets us know how we fit into our society. Sociologists and psychologists have studied how people become socialized, which has led to the development of several theories of socialization.

Socialization theory claims that the person we become is the result of our environment. According to sociologist Talcott Parsons, introduced in Chapter 1, socialization requires people to learn and internalize society's values.[2] In other words, we accept and integrate the values of the group as our own. These social values constantly surround us, but they often go unexamined.

At what point in our lives does socialization take place? Parsons argues that most socialization occurs during childhood.[3] Orville Brim refers to this early socialization as **primary socialization**.[4] Parents are their children's first teachers; they pass on values, language, beliefs, and an unending list of social norms. However, socialization is reciprocal because children also influence their parents. Before I had children, I thought I knew about parenting, but each child teaches me something new as I try to socialize them. Because socialization is an unending cycle, we are at times the "socializer" and at other times the "socialized."[5] This dynamic whereby socialization continues throughout our lives is considered **secondary socialization**.[6] As you experience life-changing events—like going to college, beginning a career, or getting married—new socialization occurs. At each stage of life, we encounter new norms, values, and expectations. We learn to accept and integrate them as we adapt to our environment. In a significant way, the socialization process makes us who we are.

The Nature vs. Nurture Debate—What Makes Us Who We Are?

As one theorist said, "We, and all other animals, are machines created by our genes."[7] This statement reflects the **nature theory**, the belief that the genes we get from our parents are the primary causes of human behaviour; in short, the nature theory says that our genetic makeup determines who we are. The field of sociobiology emerged in the mid twentieth century, and as the name implies, it is a combination of biology and sociology. The main premise of sociobiology is that some behaviours are at least partly inherited and result from natural selection. Just as physical traits are thought to have evolved because they gave an evolutionary advantage, social behaviours may also be more or less adaptive. One of the most well-known books on sociobiology is Edward O. Wilson's *Sociobiology: The New Synthesis*, published in 1975.[8]

Those who believe in **nurture theory**, like philosopher John Locke, propose that our environment is the primary influence on the way we think, feel, and behave.[9] Supporters of this idea assert that socialization moulds us like pieces of clay, particularly during early childhood. Many nurture theorists believe that a social process teaches people who they are and how they fit into their world. Without such nurturing, a person's ability to cope within society could be greatly affected.

Proponents on both sides of the nature/nurture debate have difficulty sorting out this issue. Noted biologist and author Paul Ehrlich supports a blended point of view. He notes, "We can't partition the responsibility for aggression, altruism, or charisma between DNA and upbringing. In many such cases, trying to separate the contributions of nature and nurture to an attribute is rather like trying to separate the contributions of length and width to the area of a rectangle, which at first glance also seems easy. When you think about it carefully, though, it proves impossible."[10]

PRIMARY SOCIALIZATION is socialization that occurs during childhood.

SECONDARY SOCIALIZATION is socialization that continues throughout our lives.

NATURE THEORY states that the genes we get from our parents are the primary cause of human behaviour.

NURTURE THEORY states that our environment is the primary influence on the way we think, feel, and behave.

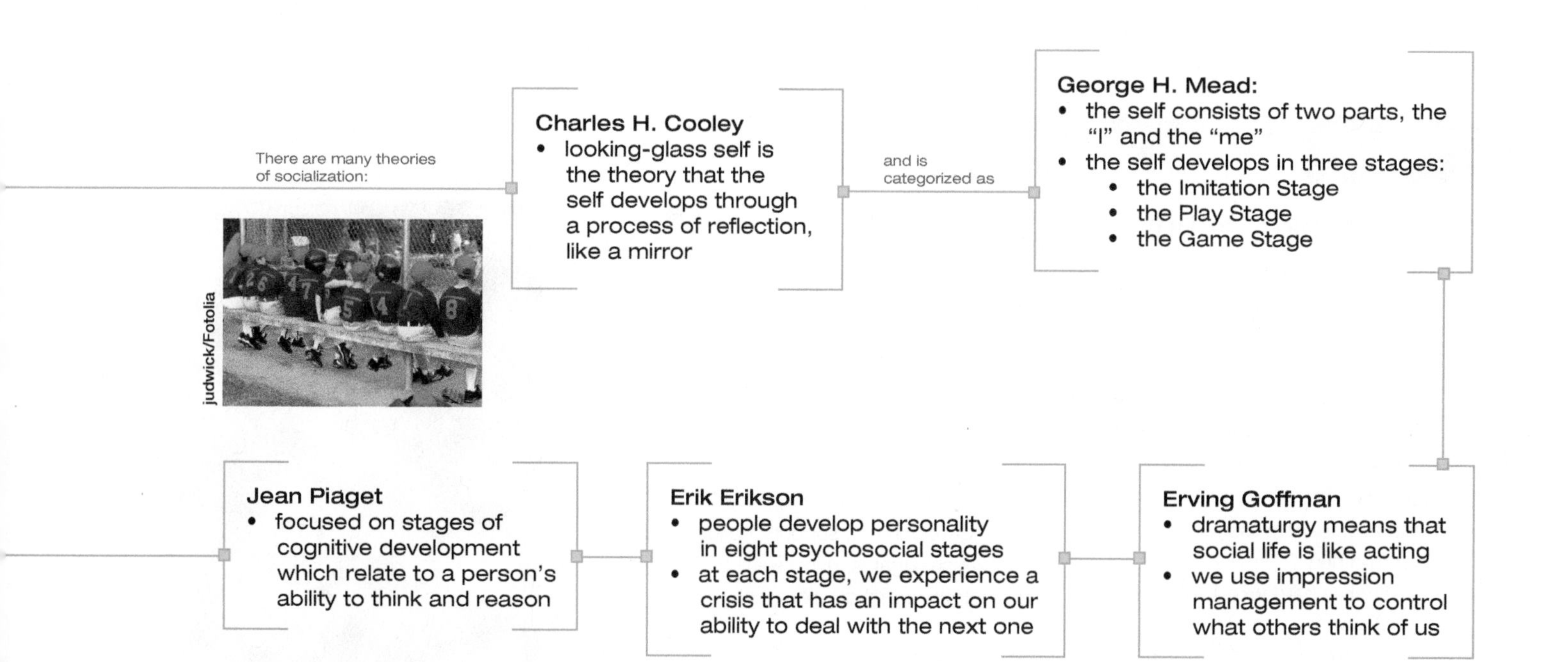

There are many theories of socialization:
Charles H. Cooley
• looking-glass self is the theory that the self develops through a process of reflection, like a mirror
and is categorized as
George H. Mead:
• the self consists of two parts, the "I" and the "me"
• the self develops in three stages:
• the Imitation Stage
• the Play Stage
• the Game Stage
Erving Goffman
• dramaturgy means that social life is like acting
• we use impression management to control what others think of us
Erik Erikson
• people develop personality in eight psychosocial stages
• at each stage, we experience a crisis that has an impact on our ability to deal with the next one
Jean Piaget
• focused on stages of cognitive development which relate to a person's ability to think and reason
judwick/Fotolia

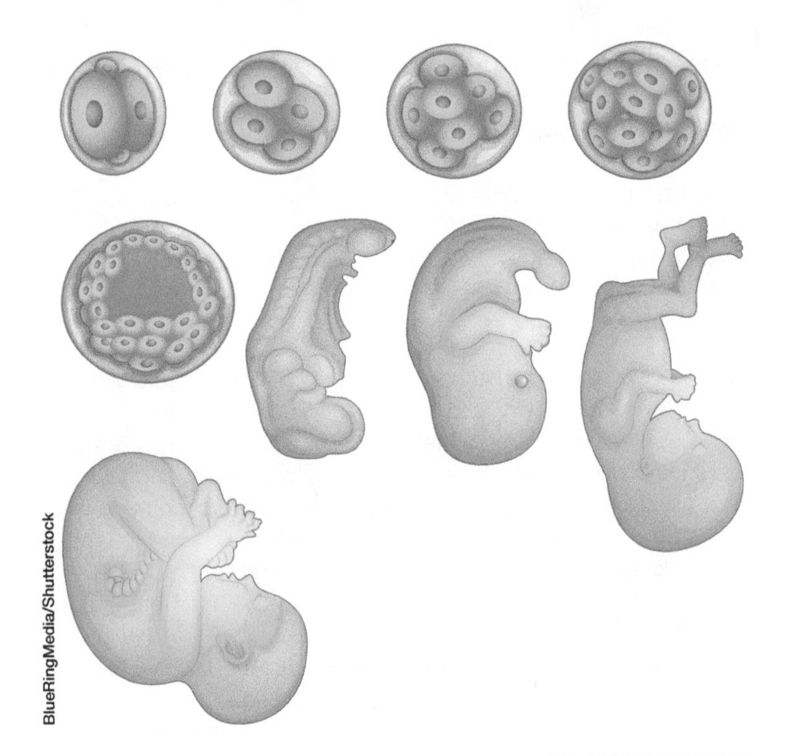
BlueRingMedia/Shutterstock

Does our genetic makeup really determine who we will become? Or do other factors come into play, such as the way our parents care for us? Where do you stand on the nature vs. nurture debate?

Theories of Socialization

Socialization is a process that theorists have been studying for decades. Many of these theorists, from sociologists to psychologists, have made significant contributions to our understanding of the development of self and the development of morality. Like a never-ending college course, we're enrolled in "socialization" until the day we die. In that sense, we're constantly learning about ourselves.

COOLEY'S LOOKING-GLASS SELF

Charles H. Cooley is one of the central theorists of the development of the self. His notion of the **looking-glass self** proposes that the self develops through a process of reflection, like a reflection in a mirror. That said, one's self is also established through interactions with others. According to Cooley, this process contains three steps:

1. We imagine how our behaviours will look to others.
2. We interpret others' reactions to our behaviours.
3. Based on our interpretation, we develop a self-concept.[12]

Although Cooley's ideas were developed more than a century ago, modern scholars remain interested in them. King-To Yeung and John Levi Martin, contemporary sociologists who study the processes of the looking-glass self, used Cooley's theory to test the internalization of self-understanding.[13] Their research found general support for the theory that our self-concept involves interpreting and internalizing others' perceptions about us. Yeung and Martin showed that the importance of our relationships is the key factor in determining how we internalize others' perceptions of us. This is why our parents influence us more than, say, the clerk at the convenience store.[14]

GEORGE HERBERT MEAD—THE THREE STAGES OF THE "I-ME" SELF

Another theory about how humans develop the self was explored in symbolic interactionist George Herbert Mead's *Mind, Self, and Society*. For Mead, the self is that part of personal identity that has both self-awareness and self-image.[15] Like Cooley, Mead agreed that the development of self involves interaction with others.

For Mead, though, the self consists of two parts: the "I" and the "me." These two parts essentially create the self through their interaction. The **"I" self** is the part of us that is an active subject, our subjective sense of who we are. It seeks self-fulfillment, asking, "What do *I* want?" In contrast, the **"me" self** is the objective part of the self, the part of our self-concept that questions how others might interpret our actions. The "me" understands the symbols that others give us and seeks to find favourable reactions to our behaviours from others.[16]

According to Mead, the self develops in three stages. The first is the **imitation stage**, which is the period from birth to about age 2. At this stage, children merely copy the behaviours of those around them. They

THINK SOCIOLOGICALLY

Rhesus Monkey Study

Which is more important to our survival—nature or nurture? To find out, researchers Harry and Margaret Harlow conducted numerous experiments with rhesus monkeys.[11] One of the most famous was designed to test which need is greater: the need for physical contact or the need for biological sustenance. The Harlows raised monkeys in isolation and eventually presented them with two artificial "mothers." The first "mother"—which was simply a hard wire frame with a wooden head—provided food. The other "mother" provided no food at all but was made of soft, cuddly material. The Harlows noticed that frightened baby monkeys sought comfort with the soft "mother" and not with the "mother" that fed them. They drew the conclusion that the key component of infant-mother bonding is not the providing of food but the presence of comfort. The Harlows' findings, while not directly applicable to human development, support the idea that socialization—that is, nurture—is a key building block in normal development.

Andrey Armyagov/Fotolia

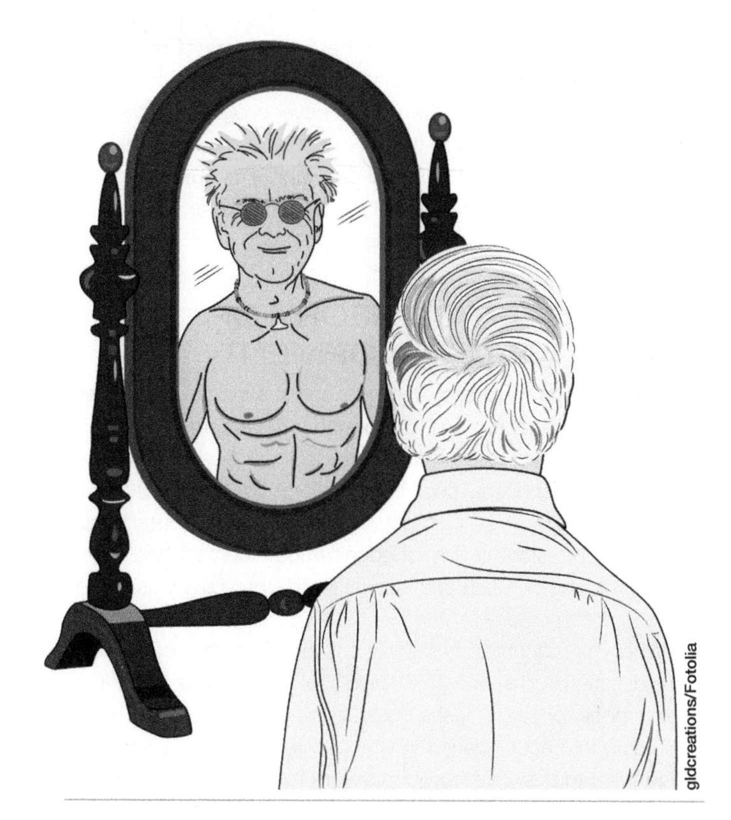
gldcreations/Fotolia

> Looking-glass self is the theory that the self develops through a process of reflection, like a reflection in a mirror.

don't attribute meaning to their actions, nor do they understand the implications of their behaviour. For instance, when you see your baby sister clapping her hands, she's probably just imitating something she's seen and not actually giving you a round of applause.

Children enter the **play stage** around the ages of 2–4 years. Here, children play roles and begin to take on the characteristics of important people in their world. The people we consider to be important and who we want to impress are called **significant others**. By playing roles, children see others as separate from themselves. They understand that their actions can affect other people and vice versa. Mead claimed that, through play, children learn to find a sense of who they are and how best to interact with others in their society. At this stage, you're likely to see little boys tie blankets around their necks and pretend to be superheroes.

During our early school years, we enter what Mead called the **game stage**, a stage that never truly ends. It is in the game stage that we begin to understand that others have expectations and demands placed upon them. Mead termed this sense of the norms, beliefs, and expectations specific to our culture the **generalized other**.

Through understanding our cultures norms, beliefs, and expectations, we are able to adjust or evaluate our own behavior. Developing a concept of the generalized other helps us understand other people's roles, norms, and expectations. This concept is important if we are to fit into society and live intimately with others.[17]

ERVING GOFFMAN—DRAMATURGY AND THE PRESENTATION OF SELF

"All the world's a stage," Shakespeare wrote in *As You Like It*. Though he wasn't technically a sociologist, the Bard may have been more accurate than he realized. Canadian sociologist Erving Goffman developed a theory of interaction called dramaturgy, which suggests that life is like acting.[18]

LOOKING-GLASS SELF is the theory that the self develops through a process of reflection, like a reflection in a mirror.

I SELF is the subjective part of the self.

ME SELF is the objective part of the self.

IMITATION STAGE is Mead's first stage of development, which is the period from birth to about age 2, when children merely copy the behaviours of those around them.

PLAY STAGE is Mead's second stage of development, which occurs around the ages of 2–4 years, during which children play roles and begin to take on the characteristics of important people in their world.

SIGNIFICANT OTHERS are the people we consider to be important and who we want to impress.

GAME STAGE is Mead's third stage of development, which never truly ends, and is the stage in which we begin to understand that others have expectations and demands placed upon them.

GENERALIZED OTHER is a sense of the norms, beliefs, and expectations specific to our culture.

IMPRESSION MANAGEMENT is management of the impression that a performer makes on others.

FRONT STAGE is what the audience sees, or the part of ourselves that we present to others.

BACKSTAGE is the demeanour that incorporates our true feelings and beliefs.

FACE-SAVING WORK is a reaction to embarrassment in the form of either humour, anger, or retreat.

Social actors enter every situation with two selves. The character may be thought of as the image that we want others to accept, while the performer attempts to manage the impressions that we make on others. Goffman termed this effort **impression management**.

For example, if you think someone having an iced mocha at the corner coffee shop is attractive, you might want to make contact with him or her. As you approach, hoping to look "cool," you are entering the **front stage**. This is what the audience sees. Most of us live our lives on the front stage.

Of course, we are more than our front stage acts. **Backstage** demeanour incorporates our true feelings and beliefs. Most people do not show their backstage personas very often. We usually save that version of ourselves for our very closest family members and friends.

Returning to our coffee shop example, let's assume that as you approach this person, you trip and fall. Obviously, you'll be embarrassed. Embarrassment occurs when we realize our act has failed. It's hard to pull off looking cool and tripping at the same time. When this type of mismatch happens, we engage in **face-saving work**. People generally choose one of three different options when they engage in face-saving work: humour, anger, or retreat.

Using humour, you can turn an embarrassing situation into a self-deprecating joke. This gives you the chance to impress upon the person that you have your act together because you can laugh at yourself.

In an angry reaction to this embarrassing situation, you may start cussing. This reaction is an attempt to say to the audience, "I'm powerful, even though I'm on the floor."

Efforts to retreat when we become embarrassed involve simply an attempt to escape. After all, our act has failed, and we want to leave the stage as soon as possible.

When children are involved in a team sport like baseball or hockey, they must understand each position's roles and responsibilities in order to play the game. Not everyone can hit or shoot; everyone has a job to do, or we can't play the game.

PSYCHOSOCIAL CRISIS is a crisis occurring during each of Erikson's stages that will be resolved either positively or negatively, and each outcome will have an effect on our ability to deal with the next one.

COGNITIVE DEVELOPMENT is a person's ability to think and reason.

SENSORIMOTOR STAGE is the stage (birth to 2 years) at which infants learn to experience and think about the world through their senses and motor skills.

ERIK ERIKSON'S EIGHT STAGES OF DEVELOPMENT

Erik Erikson proposed that humans develop a personality in eight psychosocial, or psychological and social, stages. (See page 73 for a complete list of the stages.) During each stage, we experience a particular **psychosocial crisis** that will be resolved either positively or negatively, and each outcome will have an effect on our ability to deal with the next one.[19]

According to Erikson, the crisis at each stage of development must be resolved positively before we can successfully master subsequent stages. An example is found in the sad story of Genie, who was discovered in Los Angeles in 1970 at the age of 13. The news media said she had been locked in a room and tied to a potty chair for most of her life, with little to look at and no one to talk to for more than 10 years. A group of experts, known as the "Genie team," observed that Genie could not walk normally and understood only a few words. Additionally, she had problems eating solid food and still needed diapers. However, after her rescue, Genie made rapid progress. She quickly learned to dress and go to the toilet herself. She also learned to walk more normally. Her language skills began to develop, and within a few months her vocabulary of only five to ten words had expanded to more than 100 words. Unfortunately, despite the massive efforts to help Genie, she never caught up with her peers. The Genie team concluded that her delayed progress was the result of missing key points in her social development.[21] Genie's case helps illustrate Erikson's theory that failing to master one stage can mean that a person will fail the subsequent stages.

JEAN PIAGET'S THEORY OF COGNITIVE DEVELOPMENT

Whereas Erikson's research focused on personality development, the work of Jean Piaget focused on **cognitive development**, which relates to a person's ability to think and reason. Since the way we think helps shape our self-concept, cognition (thinking) plays a significant role in socialization. Simply put, Piaget found that children don't think like adults. His four-stage theory of cognitive development has become an important basis for much educational theory, particularly as it applies to teaching young children.

When my daughter was an infant, nearly everything she touched went directly into her mouth. It didn't matter if it was a stuffed teddy bear, a book, or a bug. If she could reach it, it was going in her mouth. According to Piaget, this is the way babies learn. At the **sensorimotor stage** (birth to age 2 years), infants learn to experience and think about the world through their senses and motor skills. During this period, children develop a sense of "object permanence," the understanding that objects outside themselves still exist, even when they are not in view.[22] For example, play "peek-a-boo" with an infant, and you'll notice that the baby expresses surprise when you cover your face, followed by great joy when you reveal it. Near the end of the sensorimotor stage, peek-a-boo loses its allure, and object permanence exists.

Sun Media Corp

<<< **In September 2010, Manitoba judge Lori Douglas stepped down from active duty to await results of a federal review—immediately after news broke that naked photos of her engaged in bondage had appeared on the Web.[20] Politicians try to craft their front stage selves to appear family-oriented and honest; however, their backstage selves may tell a different story.** What other types of occupations require a person to have a highly controlled front stage demeanour?

ERIKSON'S EIGHT STAGES OF DEVELOPMENT
1
Trust vs. Mistrust
When all an infant's needs are met, trust develops. Although Erikson argued that some mistrust is necessary to exist in the world, infants who learn mistrust lack self-confidence and eventually become frustrated, withdrawn, suspicious adults. During infancy, Genie did not resolve this crisis positively, as her basic needs were not met. As a result, she was left unprepared to resolve the next life stages positively.
Infancy (birth to 1 year)
Tom Wang/Fotolia
2
Autonomy vs. Shame and Doubt
Parents who create supportive environments allow toddlers to learn self-sufficiency and gain confidence. Overprotective or disapproving parents can lead to children who second-guess themselves.
Toddlerhood (2 to 3 years)
Aletia/Shutterstock
3
Initiative vs. Guilt
Children who receive encouragement and consistent discipline gain esteem while learning to take chances. If children receive nothing but scolding, they may develop an overriding sense of guilt. Children at this stage improve their motor skills and become more interested in social interaction. Because Genie was locked in a room, she was not given this opportunity, which is why experts found her motor skills severely lacking. Genie's walk was often compared to a bunny rabbit's hop.
Preschooler (4 to 5 years)
Thomas Perkins/Fotolia
4
Industry vs. Inferiority
Doing well in school and making friends help children develop a sense of competence or industry. If, however, children have difficulty socializing, they will likely feel a sense of inadequacy.
Elementary School (6 years to puberty)
Andres Rodriguez/Fotolia
5
Identity vs. Role Confusion
If teens successfully answer the question "Who am I?" they develop a strong sense of self. If, however, they remain confused about their identity, they will likely grow up with an inability to make crucial decisions.
Adolescence (teen years into 20s)
arekmalang/Fotolia
6
Intimacy vs. Isolation
Intimacy (both sexual and nonsexual) is possible with a more-or-less solid sense of identity gained in earlier stages. If young adults still harbour doubts about who they are, then they are likely to become isolated, fear commitments, and root themselves in egocentrism.
Young Adulthood (20s to early 40s)
Stephen Derr/Getty Images
7
Generativity vs. Stagnation
Adults in this stage may dedicate their lives to rearing children, to their work, or to some special cause, all in hope of leaving a "mark" on the world. People resolve the conflict of generativity versus stagnation by giving something of themselves to future generations. If adults fail to make a contribution to the world, then they remain mired in egoism and a self-centred lifestyle.
Middle Adulthood (40s to early 60s)
kolotype/fotolia
8
Integrity vs. Despair
At this time of life, adults look back on their lives and evaluate their effect on the world. If the previous stages have been resolved positively, adults are able to approach their deaths from a healthy point of view. If, however, they have failed to resolve the conflicts of the previous developmental stages, then they may fear death and regret their lives.
Late Adulthood (late 60s to early 80s)
Lisa Eastman/Fotolia

Source: Based on *Childhood and Society* by Erik Erikson.

MAKE CONNECTIONS

Using Impression Management to Get Ahead in the Workplace

No matter where you start your career, you probably hope to climb the ladder of success while you're there. You can impress your boss and chart your course to the corner office of your dreams by following the simple steps below.

Sandy J. Wayne and Robert C. Liden showed that successful impression management techniques positively affect an employee's performance rating.[23] They found three components that influence successful performance reviews: demographic similarity, supervisor-focused impression management, and self-focused impression management. *Demographic similarity* means that you share characteristics such as race, gender, or age with your boss, co-workers, or others you encounter. *Supervisor-focused impression management* techniques involve flattering your boss and agreeing with your boss's opinions (or at least avoiding disagreements whenever possible). *Self-focused impression management* techniques include acting modest about your accomplishments (even if that modesty is false), boasting occasionally about your successes, and showing your friendliness and self-assuredness through smiles and eye contact.

Most of us like people who are like us, and this includes bosses. By using either self-focused or supervisor-focused impression management techniques, you can advance your career and look forward to the day when your employees use impression management techniques to impress *you*.

>>> **ACTIVITY** The next time you hang out with a friend, act as though your friend is your boss and use the impression management techniques listed above. Record how he or she responds and share it with your class.

PREOPERATIONAL STAGE is the stage (ages 2 through 7 years) at which the ability to speak grows rapidly.

CONCRETE OPERATIONAL STAGE is the stage (ages 7 through 12 years) at which children can think about objects in the world in more than one way and start to understand causal connections in their surroundings.

FORMAL OPERATIONAL STAGE is the stage (ages 12 years and above) at which people become able to comprehend abstract thought.

At the **preoperational stage** (ages 2 through 7 years), the ability to speak grows rapidly. Although children have already learned some words and phrases, their ability to use and interpret symbols is limited. Children will generally identify objects by a single characteristic. If you show a child the letters *C-A-T*, for example, the child is likely to read each individual letter aloud. It is unlikely that she will link them together into the word *cat*. Linking multiple symbols together is difficult for a preoperational thinker. By the end of this stage, however, a child can say the word *ball*, draw a picture of a ball, point to a ball on the floor, and understand that all of these mean the same thing.[24]

During the **concrete operational stage** (ages 7 through 12 years), children can think about objects in the world in more than one way and start to understand causal connections in their surroundings. They can think logically about some objects and events. For example, they learn that even though a plain sheet of white paper is folded into a paper airplane, it is still that same piece of white paper. Children at this stage can also imagine what other people might be thinking or feeling. Piaget believed we can't understand the "position" of others until we have passed through some developmental state. Children gain this ability during the concrete operational stage.[25]

Only at the **formal operational stage** (ages 12 years and above) do people become able to comprehend abstract thought. Because they're testing their ability to reason and comprehend the complexities of their world, children at this stage often argue with those in authority. Unsure of themselves, they test their thinking. Understanding abstract mathematical principles, such as algebra, becomes possible at this stage, and we become able to understand more deeply the interactions of concrete reality with abstract ideals.[26]

Piaget argued that it can be frustrating and traumatizing to force children to learn ahead of their cognitive capacities. In other words, it serves no purpose to try to teach geometry to a child in grade 1. Expecting a child to act like an adult is both impossible and unfair.[27]

Each of the theorists—Cooley, Mead, Erikson, and Piaget—provides a different view of the development of self. **All these theorists agree that a person's development continues throughout life. These theories present human development as a type of staircase process.** Children who miss one or more stages of socialization generally fail to reach successful completion of their development, as was the case for Genie.

Theories of Moral Development

How do we know what's right and what's wrong? Do girls learn about morals differently from boys? These are just two of the questions that theories of moral development seek to answer.

KOHLBERG'S THEORY OF MORAL DEVELOPMENT

Building upon the work of Piaget, the prominent theorist Lawrence Kohlberg suggested that moral reasoning occurs on three specific levels: preconventional, conventional, and postconventional. Each level describes different ways in which we make moral decisions.[28]

During the **preconventional level**, which lasts through the elementary school years, children make their moral judgments within a framework of **hedonism**—seeking pleasure over pain.[29] In other words, children judge right from wrong on the basis of what feels good or right to them. If a little boy notices that drawing on the walls results in a visit to the "naughty stool," chances are he won't take the crayons to the walls again.

The **conventional level** arises before puberty and uses the lens of norms and rules to determine what is right and wrong.[30] Basically, what is "right" is obedience to the rules. Rather than question the logic behind why those rules were established, a child simply does what he or she is told. The child may not understand *why* kicking his sister is wrong; he just understands that he shouldn't do it because "Mommy says so." Following the expectations of the family or group is valuable in and of itself. Doing your duty and respecting authority are the hallmarks of this level of development.

Kohlberg's third stage of moral development, the **postconventional level**, refers to a morality based on abstract principles. These may be rooted in political beliefs, religious beliefs, or a combination of both. Kohlberg suggests that the "good" includes adherence to agreed-upon principles rather than rules.[31] Such principles guide all decisions and provide a seamless web of morality for us all. For example, during the civil rights movement of the 1950s and 1960s, countless African American college students held sit-ins at segregated lunch counters, museums, libraries, and many other public places. Although their behaviour broke the Jim Crow laws of the time, these students believed their behaviour was "right" because they were drawing attention to laws that were morally wrong. ("Jim Crow" was the name of a man in a nineteenth-century song and is used as shorthand for segregation in the United States.[32])

Although Kohlberg's own research supported his theory, more recent scholars question some of his assumptions. For example, Charles Helwig and Urszula Jasiobedzka found that children's moral judgments about law and lawbreaking occur earlier in life than Kohlberg's theory proposed.[33] Preschoolers may abide by the rules because they believe rule-breaking is wrong. In addition, moral reasoning doesn't always correlate with moral behaviour. Using Kohlberg's schema, Colby and Damon showed that people at the highest levels of moral development act the same as people at lower levels of moral development. Instead, the situation influences people's behaviour.[34] Take speeding, for example. Although everyone knows it's against the law, many people speed when they believe they won't be caught. These and other questions about Kohlberg's theory of moral development led Carol Gilligan to propose another point of view in 1982.

PRECONVENTIONAL LEVEL is the first stage of moral development that lasts through the elementary school years; at this level, children make their moral judgments within a framework of hedonistic principles.

HEDONISM is seeking pleasure over pain.

CONVENTIONAL LEVEL is the second stage of moral development that arises before puberty and uses the lens of norms and rules to determine what is right and wrong.

POSTCONVENTIONAL LEVEL is the third stage of moral development that refers to a morality based on abstract principles.

CAROL GILLIGAN AND THE "MORALITY OF CARE"

Carol Gilligan suggested that Kohlberg's theories were valid, though only when discussing the development of male morality. To Gilligan, his conclusions were biased against women because Kohlberg studied only men initially.[35] Without actually studying women, he erroneously assumed that men and women develop moral decisions similarly. Do men and women approach moral decisions differently?

I recently faced a moral decision while shopping at my local discount store. The cashier gave me $10 too much change. Being a bit of a miser, I immediately noticed her mistake. I'm human, so I considered keeping the money, but then I began to wonder what might happen if I took the money. Was it my fault that the cashier made a mistake? Did anyone else notice? What would happen if I got caught? All these thoughts ran through my mind. Of course, I gave the money back to her. Gilligan would argue that my gender influenced the way I approached my decision; a woman might have done the same thing but would have followed a slightly different moralizing process.

>>> It's hard to imagine that the simple act of sitting at a lunch counter could be illegal. **The unfairness of laws** such as these **led many students of all races to hold peaceful sit-ins across the southern United States in hopes of abolishing segregation laws.**

Bettmann/Corbis

MORALITY OF JUSTICE is morality based on the rule of law.

MORALITY OF CARE is morality decided by a standard of how best to help those who are in need.

AGENTS OF SOCIALIZATION is a measure of an individual's or family's position within the social structure.

After investigating women's experiences with morality, Gilligan concluded that moral decisions arise from two different principles: the morality of justice and the morality of care. She agreed that boys primarily follow what she called a **morality of justice**, a morality based on the rule of law. However, girls learn a **morality of care**, which enables them to make moral decisions by a standard of how best to help those who are in need.[36]

To study the differences between moral development in boys and girls, Gilligan proposed a real-life moral dilemma to young male and female subjects. Gilligan used the story of "Mr. Heinz and the Druggist," a tale that Kohlberg also used in his research. The general idea of the story is this: Mr. Heinz's wife is sick with a potentially fatal disease. Luckily, their small-town pharmacy is the only place around that carries the life-saving medication that his wife needs. The problem is the drug costs an astronomical $10 000, and the druggist refuses to sell it for any less. Should Mr. Heinz steal the drug?

Gilligan found that most male subjects used logic when answering the question. Many boys believed that Mr. Heinz should steal the medication, even though it's legally wrong. Boys reasoned that the judge would likely be lenient on Mr. Heinz because of the circumstances. In short, the boys answered the question like a math problem: $x + y = z$. The girl subjects, however, considered the personal relationships involved. Girls worried that Mr. Heinz might go to jail, which could make his wife sicker and leave no one around to care for her or provide her with medicine. They also tried to think of other ways for Mr. Heinz to get the drug so that he would not have to leave his wife. Girls were more concerned about how Mr. Heinz's actions would affect the dynamic between him and his wife.

Modern research provides mixed support for Gilligan's assertion of gender differences in moral reasoning. In short, it appears that girls and boys learn *both* morality of care and morality of justice. The two types of morality are not exclusive to one gender over the other. Some findings show that since girls advance through the stages of moral development faster than boys, they actually develop postconventional morality at earlier ages.[37] The most important aspect, perhaps, is the link between ego development and the moralities of care and justice. Because girls develop faster than boys, they present a morality of care more quickly than boys.[38]

Either way, Gilligan and Kohlberg agree that moral reasoning follows a developmental process and that the surroundings affect that process. Although the precise gender differences may not be as clearly distinguished as Gilligan initially believed, and Kohlberg's age groups may be more flexible than he proposed, both theories show that we learn to make moral decisions in different ways.

KOHLBERG AND GILLIGAN'S THEORIES OF MORAL DEVELOPMENT

"Both boys and girls go through the same three stages—preconventional, conventional, and postconventional—to develop their morality."
— Lawrence Kohlberg

Lee Lockwood/Time & Life Pictures/Getty Images

"Boys and girls develop their morality differently. Boys generally develop a morality of justice, while girls develop a morality of care."
— Carol Gilligan

Paul Hawthorne/Getty Images

Agents of Socialization

We learn about our culture with outside help from different **agents of socialization**. These are the people, groups, and institutions that shape our self-concept, beliefs, and behaviour. You are being socialized when you attend a religious service, when you go to work, and when you play sports, and if you attended a daycare as a child, you were socialized there as well. However, the four primary agents of socialization are the family, peers, schools, and the media.

SOCIOECONOMIC STATUS are the people, groups, and institutions that shape our self-concept, beliefs, and behaviour.

PEERS are people who are similar in age and who share many common interests.

MASS MEDIA are forms of communication such as television, newspapers, radio, and magazines that are designed to reach a large audience.

SOCIAL MEDIA are forms of electronic communication such as blogs, forums, podcasts, and sites for social networking through which users create and share information, ideas, personal messages, and other content.

THE FAMILY

Few things in life shape us more than our parents. Because both my parents worked full time, I learned at an early age that one must work to live. I started working at 13 and am still working today, as evidenced by my writing this book on nights, weekends, and summer vacations. My parents also valued education. My sister, my brother, and I all went to university. Sometimes, I wonder what my life would have been like if I had had different parents. What if my parents had been drug addicts? Or illiterate? Or members of the wealthiest elite in the country (my personal favourite)? My point is that children don't select their parents, and yet family is one of the most important agents of socialization.

Because they are small, intimate groups, families are very effective at primary socialization. Families instill the values, beliefs, and behavioural norms that tend to persist. From our family, we are also given our **socioeconomic status**, our race and ethnic identity, and our religious and moral beliefs.

PEERS

When you were a young child, your family was probably the most important socializer in your life. As you got older, you probably met other people from outside your family, who became your friends. Your **peers** are people who are similar in age and who share many common interests with you. One of the most important purposes of the peer group is to help you separate from your family and become involved in the wider society. A distinctive feature of the peer group, at least among children, is that it is the only agent of socialization not controlled by adults. For many people, during the period from mid-childhood to early adulthood, the peer group is the most powerful agent of socialization.

SCHOOLS

If you are reading this textbook, chances are that you have spent many years in schools. In fact, you probably learned how to read in school. Schools have the formal task of passing on the dominant culture's knowledge, values, and beliefs. They also prepare people for the job market by transmitting academic, technical, and scientific knowledge. But in addition to the official academic curriculum, schools teach other things. If you think back to elementary school, you may remember that you learned all kinds of things that were unrelated to academics, like sharing, waiting your turn, and standing in line. You probably also learned that in school, you were rewarded for what you did and not for who you were. Schools also teach about competition, materialism, and obedience to authority.

THE MEDIA

I recently rediscovered a set of my teaching notes from 10 years ago. In the section about mass media as an agent of socialization, I had this sentence: "TV watching is the most time-consuming free-time activity of Canadians." That was in 2003. By 2012, internet usage had moved ahead of watching television in terms of the number of hours spent. Overall, Canadians spend more than 18 hours a week online, compared to 16.9 hours watching television.[43] Other media, such as newspapers, radio, and magazines, have all remained relatively stable. **Mass media** are forms of communication such as television, newspapers, radio, and magazines that are designed to reach a large audience. In the mass media model, a few people produce the content, which is distributed and consumed by a mass audience. While there are various theories about how mass media affect individuals and groups, there is no doubt of the powerful socializing effect of mass media. In part, in order to have mass appeal, the content often reflects widespread societal values. But the pervasiveness of mass media also shapes, perpetuates, and changes those societal values.

Since the early 1990s, the traditional mass media have been challenged by social media. **Social media** are forms of electronic communication such as blogs, forums, podcasts, and sites for social networking such as Facebook and Twitter through which users create and share information, ideas, personal messages, and other content.

Some see this change as dramatic, fundamental, and revolutionary. In contrast to the traditional and passive mass audience, today's interactive audiences expect to be able to choose what they see and read, and

GO GLOBAL

Parenting in Asian Cultures

Do parents in all cultures raise their kids the same way? Ruth Chao studied how the parenting styles of Chinese families affect children.[39] In order to explore the stereotype of Chinese schoolchildren as successful and well behaved, Chao observed how parents interacted with their children.[40] The mothers she observed provided high levels of control but also high levels of sacrifice and personal closeness to their children. Parents in China expect their children to meet high standards of both individual achievement and social conformity. In general, Chinese children meet these standards. The parents in that culture are authoritative; children receive adequate emotional support and know that their hard work will gain the family's approval.

In another study, sociologist Min Zhou proposed that Confucian philosophy, with its emphasis on family loyalty, acts as a social control mechanism that supports Asian children's success.[41] Studies of Vietnamese immigrant children living in enclaves in the United States show similar findings to those of Chao. They show that second-generation immigrant children who remain linked to their families and culture have better outcomes with regard to educational attainment and the likelihood that they will stay in school.[42] Culture plays an important role in psychologists' and sociologists' interpretations about family socialization.

CITIZEN MEDIA refers to content produced, collected, and shared by private citizens.

RESOCIALIZATION is the process of learning new norms, values, attitudes, and behaviours and abandoning old ones.

TOTAL INSTITUTIONS are places in which the most effective forms of resocialization can occur because they isolate people from outside influences so they can be reformed and controlled.

most believe they should be able to contribute content and opinions, too.[44] The term **citizen media** refers to content produced, collected, and shared by private citizens. At first it seemed that the advent of social media would require a new media paradigm—one in which users would usurp the absolute control of corporations and other commercial interests and that content would be more democratic and diverse. However, some believe that social media is more a permutation of mass media than an alternative to it.[45] Whatever the form, the media still remains an important agent of socialization.

Can We Be "Resocialized"? Experiencing the Total Institution

Resocialization is the process of learning new norms, values, attitudes, and behaviours and abandoning old ones. This process involves more than the kinds of secondary socialization that occur when we marry or take a new job. Yoda, the noted Jedi philosopher, says it well in the film *The Empire Strikes Back*, when he says that sometimes "you must unlearn what you have learned."

The most effective forms of resocialization occur in **total institutions** that isolate people from outside influences so they can be reformed and controlled.[46] People may enter total institutions voluntarily, as in the case of non-draftees that enlist in military boot camps, or involuntarily, as in the case of inmates in prisons. All total institutions have certain characteristics:

1. There is one authority, and activities take place in specific locations.
2. Carefully structured activities control the participants.
3. Authorities carefully screen all information from outside the institution.
4. Rules and roles are clearly defined.
5. A strict hierarchy exists within the institution.
6. Total institutions restrict individual choice.

How might development inside a total institution affect a person's sense of self? Look back to the opening of this chapter and consider the implications of the reference to the "hasty rituals" (like being shaven to the scalp) that young recruits to the Marines go through at the start of basic training.

Sociologist Harold Garfinkel explored the similarities in the ways prison inmates and military enlistees are resocialized upon entering those total institutions.[50] Garfinkel points out that these institutions "welcome" new members through some form of degrading ceremony designed to humiliate the person. This humiliation is required to "break them down" so that resocialization is possible. Inmates and enlistees may both have their heads shaved and their "street clothes" taken away. After putting on uniforms, their individual style of dress is erased in order for them to look like everyone else. In boot camp and under the control of the institution, the new recruit has no choice in when he or she will eat, sleep, or bathe. Similarly, inmates receive numbers to replace their names, are given uniforms to wear, and are told where they will sleep, when they will eat, and how they will spend their allocated "free" time. In both cases, the goal is to strip away former identity and resocialize the person into someone who will be obedient to commands.

Through resocialization, the institution controls all aspects of a person's life.[51] The techniques that total institutions use change the inmate's or soldier's internal thinking, which in turn changes his or her sense of self.

MAKE CONNECTIONS

Gender Bias in the Media

Kim Campbell, who for a few months in 1993 served as Canada's first female prime minister, has been quoted as saying that if she were to do it all again, she would address the issue of gender bias in the media's political coverage head-on instead of letting it take her by surprise in the election that ended her brief time in power.[47] Campbell said she realized later that, although the media had not schemed to oust her from office, reporters had reacted to their unconscious ideals and expectations of women during her disastrous re-election campaign.[48]

Consider the effect the media have in determining gendered stereotypes through sexual imagery. Kirstie Farrar and her colleagues reviewed the sexual images that aired during prime-time television hours. They found that images on shows like *The Bachelor* and *One Tree Hill* tended to reinforce the notion that women are primarily sexual objects.[49] These and other images supported the dominant male/submissive female paradigm. They also found that 64 percent of the television shows during the 2000–2001 season contained sexual messages and that sexual intercourse occurred in 14 percent of the shows. For conflict theorists, these findings suggest that such imagery is an effort by those in power to maintain it. Men are the primary decision makers for large media corporations, so are they responsible for perpetuating these ideas about gender roles?

Because of the way gender roles are defined in society, it can take several years to see through the generalizations. I can remember realizing during my first year in college that my father and I had never hugged, primarily because of gender ideals about men touching each other. The next time I returned home, I gave him a big hug as soon as he answered the door. From that day forth, hugging was no longer taboo at our house. In this simple way, my father and I changed our gender socialization.

>>> **Prison inmates are stripped of their individual identities so that they can be transformed into people who willingly follow the orders** of those in authority.

GooDAura/Fotolia

think sociologically: HOW DO THE FOUR THEORETICAL PERSPECTIVES VIEW SOCIALIZATION?

Symbolic Interactionism

We've seen how symbolic interactionists focus on individuals and small-group interactions. It is through these interactions that people learn about their culture and create a sense of self. The symbolic interactionist perspective would focus on how the process of socialization takes place between individuals and within small groups. Symbolic interactionists would highlight the communication, the use of symbols, and the interpretation of the messages by individuals as they internalize the various aspects of culture and create an identity, a sense of self. Without socialization, we would all be like Genie, unable to fit in to our society.

If a symbolic interactionist were studying the socialization that takes place in schools, he or she might look at the interactions between teachers and students. He or she would focus on how teacher expectations influence student performance and self-image. What is the teacher doing to teach students? What kinds of interactions are occurring in the classroom? How does the teacher adapt his or her teaching methods to deal with different kinds of students? What kind of socialization is happening between students? What is going on in each of the groups of friends in the schoolyard? These are the kinds of questions that a symbolic interactionist might ask regarding socialization at school.

Functionalism

Whereas symbolic interactionists study the effect of interactions on individuals, functionalists examine how certain institutions, such as religion and education, also perform a socialization function in society. An institution's function, and the individual's relationship to that institution, helps determine what role it plays in the development of self. For functionalists, socialization is important to society because it helps pass on cultural norms and values. Therefore, it maintains social stability. Without socialization, there would be no common or shared culture, and society would not work.

Functionalists would focus on the formal curriculum that is taught in schools. Which subjects are taught? How are they taught? What is the content of the courses? Functionalists focus on how schools transmit the formal and common knowledge, norms, and values of a particular society. This is important for maintaining social stability. The functionalist perspective would examine how effectively the educational system transmits these components of culture.

Conflict Theory

Whereas functionalists highlight the positive function of socialization in teaching all members of a society how to live and survive in that society, conflict theorists take the view that socialization also teaches and therefore reproduces the inequalities between different classes, religions, ethnicities, and other social groups. Socialization maintains the social, political, and economic advantages of the dominant classes. In this way, it can slow or even work against social change.

A conflict theorist would look at the educational system as a social institution that largely reflects the interests and values of the dominant classes in society. Because conflict theory also uses a macro level of analysis, it focuses on many of the same functions of education as functionalism. Both functionalists and conflict theorists agree that the educational system practises sorting, but while functionalists

GENDER SOCIALIZATION teaches us about the attitudes and behaviours that a society defines as appropriate for each sex.

claim that schools sort based upon merit, conflict theorists argue that schools sort along class lines. According to conflict theorists, schools socialize those in the working classes to accept their position as lower-class members of society.

Feminist Theory

Feminist theory focuses on the inequalities between men and women. This inequality is not natural, and it is not inevitable. It is a result of socialization; most societies teach their members that men and women are not only different but that what men do is more important. **Gender socialization** teaches us about the attitudes and behaviours that a society defines as appropriate for each sex. We learn about gender from our family and friends. However, a patriarchal social structure also has a powerful influence on all of us.

A feminist theorist would look at how education is a gendered institution. At a micro level, a feminist theorist would look at how gender socialization occurs in the classroom. Does the teacher treat boys and girls differently? The schoolyard is also a powerful site for gender socialization. At the macro level, a feminist theorist might look at the number and distribution of males and females in different fields of study. In 2010, females represented 58.2 percent of all post-secondary graduates. In fact, female degree-holders outnumbered males in every field of study except mathematics, computer sciences, architecture, engineering, transportation services, agriculture, natural resources and conservation, and leisure studies. However, males accounted for a higher proportion of doctorate recipients.[52]

THE PROPORTION OF MALE AND FEMALE POSTSECONDARY GRADUATES

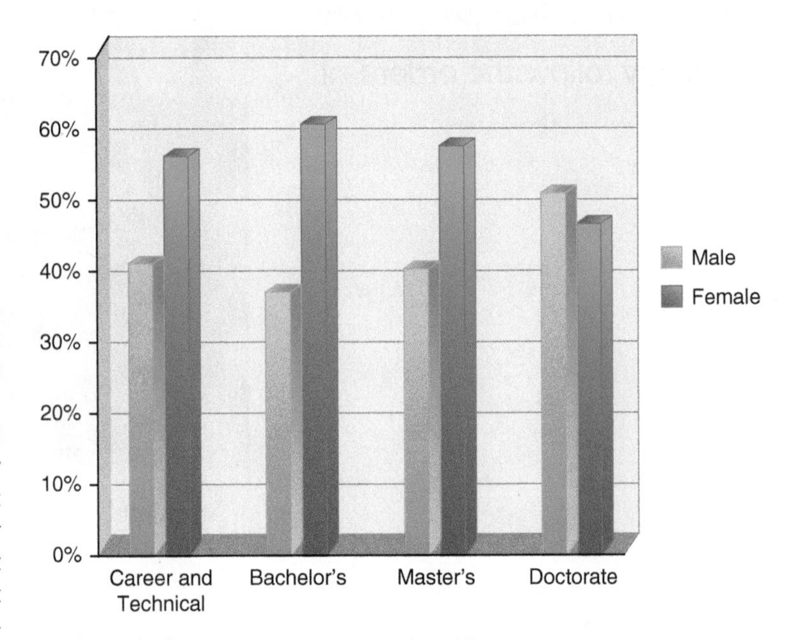

Source: Statistics Canada. (2013). Table 477-0020: Public postsecondary graduates, by Pan-Canadian Standard Classification of Education (PCSCE), Classification of Instructional Programs, Primary Grouping (CIP_PG), sex and immigration status annual (number). http://www5.statcan.gc.ca/cansim/a47. This does not constitute an endorsement by Statistics Canada of this product.

MAKE CONNECTIONS

Fictional Tales and Gender

From *Aesop's Fables* to the brothers Grimm, folktales symbolize the innocence of childhood. But a closer analysis shows how these folktales shape how children perceive gender. Most folktales follow a typical pattern in which a dependent woman relies exclusively on a strong man to save her from harm. Think about the story of Rapunzel—the girl with the long, golden hair who is trapped in a tower by a witch. In the story, Rapunzel is merely a piece of property, given away by her father in exchange for his life. While trapped in the tower, Rapunzel is dependent on the witch and unable to escape. Rapunzel, afraid of the witch's wrath, remains in the tower alone and refuses the prince's help to escape. The prince goes blind because he is unable to save the beauty. Young children, especially young girls, who read these tales internalize the idea that being submissive and reliant on men is a desired trait.

These stereotypes are not just a part of archaic folktales; they also appear in modern works of fiction. Television programs like *Grey's Anatomy* and *Desperate Housewives* feature female characters who reinforce generalizations about gender roles. That said, there are a number of stereotype-breaking characters, like those featured on *Buffy the Vampire Slayer* and *Lost*. Even in the *Harry Potter* series, Hermione Granger, Harry's sidekick, is a secondary character and yet she is always saving the day. Real life does not work as it does in fiction. Not all men can be heroes, and passivity and dependency rarely bring women success in the modern world.

>>> **ACTIVITY** Think about a movie or TV show you've seen or a book you've read recently. What gender stereotypes, if any, are depicted on the screen or the page? Does the work defy any traditional gender stereotypes? Write a paragraph analyzing the work you chose.

WRAP YOUR MIND AROUND THE THEORY

In order for a society to function, **functionalists argue that people need to be socialized into the norms and values of that society.**

Gunter Marx/Dorling Kindersley

FUNCTIONALISM

For functionalists, socialization is important to society because it helps to pass on cultural norms and values. Without socialization, there would be no common or shared culture, and society would not work. Functionalists examine how certain institutions, such as education, perform a socialization function in society. Functionalists focus on the formal curriculum that is taught in schools and how schools transmit the common knowledge, norms, and values of a particular society. This is important for maintaining social stability. The functionalist perspective examines how effectively the educational system transmits these components of culture.

CONFLICT THEORY

Conflict theorists take the view that socialization teaches and therefore reproduces the inequalities between different classes, religions, ethnicities, and other social groups. In this way, it can slow or even work against social change. A conflict theorist looks at the educational system as a social institution that largely reflects the interests and values of the dominant classes in society. Conflict theorists argue that schools sort along class lines and socialize those in the working classes to accept their position as lower-class members of society.

SYMBOLIC INTERACTIONISM

The symbolic interactionist perspective focuses on how the process of socialization takes place between individuals and within small groups. Symbolic interactionists highlight the types of communication, the use of symbols, and the interpretation of the messages by individuals as they internalize the various aspects of culture and create an identity, a sense of self. Symbolic interactionists look at the interactions between teachers and students in schools and how teacher expectations can influence student performance and self-image.

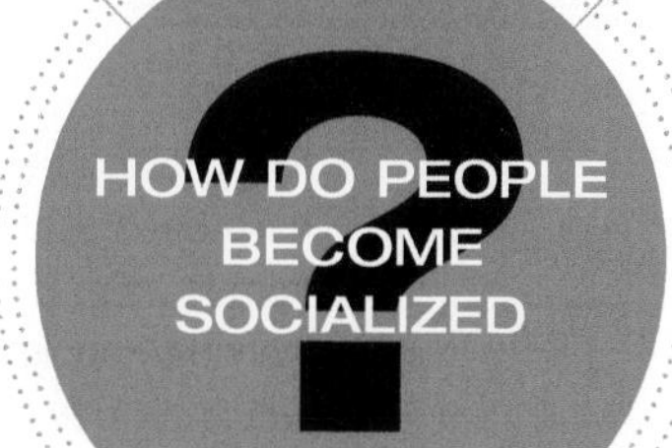
HOW DO PEOPLE BECOME SOCIALIZED

FEMINIST THEORY

Feminist theorists believe that the inequalities between men and women are not natural and not inevitable; they are the result of socialization. Gender socialization teaches us about the attitudes and behaviours that a society defines as appropriate for each sex. We learn about gender from our family members and friends. However, a patriarchal social structure also has a powerful influence on all of us. From the feminist perspective, education is a gendered institution. At a micro level, gender socialization occurs in the classroom when the teacher treats boys and girls differently. At the macro level, the number and distribution of males and females in different fields of study shows differences.

Gender socialization teaches us about the attitudes and behaviours that a society defines as appropriate for each sex. What have you learned about gender from your parents, friends, schools, and the media?

Bst2012/Fotolia

Erik Isakson/Tetra Images/Corbis

If the students in class snicker and whisper while the child gives his report, how might the child interpret these symbols? How might he feel about himself?

discover sociology in action: HOW DOES UNDERSTANDING SOCIALIZATION HELP US IMPROVE OUR SOCIETY?

Applying Sociological Thinking in the World, Social Policy, and the Canadian Charter of Rights and Freedoms

Auguste Comte, the founder of sociology, urged us to use our knowledge about society to improve society. Lawmakers have used that philosophy to enact various **social policies**, deliberate strategies designed to correct recognized social problems. The 1982 *Canadian Charter of Rights and Freedoms* might be considered one such attempt to implement sociological knowledge.

The *Charter* is part of the Canadian Constitution, the top law in the country. It has a wide impact, because:

- Governments across the country use the *Charter* as a guide in making laws.
- Courts across the country use it as a guide in applying laws.
- Individuals, associations, or the government can ask courts to rule on how it applies in particular cases.[53]

The *Charter* is regarded as the biggest achievement of then Prime Minister Pierre Trudeau. In September 2010, a decade after Trudeau's death, his politician son Justin noted: "When my father was fighting for the just society, it was about recognizing the rights of all individuals and that was (enshrined) with the *Charter of Rights and Freedoms*."[54]

ACTIVITIES

1. What agents of socialization influenced you the most when you were growing up? What influences you the most now?
2. Read stories of feral children, such as Genie. What is the importance of early socialization on development? Have researchers made any strides in socializing feral children?
3. Visit a developmental disability hospital in your area and talk to the staff and parents. Can the best efforts at socialization overcome nature? Write about your findings.

SOCIAL POLICIES are deliberate strategies designed to correct recognized social problems.

From 1867, when Canada was founded, until 1982, the Canadian Constitution did not have a bill of rights that governments had to follow. (The federal government had introduced a Canadian Bill of Rights in 1960, but it wasn't part of the Constitution and didn't have much power.) The *Charter* had a difficult political birth, and it was decided that the easiest way to introduce it was to agree that the provinces would have a way of temporarily avoiding some parts of it for a while. The equality rights section was delayed until April 1985, allowing governments across the country time to make the necessary updates to their laws.[55]

For just one example of how important the *Charter* is, consider that if it had been in effect at the time, Japanese Canadians might not have been sent to internment camps and had their property taken away from them in 1942, during World War II.[56] The historical treatment of First Nations Peoples (some of which is described in the previous chapter) would have been very different, too.

"Of all the human rights milestones in 20th century Canada, arguably the single most significant is the passing of the *Charter of Rights and Freedoms*," the Canadian Human Rights Commission says. "With its signing, human rights became an intrinsic and irrevocable part of our Canadian identity."[57]

CHAPTER

04

WHAT IS SOCIALIZATION? 68

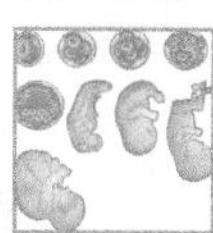

the lifelong process by which the norms, values, and other aspects of a culture are learned and internalized by group members and provides the individual with the skills necessary for participating in society

HOW DO THE FOUR THEORETICAL PERSPECTIVES VIEW SOCIALIZATION? 79

functionalism: institutions, such as religion and education, are useful in socializing individuals

conflict theory: an individual's social class can influence how she or he is socialized

symbolic interactionism: interactions between individuals and small groups teach us about our culture and give us a sense of identity

feminist theory: societies use gender socialization to teach members about the attitudes and behaviours that are appropriate for each sex

HOW DOES UNDERSTANDING SOCIALIZATION HELP US IMPROVE OUR SOCIETY? 82

through social policies that are designed to correct recognized social problems

jodi mcgee/Fotolia

get the topic: WHAT IS SOCIALIZATION?

Theories

SYMBOLIC INTERACTIONISM 79

- socialization occurs through individual and small-group interactions
- people develop their sense of self by incorporating how others interpret their behaviour
- teacher expectations can influence student performance and self-image

FUNCTIONALISM 79

- institutions, such as religion and education, perform a socialization function in society
- socialization is important to society because it maintains social stability
- schools transmit the formal knowledge, norms, and values of a particular society

CONFLICT THEORY 79

- socialization teaches and reproduces the inequalities between different social classes
- socialization maintains the social, political, and economic advantages of the dominant classes
- schools socialize those in the working classes to accept their position as lower-class members of society

FEMINIST THEORY 80

- gender socialization teaches us about the attitudes and behaviours that a society defines as appropriate for each sex
- social institutions and agents of socialization perpetuate gender stereotypes
- education is a gendered institution; teachers may treat boys and girls differently, and males and females pursue different fields of study

Key Terms

socialization is the lifelong process by which the norms, values, and other aspects of a culture are learned and internalized by group members and provides the individual with the skills necessary for participating in society. *68*

primary socialization is socialization that occurs during childhood. *69*

secondary socialization is socialization that continues throughout our lives. *69*

nature theory states that the genes we get from our parents are the primary cause of human behaviour. *69*

nurture theory states that our environment is the primary influence on the way we think, feel, and behave. *69*

looking-glass self is the theory that the self develops through a process of reflection, like a reflection in a mirror. *71*

I self is the subjective part of the self. *71*

me self is the objective part of the self. *71*

imitation stage is Mead's first stage of development, which is the period from birth to about age 2, when children merely copy the behaviours of those around them. *71*

play stage is Mead's second stage of development, which occurs around the ages of 2–4 years, during which children play roles and begin to take on the characteristics of important people in their world. *71*

significant others are the people we consider to be important and who we want to impress. *71*

game stage is Mead's third stage of development, which never truly ends, and is the stage in which we begin to understand that others have expectations and demands placed upon them. *71*

generalized other is a sense of the norms, beliefs, and expectations specific to our culture. *71*

impression management is management of the impression that a performer makes on others. *71*

front stage is what the audience sees, or the part of ourselves that we present to others. *71*

backstage is the demeanour that incorporates our true feelings and beliefs. *71*

face-saving work is a reaction to embarrassment in the form of either humour, anger, or retreat. *71*

psychosocial crisis is a crisis occurring during each of Erikson's stages that will be resolved either positively or negatively, and each outcome will have an effect on our ability to deal with the next one. *72*

cognitive development is a person's ability to think and reason. *72*

sensorimotor stage is the stage (birth to 2 years) at which infants learn to experience and think about the world through their senses and motor skills. *72*

preoperational stage is the stage (ages 2 through 7 years) at which the ability to speak grows rapidly. *74*

concrete operational stage is the stage (ages 7 through 12 years) at which children can think about objects in the world in more than one way and start to understand causal connections in their surroundings. *74*

formal operational stage is the stage (ages 12 years and above) at which people become able to comprehend abstract thought. *74*

preconventional level is the first stage of moral development that lasts through the elementary school years; at this level, children make their moral judgments within a framework of hedonistic principles. *75*

hedonism is seeking pleasure over pain. *75*

conventional level is the second stage of moral development that arises before puberty and uses the lens of norms and rules to determine what is right and wrong. *75*

postconventional level is the third stage of moral development that refers to a morality based on abstract principles. *75*

morality of justice is morality based on the rule of law. *76*

morality of care is morality decided by a standard of how best to help those who are in need. *76*

agents of socialization are the people, groups, and institutions that shape our self-concept, beliefs, and behaviour. *76*

socioeconomic status is a measure of an individual's or family's position within the social structure. *77*

peers are people who are similar in age and who share many common interests. *77*

mass media are forms of communication such as television, newspapers, radio, and magazines that are designed to reach a large audience. *77*

social media are forms of electronic communication such as blogs, forums, podcasts, and sites for social networking through which users create and share information, ideas, personal messages, and other content. *77*

citizen media refers to content produced, collected, and shared by private citizens. *78*

resocialization is the process of learning new norms, values, attitudes, and behaviours and abandoning old ones. *78*

total institutions are places in which the most effective forms of resocialization can occur because they isolate people from outside influences so they can be reformed and controlled. *78*

gender socialization teaches us about the attitudes and behaviours that a society defines as appropriate for each sex. *80*

social policies are deliberate strategies designed to correct recognized social problems. *82*

Sample Test Questions

These multiple-choice questions are similar to those found in the test bank that accompanies this textbook.

1. During which of Erikson's eight stages would a person develop a strong sense of self?
   - **a.** Trust vs. mistrust
   - **b.** Initiative vs. guilt
   - **c.** Industry vs. inferiority
   - **d.** Identity vs. role confusion
2. According to Piaget, at what stage of cognitive development does a child's ability to speak grow rapidly?
   - **a.** Sensorimotor stage
   - **b.** Preoperational stage
   - **c.** Concrete operational stage
   - **d.** Formal operational stage
3. The preconventional level, conventional level, and postconventional level are stages of
   - **a.** moral development.
   - **b.** social development.
   - **c.** creative development.
   - **d.** language development.
4. Which of the following is *not* an example of a total institution?
   - **a.** A prison
   - **b.** The military
   - **c.** A university
   - **d.** A rehabilitation clinic
5. Which researcher developed the principles of the morality of care and the morality of justice?
   - **a.** Erik Erikson
   - **b.** Carol Gilligan
   - **c.** Lawrence Kohlberg
   - **d.** George Herbert Mead

ANSWERS: 1. d; 2. b; 3. a; 4. c; 5. b

ESSAY

1. How did Piaget describe the stage at which a child learns to speak?
2. How does each theoretical perspective explain socialization?
3. Why is resocialization important in total institutions?
4. Feminist theorists often argue that men use their power to dominate and limit women. Provide an example of gender bias in the media and explain how it supports this theory.
5. In terms of Erikson's theory, how was Genie's development stunted?

WHERE TO START YOUR RESEARCH PAPER

For more information on the U.S. Marine Corps and basic training: www.marines.com/becoming-a-marine/recruit-training.

For more on socialization theories: www.boundless.com/sociology/understanding-socialization/theories-of-socialization/theories-of-socialization/.

To find data on child socialization, go to www.childdevelopmentinfo.com.

For information on early childhood learning and development, go to www.eccdc.org.

To learn more about how media influences society (particularly the sociological perspective on media and society), go to www.theory.org.uk/resources.htm.

Remember to check www.thethinkspot.ca **for additional information, downloadable flashcards, and other helpful resources.**

SOCIAL STRUCTURES AND INTERACTION

anandkrish16/Fotolia

WHAT ELEMENTS CREATE THE SOCIAL STRUCTURES?
WHAT ARE THE CHARACTERISTICS OF SOCIAL INTERACTION?
HOW DO THE FOUR PERSPECTIVES VIEW THE SOCIAL STRUCTURES AND SOCIAL INTERACTION?
HOW CAN SOCIAL POLICIES IMPROVE SOCIETY?

"Many immigrants, refugees, and international students have come to Canada with the belief that the hard work, intelligence, ambition, tenacity, maturity, and other personal qualities that made them successful in their old countries and helped them survive what might have been a treacherous journey would also help them to succeed in Canada. Unfortunately, this has not always been the case. Such overconfidence has been the undoing of many an immigrant, refugee and international student. Far too many have been blindsided in the benign looking environment of Canada, forcing them to abandon their dreams and to accept conditions of life that they would never have imagined a few years before.

"Not taking the time to understand the Canadian system, the underlying rules that govern life, and strategic resources that facilitate success can be pricey in the long run. . . . The point is that it takes strategic resources to enhance one's hard work, intelligence, talents, abilities and ambition to make the stories about Canada as land of milk and honey a reality.

"Although Canada claims to be a multicultural country, the reality is that conventional rewards are located in the upper/middle class Anglo and Franco cultures of both the larger society and academia. Those who have access to strategic resources to effectively connect with the opportunity structures of the mainstream culture and/or academia are those who get most conventional rewards. New entrants to Canada who remain disconnected from strategic resources remain secluded in their minority cultures and tend to experience trapped socio-economic mobility. Real life experiences of immigrants, refugees and international students support this claim. The fact is connecting with the opportunity structures in the mainstream Canadian culture and academia from a culture on the margins requires appropriate information and knowledge, definitive decisions on the choices the information presents, mentoring, relevant networking and a strong support system. . . .

"For new immigrants, refugees, and international students, basic skills are not enough because of the reality that unequal opportunity structures exist in Canadian society and academia that tend to work against minorities because of racism, ethnocentrism and other social injustices embedded in the Canadian social structure. Therefore racial and ethnic minorities are located in the margins of Canadian society and their success may not be determined by hard work, individual intelligence and personal ambition. Should new immigrants, refugees and international students despair and lose faith in themselves because of racism, ethnocentrism and injustices in Canadian society and academia? No! There is a way out! Many immigrants, refugees and international students have proven that there is some wisdom in the popular notion in the minority communities that says because of racism and ethnocentrism in Canada minorities need higher than average qualifications, abilities, skills, mentors, and support systems in order to achieve success. . . . The reality is that new immigrants, refugees and international students can succeed in Canadian society and academia despite the prevalence of racism, ethnocentrism and other barriers they face. *Chocolate can thrive in a Vanilla World!*"[1]

Macro *and* Micro Orientations

CHAPTER 05

By focusing on how racial and cultural minorities within Canada can succeed, Francis Adu-Febiri and Everett Ofori illustrate that there is a clear link between the small-scale and large-scale components of a society.

CCB Publishing

While I was a student, I also worked at the university cafeteria. One day, I came in to work to find that a new person had been hired to work in the dishroom. He ended up telling me his story. He had just recently arrived from Burma (also known as Myanmar), and he had a degree in engineering. However, his degree was not recognized in Canada, so he was obliged to take engineering courses at the university. Because his degree was not recognized, he was unable to find a job in his field, and so the engineer was working as a dishwasher.

That is the kind of social barrier that Adu-Febiri and Ofori write about overcoming in *Succeeding from the Margins of Canadian Society: A Strategic Resource for New Immigrants, Refugees and International Students.*

When you take note of differences between the lives of minority and established segments of Canadian society, you are really looking at ways in which small and large components combine to create the social world.

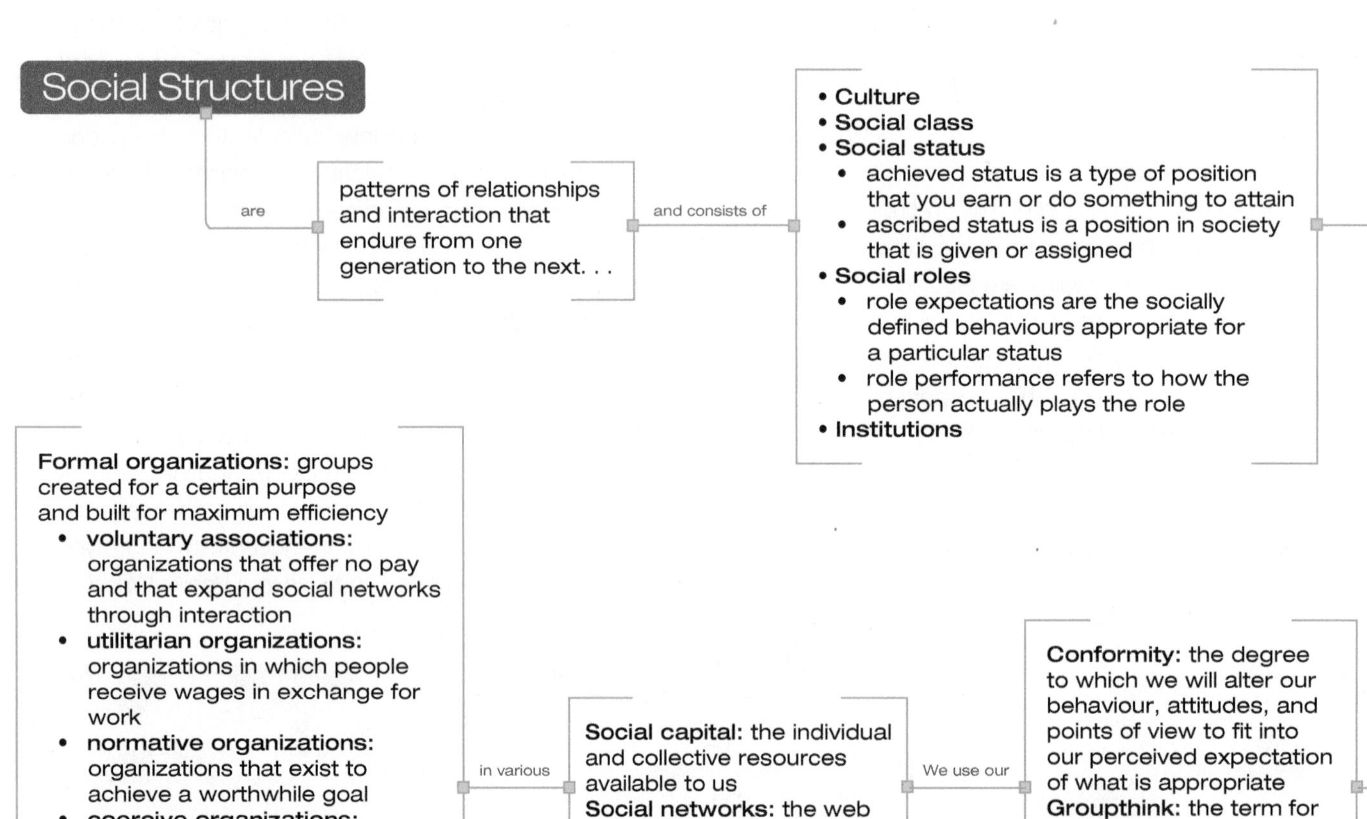
Social Structures
are
patterns of relationships and interaction that endure from one generation to the next. . .
and consists of
• Culture
• Social class
• Social status
• achieved status is a type of position that you earn or do something to attain
• ascribed status is a position in society that is given or assigned
• Social roles
• role expectations are the socially defined behaviours appropriate for a particular status
• role performance refers to how the person actually plays the role
• Institutions
Formal organizations: groups created for a certain purpose and built for maximum efficiency
• voluntary associations: organizations that offer no pay and that expand social networks through interaction
• utilitarian organizations: organizations in which people receive wages in exchange for work
• normative organizations: organizations that exist to achieve a worthwhile goal
• coercive organizations: organizations that people are forced to join
• bureaucracies: formal organizations that are organized into a hierarchy of smaller departments
in various
Social capital: the individual and collective resources available to us
Social networks: the web of ties we have with others
We use our
Conformity: the degree to which we will alter our behaviour, attitudes, and points of view to fit into our perceived expectation of what is appropriate
Groupthink: the term for group decisions that are made without objective thought

get the topic: WHAT ELEMENTS CREATE THE SOCIAL STRUCTURES?

In Chapter 1, you learned that macrosociology focuses on the social structures that exist within a society and examines how those structures create the social world. Microsociology deals primarily with the intimate, face-to-face interactions of daily social life. In this chapter, you will learn how sociologists use both of these levels of analysis in order to understand *what* the social structures are made of and *how* social interactions work.

Social Structures

You've probably never had to think too hard about what society is. That's because we often have an inherent understanding of how our society is structured. **Social structures** are patterns of relationships and interaction that endure from one generation to the next. A social structure determines who does what and how things get done.

When you were in high school, you quickly learned that the guidance counsellor could help you choose your courses but was probably not much help with your math homework. You didn't expect the principal to clean the blackboards, and you would have been surprised if the janitor had given you a detention. The pattern of these relationships does not change much over time, and it guides your expectations of how things work. Social structures are made up of different elements—culture, social class, status, roles, and social institutions.

SOCIAL STRUCTURES are patterns of relationships that endure from one generation to the next.

SOCIAL CLASS refers to a group of people with similar access to power, wealth, and prestige.

CULTURE

Culture, discussed in depth in Chapter 3, is the symbols, values, norms, and material objects that societies create. The unique components of culture touch every aspect of our lives and are a large part of our society. Culture is what makes a social structure come alive.

SOCIAL CLASS

Social class, which will be discussed in more detail in Chapter 6, refers to a group of people with similar access to power, wealth, and prestige. The main determinants of social class are wealth, income, education, and occupation. The importance of social class varies, depending upon the society. In Canada, for example, about 30 percent of the population can be considered working class.[2] Members of this social class are often the swing voters in elections.

and is held together by

Solidarity:
- **mechanical:** usually found in traditional societies; people share beliefs and values
- **organic solidarity:** society with a diverse division of labour
- **Gemeinschaft:** community connections involving personal relationships
- **Gesellschaft:** social connections that are more formal and impersonal

Social Interaction

involves

Social groups:
- primary groups are groups that are small, intimate, and enduring
- secondary groups are groups that are formal, superficial, and temporary
- in-group is a group to which we feel an affinity or closeness
- out-group is a group from which we are disconnected
- reference group is the group that you use to evaluate yourself

and have

A. Ramey/PhotoEdit,Inc

and

Leadership styles: behavioural modes that leaders use to influence group members
- **autocratic leaders** are leaders who determine the group policies and assign tasks
- **democratic leaders** are leaders who strive to set group policy by discussion and agreement
- **laissez-faire leaders** are leaders who lead by absence and may in fact not want to be leaders at all

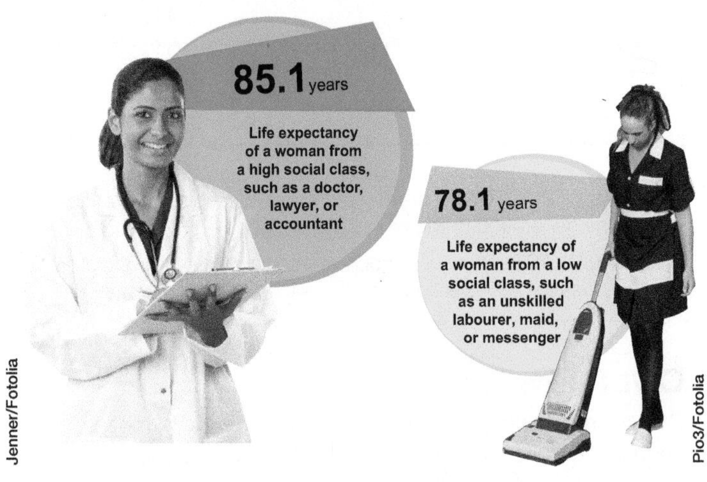

85.1 years
Life expectancy of a woman from a high social class, such as a doctor, lawyer, or accountant
78.1 years
Life expectancy of a woman from a low social class, such as an unskilled labourer, maid, or messenger
Jenner/Fotolia
Pio3/Fotolia

Source: Data from Jill Sheerman, "Wealthy, Healthy, and Aged 85: The Women Living Even Longer"

Social class not only differentiates groups of people; it ranks them. Your social class can have a profound impact on your life, especially the length of it. Studies have shown that your social class can affect your health, happiness, and life span.[3]

SOCIAL STATUS

If you look around you, society seems to be generally ordered. People know what they have to do and how to do it. Maybe you took the bus to school this morning. When you boarded the bus, you did not expect to drive the bus; there was a driver to do that. When you walked into class, you probably sat at a desk and prepared to take notes. You did not stand at the front of the class and prepare to give a lecture—you waited for your instructor to do that. When I walk into a classroom at Vanier College, I *do* stand at the front and prepare to explain what social status is. However, I am also a student at Sherbrooke University, and when I walk into one of those classes, I *don't* stand at the front; I sit at one of the desks.

In our daily social life, we do many different things. Sociologists use the term **social status** to refer to socially defined positions that are characterized by certain expectations, rights, and duties. For example, bus driver and passenger, student and teacher are different social statuses. They define different positions that people occupy in society. Each status is part of the larger social structure and exists independently of the individual.

SOCIAL STATUS refers to socially defined positions that are characterized by certain expectations, rights, and duties.

ACHIEVED STATUS is a type of position that you earn or do something to attain.

ASCRIBED STATUS is a position in society that is given or assigned.

STATUS SET is all the statuses we occupy.

MASTER STATUS is the most important status.

Sociologists divide status into two different types: achieved and ascribed. **Achieved status** refers to a type of position that someone earns or does something to attain. When you finish your college degree, you'll have *achieved* the position of college graduate. **Ascribed status** describes a position in society that is given or assigned. For example, socialite Kim Kardashian's fame is an ascribed status. Because she was born into a wealthy and famous family, she draws attention at red-carpet events and enjoys the privileges of a celebrity. Kardashian didn't choose to be wealthy, just like you didn't choose your gender, race, or ethnicity. Ascribed statuses are given to us at birth; we do not make a decision to choose them.

We occupy many statuses. For example, I am an author, a college professor, a Canadian, a father, a son, and a brother, just to name a few. All our statuses together make up our **status set**. Since we all occupy more than one status in life, we will often gravitate toward one, which we call a **master status**. The master status may be what is most important to us, such as our status as a parent, or what is most important to others, such as one's ethnicity or social class.

Statuses are important in society because they tell us what positions we hold in the social structure. We also look at other people's statuses in order to know what to expect from them. Because statuses are so

GO GLOBAL

Social Class in China

While some cultures don't have a rigid social class system, others have a well-established system. Take, for example, the Hukou system used in China immediately after the Communist Revolution. Under this system, once a person registered in a specific geographic area—rural or urban—he or she was not allowed to move far beyond the area. This fixed system gave city dwellers the advantages of better access to education and more opportunity for advancement than those living in rural areas.

Today, groups of workers in rural areas are predominantly male and make up emerging social classes. In the rural areas of modern China, being connected to the government is far less important than it is in urban areas, where Communist party membership can be vital to a person's success. Therefore, in urban areas, class systems are significantly different than they are in rural areas. For one thing, they're much more fluid and allow for more movement than rural divisions do.

In the rigid rural class system, people do not have much freedom to move up and down the hierarchy. The rural system from top to bottom includes cadres, capitalists, managers, household business owners, professionals, wage labourers, and peasants.

For the urban class, the system is more flexible. The urban social class system from top to bottom includes capitalist entrepreneurs, intellectuals and professionals, members of the middle and working class, and the poor.

Because of the increasing fluidity of China's social systems, people are able to change the social class to which they belong. Receiving an education and owning a business are two ways that people raise their social standing.[4]

THINK SOCIOLOGICALLY

Social Class and Character Traits

Many people believe that a person's social class implies specific traits. A story in a 1994 book on Upper Canada College by Toronto writer James FitzGerald illustrates the point.[5] UCC is an exclusive boys' school whose students have included the sons of the rich and famous upper class in Canada, and some people regard it as snobbish. (Indeed, FitzGerald quotes author James Bacque as saying, "In my day, UCC was very snobbish."[6]) Trial judge Frank Kelso Roberts recalls in the book that when he was a young lawyer, another young lawyer—after being scolded by senior partners in their firm for making a mistake—confided that he had come up "through a poor family." The young lawyer used derogatory terms for the senior partners and mentioned in the same sentence that the senior partners were "all Upper Canada College graduates." Roberts didn't mention that he too had attended UCC. Instead, he agreed with the young lawyer's assessment.[7]

It's clear that the lawyer from a poor family regarded everyone who had graduated from the privileged halls of UCC as uniformly snobbish. He was so sure of it that he didn't even consider that a lawyer he looked up to might have attended the same school.

When people hear the terms *working class*, *middle class*, and *upper class*, they don't always think about character right away. They typically first associate the terms with occupation and salary. Do you think these terms also imply specific personal characteristics?

STATUS SYMBOLS are material signs that represent a specific status.

ROLE is the behaviour associated with a specific status.

ROLE EXPECTATIONS are the socially defined behaviours appropriate for a particular status.

important, we often use symbols in order to identify our statuses and to recognize the statuses of others. **Status symbols** are material signs that represent a specific status. For example, a wedding ring is a symbol that someone has the status "married"; a high school diploma is a symbol that that someone has the status "high school graduate"; and a uniform at a restaurant indicates that someone is an employee and not a customer.

In everyday usage, we often use the term *social status* to refer not just to different positions that people hold but also to the ranking of those positions. It then follows that "status symbols" do not simply represent different positions but are objects that represent better positions. Some sociologists prefer to use the terms *social status* and *status symbol* in a more neutral sense and to use the term *social class* to refer to the relative ranking of the different statuses within a society.

Status is an important social construct because **the positions we occupy lead to the roles we play.**

SOCIAL ROLES

As you saw above, when you enter a classroom, you sit in the chairs designated for students. You don't go to the front of the room and prepare to teach. You understand that your status is that of a student, and so you play the role of student, not teacher. A **role** is the behaviour associated with a specific status. If the professor asked you to lecture without any advance notice, you'd probably think something was wrong. This is because the statuses we occupy come with certain expectations about how to act while we occupy those statuses.

Role expectations are the socially defined behaviours appropriate for a particular status. They are like a set of instructions about how to act in social situations. When you go to the doctor, you probably do as the doctor says, even if you have never met him or her before.

Westend61/Corbis

>>> Here, the roles seem to have reversed. We'd normally expect the adult to play the role of the doctor and the child to play the role of the patient.

This is because the statuses of doctor and patient define the roles. However, if the doctor is rude or obviously uninterested in your care, you'll say he or she has a "bad bedside manner." We tend to view people as less capable when they do not fill their role as we would expect.

Role performance refers to how a person actually plays a role; when this is far from the role expectation, we call it deviance, which you will look at in Chapter 12. We evaluate role performance based on whether a person plays the role in a manner we expect.

Robert Merton clarifies other important components of roles.[8] Because we all have a complex status set, we all play a variety of roles. As a college student, you might also be a child, an employee, a parent, or a spouse, and when playing these multiple roles, you might find you have to choose among the competing demands of those roles—a phenomenon known as **role conflict**. This happens when you need to study for a final exam to satisfy your role as a student the same night you need to attend your dad's retirement party to satisfy your role as a child.

At other times, we may feel **role strain**. This occurs when the demands and expectations of one role are impossible for us to satisfy. You might feel role strain when deciding whether to go out to a party on Saturday night or to cram for your midterm that Monday.

The ways in which status and roles influence our lives often go unnoticed. We expect the cashier at the grocery store to take our money and send us on our way. If he or she talks too much, we might get annoyed. The setting influences our expectations. The variety of statuses and roles depends on the type of society.

***Succeeding from the Margins of Canadian Society*, Adu-Febiri and Ofori describe how racism and ethnocentrism in Canada stigmatize certain social statuses—immigrants, refugees, and international students.** The authors believe newcomers who understand what's going on can overcome social barriers and succeed in Canada.

SOCIAL INSTITUTIONS

Another element of the social structure is social institutions. **Social institutions** are structures that provide for patterned relationships and that are organized around a central activity or social need. A more detailed definition is that social institutions are:

> "a complex of positions, roles, norms and values lodged in particular types of social structures and organizing relatively stable patterns of human activity with respect to fundamental problems in producing life-sustaining resources, in reproducing individuals, and in sustaining viable societal structures within a given environment."[9]

In other words, the statuses and roles are already established and the members of society merely need to step into them. It's important to note that the specifics of these institutions change with the type of society and the culture of the people being studied. Let's look at some of the most important social institutions.

ROLE CONFLICT is a phenomenon that occurs when one is forced to choose between the competing demands of multiple roles.

ROLE STRAIN occurs when the demands and expectations of one role are impossible for us to satisfy.

SOCIAL INSTITUTIONS are structures that provide for patterned relationships and that are organized around a central activity or social need.

ROLE PERFORMANCE refers to how a person actually plays a role.

Family

Families are a cultural universal. The form of the family may have changed a great deal throughout human history, but the institution of family has remained constant.[10] As a social institution, the family fulfills several social functions. It provides a legitimate context for reproduction, which is necessary for the continuation of society. Families also serve to regulate sexual behavior. Because they are small, intimate groups, families are very effective at primary socialization. Families instill in us the values, beliefs, and behavioural norms that tend to persist. From our family, we are also given many of our social statuses, such as our race and ethnic identity, our religious and moral beliefs, and our social class. Finally, the family is ideally a situation that provides protection, affection, companionship, and economic and emotional support.

Educational and Religious Systems

Two more cultural universals, education and religion, also assist in socialization. Educational systems transfer the knowledge and information of a society to new members both formally and informally.

Religious practice varies a great deal, depending upon the culture, but most religions unify people through an organized system of beliefs. By bringing people together, religion stabilizes society and provides a framework for people to live their lives.

Economic Systems

From the time of the earliest hunters and gatherers to today, societies have required a system that helps people get what they need to survive. Economic systems allow for the consumption, production, and orderly transition of goods from one person to another. If, for example, you want a new cell phone, you understand how to work to earn the money to get it.

Early economic systems involved bartering—the trading of goods from one person to another. As societies became more complex, the currency system of coins and money allowed for quicker and easier transitions of goods and services. Although bartering is often thought of as an ancient system, there are modern-day examples of the barter system on websites such as Craigslist. Craigslist gives users a forum to post free classified ads for jobs, internships, housing, and personals.

To keep a society's economic system running smoothly and efficiently, rules must be established. That's why every society has political and legal systems to help establish rules for society at large.

Political and Legal Systems

Ever since the first chief in the first hunter-gatherer tribe was named, people have been involved in politics. Political systems distribute power in a society, and power is a key component of any political

Every country has some type of educational system, even though every child does not always participate in that system.

SECONDARY SCHOOL NET ENROLLMENT RATE IN SELECTED COUNTRIES, 2011

Country	Rate
Niger	12%
Pakistan	35%
Mexico	73%
Thailand	74%
Switzerland	82%
Cuba	87%
Hungary	92%
Finland	93%
France	99%

Source: Data from the United Nations, The Millennium Development Goals Report, 2010.

system, whether a dictatorship or democracy. As you consider the importance of political systems, it's crucial to understand how power is used.

Political power is used to create laws or rules that dictate right and wrong in society. So, the political and legal systems are integrally linked. When someone with power sees something that's wrong, he or she is likely to create a law to fix it. The legal system serves the vital function of enforcing those laws to maintain social order and promote unity.

Although the forms may vary, family, education, religion, economics, politics, and legislation exist in every form of society. That makes these institutions social facts. As we have seen, societies become more complex as they develop; this complexity results in the replacement of many of the old ways of living and thinking.

Holding Society Together

In January 1998, icy rain fell on Quebec and surrounding areas for five days, in what came to be known as the ice storm of the century. In Quebec alone, 900 000 households lost power, and damage was estimated to be in the billions of dollars. At least 25 people died. The extreme weather forced about 100 000 people to leave their homes and take refuge in temporary shelters.[11] As a sociologist, I was amazed to see people's generosity; we learned that throughout the affected area, friends and family members threw open their doors and otherwise helped thousands of people stay warm. What exactly holds a society together? Solidarity. That's the "glue" that binds a society.

MECHANICAL SOLIDARITY refers to the type of community bonding usually found in traditional societies, in which people share beliefs and values and perform common activities.

ORGANIC SOLIDARITY occurs when people live in a society with a diverse division of labour.

GEMEINSCHAFT refers to community connections involving personal relationships based on friendship and kinship ties, such as family.

GESELLSCHAFT refers to social connections that are more formal and impersonal.

MECHANICAL AND ORGANIC SOLIDARITY

Émile Durkheim described two different types of solidarity: mechanical and organic. **Mechanical solidarity** refers to the type of community bonding usually found in traditional societies, in which people share beliefs and values and perform common activities. It's this bond that works to keep society running smoothly.[12] As societies become more complex, their type of solidarity changes from mechanical to organic. **Organic solidarity** occurs when people live in a society with a diverse division of labour. Division of labour refers to the many different jobs we have today; the division forces people to depend on one another for survival. When was the last time you ate something you either grew or killed yourself? For most of us, the answer is never. Food is essential for survival, and yet most of us require a complex division of labour to feed ourselves. Farmers, truckers, and grocers all must do their part so we can eat.[13] This organic connection ensures that we get the things we need and holds society together. Beliefs remain important in a modern society, but what binds people together is their organic solidarity.[14]

Durkheim's idea led German sociologist Ferdinand Tönnies to investigate how the form of social grouping affects the interactions that we might have.

GEMEINSCHAFT AND *GESELLSCHAFT*

Social groupings can be classified into two distinct groups: *Gemeinschaft* (or community) and *Gesellschaft* (or society).[15] ***Gemeinschaft*** connections involve personal relationships based on friendship and kinship ties, such as family. A society's form can also influence the type of group. For example, small bands of hunters and gatherers live in communal societies because they have very little division of labour. This creates a group that exists with shared values, goals, and beliefs.

Often we also engage in groups considered as ***Gesellschaft***. These relationships are more formal and impersonal. Urban life is filled with many impersonal interchanges, so groups living here are more likely to occur in industrial and postindustrial societies. In such a society, social status, role, and social class become very important. Are you interested in knowing the janitor who cleans the classroom? You're probably only aware that the seats and floor are clean. Tönnies suggested that as societies grow more complex, many of our interactions invariably become more impersonal.

As you review these ideas, you can see that large cities tend toward *Gesellschaft* relationships, while smaller ones tend to be more *Gemeinschaft.* That means the size of your immediate area influences your daily life.[16] This idea leads sociologists to look for other common behaviour patterns. To do this, we turn from large-scale observations and review the sociological study of small orientations.

Since people have virtually the same job, mechanical solidarity creates a common moral order that holds people together.

get the topic: WHAT ARE THE CHARACTERISTICS OF SOCIAL INTERACTION?

On March 20, 2010, an estimated 75 000 public-sector workers from all across Quebec took to the streets in downtown Montreal to protest lagging contract talks. The crowd included nurses, teachers, and other public-sector workers. Among the crowd were about 30 teachers (including me) from the college where I teach. We all knew each other and saw each other quite often. Within the larger crowd, we were a **social group**. While I did stop to talk with others who were there, I noticed that I was acting differently with the people I knew. **Social interaction** refers to all the ways people behave and communicate in social situations.

SOCIAL GROUP is any number of people with similar norms, values, and behaviours who frequently interact with one another.

SOCIAL INTERACTION refers to all the ways people behave and communicate in social situations.

PRIMARY GROUPS are groups that are small, intimate, and enduring.

SECONDARY GROUPS are groups that are formal, superficial, and temporary.

BOUNDED RELATIONSHIPS are relationships that exist only under specific conditions.

Social Groups

Whether we're aware of it or not, we all belong to a social group in some way or another: Families, close friends, teammates, classmates, clubs, and organizations are all examples of groups to which we belong. Few of us could live totally self-reliant lives, so we find groups on which to depend. Of course, not all groups are the same. For all intents and purposes, your membership in your family is permanent, but you might not work with the same people for the rest of your life. Although no two groups are alike, they do have two commonalities: The members of the group share something in common, and they identify each other as members of that group.

PRIMARY AND SECONDARY GROUPS

Sociologist Charles H. Cooley suggests that we divide ourselves into two types of groups: primary and secondary.[17] **Primary groups** are small, intimate, and enduring. Your family and close friends are primary groups to which you belong. Primary groups help us determine who we are. Because our primary groups are usually made up of our relatives and closest friends, their presence and influence are constant reminders of how we see ourselves. It is through these relationships that we create our "looking-glass selves" (see Chapter 4). By reflecting their perceptions back to us, primary relationships provide valuable feedback.

Secondary groups are formal, superficial, and temporary, lasting for a short or fixed time.[18] The line between primary and secondary groups is not always clear-cut, but we have far more secondary groups than primary ones. Secondary groups generally come together to meet some specific goal or purpose. The group of you and your classmates is probably a secondary group. Such groups provide **bounded relationships** that exist only under specific conditions. For example, you and your co-workers might "do lunch," but you probably wouldn't invite them to a family function. Co-workers form a group that is probably of secondary importance to you.

Keith Brofsky/Photodisc/Getty Images

<<< **These people work in the same building, maybe even in the same office. But are these people a social group?**

Nagy-Bagoly Arpad/Shutterstock

We may point out the negative differences in others to elevate our own identity, even if the differences are insignificant. By poking fun at others, members of a group make themselves feel superior.

Formal types of social norms heavily influence the way we interact in secondary groups. These norms direct our actions and frame our communication. For example, you might ask the person who brings your mail about the weather, but you probably wouldn't get into a discussion about your relationship problems. Moreover, the types of norms we follow when interacting affect the way we feel about the group. If we are close and informal, we may fit in with the group, making it feel more like a primary one. If not, we can easily feel like outsiders.

IN-GROUP is a group to which we feel an affinity or a closeness.

IN-GROUP BIAS is the feeling that a person's in-group is superior to others.

OUT-GROUP is a group from which we are disconnected.

IN-GROUPS AND OUT-GROUPS

If you've ever waited for what seemed like hours on the sidelines while all the popular kids were getting chosen for the team, you've hoped to be welcomed into the in-group of people who don't have to wait until last to be chosen.

An **in-group** is a group to which we feel an affinity or closeness. For this reason, we often have a strong sense of loyalty to an in-group. Most people hold an **in-group bias**, the feeling that their in-group is superior to others.[19] The reality series *Wife Swap* perfectly illustrates how some families engage in in-group bias. The show, in which the mothers of two very different families change places for a period of time, usually features participants who believe theirs is the best way to raise a family. The mothers are then confronted by the strange interactions of another's family. Each mother considers the other family an out-group.

An **out-group** is a group from which we are disconnected. We often hold negative biases toward out-groups and may even feel very competitive toward them. We see this all the time in sports. Ask an Edmonton Oilers fan about the Calgary Flames, and you may well face unvarnished vitriol. The same will probably happen if you ask a Flames fan about the Oilers. In both cases, the respective fan group holds an out-group bias toward the other fan group. This is especially true in partisan politics, in which skirmishes among Conservatives, Liberals, and New Democrats can erupt over even mundane issues.

Sociologist Robert Merton suggests that our biases come from our position in society.[20] We see the traits of our group as acceptable, while we hold the views of out-groups as unreasonable. Generally, people hold a bias toward out-groups; however, a number of factors impact whether these biases are positive or negative.[21] For example, social outcasts in high school can hold either a positive or negative bias toward the "popular" group. If the outcasts know that nothing can change their outsider status, then they're likely to hold the cool kids in contempt. If, on the other hand, an outcast hopes to one day penetrate the cool group, he or she holds a positive bias toward them. In a sense, outcasts place the in-group on a pedestal if they think they can join them, and they knock this group down if they feel that joining the group is impossible.[22]

Sociologists Henry Tajfel and John Turner suggest that everyone seeks a positive social identity.[23] This pursuit is the root cause of in-group and out-group biases.

Position and power are other factors that can impact our perception of in-groups and out-groups. The workplace is common ground for these biases. Courtney Von Hippel studied temporary employees' out-group biases.[24] Temps who actually wanted a full-time job desired their co-workers' acceptance.[25] Meanwhile, temps who didn't expect permanent employment resented full-time employees because they didn't need to feel accepted.[26] In other words, it was highly unlikely that full-timers were taking these temps out to lunch.

REFERENCE GROUPS

In nearly every situation, we compare ourselves to another person or group. For example, you might not have a need for a new cell phone, but if one of your best friends keeps going on and on about his new iPhone, you might find yourself visiting your local phone dealer so you're not left

>>> **Reference groups** are not necessarily in-groups because we don't have to belong to them. **If, for example, you are studying to be a family therapist,** you might talk to therapists at your local community centre **about the duties and challenges of the career.** But simply thinking like a therapist doesn't make you one. **The therapists at the centre are just a reference group to help guide who you are and who you will become.**

Olimpik/Shutterstock

Vasiliy Koval/Fotolia

REFERENCE GROUP is the group that you use to evaluate yourself.

DYAD is a group consisting of only two people.

TRIAD is a group consisting of three people.

out. Since we cannot make judgments about our own behaviour in isolation, we often use others to assess our behaviour.[27] Sociologists refer to the group you use to evaluate yourself as a **reference group**.

GROUP SIZE, STRUCTURE, AND INTERACTION

Groups come in all shapes and sizes. As a group gets larger, maintaining in-group feelings becomes harder. Smaller groups tend to be more intimate and less official, which makes them easier to maintain.

The smallest and strongest form of a group is a **dyad**, a group consisting of only two people. The two members become very close, intimate, and connected. Think of a happy marriage as an example of a strong dyad. Such closeness is not possible in larger groups. Paradoxically, a dyad can also be unstable because either member can unilaterally decide to dissolve the group.[28] If someone has ever dumped you, you probably understand this principle.

When a third member enters a twosome, a **triad**, or group of three, forms. In a triad, mediation, alliances, and competition are likely. For example, if two members of the triad are at odds, the third member can act as a mediator to resolve the conflict. Triads can also allow for alliances between two of the members—potentially against the third, which weakens the group. If two friends ever teamed up against you, then you understand this principle. When alliances occur, the chance for competition among the members increases, which can lead to dissolution of the group. As a result, sociologist Georg Simmel referred to the triad as the weakest group size.[29]

As group size grows, there are greater opportunities for potential interactions, but also more formality and less intimacy. Family gatherings are great places to see this theory play out in real life. At a recent family gathering, I closely watched the interactions taking place as people slowly began to arrive. When the group size was small, people remained together, sitting in the same room and holding a single conversation. However, as the size grew to greater than 10, having one large conversation became impossible. I noticed people breaking off into subgroups. Some played games, others went outside, and still others stayed in the kitchen, sampling the holiday goodies. Such divisions are normal even among close families. The group was simply too large to allow for one conversation.

GO GLOBAL

In and Out in Japan

Xenophobia, the fear of outsiders, is a powerful example of out-group bias. In Japan, only those with 100 percent Japanese lineage are considered Japanese.[30] Foreigners who move to Japan and live there for years might eventually be able to gain citizenship, but they will never "become Japanese," nor will their children.[31] In this way, Japanese society alienates itself from other cultures. "True" Japanese people in Japan form an in-group, whereas all other non-native or different peoples form an out-group.

Throughout history, it's been customary for the Japanese to create out-groups, ostracize them, and then hold those groups responsible for current social problems.[32] During the early 1900s, many Korean people were brought into Japan as migrant workers to meet the nation's industrialization needs.[33] Japanese society immediately began to look at the Korean population as outsiders. Association with the population was frowned upon, and cultural integration was impossible. In fact, in present-day Japan, Koreans cannot gain full citizenship. However, leaders are working to change laws in order to recognize Koreans as full-fledged Japanese citizens.

>>> **ACTIVITY** Research a country other than Japan. What in-groups and out-groups are part of that country's society? How are members of the out-groups treated? Discuss your findings with a classmate.

THINK SOCIOLOGICALLY

Leadership in Canada

Pierre Elliott Trudeau—who was Canada's prime minister for a total of 16 years—displayed each of Maxwell's levels of effective leadership.

The charismatic Quebecker was first swept to power in a 1968 federal election, soon after winning the Liberal Party leadership in a wave of "Trudeaumania" that had turned him into a political star.[34] At this point he was a positional leader, but already showed signs of rising to Maxwell's "personhood" level.

Trudeau made bold and dramatic gestures on and off the political stage. He pirouetted behind the queen's back and made news because of the famous women he dated and the young woman he married. As prime minister, he brought in the *Official Languages Act* (1969), invoked the *War Measures Act* (1970, after several bombing attempts and kidnappings by the Front de libération du Québec), appointed the first female speaker and governor general in Canada (Jeanne Sauvé on both counts), supported the enactment of the *Canadian Charter of Rights and Freedoms* (1982), and "patriated"—or brought home—the Canadian Constitution from Britain (1982).[35]

He continued to be elected to power as people were following him because it was their choice, because of what he was accomplishing, and because they were empowered. He clearly reached Maxwell's fifth level of leadership and is remembered, in the words of the CBC, as having "helped shape Canada with his vision of a unified, bilingual, multicultural 'just society.'"[36] Pierre Elliott Trudeau died in 2000.

According to Henry Hamburger and colleagues, **the size of a group affects the group's ability to cooperate in a task.**[37] This phenomenon explains why reducing class size in public schools is a major issue in education policy. **Smaller groups accomplish more in less time than larger ones do.**

LEADERSHIP STYLE is a behavioural mode that leaders use to influence group members.

AUTOCRATIC LEADERS are leaders who determine the group policies and assign tasks.

DEMOCRATIC LEADERS are leaders who strive to set group policy by discussion and agreement.

LAISSEZ-FAIRE LEADERS are leaders who lead by absence and may in fact not want to be leaders at all.

If you attend a concert in a large arena, you'll probably talk to only the friends you came with, right? You and others are sandwiched into tight surroundings, and you may be actually physically touching someone you don't know, yet you probably won't talk to that person. Ironically, our sense of group often gets smaller when we're in large crowds. As a population increases in size and becomes denser, our perception of group size becomes smaller.[38] As crowds get larger, they become more stressful to us. In order to reduce the stress, we retreat into smaller, safer groups, thus limiting the interactions in the group and the stress of being in the crowd.

LEADERSHIP STYLES

In many groups, there are individuals who always stand apart from the crowd and become leaders, either officially or unofficially.

According to Kurt Lewin and colleagues, leadership can be summarized by three distinct styles.[39] **Leadership style** refers to a behavioural mode that leaders use to influence group members. Leadership style varies among autocratic, democratic, and laissez-faire styles. **Autocratic leaders** determine the group policies and assign tasks.[40] These strict authoritarians inform you, "It's my way or the highway." Conversely, **democratic leaders** strive to set group policy by discussion and agreement.[41] They hope for consensus and are likely to ask for your opinion on matters. Finally, **laissez-faire leaders** lead by absence and may in fact not want to be leaders at all.[42] They set few goals and do only what must be done.

What makes someone a good leader? The true measure of leadership is influence on others. If you lack this ability, no one will follow you. The style of leadership—autocratic, democratic, or laissez-faire—you employ does not directly affect your level of leadership. An autocratic leader can be just as influential as a democratic leader. Influential functionalism theorist John C. Maxwell provides a model of leadership made up of five levels.[43] As you read, think about leaders you know who exhibit these qualities.

Level 1: Positional Leaders: People Following the Leader because They Must

This level serves as the most basic type of leadership. Simply put, other people give positional leaders the reins of leadership. They don't rely on vision or charisma to lead others; instead, people follow them because of their title. When you enter the workforce, the hierarchy of your company determines who your supervisor will be, and it is part of your job to follow that person's lead. In the overall scheme of things, though, the positional leader and the people he or she oversees are just cogs in a machine. This type of leader has the least amount of influence.

Level 2: Permission Leaders: People Following because They Want To

Although positional leaders often lack personal relationships with their followers, permission leaders take the opposite tack. These leaders generate followers willingly precisely because they develop personal relationships with them. A permission leader doesn't merely view workers as a means to an end; instead, the leader and workers work together because they enjoy each other's company. Such a leader has considerably more influence because his or her followers are actually invested in the relationship, and, by extension, the task that is to be completed.

Successful leaders eventually understand that there is more to leadership than merely being the boss.

designsstock/Fotolia

<<< When you're with a crowd, **do you** find that you **change your behaviour to match everyone else? Or do you march to your own drummer?**

Level 3: Production Leaders: People Following because of What You Have Done

At this level of leadership, goals are met with minimum effort because the leader sets the example. Production leaders spur a sense of accomplishment in the people who follow them and clearly communicate a vision of what can be. They then go out and perform just as hard as everyone else. Production leaders are also willing to make difficult decisions and take the blame for failures.

Level 4: People Development: People Following because They Are Empowered

Rather than demonstrate their own skills to set an example, empowering leaders help people meet their potential by encouraging them to accomplish tasks they might have previously felt were impossible. By developing people, an empowering leader accomplishes tasks more easily because the team members feel they are capable and competent.

Level 5: Personhood: People Following because of Who You Are

It can take many years for people to attain this highest level of influence. Such leaders must spend a lot of time cultivating relationships with people and developing communication skills. But once this level is reached, these leaders will be able to inspire their followers to exceed their potential and willingly sacrifice for them.

CONFORMITY is the degree to which we will alter our behaviour, attitudes, and points of view to fit into our perceived expectation of what is appropriate.

GROUPTHINK is the term for group decisions that are made without objective thought.

Maxwell suggests that all leaders have the potential to climb this ladder of influence, but every new leader starts at the first level. Successful leaders eventually understand that there is more to leadership than merely being the boss.

CONFORMITY

Because it takes a rare individual to stand out and be a leader, most members of a group are followers in some way. **Conformity** refers to the degree to which we will alter our behaviour, attitudes, and points of view to fit into our perceived expectation of what is appropriate. Everyone hopes to "fit in," but would you change your opinion of what you think is true in order to fit into a group?

Psychologist Solomon Asch wanted to test the impact of groups on people's perception in 1952.[44] Asch set up groups so that only one member was not aware that the rest were actors. Then he showed the pseudo-group a series of cards like those shown below. He asked them to match the lines on card 2 to the line they saw on card 1. At first, the confidants chose correctly, and the group could easily make unified decisions. However, over time the confidants began to make deliberate mistakes in order to test the desire to achieve group conformity. Amazingly, about a third of the participants went along with the group, even though it was in error. Such a phenomenon is more common than you might think. When people are in a group, they often want to conform to the majority and don't offer an opinion that goes against the grain.

Groupthink

At times, group conformity becomes so strong that a group will not consider other ideas or influences. Extremely cohesive groups or ones with very strong leaders might make decisions using groupthink.[45] **Groupthink** is the term for group decisions that are made without

ASCH'S CARDS

CARD 1

CARD 2

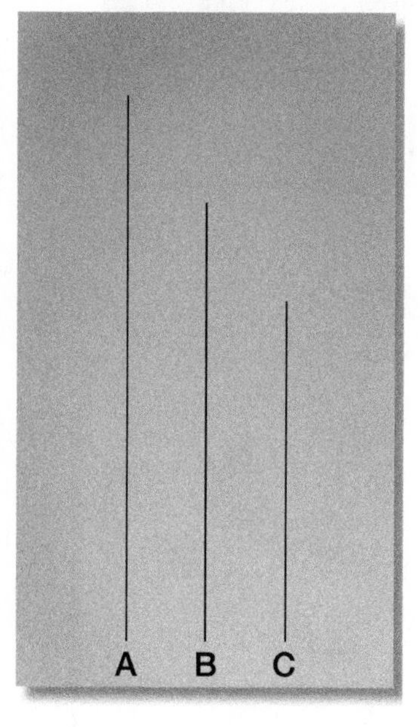

objective thought. When a group is in this mode, people conform to what they believe is the consensus of the rest of the group. They often make decisions that they would not make as individuals. Extreme group conformity leads to groupthink. It frequently results in decisions that people later agree were a mistake. Groupthink is more likely when the following conditions are present:

- **Cohesiveness:** Groups that are highly connected are especially likely to engage in groupthink. If, for example, you join a board of directors that the same people have led for 10 years, odds are groupthink is occurring. This group is likely to be very interconnected and to think it has ironed out all the possible solutions to the potential problems.
- **Threats:** When groups encounter an external threat, solidarity increases because common enemies unify groups.
- **A strong leader:** If the leader has a domineering style or is charismatic enough, the group is likely to accept the leader's will. Although a strong leader is important to a group's progress, it can also increase the odds of groupthink because few will want to disagree with the leader.[46]

SOCIAL CAPITAL AND SOCIAL NETWORKS

When you think of all the possible things that brought you to this point in your life, you're basically thinking about social capital. **Social capital** is a sociological concept that refers to the individual and collective resources available to a person. Social capital includes the institutions, relationships, attitudes, and values that influence interactions among people and contribute to economic and social development. Sociological theorist James S. Coleman suggested that social capital impacts all aspects of our lives and affects the choices and options available to us.[47]

SOCIAL CAPITAL is a sociological concept that refers to the individual and collective resources available to a person.

SOCIAL NETWORK is the web of ties you have with others.

Most of us use this kind of capital to find jobs, get into colleges, and deal with other opportunities. For example, my first job was repairing bicycles in a local bike shop. I got the job because my mother knew the owner. Later on, a friend helped me find my second job at a fast-food chicken restaurant. Of course, I had to do the work and keep the job, but my friends and family members were a part of my social capital that helped me gain employment.

Whereas Coleman suggests that social capital is functional for society and individuals, Pierre Bourdieu, a conflict theorist, views it as an economic resource.[48] Consider legacy admissions—a policy in which applicants to a highly touted private school are admitted based on their family's history with the school. Such a practice tends to benefit wealthier students because they are more likely to have family members who are alumni. In short, our social and familial contacts can help us get a foot in the door of a place to which we might otherwise be denied access.

The social contacts that people make, when pulled together, comprise a social network, which is one component of social capital. Basically, a **social network** is the web of ties you have with others. Networks usually include people with similar values, beliefs, and identities. They allow us to gain important information and may even open doors of opportunity. In the twenty-first century, social networking has taken on an even greater importance for Web-savvy individuals. Sites such as Facebook and LinkedIn serve as virtual alternatives to traditional networks. The power of the internet allows people to expand their network exponentially.

To see the value of social networks, look at how recent immigrants are able to use them to their advantage. The Longitudinal Survey of Immigrants to Canada surveyed immigrants who arrived in Canada between October 2000 and September 2001 and who were over 15 years of age. The survey found that immigrants rely on three types of social networks:

1. **Kinship networks:** networks that consist of relatives and family members
2. **Friendship networks:** networks that include friends and acquaintances
3. **Organizational networks:** various formal and informal groups and organizations, such as community groups, religious groups, and sports clubs

The study confirmed previous findings that social networks are very important. Six months after landing, immigrants without social networks faced worse situations than those who had some networks upon landing.[49]

Sometimes, you don't have to depend on a strong network to succeed. Even weak ties can also be immensely valuable to us. For example, you may hear about a job opening from someone sitting next to you in class. Even though your classmate isn't necessarily in your primary group, this tip could prove much more valuable than information from your family or friends. Mark S. Granovetter suggests that weak ties play a vital role in social capital because they expand our networks, thus expanding our possibilities.[50]

SOCIAL CAPITAL

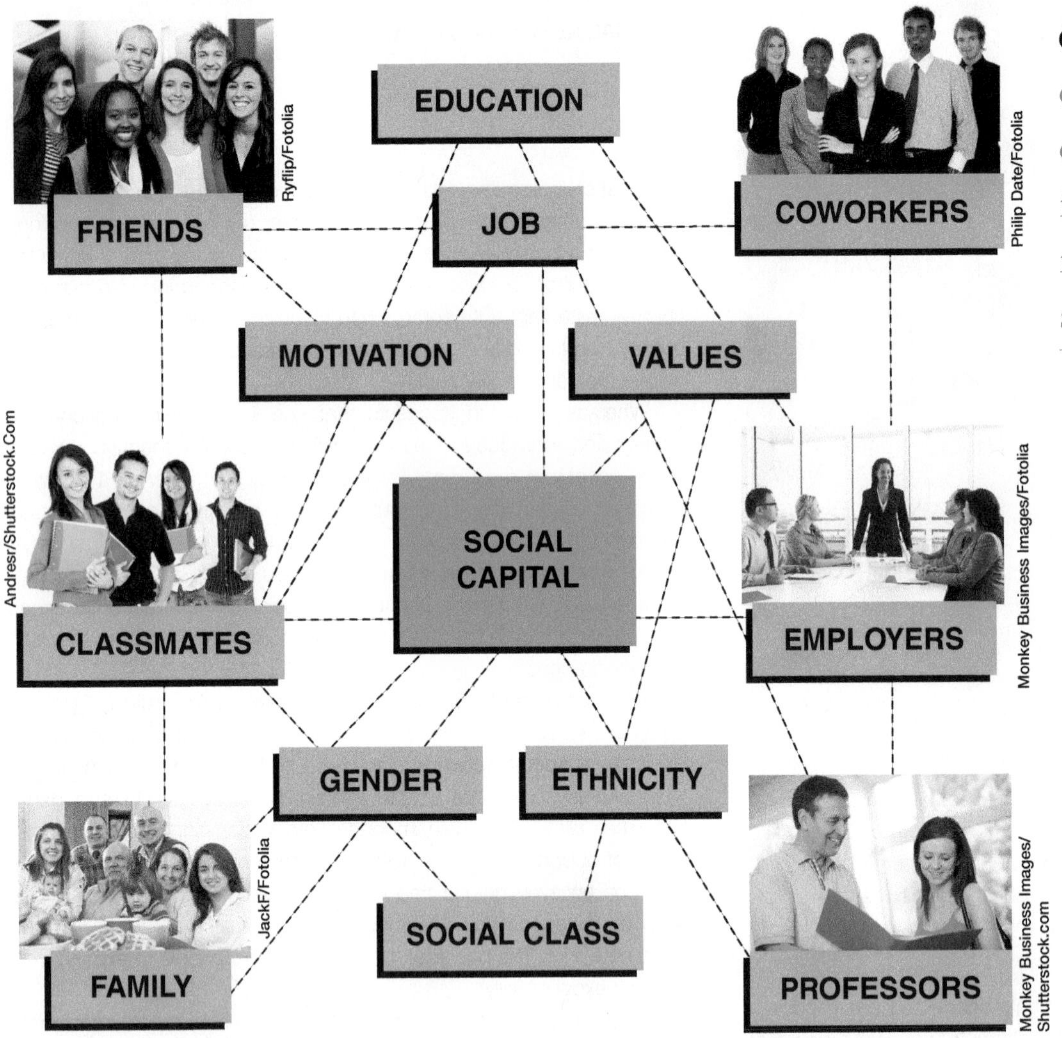

EDUCATION
FRIENDS
JOB
COWORKERS
MOTIVATION
VALUES
SOCIAL CAPITAL
CLASSMATES
EMPLOYERS
GENDER
ETHNICITY
SOCIAL CLASS
FAMILY
PROFESSORS

Ryflip/Fotolia
Philip Date/Fotolia
Andresr/Shutterstock.Com
Monkey Business Images/Fotolia
JackF/Fotolia
Monkey Business Images/Shutterstock.com

<<< **Your social capital is a** network of personal characteristics, institutions, relationships, and social statuses.

FORMAL ORGANIZATIONS are groups created for certain purposes and built for maximum efficiency.

VOLUNTARY ASSOCIATION is the act of joining an organization that offers no pay and that expands social networks through interaction.

ORGANIZATIONS are formal groups that exist to achieve desired goals.

FORMAL ORGANIZATIONS

When you hang out with friends or family members, you let your guard down and forget about all the formal rules. That's because these social groups are informal. Other groups you're affiliated with, such as your local bowling league or hockey team, are probably formal organizations. **Formal organizations** are groups created for certain purposes and built for maximum efficiency.

Voluntary Associations

Through joining a team, singing in a choir, or helping in a soup kitchen, you can make a **voluntary association**. In 1995, political scientist Robert Putnam showed that participation in these kinds of associations is declining.[51] Take bowling leagues, for example. The number of bowling leagues is decreasing, while the number of people bowling has not changed. People are joining organizations less frequently, creating a more individual and isolated society. The social capital of our entire society may be suffering from shrinking social networks, despite our using networks to increase our outcomes and improve our lives.

Voluntary associations have life-changing effects on communities. For example, in an area of Nepal where high fertility rates were an increasing problem, more individuals became involved in voluntary associations—like credit bank groups, women's groups, agricultural groups, and youth groups. As memberships increased, the likelihood of Nepalese people using contraception also increased.[52] People who lived in neighbourhoods that had a number of possible voluntary associations were more likely to use contraceptives than people who lived in relatively isolated communities. Through fostering a better sense of community among individuals, voluntary associations helped control fertility rates.

Organizations and Bureaucracies

Organizations come in a variety of types and sizes. Some organizations are formed to help a cause, such as Greenpeace. Others, like the popular furniture store IKEA, serve to make money. All organizations are alike in that they are formal groups that exist to achieve desired goals.

Sociologist Amitai Etzioni suggested that the type of organization ultimately determines our membership in it.[53] For example, when you get a job at a department store or office building, you're joining a **utilitarian organization.**[54] Members join utilitarian organizations because they receive wages in exchange for work. **Normative organizations** exist in order to achieve a worthwhile goal.[55] If you volunteer at a normative organization, such as a soup kitchen, you do so because you believe feeding the homeless serves an essential purpose in society.

While we willingly join utilitarian and normative organizations, we do not join **coercive organizations** by choice.[56] Members of coercive organizations, like prison inmates or rehab patients, don't join voluntarily; outside forces of authority bring them into the organization.

Whether utilitarian, normative, or coercive, organizations have some important qualities that keep them running smoothly:

- **Division of labour:** Tasks are clearly defined and divided, and members understand their roles and expectations.
- **Concentration of power:** Organizations concentrate power in the hands of a few, who can then use that power to control the institution.
- **Methods of succession:** Membership in the organization allows for the replacement of all roles, including leaders.[57]

UTILITARIAN ORGANIZATION is an organization in which people receive wages in exchange for work.

NORMATIVE ORGANIZATION is an organization that exists to achieve a worthwhile goal.

COERCIVE ORGANIZATION is an organization that people are forced to join.

FORMAL STRUCTURES are the explicit rules, goals, and guidelines of an organization.

INFORMAL STRUCTURES are friendships, allegiances, and loyalties among members of an organization.

A structure exists within all organizations, though some structures may be more formal than others. **Formal structure** refers to the explicit rules, goals, and guidelines of an organization. Organizational charts, policy and procedure manuals, and established titles and roles are part of the formal structure of an organization. You can see such formal structures develop in any student organization that elects presidents, vice presidents, and other officers. **Informal structures** consist of friendships, allegiances, and loyalties among members of an organization. All organizations have informal structures, and these often make the organization run smoothly.

Our view of an organization depends on our involvement with it. For example, **a prison can be a utilitarian organization** for the prison guards, **a normative organization** for people who volunteer to lead Alcoholics Anonymous groups with the inmates, **and a coercive organization** to the inmates themselves.

Ramey/PhotoEdit,Inc

BUREAUCRACY is a formal organization that is organized into a hierarchy of smaller departments.

FORMAL RATIONALITY is the reasonable actions that organizations and bureaucracies take to achieve goals in the most effective way.

IRON CAGE is a concept introduced by Max Weber that refers to the way in which bureaucracies make workers feel trapped and turn them into little more than robots accomplishing tasks.

Characteristics of Bureaucracy

If you've ever had to wait in line for hours to renew your driver's licence, only to hear "I can't help you. You'll have to wait over there," then you know some of the frustrations that come with a large bureaucracy. A **bureaucracy** is a formal organization that is organized into a hierarchy of smaller departments. Bureaucracies often have an impersonal feel when one department doesn't have much contact with another. Since a better method of organization has not yet been found, it looks like they are here to stay.

Max Weber was one of the early sociologists to discuss the idea of bureaucracy.[58] Weber proposed that no matter what a formal organization's purpose might be, all ideal bureaucracies display certain characteristics.

Weber and the Iron Cage

For Weber, bureaucratization was a logical extension of formal rational thought.[59] **Formal rationality** refers to the reasonable actions organizations and bureaucracies take to achieve goals in the most effective way.

According to Weber, any organization that grows large enough will inevitably strive toward formal rationality and bureaucracy. However, such a highly structured bureaucracy can cause the members to feel trapped in a dehumanizing **iron cage** that turns them into little more than robots accomplishing tasks. Weber proposed that this iron cage, while problematic from a personal level, is actually a good thing because it helps the organization thrive and places its needs above the needs of the individual.

The power of the bureaucracy often moves from the top down, meaning that the leaders of the group make decisions, and those lower on the organizational chart complete these tasks. This setup forces leaders to be accountable for the actions of the bureaucracy and increases their control. However, this hierarchy strips workers of having a say in decision making.

With all the decision-making power at the top, inefficiencies can occur. If leaders don't understand what is happening at the lower levels of the organization, they can easily lead it astray. For example, while I was working as a grill cook, I knew that the biggest line-up was for club sandwiches. However, my bosses thought that people wanted healthier choices, so they spent a lot of money to build a large salad bar. After a few days, it became quite obvious that few people were taking salad, but the line for club sandwiches was longer than it ever had been before.

The division of labour in a bureaucracy can also have a negative impact. Workers may become alienated from the organization's purpose and focus only on their specific tasks. For example, a factory worker who spends hours putting tires on cars might notice a broken windshield but not say anything because "it's not my job." Such a feeling arises from an impersonal organizational culture.

Although written rules and regulations let workers know what is expected of them, strict enforcement of these rules stifles creativity and imagination. Workers might not be inclined to speak up in order to implement a new idea or to perform tasks that do not fall under their job description.

Now that we have discussed the role of groups and group interaction in society, it's time to think sociologically about these groups.

WEBER'S CHARACTERISTICS OF BUREAUCRACY

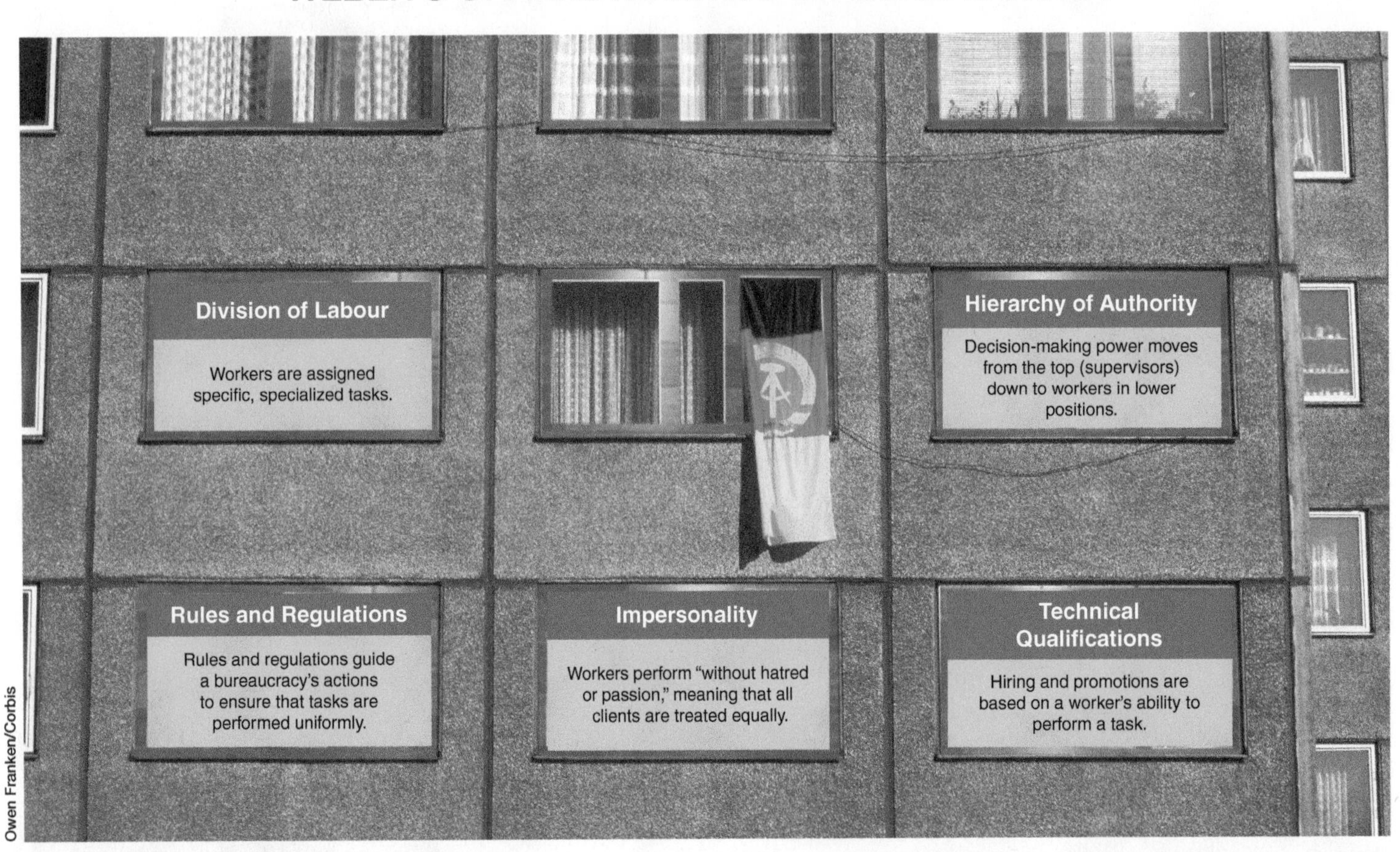

Division of Labour
Workers are assigned specific, specialized tasks.
Hierarchy of Authority
Decision-making power moves from the top (supervisors) down to workers in lower positions.
Rules and Regulations
Rules and regulations guide a bureaucracy's actions to ensure that tasks are performed uniformly.
Impersonality
Workers perform "without hatred or passion," meaning that all clients are treated equally.
Technical Qualifications
Hiring and promotions are based on a worker's ability to perform a task.

Owen Franken/Corbis

think sociologically: HOW DO THE FOUR PERSPECTIVES VIEW SOCIAL STRUCTURES AND SOCIAL INTERACTION?

Functionalism—The Essential Features of Social Structures

When functionalists study society, they often ask how the various elements fit together. Social institutions and structures serve essential functions in a society. As you study various social structures in later chapters, you will see a general functional framework that applies in virtually all cases. Durkheim called these essential features "functional requisites."[60]

Consider the five primary tasks of society that create social structures: adaptation and replacement, socialization and orientation, production and exchange, social order, and unity and purpose.

ADAPTATION AND REPLACEMENT

Effective and functional societies must get their needs met to survive. Jared Diamond suggests that societies collapse unless they can accomplish certain tasks, including adapting to changes in the environment.[61]

>>> **According to Durkheim, there are "functional requisites" that hold society together.** Think of the five tasks listed as puzzle pieces; if you're missing one, the puzzle isn't complete.

Thinglass/Fotolia

Adaptations are also essential for accommodating the changing relationships that a society has with the world around it.

Besides adapting to environmental and political changes, societies must also replace people who either die or leave the group. Without continually replacing people, societies cannot carry on.

SOCIALIZATION AND ORIENTATION

Closely tied to replacement are socialization and orientation of new members. When children are born, they need to be socialized into the group. Socialization and orientation are vital to the continuation of a society because these processes allow new members to join and assign them roles. In "traditional societies," this assigning of roles might include gender-specific tasks such as men hunting or women caring for children. In a postindustrial society, socialization and orientation can be much more formal and include teaching related social norms.

Socialization is not possible without some means to communicate. Societies create language to teach new members and to pass on information to the next generation. Socialization takes place in schools and families as well as through media, religion, and other structures found in various forms of society.

PRODUCTION AND EXCHANGE

The ability of a society to meet its needs through its environment is the most important idea associated with this task. Simple societies create a material culture based on the resources at hand, whereas more complex societies trade with other groups to get the goods and services they need.[62] Complex societies require an economic system to regulate the trading of goods and services. Although the exact nature of the economic system differs between societies, people always need a way to make or acquire the goods and services they need.

SOCIAL ORDER

Because every society has people who do not follow the rules, sanctions must be created to deal with these lawbreakers. In simple societies, force and strength might rule the day, whereas in complex societies, people settle disputes through legal battles. Not all societies have written laws, but they all socialize their members to promote social order.

UNITY AND PURPOSE

Unity is achieved through common thoughts, beliefs, and attitudes. Canada is built on common ideals, not a common heritage. Those shared thoughts united people, leading them to create a new country. Unity is also achieved through a sense of purpose, which gives a society some goal to achieve. This purpose holds people together, allowing them to work together in times of trial.[63]

Conflict Theory—Worker Participation

While Weber saw both the positive and the negative aspects of bureaucracy, Karl Marx believed that "bureaucracy [was] a circle from which one [could not] escape."[64] For Marx, bureaucracy provided no essential function for society. It was just another way for the bourgeoisie to exploit workers more efficiently and gain more wealth and control for themselves.

You'd probably expect workers to fight against bureaucratic systems. However, Marx's theory suggests that employees who oppose a bureaucracy's leadership are easily discovered, reprimanded, or fired. Is this beneficial for productivity? Studies show that a democratic, instead of an autocratic, leadership style actually increases worker productivity. Democratic leaders encourage workers to participate in production decisions, and this participation increases profits and productivity.[65] It seems that a more inclusive leadership style helps both the workers and the owners.

Greater labour participation in leadership roles does not necessarily mean that the company will succeed. In studies by Tove H. Hammer and colleagues, increased labourer participation on boards of directors does not translate to increased profits.[66] In fact, such involvement is sometimes counterproductive for future planning because workers and management tend to have differing points of view. Workers focus primarily on job protection, while managers are interested in appeasing shareholders.

Feminist Theory—The Gender Wage Gap in Canada

In August 2010, in Canada the average hourly wage for a man was $24.07; for a woman, it was $20.56.[67] Why is there a difference? Feminist theory argues that in Canada, as in most other countries, the social structure is patriarchal; that is, it benefits men more than women. One area in which women have long been disadvantaged—and still are—is in the wages they earn. Despite a growing number of women participating in the labour force, and increases in women's levels of skill, educational attainment, and work experience, there is still a noticeable and persistent difference in wages. One explanation for the difference is that women are more likely to work in lower-paying jobs, such as retail or childcare. Of course, this leads to the question, Which came first? Are these jobs lower paying because they have traditionally been held by women, or are women's wages lower than men's because they are more likely to choose jobs that pay less?

Because the Canadian social structure has developed according to a patriarchal ideology, the differences in pay that have been deeply entrenched in the employment system reflect gender bias. The social structure is fundamentally designed so that work done mainly by women is paid less than work done mainly by men. Occupational segregation ensures that males will generally earn more than females.[68]

What about when men and women work in the same job? There is still a discrepancy in their earnings, with men earning slightly more than their female co-workers. Part of the explanation comes from the fact that it is women who have babies. When a man and a woman start a new job together, they will probably earn the same salary. However, it is more likely that the woman will at some time have to leave her job if she has a child. This will have long-term consequences on her earnings. While a woman is off on maternity leave, she is probably not developing her work skills. But her male co-worker will likely continue to acquire more skills, which will result in promotions and raises for him.[69]

As a society, we can choose how we view women who leave the workforce to have children. In Canada, there is a growing trend toward offering "parental" leave rather than "maternity" leave. With both mothers and fathers eligible to take the same amount of time off when a child is born, what impact might this have on the gender wage gap?

Symbolic Interactionism—Personal Space

How do you feel when someone stands very close to you during a conversation? It's a little uncomfortable, right? Even if the person is a friend, your natural impulse is to back away.

Our feelings about **personal space** often depend on the setting and the person with whom we are interacting. For example, in order for a doctor to properly examine you, she needs to enter your personal space. In a different setting, you would never allow such behaviour. Although socially appropriate amounts of personal space vary between cultures, sociologist Edward Hall suggests that people in North America have four discrete zones of personal space[70]:

1. We reserve **intimate distance** for those with whom we are very close. This zone covers roughly from 0 to 45 centimetres. We generally reserve this distance for intimate encounters, but these conditions may vary depending on setting.
2. **Personal distance** ranges from 45 centimetres to 1.2 metres. Normal conversations occur at a personal distance. When you share secrets with a friend, you automatically lean in to an intimate distance. Once the whispering is over, though, you automatically return to a personal distance.
3. **Social distance** ranges from about 1.2 metres to 3.6 metres and is usually reserved for formal settings. When you go on a job interview, for instance, you generally sit at what Hall called "social distance."[71] Social encounters at this distance are not very personal. This distance allows the speaker to be heard but does not presume any friendship.
4. **Public distance** refers to the zone of interaction that is used in highly formal settings. This distance includes everything greater than 3.6 metres. When you sit in the back of the classroom, you guarantee that you will maintain a public distance from your professor. Public distance also occurs during political speeches, at churches, and at formal events. Speakers are separate from the listener, and, generally, the audience shows respect and deference to the speaker.

Just as you adjust the personal distance between yourself and others depending on the situation, you probably also adjust your behaviour so that it's appropriate for the setting you're in. When you're in public, you often show off your best self to others and hide what you don't want them to see.

PERSONAL SPACE is the invisible bubble that each of us has around us that insulates us from others.

INTIMATE DISTANCE is distance reserved for those with whom we are very close.

PERSONAL DISTANCE is distance that ranges from 45 centimetres to 1.2 metres; this distance is for normal conversations.

SOCIAL DISTANCE is distance that ranges from about 1.2 metres to 3.6 metres and is usually reserved for formal settings.

PUBLIC DISTANCE is the zone of interaction that is used in highly formal settings; this distance includes everything greater than 3.6 metres.

ZONES OF PERSONAL SPACE

WRAP YOUR MIND AROUND THE THEORY

Functionalists claim that unity is achieved through a sense of purpose. **This purpose holds people together, allowing them to work together.**

Monkey Business/Fotolia

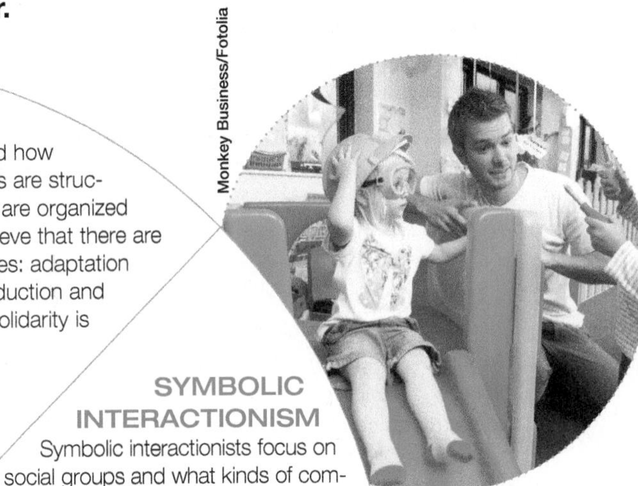

Monkey Business/Fotolia

HOW DO THE FOUR PERSPECTIVES VIEW SOCIAL STRUCTURE AND SOCIAL INTERACTION?

FUNCTIONALISM

Since functionalism is a macro perspective, it focuses on the social structure and how it is made up of social institutions. Social institutions are structures that provide for patterned relationships and that are organized around a central activity or social need. Functionalists believe that there are five primary tasks of society that create social structures: adaptation and replacement, socialization and orientation, production and exchange, social order, and unity and purpose. Solidarity is the "glue" that binds a society.

CONFLICT THEORY

Conflict theorists look at the social structure as an arrangement that benefits the dominant class and maintains stratification and inequality. Rather than focus on social institutions, conflict theorists believe that the main components of the social structure are the various social classes. The main determinants of social class are wealth, income, education, and occupation. Social class not only differentiates groups of people, it ranks them. Your social class can have a profound impact on your life. It can determine how much education you acquire, what job you get, and even who your friends are and how long you will live.

SYMBOLIC INTERACTIONISM

Symbolic interactionists focus on social groups and what kinds of communication and interactions occur in different kinds of groups. Primary groups are small, intimate, and enduring, while secondary groups are formal, superficial, and temporary. Much of our social interaction is based on conformity—the degree to which we will alter our behaviour, attitudes, and points of view to fit into our perceived expectation of what is appropriate. Our feelings about personal space often depend on the setting and the person with whom we are interacting. When in public, we often show off our best self to others and hide what we don't want them to see.

FEMINIST THEORY

Feminists perceive the social structure to be overtly patriarchal. More opportunities are available to men within the structure because the structure has been built to benefit men. If it were mainly men who worked in childcare facilities, childcare workers would probably earn as much as bus drivers. The gender wage gap in Canada is evidence that the social structure of work in Canada benefits men more than women.

Our feelings about personal space often depend on the setting **and the people with whom we are interacting.**

Micromonkey/Fotolia

Does this image tell you anything about the **social status of this person?**

Ian Paterson/Alamy

discover sociology in action: HOW CAN SOCIAL POLICIES IMPROVE SOCIETY?

In our culture, social policies are applied in an effort to improve society. High-quality preschool is one area that is still going through much change in Canada.

Social Policy—Childcare in Canada

Preschool childcare is a controversial subject in Canada. It's widely used, and levels of funding vary across the country.

Seven out of 10 preschool children with an employed or studying mother now use regulated childcare (including kindergarten) in Quebec, and 4 out of 10 do so in the rest of the country, according to a major report prepared for the nonprofit Institute for Research on Public Policy in 2008. The Quebec figures tripled, and the figures for the rest of Canada doubled, to 72 percent and 40 percent, respectively, in the space of a decade.[72]

This gives you a good idea of how important high-quality preschool childcare has become in Canada. It also reflects the fact that Quebec is regarded as a leader in providing universal daycare (even though there have been some problems with waiting lists to get into subsidized daycare programs in Quebec).[73]

When kindergarten is not counted, just over a third of all Canadian preschool children with employed or studying mothers now attend regulated care services, and just under a third receive exclusively parental care, the IRPP report said.[74] Kindergarten is part of the compulsory school system only in New Brunswick.[75] It is free for 5-year-olds, and in Ontario also for 4-year-olds. Most regulated childcare is expensive, the IRPP report notes, adding that "Low-income (particularly single-parent) families in Canada may be eligible for childcare subsidies for children of any age. As a result, those in the lowest income quintile are not less likely to use regulated care than those with middle incomes."[76]

The federal government has been proposing to make some changes to its childcare benefits.[77] However, in 2009, the Child Care Advocacy Association of Canada said the government had "simply failed to meet the childcare needs of Canadian families."[78]

ACTIVITIES

1. Visit a childcare centre in your area. Talk to the staff and the clients and learn why early intervention is important. Consider spending some time helping them as a student volunteer.
2. What type of public funding does your province or territory provide for preschool education? Does the province or territory rank daycare centres based on quality? If so, how?
3. Aside from preschool, what features act to strengthen Canadian society? What features weaken it?

CHAPTER

WHAT ELEMENTS CREATE THE SOCIAL STRUCTURES? 89

Social structures are made up of different elements—culture, social class, status, roles, and social institutions.

WHAT ARE THE CHARACTERISTICS OF SOCIAL INTERACTION? 94

Social interaction refers to all the ways people behave and communicate in social situations.

HOW DO THE FOUR PERSPECTIVES VIEW THE SOCIAL STRUCTURES AND SOCIAL INTERACTION? 103

functionalism: social institutions serve essential functions in a society
conflict theory: the structure and culture of society generally benefit the dominant group
symbolic interactionism: society is created and defined through communication and social interaction
feminist theory: the social structure is patriarchal and benefits men more than women

HOW CAN SOCIAL POLICIES IMPROVE SOCIETY? 107

High-quality preschool programs improve the lives of the participants and decrease the amount of funding needed for other social programs (special education, welfare).

get the topic: WHAT ARE SOCIAL STRUCTURES AND SOCIAL INTERACTION?

Theories

FUNCTIONALISM 103

- focuses on the social structure and how it is made up of social institutions
- social institutions are structures that provide for patterned relationships and that are organized around a central activity or social need

CONFLICT THEORY 104

- looks at the social structure as an arrangement that benefits the dominant class and maintains stratification and inequality
- social class not only differentiates groups of people, it ranks them

FEMINIST THEORY 104

- in most societies, the social structure is patriarchal
- more opportunities are available to men within the structure because the structure has been built to benefit men

SYMBOLIC INTERACTIONISM 105

- focuses on social groups and what kinds of communication and interactions occur in different kinds of groups
- when in public, we often show off our best self to others and hide what we don't want them to see

Key Terms

social structures are patterns of relationships that endure from one generation to the next. *89*

social class refers to a group of people with similar access to power, wealth, and prestige. *90*

social status refers to socially defined positions that are characterized by certain expectations, rights, and duties. *90*

achieved status is a type of position that you earn or do something to attain. *90*

ascribed status is a position in society that is given or assigned. *90*

status set is all the statuses we occupy. *90*

master status is the most important status. *91*

status symbols are material signs that represent a specific status. *91*

role is the behaviour associated with a specific status. *91*

role expectations are the socially defined behaviours appropriate for a particular status. *91*

role performance refers to how a person actually plays a role. *92*

role conflict is a phenomenon that occurs when one is forced to choose between the competing demands of multiple roles. *92*

role strain occurs when the demands and expectations of one role are impossible for us to satisfy. *92*

social institutions are structures that provide for patterned relationships and that are organized around a central activity or social need. *92*

mechanical solidarity refers to the type of community bonding usually found in traditional societies, in which people share beliefs and values and perform common activities. *93*

organic solidarity occurs when people live in a society with a diverse division of labour. *93*

Gemeinschaft refers to community connections involving personal relationships based on friendship and kinship ties, such as family. *93*

Gesellschaft refers to social connections that are more formal and impersonal. *93*

social group is any number of people with similar norms, values, and behaviours who frequently interact with one another. *94*

social interaction refers to all the ways people behave and communicate in social situations. *94*

primary groups are groups that are small, intimate, and enduring. *94*

secondary groups are groups that are formal, superficial, and temporary. *94*

bounded relationships are relationships that exist only under specific conditions. *94*

in-group is a group to which we feel an affinity or a closeness. *95*

in-group bias is the feeling that a person's in-group is superior to others. *95*

out-group is a group from which we are disconnected. *95*

reference group is the group that you use to evaluate yourself. *96*

dyad is a group consisting of only two people. *96*

triad is a group consisting of three people. *96*

leadership style is a behavioural mode that leaders use to influence group members. *97*

autocratic leaders are leaders who determine the group policies and assign tasks. *97*

democratic leaders are leaders who strive to set group policy by discussion and agreement. *97*

laissez-faire leaders are leaders who lead by absence and may in fact not want to be leaders at all. *97*

conformity is the degree to which we will alter our behaviour, attitudes, and points of view to fit into our perceived expectation of what is appropriate. *98*

groupthink is the term for group decisions that are made without objective thought. *98*

social capital is a sociological concept that refers to the individual and collective resources available to a person. *99*

social network is the web of ties you have with others. *99*

formal organizations are groups created for a certain purpose and built for maximum efficiency. *100*

voluntary association is the act of joining an organization that offers no pay and that expands social networks through interaction. *100*

organizations are formal groups that exist to achieve desired goals. *100*

utilitarian organization is an organization in which people receive wages in exchange for work. *101*

normative organization is an organization that exists to achieve a worthwhile goal. *101*

coercive organization is an organization that people are forced to join. *101*

formal structures are the explicit rules, goals, and guidelines of an organization. *101*

informal structures are friendships, allegiances, and loyalties among members of an organization. *101*

bureaucracy is a formal organization that is organized into a hierarchy of smaller departments *102*.

formal rationality is the reasonable actions that organizations and bureaucracies take to achieve goals in the most effective way. *102*

iron cage is a concept introduced by Max Weber that refers to the way in which bureaucracies make workers feel trapped and turn them into little more than robots accomplishing tasks. *102*

personal space is the invisible bubble that each of us has around us that insulates us from others. *105*

intimate distance is distance reserved for those with whom we are very close. *105*

personal distance is distance that ranges from 45 centimetres to 1.2 metres; this distance is for normal conversations. *105*

social distance is distance that ranges from about 1.2 metres to 3.6 metres and is usually reserved for formal settings. *105*

public distance is the zone of interaction that is used in highly formal settings; this distance includes everything greater than 3.6 metres. *105*

Sample Test Questions

These multiple-choice questions are similar to those found in the test bank that accompanies this textbook.

1. A position in society that is given or assigned is called
   - a. achieved status.
   - b. formal structure.
   - c. ascribed status.
   - d. master status.
2. The type of community bonding in traditional societies is called
   - a. organic solidarity.
   - b. formal rationality.
   - c. mechanical solidarity.
   - d. social network.
3. Which of the following systems distributes power in a society?
   - a. Legal
   - b. Political
   - c. Economic
   - d. Educational
4. Which of the following groups is the best example of a *Gemeinschaft* relationship?
   - a. A large city
   - b. A soccer team
   - c. A government
   - d. A large corporation
5. Which of the five tasks of society allows new members to join and assigns roles to the new members?
   - a. Socialization and orientation
   - b. Adaptation and replacement
   - c. Production and economy
   - d. Unity and purpose

ANSWERS: 1. c; 2. c; 3. b; 4. b; 5. a

ESSAY

1. What are the differences between ascribed status and achieved status?
2. How do societies demonstrate adaptation and replacement for survival? Give examples.
3. Why is it important to observe the conventions of personal space?
4. Explain how a group might change from a *Gemeinschaft* to *Gesellschaft* type of organization.
5. Which systems would a conflict theorist target when addressing the issue of cultural integration? Why?

WHERE TO START YOUR RESEARCH PAPER

For information and resources related to social structure and social interaction:

www.mhhe.com/socscience/sociology/resources/social.htm.

To learn more about how elevated social status may affect body weight, go to

www.statcan.gc.ca/pub/82-003-x/2009004/article/11020-eng.pdf.

For more on status and roles:

www.sociologyguide.com/basic-concepts/Status-and-Role.php.

For more on childcare in Canada:

www.childcarecanada.org.

Remember to check www.thethinkspot.ca for additional information, downloadable flashcards, and other helpful resources.

SOCIAL STRATIFICATION

dbimages/Alamy

WHAT IS SOCIAL STRATIFICATION?
WHAT IS GLOBAL STRATIFICATION?
WHAT CAUSES GLOBAL STRATIFICATION?
WHAT IS BEING DONE TO ASSIST POOR COUNTRIES?

"In July 2005,

I was travelling in Kenya, visiting an association of women living with AIDS in a slum suburb of the city of Nairobi. The slum was teeming with orphans, being cared for by the women left alive. In every such instance, there's always some kind of 'performance' for the visitors, as though the encounter would be incomplete or marred without it. We gathered outside one of the crumbling homes, where six children, ranging in age from five to twelve, wearing ragged green school uniforms, chanted the largely tuneless, funereal dirge of their own composition: 'Here we are, the orphans, carrying our parents in their coffins to their graves.' The song ended with the words 'Help, Help, Help.' And then there came forward a girl of ten, a translator at her side, to describe the last remnants of her mother's life. It was awful. The mother had clearly died only a few days before, and as the young girl described the journeys in and out of hospital, and her mother's final hours, she wept so uncontrollably, her words strangled in loss, the tears gushing—not falling, or streaming, or pouring, but gushing—down her cheeks and onto her sweater and then to the ground. . . .

"I have to say that the ongoing plight of Africa forces me to perpetual rage. It's all so unnecessary, so crazy that hundreds of millions of people should be thus abandoned. . . . It's important to remember that Africa was left in dreadful shape by the departing colonial powers, and was subsequently whip-sawed between ideological factions in the Cold War. But rather more decisive, it was also delivered to the depredations of the so-called IFIs—the collection of International Financial Institutions dominated by the World Bank and the International Monetary Fund (colloquially known as 'the Bank' and 'the Fund'), and including the African Development Bank and other regional development banks. The result of the IFIs' destructive power over Africa was to compromise the social sectors, particularly the health and education sectors of the continent to this day."[1]

Wealth and Poverty *in the* World

CHAPTER 06

In *Race against Time*, Stephen Lewis gives a stark description of the terrible situation confronting the majority of people living on the African continent.

Stephen Lewis saw the poverty in Africa firsthand as Canada's ambassador to the United Nations between 1984 and 1988 and, later, as the United Nations secretary-general's special envoy for HIV/AIDS in Africa. He also saw the United Nations from an insider's perspective, and he sadly realized that the very organization that professed to be helping the people in Africa was, in many ways, responsible for their dire situation.

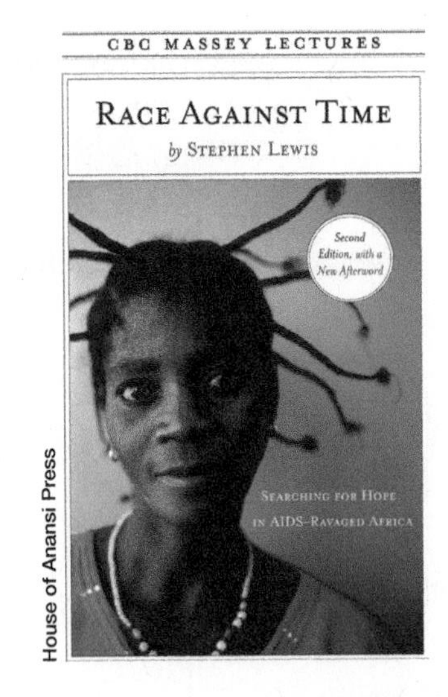

House of Anansi Press

get the topic: WHAT IS SOCIAL STRATIFICATION?

It seems that it's in our nature to rank things. Pick up any magazine at the end of a given year, and you're sure to find "top 10" lists ranking that year's best (or worst) movies, albums, or books. Similarly, David Letterman has made the Top Ten List his signature bit on the *Late Show with David Letterman*. **Social stratification** refers to the ranking of people and the rewards they receive, based on social factors, often including wealth, power, and/or prestige. Social stratification is a feature of society, not simply a ranking of individual differences. Every society has some

SOCIAL STRATIFICATION refers to the ranking of people and the rewards they receive, based on social factors, often including wealth, power, and/or prestige.

Social Stratification

is

a system of ranking of people and the rewards they receive based on social factors, often including wealth, power, and/or prestige

and has different forms such as

Slavery: a stratification system in which one person has complete control over another
- **Chattel slavery:** a form of slavery in which a slave is considered property
- **Debt bondage:** a form of slavery in which someone borrows money in order to repay a different debt and works to pay off the new debt
- **Contract slavery:** a form of slavery in which a person signs a work contract and receives food and shelter from an employer but is threatened when he or she tries to leave the contract

Caste systems: a person's position is permanently fixed
Class systems: allow social mobility

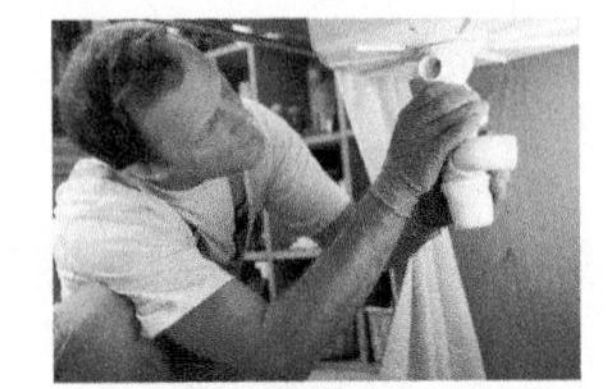

Absolute poverty is poverty so severe that one lacks resources to survive
Relative poverty is based on comparing ourselves to those around us

and poverty has different meanings, such as

Global stratification refers to the ranking of countries which highlights social and economic inequality throughout the world

system of social stratification, and each system of stratification tends to endure from generation to generation. Stratification persists because it is supported by an ideology. **Ideology** is a set of cultural beliefs that justifies various social arrangements, including inequality.

Social Stratification Systems

All societies have systems by which they stratify, or rank, their members and by which those people receive the rewards of that society. Some societies may use political power to separate people by giving certain groups special privileges that are unavailable to others. Societies might use wealth to stratify people into social classes as well; in this case, the more money you have, the higher your status. Still others use birth status and family of origin as a means to divide people; certain families regarded as "nobility" hold privileged positions. Societies use **social stratification systems** to rank different groups. The three most common social stratification systems are slavery, caste, and class systems.

SLAVERY

Slavery is a stratification system in which one person has complete control over another. You may believe that slavery is a thing of the past; however, estimates suggest that there are currently as many as 27 million slaves worldwide.[2] That number equals more than 80 percent of the total population of Canada.[3] This staggering figure is probably difficult to believe, but the important thing to remember is that today's slavery hardly resembles the slavery of the past.

IDEOLOGY is a set of cultural beliefs that justifies various social arrangements, including inequality.

SOCIAL STRATIFICATION SYSTEMS are systems societies use to rank different groups.

SLAVERY is a stratification system in which one person has complete control over another.

In *Disposable People*, Kevin Bales discusses "old" slavery and "new" slavery.[4] **Under old systems, slavery was legal, and slaves were never paid. Today, slavery is illegal,** but today's slaves may be bound by debts, rarely earning enough to repay them.

Slaves were once expensive; in 1850, a field slave sold for approximately \$1000 to \$1800, or about \$50 000 to \$100 000 today. Because of their expense, slave owners viewed slaves as long-term investments. The high price and required care of slaves meant annual profits might have been only 5 percent of the initial investment. Today, slaves are much cheaper and virtually disposable. Once "used up," they are sent away, which increases profits. Bales estimates annual profits from modern slaves are about 50 percent of the initial investment. Owners of modern slaves are in a win–win situation: They have a continuous supply of labour and stand to make a huge profit.

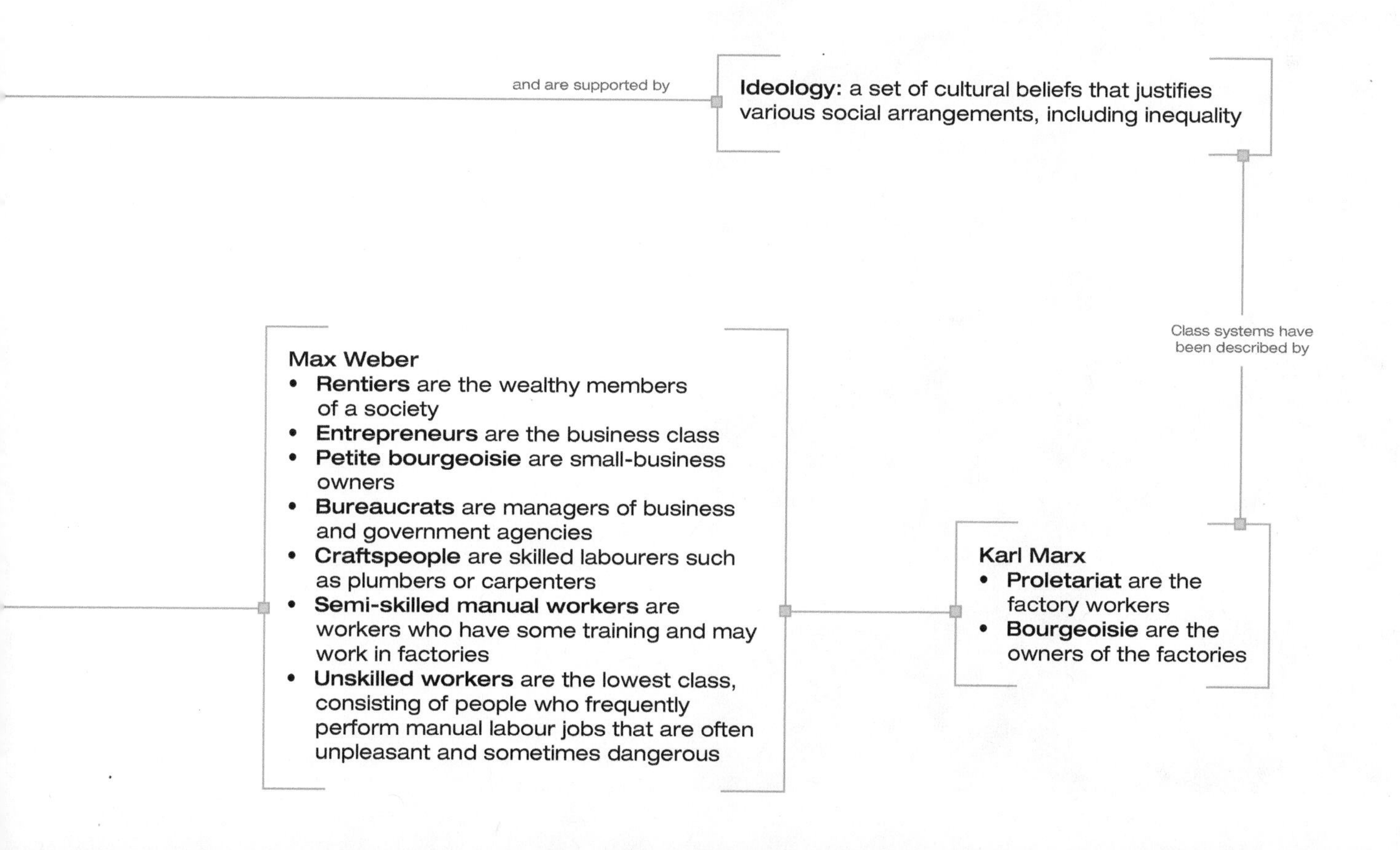

and are supported by
Ideology: a set of cultural beliefs that justifies various social arrangements, including inequality
Class systems have been described by
Max Weber
• Rentiers are the wealthy members of a society
• Entrepreneurs are the business class
• Petite bourgeoisie are small-business owners
• Bureaucrats are managers of business and government agencies
• Craftspeople are skilled labourers such as plumbers or carpenters
• Semi-skilled manual workers are workers who have some training and may work in factories
• Unskilled workers are the lowest class, consisting of people who frequently perform manual labour jobs that are often unpleasant and sometimes dangerous
Karl Marx
• Proletariat are the factory workers
• Bourgeoisie are the owners of the factories

Bales suggests that several new factors drive slavery today. Apart from rapid population growth and extreme poverty, weak governments, worldwide desire for cheap labour, and capital investment can support slavery. Weak governments may tolerate bribery or may not be able to control the behaviour of local warlords and wealthy landowners. With rapid population growth, potential slaves abound. Many countries use their abundant labour supply to attract foreign investment, which can easily lead to slavery.

Forms of Slavery

Modern slavery takes three forms: chattel, debt bondage, and contract slavery. **Chattel slavery** is the closest to the old form of slavery because the slave is considered property. A chattel slave may work a lifetime for one family. Future generations will also become servants of the "owner."

CHATTEL SLAVERY is a form of slavery in which a slave is considered property.

DEBT BONDAGE is a form of slavery in which someone borrows money in order to repay a different debt and works to pay off the new debt.

Debt bondage occurs when a debtor is housed and fed by his or her lender. Debtors' wages are never enough to cover their expenses or debt. This form of slavery usually begins when someone borrows money in order to repay a different debt. The borrower then promises to work for the lender. Of course, the pay for the work is never high enough to decrease the debt while covering expenses for food and shelter. Thus, the person remains enslaved by his or her debt.

Bettmann/CORBIS

Malcolm Linton/Liaison/Getty Images

<<< **Contrary to popular belief, slavery is not a thing of the past.** Modern-day slaves exist in countries all around the world. How do you think the slaves in these pictures differ?

Source: (top image) *Returning from the Cotton Fields in South Carolina*, ca. 1860, stereograph by Barbard, negative number 47843. © Collection of The New-York Historical Society.

Contract slavery occurs when a person signs a work contract and receives food and shelter through an employer. This is different from debt bondage because it is conducted under the façade of a legal contract. Workers sign contracts to work, often in another country, and the employer transports them to a job site. The employer also feeds and houses them. Employers deduct these costs, which often exceed the pay, and use fear and intimidation to keep workers from running away.[5]

CONTRACT SLAVERY is a form of slavery in which a person signs a work contract, receives food and shelter from an employer, but is threatened when he or she tries to leave the contract.

CASTE SYSTEM is a system in which a person's position may be a position of power and privilege or of disadvantage; his or her place is permanently fixed.

CLASS SYSTEM is a form of stratification that allows social mobility.

CASTE SYSTEMS

Caste systems are similar to slave systems in that people have an ascribed status. However, unlike with most slave systems, people are born into a caste system, and the status is lifelong. Within **caste systems**, a person's position may be a position of power and privilege or of disadvantage, but in either case, his or her place is permanently fixed. Caste systems do not allow people to move up and down the ranks, as the Canadian class system does. A person who is born to the lower class in a caste system will never have an opportunity to move vertically and join a higher class.

Perhaps the most widely known caste system is in India. Although now illegal, the caste system remains a powerful force in India today, especially in rural areas, where the system decides whom you marry, what job you have, and where you live.[6] The Go Global box on page 116 provides a brief overview of the Indian caste system.

CLASS SYSTEMS

Unlike caste systems, **class systems** represent a form of stratification that allows social mobility. In fact, North Americans like to think of themselves as having a classless society. In 2000, for example, 20 percent of Americans thought they would make it into the top 1 percent of income earners during their lifetime. Another 19 percent thought they were already there, which means that a whopping 39 percent of people thought they could become rich or were already rich.[7] Sociologically speaking, there is no "official" agreement on the number and kind of social classes within Canada. However, as we will see in Chapter 7, it's unlikely for a person from the lower class to climb very high on the social class ladder. If a person does manage to climb vertically, he or she usually goes up only a few rungs.

Karl Marx on Class Systems

Recall from Chapter 1 that Karl Marx suggested that the class structure of western Europe consisted of three groups: the proletariat, the bourgeoisie, and the petite bourgeoisie.[14] The *proletariat* were the factory workers, the *bourgeoisie* were the owners of the factories, and the *petite bourgeoisie* had their own small businesses.

Marx suggested that the owners foster this ideology in order to maintain their powerful position in society. Let's say you have a lower-rung job at a major corporation and receive a bonus each year because of what your manager calls "profit sharing"; you would be operating under false consciousness if you thought you were going to get rich as long as the corporation continued to make millions of dollars in profits each year. Only through class consciousness, or an understanding of one's position in the social system, will workers unite and eventually benefit from their labour. The bourgeoisie promote false consciousness to further exploit workers for their own benefits. The only way to break through this façade is for the exploited to unite and take power from the dominant class.[15]

According to Marx, class consciousness begins the revolution whereby the proletariat usher in a perfect society and everyone shares resources equally.[16]

Marx pointed out that **workers willingly participate in their own exploitation because they have a false consciousness,** or a false sense of their place in society.

THINK SOCIOLOGICALLY

Slaves in Canada

Your first instinct may be to associate slavery in Canada with another century. After all, slavery was abolished throughout the British Empire in the 1830s.[8] But even as this textbook was being put together, modern-day slavery was in the news in Canada: In October 2010 police arrested and charged a man with running several brothels in Metro Vancouver, where police said women had been forced to work as sex slaves after being lured from Hong Kong.[9]

Slavery first raised its head in Canada hundreds of years ago. Its presence has taken different forms. For example:

- A number of aboriginal tribes practised slavery long before Canada came into existence as a country.
- Portuguese explorer Gaspar Corte-Real may have been the first European to practise slavery in this part of the world. He is known to have enslaved 50 aboriginal men and women in Newfoundland in 1500.[10]
- Oliver Le Jeune was the first black slave officially recorded in Canada, in 1628. After being captured in Africa at age 6, he was brought to Canada by an Englishman and then sold to a Canadian resident in 1629. A total of 1132 slaves of African descent were taken to the part of Canada known at the time as New France.[11]

If there is a bright spark in a discussion of slavery in Canada, it has to be the existence of the so-called Underground Railroad, which helped escaping American slaves find freedom in Canada from about 1835 until 1865, when slavery was abolished in the United States. As many as 40 000 "freedom seekers" made it to Canada.[12]

C. Malhotra/Hulton Archive/Getty Images

^^^ *Dalit* protestors call for equal opportunities and treatment. **Although there are laws to protect the rights of *Dalits*, much of Indian society still treats them poorly.**

The Indian Caste System

India is often referred to as a land of castes. India's caste system has five different levels: *Brahmin*, *Kshatriya*, *Vaishya*, *Shudra*, and the *Harijans* (*Dalit*). Citizens are born, live, work, marry, and die within their caste. There is no room for movement up or down in the hierarchy of the system, and social order dictates that castes remain separate.

In India, *Brahmins* make up the priest and scholar caste. *Kshatriyas* represent the warrior caste, the political leaders who protected the people and fought wars. Merchants, artists, and traders come from the *Vaishya* caste. Mohandas Gandhi, the "father" of the Indian nation, was part of this caste. The *Shudra* caste represents the country's workers, such as labourers from the fields and cities. The lowest caste is "the untouchables." Gandhi referred to them as the *Harijans*, or the people of God. Today, they are known as the *Dalit*. They were seen as unsanitary people who performed the lowest form of labour in the society. In such a system, *Harijans* were socially unacceptable. They lived outside the mainstream, remaining separate from the rest of society.[13]

RENTIERS are the wealthy members of a society, as identified by Weber.

ENTREPRENEURS are the business class, as identified by Weber.

PETITE BOURGEOISIE are small-business owners in Weber's class system.

BUREAUCRATS are managers of business and government agencies.

CRAFTSPEOPLE are skilled labourers such as plumbers or carpenters.

SEMI-SKILLED MANUAL WORKERS are workers who have some training and may work in factories.

UNSKILLED WORKERS are the lowest class, consisting of people who frequently perform manual labour jobs that are often unpleasant and sometimes dangerous.

Max Weber's Class System

Max Weber expanded Marx's idea that property is the sole determinant of social class. Weber's class system includes class, status, and party. When Weber discussed class, he referred to wealth, much as did Marx. However, for Weber, a person's position in society is not determined by only one factor. Status or prestige includes people with fame or important positions.[17] Status matters in society. Party refers to the political dimension of power. Power elevates a person's importance, which in turn causes his or her rank to rise.

Weber's class system is more detailed than that of Marx. For Weber, **rentiers** are the wealthy of a society. They come from a privileged class who own businesses and land; they are the people with "old money." **Entrepreneurs** are the business class. They, too, may have a great deal of money, but they must work to maintain their place. They are "new money." These two groups make up social classes similar to what Marx called the bourgeoisie.

The **petite bourgeoisie** own small businesses. The people who own your local convenience store might be considered members of this group. Although they own a business and have power similar to the that of entrepreneurs, they do not have the same wealth, prestige, or power.

Bureaucrats make up a separate class. They are the managers of business and government agencies. They own nothing, but they have great power in the corporate structure. Corporations hire accountants and middle managers to oversee their business, often with high salaries. Weber felt this class would grow along with society's tendency to become more bureaucratic.

Next, Weber describes three categories of labourers. Craftsmen, or **craftspeople**, are skilled labourers, such as plumbers or carpenters. They hold a special position in society because they have a needed skill that is unusual. **Semi-skilled manual workers** have some training and may work in factories. I was a semi-skilled worker when I was a bicycle mechanic. Without at least a little training, I would not have been able to perform well at my job. **Unskilled workers** make up the lowest class. They are an unorganized group who frequently perform manual labour jobs that are often unpleasant and sometimes dangerous. When I fried chicken at a fast-food restaurant, I was doing unskilled labour. The work was hot, dirty, and dangerous because the hot grease often burned me. However, it didn't take any specialized skills for me to fry chicken. Unskilled labour pays the least and frequently places the heaviest physical demands on the worker.

For Weber, people have differing levels of wealth, power, and prestige. Those with the most of all three components make up the upper class, or the rentiers. While Weber linked social class to job type, class is also related to these other factors. Marx, on the other hand, primarily linked social class to business ownership. **According to Marx, you are either a worker or an owner. Only through class consciousness will the poor rise up and create an egalitarian society.[18]**

Now you have a solid framework for discussing global stratification and its effect on citizens around the world. Why do you think global stratification occurs?

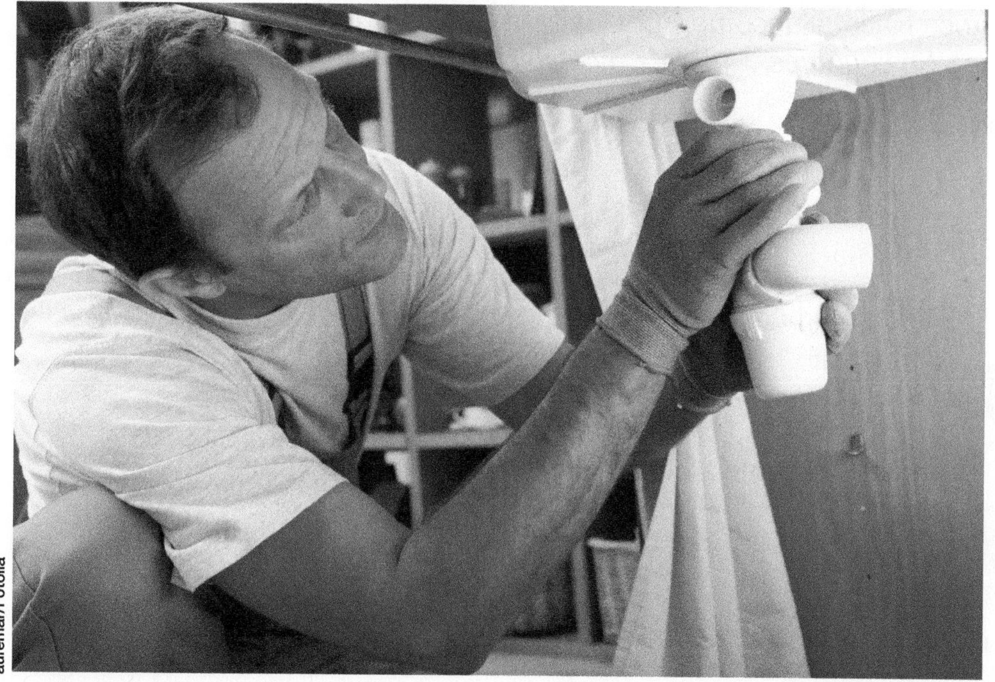
auremar/Fotolia

<<< **Weber divided the labourer group into three classes: craftspeople, semi-skilled manual workers, and unskilled workers.** Craftspeople, like the plumber shown here, have unique skills that make them valuable members of society.

get the topic: WHAT IS GLOBAL STRATIFICATION?

Global Stratification—No Longer Three Worlds

When I was in university, I was told the world was divided into three parts: the first, second, and third worlds. The first world was the United States and its allies—including Canada and western European nations; the second world consisted of the Soviet Union and its allies; and the third world was made up of everyone else. Of course, this system bases its divisions on political and economic ideologies. Sociologists rarely use this system today. First, it's ethnocentric, inferring that the West should be first. Second, the "second world" no longer exists; the Soviet bloc has dissolved. Finally, lumping more than 60 percent of the world into one category called the third world hardly provides an accurate description of the included countries.

Nearly 2.5 billion people live on less than $2 a day.[19] The loaf of bread on my kitchen counter costs double that. Although poverty exists in Canada and countries all around the world, the widest gap in social inequality is not within nations but between them. Thus, when you look at the standard of living in a wealthy country, such as Canada, and compare it to a poorer nation, such as Liberia, you see great disparity in the way people live. **Global stratification** refers to the ranking of countries that highlights social and economic inequality throughout the world.

MEASURES OF STRATIFICATION

The World Bank uses **gross national income (GNI)** per capita to classify countries, according to these groups: low income, $1025 or less; lower-middle income, $1026–$4035; upper-middle income, $4036–$12 475; and high income, $12 476 or more.[20]

As you can see in the table, the average annual income of a resident of Qatar is 254 times that of a resident of the Democratic Republic of Congo.

This clearly illustrates one component of global stratification: The gulf between the richest countries and the poorest countries is extremely wide.

GLOBAL STRATIFICATION refers to the ranking of countries that highlights social and economic inequality throughout the world.

GROSS NATIONAL INCOME (GNI) is a measure of the value of goods and services produced by a country.

GINI INDEX is a measure of income inequality.

HUMAN DEVELOPMENT INDEX (HDI) is a new way of ranking countries by combining indicators of life expectancy, educational attainment, and income.

In 2011, Canada ranked 15th, with a gross national income per capita of $39 710.[21] To determine a country's per-capita GNI, you must divide the country's total GNI by the number of people in that country and assume that it is equally distributed—which, of course, it is not. However, the per-capita income can provide interesting comparisons. Look at the top and bottom income-producing countries in the table. Most of the top income-producing countries are located in Europe, while most of the bottom income-producing countries are located in Africa.

The **Gini index** is the most commonly used measure of income inequality. Named after the Italian statistician Corrado Gini, the Gini index tells us to what extent the distribution of income deviates from a perfectly equal distribution. It ranges from 0 to 1. A Gini index of 0 represents exact equality (that is, everybody has the same amount of income), and a Gini index of 1 represents total inequality (that is, one person has all the income, and the rest of the society has none).

In 1990, the United Nations Development Program published the first Human Development Report. This report introduced a new way of ranking countries by combining indicators of life expectancy, educational attainment, and income into a composite **human development index (HDI)**. This is based on the premise that "people are the real wealth of a nation."[22] By presenting a new way of thinking about and measuring development, the Human Development Index has had a profound impact on policies around the world.[23]

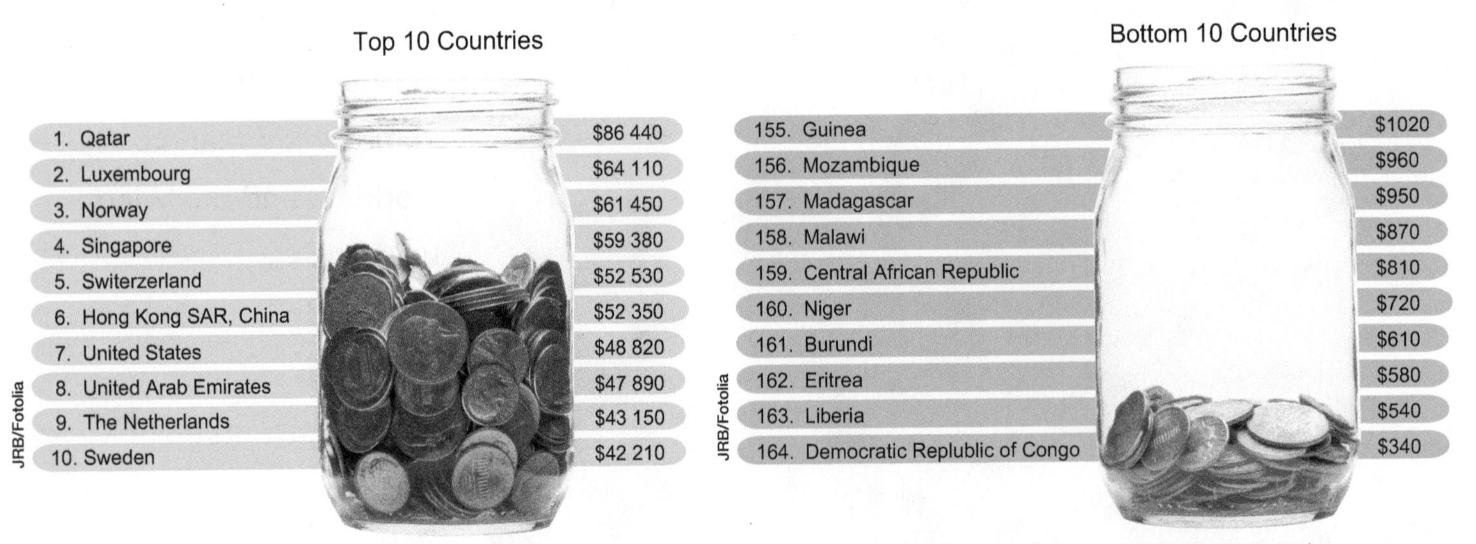

Gross National Income Per Capita in 2011
(*in countries with data available*)

Top 10 Countries

1. Qatar	$86 440
2. Luxembourg	$64 110
3. Norway	$61 450
4. Singapore	$59 380
5. Switerzerland	$52 530
6. Hong Kong SAR, China	$52 350
7. United States	$48 820
8. United Arab Emirates	$47 890
9. The Netherlands	$43 150
10. Sweden	$42 210

JRB/Fotolia

Bottom 10 Countries

155. Guinea	$1020
156. Mozambique	$960
157. Madagascar	$950
158. Malawi	$870
159. Central African Republic	$810
160. Niger	$720
161. Burundi	$610
162. Eritrea	$580
163. Liberia	$540
164. Democratic Replublic of Congo	$340

JRB/Fotolia

Source: GNI per Capita, PPP (Current International $), *The World Bank Group*, 2013. http://data.worldbank.org/indicator/NY.GNP.PCAP.PP.CD/countries?display=default, accessed August 16, 2013.

PROFILES OF COUNTRIES BY WORLD BANK INCOME CATEGORIES

Income categories	Income classification criteria: gross national income per capita in 2009 (US$)*	Number of countries	Country examples	Total population	Average income in 2010 (constant ppp 2005 international $)	Secondary school enrolment rate, 2010**	Life expectancy at birth (years, 2009)	Infant mortality rate (per 1,000 live births, 2009)
High-income countries (rich countries)	and high income, $12 476 or more	70	Canada, Poland, U.S.	1.1 billion	$33,232	100%	79.8	5.8
Upper-middle-income countries	upper middle income, $4 036–$12 475;	54	Brazil, China, Russia	2.5 billion	$8,731	90%	71.5	17.5
Lower-middle-income countries	lower middle income, $1 026–$4 035;	56	Guatemala, India, Nigeria	2.5 billion	$3,287	64%	64.8	51.7
Low-income countries (poor countries)	low income, $1 025 or less;	35	Bangladesh, Cambodia, Kenya	817 million	$1,099	39%	57.5	76.5

*The World Bank calculates gross national income using the Atlas conversion factor, which reduces the impact of exchange rate fluctuations when comparing national incomes across different countries.

**Ratio of enrolment in secondary school (regardless of age) to the population of the age group that corresponds to that level of education.

Source: Profile of Countries by World Bank Income Categories, *The Conference Board of Canada*, 2013. http://www.conferenceboard.ca/hcp/hot-topics/worldinequality.aspx

ABSOLUTE POVERTY is poverty so severe that one lacks resources to survive.

RELATIVE POVERTY is based on comparing ourselves to those around us.

Poverty means different things to different people. A person who experiences **absolute poverty** is so poor that he or she doesn't have resources to survive. The people who are starving to death in the Darfur region of the Sudan are living in absolute poverty. **Relative poverty** is based on comparing ourselves to those around us. You might experience relative poverty if you feel like your cell phone is old and insufficient compared with your friend's phone, and you cannot afford a new one.

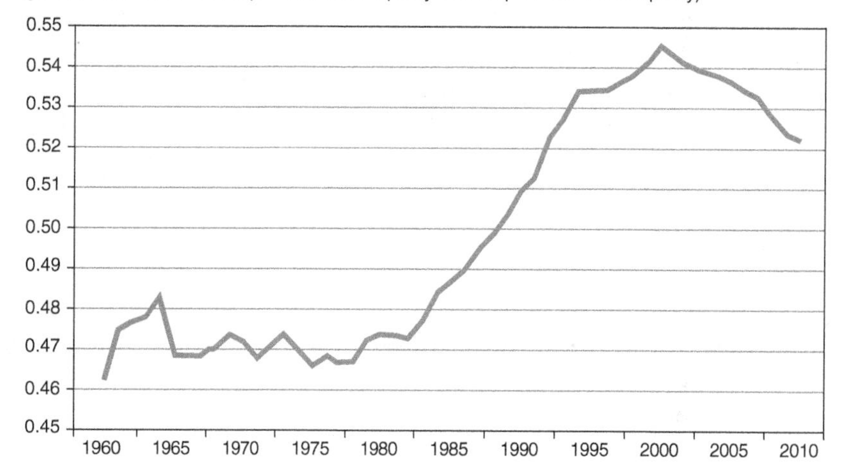

Source: World Income Inequality, *The Conference Board of Canada*, 2013. http://www.conferenceboard.ca/hcp/hot-topics/worldinequality.aspx

Absolute poverty is deadly serious. In the words of one charity foundation: "Extreme poverty is not an inconvenience. It is a death sentence. Millions of people die from malnutrition and disease."[24] However, in a world where the disparities between rich and poor are so great, relative poverty is also an important issue. At the 2011 World Economic Forum in Davos, Switzerland, income inequality was identified as one of the most serious challenges facing the world.[25]

According to international stratification measures, sub-Saharan Africa is the most disadvantaged region of the world. This region has the highest rates of childhood death, hunger, and people living on less than $1 a day. Sub-Saharan Africa also has the lowest rates of sanitation, which leads to increased rates of illness and death.[26]

Disadvantaged regions illustrate disparity between wealthy countries and poor ones. A striking 99 percent of all maternal deaths occur in developing regions—57 percent of them in sub-Saharan Africa, and 30 percent in South Asia.[27] Examples of the lifetime risk of maternal death in different regions include:

- **Sub-Saharan Africa:** 1 in 31
- **South Asia:** 1 in 110
- **High-income countries:** 1 in 3900.[28]

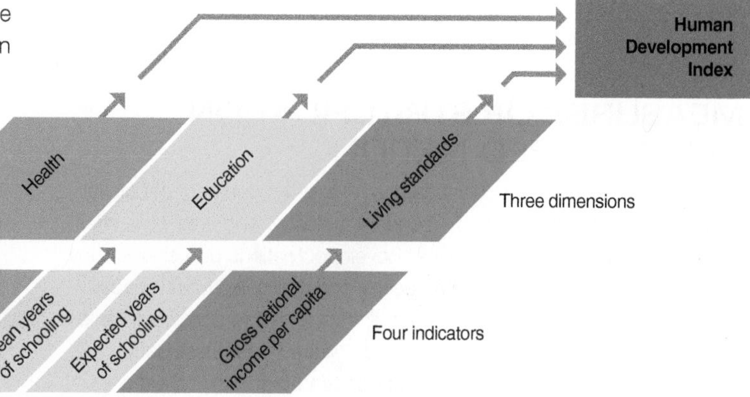

Source: UNDP, "Human Development Index (HDI)," accessed August 24, 2013.

MAKE CONNECTIONS

Access to Communication and Literacy

Think about different media and electronic communication devices you use every day, such as email, texting, and cell phones. You may be surprised to learn that much of the world doesn't have the same access to these communication devices as you do. These figures show selected countries' access to cell phones and the internet, as well as their literacy rates.

People living in underdeveloped countries who aren't able to read or write are often forced to take unskilled, labour-intensive jobs and work long hours to help support their families. As a college student in Canada, you probably can't imagine living under these conditions. But for many people around the world, other options aren't available.

>>> **ACTIVITY** Spend a day without using any type of communication device. This means no cell phones, computers, books, magazines, televisions, radios, journals, and so on. After spending a day without using a communication device, think about your experience. What did you spend your day doing? How did you feel? Bored? Appreciative? Peaceful? How do you think your life would be different without these items?

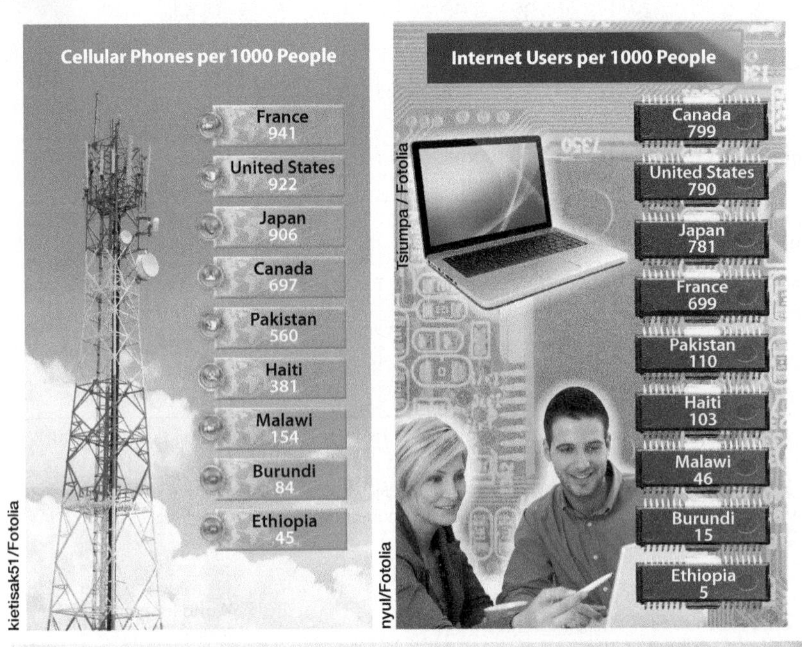

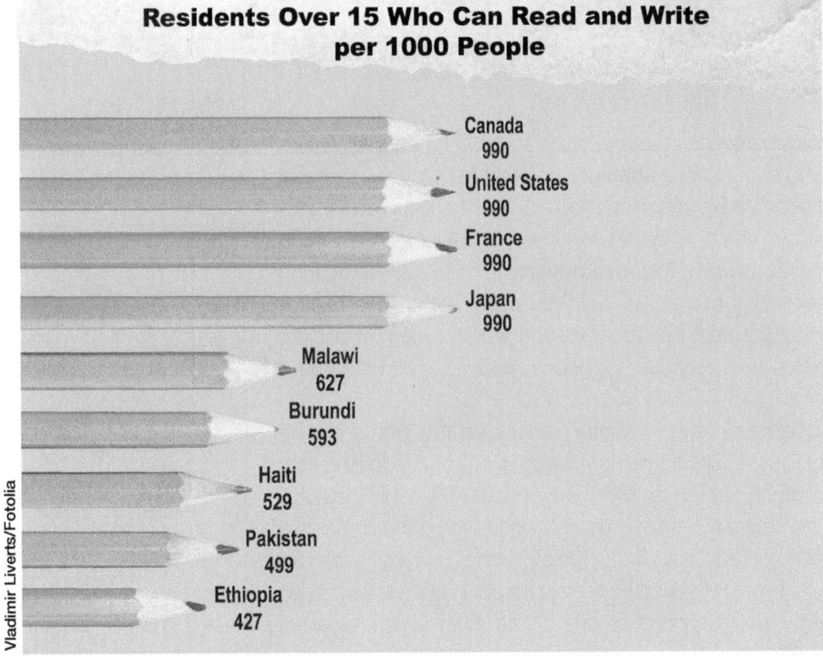

Source: Data from *The World Factbook*, 2008 and 2010.

MEASURES OF STRATIFICATION IN DEVELOPED NATIONS

Developed countries, like Canada, have a well-educated population, regular elections, diverse and abundant industry, and free enterprise. Germany, Japan, and Britain are all developed nations and share many of the same characteristics, both socially and politically, with Canada.

When studying global stratification, it's important to consider international comparisons of poverty among developed countries. Before you look at the numbers, you'll need to understand that U.S. dollars are the standard measure of income and that poverty definitions vary, depending on the country. As a result, our data use half of the median income of the country as the definition for poverty, which allows for a more standardized comparison among nations. The table below shows how the poverty rates of 10 developed countries stack up against one another.

Clearly, there are relatively high percentages of poverty in North America as a whole, even though Canada ranks 5.6 percentage points lower than its list-topping neighbour, the United States. The U.S. showing reflects the fact that the United States has the greatest gap between the rich and the poor of all high-income countries. What does that mean? Of the top 21 nations in the world by income, the distance between the top 10 percent of incomes and the bottom 10 percent is greatest in the United States.[29] Note that the poverty figures are consistently lower

POVERTY RATES OF 10 DEVELOPED COUNTRIES

Country	Percentage of Total Population in Poverty (Rank)	Percentage of Children in Poverty	Percentage of Children in Poverty after Taxes and Welfare Transfers	Percentage of Elderly in Poverty
United States	17.0% (1)	26.6%	21.9%	24.7%
Ireland	16.5% (2)	24.9%	15.7%	35.8%
United Kingdom	12.4% (3)	25.4%	15.4%	20.5%
Canada	11.4% (4)	22.8%	14.9%	5.9%
Denmark	9.2% (5)	11.8%	2.4%	6.6%
Germany	8.3% (6)	18.2%	10.2%	10.1%
France	8.0% (7)	27.7%	7.5%	9.8%
Belgium	8.0% (8)	16.7%	7.7%	16.4%
Austria	7.7% (9)	17.7%	10.2%	13.7%
Switzerland	7.6% (10)	7.8%	6.8%	18.4%

Source: Reprinted from *The State of Working America*, 2004/2005, by Lawrence Mishel, Jared Bernstein, and Sylvia Allegretto Copyright © 2005. Used by permission of the publisher, Cornell University Press.

in continental Europe than in Canada. The area where Canada stands out most positively is the percentage of the country's elderly living in poverty—5.9 percent. But when it comes to child poverty, the percentage in Canada drops nearly 8 percent when taxes and welfare transfers are taken into account; still, the end result, 14.9 percent of children in poverty, is far above the lowest on the list shown here; Danish taxes and welfare transfers reduce child poverty by more than 9 percent, to 2.4 percent.

QUALITY OF LIFE

Which world city offers the best quality of life? A 2010 study shows that Vienna, Austria, is the best city to live in, and the same study ranks five Canadian cities among the top 30: Vancouver (4th), Ottawa (14th), Toronto (16th), Montreal (21st), and Calgary (28th).[30] The Swiss cities of Zurich and Geneva are 2nd and 3rd, respectively, and the highest-ranking U.S. cities are Honolulu (30th) and San Francisco (32nd).

An associated eco-city ranking places Calgary 1st in the world and Ottawa 3rd, with Montreal and Vancouver tied for 13th spot, and Toronto in 39th position. This index is based on ecological factors such as water availability, water potability, waste removal, sewage, air pollution, and traffic congestion.[31]

So, how might one measure the quality of life in one country or another? Many use measures of health and longevity to determine a location's quality of life. Common sense says that the quality of life must be highest in the countries in which fewer babies die and people live longer. The small Asian nation of Macau boasts the highest life expectancy (84.36 years), while Angola has the lowest (38.20 years), in an estimate of 2010 figures.[32] We discussed earlier in this chapter that sub-Saharan Africa has the highest rate of childhood deaths. These numbers, though, tell only part of the story about a country's quality of life.

Sociologists and economists look for variables to make international comparisons.[33] Kai Müller created a list that ranks world economic and social development using a variety of measures.[34] Although income is important, it is only one of many factors to be considered. Other measures include access to telephones, televisions, and newspapers. Structural measures such as the country's debt ratio and the gross national product are also included. Finally, infant mortality, life expectancy, and literacy round out a series of items. By this method, Müller proposes that Norway is the best country in the world to live and the Congo is the worst.

Outside of Japan (2nd), New Zealand (20th), Australia (17th), and Canada (11th), all of the top 20 countries in Müller's list are located in western Europe. Furthermore, the bottom-ranked 20 countries are all in Africa. Clearly, quality of life is not equal throughout the world. Students are often surprised to see that the United States is not in the top 20. Of course, methods of weighing the factors can significantly change the ranking. For example, using older data but similar variables, Daniel J. Slottje found that Canada ranked 6th and Switzerland placed 1st.[35]

Li Lian Ong and Jason D. Mitchell provide a slightly different list.[36] By ranking 21 different countries on four criteria—economic, social, cultural, and political—they provide another view of how to compare countries. These rankings showed that some countries might rank very high in one area but lower in others. For example, Canada ranks 8th in social and cultural components but 19th in economic aspects and 14th overall. Ong and Mitchell combined all the tested areas to compile their quality-of-life list.

Efforts to compare and contrast different countries and measure quality of life often involve subjectivity. If you were to develop a schema, what variables would you use? The amount of air pollution is easy to measure, but any assertion that one country has more beauty than another is very much open to debate.

think sociologically: WHAT CAUSES GLOBAL STRATIFICATION?

As we have seen, there is much disparity between countries. As sociologists, we want to understand how and why countries have different levels of economic and social development.

Walter Rostow's Modernization Theory

Based on a historical analysis of how western European and North American countries became industrialized, in 1962 Walter Rostow proposed the modernization theory, in which he suggested that economic growth occurs in five consecutive stages.

1. The first stage is called traditional society, and it is characterized by subsistence agriculture or hunting and gathering. There is primitive technology, and while some change does occur, it is often slow and modest.
2. The second stage is called preconditions to take-off. In this stage, scientific developments allow for greater agricultural production, which generates a surplus. This surplus can be invested for further economic growth. Along with greater economic prosperity, there are social changes as well. Social mobility increases, and a sense of national identity begins to emerge.
3. The third stage is called the take-off, when manufacturing becomes industrialized and goods are produced both for export and for domestic consumption. Growth and expansion become essential features of the economy during this stage.
4. The fourth stage is called the drive to maturity. During this stage, manufacturing becomes more diversified, and more consumer goods are produced. A large percentage of the population receives some level of education, and political power is more equally divided.
5. In the final stage, the age of mass consumption, there is widespread consumption of basic consumer goods, such as processed foods, and high-value consumer goods, such as cars. Most people have some disposable income, beyond that needed for satisfying their basic needs, and so are able to continue to buy these consumer goods.[37]

Functionalism

Remember that functionalism studies how social structures affect society. Modernization theory looks at how resources and institutions within a society can lead to economic development. In 1997, Jared Diamond published *Guns, Germs, and Steel*, in which he explained how the Western world advanced so quickly while other regions of the world were left behind. Diamond points out that there was a time in history when all people on the earth were poor and lived in underdeveloped conditions. So why did some regions advance while others did not?[38]

Simply put, the fastest-developing regions of the world had the climate, geography, and available natural resources that allowed them to advance. Other areas did not possess such advantages. The dawn of agrarian civilization occurred in the Fertile Crescent, an area that is present-day Iraq. The land in this region is fertile and easy to traverse. Most mountain ranges there are passable, allowing for travel and trade among peoples. Goods and knowledge were shared throughout the region. With knowledge, civilizations became more organized, complex, and powerful because they used information to improve the quality of life. This led to greater power and wealth, which allowed for more trade.[39]

Tribal groups in Europe competed for many centuries, which built up the region's military know-how. Internal struggles led to alliances between groups, increasing trade and the transmission of information.[40]

Tribes in Europe and Asia were able to domesticate a number of animals and plants. Herders raised sheep and goats, while farmers grew grains. Domesticated animals and plants allowed groups to amass more wealth and knowledge, which left people available to specialize as teachers, craftspeople, artists, and warriors.[41]

Unlike in Europe and Asia, native animals that live in sub-Saharan Africa defy domestication. Although native plants can be eaten, the Africans did not have the long grains that grew in the Fertile Crescent. In addition, because the diverse African landscape ranges from desert to mountainous, regions could not share the same technologies used to grow food.[42]

An abundance of food allowed Europeans to thrive. They created cities where they faced another hardship, which actually helped them more than hurt them. Open sewers spread disease and created high death rates for city dwellers. Consequently, their descendants developed strong immune systems and were genetically hardier than their ancestors.[43]

The areas with great natural resources were able to acquire the power needed to function as the wealthy power brokers in the world. Diamond believes that Europeans and Asians advanced because they had abundant resources, strong military skills, set trade routes, and strengthened immune systems. Geographic areas with fewer advantages developed at a much slower place.[44]

Immanuel Wallerstein's World Systems Model

Whereas Rostow's theory focused on individual countries as the agents of their own growth, Immanuel Wallerstein's world systems model suggests that the world is divided into regions, and states either use or are used by countries in other regions. This model is based on the division of labour—not between social groups but between regions.[45] At the centre of the system are the core nations that focus on highly skilled, capital-intensive production. They are constantly trying to expand their markets, decrease costs, and increase profits. The economies of these nations influence the actions of others.

Because the core nations eventually run out of natural resources, they constantly seek expansion, and they find ways to enter *periphery* countries. Historically, core nations made colonies of periphery nations in order to expand their influence. For example, Britain used its Indian colony to expand its market and gain access to resources. Indians had to buy salt from British companies because it was illegal to make and use sea salt. Today, core nations do not have colonies. Instead, they use multinational corporations, trade treaties, and other techniques in order to access the periphery's resources and send the wealth home. Periphery nations hope to generate wealth through the sale of their human and natural resources. Countries like Nigeria and Iraq are periphery nations because of their rich natural resources, such as natural gas and petroleum.[46]

If a periphery nation can use some of its wealth to build its own economy, a small group of elites will arise who build industries of their own. In that way, the country becomes *semi-periphery*. Semi-periphery nations are developing nations that use their raw materials to manufacture goods that can be sold to the core nations while keeping more wealth in the country. Investments in future services and industries mean that the country has the chance to move closer to the core. Countries like Brazil and South Korea are semi-periphery nations.

External nations are underdeveloped nations that have little interaction with the rest of the system. They have few national resources and little ability to attract investment or interest from core nations. Burundi, Chad, and many of the nations of sub-Saharan Africa fit this category. From the perspective of the world systems model, they exercise little or no impact on other countries.

Conflict Theory

Wallerstein's world systems model reflects the conflict perspective because it focuses on inequality and exploitation, although not between different social classes but on a global scale between countries and regions. Nations are dependent because they have no other choice but to borrow from wealthy places, but this often leaves them with nothing.

>>> Wallerstein's model suggests that **core nations are at the centre of the "universe" and affect all surrounding nations.** External nations, however, are unaffected because they are seen as having little to offer to the rest of the system.

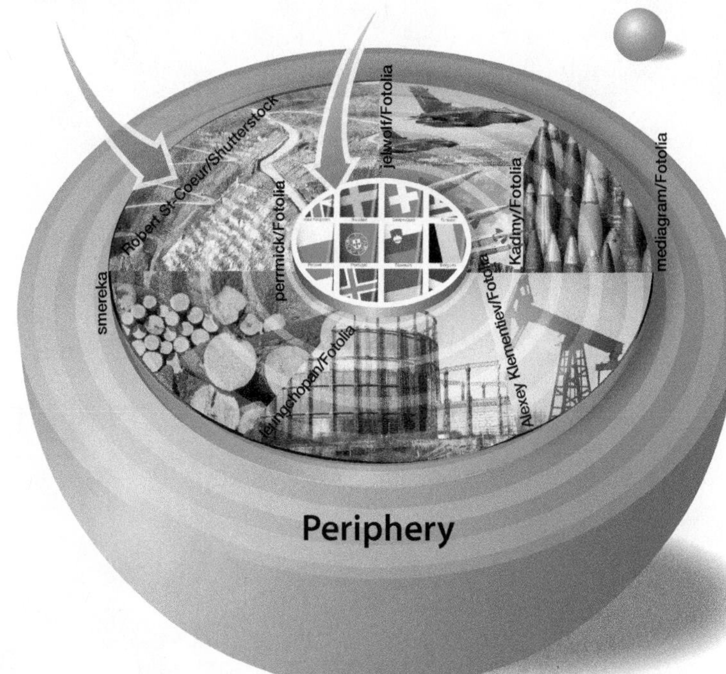

Source: Adapted from Immanuel Wallerstein's *The Modern World-System*, 1974.

NEOCOLONIALISM is a process in which powerful nations use loans and economic power to maintain control over poor nations.

GLOBALIZATION is a complex process by which the world and its international economy are becoming more and more intertwined.

We will now look at two more models of global stratification which arise from the conflict perspective—neocolonialism and globalization.

Neocolonialism

Much of the world was once under the colonial rule of various European powers. Over time, however, it became difficult to stop rebellions, so many countries gave up their colonies.[47]

Michael Harrington says countries now use **neocolonialism**, a process in which powerful nations use loans and economic power to maintain control over poor nations.[48] Through loans for food, weapons, and development, poor nations become dependent on rich ones. Once in debt, poor countries often cannot repay the loans and so agree to alliances, sale of natural resources, and trade agreements that primarily benefit the wealthy nation.[49]

Extending the ideas of neocolonialism, some propose that wealthy nations now use multinational corporations to control poorer nations.[50] Multinational corporations offer jobs, income, and potential riches to poor nations. The corporations benefit because they may gain tax-free status, weak environmental oversight, or some other concession that may not be in the best interest of the country. These corporations may create working conditions that lead to the enslavement of the native people. Bales points out that although company executives might not want to be involved in slave labour, they probably want to maximize their profits.

Through multinational corporations, wealthy countries continue to control weaker ones with corporate investment. This may, in effect, lead countries to engage in a "race to the bottom." To win the prize of foreign investment, they cut local regulations and salaries. This "race" can lead to wage and gender discrimination and less worker safety.[51] Of course, there is another side of this: They provide jobs and incomes to workers who have few other opportunities.

Globalization

Globalization refers to a complex process by which the world and its international economy are becoming more and more intertwined. Globalization connects the world through business, travel, immigration, and the production of goods and services.[52] Bales argues that every consumer in the world is linked to modern-day slavery in one way or another. Workers in China put together shoes made from leather tanned in Brazil, with rubber soles from Indonesia. Frequently, rich countries recruit the best and brightest from poor countries to become doctors, scientists, and other vital occupations. This is brain drain: The best talent leaves poor countries and thereby provides an even greater advantage to wealthy countries.[53]

Some argue that an aspect of globalization is exploitation. Others say that globalization is the only hope for poor nations. As the world becomes more interconnected, are the various cultures around the world becoming more similar or less so? Those who believe cultures are becoming more similar suggest that the world's cultures are adopting more Western values. On the other hand, some suggest that globalization will have the opposite effect on culture, as local groups work hard to maintain their own religions, customs, and languages.[54]

Max Weber's Protestant Ethic

In 1905, Max Weber wrote a series of essays that were published as the book *The Protestant Ethic and the Spirit of Capitalism*. In this book, Weber suggested that capitalism in northern Europe developed because the Protestant ethic encouraged people to develop their own businesses, to engage in trade, and to accumulate wealth for investment. The spirit of capitalism that Weber described may be traced to the Reformation. During the Middle Ages, the Roman Catholic Church assured salvation to individuals who accepted the church's sacraments and submitted to the clerical authority. However, the Reformation, in which several Protestant sects emerged and split from the Roman Catholic Church, effectively removed such assurances. The average person had difficulty adjusting to this new worldview, and in the absence of assured salvation from religious authority, Weber argued that Protestants began to look for other signs that they were saved. Calvin and his followers taught a doctrine that espoused the absolute duty to believe that one was chosen for salvation and to dispel any doubt about that. Worldly success became one measure of that self-confidence.[55]

Some theorists say that globalization polarizes the world and creates gaps between groups. They predict more war, terrorism, and unrest as Western countries continue to expand. Do you share this view on globalization?

Symbolic Interactionism

Like all other social events, economic development can be more fully understood if we look at the historical context and appreciate that human behaviour is intrinsically meaningful and can be interpreted or understood. The cultural values that lend meaning to human life are created by and can create the specific processes of social development.

Sociologist Thorstein Veblen used the term **conspicuous consumption** in his book *The Theory of the Leisure Class: An Economic Study in the Evolution of Institutions.* This term described a behavior that Veblen observed primarily among the "nouveau riche" social class that emerged in the United States at the end of the nineteenth century. People of this class would often spend their immense wealth not on practical investments but on lavish and highly conspicuous goods and services as a means of publicly flaunting their economic power and social prestige.[56]

CONSPICUOUS CONSUMPTION is the purchase of goods or services for the specific purpose of displaying one's wealth.

>>> **Multinational corporations** often set up factories in countries where they can **pay lower wages to the workers in order to make a heftier profit.** The Chinese women in this image are workers in the Reebok shoe factory.

Michael S. Yamashita/Corbis

Feminist Theory

Around the world, women and girls suffer disproportionately from poverty, hunger, abuse, and lack of basic human rights. Each year, half a million women die from complications related to pregnancy and birth. The majority of these women live in poor countries. In some countries in sub-Saharan Africa, 1 woman in 50 dies during childbirth. Compare this to Canada, where the rate is less than 1 per 10 000. [57]

Women are increasingly the sole heads of households. Unfortunately, these families, especially those with younger children, are overrepresented among the poor, despite the fact that women on average work more than men. Persistent sexual discrimination in terms of work and wages leads to a vicious cycle of poverty and, as a result, children get less food and maternal care.

Breaking the vicious cycle of poverty will require significant social changes and targeted social policies. One requirement is to expand the access of poor women to family planning and reproductive health services. Another important strategy involves expanding access to education for girls. Women who are educated tend to have fewer and healthier children, and their children are more likely to attend school. Yet in all regions of the world except North America and western Europe, women's literacy rates are less than men's. Two-thirds of illiterate people around the world are women. Because education improves health, autonomy, and income, strategies aimed at improving access to education for girls would yield future benefits for these women and for their children. As former World Bank Vice President Mieko Nishimizu has said, "If you educate a boy, you educate a human being. If you educate a girl, you educate generations."[58]

Working Hours Around the World 2012

	Annual hours	Average per week
Mexico	2226	43.6*
United States	1790	NA
Australia	1728	36.0
Japan	1745	NA
Canada	1710	36.5**
United Kingdom	1654	36.6
Italy	1752	38.0
Sweden	1621	36.3
Germany	1397	35.7
France	1479	38.0
Norway	1420	33.9

Note: * 2004 data, ** 2006 data,
NA = not available

samantha grandy/Shutterstock

<<< **On average, Europeans work fewer hours and have more paid vacation time than Canadians.** Why do you think Canadian workers spend more hours at the office?

Valua Vitaly/Fotolia

Source: Based on data from "Hourly Earnings under Earnings under Labour from OECD Stat Extracts," assessed at http://stats.oecd.org.Index.aspx?DatasetCode=EAR_MEI, August 16, 2013.

WRAP YOUR MIND AROUND THE THEORY

Globalization means that some companies operate around the world. McDonald's is the world's leading food-service retailer, with more than 33,000 restaurants serving more than 64 million people in 119 countries every day.[59] **But what effect does this have on different cultures?**

dailin/Shutterstock

Patti McConville / Alamy

WHAT CAUSES GLOBAL STRATIFICATION BETWEEN COUNTRIES?

FUNCTIONALISM

Functionalism studies how social structures affect society. Modernization theory looks at how resources and institutions within a society can lead to economic development. Rostow's model proposes five stages that societies pass through as they develop and become fully industrialized. In the final stage, the age of mass consumption, there is widespread consumption of basic consumer goods, such as processed foods, and high-value consumer goods, such as cars. Most people have some disposable income, beyond that needed for satisfying their basic needs, and so are able to continue to buy these consumer goods.

CONFLICT THEORY

Immanuel Wallerstein's world systems model reflects the conflict perspective because it focuses on inequality and exploitation, although not between different social classes but on a global scale between countries and regions. Much of the world was once under the colonial rule of various European powers. Michael Harrington says countries now use neocolonialism, a process in which powerful nations use loans and economic power to maintain control over poor nations. Globalization is a complex process by which the international states and economies are becoming more and more intertwined. Some argue that an aspect of globalization is exploitation. Others say that globalization is the only hope for poor nations.

SYMBOLIC INTERACTIONISM

Like all other social events, economic development can be more fully understood if we look at the historical context and appreciate that human behaviour is intrinsically meaningful and can be interpreted or understood. Weber suggested that capitalism in northern Europe developed because the Protestant ethic encouraged people to develop their own businesses, to engage in trade, and to accumulate wealth for investment. The spirit of capitalism is based on the premise that worldly success is a measure of salvation. Thorstein Veblen used the term conspicuous consumption to describe a behavior of the "nouveau riche" in the United States at the end of the nineteenth century.

FEMINIST THEORY

Feminist theory focuses on the poverty of women around the world. Since women are largely responsible for the care of children, their poverty results in a vicious cycle in which their children suffer from malnutrition, poor health, lack of access to education, and a grim future. Social policies that serve to reduce the poverty of women, give them better access to health care, and improve access to education for all children, especially girls, would go a long way toward reducing poverty.

Poor countries and their workers are exploited by richer, more powerful countries. These workers work long, hard hours for a fraction of what workers in a richer country would be paid.

Julio Etchart / Alamy

XtravaganT/Fotolia

Core nations have markets with local goods, but many of the cheaper items are made by slave labour in foreign countries. **Developed nations enjoy the best standards of living in the world, but what is the cost to other nations?**

discover sociology in action: WHAT IS BEING DONE TO ASSIST POOR COUNTRIES?

Social Policy: Foreign Aid

Some students get angry about foreign aid. They oppose the idea of paying huge amounts of tax dollars to help other nations when there are people in Canada in need.

"Helping the world's poor is a strategic priority and a moral imperative. Economic development, responsible governance, and individual liberty are intimately connected."[60]

The main aim of Canadian foreign aid is to promote popular welfare and overall economic improvement of underdeveloped countries around the world.[61] The world's rich countries agreed in 1970 at the United Nations General Assembly to provide 0.7 percent of their gross national product (GNP) for international development aid each year. They have since rarely met their targets, and the European Union has set a new target date of 2015.[62]

The countries' donations depend on a percentage of the wealth of the country. An example may help you understand the difference. If you and I both donate $10 to charity, but you only have $100 in the bank and I have $1000, who has actually given more? We both gave the same amount, but you gave 10 percent of your wealth, while I gave only 1 percent of mine.

In 2009, Canada donated 0.3 percent of its GNP, or $4.5 billion.[63] The Organisation for Economic Co-operation and Development (OECD) said that five countries exceeded the 0.7 percent target in 2009: Denmark, Luxembourg, the Netherlands, Norway, and Sweden.[64]

ACTIVITIES

1. Check the tags of your clothes and shoes. Where were they made? Do you have any assurances that slaves were not used to make your apparel?
2. Discuss with a partner what can be done to combat slavery. If almost everything is connected to slavery, what can be done?
3. Take an internet trip to www.antislavery.org. Surf the website. Write a paragraph explaining what you learned about modern slavery, how to stop human trafficking, and the lengths to which people are going to stop slavery.

CHAPTER

06

WHAT IS SOCIAL STRATIFICATION? 112

the ranking of people and the rewards they receive based on social factors, often including wealth, power, and/or prestige.

WHAT IS GLOBAL STRATIFICATION? 118

the ranking of countries that highlights social and economic inequality throughout the world.

WHAT CAUSES GLOBAL STRATIFICATION? 122

world systems theory: the world is divided by its connection to economic power
neocolonialism: powerful nations use loans and economic power to maintain control over poor nations
globalization: a complex process by which the world and its international economy are becoming more and more intertwined; some argue that an aspect of globalization is exploitation. Others say that globalization is the only hope for poor nations

WHAT IS BEING DONE TO ASSIST POOR COUNTRIES? 127

get the topic: WHAT IS SOCIAL STRATIFICATION?

Theories

FUNCTIONALISM 122

- modernization theory looks at how resources and institutions within a society can lead to economic development
- Rostow's model proposes five stages that societies pass through as they develop and become fully industrialized
- in the final stage, there is widespread consumption of basic consumer goods, and most people have some disposable income

CONFLICT THEORY 123

- Immanuel Wallerstein's world systems model focuses on inequality and exploitation on a global scale between countries and regions
- much of the world was once under the colonial rule of various European powers; powerful countries now use neocolonialism to maintain control over poor nations
- globalization is a complex process by which the international states and economies are becoming more and more intertwined

SYMBOLIC INTERACTIONISM 124

- economic development can be more fully understood if we look at the historical context and appreciate that human behaviour is intrinsically meaningful
- Weber suggested that capitalism in northern Europe developed because the Protestant ethic encouraged people to develop their own businesses, to engage in trade, and to accumulate wealth for investment
- Thorstein Veblen used the term conspicuous consumption to describe a behavior of the "nouveau riche" in the United States at the end of the nineteenth century

FEMINIST THEORY 124

- globally, women are more likely than men to live in poverty
- since women are also the primary caregivers to children, this results in a vicious cycle of poverty
- social policies that reduce the poverty of women would go a long way toward reducing global poverty

Key Terms

social stratification refers to the ranking of people and the rewards they receive, based on social factors, often including wealth, power, and/or prestige. *112*

ideology is a set of cultural beliefs that justifies various social arrangements, including inequality. *113*

social stratification systems are systems societies use to rank different groups. *113*

slavery is a stratification system in which one person has complete control over another. *113*

chattel slavery is a form of slavery in which a slave is considered property. *114*

debt bondage is a form of slavery in which someone borrows money in order to repay a different debt and works to pay off the new debt. *114*

contract slavery is a form of slavery in which a person signs a work contract, receives food and shelter from an employer, but is threatened when he or she tries to leave the contract. *115*

caste system is a system in which a person's position may be a position of power and privilege or of disadvantage; his or her place is permanently fixed. *115*

class system is a form of stratification that allows social mobility. *115*

rentiers are the wealthy members of a society, as identified by Weber. *117*

entrepreneurs are the business class, as identified by Weber. *117*

petite bourgeoisie are small-business owners in Weber's class system. *117*

bureaucrats are managers of business and government agencies. *117*

craftspeople are skilled labourers such as plumbers or carpenters. *117*

semi-skilled manual workers are workers who have some training and may work in factories. *117*

unskilled workers are the lowest class, consisting of people who frequently perform manual labour jobs that are often unpleasant and sometimes dangerous. *117*

global stratification refers to the ranking of countries that highlights social and economic inequality throughout the world. *118*

gross national income is a measure of the value of goods and services produced by a country. *118*

Gini index is a measure of income inequality. *118*

human development index (HDI) is a new way of ranking countries by combining indicators of life expectancy, educational attainment, and income. *118*

absolute poverty is poverty so severe that one lacks resources to survive. *119*

relative poverty is based on comparing ourselves to those around us. *119*

neocolonialism is a process in which powerful nations use loans and economic power to maintain control over poor nations. *123*

globalization is a complex process by which the world and its international economy are becoming more and more intertwined. *123*

conspicuous consumption is the purchase of goods or services for the specific purpose of displaying one's wealth. *124*

Sample Test Questions

These multiple-choice questions are similar to those found in the test bank that accompanies this textbook.

1. Which social stratification system allows social mobility?
  a. Contract slavery
  b. Caste system
  c. Class system
  d. Debt bondage

2. Which citizens exhibit what Marx would call an ideology of false consciousness?
  a. Petite bourgeoisie
  b. Bourgeoisie
  c. Proletariat
  d. Rentiers

3. Which of the following is *not* one of the three labour groups described by Weber?
  a. Craftspeople
  b. Bureaucrats
  c. Unskilled workers
  d. Semi-skilled manual workers

4. According to Weber, what encouraged people to develop their own businesses, to engage in trade, and to accumulate wealth for investment?
  a. False ideology
  b. The Protestant ethic
  c. Conspicuous consumption
  d. Relative poverty

5. Nations that have wealth, technology, and strong military power, which they use to influence the entire global system, are called
  a. core nations.
  b. external nations.
  c. periphery nations.
  d. semi-periphery nations.

ANSWERS: 1. c; 2. c; 3. b; 4. b; 5. a

ESSAY

1. What are the positive and negative effects that globalization can have on underdeveloped nations?
2. What are the differences between a caste system and a class system?
3. According to Marx, how do the bourgeoisie successfully promote false consciousness?
4. What characteristics does Weber use to determine social class?
5. How could wealthy nations be using multinational corporations to control poorer nations?

WHERE TO START YOUR RESEARCH PAPER

To learn more about efforts to curb slavery throughout the world, go to www.antislavery.org.

For more information on the World Bank Group, go to www.worldbank.org.

For interactive maps and data to visualize world issues, go to www.gapminder.org.

For information regarding health, crime, and standards of living, go to www.nationmaster.com/index.php.

To learn more about the OECD and read its reports on economic development throughout the world, go to www.oecd.org.

For more information regarding the use of cheap labour and child labour in the garment industry, go to www.freethechildren.com

To learn more about international aid funded by the federal government, go to www.acdi-cida.gc.ca/index-e.htm.

For more information about hunger and poverty in the world, go to www.undp.org/poverty/ and www.poverty.com.

For information on the nongovernmental organizations (NGOs) Canada works with to give international aid, go to www.ccic.ca.

To learn more about bilateral and multilateral methods and how Canada distributes aid, go to www.acdi-cida.gc.ca/acdi-cida/ACDI-CIDA.nsf/eng/JUD-112911931-LY2.

For national statistics and reports from Statistics Canada, go to www.statcan.gc.ca.

For more information about the United Nations, go to www.un.org/english.

For more information about the World Food Programme, go to www.wfp.org.

For more information about the World Health Organization and its data, including issues of hunger, HIV/AIDS, and other statistics from a variety of countries throughout the world, go to www.who.int/en.

To learn more about Canada's economic, financial, and trade-based relationships with the rest of the world, and how the country's foreign policy is used, visit Foreign Affairs, Trade and Development Canada, at www.international.gc.ca/international/index.aspx.

Remember to check www.thethinkspot.ca for additional information, downloadable flashcards, and other helpful resources.

SOCIAL CLASS IN CANADA

Forestpath/Fotolia

HOW IS POVERTY DEFINED IN CANADA?
WHAT IS THE CLASS STRUCTURE IN CANADA?
WHAT SOCIAL POLICIES HAVE BEEN CREATED TO EASE POVERTY?

"One of the most persistent images that Canadians have of their society is that it has no classes. This image becomes translated into the assertion that Canadians are all relatively equal in their possessions, in the amount of money they earn, and in the opportunities which they and their children have to get on in the world. An important element in this image of classlessness is that, with the absence of formal aristocracy and aristocratic institutions, Canada is a society in which equalitarian values have asserted themselves over authoritarian values. Canada, it is thought, shares not only a continent with the United States, but also a democratic ideology which rejects the historical class and power structures of Europe.

"In a society which is made up of many cultural groups there is usually some relationship between a person's membership in these groups and his class position and, consequently, his chances of reaching positions of power. Because the Canadian people are often referred to as a mosaic composed of different ethnic groups, the title, 'The Vertical Mosaic,' was originally given to the chapter which examines the relationship between ethnicity and social class. As the study proceeded, however, the hierarchical relationship between Canada's many cultural groups became a recurring theme in class and power. For example, it became clear that the Canadians of British origin have retained, within the elite structure of the society, the charter group status with which they started out, and that in some institutional settings the French have been admitted as a co-charter group whereas in others they have not. The title, 'The Vertical Mosaic,' therefore seemed to be an appropriate link between the two parts of the book."[1]

Stratification *in a* Modern Society

CHAPTER 07

In *The Vertical Mosaic: An Analysis of Social Class and Power in Canada*, John Porter described the features of class and stratification in Canadian society.

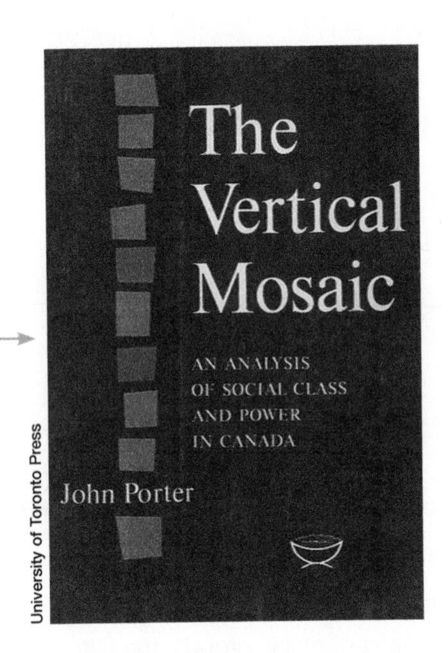

University of Toronto Press

Although this book was researched and written nearly 50 years ago, much is still relevant in Porter's analysis of the Canadian social structure. The term *mosaic* refers to the rich diversity of languages, cultures, ethnicities, and religions that make up Canadian society. However, as Porter pointed out, not all groups enjoy the same power and status. There is a hierarchy, and so the mosaic is also "vertical," with some groups higher than others. Being higher means having better income, better health, better education—overall, a better life. In Canada, those of British ancestry enjoy the greatest privileges, while aboriginal peoples are the most disadvantaged. How does social position affect a person's life? As sociologists, we want to find out.

Social Class

in Canada is based on

Income: the money received for work or through investments
Wealth: all of your material possessions
Power: the ability to carry out your will and impose it on others
Prestige: the level of esteem associated with one's status and social standing

and is measured using

Low income cut-off (LICO): families that spend at least 20 percentage points more of their after-tax income on food, clothing, and shelter than the average family of the same size are counted as low-income
Low income measure (LIM): defines low-income Canadians as those living in families that have an after-tax income lower than 50 percent of the median income for all Canadian families
Market basket measure (MBM): estimates the cost of a specified set of goods and services in 48 geographic regions across Canada
Quintile: one of five groups of households, ranked by income

- **Social mobility:** the ability to change social classes
- **Horizontal mobility:** ability to move within the same status category
- **Vertical mobility:** ability to move from one social status to another
- **Intragenerational mobility:** occurs when an individual changes social standing, especially in the workforce
- **Intergenerational mobility:** the change that family members make from one social class to the next through generations
- **Structural mobility:** occurs when social changes affect large numbers of people
- **Exchange mobility:** a concept suggesting that, within a country, each social class contains a relatively fixed number of people

get the topic: HOW IS POVERTY DEFINED IN CANADA?

INCOME is the money received for work or through investments.
WEALTH is all of your material possessions.
QUINTILE is one of five groups of households, ranked by income.

In Canada, we tend to divide groups by their access to wealth and/or income. **Income** refers to the money received for work or through investments. Whether it's the pay cheque you get every two weeks or the dividends you receive from your stock investments, the money you receive regularly is considered income. **Wealth**, on the other hand, refers to all your material possessions. If you were to take everything you own—your car, your laptop, your clothes, and so on—and sell it all at a fair market value, you could probably raise a considerable sum that would be more than your monthly income. It's important to know the difference between the two and to understand how each of these factors can affect your social standing.

Income Distribution

When I was a college student, everything I owned was in my one-room apartment. I worked for minimum wage, and I had few expenses. I earn much more now than I did in college, but my expenses have also increased significantly because I married, bought a house, and started a family. Statistics Canada conducts an annual survey of Canadian households that measures the distribution of income. All households are listed, from poorest to richest, and then divided into five groups called **quintiles**. If income distribution trends continue, the rich are going to get richer and the poor are going to get poorer. In 1989, the lowest quintile received 4.8 percent of total income and the highest quintile received 43 percent. Compare these percentages with 2008, when the poorest 20 percent of the country's earners received only 4.2 percent of the total income, whereas the top 20 percent received 47.3 percent.[2] The median, or midpoint, household income for Canadian families of two or more persons in 2010 was $65,500. However, Canadian households in the lowest quintile had incomes of just $15 200 or lower, while the top 20 percent of all households earned more than $171 900.[3] Between 1980 and 2010, the share of income of the highest quintile increased from 41.8 percent to 47.3 percent; the share of all other quintiles fell during the same period.[4]

There are six social classes

Upper or elite class: very small in number and holds significant wealth
Upper middle class: consists of high-income members of society who are often well educated but do not belong to the elite membership of the super wealthy
Middle class: consists of those who have moderate incomes
Working class: generally made up of people with high school diplomas and lower levels of education
Lower class: people living in poverty
Underclass: includes the homeless and people living in substandard housing

There are different types of poverty

and various kinds of social mobility

Transitional poverty: a temporary state of poverty that occurs when someone loses a job for a short time
Marginal poverty: a state of poverty that occurs when a person lacks stable employment
Residual poverty: is chronic and multi-generational poverty
Cycle of poverty: refers to the vicious circle in which poor children are more likely to be poor as adults
Feminization of poverty: refers to the fact that around the world, women experience poverty at far higher rates than men

TRANSITIONAL POVERTY is a temporary state of poverty that occurs when someone loses a job for a short time.

MARGINAL POVERTY is a state of poverty that occurs when a person lacks stable employment.

RESIDUAL POVERTY is chronic and multigenerational poverty.

Wealth Distribution

For most Canadians, their most significant asset is their house. Other kinds of assets are cars, other belongings, and personal pension funds, including registered retirement savings plans (RRSPs). The median wealth of Canadian families was $148 400 in 2005. We do not have more recent figures because that was the last year Statistics Canada collected data on the distribution of wealth in Canada. A recent private-sector study showed that by the end of 2009, 3.8 percent of Canadian households controlled $1.78 trillion of financial wealth, or 67 percent of the total wealth in Canada.[5] Since 1999, all Canadian families have seen an increase in wealth, except for families in the lowest quintile. Increases were highest in the fourth and fifth quintiles, which indicates a growing inequality in Canada's wealth distribution. In Chapter 6, you saw that the Gini index is a measure of inequality in a society. In 2012, Canada's Gini coefficient was 0.43, which is lower than that of the United States but higher than those of most other comparable countries, such as those in western Europe and Australia. There are two reasons for the growing inequality. One explanation involves changing market forces. Because of technical changes and increased globalization, there is increasing demand for highly skilled labour. Workers who are educated and highly skilled are earning more than ever before, while unskilled workers and those in many service-sector jobs are earning less. Another explanation is that the increase in inequality can be attributed to institutional forces, such as declines in unionization rates, stagnating minimum wage rates, and policies, such as tax breaks, that favour the wealthy.[6]

The wealth distribution of Canada shows other trends as well. Generally, men have more wealth than women do. In 2005, Canadian families headed by a woman had a median wealth value of $105 470 compared to $184 964 for families headed by a man. Families with an older family head typically have more wealth. After 65 years of age, though, wealth starts to decline because retired people often draw on their assets to supplement their income when they retire. In 2005, older families had the highest median wealth. This is mainly because they are more likely to live in a mortgage-free home and their pension assets are higher. Single individuals, including the elderly living alone, had the lowest median wealth.[7]

Richest Group Accounts for the Largest Share of Canadian National Income, 2010
(share of the national adjusted after-tax income by income quintile, percent)

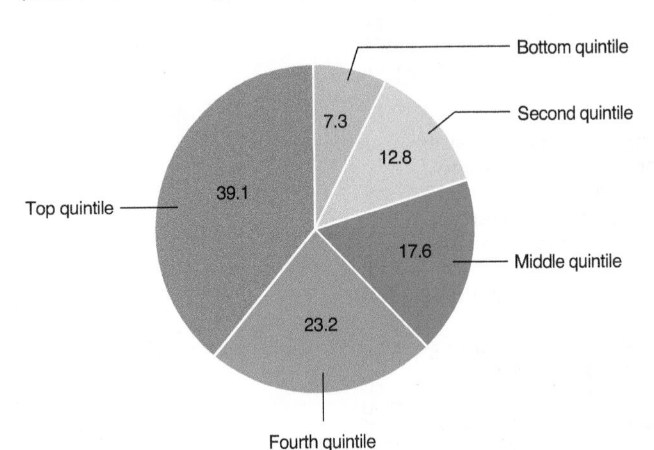

Source: Conference Board of Canada, "Income Inequality," www.conferenceboard.ca/hcp/details/society/income-inequality.aspx, accessed August 18, 2013.

Geoffrey Robinson/Alamy

Some societies use birth as a way to stratify their people. **Although Great Britain is a democracy with a prime minister, the royal family is among that society's most elite and wealthy members.**

How Is Poverty Defined in Canada?

Sociologists have several different ways of defining poverty. **Transitional poverty** is a temporary state that occurs when someone loses a job for a short time. **Marginal poverty** occurs when a person lacks stable employment. For example, if your job is lifeguarding at a pool during the summer season, you might experience marginal poverty when the season ends. The next, more serious level, **residual poverty**, is chronic and multigenerational. People who live in a seemingly never-ending cycle of poverty that passes on to their children and grandchildren experience this type of poverty.

While there is no "official" definition of poverty in Canada, Statistics Canada uses three measures of low income. The first is the *low income cut-off* (LICO). Families that spend at least 20 percentage points more of their after-tax income on food, clothing, and shelter than the average family of the same size are counted as low income. Since it is a comparative measure, the LICO is more of a measure of inequality or relative poverty than of absolute poverty.

The *low income measure* (LIM) defines low-income Canadians as those living in families that have an after-tax income lower than 50 percent of the median income for all Canadian families. This measure is often used to make international comparisons. One of the main criticisms of the LICO and the LIM is that they do not account for regional differences in the cost of living. The *market basket measure* (MBM) estimates the cost of a specified set of goods and services in 48 geographic regions

LOW-INCOME CUT-OFFS (1992 BASE), 2011 AFTER TAX

	Community Size				
	Rural Areas	Less Than 30 000	30 000–99 999	100 000–499 999	500 000+
1 person	$12 629	$14 454	$16 124	$16 328	$19 307
2 persons	$15 371	$17 592	$19 625	$19 872	$23 498
3 persons	$19 141	$21 905	$24 437	$24 745	$29 260
4 persons	$23 879	$27 329	$30 487	$30 871	$36 504
5 persons	$27 192	$31 120	$34 717	$35 154	$41 567
6 persons	$30 156	$34 513	$38 502	$38 986	$46 099
7 or more persons	$33 121	$37 906	$42 286	$42 819	$50 631

Source*:* Statistics Canada, "Low Income Cut-offs (1992 base) after Tax," Catalogue No. 75F0002MWE. Found at: http://www.statcan.gc.ca/pub/75f0002m/2012002/tbl/tbl01-eng.htm, accessed March 26, 2013. This does not constitute an endorsement by Statistics Canada of this product.

across Canada.[8] This measure accounts for regional variations. For example, in 2010, the MBM for a family of two adults and two children in Regina was $29 875, in Ottawa $32 155, and in Halifax $32 303.[9]

Three factors that influence the impact of poverty on families are its depth, its breadth, and its duration. The depth of poverty refers to how far a family or individual income is below the poverty line. The further below, the more difficult it is to provide for the basic needs. Breadth refers to other aspects associated with poverty, such as illiteracy, living in a poor neighbourhood, and poor health. Duration refers to how long the poverty lasts. A temporary and short-term drop in income is easier to weather than prolonged periods because individuals usually have some resources to help tide them over a bad period. When poverty is prolonged, however, all accumulated resources (such as savings) are eventually depleted and need to be renewed.[10]

CANADA INCOME DISTRIBUTION, 2008

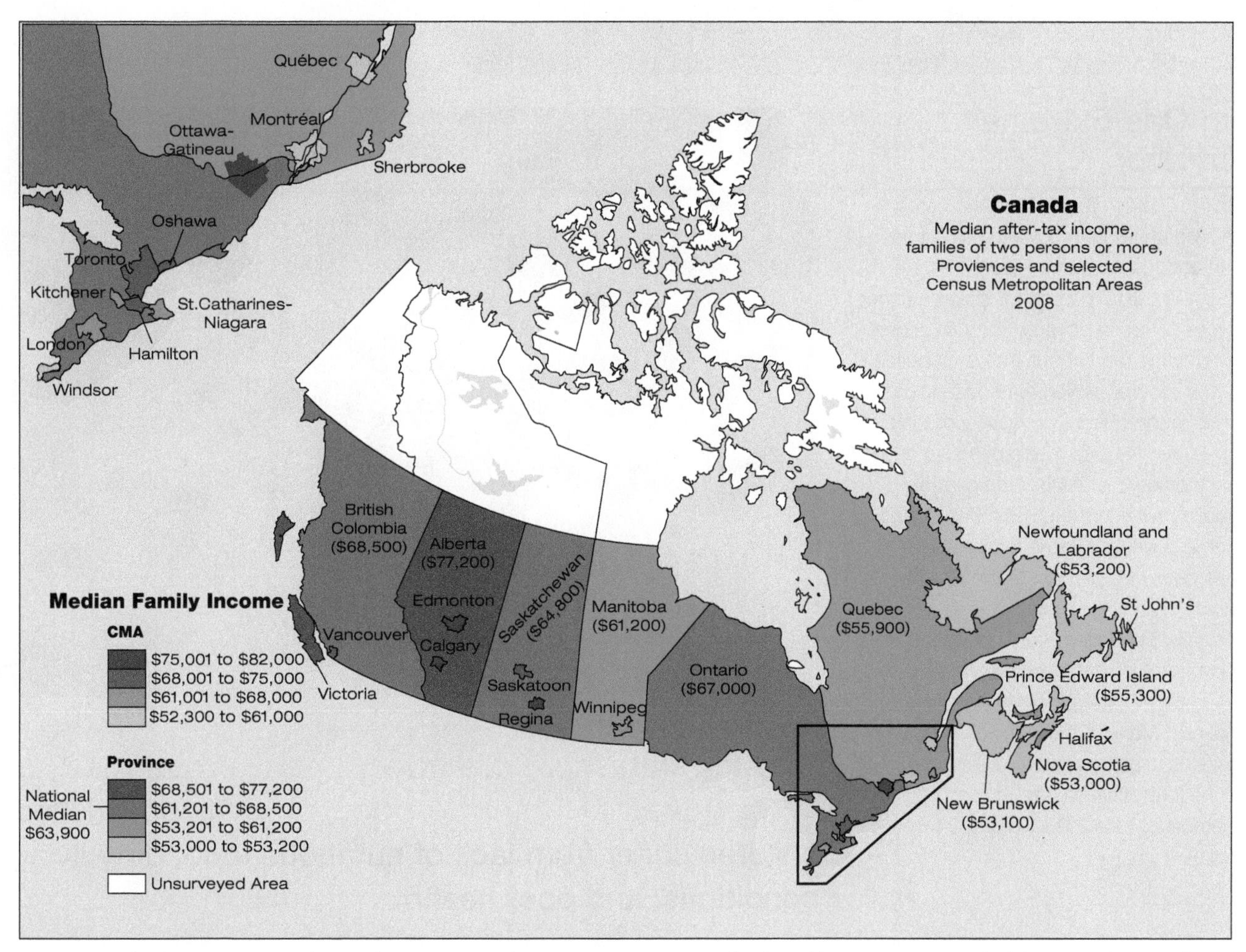

Source: Statistics Canada, "Income in Canada, Catalogue 75-202-X, 2008," Figure 1, accessed at http://www.statcan.gc.ca/pub/75-202-x/2008000/analysis-analyses-eng.htm, August 18. 2013. This does not constitute an endorsement by Statistics Canada of this product.

POWER

Another measure of stratification is **power**—the ability to carry out your will and impose it on others. Individuals have varying amounts of power, as do certain social groups. C. Wright Mills suggested that within the United States, a small group called the **power elite** holds immense power.[11] Canada has its own version of a power elite. The power elite come from three distinct but related groups: the economic elite, the state elite, and the media elite. They decide what information and knowledge to share with the rest of us, and they use their social position and influence to direct the country's decisions. For example, in Canada, six families control 723 companies: the Westons (123), the Blacks (123), the Desmaraises (121), the Irvings (121), and two branches of the Bronfmans (Charles Rosner, with 118, and Edward and Peter, with 117).[12]

Most politicians must be voted into power, but not all eligible voters exercise their right to vote. People with high incomes and people who have achieved high levels of education are more likely to vote than their less wealthy, less-educated neighbours.[13] So what does this mean? Older, wealthier, educated people are making key decisions for the entire country. How does this affect the kinds of politicians we elect, the social measures we pass, and the economic packages we approve?

PRESTIGE

Prestige refers to the level of esteem associated with one's status and social standing. Most of us want others to hold us in high regard, but various types of jobs hold differing levels of prestige. Occupational prestige refers to how well a job is regarded by society. It may be based on how much the job pays but also includes other factors, such as the level of education required to gain entry to the job, the sector, the degree of autonomy, or even the perceived "social usefulness" of the job.[14] We often judge people by the job they do. When I worked as a cafeteria manager, I made pretty good money, but when I told people what I did for a living, they were not impressed. When I became a college teacher, people were much more interested in knowing more about me and what I did (although I knew that my salary was lower). Occupational prestige varies a great deal among jobs and shows the general respect our society has for certain kinds of work.

Occupational prestige is generally ranked on a scale from 0 to 100, with 0 being the lowest. Because occupational prestige is socially defined, job rankings can change over time. In 2000, John Goyder replicated a study done in 1975 in Kitchener-Waterloo. In 1975, the lowest-ranked jobs in the survey were worker in a dry-cleaner (16.7) and filling-station attendant (17.2), while physician (93.6) and architect (90.3) were the highest ranked. In 2000, some of these jobs had changed a lot

POWER is the ability to carry out your will and impose it on others.

POWER ELITE is a small group of people who hold immense power.

PRESTIGE is the level of esteem associated with one's status and social standing.

GO GLOBAL

From One Extreme to Another

The United States has the greatest percentage of children living in poverty compared with other industrial democracies.[15] In the United States, 20.7 percent of children under the age of 18 live in poverty,[16] and 21.3 percent of children live in households classified as "food insecure," which are households that change the quantity or quality of their food or frequently skip meals because of limited incomes.[17] In 2005, 7 percent of the children living in the United States lived in extreme poverty.[18] These families have incomes below 50 percent of the poverty threshold.[19]

Ironically, the United States leads the world in the total number of millionaires as well as the highest percentage of new millionaires.[20] Many of these millionaires run for positions in government or contribute large donations to political causes. In fact, of the 100 members in the 2010 Senate, 54 were millionaires.[21]

Nathan Benn/Alamy

Although there are government programs designed to help the poor, many **impoverished children suffer from lack of nutritious food, dirty living conditions, and poor health.**

UPPER, OR ELITE, CLASS is a social class that is very small in number and holds significant wealth.

UPPER MIDDLE CLASS is a social class that consists of high-income members of society who are often well educated but do not belong to the elite membership of the super wealthy.

in their ranking. Architects had fallen to 74.5, while hospital attendants had increased from 30.8 to 55.5.[22]

In 2001, Canadians ranked physicians, dentists, and judges and lawyers as the top occupations. Trappers and hunters, sports referees, and door-to-door vendors were ranked the lowest.[23] A prestigious job may carry its benefits into other areas of life. For example, you might take a stock tip from the CEO of a successful start-up, but I doubt you'd take the advice of a minimum-wage-earning grocery bagger. You don't expect someone who works as a bagger to be able to give you a great stock tip; if the person really knew stocks, why would he or she be working in such a low-status job? Occupational prestige varies a great deal among jobs and shows the general respect we have for certain kinds of work. Few people look at their newborn baby and hope she'll grow up to become a fry cook rather than a doctor.

Wealth, power, and prestige are the basis for the stratification system, so these three components can also be used to analyze the class system of Canada.

CLASS STRUCTURE IN CANADA

If someone asked you what your social class is, what would you say? You have already seen in this chapter that social class is in fact a complicated mix of income, wealth, and occupation. It also includes things like education and political ideology. Sociologists have varying opinions on how many classes there should be and what constitutes each class. For our discussion, however, let's look at six different social classes in Canada: upper class, upper middle class, middle class, working class, lower class, and underclass. Ask yourself how your membership in one class or the other might influence your perspective, opportunities, and long-term outcomes in life.

Upper/Elite Class

The **upper, or elite, class** is very small in number and holds significant wealth. The upper class possesses much of the country's "old money," which affords them great access to the three components of class: wealth, power, and prestige. The Bronfmans, Thomsons, Molsons, and Westons have been rich for generations. This class also includes the "new rich," people such as Jim Balsillie, who made billions selling the BlackBerry, or Wayne Gretzky, the hockey superstar turned astute businessperson.

In *The Vertical Mosaic*, John Porter describes the Canadian elite:

> At the high end of the social class spectrum are the families of great wealth and influence. They are not perhaps as ostentatious as the very wealthy of other societies, and Canada has no "celebrity world" with which these families must compete for prestige. . . . Almost every large Canadian city has its wealthy and prominent families of several generations. They have their own social life, their children go to private schools, they have their clubs and associations, and they take on the charitable and philanthropic roles which have so long been the "duty" of those of high status.[24]

The upper class's money affords them opportunities that most people only dream of having. However, members of the upper middle class come pretty close to matching the elite's status.

Upper Middle Class

As with all other distinctions of class, the definition of the upper middle class is fairly subjective. For the purposes of our discussion, the **upper middle class** consists of high-income members of society who are often well educated but do not belong to the elite membership of the super wealthy. These people occupy professional positions and have achieved a level of income that makes their lives very comfortable. They own property, have high occupational prestige, and often hold positions of authority within their jobs.[25]

Middle Class

Most Canadians claim that they are members of the middle class. If you're trying to decide where you fall along the country's economic spectrum, you might think, "Well, I'm not poor, and I'm not rich, so I must be somewhere in the middle. That's middle class, right?" However, the sociological definition for middle class is a bit more complex.

Images Distribution-Pierre Roussel/Newscom

>>> **Geoff Molson was born into one of the richest families in Canada.** Do you think he would have been as successful if he had been born into a poor family?

THINK SOCIOLOGICALLY

Ashbury College

One of the luxuries that elite students enjoy is attending a high-quality preparatory school such as Ashbury College in Ottawa. Founded in 1891, Ashbury College is a co-educational boarding school with slightly more than 500 students in grades 4 through 12. Students enjoy a variety of educational opportunities, from anatomy to German, and can participate in many different sports, including downhill skiing and rowing. The average class size is 17 students. Students who wish to attend pay up to $44 250 a year for the privilege.[26]

This kind of education gives the upper class the edge they need to succeed. In recent years, 100 percent of graduates from Ashbury College have been accepted at universities such as McGill, Queen's, and the University of Toronto. The exclusive education they received ensures that they are groomed for top-paying positions that come with great power.

The two primary components of this group are occupational prestige and education. Owning a small business, having a professional career, or holding a high-status job often propels a person into this group. Your dentist, your lawyer, or the owner of a successful business may belong in this group.[27]

MIDDLE CLASS is a social class that consists of those who have moderate incomes.

WORKING CLASS is a social class generally made up of people with high school diplomas and lower levels of education.

LOWER CLASS is a social class living in poverty.

In general, **middle class** people have moderate incomes. They may be lower-paid white-collar workers, such as schoolteachers, or well-paid blue-collar workers, like factory supervisors. Middle-class workers generally aren't involved in manual labour, but they may be skilled labourers (such as electricians). In many middle-class families, if there are two parents present, both must work in order to have a comfortable life. Most middle-class members have at least a high school diploma, and many have technical training or college credits. Such attainment affords them a moderate level of occupational prestige. When you graduate from college and get your first job, you are likely to start out in the middle class. Members own property but generally hold much less wealth than the previously discussed groups.

Working Class

The **working class** is generally made up of people with high school diplomas and lower levels of education. They often hold jobs that involve manual labour or clerical skills. Blue-collar factory workers and white-collar clerical workers make up most of the working class. Unlike those in the middle and upper middle classes, members of the working class earn an hourly wage instead of a salary. Because they work by the hour and lack formal education, the working class has very limited opportunities for job improvement. Many nontraditional college students come from the working class. They understand that "good jobs" are increasingly rare and that education opens doors. However, their ability to raise their social class is hindered by the increasing number of blue-collar and even white-collar jobs that are moving overseas. There is an increasing amount of competition for work, which is a further motivation for workers to boost their marketable skills.

Lower Class

A notch below the working class are the members of society who truly feel the effects of poverty: the **lower class**. Because of the skyrocketing costs

>>> **Many nontraditional students are working-class adults who want to gain more skills through education.** More and more adults are going back to school for additional training and new careers.

Pressmaster/Shutterstock

LOW-INCOME RATES AMONG WORKING-AGE MAIN INCOME RECIPIENTS, VARIOUS GROUPS, 2010

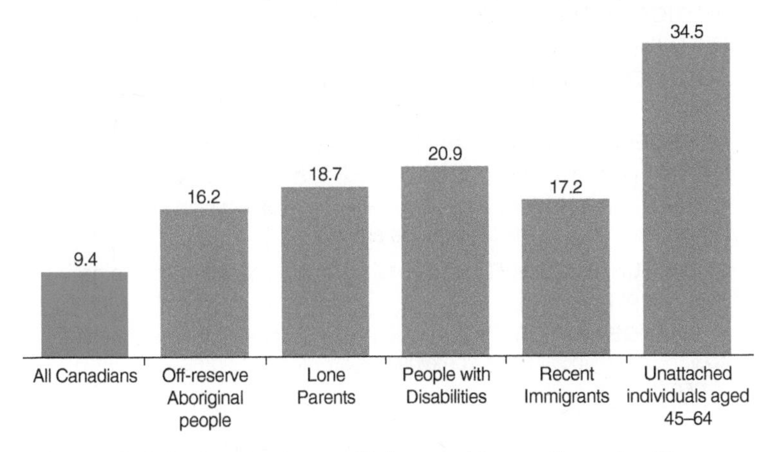

Source: Statistics Canada, *Survey of Labour and Income Dynamics*. Ottawa: Statistics Canada, 2012. Reproduced and distributed on an "as is" basis with the permission of Statistics Canada.

of tuition, food, and rent, many college students might think they understand what it means to be poor. In most cases, though, the relative poverty of their situation pales in comparison to the experiences of the working poor. After all, the privileges of attending a college or university and receiving a higher education are designed to lead students to employment that will land them in the middle class. When I was in university, I worked at a cafeteria as a grill cook. Our pay was low, and the hours were long. But for me, a university student living alone in a one-room apartment, it was a good job.

The Underclass

Despite our country's prosperity, there are homeless people in Canada. They belong to the **underclass** of Canadian society. Other members of this group live in substandard housing and may be receiving government assistance. They often lack a high school diploma, and if they find a job, it's usually a minimum-wage position that propels them no higher than the poorest of the working class.

However, what makes them truly disadvantaged is that they are often socially isolated and lack conventional role models. These issues make life significantly more difficult for the residents and children who live in these ghettos.

UNDERCLASS includes the homeless and people living in substandard housing.

NEIGHBOURHOODS AND SOCIAL CLASS

Sociologists have observed how neighbourhoods influence behaviour. Their findings have demonstrated an increase in the geographic concentration of poverty and affluence especially in large cities. Over time, poor people congregate in neighbourhoods densely populated by other poor people. Simultaneously, the well-off members of society, particularly those who live in cities, tend to cluster in economically affluent neighbourhoods, such as Westmount in Montreal, Rosedale in Toronto, and Shaughnessy in Vancouver. Looking at each end of the spectrum gives us a clear vision of the dynamics between poverty and affluence in Canada.

The concentration of poverty in a single geographic area is correlated to various issues, such as high crime rates, increased drug use, and increasing numbers of lone-parent homes. Often, people who achieve any sort of economic advantage move out of these poor neighbourhoods. This sort of residential segregation increases the disadvantages for those left behind.[28] Children who grow up in such neighbourhoods are at increased risk for lower birth weights, poorer health, lower levels of educational attainment, and higher dropout levels.[29]

Conversely, children growing up in affluent neighbourhoods do better in school, have lower rates of teen pregnancy, and have higher test scores. Interestingly, when a poor child is raised in a more affluent neighbourhood, due to foster care or some type of rent control supplement, the child tends to do better than his or her peers who remain living in poor neighbourhoods. In short, living in a more affluent neighbourhood seems to decrease the power of the negative effect that poverty has on children. Why do you think this is the case? Apparently being "the poor kid on the block" is better for a child than being another poor kid on the block.[30] Why?

In Canada, the labour market has changed immensely. When was the last time you bought something that was labelled MADE IN CANADA? **Canadian citizens who previously performed this type of work find themselves out of jobs, which in turn slows upward mobility.**

PERCENTAGE OF PERSONS IN LOW INCOME (1992 BASE AFTER-TAX INCOME LOW INCOME CUT-OFFS)

	2000	2001	2002	2003	2004	2005	2006	2007	2008	2009	2010
All persons	**12.5**	**11.2**	**11.6**	**11.6**	**11.4**	**10.8**	**10.3**	**9.1**	**9.3**	**9.5**	**9.0**
Under 18 years old in economic families	13.8	12.1	12.3	12.5	12.9	11.6	11.0	9.4	8.9	9.4	8.1
In two-parent families	9.5	8.3	7.4	7.9	8.4	7.8	7.5	6.5	6.4	7.3	5.7
In female lone-parent families	40.1	37.4	43.0	41.4	40.4	32.9	31.2	26.7	23.3	21.5	21.8
18 to 64 years old	12.9	11.7	12.0	12.2	11.9	11.4	11.1	9.9	10.1	10.4	10.1
65 and over	7.6	6.7	7.6	6.8	5.6	6.2	5.3	4.8	5.8	5.1	5.3

Source: Statistics Canada, May 23, 2013. Found at: http://www.statcan.gc.ca/daily-quotidien/120618/t120618b003-eng.htm, December 31, 2010. This does not constitute an endorsement by Statistics Canada of this product.

Social Mobility

Wherever we are in life, there's always the chance that something could happen to us that would change our status. Whether it's winning the lottery or investing in the wrong stocks, our social class could change in an instant. Social events, such as the recent recession and corporate downsizing have sent many middle-class families plummeting into poverty. **Social mobility** is a term that describes this ability to change social classes. If social class is a ladder, social mobility occurs when we climb either up or down it. Several patterns of social mobility are possible.

Horizontal mobility, as the name suggests, refers to moving within the same status category. For example, when a teacher leaves one school to take a position at another school, horizontal mobility has occurred. The teacher is earning the same amount of money and performs the same tasks; she just happens to be doing these things at a different location. Her movement is lateral, not vertical. **Vertical mobility** involves moving from one social status to another. This type of mobility can either be upward, in the form of a promotion at work, or downward, in the form of a demotion at work. For example, if the same teacher gets a master's degree and becomes a principal, then vertical mobility has occurred.

Intragenerational mobility occurs when an individual changes social standing, especially in the workforce. Climbing the corporate ladder is a prime example of this type of mobility. For instance, if you begin your working career as an unskilled labourer doing construction work and then 10 years later own a construction company, you are experiencing intragenerational mobility.

Intergenerational mobility refers to the change that family members make from one social class to the next through generations. If you hope to live a better life than your parents did, then you hope for upward intergenerational mobility. However, if you expect to do much better than your parents, the odds are probably stacked against you. A number of researchers have found that while intergenerational mobility does occur, children tend to climb only a little higher on the social class ladder compared with their parents, if they climb at all.[31]

The likelihood of this kind of mobility is even less for children born into poor families. Their parents probably lack the education, skills, social networks, and other resources that would provide them with the social capital that would make mobility upward easier. Children raised in poor homes are more likely to experience poverty in adulthood. In a vicious circle called the **cycle of poverty**, poor children are more likely to remain poor in adulthood than are other children who are not raised in poverty.

SOCIAL MOBILITY is the ability to change social classes.

HORIZONTAL MOBILITY refers to moving within the same status category.

VERTICAL MOBILITY refers to moving from one social status to another.

INTRAGENERATIONAL MOBILITY occurs when an individual changes social standing, especially in the workforce.

INTERGENERATIONAL MOBILITY refers to the change that family members make from one social class to the next through generations.

CYCLE OF POVERTY refers to the vicious circle in which poor children are likely to remain poor as adults.

STRUCTURAL MOBILITY occurs when social changes affect large numbers of people.

EXCHANGE MOBILITY is a concept which suggests that, within a country, each social class contains a relatively fixed number of people.

Structural mobility occurs when social changes affect large numbers of people. During economic booms, some climb the ladder and benefit from changes in the economy. The Great Depression of the 1930s was a very significant event that resulted in millions of people experiencing downward mobility due to structural changes. More recently, the dot-com boom (and then bust) of the late 1990s is another example of structural mobility for many.

The concept of **exchange mobility** suggests that, within a country, each social class contains a relatively fixed number of people. If you move upward into a class above you, someone else must move down. When you consider the changes in income over time that we talked about earlier, you can see that such data generally support the idea that social stratification levels do not change much, though the people who make up each layer may be different.

When the economy heads into a recession, workers who have lost their jobs to outsourcing experience downward structural mobility. Canadian business executives see outsourcing as one of the best ways to reduce costs. But for workers such as those at RBC who lost their jobs to temporary foreign workers, the results can be devastating.

MAKE CONNECTIONS

Nickel and Dimed into Poverty

Before writing the book *Nickel and Dimed*, Barbara Ehrenreich spent a year living among the working class in the United States. Going from state to state, she worked as a waitress, a maid, a nursing home aide, and a Walmart salesperson. Ehrenreich's experiences led her to dispute the idea that these jobs require low-level skills. Instead, she believes that such low-wage jobs are physically demanding and actually require a great deal of interpersonal and technical skills. These jobs don't normally provide health care or sick leave, so workers who fall ill have to choose between their health and their pay. Yet despite the hurdles society has placed in their way, these workers are actually more motivated to succeed and are not depressed by a system of low wages and long hours.

>>> **ACTIVITY** Recent college graduate Adam Shepard wrote *Scratch Beginnings: Me, $25, and the Search for the American Dream* in rebuttal to Ehrenreich's book. By undertaking a self-imposed experiment, Shepard tried to demonstrate that an individual can overcome the structural obstacles to success. Read Shepard's book or search the internet to learn his findings. Which author paints a more accurate picture of life for the working poor? Why?

think sociologically: WHAT IS THE CLASS STRUCTURE IN CANADA?

Functionalism

Functionalists believe that systems find equilibrium, or balance, so stratification must be the result of some kind of functional balance. Theorists Kingsley Davis and Wilbert Moore summarized the common argument that a stratification system is inevitable and aids in the smooth functioning of society.[32] This **meritocracy argument** states that those who get ahead do so based on their own merit.

Davis and Moore believed that each society has important positions that must be filled. The more important the position, the more we reward those who choose to pursue it. Doctors in Canada generally get hefty pay cheques because everyone needs a doctor to tend to his or her health care needs. Society offers rewards to those who are willing to fill important positions. The rarer the skill or the longer the training period, the greater the rewards can be. If you faint at the sight of blood or if you can't stand the thought of spending a good portion of your life in school, you probably shouldn't become a doctor.

On the other hand, KFC (or PFK in Quebec) is able to pay its employees minimum wage because they can learn to fry chicken in about two hours. I should know; I once cooked chicken for the Colonel. But why would anyone become a medical doctor, considering the stress and training involved? Davis and Moore said that society has to offer greater rewards to entice people to take particularly tough or stressful jobs. To sum up the functionalist view, stratification inevitably happens because people have different abilities, and those abilities are more or less important to society. The unequal rewards given to different positions ensures that the most capable and qualified people fill those positions, and this is a benefit to society as a whole.

Therefore, if you get ahead, it is based on some ability or drive you have that pushes you to get there. Delayed gratification, or the ability to wait to get something you want, can also determine your success. If you're willing to put in the time to go to school and work hard, you're likely to be successful.

In this sense, stratification is inevitable, since we do not all have the same intelligence, drive, and desire.

Those who get ahead in this country tend to be those who use these individual forces to reap society's rewards.

After teaching sociology for many years, John Carl (one of the authors of this book) believes that most of his students are functionalists. They support the idea that people succeed or fail based on their own merit.

The graphic on the right provides information from student surveys that he has used in his classes. This nonscientific study yields the same results virtually every year. He asked students if they "agree with the following reasons," and the percentages show those who agree with each reason. What do you think? Do individuals determine their own success?

Conflict Theory

Unlike functionalists, conflict theorists focus on the role of conflict as the basis of stratification. Every society has limited resources to go around, and groups struggle with one another for those resources. Melvin Tumin offered a critique of Davis and Moore that supports the conflict point of view. For Tumin, social inequality is rooted in a system that is more likely to reward you based on where you start—not solely based on the abilities you have.[36] There is nothing inevitable about inequality; it is merely those

MERITOCRACY ARGUMENT states that those who get ahead do so based on their own merit.

John Carl's students are American. **Take a survey of students in your class and see if the percentages are different from those shown above.**

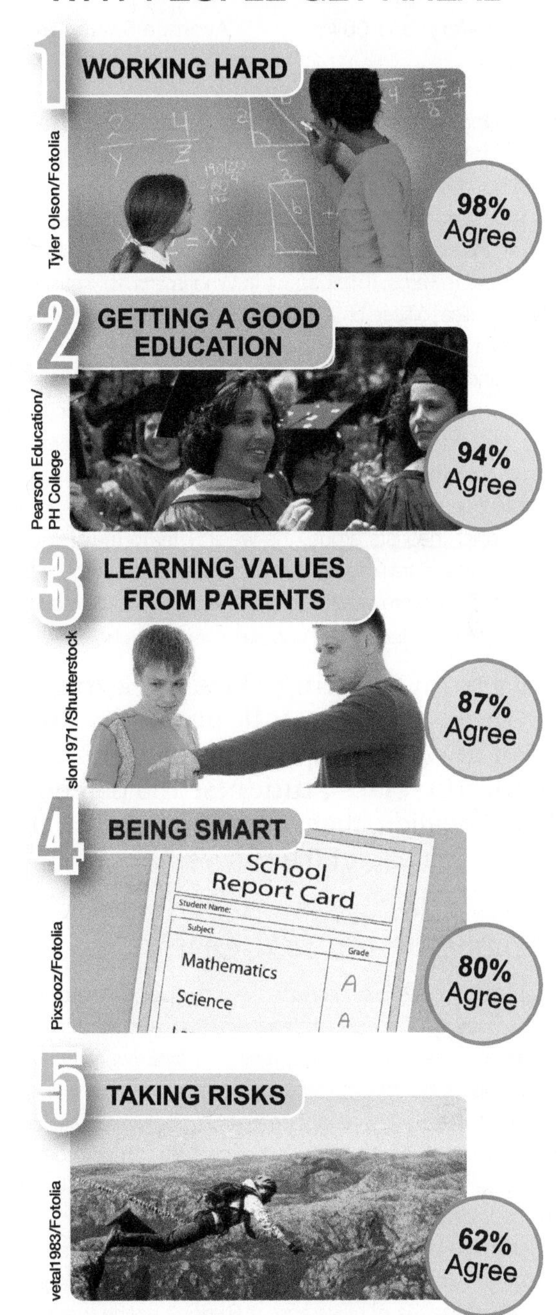

Source: Based on informal surveys by John D. Carl of American sociology students on the reasons people get ahead in the United States.

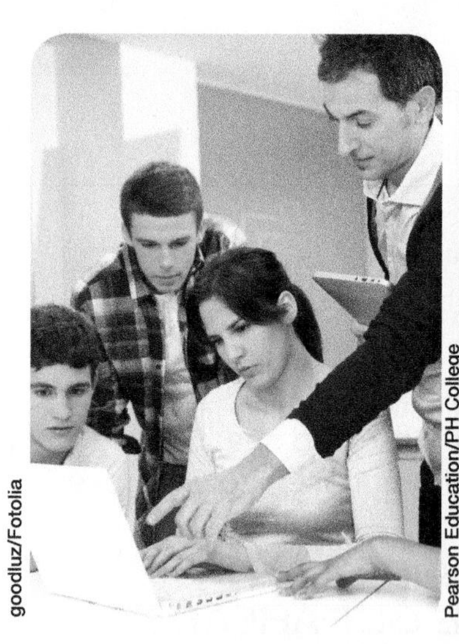
goodluz/Fotolia
Average Salary: $51 064[33]

Pearson Education/PH College
Average Salary: $73 582[34]

Greg Fiume/NewSport/ZUMA Press, Inc/Alamy
2013 Salary: $12 million[35]

<<< Teachers and police officers are essential for society, but professional athletes, like Sidney Crosby, are not. **Why do you think there is such a discrepancy between salaries?**

with wealth doing the best they can to keep that wealth and pass it on to their children. In this way, social inequality is rooted in the unjust capitalist system and not the people who live under it.

Tumin also suggests that stratification is not as simple as some might suggest. First, the societal importance of a job does not seem to be the only basis for financial rewards. Think about it: Who is arguably more important to society: a police officer or a professional athlete? Who makes more money? Being a soldier, firefighter, police officer, or teacher requires dedication, training, and unique skills. But these groups are actually paid very little in comparison to entertainers, corporate CEOs, and professional athletes.

Conflict theorists point out that groups with power will extract what they can from the groups beneath them. The dominant group takes control of social institutions in order to preserve the best resources for itself. By extension, conflict theorists argue, the wealthy try to maintain the status quo so that access to training will remain limited to their group, thus helping them gain even more wealth and power. Why do doctors make so much money? People need them and have very little choice about it.

Students from working-class backgrounds are far more likely to talk about social class as an issue on college campuses than are upper middle-class students. **The perception of social stratification, then, comes primarily from the "have-nots" instead of the "haves."**

Symbolic Interactionism

Symbolic interactionists are interested in how people perceive poverty and wealth. They seek to understand whether people actually have a sense of social class. According to research by Edward G. Grabb and Ronald D. Lambert, our particular social class impacts how we talk about class in general. In a survey, respondents from the lower class were more likely to identify class as being based exclusively on economic criteria, while the upper-class respondents were more likely to include non-economic considerations.[37]

The higher our socioeconomic status (SES), the less we believe that social class matters. For example, upper middle-class college students tend to disregard issues of class and often don't notice that others cannot do what they can do financially. They may be socialized not to care about social class, or they might not have thought much about it.

FEMINIZATION OF POVERTY refers to the fact that, around the world, women experience poverty at far higher rates than men.

This could be because working-class students must make financial choices that upper middle-class students don't even have to consider. In addition, students from the working class have lower expectations about future earnings and successes. Basically, the disparity in these college students' social status demonstrates how ascribed positions affect expectations.

The perception of class differences is most pronounced in the dichotomous way that people look at welfare recipients. Some students in my classes become angry when discussing the social welfare system. As one young woman put it, "If they really wanted to, they could just get a job and make money like everyone else." Putting aside the obvious problems with this statement, this woman's words certainly illustrate the difference between what the general public perceives and the reality of welfare.

Feminist Theory

Feminist theorists talk about the **feminization of poverty**—the term used to describe the fact that, around the world, women experience poverty at far higher rates than men. For example, median annual earnings for Canadian men in 2010 were $35 000, whereas the median earnings for Canadian women were $23 900.[38] By this measure, women earn 68 cents for every dollar that men earn.

In *So You Think I Drive a Cadillac?* Karen Seccombe investigates how female welfare recipients view the welfare system and deal with the associated stigma. Some of their coping strategies include distancing and denial. Women who avoid any discussion about their situations are distancing themselves from the fact that they receive assistance at all. Others who come up with plausible excuses—such as losing a job or fleeing an abusive marriage—are denying that they are similar to other welfare recipients. But, when they viewed other women on welfare, they restated common stereotypes that echoed my student's anti-welfare tirade.

Poor women realize that society views them negatively, so they see accepting welfare as a last resort. Seccombe specifically shows that low wages and a lack of financial support from men are the driving factors behind female poverty. The reason many of these individuals are poor is that they cannot earn enough to make ends meet or they're not receiving court-ordered child support from their ex-husbands.

WRAP YOUR MIND AROUND THE THEORY

The average salary for a physician is over $200 000.[39] On the other hand, **the average salary for someone earning a minimum wage of $10 per hour would be approximately $18 000 a year. What factors might have influenced such different outcomes** for these two people?

Tim Cuff/Alamy

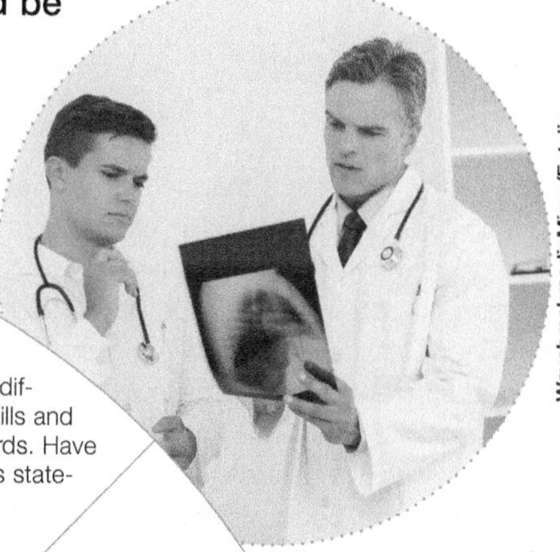

WavebreakmediaMicro/Fotolia

FUNCTIONALISM

Functionalists suggest that social class is connected to a person's ability to negotiate the social world. Therefore, intelligence, drive, and personal choice influence a person's social class. All people are different, so it makes sense that differences in social class exist in Canada. Some people simply have more skills and abilities than others, and these skills naturally help them reap economic rewards. Have you ever heard the phrase "The cream rises to the top"? In many ways, this statement explains why stratification continues to occur.

CONFLICT THEORY

Conflict theorists believe that social mobility rarely occurs in a dramatic way, largely because the Canadian system doesn't allow it. Generally, one's parents and the opportunities they can provide determine social class. Parents in positions of wealth wish to make sure their children keep that advantage, so they pass wealth to their children in the form of an inheritance, they make sure their children attend the "best schools," and they use their social prestige to help their children succeed. Children who lack such things generally remain poor.

WHAT FACTORS INFLUENCE SOCIAL CLASS IN CANADA?

SYMBOLIC INTERACTIONISM

Social class and our understanding of it are relative to our personal belief system. In "The Subjective Meanings of Social Class among Canadians," Grabb and Lambert used a different strategy to study social class in Canada. Rather than use the traditional sociological approach in which the researcher classifies individuals based on objective social conditions, they asked ordinary Canadians to give their own subjective definitions of class. Because people in the lower class have fewer financial resources, they are probably more concerned with "bread and butter" issues. More prosperous individuals might try to legitimize their prosperity by pointing to cultural and psychological explanations for their success. Because of these different perspectives, lower-class respondents were more likely to identify class as being based exclusively on economic criteria, while the upper-class respondents were more likely to include non-economic considerations.[40]

FEMINIST THEORY

Feminization of poverty is the term used to describe the fact that women are far more likely than men to experience poverty. The poorest families in Canada are those headed by a single mother. Elderly women living alone are also more likely to be living in poverty. It is not that women are less capable than men. There are more women living in poverty because the social structure is designed so that it is more difficult for a woman to earn the same income as a man. Since most lone-parent households are headed by women, a significant number of Canadian children also live in poverty.

Aletia /Shutterstock

Affluent parents often give their children opportunities, such as music lessons and access to organized sports, **which can influence their social class later in life.**

Shepard Sherbell/CORBIS SABA

What future might lie in store for the children of these unwed **young mothers?**

discover sociology in action: WHAT SOCIAL POLICIES HAVE BEEN CREATED TO EASE POVERTY?

Social Policy: Welfare for the Poor

You saw in Chapter 3 that compassion and generosity are defining values of the Canadian culture. You might expect that in a country with such values, everyone would be taken care of, and no one would really be poor. The truth is that some people in Canada do suffer from poverty. If you were to make a plan so that no Canadian would suffer from poverty, what would you recommend?

This was the challenge given to the Standing Senate Committee on Social Affairs, Science and Technology. In late 2009, the committee published a report called "In from the Margins: A Call to Action on Poverty, Housing and Homelessness." The report examined how governments, businesses, and volunteer organizations could help poor Canadians escape poverty. In talking with various people across the country, the committee members made a startling and devastating discovery: The existing policies and programs too often trap people in a cycle of poverty. People become reliant on income security programs and even homeless shelters, making it difficult for them to escape poverty. Even when the programs are working, the resulting benefits they receive still keep people in poverty rather than lifting them into a life of full participation in the economic and social components of their communities.

On the bright side, many of the federal programs have been effective. The Working Income Tax Benefit supplements the revenue of low-income workers. The National Child Benefit is designed to help families with children, and Old Age Security/Guaranteed Income Supplement provides assistance to seniors.

The committee identified certain groups in Canadian society that are particularly disadvantaged. These are unattached individuals, people with disabilities, aboriginals, newcomers to Canada (including immigrants and refugee claimants), and lone parents. In later chapters, you will see how race, ethnicity, and gender are all significant factors in social stratification. The committee found that race and gender seriously complicated the challenge for people already in these disadvantaged groups.

The final report made 74 recommendations on how to deal with poverty in Canada. Here are a few highlights from the recommendations[41]:

- Adopt a goal that all programs dealing with poverty and homelessness are to lift Canadians out of poverty rather than make living within poverty more manageable (Recommendation 1).
- Implement a federal minimum wage of $10 per hour, indexed to the consumer price index (Recommendation 6).
- Analyze gender-based differences in designing policies (Recommendation 32).

Senate
Sénat
CANADA
IN FROM THE MARGINS:
A CALL TO ACTION ON
POVERTY, HOUSING
AND HOMELESSNESS
The Standing Senate Committee
on Social Affairs, Science and Technology
Report of the Subcommittee on Cities
The Honourable Art Eggleton P.C., Chair
The Honourable Hugh Segal, Deputy Chair
December 2009
PWGSC

Source: Reprinted with permission by the Senate of Canada.

The report "In from the Margins: A Call to Action on Poverty, Housing and Homelessness" examines how **governments, businesses, and volunteer organizations could help poor Canadians escape poverty.**

- Increase the Guaranteed Income Supplement to seniors (Recommendation 33).
- Increase the National Child Benefit to $5000 by 2012 (Recommendation 34).

Social Policy: Minimum Wage

When you were in high school, your first job might have consisted of flipping burgers at McDonald's or stocking the cereal aisle at a grocery store. Whatever the case, that job probably earned you the minimum wage.

Many of us have probably held a minimum-wage job at some point in our lives, but who really are the minimum-wage workers? The demographics that make up this particular workforce might surprise you. In 2008, more than 750 000 Canadians worked at or below minimum wage, representing 5.2 percent of Canadian workers. Women accounted for 60 percent of workers who earned minimum wage. Only about 35 percent of teens aged 15 to 19 worked for minimum wage. People who did not complete high school were five times more likely than those with some postsecondary training to earn minimum wage or less. Nine percent of workers who received a minimum wage belonged to a union or were covered by a collective agreement. I saw this firsthand when I used to work in the food-service business. Although the cafeteria was unionized, many of the workers earned only minimum wage.

The first Canadian minimum-wage law was passed in 1918 in British Columbia and Manitoba, followed two years later by Ontario, Quebec, Nova Scotia, and Saskatchewan. Minimum wage is intended to reduce poverty by ensuring that full-time workers can live off the income they receive. But just about everyone agrees that a minimum wage is not a living wage. Even two minimum wages in a household will not protect it from the short-term and long-term consequences of poverty.[42]

ACTIVITIES

1. Get to know some of the homeless and poor people in your community. Visit or take a tour of a shelter in your community.
2. Check with your province to find out the monthly welfare payments for a mother and two children. Do you think you'd be able to live on that?
3. Create a household budget for two parents who are both working minimum-wage jobs. Budget for rent, utilities, food, childcare, and transportation for a family of four living in your local area. Don't make up expenses. Research the minimum wage and prices in your area and provide your sources. How difficult is it to survive even with two incomes?

Maybe reading about wealth and poverty has made you think about how you might use these ideas in your everyday life. One major way in which you can take action is working at a community homeless shelter. Students who lend a hand at shelters and soup kitchens get firsthand knowledge about the complexities of poverty in Canada.

While you might categorize a minimum-wage job as something limited to teenagers venturing into the workforce for the first time, **in fact a large percentage of minimum-wage workers (29 percent) are over 25 years old.**[43]

CHAPTER

07

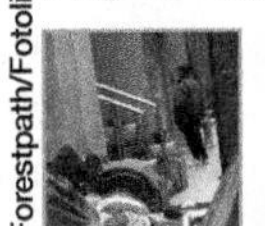
Forestpath/Fotolia

HOW IS POVERTY DEFINED IN CANADA? 133

while there is no "official" definition of poverty in Canada, Statistics Canada uses three measures of low income—the *low income cut-off* (LICO), the *low income measure* (LIM), and the *market basket measure* (MBM).

WHAT IS THE CLASS STRUCTURE IN CANADA? 141

there are six different social classes in Canada: upper class, upper middle class, middle class, working class, lower class, and underclass.

WHAT SOCIAL POLICIES HAVE BEEN CREATED TO EASE POVERTY? 144

Working Income Tax Benefit, Old Age Security/Guaranteed Income Supplement, National Child Benefit, minimum wage

get the topic: WHAT IS SOCIAL STRATIFICATION?

Theories

FUNCTIONALISM 141

- social class is connected to a person's ability to negotiate the social world
- intelligence, drive, and personal choice influence a person's social class
- all people are different, so it makes sense that differences in social class exist

CONFLICT THEORY 141

- social mobility rarely occurs in a dramatic way
- generally, one's parents and the opportunities they can provide determine social class
- the higher our socioeconomic status, the less we believe social class matters

SYMBOLIC INTERACTIONISM 142

- social class and our understanding of it are relative to our personal belief system
- because people in the lower class have fewer financial resources, they are probably more concerned with "bread and butter" issues
- more prosperous people might try to legitimize their prosperity by pointing to individual explanations for their success

FEMINIST THEORY 142

- poverty is more frequent among women than among men
- the social structure, which is patriarchal, makes it more difficult for women to earn as much as men

Key Terms

income is the money received for work or through investments. *133*

wealth is all of your material possessions. *133*

quintile is one of five groups of households, ranked by income. *133*

transitional poverty is a temporary state of poverty that occurs when someone loses a job for a short time. *134*

marginal poverty is a state of poverty that occurs when a person lacks stable employment. *134*

residual poverty is chronic and multigenerational poverty. *134*

power is the ability to carry out your will and impose it on others. *136*

power elite is a small group of people who hold immense power. *136*

prestige is the level of esteem associated with one's status and social standing. *136*

upper, or elite, class is a social class that is very small in number and holds significant wealth. *137*

upper middle class is a social class that consists of high-income members of society who are often well educated but do not belong to the elite membership of the super wealthy. *137*

middle class is a social class that consists of those who have moderate incomes. *138*

working class is a social class generally made up of people with high school diplomas and lower levels of education. *138*

lower class is a social class living in poverty. 138

underclass includes the homeless and people living in substandard housing. 139

social mobility is the ability to change social classes. 140

horizontal mobility refers to moving within the same status category. 140

vertical mobility refers to moving from one social status to another. 140

intragenerational mobility occurs when an individual changes social standing, especially in the workforce. 140

intergenerational mobility refers to the change that family members make from one social class to the next through generations. 140

cycle of poverty refers to the vicious circle in which poor children are likely to remain poor as adults. 140

structural mobility occurs when social changes affect large numbers of people. 140

exchange mobility is a concept which suggests that, within a country, each social class contains a relatively fixed number of people. 140

meritocracy argument states that those who get ahead do so based on their own merit. 141

feminization of poverty refers to the fact that, around the world, women experience poverty at far higher rates than men. 142

Sample Test Questions

These multiple-choice questions are similar to those found in the test bank that accompanies this textbook.

1. People with seasonal jobs most likely experience
   a. residual poverty.
   b. absolute poverty.
   c. marginal poverty.
   d. transitional poverty.
2. Which of the following is *not* a member of the Canadian power elite?
   a. Economic elite
   b. State elite
   c. Sports elite
   d. Media elite
3. Which of the following is true of the upper, or elite, class?
   a. Most members are newly wealthy.
   b. They have higher rates of teen pregnancy.
   c. They make up 1 percent of the country's population.
   d. They are generally regarded highly for their specialized skills.
4. A doctor transferring from one hospital to another is an example of
   a. intergenerational mobility.
   b. horizontal mobility.
   c. vertical mobility.
   d. exchange mobility.
5. A high school graduate who works on an assembly line in a manufacturing plant is most likely a member of which social class?
   a. Urban underclass
   b. Working class
   c. Middle class
   d. Lower class

ANSWERS: 1. c; 2. c; 3. c; 4. b; 5. b

ESSAY

1. How does prestige affect one's social standing?
2. How is mobility restricted in Canadian society?
3. What is the relationship between social class and education?
4. Which social policies are available to Canadians with low income?
5. How does the concept of exchange mobility conflict with the beliefs of conflict theorists?

WHERE TO START YOUR RESEARCH PAPER

For more information on current poverty in Canada:

www.campaign2000.ca.

www.ccsd.ca/pubs/recastin.htm.

To see what people are doing to break the cycle of poverty, go to www.makepovertyhistory.ca.

For a report on income inequality in Canada:

www.conferenceboard.ca/hcp/details/society/income-inequality.aspx.

For more information on working in homeless shelters, including a complete list of shelters, go to www.raisingtheroof.org.

For more information about minimum wage, go to Service Canada, at srv116.services.gc.ca/dimt-wid/sm-mw/menu.aspx?lang=eng.

For an article about minimum wage in Canada—now and historically—go to www.cbc.ca/money/story/2009/01/23/f-money-minimum-wage.html.

Remember to check www.thethinkspot.ca for additional information, downloadable flashcards, and other helpful resources.

POPULATION AND ENVIRONMENTAL IMPACT

maxstockphoto/Shutterstock.com

WHAT IS DEMOGRAPHY?
WHAT IS ENVIRONMENTAL SOCIOLOGY?
CAN GOVERNMENTS CONTROL POPULATION GROWTH?

"Demographic changes in Canada have contributed to a greater concern for the maintenance of environmental quality. . . . The size of the Canadian population, its distribution, and its density all affect the quality of the environment. Approximately 140 years since Confederation, the Canadian population has grown from 3.7 million to over 31 million persons. Although the fertility rate has generally declined and stabilized over the last century, immigration has contributed significantly to population growth. . . .

Acceleration in rates of population growth and economic activity puts pressure on the amount and quality of resources upon which these activities are based. . . . The accelerated pace and consequences of social impacts on environmental quality, their often irremediable character, as well as the lack of preventative measures to forestall these problems are perceived increasingly as a crisis of governance. . . .

The evolution of Canadian policy reflects part of a global shift toward concern for the greater conservation of the environment and the sustainability of existing resource bases . . . [it] has shifted to a concept of resource management, but it is still located within the context of economic activity. . . . The entry of environmental groups into policy processes in the 1960s and 1970s and the continued efforts of women, First Nations, and others to gain entry into resource and environmental policy communities and networks have generated new ideas and policy discourses that are challenging the traditional economic concerns that underlie the resource management paradigm. . . ."[1]

Growth *and* Sustainability

CHAPTER 08

In their 2005 book *Canadian Natural Resource and Environmental Policy: Political Economy and Public Policy*, Melody Hessing, Michael Howlett, and Tracy Summerville provide a historical description of the changes and evolution of Canadian resource and environmental policy.

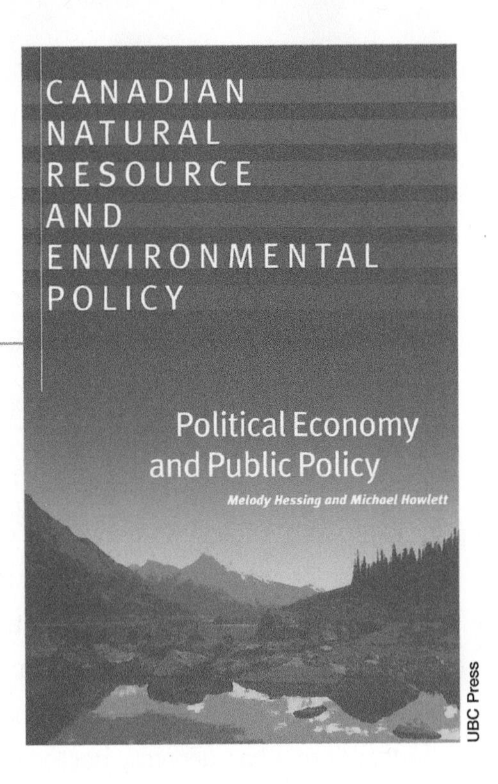

UBC Press

They also provide a framework to evaluate these policies. Above all, the authors recognize that the use of natural resources and environmental problems are strongly tied to political and economic policies. It is vitally important to understand the influence of population growth and environmental changes and the dramatic effects they have on society. We must also understand that what we do as a society has a powerful and often detrimental impact on our natural environment.

Demography

is

the study of population size and composition

and uses measures such as

- **Crude birth rate:** the number of births for every 1000 people each year
- **Total fertility rate:** the number of children that a woman would have over the course of her reproductive life
- **Generational replacement level:** the fertility rate (2.1 children per woman) that must be maintained to replace the population in the absence of migration
- **Mortality rate:** the number of deaths that occur in a population
- **Crude death rate:** the number of deaths for every 1000 people each year
- **Age-specific death rate:** the number of deaths in a particular age group during a given year
- **Infant mortality rate:** the number of deaths of children less than 1 year of age per 1000 live births in the same year
- **Life expectancy:** the average number of years a person is expected to live
- **Rate of natural increase:** the crude birth rate minus the crude death rate of a population
- **Doubling time:** the number of years it takes for a population to double

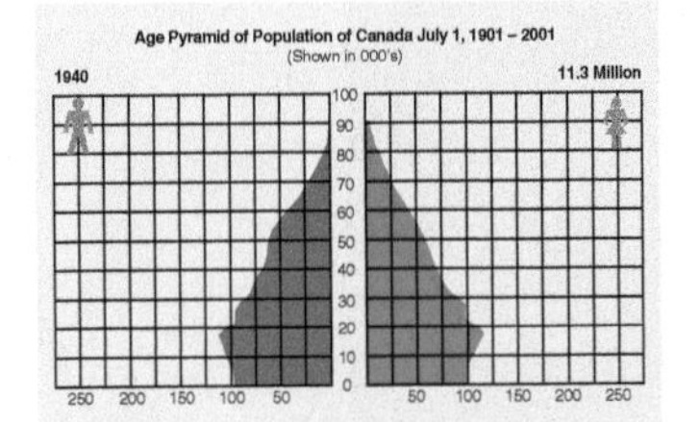

- **Human ecology:** recognizes that the natural environment performs many services for human beings
- **The sustainable development model:** model based on the premise that economic development and environmental protection are compatible goals
- **Deep ecology:** a perspective based on the belief that we are just one species among many, that our role and our activities are no more important than any other species', and that our primary concern should be ecological viability and preservation rather than economic growth
- **Ecofeminist theory:** a merging of ecological and feminist thought that focuses on the common experiences of women and nature
- **Resource management approach:** focuses on negotiating and regulating the extraction of resources and the disposal of hazardous waste

and uses theories such as

get the topic: WHAT IS DEMOGRAPHY?

DEMOGRAPHY is the study of population size and composition.

TOTAL FERTILITY RATE refers to the number of children that a woman would have over the course of her reproductive life.

Population by the Numbers

Demography is the study of population size and composition. Sociologists, market researchers, and virtually all other social scientists use demographic variables such as population size, age distribution, ethnic composition, and birth rates and death rates to discuss populations.

The world's population is not evenly distributed. For example, approximately 37 percent of the world's population lives in either China or India. These two countries account for more of the world's population than the next 23 largest countries combined.[2] Canada's population at the start of 2013 was a bit over 35 million.[3] The world population was a bit over 7 billion at that time, making Canada's proportion of the world population less than 0.5 percent of the world's population. However, in terms of geographic area, Canada is the second largest country (after Russia), covering nearly 10 million square kilometers.

Tools for Studying Population

Somewhere in the world at this very moment, a family is celebrating the birth of a baby, while another is mourning the loss of a loved one. Every day babies are born and people die. When studying populations, sociologists frequently compare rates of fertility (birth) and rates of mortality (death). It's preferable to use rates and not total numbers when making comparisons between countries to ensure that a country's population size doesn't influence findings.

FERTILITY RATES

The **total fertility rate** refers to the number of children that a woman would have over the course of her reproductive life if she experienced the age-specific fertility rates observed in a particular calendar year. It is based on a compilation of the fertility experiences of many different cohorts of women in a given year. Despite sounding complicated, the

and studies changes in the population due to

- **Migration:** the movement of people from one area to another
- **Immigration:** the movement of people into an area
- **Emigration:** the movement of people out of an area

Environmental Sociology

is

concerned with the reciprocal relationship between societies and their environments

>>> **In Canada, the fertility rate has been stable since the early 1990s, at about** 1.6 children per woman.[4]

WavebreakmediaMicro/Fotolia

CRUDE BIRTH RATE is the number of births for every 1000 people each year.

GENERATIONAL REPLACEMENT LEVEL is the fertility rate (2.1 children per woman) that must be maintained to replace the population in the absence of migration.

CRUDE DEATH RATE is the number of deaths for every 1000 people each year.

AGE-SPECIFIC DEATH RATE is the number of deaths in a particular age group during a given year.

INFANT MORTALITY RATE is the number of deaths of children less than 1 year of age per 1000 live births in the same year.

LIFE EXPECTANCY is the average number of years a person is expected to live.

total fertility rate is easily calculated, allows for year-to-year as well as international comparisons, and is not affected by variations in population size or age structure. The **crude birth rate** is a measure of the number of live births for every 1000 people in a given year. Predictably, the greater the number of women of birthing age, the higher the number of births.

In Canada, the total fertility rate is below the **generational replacement level** of 2.1 children per woman—the fertility rate that must be maintained to replace the population in the absence of migration. The last year that the total fertility rate in Canada was more than the generational replacement level was 1971.

In general, birth rates are inversely connected to a woman's income and level of education. For example, women who are college graduates tend to have lower birth rates than women with less education. This may be due to women spending their primary reproductive years continuing their education and entering the workforce, the increased availability of birth control, better understanding of reproduction, and changing ideas about the role of women in society.

TOTAL FERTILITY RATE IN CANADA, 1926 TO 2010

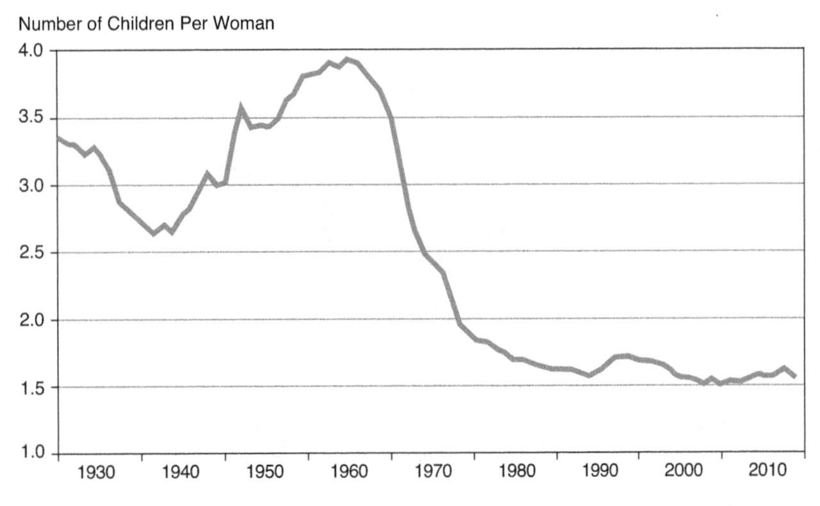

Source: Statistics Canada, 2006, "Report on the Demographic Situation in Canada 2003 and 2004"; Statistics Canada, Catalogue number 91-209-XIE, "Demography Division, and Health Statistics Division"; Statistics Canada, "CANSIM, Table 102-4505". This does not constitute an endorsement by Statistics Canada of this product.

MORTALITY RATES

The **crude death rate** is the number of deaths per year for every 1000 people. Measuring the death rate in a population gives sociologists a better perspective of the society as a whole. The **age-specific death rate** is the number of deaths in a particular age group during a given year.[5] Particular attention is paid to the **infant mortality rate**, which is the number of deaths of children less than 1 year of age per 1000 live births in the same year. In 2009, the overall Canadian infant mortality rate was 4.9, but it was three times higher in Nunavut (14.8) and in the Northwest Territories (15.5). What do you think accounts for this significant difference?[6]

Sociologists also study **life expectancy**, the average number of years of life remaining for a population at a specific age, assuming that the individuals comprising that population would experience the age-specific mortality rates observed in a given year, throughout their lives. It is a key indicator of a population's health status and is based on age-specific mortality rates.[7] Thanks to economic development and public health improvements, trends for the past 100 years show rapid increases in life expectancy.[8]

One way to compare countries is to note their different life expectancies. For example, Monaco, a tiny country bordering the Mediterranean Sea on the southern coast of France, has the longest life expectancy (89.68 years) in the world, whereas Chad, a poor country in Central Africa, has the shortest life expectancy (48.69 years). Canada ranks 12th in the world, with a life expectancy of 81.48 years.[9] Life expectancy is closely linked to health care access and environmental factors. The African HIV/AIDS epidemic, which is the leading cause of death in many African nations, contributes to that continent's low life expectancy rates.[10]

POPULATION PYRAMIDS

Population pyramids visually represent the age and sex of a country's population. The population pyramids below show data for the Canadian population from 1901 to 2000. What do you see about the distribution of the Canadian population at these different times?

You can see the changing shape of the population pyramid from 1901 to 2000.[11] The shape of this graph changes from a pyramid to a rectangular shape, which is known as "squaring the pyramid." This phenomenon occurs as people begin to live longer and as birth rates remain stable, demonstrating the dramatic impact age can have on a society. Demographers know that the number of children or elderly people in a population will affect a society's needs. For example, children require education, and societies often provide schools for them. Children place demands on a society's resources even when they grow up: They desire jobs, homes, and other resources, but they also have the potential to create more goods for the society. Large numbers of elderly people can also put a burden on a society because their need for medical care means that hospitals and nursing homes need to be built and staffed.

After World War II, Canada and many other nations experienced a rapid increase in births. We refer to this as the *baby boom*, and the children born after World War II through the early 1960s are known as baby boomers. Although this group has had fewer children than their parents, a quick review of the pyramids shows that they created a surge in growth due to the large number of people who were of birthing age. Even if the boomers had only replacement levels of children, the population still grew because the cohort was so large. Can you see the baby boomers on the pyramids?

MIGRATION is the movement of people from one area to another.

IMMIGRATION is the movement of people into an area.

MIGRATION

Another source of change in a population is **migration**, the movement of people from one area to another. Migration occurs in two directions. **Immigration** refers to the movement of people into an area. The immigration rate is a ratio of the number of immigrants admitted into a host country in a given year to the size of the national population, expressed

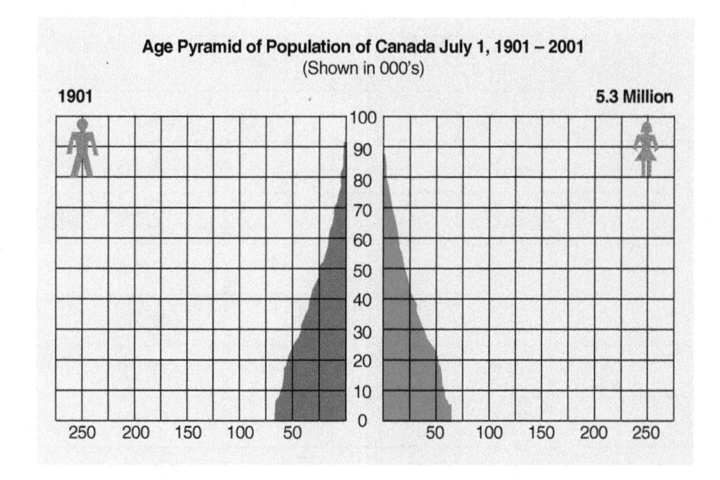

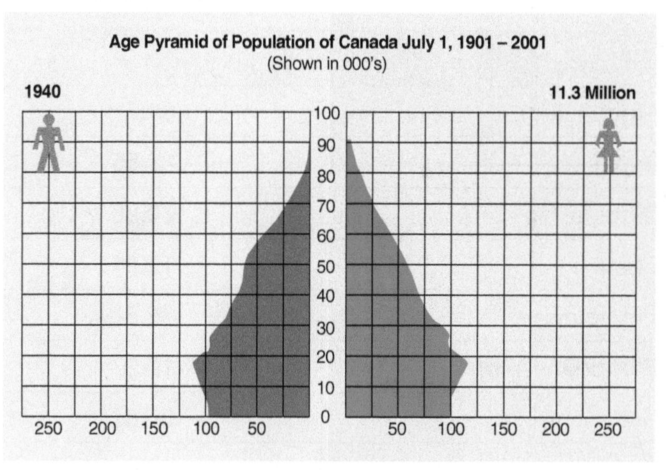

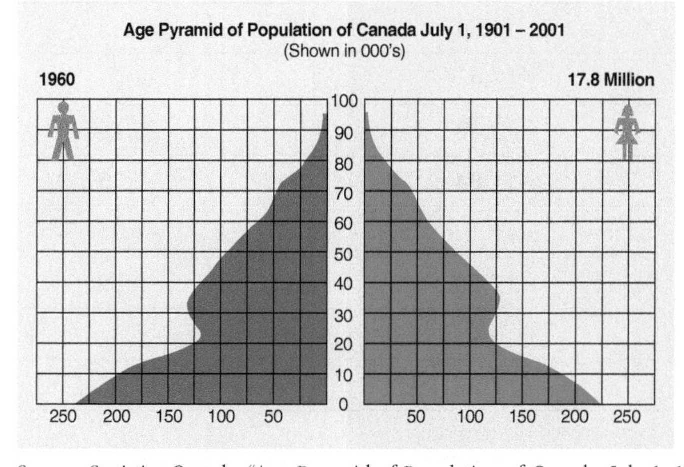

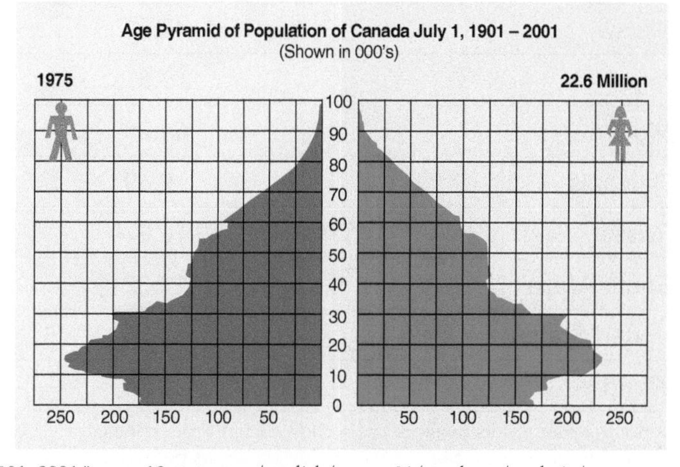

Source: Statistics Canada, "Age Pyramid of Population of Canada, July 1, 1901–2001," www12.statcan.ca/english/census01/products/analytic/Multimedia.cfm?M=1, accessed August 18, 2013. This does not constitute an endorsement by Statistics Canada of this product.

EMIGRATION is the movement of people out of an area.

PUSH–PULL, OR NEO-CLASSICAL, MIGRATION THEORY suggests that migration depends on the supply and demand for labor, both in the sending area and the receiving area.

RATE OF NATURAL INCREASE (RNI) is the crude birth rate minus the crude death rate of a population.

per 1000 people. This indicator can be used to compare the level of immigration over time as well as for international comparisons across countries. The immigration rate in Canada was 7.5 immigrants per 1000 population in 2009.[12] **Emigration** refers to the movement of people out of an area. The net migration rate is the difference between immigrants who entered Canada and emigrants who left Canada, expressed per 1000 population. The net migration rate in Canada is higher than that of most other countries. This explains why Canada's total population is growing, despite the fact that the rates of natural increase and the generational replacement levels are low. To calculate the current population of a specific area, add births and immigrants to the base population and subtract deaths and emigrants.

Push–pull, or neo-classical, migration theory is used to explain migration; it suggests that migration depends on the supply and demand for labour, both in the sending area as well as in the receiving area. When I was young, my family migrated from Montreal to Ottawa. The "push" was the lack of opportunities for advancement in my father's job in Montreal, and the "pull" was a pay raise and better work opportunities in Ottawa. As a result, we migrated. Push–pull migration theory applies both to international migration, such as immigration from China to Canada, and internal migration patterns, such as migration from rural to urban areas. Just like my father, my ancestors were "pushed" from France due to lack of work and "pulled" to Canada, where there was work.

RATE OF NATURAL INCREASE

The **rate of natural increase (RNI)** is the crude birth rate minus the crude death rate for a population. Countries with a positive RNI have a growing population, and countries with a negative one have a declining population (if we ignore the effect of migration). The table below shows the crude birth rate, crude death rate, and RNI for the world and for selected countries. As you can see, countries in Africa have the highest rates of natural increase, primarily due to their high birth rates. Romania and Russia have negative rates of natural increase, which means that without positive migration, their populations will decrease.

RATE OF NATURAL INCREASE IN VARIOUS COUNTRIES

Country	Birth Rate	Death Rate	RNI
Afghanistan	39.3	14.59	24.71
Benin	37.55	8.79	28.76
Canada	10.28	8.09	2.19
China	12.31	7.17	5.14
Ethiopia	38.5	9.3	29.2
European Union	10.27	10.05	0.22
Haiti	23.87	8.1	15.77
India	20.6	7.43	13.17
Malawi	40.42	12.84	27.58
Niger	47.6	13.4	34.2
Nigeria	39.23	13.48	25.75
Romania	9.49	11.84	–2.35
Russia	12.3	14.1	–1.8
South Africa	19.32	17.23	2.09
United States	13.7	8.4	5.3
World	19.14	7.99	11.15

Note: This rate results in about 252 worldwide births per minute, or 4.2 births every second (2012 est.).
Note: This rate results in about 107 worldwide deaths per minute, or 1.8 deaths every second (2012 est.).

Source: Data from *The CIA World Factbook*, 2013.

DOUBLING TIME refers to the number of years it takes for a population to double.

MALTHUSIAN THEOREM is a population projection that suggests the population will exceed the available food supply because populations grow at geometric rates, while food supplies grow at arithmetic rates.

DOUBLING TIME

While some countries are dealing with decreasing numbers, other populations are experiencing rapid growth. **Doubling time** refers to the number of years it takes for a population to double.

From the year 10 000 BCE, when just 1 million people inhabited the planet, it took more than 11 000 years for the population to reach 1 billion. However, after 1850, it took only nine decades to double that first billion. After that, it took 42 more years to double that number. At this rate, estimates show that by 2026, the population will have doubled once again.

A country's doubling time can radically influence its future. For example, if a country's population is expected to double in 40 years, then all its economic resources also need to double during that period.

It's important to note that projections rarely occur exactly as calculated because population increases vary from year to year. In fact, previous predictions of doubling times have rarely been completely accurate.[13] Nevertheless, the use of doubling time shows some possible trends in world population growth and helps make comparisons between countries. The population growth of Africa, South America, and Asia suggests that the population of each of these continents will probably double within your lifetime.

POPULATION PROJECTIONS

Fertility rates, mortality rates, population pyramids, migration trends, rates of natural increase, and doubling time—all these demographic tools help demographers make population projections that can be very useful to society. For example, if you project an increase in the elderly population, it makes sense to build retirement homes before they're needed. All population projections use estimates of birth, death, and migration rates and apply them to the future.

Malthusian Theory

Thomas Malthus, an English clergyman, made one of the first and most circulated population projections in history. His work *An Essay on the Principle of Population* was published in 1798. In it, Malthus theorized that populations grow at a geometric rate (2, 4, 8, 16, and so on), but food supplies increase at an arithmetic rate (1, 2, 3, 4, 5, and so on). This is often known as the **Malthusian theory**. Increases in agricultural technology can increase the food supply, but this increase cannot keep up with the population explosion. Therefore, at some point in time, the population will exceed food production. At that point, the world will experience wars over food and suffer famine and increases in disease.[14]

During Malthus's lifetime, he saw the flowering of the Industrial Revolution. Quality of life improved, leading to increased life expectancy and rapid population growth. These events caused Malthus to consider the effects of population growth on society. He believed that a rapid rise would put a severe strain on the food supply and would eventually lead to outbreaks of famine and war. He theorized that the world's population would eventually grow itself into disaster and suggested that society would come under the influence of positive checks—including war and disease—to curb the population. Positive checks are events or conditions that raise the death rate and therefore reduce the population. However, preventive checks such as birth control, delayed marriage, and sexual abstinence serve to reduce the birth rate. Preventive checks also serves to reduce the population, but in a less deleterious manner than positive checks.

Malthus's ideas remain in the minds of many who study population. Paul Ehrlich, a famous biologist who also studied population growth,

GO GLOBAL

Birth Dearth in Japan

In the period between 1947 and 1957, Japan's total fertility rate dropped from 4.54 children per woman to about 2 children per woman. After this drop, fertility rates remained somewhat stable until the 1970s. From the mid 1970s to the early 1990s, fertility dropped again, to a level of 1.46 children per woman, which is below replacement level.[15]

What caused this decline? Japan's defeat in World War II didn't just change the country's political culture; it also altered the economic culture. With the help of the United States, the Japanese rebuilt the national infrastructure and created efficient businesses. In a short time, Japan emerged from the ravages of war to become a formidable economic power. Because fertility rates tend to drop as education and wealth levels increase, Japan's push toward economic success had a negative effect on births. Although measures of family values didn't seem to change, women's labor force participation increased, as did the pressure on women to become educated. This focus on career led men and women to marry and have children later in life, which made it less likely for couples to bear many children.[16]

However, the Japanese government has serious concerns about its impending demographic future. By 2050, the number of children in Japan is estimated to have dropped by half; at the same time, the number of people of retirement age is expected to continue to climb. This impending demographic scenario has Japanese politicians scrambling to meet the needs of a new social reality. Schools are being closed and converted into senior citizen centres.[17] And without a replacement population, fewer people are entering the workforce. Shrinking numbers of workers could create problems for Japanese businesses. As the elderly grow in number, the pension systems for private business and the federal government are expected to have difficulty meeting their needs. These realities have resulted in an increase of government policies designed to increase births, including expanded childcare assistance and more liberal childcare leave laws. Lawmakers hope these policies will boost birth rates by allowing working women to keep their jobs while supporting children.[18]

DEMOGRAPHIC TRANSITION THEORY suggests that people control their own fertility as they move from agrarian to industrial societies.

wrote a book called *The Population Bomb*.[19] He suggested that there will be a point in time when the resources of the planet simply cannot keep up with the growing population. Eventually, the world's population will outgrow the world's ability to sustain it. In 1972, the publication of *The Limits to Growth* aroused renewed fears about the imminent global disaster facing humanity. The report, written by a team of Massachusetts Institute of Technology scientists, made the gloomy prediction that within 70 years, our social and economic systems would collapse unless drastic changes were made.[20]

Malthus has greatly influenced the way people currently think about population growth. However, not everyone agrees with Malthus. Demographers who ascribe to the demographic transition theory believe that population growth will inevitably decline.

Demographic Transition Theory

Demographic transition theory is based on historical data of population growth in northern Europe.[21] Demographic transition theorists suggest that people control their fertility as societies move from agrarian to industrial. This transition usually occurs in five stages.

In *stage 1*, the society is not industrialized. Birth rates and death rates are high, life expectancy is short, and infant mortality is high. Economically, it's beneficial to have large numbers of children, so they can assist you in day-to-day physical labour. Having a large number of children also increases the chance that some will survive into adulthood. Population grows slowly because birth rates and death rates are similar.

Things change in *stage 2*, when a country enters the initial phase of industrialization. New technologies mean fewer people are needed for physical labour. People migrate to urban areas, seeking work in factories. Modernization brings more food, better medical care, cleaner water, and a generally higher standard of living. Birth rates remain high, and infant mortality drops.[22] A rapid decline in the death rate means that life expectancy increases. Population grows fastest at this stage because of stable birth rates and rapidly declining death rates.

Birth rates decline after a country establishes itself as an industrialized nation in *stage 3*. Even before artificial means of birth control were available, European nations that entered stage 3 had declines in birth rates. Meanwhile, life expectancy continues to improve, resulting in lower and more stable death rates. The economic and social conditions appear to influence individual choices, and people willingly control their own fertility. The rate of population growth declines, although the population is still growing.[23]

Countries with constant populations generally fit into *stage 4* of the transition. Once a nation enters into a postindustrial economy, the population growth stabilizes. Typically, birth and death rates are low. This theory suggests that industrialization actually improves people's quality of life. Since the people are healthier and live longer, the population grows rapidly at first. However, with development, the population stabilizes. Therefore, as underdeveloped parts of the world go through this transition, the theory suggests that world population will once again stabilize.[24]

A fifth stage has been added to the model, based on recent observations. In *stage 5*, countries actually experience population decline, as both birth rates and fertility rates fall below the replacement rate. This,

THE DEMOGRAPHIC TRANSITION MODEL

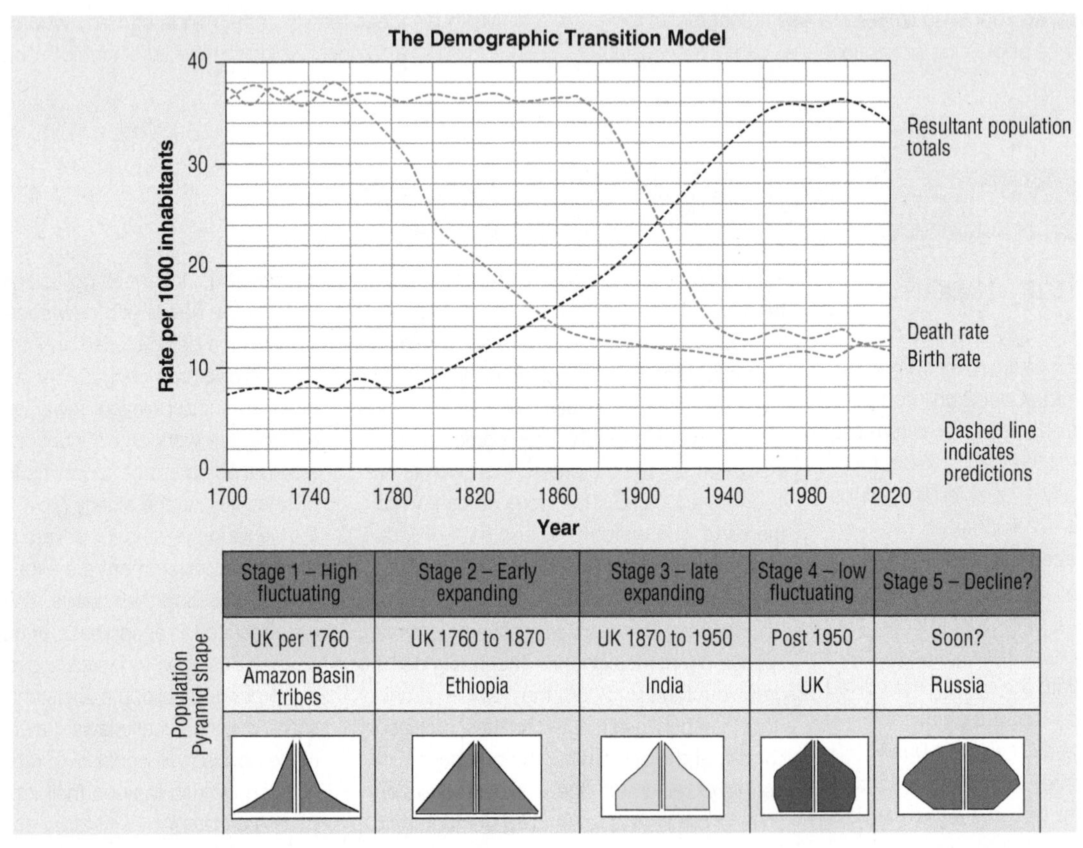

Stage 1 – High fluctuating	Stage 2 – Early expanding	Stage 3 – late expanding	Stage 4 – low fluctuating	Stage 5 – Decline?
UK per 1760	UK 1760 to 1870	UK 1870 to 1950	Post 1950	Soon?
Amazon Basin tribes	Ethiopia	India	UK	Russia

Source: Robert Gamesby

TOTAL FERTILITY RATE ACROSS AN URBAN-TO-RURAL GRADIENT, CANADA, 1971–2001

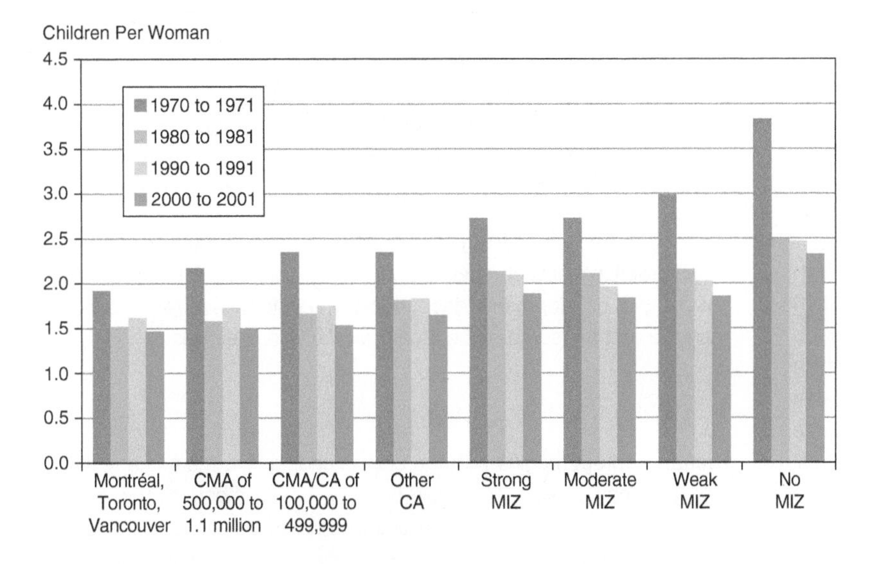

Source: Statistics Canada, 2007, http://www.statcan.gc.ca/pub/91f0015m/2007008/figures/4144740-eng.htm. This does not constitute an endorsement by Statistics Canada of this product.

together with increased life expectancy, results in aging populations for these countries.[25]

You can see the theory in action today. Agriculture-based communities, such as many rural families in Canada, tend to have more children as a means of acquiring wealth and income. However, people in urban areas may consider multiple children a liability. More children equal more mouths to feed, which can strain a family's finances. Families in rural areas having more children has been the general rule of thumb. The figure below seems to confirm this for Canada.

Demographic transition theory can be questioned for a number of reasons. First, although fertility declined in Europe, it may not have done so only as a product of economic incentive; it may have been due to other reasons, such as a delay in marriage and changing social norms.[26] Furthermore, fertility decline in Europe does not necessarily mean that fertility will decline in non-European countries around the world. The Eurocentric perspective of demographic transition theory is probably its greatest limitation because it ignores cultural differences around the world.

People from different cultures might behave differently. For example, the value of children and the attitude toward marriage and reproduction vary from place to place. The status of parenthood may outweigh the costs of having a large family.[27]

Many demographers estimate that the entire world population growth will begin to slow by 2050 and that overpopulation will no longer be an issue by the end of the twenty-first century.[28] **Trends show that fertility decline is already occurring worldwide, which gives credibility to the demographic transition theory.**

Vova Pomortzeff/Alamy

get the topic: WHAT IS ENVIRONMENTAL SOCIOLOGY?

When Hurricane Katrina ravaged the U.S. Gulf Coast and submerged New Orleans under water, the public saw how intimately the environment and society are linked together. The force of the hurricane could not be controlled. However, the reactions and responses of the U.S. government and other organizations clearly showed that the race and class of the victims both played important roles in shaping these responses.

Environmental sociology is concerned with the reciprocal relationship between societies and their environments. Canadian research on the environment and society has focused on the social dimensions of natural resource use, global climate change, environmental health risks, environmental movements, gender and the environment, media representations of nature, and political decision making related to the environment.[29] Although humans have always interacted with the natural environment, it was only in the 1970s that environmental sociology really emerged and established itself as a significant topic of study. This in itself is a reflection of the context in which sociology developed. In the process of developing distinct explanations for human social behaviour, sociologists downplayed the effects of nature and biology and focused on sociocultural causes.[30]

ENVIRONMENTAL SOCIOLOGY is concerned with the reciprocal relationship between societies and their environments.

HUMAN ECOLOGY recognizes that there is a relationship between people and their physical environments.

Environmental sociology has produced various theories regarding the interaction between society and the environment. Human ecology, sustainable development, deep ecology, ecofeminism, and resource management are some of the most prevalent perspectives.

Human Ecology

Human ecology begins with the understanding that there is a relationship between people and their physical environments.[31] The natural environment performs many services for human beings, and these can be summarized into three general functions. First, the environment provides us with the resources necessary for life—most importantly clean air and water, food, and shelter. Second, when we consume resources, we produce waste products; in fact, humans produce more waste products

Â© Sunny studio-Igor Yaruta/Shutterstock.com

<<< We must find ways to meet the needs of the present without compromising the ability of future generations to also meet their needs.[32]

than do any other species. The environment serves as a repository for these wastes, either absorbing or recycling them into useful or at least harmless substances. When the waste products exceed an environment's ability to absorb them, the result is pollution. Finally, like all other species, humans must also have a place to live, and the environment provides our home—where we live, work, and play. Environmental sociologists have focused on a variety of living space issues, ranging from housing to urban design but also addressing issues such as the impacts of deforestation, desertification, and climate change on human societies.[33]

SUSTAINABLE DEVELOPMENT is based on the premise that economic development and environmental protection are compatible goals.

DEEP ECOLOGY is a perspective based on the belief that we are just one species among many, that our role and our activities are no more important than any other species', and that our primary concern should be ecological viability and preservation rather than economic growth.

ANTHROPOCENTRIC BIAS is the belief that humans are the most significant species in nature.

ECOFEMINIST THEORY is a merging of ecological and feminist thought that focuses on the common experiences of women and nature.

RESOURCE MANAGEMENT focuses on negotiating and regulating the extraction of resources and the disposal of hazardous waste.

Sustainable Development

Economic development has produced greater wealth and comfort for many people. However, we have also seen the problems and damage it has produced in the natural environment. The **sustainable development** model is based on the premise that economic development and environmental protection are compatible goals. Sustainable development can occur if resources that are needed and used are recycled and replenished and if waste is properly managed so that is does not cause irreparable damage to the natural environment. The sustainable development approach holds that resources must be treated on the basis of their future value as well as their present value.

Deep Ecology

Deep ecology is a perspective based on the belief that we are just one species among many, that our role and our activities are no more important than any other species', and that our primary concern should be ecological viability and preservation rather than economic growth. Deep ecology is a critique of the **anthropocentric bias** that permeates all our current institutions and policies. As humans, we must recognize and respect our connections to the natural ecosystem rather than see the environment as simply a source of resources to be exploited for our own unsustainable growth. The deep ecology model calls for a radical shift in how we perceive, talk about, and treat the natural environment.[34] The environmental problems we now see are not so much the result of changes in the objective conditions of the environment but are more visible because we have reconstructed and changed how we look at nature.[35]

Ecofeminism

The **ecofeminist** theory is a merging of ecological and feminist thought.[36] If you think about some of the terms we use to refer to the ecological environment—such as "Mother Earth" and "Mother Nature"—you can see the feminization of the natural world. Women are most hurt by the exploitation of the earth because in a patriarchal society, they are the most vulnerable.

The ecofeminist call is for women to act directly at the local level to stop pollution and destruction. The goal is not to return to prehistory but rather to develop a healthier relationship with nature, based on the needs of all people. The future requires the creation of a new consciousness where development and progress are not necessarily required and where people and the quality of their lives are foremost. Instead of exploiting the ecosystem of the earth for our needs, we need to change our lives to live within the system.[37]

Resource Management

The **resource management** approach to environmental issues recognizes the interdependence of humans and the natural environment and is concerned about the impact that humans have on the natural environment, but in a limited way.

THINK SOCIOLOGICALLY

What Is Environmental Sociology?

Because it recognizes the interrelatedness of society and the natural environment, and because it examines the functions of the environment for humans, the human ecology theory is most associated with the functionalist perspective. The sustainable development model also focuses on structural changes in order to achieve its goals. As such, it too reflects the functionalist perspective.

Proponents of the deep ecology movement often advocate change on an individual level. They say that each of us changing our view of our relationship with nature would do more to protect the environment than trying to get governments and industries to change how they operate. In this way, deep ecology reflects the symbolic interactionist perspective. If we change the way we talk about nature, and if each of us changes how we interact with nature, then we come closer to meeting the goals of deep ecology.

The ecofeminist theory is a merging of ecological and feminist thought. This theory focuses on the common experiences of women and nature. Both share productive and reproductive functions, and both have been subordinated and controlled by patriarchal systems of power.[38]

The resource management model is preferred by the powerful groups in society that benefit under the existing system. They use their influence to determine policies that will allow them to continue to profit from the careless extraction and exploitation of resources and that minimize the penalties imposed on them for creating pollution and squandering the supply of natural resources. This model is best explained from the conflict perspective.

Taina Sohlman/Shutterstock

Resource management includes negotiating and regulating the extraction of resources **and the disposal of hazardous waste.**[39]

However, resource management policies are usually kept out of the public forum of debate because such exposure seldom serves the interests of either the government or the corporations involved. While resource management policies claim to be based on "applied" science, in fact, much of the research on which these policies have been based has been done by industries and private companies who have vested interests.

MAKE CONNECTIONS

Carpooling for the Environment

With gas prices increasing so much in recent years, many of my students were complaining about their decreasing funds. Some students decided that biking to school would be their best money-saving option. Devante, who drove 20 minutes to get to class, suggested a campus-wide carpool. Using the school's online community board, he set up a page where commuters could find other students in their area.

"I wanted 1 or 2 other people to share the cost of travel. I didn't expect to hear back from more than 20 people. The online community board made it easy for us to get in touch and figure out scheduling details. It also helped us form a commuter community on campus. We ended up creating a commuter's lounge where students could relax between classes and wait for their rides.

"Then, the campus's conservation club wrote an article for the school newspaper about how carpooling helps the environment by decreasing pollution. Even more students joined our online group. It was great to see so many people in one group for so many different reasons. I got to meet a lot of really interesting people, and I felt closer to our school community. By the end of the semester, the money I had saved on gas was just one of the many perks I received by starting this group."

>>> **ACTIVITY** Is there a carpooling project at your school? What other programs exist at your school, or in your community, to help commuters while decreasing pollution due to emissions?

think sociologically: CLIMATE CHANGE

All human activities, big and small, leave some mark. Sociologists have developed a formula to describe a population's *environmental footprint*, or impact on the environment. The *IPAT formula* (Impacts = Population × Affluence × Technology) determines the environmental impact that population, wealth, and technology have on a society.[40] Hunter-gatherer societies generally live off the land and do not produce much of a footprint.[41] However, a complex postindustrial society such as Canada has a significant environmental footprint. Of course, advanced societies have a variety of technologies that can either increase or decrease their footprint.

The issue of climate change is not just on the minds of scientists, politicians, and bloggers; it's an area that is often discussed in environmental sociology as well. How might changing climates affect society?

The chief suspect for climate change is increasing levels of greenhouse gases in the atmosphere. One primary greenhouse gas, carbon dioxide, is sent into the air every time you exhale. But it also occurs when fossil fuels, like the gasoline that propels the millions of cars on the road, are burned. In the atmosphere, carbon dioxide acts like a piece of glass on a greenhouse: allowing in the sun's heat and keeping its warmth from escaping.[42]

The sociological issue is how climate change might influence the social world. Global warming has been blamed for melting the polar ice cap and raising sea levels. As the oceans continue to rise, people who live in low-lying areas are likely to experience more and more problems with issues such as storm surges and the erosion of coastlands. One country, the small island nation of the Maldives, located off the southern coast of India, is rapidly disappearing. "If carbon emissions were to stop today, the planet would not see a difference for 60 to 70 years," said Mohamed Nasheed, president of the Maldives from 2008 to 2012. "If carbon emissions continue at the rate they are climbing today, my country will be underwater in seven years."[43] As the world becomes more aware of environmental concerns—especially in wealthy, developed nations—this example gives us hope that these trends can be reversed.[44]

Dustie/Shutterstock

^^^ We can minimize our environmental footprint by reducing what we use and recycling materials.

CB2/ZOB/WENN.com/Newscom

<<< In 2009, then President Mohamed Nasheed held a 30-minute cabinet meeting 6 metres below sea level to show what the future could hold for the Maldives.

Source: "Maldives Cabinet Holds Underwater Meeting," *CBC News*, www.cbc.ca/news/world/story/2009/10/17/maldives-climate-change.html, accessed August 6, 2013.

discover sociology in action: CAN GOVERNMENTS CONTROL POPULATION GROWTH?

Population Control Programs

Government officials often consider population when planning for the future. Nations that promote fertility among their populations are considered pro-natalist. The United States is a pro-natalist country because it provides tax deductions to couples who have children. The more children you have, the less income tax you pay. On the opposite end of the spectrum are anti-natalist countries, or countries that do not promote fertility. Countries such as China have laws and tax penalties for people who have multiple births. This is an example of how public policy can influence population.

Consider different countries and the percentages of women of birth-ing age in those nations who use modern means of birth control. In wealthy nations such as Canada or the United States, the rate is quite high, while poorer nations have much lower rates.

In China, however, the rate of birth control use is also quite high. Chinese fertility patterns have often differed from those in the Western world. In 1979, China began what is often called the "one-child" policy.[45] The policy was established after the Chinese government saw population projections that foreshadowed many problems, such as hunger, lack of economic opportunity, and an inability to sustain the population in the future without quick and drastic measures.

The one-child policy is not as simple as it sounds, though. For example, China's family planning policy includes delaying marriage and improving access to contraception. Critics of the policy paint a dark picture of the policy, suggesting that it has led to forced abortions and sterilizations.[46] In addition, the Chinese preference for sons has led some mothers to purposefully abort female fetuses, which has led to an extremely imbalanced sex ratio.[47] China's official policy also varies based on a person's geographic location. In highly concentrated urban areas, the one-child-per-couple standard is enforced, but in more rural areas, the policy allows a couple to have a second child.[48]

China's policy basically follows the logic that bigger families use more state resources. In some areas, having only one child can give the parents bonuses in income, better health care benefits, priority for housing and school choice, and longer maternity leave. After the birth of their first child, a couple pledges to have no more children and thus can reap these benefits as long as they comply. If a couple decides to disobey the policy, the government may impose a tax penalty on their earnings.[49]

ACTIVITIES

1. How do you think your home town would change if the population increased by 100 000 people? How about 1 000 000 people?
2. Contact a city official and ask what type of data the city uses from Statistics Canada or from other sources to help determine future needs.
3. How might population growth influence the balance of global power?
4. Go to the Statistics Canada website and check out the sections on the environment and on population and demography.

WRAP YOUR MIND AROUND THE THEORY

CB2/ZOB/WENN.com/Newscom

What is this the future for populations living close to sea-level?

FUNCTIONALISM

Functionalists look at structural factors, such as economic wealth, education, and government policies, that may influence population growth. Functionalists want to know what part a growing population plays in society. They also try to understand how changes in the population affect the various social institutions. Functionalism recognizes the interrelatedness of society and the natural environment, and it examines the functions of the environment for humans. The sustainable development model focuses on how structural changes can result in economic growth without compromising the ability of future generations to also enjoy growth.

CONFLICT THEORY

Conflict theorists might view population growth using the Malthusian point of view. More people need more resources, such as food, clean water, and space. Although advancements in technology can increase the food supply, at some point the population will outgrow the availability of food, causing a clear difference between the "haves" and "have-nots." The haves will obtain the necessary goods and power, while the have-nots will have fewer goods, less wealth, and, therefore, less power. This imbalance will lead to conflict and cause war and discord. The resource management model allows powerful groups in society to use their influence to determine policies that will allow them to continue to profit from the careless extraction and exploitation of resources and that minimize the penalties imposed on them for creating pollution and for squandering the supply of natural resources.

WHAT IS THE CONNECTION BETWEEN POPULATION, SOCIETY, AND THE ENVIRONMENT?

SYMBOLIC INTERACTIONISM

Symbolic interactionism looks at how a society's culture influences that society. Although health and economic factors influence birth rates as well, interactionists study how people's attitudes toward children influence birth rates. Changing attitudes about the use of birth control and the delay of marriage result in fewer births and decreased population growth. Changes on an individual level also influence our interactions with the environment. Symbolic interactionists say that each of us changing our view of our relationship with nature would do more to protect the environment than trying to get governments and industries to change how they operate.

FEMINIST THEORY

Because it is women who have babies, feminists focus on women as the key to understanding population growth. In industrial and postindustrial societies, the changing definitions of men's and women's roles in society have influenced the education of women and have resulted in more women entering the workforce. Delaying childbearing leads to fewer births and decreased population growth. The ecofeminist theory is a merging of ecological and feminist thought that focuses on the common experiences of women and nature. This theory recognizes that both share reproductive functions, and both have been subordinated and controlled by patriarchal systems of power.

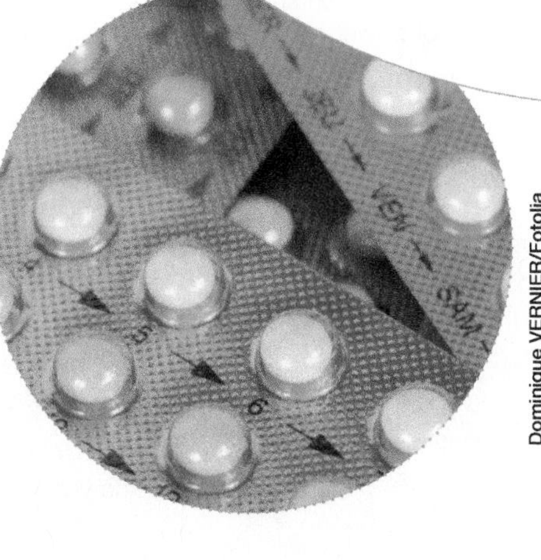

Dominique VERNIER/Fotolia

The birth control pill has had an enormous impact on population growth.

Rohit Seth/Fotolia

Feminists focus on women as the key to understanding population growth.

CHAPTER

08

WHAT IS DEMOGRAPHY? 151

the study of population size and composition

WHAT IS ENVIRONMENTAL SOCIOLOGY? 158

a new sociological paradigm that evaluates how the environment influences society and vice versa

CAN GOVERNMENTS CONTROL POPULATION GROWTH? 162

they can promote or discourage fertility, create fertility policies, and implement tax deductions

get the topic: WHAT IS DEMOGRAPHY?

get the topic: WHAT IS ENVIRONMENTAL SOCIOLOGY?

Theories

FUNCTIONALISM 163

- the functionalist perspective looks at the structure of society and how all the different parts are interrelated
- the human ecology theory is most associated with the functionalist perspective
- the sustainable development model focuses on structural changes in order to achieve its goals, and it also reflects the functionalist perspective

CONFLICT THEORY 163

- conflict theorists look at how different social groups and classes struggle to have their interests met
- powerful groups in society that currently benefit under the existing system prefer the resource management model
- those powerful groups use their influence to determine policies that will allow them to continue to profit from natural resources

SYMBOLIC INTERACTIONISM 163

- symbolic interactionism looks at how individuals and small groups give meaning to and interpret issues
- proponents of the deep ecology movement often advocate changing our view of our relationship with nature
- if we change the way we talk about nature and if each of us changes how we interact with nature, we get closer to meeting the goals of deep ecology

FEMINIST THEORY 163

- feminist theorists are concerned about how social issues affect women
- the ecofeminist theory is a merging of ecological and feminist thought and focuses on the common experiences of women and nature
- both women and nature share productive and reproductive functions, and both have been subordinated and controlled by patriarchal systems of power

Key Terms

demography is the study of population size and composition. *151*

total fertility rate refers to the number of children that a woman would have over the course of her reproductive life. *151*

crude birth rate is the number of births for every 1000 people each year. *152*

generational replacement level is the fertility rate (2.1 children per woman) that must be maintained to replace the population in the absence of migration. *152*

mortality rate is the number of deaths that occur in a population.

crude death rate is the number of deaths for every 1000 people each year. *152*

age-specific death rate is the number of deaths in a particular age group during a given year. *152*

infant mortality rate is the number of deaths of children less than 1 year of age per 1000 live births in the same year. *152*

life expectancy is the average number of years a person is expected to live. *152*

migration is the movement of people from one area to another. *153*

immigration is the movement of people into an area. *153*

emigration is the movement of people out of an area. *154*

push-pull, or neo-classical, migration theory suggests that migration depends on the supply and demand for labor, both in the sending area and the receiving are. *154*

rate of natural increase (RNI) is the crude birth rate minus the crude death rate of a population. *154*

doubling time refers to the number of years it takes for a population to double. *155*

Malthusian theory is a population projection which suggests that the population will exceed the available food supply because populations grow at geometric rates, whereas food supplies grow at arithmetic rates. *155*

demographic transition theory suggests that people control their own fertility as they move from agrarian to industrial societies. *156*

environmental sociology is concerned with the reciprocal relationship between societies and their environments. *158*

human ecology recognizes that there is a relationship between people and their physical environments. *158*

sustainable development is based on the premise that economic development and environmental protection are compatible goals. *159*

deep ecology is a perspective based on the belief that we are just one species among many, that our role and our activities are no more important than any other species', and that our primary concern should be ecological viability and preservation rather than economic growth. *159*

anthropocentric bias is the belief that humans are the most significant species in nature. *159*

ecofeminist theory is a merging of ecological and feminist thought that focuses on the common experiences of women and nature. *159*

resource management focuses on negotiating and regulating the extraction of resources and the disposal of hazardous waste. *159*

Sample Test Questions

These multiple-choice questions are similar to those found in the test bank that accompanies this textbook.

1. Which of the following refers to the number of children that a woman would have over the course of her reproductive life if she experienced the age-specific fertility rates observed in a particular calendar year?
   a. Crude birth rate
   b. Fertility rate
   c. Generational replacement rate
   d. Crude demographic rate
2. Countries entering the first stage of transition in the demographic transition theory are
   a. not yet industrialized.
   b. in a postindustrial economy.
   c. established as industrialized nations.
   d. entering the initial phase of industrialization.
3. The movement of people into an area is called
   a. emigration.
   b. rate of natural increase.
   c. migration.
   d. immigration.
4. Which theory recognizes that the natural environment performs many services for human beings?
   a. Human ecology
   b. Ecofeminism
   c. Deep ecology
   d. Resource management
5. Which term refers to the belief that humans are the most significant species in nature?
   a. Deep ecology
   b. Anthropocentric bias
   c. Human environmentalism
   d. Primary environmental significance

ANSWERS: 1. b; 2. a; 3. d; 4. a; 5. b

ESSAY

1. Why doesn't population growth generally affect the income and wealth of developed countries?
2. How do sociologists describe a population's environmental footprint?
3. How can reducing one's environmental footprint help reduce climate change and global warming?
4. Describe the arguments for and against anti-natalist policies such as China's.
5. How do social factors affect birth rates?

WHERE TO START YOUR RESEARCH PAPER

To find more facts and figures for countries around the world, go to www.cia.gov/library/publications/the-world-factbook/.

For Canadian statistics and reports, go to www.statcan.gc.ca/start-debut-eng.html and look at the sections Environment and Population and Demography.

www5.statcan.gc.ca/subject-sujet/theme-theme.action?pid=1762&lang=eng&more=0&HPA.

www5.statcan.gc.ca/subject-sujet/theme-theme.action?pid=3867&lang=eng&more=0&HPA.

To see the world population clock and more international demographic graphs, go to www.census.gov/population/international/.

For more information on immigration to Canada, go to www.cic.gc.ca/english/index-can.asp.

To learn more about the world population and issues that arise with growing numbers, go to www.overpopulation.org and www.prb.org.

To find out more about what countries are doing to control their populations, go to www.popcouncil.org.

To see what people do to celebrate Earth Day, go to www.earthday.net and www.epa.gov/earthday/.

Remember to check www.thethinkspot.ca for additional information, downloadable flashcards, and other helpful resources.

RyFlip/Shutterstock

RACE AND ETHNICITY

Is It a Question *of* Colour?

CHAPTER 09

WHAT IS THE DIFFERENCE BETWEEN RACE AND ETHNICITY?
WHAT CAUSES RACIST ATTITUDES, AND HOW DO THESE ATTITUDES AFFECT PEOPLE?
HOW DOES AFFIRMATIVE ACTION HELP MINORITY GROUPS IN CANADA?

"The territory now called Canada was originally occupied by diverse, plural groups of aboriginals. By 1867, the time of the confederation of four provinces, Ontario, Quebec, Nova Scotia and New Brunswick, Canadian censuses showed that the British comprised almost two-thirds of the population of the federated territory and the French one-third, and that the Germans (who likewise were north Europeans), were the third largest group. The aboriginals were not counted in the vast stretches of space north and west of this tiny new nation, known as the Northwest Territories. The confederation of provinces called Canada remained largely north European and white for a century. By 1991, however, Canadians of non-European origin had doubled to ten percent, so that they were very visible in the European sea of white faces. Among Canadian cities Toronto and Vancouver, especially, began to see that "visible minority" numbers would double in a generation or two. Estimates are that "people of colour" will make up twenty percent of Canada by 2016. Immigration laws which had favored north Europeans were changed in the 1960s, when more equitable laws were passed which, especially for Asians, increased the chances of coming to Canada. . . .

"Stratification by race is a fairly recent phenomenon, maintained in existence especially during the last several hundred years by white Europeans and their ancestors. . . . Race, and its meaning, has evolved and changed over time. Explorers and traders were finding people who looked and behaved somewhat differently from themselves, so they became interested in common and distinctive features and invariably began to wonder about the origin of these differences in colour and physical characteristics. . . . "Race" today is defined as an arbitrary biological grouping of people on the basis of physical traits…While "racism" is a negative concept, based on the belief that some races are inferior to others, the concept of inequality is an attempt at ranking people more objectively on the basis of opportunities to compete in the social, economic, and political spheres of our society . . . Inequality is a part of the social structure of a society, rather than a form of biological determinism. While biological features are difficult to change, social structures can be changed, although not easily."[1]

In *Race and Racism: Canada's Challenge,* Leo Driedger and Shiva S. Halli have gathered together a wonderful set of essays on the complex and fascinating issue of race and ethnicity in Canada. The excerpt above was taken from Chapter 1, "The Race Challenge 2000".

McGill-Queen's University Press, 2000.

Race is a word that has many powerful meanings. We might try to act like it doesn't exist, or pretend that it doesn't really mean anything, especially in a country as tolerant as Canada. And yet, there is a lot of evidence that shows that race and ethnicity (which are not the same thing) *are* still important, even in Canada. Your race or ethnicity determines your chances of finishing high school, what kind of job you will likely get, whether or not you will go to prison, and even how long you can expect to live.

According to recent science, race is purely a social construct, not a biological one. And yet, people often seek to define race solely in biological terms. Often, this mentality is instilled at an early age because we often teach children, who don't even have a concept of race, about racial differences that do not really exist. This is how we learn about race: from our social experiences. Evidence from the analysis of DNA indicates that most physical variation, about 94 percent, lies within so-called racial groups. Conventional racial groupings differ from one another only in about 6 percent of their genes. This means that there is greater variation *within* racial groups than *between* them. Throughout history, whenever different groups have come into contact, they have interbred. The continued sharing of genetic materials has maintained all of humankind as a single species. Physical variations in the human species have no meaning except the social ones that humans put on them.[2]

Race

is

the socially defined classification of people based on certain physical characteristics

and differs from

Ethnicity: the classification of people based on a common cultural, linguistic, or ancestral heritage

and different types of minorities such as

Militant minorities: groups that seek to overthrow the existing system because they see it as unjust
Pluralistic minorities: groups that enter into an area voluntarily but seek to maintain their own culture while also integrating into the dominant group
Assimilationist minorities: groups that seek to shed their old ways and integrate themselves into mainstream society
Secessionist minorities: groups that voluntarily separate themselves from the dominant group and view the dominant group with disdain, believing that it will corrupt the group's belief system

Voluntary migration: the willing movement of people from one society to another
Expulsion or confinement: the dominant group expels or forcibly confines a minority group
Genocide: the attempt to destroy or exterminate a people based on their race or ethnicity
Ethnic cleansing: persecution through imprisonment, expulsion, or murder of members of an ethnic minority by a majority to achieve ethnic homogeneity in majority-controlled territory
Multiculturalism: a concept that supports the inherent value of different cultures within society
Assimilation: the process by which minority groups adopt the patterns of the dominant culture

get the topic: WHAT IS THE DIFFERENCE BETWEEN RACE AND ETHNICITY?

If you walk down any street, you'll find people with different hairstyles, fashion sense, age, body type, and, yes, skin colour. **Race** refers to the socially defined classification of people based on certain physical characteristics. The most prominent of these characteristics is skin colour. Examples of racial categories include white and black, or Caucasian, Negroid, and Asian. **Ethnicity** is a little more complex than race because it usually involves grouping people who share a common cultural, linguistic, or ancestral heritage. Thus, there are many more ethnic than racial categories. Examples of ethnic groups in Canada include those from Chinese, Ukrainian, Italian, or Haitian backgrounds.

As the population grows and intermarriage becomes more common, traits like skin colour may no longer be such a simple signifier of identity. However, sociological questions regarding race are not fixated on the differences in looks. Instead, these questions focus on how society interprets those differences in appearance and how those interpretations affect an individual's opportunities.

Census Definitions

At the time of Confederation in 1867, Canada was already a multicultural society. The first Canadian census was conducted in 1871, and it asked questions about people's age, sex, religion, and race. Since that first census, the choices for "race," "ethnicity," and "ancestry" have changed many times. In the 1891 census there was no question about race, but in the next census it reappeared, and from 1901 until 1941 Canadians were asked to identify their race. The race question was mysteriously dropped in 1951. By 1991, Canadians were being asked to identify their "ethnic origin" and could select from a list of 11 choices. In the 1996 census, respondents were asked to identify themselves according to population group. This data was used to derive counts of the **visible minority** population in Canada. Of course, the term *visible minority* is a relative term that reflects certain social and political perspectives. In Canada, a visible minority is someone, other than an Aboriginal person, who is non-Caucasian in race or non-white in colour.[3] An **aboriginal** is a person who is Indian, Inuit, or Métis.[4] The 1996 census was also the first time "Canadian" was included as one of the ethnic origin choices.[5]

RACE is the socially defined classification of people based on certain physical characteristics.

ETHNICITY is the classification of people based on a common cultural, linguistic, or ancestral heritage.

VISIBLE MINORITY is a person, other than an aboriginal, who is non-Caucasian in race or non-white in colour.

ABORIGINAL is a person who is Indian, Inuit, or Métis.

These constant changes are good evidence that race and ethnicity are social constructs rather than biological categories. The census people at Statistics Canada are good sociologists because on their website they state, "It must be noted that the measurement of ethnicity is affected by changes in the social environment in which the questions are asked, and changes in the respondent's understanding or views about the topic."[6]

Racial Stratification in Canada

Now that we have a context in which to look at race and ethnicity, let's turn our attention to how these characteristics stratify our society. Although we live in a free society that claims to be equal, there are still injustices that occur because of race and ethnicity. How does the well-being of different racial and ethnic groups compare? Read on to find out.

Statistics Canada identifies

Visible minority: a person, other than an aboriginal, who is non-Caucasian in race or non-white in colour
Aboriginal: a person who is Indian, Inuit, or Métis

Stratification based on race and ethnicity can lead to

Minority group: any group that holds less power than the majority group
Dominant group: the group that has the greatest power but not necessarily the greatest numbers
Racism: an ideology that maintains that one racial group is inherently superior to another
Prejudice: negative attitudes about an entire social category of people
Stereotypes: simplified perceptions people have of an entire group, usually based on a false assumption
Discrimination: the unfair treatment of people based on their social category membership rather than on merit

and different patterns of interaction such as

Segregation: forced separation because of factors such as race, gender, or ethnicity
Ethnic enclaves: neighbourhoods where people from similar cultures live together and assert cultural distinction from the dominant group
Migrant superordination: the conquest of a native population by a more powerful group
Indigenous superordination: the subordination of an immigrant group to adominant group

SELF-IDENTIFIED ETHNIC ORIGINS OF ANCESTORS (2011 NATIONAL HOUSEHOLD SURVEY)

Ethnic Origin	Number of Respondents
British Isles	11 343 710
Canadian	10 563 805
French	5 077 215
European (excluding British and French)	3 737 040
East/Southeast Asian	2 650 000
Aboriginal	1 836 035
South Asian	1 615 925
West Central Asian and Middle Eastern	778 465
African	766 735
Caribbean	627 590
Latin/Central/South American	544 380
Oceania	74 875

Source: Statistics Canada, "2011 National Household Survey: Data Tables," Statistics Canada Catalogue no. 99-010-X2011028. May 28, 2013, www12.statcan.gc.ca/nhs-enm/2011/dp-pd/dt-td/Rp-eng.cfm?LANG=E&APATH=3&DETAIL=0&DIM=0&FL=A&FREE=0&GC=0&GID=0&GK=0&GRP=1&PID=105396&PRID=0&PTYPE=105277&S=0&SHOWALL=0&SUB=0&Temporal=2013&THEME=95&VID=0&VNAMEE=&VNAMEF=, accessed August 23, 2013. This does not constitute an endorsement by Statistics Canada of this product.

Note: Figures add up to more than the total number of respondents (32 852 320) because respondents may identify multiple origins.

Although these women differ in physical appearance, they are very much the same biologically. **Why does society see fit to place them in separate racial categories?**

Philip Date/Fotolia

INCOME

In Canada, minorities tend to be overrepresented in poverty statistics, particularly aboriginals and visible minorities. In 2009, the unemployment rate for aboriginals was 13.9 percent, significantly higher than the Canadian rate of 8.1 percent.[7] In 2006, the median income for aboriginals ($18 962) was much lower than the Canadian median income ($25 615).[8] A study by Feng Hou and Simon Coulombe found that in the public sector, whites and visible minorities received similar pay for similar jobs, but in the private sector, visible minorities earned significantly less than whites doing comparable jobs.[9] Overall, Canadian-born visible minorities are not more likely than others born in Canada to experience low income. However, visible minority immigrants are more likely than other immigrants to be poor. This may be because they have lower levels of education or because they do not speak either English or French. It also suggests that there is persistent exclusion and discrimination in the labour market.

EDUCATION

One of the most important factors in determining income is education. Without formal education, it's difficult to get a well-paying job and advance in the workplace. There is a strong correlation between level of education and income, with people who have advanced degrees earning the most money. But who exactly is earning these advanced degrees? The graphs below

INEQUALITY IN CANADA

	Population Size (15 years and older)	Income	Labour Force: Unemployment Rate
Visible Minorities	**5 069 095**	**Median $22 395** **Mean $30 385**	**8.6%**
Aboriginals	**1 172 785**	**Median $18 962** **Mean $25 961**	**14.8%**
Canada	**31 241 030**	**Median $25 615** **Mean $35 498**	**6.6%**

Source: Adapted from Statistics Canada, "2006 Census of Population," www12.statcan.gc.ca/census-recensement/2006/dp-pd/tbt/Rp-eng.cfm? LANG=E&APATH=3&DETAIL=0&DIM=0&FL=A&FREE=0&GC=0&GID=0&GK=0&GRP=1&PID=94183&PRID=0&PTYPE=88971,97154&S=0&SHOWALL=0&SUB=0&Temporal=2006&THEME=80&VID-=0&VNAMEE=&VNAMEF=">www12.statcan.gc.ca/census-recensement/2006/dp-pd/tbt/Rp-eng.cfm? LANG=E&APATH=3&DETAIL=0&DIM=0&FL=A&FREE=0&GC=0&GID=0&GK=0&GRP=1&PID=94183&PRID=0&PTYPE=88971,97154&S=0&SHOWALL=0&SUB=0&Temporal=2006&THEME=80&VID=0&VNAMEE=&VNAMEF=, accessed February 17, 2011; adapted from Statistics Canada, "Aboriginal Population Profile," January 15, 2008, www12.statcan.ca/census-recensement/2006/dp-pd/prof/92-594/index.cfm?Lang=E">www12.statcan.ca/census-recensement/2006/dp-pd/prof/92-594/index.cfm?Lang=E, accessed February 17, 2011.

show the educational attainment of visible minorities and aboriginals in Canada. Visible minorities are more likely than the average Canadian to have a university degree. Unfortunately, the picture is not so good for aboriginals. They are more than twice as likely to not finish high school, and only 6 percent complete a university degree.

MINORITY GROUP is any group that holds less power than the majority group.

DOMINANT GROUP is the group that has the greatest power but not necessarily the greatest numbers.

MINORITY AND DOMINANT GROUPS

In Chapter 3, you learned that a **minority group** is any group that holds less power than the majority group. Louis Wirth states that minority group status is assigned to people who are singled out for unequal treatment. Minorities also have a collective sense of being discriminated against.[10]

In some societies, having a numeric majority isn't necessarily required to wield power or practise discrimination. Sociologists refer to those who are more powerful as the **dominant group** because even if they may not have greater numbers, they have greater power. Apartheid, the five-decades-long system of oppression in South Africa, showed how a group's numbers don't necessarily reflect a group's political and economic power. In the era of apartheid, whites, who were the numeric minority of South Africa, passed laws that forced blacks, the native majority, into segregated housing, took away their right to vote, and generally treated them like second-class citizens.[11] Politically, the situation of a minority group ruling over a majority population, especially in periphery nations, is almost always a direct result of colonialism, in which more powerful countries impose their will on weaker nations. More often than not, though, dominant groups tend to be a country's numeric majority as well.

In 2011, more than 6 million Canadians identified themselves as members of the visible minority population. This represents 19.1 percent of Canada's total population, compared with 16.2 percent in the 2006 census. Migration patterns certainly influence these figures. Visible minorities accounted for 78.0 percent of the immigrants who arrived

Educational Attainment Distribution of Visible Minorities
Aged 15 Years and Over

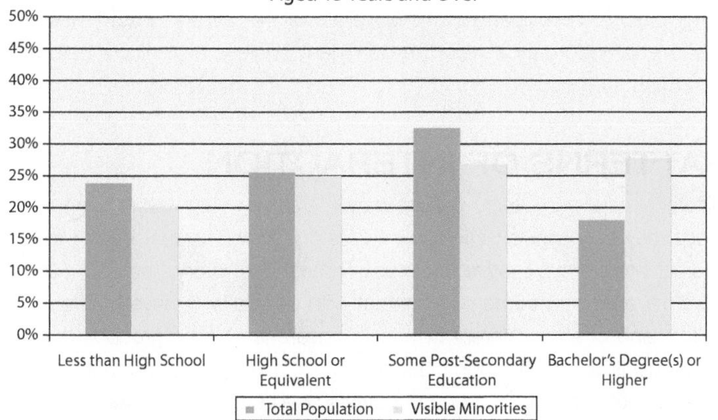

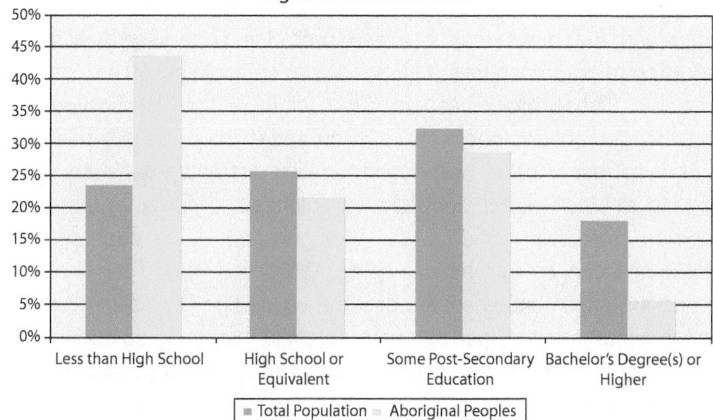

Adapted from Statistics Canada, 2006 Census of Canada. This does not constitute an endorsement by Statistics Canada of this product.

MAKE CONNECTIONS

Justice Denied—The Donald Marshall Story

In the Canadian justice system, the accused is always presumed innocent until proven guilty. At least this is the principle. But in 1971, Donald Marshall wrongly received a life sentence for the murder of Sandy Seale in Sydney, Nova Scotia. He was just 17 years old when he was convicted. He was also a Mi'kmaq.

Marshall served 11 years in prison before a re-examination of the evidence led to the arrest and conviction of Roy Ebsary. Marshall was acquitted in May 1983, but his case had received much attention, and his name had become synonymous with the term *wrongful conviction*. There were powerful suggestions that prejudice may have been a factor.

In 1989, a royal commission completed its two-year investigation into the Marshall case. The commission concluded that "the criminal justice system failed Donald Marshall at virtually every turn," and that racism was a factor in the wrongful conviction. In compensation, Donald Marshall was awarded a lifetime pension, which he received until he died in 2009.

While the Canadian justice system let Donald Marshall down, it did learn something from its mistakes. The royal commission that investigated his case recommended changes to the *Evidence Act*, such that the crown attorney is now obliged to present all evidence at a trial—rather than choosing to present only evidence that supports the Crown's case, as was done at Donald Marshall's trial. Sometimes it takes a dramatic travesty before changes are made to unfair practices.[12]

RACISM refers to an ideology that maintains that one racial group is inherently superior to another.

PREJUDICE refers to negative attitudes about an entire social category of people.

STEREOTYPES are simplified perceptions people have of an entire group, usually based on a false assumption.

DISCRIMINATION is the unfair treatment of people based on their social category membership rather than on merit.

between 2006 and 2011. In contrast, they made up Just 12.4 percent of immigrants who arrived before 1971.[13] In the future, minority group members will have greater representation in the population.

RACISM

Race and ethnicity are important social concepts, not only because they describe social diversity but also because they are often the basis for social stratification. The simplest definition of **racism** is that it refers to an ideology that maintains that one racial group is inherently superior to another. As we have seen, racism is still a social problem in Canada. But how did all this get started? To better think like sociologists, we need to understand the origins of racial and ethnic stratification.

PREJUDICE VS. DISCRIMINATION

To truly understand the complexity of race relations, it is vital to understand the differences between prejudice and discrimination. **Prejudice** refers to negative attitudes about an entire social category of people. These prejudices are often reinforced by **stereotypes**: simplified perceptions people have of an entire group, usually based on a false assumption. Although negative stereotypes—such as believing all black people are prone to violence and crime, or that all Arabs are terrorists—are absolutely wrongheaded, so-called positive stereotypes can be just as damaging. While you may think you're offering a compliment when you assume your Asian Canadian classmate is a mathematical genius, the problem is that doing so confines that individual to a box that you have constructed in your mind. That is the danger of stereotypes. If we aren't careful, we might allow our prejudices to overtake our common sense.

These attitudes, if left unchecked, may lead to **discrimination**, or the unfair treatment of people based on their social category membership rather than on merit. Essentially, prejudice is an attitude, while discrimination is an action that stems from that attitude. The apartheid laws of South Africa were perpetuated by whites' attitudes toward black people. However, discrimination doesn't always have to be as blatant as the segregated water fountains and restaurants. A teacher with a prejudice against African Canadians may treat black students with contempt in the classroom. Similarly, a teacher who assumes that the Asian Canadian student in class is a naturally studious person could overlook the fact that the student might actually need help.

Essentially, prejudice is an attitude, while discrimination is an action that stems from that attitude.

Many of these prejudices and stereotypes are so prevalent that it's difficult to trace exactly where they come from. Generally, sociologists agree that while we aren't born with prejudiced attitudes, we often learn prejudice from those around us.[14] We can even learn a prejudice against a group to which we belong. This self-loathing occurs when we internalize the values of the dominant group.[15] In my classes, I often have my students take an online test designed to measure biases. Generally, minorities hold similar beliefs to their non-minority counterparts. Recently a black student took the "Know Your Bias" test and was shocked to find that she held negative attitudes toward other blacks. This illustrates how we are all socialized to hold biases that are in accordance with the dominant society, even if we belong to a minority group.

PATTERNS OF INTERACTION

Different racial and ethnic groups can interact in many ways. Some of these may be positive; unfortunately, history shows us that often these interactions are exploitative and cruel. Throughout history, human groups have travelled and come into contact with people who have a different culture and often a different physical appearance. If one group is more powerful, it will try to dominate the other. During the sixteenth and seventeenth centuries, European powers used their superior technology and military strength to colonize Africa, Asia, and the Americas.[16]

VOLUNTARY MIGRATION refers to the willing movement of people from one society to another.

EXPULSION OR CONFINEMENT occurs when the dominant group expels or forcibly confines a minority group.

GENOCIDE is the attempt to destroy or exterminate a people based on their race or ethnicity.

Migration

One event that can create racial and ethnic interaction is migration, which was discussed in Chapter 8. **Voluntary migration** refers to the willing movement of people from one society to another. However, the countries receiving these people may not always welcome the new immigrants with open arms. Discrimination is most likely when the immigrants are from a different race than the dominant group. In 1871, construction of the Canadian transnational railway began, and thousands of Chinese men came to Canada to fill the need for workers. However, when the railway was completed in 1885, the federal government tried to stop the flow of Chinese immigrants. That same year, a head tax was imposed on every Chinese immigrant. No other group of immigrants was targeted in this way. The *Chinese Exclusion Act* was passed in 1923, making it virtually impossible for anyone from China to immigrate to Canada. This law was in effect until 1947.[17]

Expulsion or confinement occurs when the dominant group expels or forcibly confines a minority group to a particular area. Forcing First Nations peoples onto reservations and imprisoning thousands of Japanese Canadians in detention camps during World War II are both examples of confinement in Canadian history.

Genocide

An extreme example of interaction is **genocide**, the attempt to destroy or exterminate a people based on their race or ethnicity. The most well-known example is the Holocaust during World War II. The Nazis slaughtered millions of Jews, Roma, and people with mental or physical disabilities in an attempt to cleanse Europe of people they felt were inferior. Extreme racism is not a thing of the past, either. The film *Hotel Rwanda* depicted the events of 1994, when members of two Rwandan political parties began killing opposition leaders and journalists. Quickly, the violence spread to rural areas, where members of the majority Hutu tribe slaughtered members of the Tutsi tribe. Don Cheadle received an Oscar nomination for his portrayal in the film of Paul Rusesabagina, a hotel manager who heroically saved the lives of nearly 1300 Rwandans. Demographic data show that gender made little difference in predicting who might survive; men, women, children, and the elderly were all killed.[18]

The idea of racial purity has not just been the dominion of Nazi Germany or tribal Rwanda. The history of Canada is stained by similarly horrible acts, starting with the appalling treatment of First Nations peoples but also including the Chinese Head Tax and Japanese internment camps during World War II. Most people associate slavery with the American pre–Civil War South, but slavery was also legal in Canada until it was formally abolished in 1834—just 31 years before abolition in the United States.[19]

Such behaviour has a long history and still continues today. There is an increasing use of the internet by hate groups in Canada and around the world. These groups are organizations that promote

Shanawdithit, the last known member of the Beothuk culture, died in St. John's, Newfoundland, in 1829.

Kevin Van Paassen/The Globe an Mail/Canadian Press Images

GO GLOBAL

Ethnic Cleansing—Bosnia

Following the breakup of the former country of Yugoslavia in 1990, the Serbian majority seized control and forced large numbers of minority group members, particularly Bosnian Muslims, or Bosniaks, to leave their lands or face extermination. In 1992, the Serbian army launched an ethnic cleansing campaign against Bosniaks in eastern Bosnia. **Ethnic cleansing** refers to persecution through imprisonment, expulsion, or murder of members of an ethnic minority by a majority to achieve ethnic homogeneity in majority-controlled territory. Bosniak civilians were rounded up and detained in camps; Bosnian civilians, men and women, were rounded up and detained in separate camps. Many were beaten or killed during capture. The surviving men were sent to concentration camps, and the women were sent to detention centres known as rape camps. In July 1995, near the end of the war, the Serbs rounded up and killed an estimated 8000 Bosniaks in the region of Srebrenica. This act of genocide, known as the Srebrenica Massacre, is the largest mass murder in Europe since World War II.[20] The Serbian and Croatian forces carried out these tactics of torture and murder in the hope of creating ethnically pure states. During this war, armies used ethnic differences as a justification for thousands of deaths and the forced removal of millions of people from their homes.[21]

These crimes, however, have not gone unnoticed by the rest of the world. In 1995, the International Criminal Tribunal for the former Yugoslavia in The Hague indicted former Bosnian Serb leader Radovan Karadzic. Charged with multiple counts of genocide, war crimes, and crimes against humanity, Karadzic went into hiding for more than 12 years before he was eventually captured in 2008. His trial is still ongoing. If convicted, Karadzic could face a possible life sentence for crimes committed during the Bosnian War.[22]

ETHNIC CLEANSING refers to persecution through imprisonment, expulsion, or murder of members of an ethnic minority by a majority to achieve ethnic homogeneity in majority-controlled territory.

SEGREGATION is forced separation because of factors such as race, gender, or ethnicity.

MIGRANT SUPERORDINATION is the conquest of a native population by a more powerful group.

INDIGENOUS SUPERORDINATION is the subordination of an immigrant group to a dominant group.

hostility or violence toward others based on race and other factors. They include white supremacists, neo-Nazis, and other groups that advocate hate against immigrants, gays, and other minorities. In Canada, the most active hate groups are Northern Alliance, Heritage Front, and Western Canada for Us.[23]

It's not just openly racist groups that can have significant impacts on minority groups. European settlers in Canada may not have deliberately tried to exterminate the indigenous peoples they met, but their actions often had serious consequences. The Beothuk were the original inhabitants of Newfoundland. For hundreds of years before the arrival of the Europeans, the Beothuk hunted and fished along the coast of the island. In contrast to many other First Nations peoples, the Beothuk generally avoided any kind of interaction with the Europeans. In the late 1700s and early 1800s, there was an increase in European settlers throughout Newfoundland. The Beothuk, already very few in number (perhaps just 1000 people), were displaced from their traditional hunting and fishing territories and forced into armed disputes with the settlers. By the 1820s, the Beothuk had been practically wiped out. In 1829, Shanawdithit, the last known remaining Beothuk woman, died. While the extermination of this peaceful culture was not intentional, in the territorial disputes with the Europeans, the already tiny and fragile Beothuk culture was sadly lost.[24]

Segregation

People who are discriminated against are often separated from the dominant group in terms of housing, workplace, and social settings. This enforced separation is called **segregation** when factors such as race, gender, or ethnicity are involved. Blacks and whites had separate schools, neighbourhoods, restaurants, and public restrooms in the southern United States in the 1960s and earlier. Although these and other forms of segregation are no longer legal, issues such as unofficial segregation continue to this day.

In a study of Canadian housing segregation, Harald Bauder and Bob Sharpe found that racial or ethnic segregation is linked to a number of factors. There may be "good segregation" and "bad segregation." Sometimes, minorities prefer to live in areas that are populated by their own groups. This is "good segregation," and is deliberately chosen because it is a protective measure that benefits the minority population. On the other hand, "bad segregation" is the result of racism and discrimination, and it does not benefit the minority group. A third explanation is that residential segregation is simply a reflection of socioeconomic status. Because some new immigrants are more likely to have lower incomes, they are also more likely to live in poor neighbourhoods.[25]

Superordination

Some predictable patterns of interaction can occur when people come into contact with unfamiliar groups. **Migrant superordination** occurs when a more powerful group enters an area and conquers the native population. In the sixteenth century, Spain used military strength to dominate Central and South America and to elevate their own culture above the native culture. In this case, the migrants' status was elevated, or superordinated. The opposite of this is **indigenous superordination**. When arriving immigrants enter Canada today, they are expected to learn English and subordinate their old ways to their new country. In other words, they must become subordinate to the dominant group. In the province of Quebec, French has been the only official language since 1974, when the provincial government passed Bill 22, *la Loi sur la langue officielle*. In Chapter 3, you read about Bill 101, the infamous language law, which states that immigrants must send their children to French schools. This is because the Quebec government wants new immigrants to adopt the Québécois culture.[26]

THINK SOCIOLOGICALLY

They're Coming to Canada

For centuries, immigrants have come to Canada. This trend continues to this day, constantly changing the face of the country.

Researchers are interested in what helps these immigrants not only survive but also thrive in a new country. They note that one key component of immigrant success is a successful neighbourhood, or *enclave*, in which they can live. Eric Fong and Milena Gulia studied different ethnic neighbourhoods in 20 Canadian cities. They found that new immigrants often form enclaves—that is, they all tend to live in the same neighbourhood. This is why there are Chinatowns, Little Italys, and Little Indias in cities across Canada. If new immigrants lack information about the new country and have low levels of language and work skills, they have a higher incentive to stay close to their countrymen for social, financial, and emotional support. Groups in which a large proportion of members are recent immigrants also have a greater tendency to live close together. This is particularly important to groups with cultures which are significantly different from that of the dominant group, for example Southeast Asian immigrants.

British, northern Europeans, and western Europeans tend to live in relatively better neighbourhoods. These are characterized by households with a lower average number of residents per room, a higher percentage of neighbours who have completed university education, a higher median household income, a lower percentage of persons who do not speak either official language, a lower percentage of low-income families, and a lower percentage of unemployed residents.

On the other hand, southern Europeans and visible minority groups, such as South Asians, Southeast Asians, and blacks, tend to live in neighbourhoods with a poorer social environment. These neighbourhoods are characterized by higher density, lower educational attainment, a higher percentage of low-income families, and a higher percentage of unemployed.[27]

As an immigrant group becomes established, members become more integrated into the dominant culture. They are more likely to speak English or French, and they probably earn a higher income. Once this happens, members of the group tend to move out into a better neighbourhood. In the late 1950s, a large number of Greek immigrants arrived in Montreal. Many settled in a district called "Park Extension," displacing the Jews who for years had been the dominant ethnic group in that area. After about 20 years, as they became more financially successful, the Greeks started moving to the more prestigious suburbs, primarily Chomedy in Laval. As they moved out of Park Extension, new waves of immigrants from Pakistan, the West Indies, and Sri Lanka moved in.[28]

>>> **ACTIVITY** Locate the nearest ethnic enclave in your city or province. To what ethnicity does it cater?

These two patterns of interaction are often justified through ethnocentric thinking. Remember, *ethnocentrism* is thinking about or defining another culture on the basis of your own. Generally, the greater the differences, the more negatively groups tend to view each other. At the same time, there is often competition between groups, which becomes more intense when resources are scarce. Consider the migrant pattern to Montreal in the first half of the twentieth century. Immigrants divided up the jobs that were available to them. Jewish immigrants took over the clothing industry, Greek immigrants established themselves in restaurants, and Italian immigrants were predominant in construction. If you were a member of one of these groups, you could find a job in those industries. But if you were a Greek immigrant who wanted to work in construction, you were unlikely to be hired. This is because ethnic groups often had differences in power. Once a group has power, it is unlikely to let it go.

MULTICULTURALISM AND ASSIMILATION

Multiculturalism is a concept that supports the inherent value of different cultures within society. Proponents of multiculturalism think that immigrants should maintain links to elements of their original culture—such as language, cultural beliefs and traditions, and religion—while also integrating into their new culture. However, opponents of multiculturalism worry that this practice keeps groups from adapting to the dominant culture. In 1971, Canada became the first country in the world to adopt multiculturalism as an official state policy.[29]

MULTICULTURALISM is a concept that supports the inherent value of different cultures within society.

ASSIMILATION is the process by which minority groups adopt the patterns of the dominant culture.

PLURALISTIC MINORITIES are groups that enter into an area voluntarily but seek to maintain their own culture while also integrating into the dominant group.

Assimilation is the process by which a minority group adopts the patterns of the dominant culture. If a minority group completely abandons its previous culture in favour of a new one, that group is likely to experience rapid assimilation. Assimilation is usually voluntary, but not always. One method by which the Canadian government tried to force rapid assimilation involved taking aboriginal children from their parents and placing them in residential schools to teach them "white ways." However, many of these students left the residential schools unprepared to live in either the dominant culture or their own culture.

TYPES OF MINORITY GROUPS

When minority groups face superordination, there are a number of ways they can choose to react. **Pluralistic minorities** are generally groups that enter into an area voluntarily. They seek to maintain their own culture but want to integrate with the dominant group as well. Thus they hope to keep their cultural ties while participating in the political and economic

byheaven/Fotolia

In 1971, Canada became the first country in the world to adopt multiculturalism as an official state policy.

ASSIMILATIONIST MINORITIES are groups that seek to shed their old ways and integrate themselves into mainstream society.

SECESSIONIST MINORITIES are groups that voluntarily separate themselves from the dominant group and view the dominant group with disdain, believing that it will corrupt the group's belief system.

system of the new society. **Assimilationist minorities**, on the other hand, seek to shed their old ways and integrate themselves into society. Groups that most closely resemble the dominant group—either racially or ethnically—are able to do this more easily.

For example, when German immigrants first came to Canada, their culture and language were generally accepted. German newspapers were printed, and there was even a town named Berlin, Ontario (it was later renamed Kitchener). However, with the beginning of World War I in 1914 came outright hostility toward almost anything German. Many German Canadians tried to camouflage their identity and to pass as Dutch, Scandinavian, or Russian. Perhaps because of this hostility, German Canadians were more likely to try to assimilate into the dominant culture. Census data confirm that even now, German Canadians are more likely than other ethnic groups to abandon their mother tongue.[30]

Sometimes, groups voluntarily decide to separate themselves from the dominant group and become **secessionist minorities**. Such a group does not seek assimilation or cultural unification. Instead, it views the dominant group with disdain, believing that it will corrupt its belief system. The Mennonites of Ontario can be considered an example of a secessionist minority. This group has carved out a lifestyle and culture in which a form of German is commonly spoken, and modern conveniences are rare. The Mennonites emphasize the importance of family, religion, and a simple lifestyle. Their children are educated at Mennonite schools, and a great deal of their life is exactly as it was 100 years ago. Although some Mennonite people are increasingly opening themselves up to other businesses besides farming, as well as allowing in a few modern technologies, their community remains secessionist.[31]

Ever since Confederation, there has been a secessionist element in the province of Quebec. Supporters of Quebec sovereignty point to the unique culture and the French-speaking majority in the province as rationales for Quebec having a unique relationship with the rest of Canada. Support for the sovereignty movement has come and gone in waves. The most recent revival was in 1995, when the provincial Parti Québécois held a referendum on the question of whether Quebec

TYPES OF MINORITY GROUPS

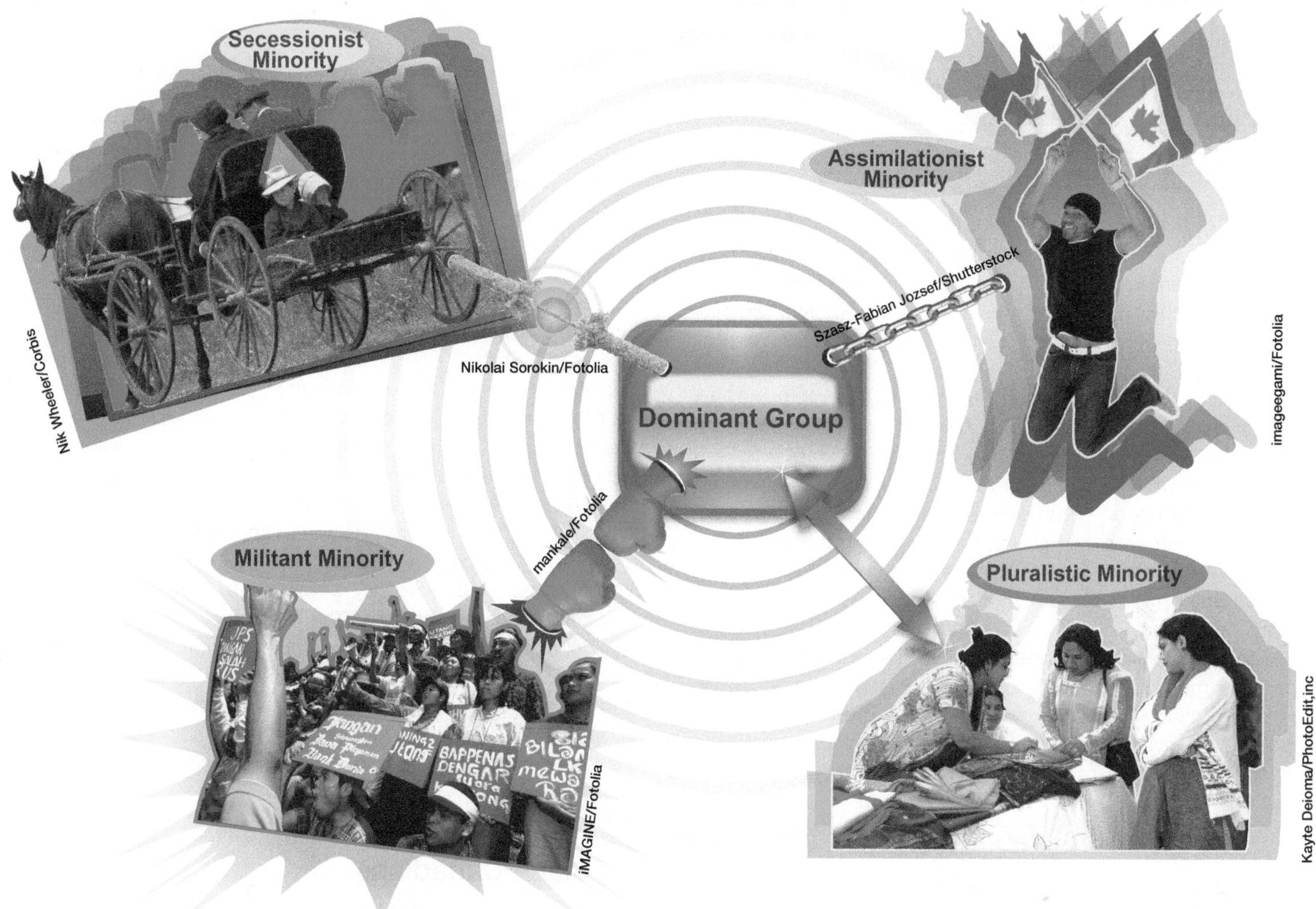

should become a sovereign nation. The "No" side narrowly won, with 50.6 percent.[32]

Sometimes, minorities react to their subordination through militancy. **Militant minorities** seek to overthrow the existing system, which they see as unjust. Often the militant minority is actually a numeric majority and may take the path of violence and war to fight perceived injustice, as was the case in Cuba in 1958, when Fidel Castro overthrew a government that he believed was corrupt.[33] Militants can also be peaceful, as when Mohandas Gandhi led a peaceful revolution that ended in 1947 and ultimately brought about the end of British occupation of India.[34]

MILITANT MINORITIES are groups that seek to overthrow the existing system because they see it as unjust.

ETHNIC ENCLAVES are neighbourhoods where people from similar cultures live together and assert cultural distinction from the dominant group.

Types of Minority Groups

Research suggests that racial and ethnic identity is related to four key factors: relative size, power, appearance, and discrimination.[35] These factors also tend to encourage a sense of solidarity among members of a single racial or ethnic group. In a sense, being different from the dominant group holds people together. The reason many minority groups tend to cluster together in neighbourhoods is because their differences from the dominant group often lead to discrimination. Furthermore, the shared values of similar people make adjustment easier. Finally, their social capital increases their chances of success. On the other hand, belonging to a group that looks like the dominant group rarely leads to discrimination. Such people often let go of their ethnic heritage because their appearance makes it easier to assimilate into the dominant culture.

This lack of privilege to belong to the dominant group is the reason many minority groups often bond together. This is especially true for new immigrants who are visible minorities. It is quite common for immigrants to live in neighbourhoods where people from similar cultures live together and assert cultural distinction, which are called **ethnic enclaves**, like a Chinatown or Little Italy. Such enclaves assist the new immigrant in making an easier transition into the new culture.

think sociologically: WHAT CAUSES RACIST ATTITUDES, AND HOW DO THESE ATTITUDES AFFECT PEOPLE?

Conflict Theory: Split Labour-Market Theory

Immigrants to Canada may experience discrimination. When their non-Canadian credentials are questioned and when their non-Canadian work experience is not recognized, immigrants are excluded from obtaining appropriate and rewarding jobs in Canada. Who benefits from this discrimination?

According to the split labour-market theory, conflict develops between three economic classes: business owners, higher-paid labour, and cheaper labour. The chief interest of the business class is to keep the cost of labour as low as possible. The cheaper labour class provides just this kind of labour, though these people also tend to be unskilled. The interest of those in the higher-paid labour class is to increase their wages and protect their jobs. One outcome, according to Edna Bonacich is a split labour market between the higher-paid workers and the cheap labour. The response of the higher-paid labour class will often manifest itself as racism against the lower-paid class. This is especially likely if the labour markets are divided along ethnic or racial lines. We still see evidence of this.[36] In 2013, the Royal Bank of Canada (RBC) faced strong public criticism after dozens of employees at the bank lost their jobs to temporary foreign workers brought in from India.[37]

Symbolic Interactionism: Colour-Blind Racism

Symbolic interactionists stress the importance of symbolism and language in the creation of society. In Canada, overtly racist language is socially unacceptable in most circles; however, sociologists don't believe that this means we have become a "colour-blind" society. In fact, **colour-blind racism**—the idea that racism still exists in more subtle ways—remains a part of Canadian society to this day. For example, there is no doubt that aboriginals in Canada remain in disadvantaged positions; they are poorer, achieve lower educational outcomes, live shorter lives, attend underfunded schools, experience problems with assimilation, and generally believe that the police and other social institutions work to increase their disadvantage.[38] Despite these facts, though, most whites in Canada claim that these outcomes have nothing to do with racism. How can that be? Furthermore, most whites claim that they are not racist.

Eduardo Bonilla-Silva suggests that this is because whites have developed a series of excuses for the status quo through four key factors: First, whites tend to hold on to ideals such as equality, individualism, and choice in an effort to explain why racial groups are disadvantaged.[39] In other words, people are only poor because they made bad choices, not because of some historical or cultural context that supports racism. Second, white people often use cultural stereotypes to explain racial inequality. Rather than understand the source of the problem, many people simply latch on to stereotypes to explain the issue. The third factor is the false belief that segregation is a personal choice. The suggestion is that it's natural for racial groups to prefer "their own kind." Often, this attitude prevents white people from understanding the complex role that institutionalized racism has on "segregated" communities. Fourth, and finally, many whites

COLOUR-BLIND RACISM is the idea that racism still exists in society in more subtle ways.

in Canada simply believe that racism is a thing of the past and deny that it has any impact on minorities' lives today.[40] Such thinking serves to defend the way things are and excuses the dominant group from any responsibility to make things better.

Although racism is not as overt as it once was, the problem has not been eradicated. Racial prejudice still exists; it's just hidden behind a series of clever language constructions. For example, white college students rarely use racist terms such as "the n-word," but they might tell racist jokes. They usually first explain that the joke doesn't really reflect their beliefs and conclude the joke with an apologetic comment in order to eliminate the perception of racism.[41]

Whites may try to prove they're not racist by claiming that some of their "best friends are not white." This is supposed to give the speaker an air of credibility for not being racist. Unfortunately, such disclaimers are usually followed by a negative stereotype. They might try to excuse a long history of structural racism or try to take all sides when it comes to matters of race. Whites may also excuse the long history of racism and a lack of equal opportunities by denying any personal responsibility for it.

Black Canadians, and other visible minorities, **often have to live in two worlds—one black and the other white.**

Stock Illustration Source

>>> **Lucien Comeau was upset that** the taxes he paid did not fund the French-language school his children attended.

David Martin/AP Images

Comments like "I didn't steal land from the Indians; it's not my fault" lead the conversation away from structural problems that continue to exist regarding race, while excusing the speaker from any possible advantage based on his or her race.

W.E.B. Du Bois suggested that African Americans have a sort of **double consciousness**, meaning black people have to keep a foot in two worlds, one white and one black.[42] Minority group members must learn to integrate into the dominant group in order to successfully live in the society. They must also learn to live within their own culture. Many visible minorities are forced to "code switch"—that is, to speak and act one way among their own group and another in white society. Du Bois considered blacks to be in a unique position because they were accountable to white culture as well as their own. This influences their sense of self and affects how they live in the world. Only through understanding this position can blacks hope to navigate the world successfully.

Du Bois's classical ideas also apply to the study of other minority groups, including Hispanics and women.[43] Generally, sociologists find that members of the dominant group do not think much about race—but, as one student put it, "When you're a minority, race is always a factor."[44]

DOUBLE CONSCIOUSNESS is the sense that a person must keep a foot in two worlds, one in the majority group's world and one in the minority group's world.

INSTITUTIONAL DISCRIMINATION maintains the advantage for the dominant group, while providing the appearance of fairness to all.

INTERSECTIONALITY is a term used to describe the fact that women experience oppression based on a number of minority statuses.

Functionalism: Institutional Discrimination in Canada

While personal biases often cause individuals to view others negatively, those attitudes can carry over into the structures of society and often go unnoticed by others who don't even hold those views. When this happens, social institutions end up supporting racial and ethnic inequality. This **institutional discrimination** maintains the advantage for the dominant group, while providing the appearance of fairness to others. At various times in Canadian history, immigration policies have reflected direct institutional discrimination against certain groups such as the Chinese, blacks, and Jews. The *Canadian Charter of Rights and Freedoms* proscribes direct institutional discrimination, yet minority groups in Canada continue to suffer from indirect institutional discrimination. Indirect institutional discrimination maintains the advantage for the dominant group, while providing the appearance of fairness to all. It occurs when members of a minority group experience unequal treatment, not because of openly discriminatory policies, but because of unfair structural factors. In June 2003, Lucien Comeau filed a complaint against the City of Halifax for unequal funding that resulted in discrimination against him as a person of Acadian descent. He argued that a change to the taxation process meant that part of his property taxes went to provide additional funding for the English-language schools of the Halifax Regional School Board (HRSB) but not to the French-language schools of the *Conseil Scolaire Acadien Provincial* (CSAP). Mr. Comeau's children attended a CSAP school. The law has been changed so that both school boards now receive the same funding.[45]

Feminist Theory: Intersectionality

While discrimination based on race or ethnicity can have powerful impacts on an individual, feminists point out that the effects are especially severe when the victim is also a woman. In the 1960s, a number of black feminists argued that, while sexism is certainly one form of discrimination, the types of oppression experienced by white, middle-class women were not representative of all women. A black woman in North America may suffer discrimination because she is a woman, but this is compounded by the fact that she is also black. In 1989, Kimberlé Crenshaw coined the term **intersectionality** to describe the fact that women experience oppression based on a variety of minority statuses, which may include not only gender, but also race, marital status, social class, religion, and sexual orientation. For example, a single black woman may have difficulty finding an apartment because many landlords believe the stereotype that she is less dependable than others for paying the rent.[46]

WRAP YOUR MIND AROUND THE THEORY

HEINZ RUCKEMANN/Newscom

These B.C. First Nations **protesters are fighting to have their** legal land rights recognized.

HOW DO THE FOUR PARADIGMS VIEW RACISM?

FUNCTIONALISM

Racist attitudes are not only observable in individuals, but they can carry over into the structures of society. When this happens, social institutions end up supporting racial and ethnic inequality. This institutional discrimination maintains the advantage for the dominant group, while providing the appearance of fairness to others. At various times in Canadian history, immigration policies have reflected direct institutional discrimination against certain groups such as the Chinese, blacks, and Jews. The *Canadian Charter of Rights and Freedoms* proscribes direct institutional discrimination, yet minority groups in Canada continue to suffer from indirect institutional discrimination. Indirect institutional discrimination maintains the advantage for the dominant group, while providing the appearance of fairness to all. It occurs when members of a minority group experience unequal treatment, not because of openly discriminatory policies, but because of unfair structural factors.

CONFLICT THEORY

Through a conflict theorist's lens, racism is the result of one group wanting to keep its advantage over another. According to the split labour-market theory, conflict develops between three economic classes: business owners, higher-paid labour, and cheaper labour. One outcome is a split labour-market between the higher-paid workers and the cheap labour. The response of the higher-paid labour class will often manifest itself as racism against the lower-paid class, especially if the labour markets are divided along ethnic or racial lines. In 2013, the Royal Bank of Canada (RBC) faced strong public criticism after dozens of employees at the bank lost their jobs to temporary foreign workers brought in from India.

SYMBOLIC INTERACTIONISM

Symbolic interactionists stress the importance of symbolism and language in the creation of society. Colour-blind racism remains a part of Canadian society to this day. This is because whites have developed a series of excuses for the status quo. Such thinking serves to defend the way things are and excuses the dominant group from any responsibility to make things better. Although racism is not as overt as it once was, the problem has not been eradicated. W.E.B. Du Bois suggested that African Americans have a sort of double consciousness, meaning black people have to keep a foot in two worlds, one white and one black. Minority group members must learn to integrate into the dominant group in order to successfully live in the society. They must also learn to live within their own culture. Many visible minorities are forced to "code switch"—that is, to speak and act one way among their own group and another in white society.

FEMINIST THEORY

Feminists point out that the effects of racism are even more severe when the victim is also a woman. In the 1960s, a number of black feminists argued that, while sexism is certainly one form of discrimination, the discrimination faced by a black woman in North America is compounded by the fact that she is also black. The term *intersectionality* is used to describe the fact that women experience oppression based on a variety of minority statuses, which may include not only gender, but also race, marital status, social class, religion, and sexual orientation.

When Japan entered World War II, **more than 20 000 Canadians of Japanese descent were sent to internment camps** by the Canadian government.

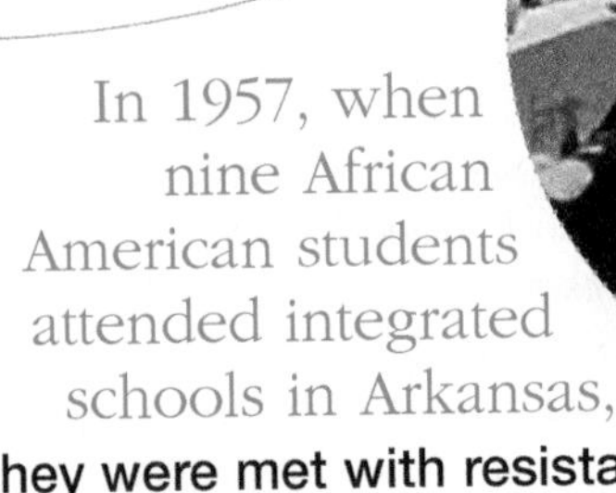

St Petersburg Times/ZUMAPRESS/Newscom

In 1957, when nine African American students attended integrated schools in Arkansas, **they were met with resistance and racial slurs from the school's white population.**

discover sociology in action: HOW DOES AFFIRMATIVE ACTION HELP MINORITY GROUPS IN CANADA?

Affirmative Action

Affirmative action is a social policy designed to help minority groups gain opportunities through employment and education. In Canada, the *Canadian Charter of Rights and Freedoms* states that every individual is equal before the law. The charter also includes a statement about affirmative action programs, which allow special provisions for individuals or groups disadvantaged because of race, national or ethnic origin, colour, religion, sex, age, or mental or physical disability. For example, in the Northwest Territories, aboriginal people are given preference for jobs and education. The logic behind this preference is based on hundreds of years of discrimination, as well as the obvious disadvantages that still exist for minorities.

A great deal of controversy surrounds affirmative action because some believe that the policy would require universities and companies to establish quotas for minority groups. The Canadian *Employment Equity Act* requires employers in federally regulated industries to give preferential treatment to four designated groups: women, people with disabilities, aboriginal people, and visible minorities. In most Canadian universities, people of aboriginal background often have lower entrance requirements and are eligible to receive exclusive scholarships. The truth is that quotas are not part of acceptable affirmative action policies since that could encourage employers to hire minority members who are not qualified.

While acknowledging the continuation of discrimination, sociologist William J. Wilson suggested that class-based policies should replace race-based ones.[47] He argued that financial needs and not race should determine advantage. This would allow poor whites, blacks, aboriginals, and so on to receive benefits—and, since visible minority groups and aboriginals are disproportionately poor, they would still reap the lion's share of these benefits. Basing the policies on class rather than on race would eliminate the perception of racial bias.

Do affirmative action policies work? Before affirmative hiring policies were introduced, visible minorities and aboriginals were underrepresented in the public service. Recent figures show that three of the four groups are now overrepresented in the federal government compared with the overall Canadian workforce. Only visible minorities are less represented in the federal government than in the workforce generally.[48]

AFFIRMATIVE ACTION is a social policy designed to help minority groups gain opportunities through employment and education.

ACTIVITIES

1. Engage someone not in this class in a conversation about race and ethnicity. See what you learn about his or her beliefs. Ask the following questions:
   - What are the different racial and ethnic groups in Canada?
   - Are there any biological differences in races?
   - Does race play a role in opportunities?
2. Find out if your school has a policy on racism and discrimination. Are there any groups that address issues of race and ethnicity?
3. Talk to your classmates about your own experiences of racial tension. Then visit this website to learn more about what you can do about racism: www.citizenequity.org/cmard/docs/How%20can%20I%20help%20combat%20racism%20and%20discrimination.pdf.

CHAPTER

09

WHAT IS THE DIFFERENCE BETWEEN RACE AND ETHNICITY? 169

RyFlip/Shutterstock

race is the division of people based on certain physical characteristics; *ethnicity* is the classification of people who share a common cultural, linguistic, or ancestral heritage

WHAT CAUSES RACIST ATTITUDES, AND HOW DO THESE ATTITUDES AFFECT PEOPLE? 178

colour-blind racism, racial stereotypes, belief that segregation is a personal choice, belief that racism is a thing of the past, which denies its impact on minorities; these lead to a feeling of double consciousness for minorities

HOW DOES AFFIRMATIVE ACTION HELP MINORITY GROUPS IN CANADA? 181

by allowing employers and educators to use minority status as a deciding factor if candidates are equal

get the topic: WHAT IS THE DIFFERENCE BETWEEN RACE AND ETHNICITY?

Theories

CONFLICT THEORY 178

- racism is the result of one group wanting to keep its advantage over another
- according to the split labour-market theory, conflict develops between higher-paid labour and cheaper labour
- if the labour markets are divided along ethnic or racial lines, this conflict may manifest itself as racism

SYMBOLIC INTERACTIONISM 178

- stresses the importance of symbolism and language in the creation of racism
- colour-blind racism remains a part of Canadian society to this day
- many visible minorities are forced to "code switch"—that is, to speak and act one way among their own group and another in white society

FUNCTIONALISM 179

- institutional discrimination maintains the advantage for the dominant group while providing the appearance of fairness to others
- at various times in Canadian history, immigration policies have reflected direct institutional discrimination against certain groups
- minority groups in Canada continue to suffer from indirect institutional discrimination

FEMINIST THEORY 179

- women who are also visible minorities suffer from multiple forms of discrimination
- Kimberlé Crenshaw coined the term *intersectionality* to refer to this intersection of multiple forms of discrimination

Key Terms

race is the socially defined classification of people based on certain physical characteristics. *169*

ethnicity is the classification of people based on a common cultural, linguistic, or ancestral heritage. *169*

visible minority is a person, other than an aboriginal, who is non-Caucasian in race or non-white in colour. *169*

aboriginal is a person who is Indian, Inuit, or Métis. *169*

minority group is any group that holds less power than the majority group. *171*

dominant group is the group that has the greatest power but not necessarily the greatest numbers. *171*

racism refers to an ideology that maintains that one racial group is inherently superior to another. *172*

prejudice refers to negative attitudes about an entire social category of people. *172*

stereotypes are simplified perceptions people have of an entire group, usually based on a false assumption. *172*

discrimination is the unfair treatment of people based on their social category membership rather than on merit. *172*

voluntary migration refers to the willing movement of people from one society to another. *173*

expulsion or confinement occurs when the dominant group expels or forcibly confines a minority group. *173*

genocide is the attempt to destroy or exterminate a people based on their race or ethnicity. *173*

ethnic cleansing refers to persecution through imprisonment, expulsion, or murder of members of an ethnic minority by a majority to achieve ethnic homogeneity in majority-controlled territory. *174*

segregation is forced separation because of factors such as race, gender, or ethnicity. *174*

migrant superordination is the conquest of a native population by a more powerful group. *174*

indigenous superordination is the subordination of an immigrant group to a dominant group. *174*

multiculturalism is a concept that supports the inherent value of different cultures within society. *175*

assimilation is the process by which minority groups adopt the patterns of the dominant culture. *175*

pluralistic minorities are groups that enter into an area voluntarily but seek to maintain their own culture while also integrating into the dominant group. *175*

assimilationist minorities are groups that seek to shed their old ways and integrate themselves into mainstream society. *176*

secessionist minorities are groups that voluntarily separate themselves from the dominant group and view the dominant group with disdain, believing that it will corrupt the group's belief system. *176*

militant minorities are groups that seek to overthrow the existing system because they see it as unjust. *177*

ethnic enclaves are neighbourhoods where people from similar cultures live together and assert cultural distinction from the dominant group. *177*

colour-blind racism is the idea that racism still exists in society in more subtle ways. *178*

double consciousness is the sense that a person must keep a foot in two worlds, one in the majority group's world and one in the minority group's world. *179*

institutional discrimination maintains the advantage for the dominant group, while providing the appearance of fairness to all. *179*

intersectionality is a term used to describe the fact that women experience oppression based on a number of minority statuses. *179*

affirmative action is a social policy designed to help minority groups gain opportunities through employment and education. *181*

Sample Test Questions

These multiple-choice questions are similar to those found in the test bank that accompanies this textbook.

1. Which term describes the process of a minority group trying to integrate itself into mainstream society?
   - **a.** Annexation
   - **b.** Migrant superordination
   - **c.** Assimilation
   - **d.** Conquest
2. Immigrants who learn their new home's language and culture while maintaining their own customs and beliefs are
   - **a.** assimilationist minorities.
   - **b.** secessionist minorities.
   - **c.** pluralistic minorities.
   - **d.** militant minorities.
3. Which term describes a social policy designed to help minority groups gain opportunities through employment and education?
   - **a.** Ethnocentrism
   - **b.** Ethnic segregation
   - **c.** Colour-blind racism
   - **d.** Affirmative action
4. A dominant group
   - **a.** always has the most in number and in power.
   - **b.** always has the least in number and in power.
   - **c.** usually has the most in number and in power.
   - **d.** usually has the least in number and in power.
5. Which term is used to describe the fact that women experience oppression based on a number of minority statuses?
   - **a.** Colour-blind racism
   - **b.** Intersectionality
   - **c.** Code-switching
   - **d.** Double consciousness

ANSWERS: 1. c; 2. c; 3. d; 4. c; 5. b

ESSAY

1. In Canada, who is considered a visible minority? Who is considered an aboriginal?
2. Why does Wilson believe that class-based affirmative action should replace our current race-based system?
3. Why do some people have a sort of "double consciousness"?
4. What is the difference between prejudice and discrimination?
5. What are some ways that Canada is trying to break the cycle of poverty for minority groups?

WHERE TO START YOUR RESEARCH PAPER

For the American Anthropological Association Statement on "Race" (May 17, 1998), go to www.aaanet.org/stmts/racepp.htm.

To see the *Canadian Human Rights Act*, go to http://laws.justice.gc.ca/en/h-6/index.html.

To find information about human rights and discrimination, go to www.chrc-ccdp.ca/eng/content/what-discrimination.

To take the "Know Your Biases" test, go to https://implicit.harvard.edu/implicit.

To learn more about the history of multiculturalism in Canada, watch archived footage, and read speeches and articles, go to http://archives.cbc.ca/society/celebrations/topics/3517/.

To read more about what people are doing to stop genocide in the world today, go to www.genocidewatch.org.

To read about how immigrants get help when settling in Canada, visit the City of Toronto's immigration help site, at www.toronto.ca/immigration/.

To find out ways countries are trying to stop discrimination, go to www.unesco.org/new/en/social-and-human-sciences/themes/human-rights/fight-against-discrimination/.

To find more information on minority groups, go to www.minorityrights.org.

To read about the World Conference against Racism, go to www.un.org/WCAR.

Remember to check www.thethinkspot.ca for additional information, downloadable flashcards, and other helpful resources.

GENDER AND SEXUALITY

Kirill Kedrinski/Fotolia

WHAT IS THE DIFFERENCE BETWEEN SEX AND GENDER?
WHAT ARE THE SOCIOLOGICAL PERSPECTIVES ON GENDER AND GENDER INEQUALITY?
WHAT POLICIES ARE IN PLACE TO PREVENT SEXUAL HARASSMENT AND ABUSE?

"She is not the same woman in each magazine advertisement, but she is the same idea. She has that working-mother look as she strides forward, briefcase in one hand, smiling child in the other. Literally and figuratively, she is moving ahead. Her hair, if long, tosses behind her; if it is short, it sweeps back at the sides, suggesting mobility and progress. There is nothing shy or passive about her. She is confident, active, 'liberated.' She wears a dark tailored suit, but with a silk bow or colorful frill that says, 'I'm really feminine underneath.' She has made it in a man's world without sacrificing her femininity. And she has done this on her own. By some personal miracle, this image suggests, she has managed to combine what 150 years of industrialization have split wide apart—child and job, frill and suit, female culture and male. "When I showed a photograph of a supermom like this to the working mothers I talked to in the course of researching this book, many responded with an outright laugh."[1]

The Social Side of Sex

CHAPTER 10

In their book *The Second Shift: Working Parents and the Revolution at Home*, sociologists Arlie Russell Hochschild and Anne Machung expound on the different expectations men and women have about women's roles in society.

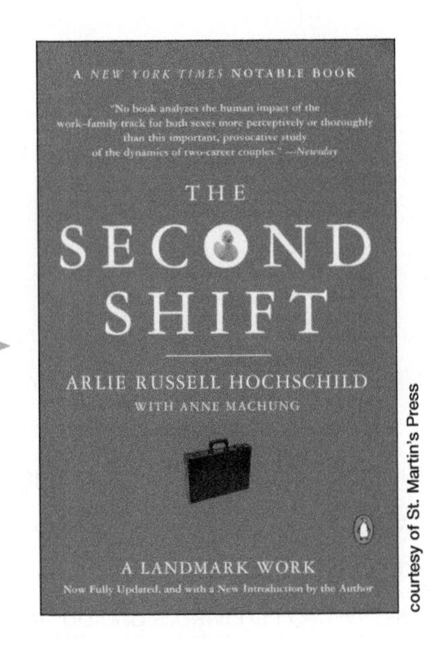

courtesy of St. Martin's Press

Nearly two decades after Dr. John Gray released *Men Are from Mars, Women Are from Venus*, it is still essential reading for anyone trying to figure out why his or her significant other is so annoying. The idea that the differences between men and women are so profound that we come from different planets may be a little extreme, but significant differences do exist between the sexes.

In *The Second Shift*, Hochschild and Machung contend that the women's liberation movement has actually created additional burdens for women.[2] The movement opened up the world of work but kept women in the world of domestic service. The image of the perfect woman involves brains, beauty, and toughness. However, as *The Second Shift* demonstrates, this image raises many problems for women. Even though women have excelled in the workforce and contributed mightily to the economy, society still expects them to fill the traditional role of mother.

In Canada, only around 8 percent of men spend 30 hours or more on housework per week, whereas up to 20 percent of women clock those hours.[3] Even in households in which the wife works full time, Hochschild shows how she is often expected to be a "supermom" when she comes home. Who created these ideas of men and women?

is

the social, cultural, and psychological traits and behaviours connected with being masculine or feminine

and gives us

Gender identity: our perception of ourselves as male or female
Gender roles: society's expectations of how males and females should think and act
- **Instrumental role:** focused on working to provide for the family in a financial way
- **Expressive role:** focused on the socialization of children and meeting the family's emotional needs

Sexism: the belief that one sex is superior to the other
Homophobia: a negative attitude toward homosexuals and homosexuality

Stratification based on sex, gender, and sexuality can lead to

get the topic: WHAT IS THE DIFFERENCE BETWEEN SEX AND GENDER?

Sex vs. Gender

Sex refers to the biological characteristics that distinguish males and females. The focus is on anatomical differences, in particular those related to reproduction, as well as differences in hormones, chromosomes, and other physiological components. We generally categorize people into one of these two groups. However, although it is rare, some people are **intersexed**, which means that their bodies have both male and female characteristics. For example, they might have both female ovaries and male testis. This is different from the term **transsexual**, which refers to people who are born as one identifiable sex and have undergone surgical modifications and hormonal interventions to become the other sex.[4]

Gender is defined as the social, cultural, and psychological traits and behaviours connected with being masculine or feminine. Gender is socially defined. For instance, in Canadian society, at formal events, wearing a fancy dress is associated with being feminine, while wearing a suit or a tuxedo is associated with masculinity. The biological differences between men and women do correlate with some behavioural differences. For example, boys may be more naturally aggressive, and girls more innately verbal. Such simple correlations support the notion that ideas about gender are based on sex.[5] However, sociologists suggest that socialization, rather than biology, is the main determinant of gender.

GENDER CONSTRUCTION

In early 2011, a baby named Storm was born in Toronto. Usually, when a baby is born, people ask "is it a boy or a girl?" In this case, the parents decided not to divulge the baby's sex because they wanted to allow the baby to develop as long as he or she could without the constraints of gender stereotypes.[6] Yet gender, like all our other social identities, is something that we learn.

SEX refers to the biological characteristics that distinguish males and females.

INTERSEXED refers to a person whose body has both male and female characteristics.

TRANSSEXUAL refers to people who born as one identifiable sex and have undergone surgical modifications and hormonal interventions to become the other sex.

GENDER is defined as the social, cultural, and psychological traits and behaviours connected with being masculine or feminine.

GENDER IDENTITY is our perception of ourselves as masculine or feminine.

TRANSGENDER individuals have a biological sex but possess a gender identity other than that typically assigned to their sex.

Sociologists Candace West and Don H. Zimmerman suggest that gender is developed in two ways: Not only do we "do gender" or participate in its construction, but we also have gender done to us as members of society.[7] Childhood is the prime time for development of **gender identity**, or our perception of ourselves as masculine or feminine. During our childhood, we learn what behaviour is "appropriate" for each gender and how to fit in with others like us. **Transgender** individuals have a biological sex but possess a gender identity other than that typically assigned to their sex.[8]

Gender is not only a set of traits or roles; it is a product of society.

To find out how children display or learn their gender, sociologist Michael Messner examined the interactions between two soccer teams—the all-boy Sea Monsters and the all-girl Barbie Girls.[9] Before a season-opening ceremony began, the Barbie Girls rallied together

and differs from

Sex: the biological characteristics distinguishing males and females
Intersexed: a person whose body has both male and female characteristics
Transsexual: people who feel like they are one sex even though biologically they are identified as the other

Sexuality is a particular kind of social interaction in which we express ourselves as sexual beings

Sexual orientation: is a reflection of a person's preference for sexual partners

- **Heterosexual:** describes people who are sexually attracted to people of the opposite sex
- **Homosexual:** describes people who are sexually attracted to people of the same sex
- **Bisexual:** describes people who are sexually attracted to people of either sex
- **Asexual:** describes people who are not sexually attracted to people of either sex

around a miniature Barbie float decorated with their team colours. A boom box on the float played music, and the girls gathered together to sing and dance. At first the little boys watched in confused awe but soon took up a chant of "No Barbie!" When this chant failed to get the girls' attention, the little boys invaded their space, and a game of chase ensued. The parents observed this behaviour from the sidelines and remarked that little boys and little girls are like members of two different species.

Messner argues that the parents easily recognized the differences but failed to recognize the similarities between the girls' and boys' teams during the rest of the season. Players on both teams regularly displayed many of the same behaviours—crying over skinned knees, racing to get snacks after the game, paying attention to birds or airplanes rather than to the coach—that would indicate a lack of major gender differences. Parents have no problem pointing out the differences between the boys and girls but have difficulty identifying similarities due to "an institutional context that is characterized by informally structured sex segregation among the parent coaches and team managers, and by formally structured sex segregation among the children."[10] In other words, the adults couldn't see the similarities because they were socialized to see boys and girls as different.

>>> During our childhood, society shapes our gender identity. **What social cues might this young girl have picked up from the world around her?**

Pegbes/Fotolia

SEXUALITY refers to a particular kind of social interaction in which we express ourselves as sexual beings.

INCEST TABOO is a cultural universal which prohibits sex between closely related individuals.

SEXUAL ORIENTATION is a reflection of a person's preference for sexual partners.

HETEROSEXUAL describes people who are sexually attracted to people of the opposite sex

HOMOSEXUAL describes people who are sexually attracted to people of the same sex.

BISEXUAL describes people who are sexually attracted to people of either sex.

ASEXUAL describes people who are not sexually attracted to people of either sex.

SEXISM is the belief that one sex is superior to the other.

Sexuality

You have seen that sex refers to biological differences and gender refers to socially defined behaviours. **Sexuality** refers to a particular kind of social interaction in which we express ourselves as sexual beings. It encompasses both the biological and the social. There is little doubt that most people have a biological sex drive; however, how this is expressed and how it is perceived by society has as much variation as culturally acceptable forms of dress or any other cultural norm. And like all other cultural norms, the social perception of sexuality changes over time and across cultures. In fact, sociological research has found that there is incredible diversity in human sexuality.

However, one cultural universal that has been observed regarding sexuality is the **incest taboo**, which appears in some form in every society and which prohibits sex between closely related individuals.[11] Under Canadian law we are barred from having sexual intercourse with certain relatives, such as parents, grandparents, and siblings (including half-brothers and half-sisters).[12]

SEXUAL ORIENTATION

Sexual orientation is a reflection of a person's preference for sexual partners. Like gender identity, it tends to be associated with biological sex, although there is much evidence that it is not. Like all other aspects of sexuality, there is much variation in how people express and experience sexual pleasure. **Heterosexual** describes people who are sexually attracted to people of the opposite sex, while **homosexual** describes people who are sexually attracted to people of the same sex. **Bisexual** describes people who are sexually attracted to people of either sex. Finally, **asexual** describes people who are not sexually attracted to people of either sex.

Patriarchy and Sexism

You learned in Chapter 1 that patriarchy is a social system that benefits men. The patriarchal system also often results in **sexism**, or the belief that one sex is superior to the other. In many societies, attitudes often suggest women are the "weaker sex." This belief system may be adopted by women who seek jobs that fulfill these views. A few years ago, a very bright female student told me she wanted to be a medical doctor. I asked, "What's your major?"

THINK SOCIOLOGICALLY

Sexual Behaviour in the Human Male

In 1948, Alfred Kinsey and his colleagues conducted landmark studies of sexual behavior among Americans. The first report was *Sexual Behaviour in the Human Male*,[13] published in 1948, followed in 1953 by *Sexual Behaviour in the Human Female*. Both these reports aroused surprise and even shock at the time they were published, but they also shed light on a previously little-studied topic of human behavior. The following passages are from the first report, and they give an interesting discussion of sexual orientation:

> Concerning patterns of sexual behavior, a great deal of the thinking done by scientists and laymen alike stems from the assumption that there are persons who are "heterosexual" and persons who are "homosexual," that these two types represent antitheses in the sexual world, and that there is only an insignificant class of "bisexuals" who occupy an intermediate position between the other groups. It is implied that every individual is innately—inherently—either heterosexual or homosexual. It is further implied that from the time of birth one is fated to be one thing or the other, and that there is little chance for one to change his pattern in the course of a lifetime . . .
>
> It is quite generally believed that one's preference for a sexual partner of one or the other sex is correlated with various physical and mental qualities, and with the total personality which makes a homosexual male or female physically, psychically, and perhaps spiritually distinct from a heterosexual individual. It is generally thought that these qualities make a homosexual person obvious and recognizable to any one who has a sufficient understanding of such matters. Even psychiatrists discuss "the homosexual personality" and many of them believe that preferences for sexual partners of a particular sex are merely secondary manifestations of something that lies much deeper in the totality of that intangible which they call the personality. . . . The characterizations are so distinct they seem to leave little room for doubt that homosexual and heterosexual represent two very distinct types of males . . .
>
> Since only 50 per cent of the population is exclusively heterosexual throughout its adult life, and since only 4 percent of the population is exclusively homosexual throughout its life, it appears that nearly half (46%) of the population engages in both heterosexual and homosexual activities, or reacts to persons of both sexes, in the course of their adult lives. If homosexual activity persists on as large a scale as it does, in the face of the very considerable public sentiment against it and in spite of the severity of the penalties that our Anglo-American culture has placed upon it through the centuries, there seems some reason for believing that such activity would appear in the histories of a much larger portion of the population.

Source: Alfred C. Kinsey, Wardell R. Pomeroy, and Clyde E. Martin, *Sexual Behavior in the Human Male* Bloomington, IN: Indiana University Press.

"Nursing" was the reply. She explained that her father, fiancé, and religious belief all dictated that women shouldn't be doctors. These patriarchal beliefs possibly prevented a great mind from becoming a great doctor.

At many different times and in many different places, sexual relationships between people of the same sex have been the cause of discrimination, both in law and according to social norms. Such discrimination is often the result of **homophobia**, a negative attitude toward homosexuals and homosexuality. In Canada, homosexual acts were considered a crime punishable by imprisonment until 1969. In 1985, the *Canadian Human Rights Act* banned discrimination based on sexual orientation, including the unequal treatment of gay men, lesbians, and bisexuals.[14]

HOMOPHOBIA is a negative attitude toward homosexuals and homosexuality.

GENDER ROLES are society's expectations of how males and females should think and act.

Gender Roles

Television's female characters have come a long way since Wilma Flintstone and June Cleaver, for whom kissing their husbands goodbye and seeing the kids off to school started off a day of cleaning, baking, and homemaking. Today, we're used to seeing women portrayed as surgeons and attorneys and men actively participating in raising their children. What makes these arrangements acceptable to us now? The prevailing culture and the socialization that parents provide to their children shape ideas about gender-appropriate behaviours.

While women are succeeding in traditionally masculine fields like medicine and business, most of our children are still socialized to fit specific **gender roles**, or society's expectations of how males and females should act and think. Children's toys are an example of socialization at a young age. Manhattan Toy makes a line of dolls called Groovy Girls, which allows girls to "celebrate their own unique personalities," with various fashion options for the dolls.[15] The Hasbro Company's Nerf toys—geared toward more aggressive play, like football and mock war situations—continue to be popular among young boys.[16]

However, gender roles in North America are in a constant state of flux. This is not to say that we now encourage males to possess feminine characteristics or vice versa, but the differences between the sexes are less pronounced than they once were. Young girls race down soccer fields or shoot hoops after school, and they're just as likely to wear jeans and T-shirts as skirts. The traditional roles of man as provider and woman as homemaker are shifting as well, since many households today have two breadwinners.

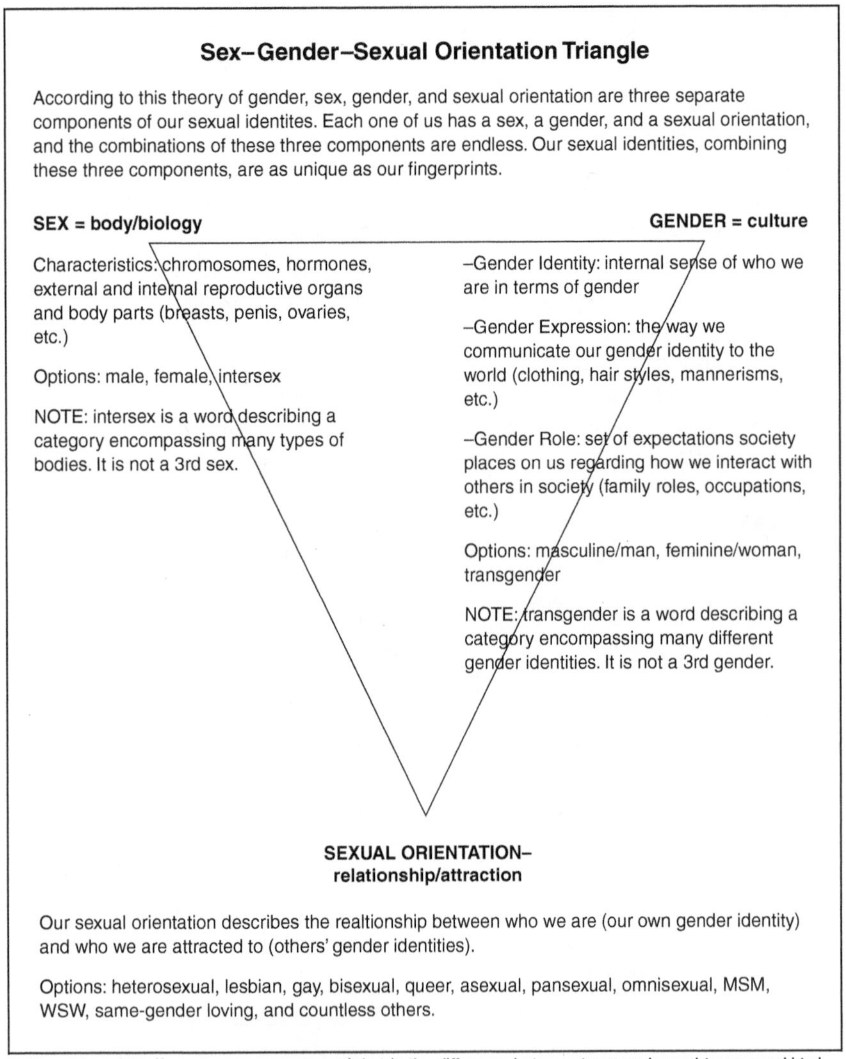

Sex–Gender–Sexual Orientation Triangle

According to this theory of gender, sex, gender, and sexual orientation are three separate components of our sexual identites. Each one of us has a sex, a gender, and a sexual orientation, and the combinations of these three components are endless. Our sexual identities, combining these three components, are as unique as our fingerprints.

SEX = body/biology

Characteristics: chromosomes, hormones, external and internal reproductive organs and body parts (breasts, penis, ovaries, etc.)

Options: male, female, intersex

NOTE: intersex is a word describing a category encompassing many types of bodies. It is not a 3rd sex.

GENDER = culture

–Gender Identity: internal sense of who we are in terms of gender

–Gender Expression: the way we communicate our gender identity to the world (clothing, hair styles, mannerisms, etc.)

–Gender Role: set of expectations society places on us regarding how we interact with others in society (family roles, occupations, etc.)

Options: masculine/man, feminine/woman, transgender

NOTE: transgender is a word describing a category encompassing many different gender identities. It is not a 3rd gender.

SEXUAL ORIENTATION–relationship/attraction

Our sexual orientation describes the realtionship between who we are (our own gender identity) and who we are attracted to (others' gender identities).

Options: heterosexual, lesbian, gay, bisexual, queer, asexual, pansexual, omnisexual, MSM, WSW, same-gender loving, and countless others.

Retrieved from http://www.transawareness.org/what-is-the-difference-between-transgender-and-transsexual.html. Reprinted by permission of Owen Marciano.

<<< **The** sex–gender–sexual orientation triangle **is helpful in understanding the distinctions and the links between these three aspects of human sexuality.**

THE FLUIDITY OF GENDER ROLES: INDONESIA'S BUGIS PEOPLE

Some cultures, like the Bugis people living on the Indonesian island of Sulawesi, have a unique view of sex and gender roles. Australian anthropologist Sharyn Davies studied the Bugis people and found that gender-specific pronouns like "he" and "she" don't exist in their language.[17] Gender stratification among the Bugis is complicated, with five different gender classifications: *oroané* (masculine male), *makkunrai* (feminine female), *calalai* (masculine female), *calabai* (feminine male), and *bissu* (embodying both male and female energies, revered as a shaman).[18] Each gender has specific behaviours, articles of clothing, social and religious roles, and sexual practices. The oroané and makkunrai genders are comparable to what we know; the calalai, calabai, and bissu are what we might call "gender benders."

The calalai are anatomical females who assume the characteristics of men. They hold masculine jobs and dress as men, practise homosexuality, and typically live with female partners to adopt children.

The calabai are anatomical males who adhere to some of the responsibilities of women. Calabai males are homosexual and dress as women, yet they don't follow all cultural suggestions for women. They do, however, take on traditionally female responsibilities, like planning weddings.

The bissu embody the perfect mixture of male and female. A bissu that is externally male is considered to be internally female, and vice versa if the bissu is female. The Bugis people believe that bissu embody the best characteristics of both sexes, so they are able to communicate with the spirits and therefore occupy a special place in the community.

The Bugis have ideas about gender that are different from our own but seem to be more accepting of different kinds of people. Men and women are allowed to live the gender role that suits them best in Bugis society.

Gender and Inequality

In many societies, the idea of gender is not as fluid as the Bugis people suggest, and a hierarchy of sorts exists between the sexes. In Canada, for example, men and women are ranked differently in terms of power and wealth. In 2010, the average total earnings for women was $31 700, and for men $46 500.[19] Because women are more likely to earn less than men, they're also more likely to live below the poverty line. Why is there such inequality between income levels and poverty status of men and women? We'll look into this further in the section relating to work. But first, let's look at a topic that should be relevant to everyone reading this book—gender and education.

GENDER AND THE WORKPLACE

These days, women make up almost half of Canada's paid labour force,[20] and two-thirds of Canadian families depend on two incomes.[21] While it's now accepted and necessary for women to work, the types of jobs as well as the compensation for these jobs remain different for men and women. Three theoretical models—the human capital model, the choice model, and the patriarchy model—attempt to explain these discrepancies.

The human capital model assumes that men and women bring different natural skills to the workplace. For example, society perceives men to have more mechanical skills and thus make better engineers. Because society considers women to be more nurturing, they are assumed to be better teachers. Under such beliefs, it is not discrimination to hire men to do jobs for which they are more suited. This explains why men seem to have advantages in higher-income professions, such as medicine, engineering, and law.[22]

The choice model explains the income gap by analyzing the kinds of jobs women choose. Many women choose to major in social work or elementary education, therefore knowingly entering fields that traditionally pay less. This argument suggests that if you choose a career that you know pays very little, you have only yourself to blame.[23]

››› GO GLOBAL

Masculine vs. Feminine Cultures

Is it possible to compare national values? This was the question posed by Geert Hofstede while he was head of the Personnel Research Department for IBM International. Between 1967 and 1973, the department collected 117 000 attitude and value surveys from IBM employees in 72 countries. After leaving IBM in 1971, Hofstede obtained permission to analyze the IBM data and, as a result, he developed the cultural dimensions theory.

In the original theory, Hofstede identified four empirical dimensions of national cultures:

1. *Power distance*, the extent to which the less powerful members of institutions and organizations within a country expect and accept that power is distributed unequally
2. *Individualism*, the extent to which the ties between individuals in a society are loose, so that everyone is expected to look after himself or herself and his or her immediate family only
3. *Masculinity*, the extent to which social gender roles in a society are clearly distinct
4. *Uncertainty avoidance*, the extent to which members of a culture feel threatened by unknown or uncertain situations[24]

For the masculinity dimension, a high score indicates that the society is driven by competition, achievement, and success. This value system starts in school and continues throughout one's working life and even in leisure pursuits.

A low score means that the dominant values in society are caring for others and quality of life. A feminine society is one where quality of life is the sign of success and standing out from the crowd is not admirable.

The fundamental issue here is what motivates people: wanting to be the best (masculine) or liking what you do (feminine).

The following are some of the common traits found in countries that score low on the masculinity scale:

- In life the main priorities are the family, relationships, and quality of life.
- Conflicts should ideally be solved through negotiation.
- Men and women should share equal positions in society.
- Professionals "work to live," meaning longer vacations and flexible working hours.

The following are some of the common traits found in countries that score high on the masculinity scale:

- Life's priorities are achievement, wealth, and expansion.
- It is acceptable to settle conflicts through aggressive means.
- Women and men have different roles in society.
- Professionals often "live to work," meaning longer work hours and short vacations.[25]

From Hofstede's research, Japan was found to be the world's most masculine society, with a rating of 95. Sweden was the most feminine, with a rating of 5. Canada scored 52 and can be characterized as a moderately "masculine" society. While Canadians value high standards of performance in both work and play, the overall cultural tone is more subdued with respect to achievement, success, and winning when compared to the United States. Canadians also tend to have a better work–life balance and are more likely to take time to enjoy personal pursuits, family gatherings, and life in general.[26]

picturelibrary/Alamy

GLASS CEILING is an invisible barrier preventing women from reaching executive-level positions in the workplace.

The patriarchy model assumes that we have a male-dominated society that doesn't allow women to hold upper-tier jobs or steers them away from such careers early in life. For example, when discussing majors with an academic adviser, students may experience stereotypical gender role expectations. Male students may be asked to consider business or engineering. Female students may be asked about education or communication fields as possible professions.

The patriarchy model also supports the idea of a **glass ceiling**, or an invisible barrier that prevents women from reaching the executive suite. For example, relatively few women become the CEOs of large companies. Women lead only 19 of the top 500 companies in Canada.[27] Sociology professor Shelley J. Correll studied labour distribution by

<<< **In most societies, choosing a feminine style of dress will make a man stand out in a crowd.** Why is it less conspicuous for calabai males to dress in a feminine style?

THINK SOCIOLOGICALLY

Culture's Effect on Gender Roles

Anthropologist Margaret Mead conducted a study of gender roles among three tribes in New Guinea: the Arapesh, the Mundgumor, and the Tchambuli.[28] She concluded that gender roles are largely dependent on culture. The men and women of the Arapesh tribe would both be considered "feminine" by our standards. The Mundgumor men and women were aggressive and violent, possessing "masculine" qualities. However, among the Tchambuli people, men stayed home and raised the children, and women provided for the household.[29] This study drew much criticism; many accused Mead of doctoring her results to show what she had hoped to find.[30] Nevertheless, this study showed that gender is culturally constructed.

Other studies of gender roles have found that, in most societies, traditional gender roles have degrees of variation for any individual task. Anthropologist George Murdock's 1937 study of more than 200 societies found that women performed farming tasks and construction of homes in almost as many societies as men. Although not every society is uniform, Murdock's findings showed definite cross-cultural similarities in the roles of men and women.[31]

Changes in gender roles have left working women with children in a tough position. In *The Second Shift*, Hochschild found that although gender roles in the working world may have changed, working women are still largely responsible for maintaining the home.[32]

INSTRUMENTAL ROLE is focused on working to provide for the family in a financial way.

EXPRESSIVE ROLE is focused on the socialization of children and meeting the family's emotional needs.

sex and found that cultural beliefs about gender shape both male and female attitudes about their abilities.[33] If this is the case, our ideas about gender may need to undergo a radical change before the income gap between men and women disappears.

GENDER AND THE FAMILY

The family is the primary site of gender socialization. Parents, siblings, and other relatives teach you about gender. Everything from the clothes you wear to the toys you play with to the chores you are expected to do teach you what is expected of females and males. Within families, roles are often divided between the sexes. Talcott Parsons and Robert Bales identified two distinct roles: instrumental and expressive roles.[34] In the traditional family form, men play an **instrumental role**, which is focused on achieving success at work and then enables them to provide for their family in a financial way. On the other hand, women have an **expressive role**, which is focused on the socialization of children and meeting the family's emotional needs. Parsons and Bales state that this division of labour is based on biology; for example, women are more naturally suited to the nurturing role.

GENDER AND POLITICS

Women are making huge political strides. Yet in 2010, Canada ranked 51st and the United States 73rd in terms of representation of women in national parliaments around the world.[35] In Canada, the lone woman who has served as prime minister did so for only a few months—Kim Campbell, in 1993. Women regularly hold high political office in other parts of the world. England has had several women in power, beginning in 1553 with Queen Mary I. Margaret Thatcher was prime minister from 1979 to 1990. Golda Meir was prime minister of Israel from 1969 to 1973, and Benazir Bhutto was prime minister of Pakistan from 1988 to 1990 and 1993 to 1996.[36] No woman has yet served as president of the United States, although Hillary Rodham Clinton received strong support in her bid for the 2008 Democratic presidential nomination.[37] Let's examine three theories that attempt to explain why women in North America are still not on an equal footing with men when it comes to the top political positions.

Theory #1: Women, by nature, are uninterested in politics. This theory has been disproved time and again by data that show that women vote more regularly than men.[38] Women have also risen to political prominence, including the three

Charly Franklin/Taxi/Getty Images

<<< **Women in the workplace often have to work twice as hard as men** to break through the glass ceiling above them.

MAKE CONNECTIONS

Men Are a Gender, Too

It's important to remember that men are a gender, too. As noted earlier, men have many advantages in North American society. Christine Williams discusses how men have a "glass elevator" when it comes to getting jobs in traditionally female-dominated occupations. Men who sought jobs in the nursing, library, and elementary education fields said they felt they had an advantage over women applying for the same job because there were fewer men in those fields.[39]

However, it's important to know that with the male gender role come gender expectations. Recently, the son of a friend was going off to college. The boy complained when his parents refused to buy him a new car. His sister got a new car when she went to college, but my friend explained, "He's a boy. It's good for him to learn how to fix a junker car."

>>> **ACTIVITY** Write out as many household tasks as you can think of, and place an M next to those done primarily by men and a W next to those done primarily by women. Do you see any gender bias in your life?

women who have been appointed governor-general in Canada: Jeanne Sauvé (1984–1990), Adrienne Clarkson (1999–2005), and Michaëlle Jean (2005–2010).[40]

Theory #2: The structure of women's lives does not lend itself to the rigours of political office. I like to call this theory the "baby bias." Similar to Hochschild's "supermom" responsibilities, the theory assumes that a woman in office would be too overwhelmed by her mothering duties to succeed in office. When Pat Carney announced in 2007 that she was resigning from her Canadian Senate seat—after more than a quarter century in Parliament—she was called "an example of how cultural and societal limitations on women were broken down, often through compelling competence, sheer acts of courage and personal will of the kind her career will always symbolize."[41] Carney played a "demanding role" in *Canada–U.S. Free Trade Agreement* negotiations and in 1991 voted against her own party to help defeat a bill that would have criminalized abortion.[42] She is also the mother of two children.[43]

Theory #3: Society forces women into a politically passive role. Traditionally, this has been the case. But women are more independent today and have an increased interest in holding political office. Furthermore, politicians tend to often be lawyers and business people, traditionally "men's" worlds. Although this is changing, female representation in politics remains disproportionately low.

VOTER TURNOUT BY GENDER IN 2011 FEDERAL ELECTION

Source: Numbers adapted from Elections Canada, "Estimation of Voter Turnout by Age Group at the 2011 Federal General Election," www.elections.ca/content.aspx?section=res&dir=rec/part/estim&document=index&lang=ee, accessed June 3, 2013.

think sociologically: WHAT ARE THE SOCIOLOGICAL PERSPECTIVES ON GENDER AND GENDER INEQUALITY?

Feminist Theory

Feminists study how gender affects the experiences and opportunities of men and women. Although feminists may not always agree about how to achieve gender equality, they do tend to adopt four general beliefs:

1 **Increasing equality in work and education.** Year after year, women are earning more professional degrees than men and entering the workforce in large numbers. However, feminists continue fighting for equality in both the workplace and schools against the gender wage gap and the glass ceiling that women commonly face in the workplace.

2 **Expanding human choice for outcomes.** In the book *Woman Hating*, feminist Andrea Dworkin comments that "Being female in this world is having been robbed of the potential for human choice by men who love to hate us."[44] Not all feminists agree with Dworkin's suggestion, but virtually all feminists work to create a society in which men and women have equal opportunities. For example, by expanding enrollment in professional and graduate schools, women have greater opportunities to choose careers they enjoy.

3 **Eliminating gender stratification.** Feminism commits itself to ensuring equal rights, equal opportunity, and equal pay for women. For example, about 15 percent of Canadian Forces personnel are women.[45]

4 **Ending sexual violence.** Feminist theorists believe that male violence against women perpetuates gender inequality in our society.[46] For example, the "rule of thumb" refers to the alleged British common law that allowed a man to beat his wife with a stick, as long as it was not any larger than the diameter of his thumb. It's important to note that this was never an actual law; however, men were allowed to punish their wives corporally.[47]

Functionalism

While feminists fight gender inequality in Canada, functionalists examine how the separation of gender roles actually functions in a society. Society places men and women in different spheres, and these differences help maintain society. Because men and women often play different roles, competition is eliminated between the sexes, and family life runs smoothly.[48] For example, if men are expected to go out and work to provide for the family, while women are expected to perform domestic tasks and care for the children, their roles are complementary to each other. Each is doing a job that must be done. As women steadily enter the workforce, the separation of gender roles becomes less distinct. Even so, women are generally expected to maintain the home.

Talcott Parsons studied the separation of gender roles in the context of the family. Parsons noted that for children, "sex discrimination is more than anything else a reflection of the differentiation of adult sex roles."[49] Girls at a young age are socialized to display expressive qualities, such as calmness and nurturing (qualities expected of many adult women), while boys are prone to be rational and competitive, which are instrumental qualities.[50]

According to Parsons, young girls are able to step into the adult feminine role early in their development.[51] These girls see their mothers performing domestic tasks and are often expected to help out. Young boys, however, have fathers who work outside the house. As a result, boys are trained to prepare for their futures in the workforce.

Conflict Theory

Conflict theorists argue that capitalism and patriarchy are deeply intertwined. In a capitalist society, women generally are at the bottom of the system, regardless of their job. Furthermore, they often engage in unpaid,

Trinette Reed/CORBIS

<<< Notice the difference in dress between these male and female cheerleaders. **Conflict theorists would argue that cheerleading is just one way that men exploit women in our society.**

domestic tasks that serve to maintain the status quo.[52] However, men devalue the work that women do, which reinforces the power that men have over women.[53]

Women in the workforce work tend to make less money than men in the workforce, so women are often subordinate to their better-paid husbands. Women are generally locked in a never-ending cycle that makes them submissive and subservient to men.

Friedrich Engels, a contemporary of Karl Marx, suggested that women are the first oppressed group in society.[54] Although he agreed with Marx that the proletariat are oppressed, Engels pointed out that women, too, are exploited. This may not seem to be a major idea in today's world, but in 1884, it was staggering.

Symbolic Interactionism

Symbolic interactionists believe that people's definition of gender develops from everyday interactions with others from the same and the opposite sex.[55] Sociologists West and Zimmerman's idea of "doing gender" best illustrates the symbolic interactionists' point of view.[56] We all "do gender" every day, which means we act in a certain way that is associated with a particular gender. The way you style your hair, the mannerisms you have, and the way you talk are all part of the way you communicate your gender to others.

Sociologist Janet Chafetz argues that "doing gender" not only "(re) produces gender difference, it (re)produces gender inequality."[57] One way this happens is through conversation. Deborah Tannen's *You Just Don't Understand: Men and Women in Conversation* argues that our lives are essentially a series of conversations, and we pass on "different, asymmetrical assumptions about men and women" in these conversations.[58]

Chafetz would argue that men and women communicate differently. Men often dominate conversations, and women struggle to follow the sometimes arbitrary rules that men impose on the dialogue. Women use "verbal and body language in ways that weaken their ability to assert themselves," which makes them appear less powerful than their male counterparts.[59] For example, while eating out one day, I noticed a men's softball team and a few of their wives/girlfriends at a nearby table. The guys were talking and laughing, but the women were passive. Gender socialization generally teaches boys to make their voice heard, while girls are taught to be "good," meaning quiet and docile.

Men and women often follow scripted behaviour, acting in ways that are associated with their gender.[60] For example, men and women use different types of language and gesture. Men tend to be more direct than women in describing their wants and desires.[61]

>>> Think about your conversations with people of the opposite sex. What patterns do you notice? **Do men and women really communicate differently?**

contrastwerkstatt/Fotolia

WRAP YOUR MIND AROUND THE THEORY

FrÃ©dÃ©ric Prochasson/Fotolia

How might these boys define masculinity in tomorrow's society? What gender roles will they have?

FUNCTIONALISM

The functionalists view society as a system of many parts, working in concert with one another to form a whole. Talcott Parsons believed that gender differences are essential in maintaining a properly functioning society. Parents socialize boys and girls for their future roles of father and mother. Boys are taught to be confident, rational, and competitive because these characteristics are instrumental qualities for men to succeed. Parents socialize girls with the primary goal of preparing them to raise children. They learn nurturing qualities that Parsons refers to as expressive qualities. These complementary roles assist in the smooth functioning of society.

CONFLICT THEORY

In the case of gender, conflict theorists see that capitalism and patriarchy are deeply intertwined. In a capitalist society, women generally are at the bottom of the system, regardless of their job. Friedrich Engels suggested that women are the first oppressed group in society. Men devalue the work that women do, which reinforces the power that men have over women. Women who work tend to make less money than men in the workforce, so women are often subordinate to their better-paid husbands. Women are generally locked in a never-ending cycle that makes them submissive and subservient to men.

WHY DOES GENDER STRATIFICATION EXIST?

SYMBOLIC INTERACTIONISM

Symbolic interactionists believe that people's definition of gender develops from everyday interactions with others from the same and the opposite sex. We all "do gender" every day, which means we act in a certain way that is associated with a particular gender. The way you style your hair, the mannerisms you have, and the way you talk are all part of the way you communicate your gender to others. Janet Chafetz suggests that men and women communicate differently. Men often dominate conversations, and women struggle to follow the sometimes arbitrary rules that men impose on the dialogue. Women use "verbal and body language in ways that weaken their ability to assert themselves," [62] which makes them appear less powerful than their male counterparts.

FEMINIST THEORY

Feminists study how gender affects the experiences and opportunities of men and women. They tend to adopt four general beliefs about gender stratification. The first is that there should be more equality in work and education. The second is that there should be greater opportunities for choices, such as in choosing a career. The third is a commitment to eliminating gender stratification. Finally, feminist theorists believe that male violence against women perpetuates gender inequality in our society and is unacceptable.

Why might capitalism give men and women **reason to fight?**

Ljupco Smokovski /Shutterstock

What are the **pros and cons of selecting a career** that falls **outside the traditional roles** for your gender?

Darrin Klimek/Riser/Getty Images

discover sociology in action: WHAT POLICIES ARE IN PLACE TO PREVENT SEXUAL HARASSMENT AND ABUSE?

Physical, sexual, emotional, economic, and psychological abuse are all forms of oppression. In Canada, the General Social Survey 2009 (GSS) found that a large number of crimes go unreported: Only 69 percent of violent victimizations (sexual assault, robbery, physical assault) are reported to police.[63] The most common reasons for not reporting sexual assaults were believing the incident was not important enough (68 percent), not believing the police could help (59 percent), feeling the incident should be dealt with in an alternative way (42 percent), and feeling the incident was personal (34 percent).[64] It has been noted that because such victims begin to internalize their emotions, the women involved either believe they deserved the assault or believe that no one can help them.[65]

Resources are available to help the victims, but victims are often too scared or ashamed to come forward. In Canada, revisions to the *Criminal Code* have lengthened minimum sentences for certain sexual assault offences.[66] Canada also has a National Sex Offender Registry that is "a national registration system for sex offenders who have been convicted of designated sex offences and ordered by the courts to report annually to police."[67] A Public Safety Canada announcement in 2010 said that the federal government "is committed to strengthening the National Sex Offender Registry and the National DNA Data Bank so that they better protect Canadians from sexual offenders. Proposed changes will also enable police to prevent and investigate crimes of a sexual nature more effectively."[68]

ACTIVITIES

1. Research your province's sex offender laws. What is the suggested penalty for first-time rape offenders? Are sex offenders required to register and inform the neighbourhood in which they reside of their status?
2. Locate a battered women's shelter in your area. How is the shelter funded? What services does the shelter provide?

Social Policy—Stopping Sexual Harassment and Abuse

Sexual harassment and abuse are persistent issues, as stories of office harassment, domestic violence, and rape are commonplace items in the news. In one of Canada's biggest recent sex murder stories, the country learned in 2010 that one of the two victims of Russell Williams, a colonel in the Armed Forces at the time, was a woman corporal who had been under his charge at CFB Trenton in Ontario. Williams was sentenced to two life terms in jail.[69]

The 2006 General Social Survey found that approximately 34 percent of women and 15 percent of men claim they were victims of sexual assault, and 51 percent of those assaults were done by a friend, acquaintance, or neighbour.[70]

Measures to help women victims include the creation of shelters for battered women, which give victims a place to stay to recuperate from domestic violence, and counselling services that help battered women with self-esteem issues and other psychological trauma brought on by abuse. It is important to help men, women, and families suffering from abuse because damages extend far beyond bruises. Abuse harms people on three levels: physical, financial, and emotional.[71]

CHAPTER 10

WHAT IS THE DIFFERENCE BETWEEN SEX AND GENDER? 187

sex: the biological makeup of a male or female
gender: the personal traits and position in society connected with being a male or female

WHAT ARE THE SOCIOLOGICAL PERSPECTIVES ON GENDER AND GENDER INEQUALITY? 194

feminist theory: feminists share the belief that equality in work and education should increase, human choice for outcomes should be expanded, gender stratification should be eliminated, and sexual violence should end
functionalism: the separation of gender roles eliminates competition between the sexes and makes family life run smoothly
conflict theory: capitalism and patriarchy are intertwined; as a result, women are locked in a never-ending cycle that makes them submissive and subservient to men
symbolic interactionism: people's definition of gender develops from everyday interactions with others from the same and opposite sex

WHAT POLICIES ARE IN PLACE TO PREVENT SEXUAL HARASSMENT AND ABUSE? 197

campaigns against sexual assault and domestic violence, shelters, and counselling services

get the topic: WHAT IS THE DIFFERENCE BETWEEN SEX AND GENDER?

Theories

FEMINIST THEORY 194

- gender affects the experiences and opportunities of men and women
- there should be increasing equality in work and education
- there should be expanding human choice for outcomes
- feminists are committed to eliminating gender stratification
- male violence against women perpetuates gender inequality in our society and is unacceptable

FUNCTIONALISM 194

- gender differences help maintain a functioning society
- parents socialize boys and girls to their future roles of fathers and mothers
- boys are taught to be competitive and confident; girls are taught to be nurturing and caring

CONFLICT THEORY 194

- gender roles are beneficial to men, as their role as main breadwinner gives them power and control
- capitalism emphasizes male domination, as women are encouraged to spend money on goods
- Engels: women are the first oppressed group

SYMBOLIC INTERACTIONISM 195

- people's definition of gender develops from everyday interactions with others from the same and opposite sex
- people "do gender" every day
- Janet Chafetz suggests that men and women communicate differently
- Men often dominate conversations, while women use verbal and body language that makes them appear less powerful than their male counterparts

Key Terms

sex refers to the biological characteristics that distinguish males and females. *187*

intersexed refers to a person whose body has both male and female characteristics. *187*

transsexual refers to people who born as one identifiable sex and have undergone surgical modifications and hormonal interventions to become the other sex. *187*

gender is defined as the social, cultural, and psychological traits and behaviours connected with being masculine or feminine. *187*

gender identity is our perception of ourselves as male or female. *187*

transgender individuals have a biological sex but possess a gender identity other than that typically assigned to their sex. *187*

sexuality refers to a particular kind of social interaction in which we express ourselves as sexual beings. *188*

incest taboo is a cultural universal which prohibits sex between closely related individuals. *188*

sexual orientation is a reflection of a person's preference for sexual partners. *188*

heterosexual describes people who are sexually attracted to people of the opposite sex. *188*

homosexual describes people who are sexually attracted to people of the same sex. *188*

bisexual describes people who are sexually attracted to people of either sex. *188*

asexual describes people who are not sexually attracted to people of either sex. *188*

sexism is the belief that one sex is superior to the other. *188*

homophobia is a negative attitude toward homosexuals and homosexuality. *189*

gender roles are society's expectations of how males and females should think and act. *189*

glass ceiling is an invisible barrier preventing women from reaching executive-level positions in the workplace. *191*

instrumental role is focused on working to provide for the family in a financial way. *192*

expressive role is focused on the socialization of children and meeting the family's emotional needs. *192*

Sample Test Questions

These multiple-choice questions are similar to those found in the test bank that accompanies this textbook.

1. What is the difference between sex and gender?
   a. Sex is social, and gender is biological.
   b. Sex is biological, and gender is social.
   c. Sex is about who you are attracted to sexually.
   d. Gender is about who you are attracted to sexually.
2. Individuals who have a biological sex but possess a gender identity other than that typically assigned to their sex are called
   a. transsexual.
   b. intersexed.
   c. transgender.
   d. homosexual.
3. The belief that one sex is superior to the other is called
   a. patriarchy.
   b. sexual orientation.
   c. gender stratification.
   d. sexism.
4. Which of the following is true about women in Canada?
   a. They generally earn as much as men.
   b. They perform less housework than men.
   c. They vote less than men.
   d. They earn more university degrees than men.
5. According to functionalist analysis, children are gender socialized in order to
   a. keep men in a dominant position in society.
   b. maintain a society that runs properly.
   c. establish a clear career path.
   d. entertain their parents.

ANSWERS: 1. b; 2. c; 3. d; 4. d; 5. b

ESSAY

1. How have gender roles in Canada changed and stayed the same since the 1950s?
2. What are the underlying causes of sexism, and will society ever be able to overcome them?
3. How might society be different if traditional gender roles were reversed?
4. Which of the three models explaining inequality in the workplace do you think is the strongest?
5. How effective do you think the feminist movement has been in championing women's equality?

WHERE TO START YOUR RESEARCH PAPER

To learn more about baby Storm, go to www.ctvnews.ca/baby-raised-without-gender-sets-off-debate-1.649286.

To learn about government's role in the status of women in Canada, go to www.swc-cfc.gc.ca/index-eng.html.

For information about December 6, the National Day of Remembrance and Action on Violence against Women in Canada, go to www.swc-cfc.gc.ca/dates/vaw-vff/index-eng.html.

For information about ending violence against women worldwide, go to www.un.org/events/women/iwd/2007/.

To learn more about the National Sex Offender Registry, go to www.publicsafety.gc.ca/prg/cor/tls/soir-eng.aspx.

To learn more about and to report homophobic violence, go to http://egale.ca/category/discrimination-and-hate-crimes/report-homophobic-violence-period/.

Remember to check www.thethinkspot.ca for additional information, downloadable flashcards, and other helpful resources.

Kurhan/Fotolia

AGING AND HEALTH

HOW DO HEALTH AND AGING AFFECT STRATIFICATION?
WHAT THEORIES EXIST ABOUT THE AGING PROCESS?
HOW DO WE TAKE CARE OF RETIRED CANADIANS?

"During my medical school years, a major topic of discussion was the embryonic development of what Canadians now commonly know as Medicare. From 1970 to 1990, universal access to hospital and physician services became a practical reality in Canada. Medical school admissions grew. People sensed that quality of care was increasing and outcomes were improving. This era might be considered the golden age of Medicare. Certainly, during this time, Medicare entered the Canadian pantheon of values, alongside such concepts as hockey and fair play, woven into the fabric of our country. It remains so.

"During the nineties, the cost of care, an important driver in the health system, became an urgent concern. Those responsible for managing health costs saw restricting access to products and services as an easy way to control costs. Thus began what might be called the restructuring era of Medicare.

"More recently, restricting access has had the unintended but adverse effect of reducing the quality of health care. The Canadian public now has a widespread perception that the quality of health care has decreased and continues to decline. This has driven several governmental task forces, the Romanow Commission most notable among them, to seek out the underlying problems and make corrective recommendations for Medicare. One common insight from these commissions is the realization that there is no single, simple legislative solution."[1]

The Greying *of* Society

CHAPTER 11

Doctor Terrence Montague takes a critical look at the health care system in Canada in the book *Patients First: Closing the Health Care Gap in Canada.*

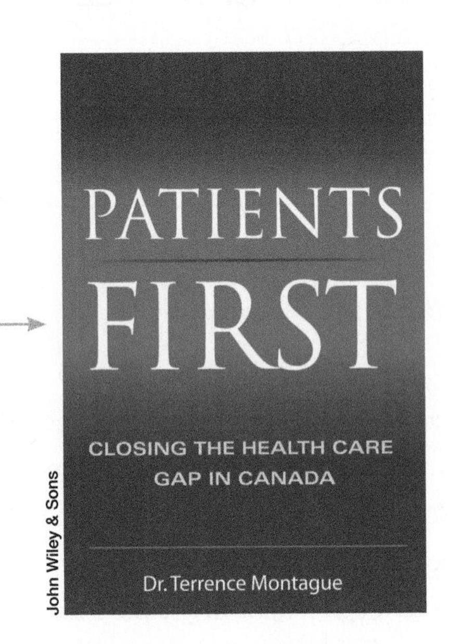

John Wiley & Sons

Most of you reading this textbook were born after the introduction of **Medicare** in Canada. Free universal health care is a powerful, almost sacred value in Canadian society. But this system has been in place only since the mid-1960s, and as Dr. Montague describes, it is now under threat because of the enormous financial costs of maintaining it.

After 50 years, anxiety is growing among Canadians about the future of our precious health care system. The issue consistently tops the polls as a primary political concern for Canadians. For patients, health care providers, academics, policy-makers, bureaucrats, and politicians alike, fixing Medicare has become an endless challenge.[2] Cracks have started to appear in the form of private clinics, in which individuals pay from their own pocket in order to receive faster care. The next few years will be a real test of our desire and ability to maintain free universal health care for all.

Canada's population is aging, placing even more strain on an already fragile system. This is true not just in Canada but all over the world. In fact, the world's elderly population is increasing by approximately 800 000 people per month.[3] The rising number of elderly people brings a new dilemma: How do we support and take care of our aging population? What does the growing elderly population mean to society as a whole?

is

a state of complete physical, mental, and social well-being and not merely the absence of disease or infirmity

and

social epidemiology is the study of the distribution of diseases and health throughout a society's population

Social determinants of health are

- Biological changes
- Gender differences
- Ageism
- Dependency ratio
- Retirement
- Pensions

concerns about aging are

get the topic: HOW DO HEALTH AND AGING AFFECT STRATIFICATION?

Health Defined

When you are asked about your health, you are likely to respond by explaining how you're feeling physically. However, there's more to health and being "healthy" than whether or not you're battling a cold or nursing a fever. According to the World Health Organization, **health** is "a state of complete physical, mental, and social well-being and not merely the absence of disease or infirmity."[4] In other words, several physical, psychological, and social factors determine one's health.

SOCIAL EPIDEMIOLOGY

In the 2007 movie *The Bucket List*, Morgan Freeman and Jack Nicholson play two elderly, terminally ill patients who jet off to exotic places to fulfill their lifelong goals. The movie entertains while teaching about patterns of health in the United States. For example, Freeman's character is a lower-middle-class African American man, and Nicholson's character is an upper-class white owner of several hospitals. Nicholson gets the best care possible, while the doctors and nurses often ignore Freeman. Age, gender, social class, and race all have an effect on health care in the United States. Do you think that this is true in Canada as well?

Social epidemiology is the study of the distribution of diseases and health throughout a society's population. Social epidemiologists look for links between health and the social environment. How does one's age affect his or her health? Are there health differences between the genders? Are race and social class connected to the treatment a patient receives? These are all questions that social epidemiologists seek to answer.

MEDICARE is Canada's government-run health care insurance program that provides health coverage for all Canadians.

HEALTH is a state of complete physical, mental, and social well-being and not merely the absence of disease or infirmity.

SOCIAL EPIDEMIOLOGY is the study of the distribution of diseases and health throughout a society's population.

Social Determinants of Health

In May 2010, Juha Mikkonen and Dennis Raphael published *Social Determinants of Health: The Canadian Facts.* In this publication, they make the bold statement that "the primary factors that shape the health of Canadians are not medical treatments or lifestyle choices but rather the living conditions they experience. These conditions have come to be known as the social determinants of health."[5]

The authors identified 14 social factors that affect the health of Canadians: aboriginal status, gender, disability, housing, early life, income and income distribution, education, race, employment and working conditions, social exclusion, food insecurity, social safety net, health services, and unemployment and job security. How important are these factors? The authors claim that each of these social determinants can have a stronger effect on a person's health than traditional risk factors such as poor diet, lack of physical activity, and even tobacco and excessive alcohol use.

As you can see, health depends on a number of factors that surround individuals, families, and whole societies. Getting to the root cause of an individual's illness or other health problem requires more than just medical knowledge—it requires a sociological understanding as well.

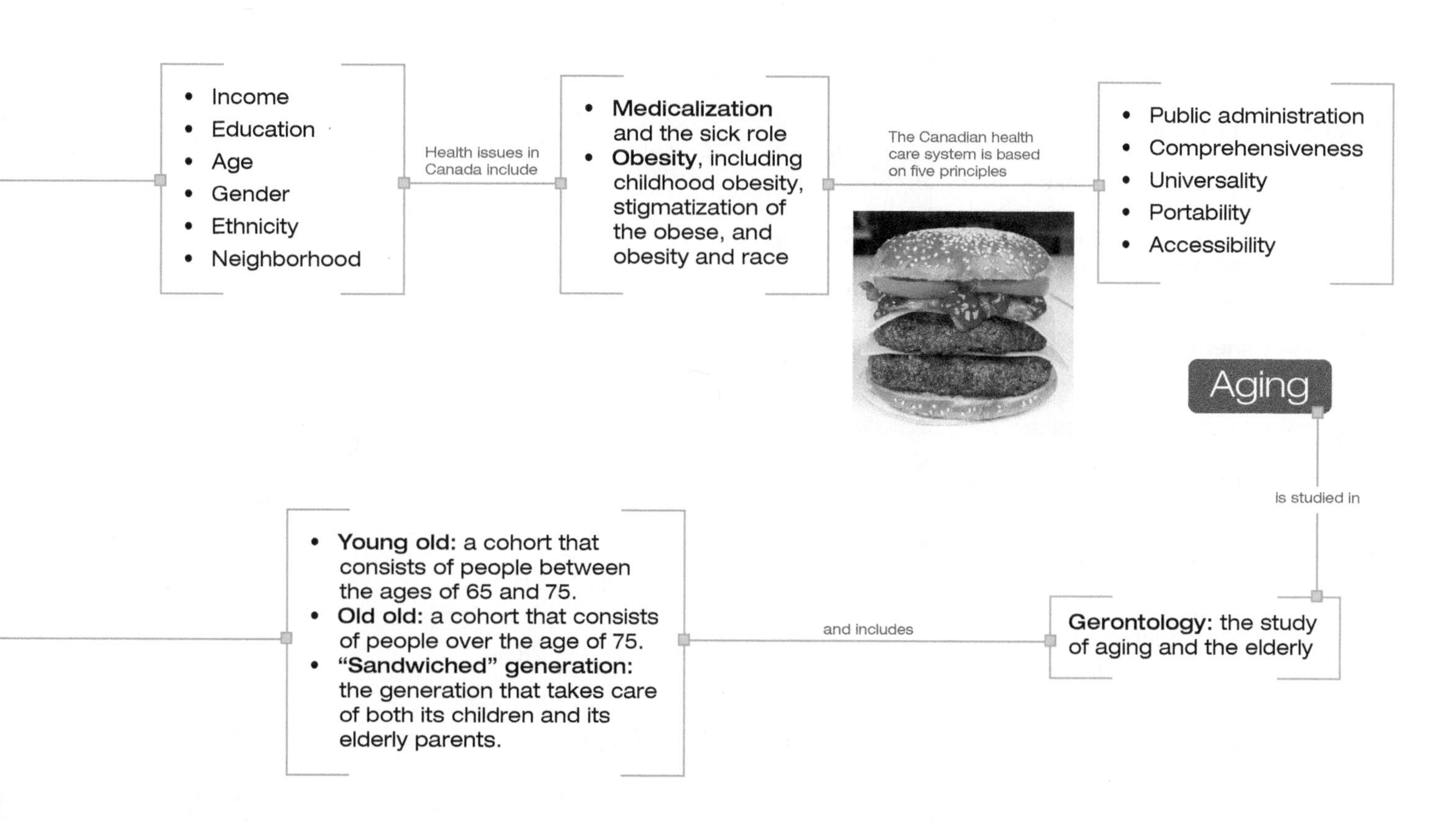

• Income
• Education
• Age
• Gender
• Ethnicity
• Neighborhood
Health issues in Canada include
• Medicalization and the sick role
• Obesity, including childhood obesity, stigmatization of the obese, and obesity and race
The Canadian health care system is based on five principles
• Public administration
• Comprehensiveness
• Universality
• Portability
• Accessibility
Aging
is studied in
Gerontology: the study of aging and the elderly
and includes
• Young old: a cohort that consists of people between the ages of 65 and 75.
• Old old: a cohort that consists of people over the age of 75.
• "Sandwiched" generation: the generation that takes care of both its children and its elderly parents.

The following story was included as part of a report titled "Toward a Healthy Future: Second Report on the Health of Canadians." It illustrates the complex set of factors and conditions that determine the health of every Canadian:

"Why is Jason in the hospital?
Because he has a bad infection in his leg.
But why does he have an infection?
Because he has a cut on his leg and it got infected.
But why does he have a cut on his leg?
Because he was playing in the junk yard next to his apartment building and there was some sharp, jagged steel there that he fell on.
But why was he playing in a junk yard?
Because his neighbourhood is kind of run down. A lot of kids play there and there is no one to supervise them.
But why does he live in that neighbourhood?
Because his parents can't afford a nicer place to live.
But why can't his parents afford a nicer place to live?
Because his Dad is unemployed and his Mom is sick.
But why is his Dad unemployed?
Because he doesn't have much education and he can't find a job.
But why ...?"

Source: The Federal, Provincial and Territorial Advisory Committee on Population Health, "Toward a Healthy Future: Second Report on the Health of Canadians," www.phac-aspc.gc.ca/ph-sp/report-rapport/toward/pdf/toward_a_healthy_english.PDF, accessed October 12, 2010. This is a copy of an official work that is published by the Government of Canada, and the reproduction has not been produced in affiliation with, or with the endorsement of the Government of Canada.[6]

Let us look in greater detail at some of these social determinants of health.

EDUCATION AND INCOME ARE KEY SOCIAL DETERMINANTS OF HEALTHY LIVING HABITS

Please indicate how often you do each of the following: (Every day, Often, Sometimes, Rarely, Never)

The percent of Canadians who do each every day or often...	National Average	Income		Education	
		Less than $30K	$60K or more	High School or less	University
Eat breakfast	81%	77%	84%	73%	89%
Leisure activity—such as gardening, walking, playing with young children or an easy bike ride—for 10 or more minutes	78%	68%	85%	67%	85%
Sleep 6 to 8 hours during the night	77%	66%	81%	73%	82%
Reduce or restrict your fast intake	63%	57%	85%	59%	65%
Eat five servings of fruit or vegetables a day	62%	50%	66%	52%	68%
Reduce or restrict your sugar intake	60%	62%	62%	54%	63%
Active outdoor activity—such as brisk walking, hiking, running or playing a sport—for 30 minutes or more	55%	52%	57%	51%	58%
Take vitamin or mineral supplements, such as Vitamin C, folic acid, or calcium	48%	53%	45%	48%	50%
Reduce or restrict your calorie intake	47%	52%	49%	40%	47%
Stretching exercises to maintain or improve flexibility	45%	41%	47%	41%	48%
Weight training to improve muscle tone and strength	27%	22%	29%	26%	28%
Active indoor activity—such as the treadmill or racquet ball—for 30 minutes or more	24%	14%	28%	16%	29%

Source: Canadian Medical Association, "12th Annual National Report Card on Health Care," August 2012, www.cma.ca/multimedia/CMA/Content_Images/Inside_cma/Media_Release/2012/reportcard/CMA-2012National-Report-Card_en.pdf, accessed August 23, 2013.

Income and Health

There is much evidence that health improves with income. The *Second Report on the Health of Canadians* found that only 47 percent of Canadians in the lowest income bracket rated their health as very good or excellent, compared with 73 percent of Canadians in the highest income group.[7]

But this is not simply a perception. Low-income Canadians are more likely to die earlier and to suffer more illnesses than Canadians with higher incomes, regardless of age, sex, race, and place of residence. Income also impacts mental health. A longitudinal study from 1995 to 2007 found that more people in lower-income households experienced episodes of high psychological distress than those in higher-income households.[8] Some research has found that the distribution of income in a given society may be a more important determinant of health than the total amount of income earned by individuals. This may be because large gaps in income distribution lead to increases in social problems and poorer health among the population as a whole.[9]

Education and Health

Stay in school! Health also improves with level of education. In 2012, 48 percent of Canadians with less than a high school education rated their health as "excellent" or "very good"; for Canadians with a university degree, 67 percent rated their health as "excellent" or "very good."[10]

Part of the explanation is that education is closely related to socioeconomic status. This increases opportunities for job and income security as well as job satisfaction. Canadians with low literacy skills are more likely to be unemployed and poor. People with higher levels of education have better access to healthy physical environments. Education also improves people's ability to access and understand information to help keep them healthy. Surveys repeatedly find that better-educated Canadians tend to smoke less, to be more physically active, and to eat healthier foods.[11]

Age and Health

In Canada—unlike in other parts of the world, particularly developing countries—death is rare among the young. The Canadian infant mortality rate is low; only about 5 infants are expected to die per 1000 births. While this may sound very good, there are 35 countries, mostly in western Europe, but also including Japan and South Korea, with lower rates. For the most part, Canadians are healthy—or at least we think we are. In 2011, 60 percent of Canadians reported their health to be "excellent" or "very good."[12] However, as people age, they experience more and more serious health problems. Chronic conditions such as arthritis, diabetes, heart disease, respiratory diseases, and mental illness are major problems for older people. These conditions limit their activities, meaning that work, socializing, and exercise are often limited or become impossible to pursue.

Gender and Health

On average, men die before women virtually everywhere in the world.[13] In Canada, women are expected to live an average of 83.9 years, while men

Look at the infant mortality rates in Nunavut in the table below. Why do you think these rates are so much higher than in the rest of the country?

INFANT MORTALITY RATES, BY PROVINCE AND TERRITORY (BOTH SEXES)

	2005	2006	2007	2008	2009
Canada	5.4	5.0	5.1	5.1	4.9
Newfoundland and Labrador	6.2	5.3	7.5	5.1	6.3
Prince Edward Island	2.2	2.1	5.0	2.0	3.4
Nova Scotia	4.0	4.0	3.3	3.5	3.4
New Brunswick	4.1	4.0	4.3	3.2	5.8
Quebec	4.6	5.1	4.5	4.3	4.4
Ontario	5.6	5.0	5.2	5.3	5.0
Manitoba	6.6	6.0	7.3	6.5	6.3
Saskatchewan	8.3	6.1	5.8	6.2	6.7
Alberta	6.8	5.3	6.0	6.2	5.5
British Columbia	4.5	4.1	4.0	3.7	3.6
Yukon	0.0	8.2	8.5	5.4	7.8
Northwest Territories	4.2	10.2	4.1	9.7	15.5
Nunavut	10.0	13.4	15.1	16.1	14.8

Note: The infant mortality rate is calculated as the number of deaths of children less than 1 year of age per 1000 live births in the same year.

Source: Adapted from Statistics Canada, "Infant Mortality Rates, by Province and Territory (Both Sexes)," May 32, 2012, www.statcan.gc.ca/tables-tableaux/sum-som/l01/cst01/health21a-eng.htm, accessed August 23, 2013. This does not constitute an endorsement by Statistics Canada of this product.

live only 78.7 years.[14] Sociologists attribute this trend to many factors. For example, young men have higher testosterone levels than young women, which may make them more likely to abuse alcohol and tobacco, drive aggressively, and engage in other life-threatening behaviours. Men often choose riskier types of work, which is also connected to men's decreased life expectancy. Studies show that women are less likely to experience life-threatening illnesses and health problems than men are.[15]

Men and women differ in their desire for health care. Women are twice as likely to get preventive care and have regular checkups,[16] while men are less likely to discuss health issues with their doctors.[17]

Despite this discrepancy in doctor visits, most past research on health was based on data collected from middle-class white men. However, recent studies show that some treatments are more effective for different races, like an AIDS drug that was tested in 1991. The study initially said the drug would help everyone, but the studied cohort was mostly gay white men. Further studies indicated that the drug worked better for white men than black men. Feminists also criticize the tendency to think that research conducted on males can be generalized to females. Today, studies are more likely to include women and visible minorities in testing, which could positively impact their health.[18]

Neighbourhoods

Neighbourhoods in particular can have an effect on health. Neighbourhoods that house poor, poorly educated, unemployed, and single mothers with little government assistance adversely affect the health of the people living there.[19] Similarly, people living in neighbourhoods with high crime and drug use also report poor health.[20] These threatening environments can lead to stress, which can in turn lead to more serious health problems.

This raises the issue of environmental justice. Environmental justice studies the impact of environmental factors on social classes. Poor people often live in environmentally dangerous areas[21] that experience regular interaction with toxins, unclean water, and/or air.[22] For example, many of Toronto's poorest residents live near industries that spew high levels of toxic chemicals and pollutants into the air. The low-income families who live in these neighbourhoods already face diminished health from stress, bad nutrition, diabetes, and poor dental care. They are placed at further risk because they breathe air contaminated with pollutants suspected of causing cancer and reproductive disorders.[23]

Aboriginal Health

When Europeans arrived in Canada, they brought with them many foreign diseases that had a devastating effect on the First Nations peoples. Because of widespread ethnocentrism and overt racism, many aboriginal people were excluded from the health care system, and at the same time, their traditional medical practices were generally regarded as inferior to those of the Europeans. This racism and discrimination has taken its toll on the aboriginal population.

While the life expectancy of all Canadians is a bit over 81 years, an aboriginal man will die about seven years earlier than a non-aboriginal man, and an aboriginal woman will die about five years earlier than a non-aboriginal woman.[24] The infant mortality rate is 1.5 times higher among First Nations peoples than among Canadians overall.

The prevalence of diabetes in the First Nations population is at least three times the national average, and tuberculosis rates are 8 to 10 times higher than those for the Canadian population. Although aboriginal peoples make up only 5 percent of the total population in Canada, they represent 16 percent of new HIV infections.[25]

Social factors go a long way in explaining this awful situation. Although the Canadian health care system has been praised as one of the best and most progressive in the world, quality health care is out of reach for many aboriginal Canadians. Jurisdictional disputes, cultural barriers, and geographic isolation have impeded aboriginal peoples'

COMPARISON: POOR NEIGHBOURHOODS VS. RICH NEIGHBOURHOODS

John A. Giordano/Corbis

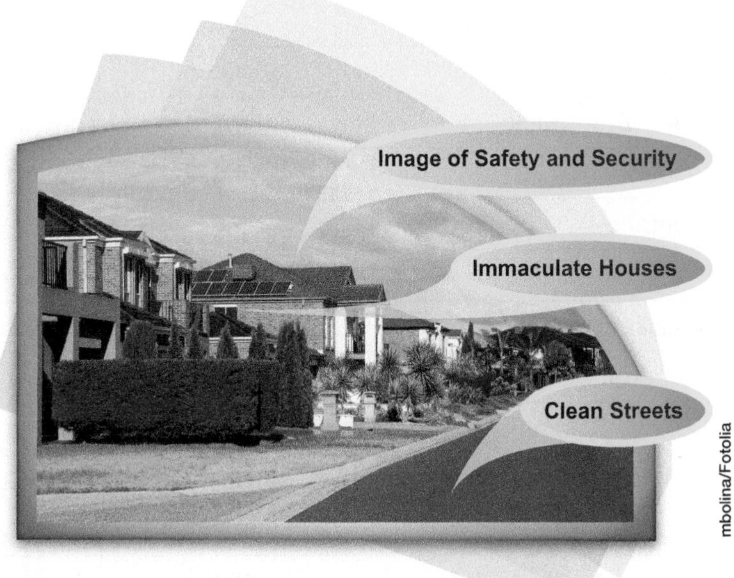

mbolina/Fotolia

Look at these two neighbourhoods. **How might each one affect the health of its residents?**

access to the health care system.[26] People who have low incomes and who live in disadvantaged neighbourhoods are at increased risk of having health problems. In many aboriginal communities, the living conditions are comparable to those of a developing nation, as measured by the United Nation's Human Development Index.

The Medicalization of North American Society

One way to consider the sociology of health is to look at how health and health care influence people's lives. Talcott Parsons believed that sickness can become a social role.[27] A **sick role** is the expected behaviours and responsibilities appropriate for someone who is ill. For example, part of an ill person's role is to go to the doctor in an attempt to get rid of the illness. Physicians have a primary position in society, allowing them to label sickness and health, which gives them great power over those with whom they come into contact.

This has led to what many consider the **medicalization** of North American society, or the idea that the medical community is the centre of many aspects of our society.[28] North Americans tend to believe that we can find the right pill for anything. I attended a funeral where the widow was quite distraught, saying, "He was my whole life." Her son, a medical professional, gave her an antidepressant. Our society believes that if you take a pill, all will be okay.

kasyge/Fotolia

If it is often not the healthiest choice, why is fast food so popular with so many people?

One of my favourite books is *The Myth of Mental Illness* by Thomas Szasz.[29] Dr. Szasz suggests that mental illness is not really a disease at all. In fact, the diagnosis of mental illness is often used as a means of social control.[30] Paula Caplan argues that the *Diagnostic and Statistical Manual of Mental Disorders*, which is used for the diagnosis of all mental illness, relies on personal ideology and political manoeuvring.[31] Over the course of 10 years, the committee added more than 70 "new" mental illnesses. In fact, according to the DSM, many women are "mentally ill" for one week a month when they menstruate.[32]

North America has many issues associated with the medicalization of our society. Keeping this in mind, let's look in depth at the epidemic of obesity.

Health in Canada: Living Off the Fat of the Land

With free health care, you would think that Canada would be a country of healthy citizens. However, all affluent nations face a host of health concerns, including obesity. Part of the problem is the foods we eat. Food options in Canada run the gamut from healthy (organic arugula) to unhealthy (bacon cheddar cheeseburgers). Many consumers, including myself, prefer the latter. Shopping for healthier food takes more time, effort, and money. Fast food is convenient and inexpensive, making it hugely popular, despite being unhealthy.

SICK ROLE is the expected behaviours and responsibilities appropriate for someone who is ill.

MEDICALIZATION is the idea that the medical community is the centre of many aspects of our society.

CHILDHOOD OBESITY

Although it's a relatively new phenomenon, Canada is in the grips of what some are calling an obesity epidemic. This is the term that was used in a report called "Healthy Weights for Healthy Kids." Canada now has one of the highest rates of childhood obesity, ranking fifth out of 34 Organisation for Economic Co-operation and Development (OECD) countries. Twenty-six percent of Canadians between 2 and 17 years old are overweight or obese. The numbers are even worse among aboriginal children, nearly half of whom are either overweight or obese.[33]

A recent study determined that the increase in childhood obesity was a direct result of the availability of energy-dense foods and drinks combined with a lack of energy expenditure.[34] That is, children are getting bigger because they are taking in more calories than they are burning. Kids today face many challenges in keeping their weight down that didn't necessarily exist before, including:

- Poor diet—only one-third of Canadian children aged 4–18 consume the number of servings of fruits and vegetables recommended by *Canada's Food Guide*.[35]
- In many dual-income and lone-parent families, children eat packaged, prepared meals, which are typically unhealthy. These busy working parents are more likely to rely on takeout to feed their families. A lack of supervision also makes it difficult to monitor how much and what their children eat.[36]
- Television, computers, and video games are many children's primary modes of entertainment, creating sedentary behaviour. This has led to a decrease in active play.[37]

STIGMATIZATION OF THE OBESE

Another consequence of childhood obesity is that overweight children are often targets of scorn and ridicule among their peers. Numerous studies have shown that people hold prejudicial attitudes about the obese. These perceptions can cause discrimination against an obese person. This loss of status could have harmful psychological, economic, and physical consequences.[38]

Sociologists Deborah Carr and Michael Friedman performed a study to determine whether obesity is in fact a stigma. They found that obese individuals believed that other members of society treated them unfairly, which contributed to their poor self-esteem and lack of psychological well-being. Carr and Friedman found that obese professional workers were 2.5 times more likely to report work-related discrimination than their thinner counterparts.[39]

MAKE CONNECTIONS

Is Keeping Kids Safe Hurting Their Health?

bikeriderlondon/Shutterstock

We know that unhealthy foods, inactivity, and lack of parental control are contributing factors to childhood obesity, but location also plays a big part in packing on the kilograms. In an article about contributing factors to childhood obesity, Arielle Concilio and colleagues assert that where a child grows up is a crucial factor in the child's health. The article explains that children growing up in poor, urban communities are more likely to suffer from obesity than kids in suburban areas. Their reasoning? It's too dangerous for kids to go outside and play.[40]

These kids are growing up in an area where fast food is cheaper than healthy food, and their parents might be working long hours. Add to this the fact that they live in neighbourhoods where space is tight and the available outdoor areas aren't safe places to play. To stay safe, kids look for indoor activities, which tend to be more sedentary. Schools may be too poor to afford physical education equipment for students, meaning that students have to find other ways to entertain themselves, and activities at home are equally limited.[41]

>>> **ACTIVITY** Do some research on youth centres where kids can go after school. What kinds of activities are available? Would these activities help or hinder a child with weight issues?

How can kids get the exercise they need when it's too dangerous to go outside and play?

OBESITY AND RACE

We saw above that in Canada, aboriginal children are nearly twice as likely to be obese as the overall Canadian average. Research in the United States has also shown that African Americans have a substantially higher rate of obesity than whites. But does this mean that certain races are more likely to be obese? We know that race is a social construct and not a biological trait. So what contributes to this statistic? One study by Jason D. Boardman and colleagues found that socioeconomic status plays a major role in the relationship between race and obesity.[42] According to this study, black communities in the United States are almost four times as likely as white communities to have obesity rates greater than 25 percent. However, when comparing black and white communities in more affluent areas, this relative risk drops. So, essentially, it appears that level of affluence, not race, is a determinant of obesity. Among Canadian First Nations children, those who live on a reservation had obesity rates of 55 percent, while those who live off reserve have rates of about 40 percent—quite a bit less.[43] An eight-year-long study on obesity in Canada found that members of the highest-income households were 40 percent less likely than those in the lowest-income households to become obese.[44] Why are the poor more likely to be obese? Part of the reason is the high cost of healthier food options. Unhealthy, inexpensive foods are often necessary for those who cannot afford healthier food options. Also, a lack of education about nutrition can lead people to make uninformed choices about what they eat.

Health Care in Canada

The Canadian health care system is often (mistakenly) called socialized medicine. In fact, it is a system of *socialized insurance* and is best described as an interlocking health insurance plan. Each of the 10 provinces and 3 territories has its own system of health insurance. The basics, however, are the same throughout Canada—universal coverage for health care services provided on the basis of need rather than the ability to pay. Known to Canadians as Medicare, the system provides access to universal, comprehensive coverage for medically necessary hospital and physician services.[45]

The system is funded through income tax: All citizens contribute according to their income rather than the benefits they expect to derive. Public health care insurance in Canada is based on the principle of transferring resources from the richer to the poorer and pooling the risks among the healthy and the less healthy. An advantage to this kind of system is that it costs less than private insurance. Public insurance eliminates the cost of marketing and selling private health care insurance policies and evaluating insurance risks. This is one of the reasons the Canadian health care system costs less to administer than the privately funded U.S. system.[46] For these reasons, Canadians have favoured public health care insurance over private insurance since 1966, the year of the first *Medical Care Act*. This does not mean, though, that the private sector is totally absent from health care in Canada. Private health care insurance exists, but it is limited to providing additional coverage for health services that are not insured by the public plan or that are only partially insured by it.[47]

GO GLOBAL

Health Care—An International Comparison

Health care in the United States operates under a very different system than ours in Canada. U.S. health care insurance is provided almost entirely by the private sector. Because the costs are very high, large numbers of Americans have no medical insurance. If they need to see a doctor, they have to pay out of their own pocket. According to the American Medical Association, people without health insurance "tend to live sicker and die younger than people with health insurance."[48] With the high numbers of uninsured persons in the United States, this trend is true for a lot of the nation's population, and many question the fairness of the U.S. system. In March 2010, the *Patient Protection and Affordable Care Act* (PPACA), commonly called *Obamacare,* was passed. This act will ensure that all Americans have access to good quality and affordable health care [49]

In 2000, the World Health Organization (WHO) released a report that identified five characteristics that a good and fair health system should have. According to WHO, a good and fair health system has:

- Overall good health (low infant mortality rates and high life expectancy)
- A fair distribution of good health (low infant mortality and high life expectancy across the entire population)
- A high level of overall responsiveness
- A fair distribution of responsiveness
- A fair distribution of financing health care (with the health care costs evenly distributed based on a person's ability to pay).[50]

The world map below shows the per-capita costs, life expectancy, and infant mortality of selected countries around the globe.

After creating a list of criteria, WHO compared the health systems of 191 of the world's countries. The United States was first in overall responsiveness, meaning that its health care system does an excellent job in responding to the desires of consumers. However, other variables present a different story.

A GLOBAL LOOK AT HEALTH CARE SYSTEMS IN 2011

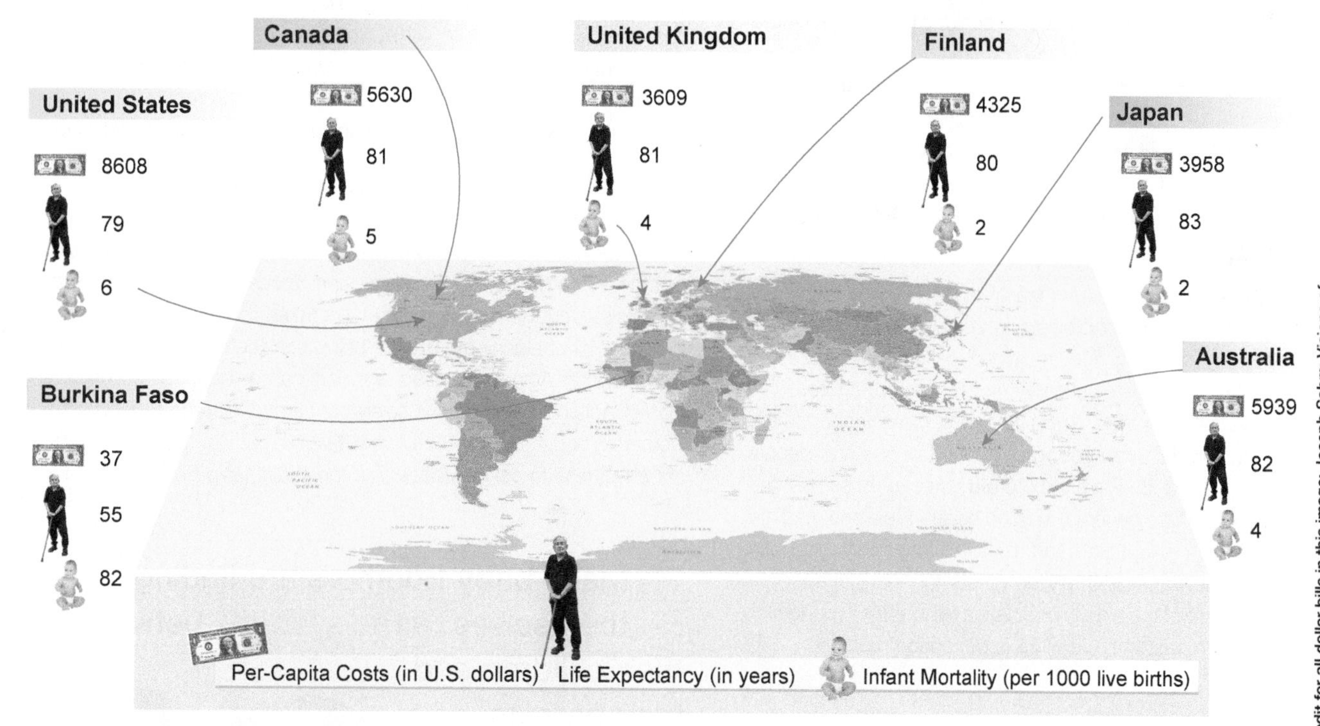

Source: The World Bank Group. (2013). Indicators. Accessed at http://data.worldbank.org/indicator.

credit for all dollar bills in this image: Joseph Sohm; Visions of America/Encyclopedia/Corbis
credit for same photo in this image: Paul Maguire/Fotolia
credit for all baby photos in this image: Olga Sapegina/Shutterstock
credit for world image: Ekler/Fotolia

	United States	Canada	United Kingdom	Finland	Japan	Australia	Burkina Faso
Per capita costs	8608	5630	3609	4325	3958	5939	37
Life expectancy	79	81	81	80	83	82	55
Infant mortality	6	5	4	2	2	4	82

The fundamental ideology behind the Canadian health care system is the principle of economic and social equity. In addition, five other specific principles define the Canadian health care system:

- *Public administration:* Each province administers a health insurance plan on a nonprofit basis by a public authority, which is accountable to the provincial government.
- *Comprehensiveness:* The health care insurance plan of a province must insure all services that are "medically necessary." Each provincial government defines what these are, so the range of insured services may vary among provinces.
- *Universality:* All residents must have access to public health care insurance and insured services on equal terms and conditions.
- *Portability:* Citizens are still insured even if they are temporarily absent from their province of residence or from Canada.
- *Accessibility:* Everyone must have reasonable and uniform access to insured health services, free of financial or other barriers. No one may be discriminated against on the basis of factors such as income, age, and health status.[51]

Aging: The Greying of Canada

The population of Canada is getting older. This trend has been called the "greying" of the population. In 1956, the median age of Canadians was 27.2 years. In 2012, it was 40 years, and by 2056, the median age is expected to reach 46.9 years.[52] The number of senior citizens could more than double, outnumbering children for the first time.[53]

The rising elderly population affects not just health care but also society as a whole. With people living longer than ever before, we have to understand the aging process and figure out what impact aging has on the individual.

AGING AND DEMOGRAPHIC CHANGE IN CANADA

Concerns about the increasing percentage of elderly people in society have drawn the attention of psychologists, medical professionals, and sociologists. The study of aging and the elderly is officially known as **gerontology**. This field of study is critically important to our future.

The elderly have been broken down into two major cohorts: the "young old" and the "old old." The **young old** cohort consists of people between the ages of 65 and 75, while the **old old** refers to those over the age of 75. The "young old" are generally in good health, live alone, and are financially independent. The "old old" tend to have failing health, live with family or in a retirement home, and rely on others for financial support. Approximately 53 percent of the elderly population fall into the "young old" category. However, living past the age of 75 is not uncommon.

Life Expectancy

Medical advances and higher standards of living dramatically increase life expectancy. At the beginning of the twentieth century, the average life expectancy was 47.3 years. In 2009, the average life expectancy in Canada was 81.23 years.[54] The development of vaccines for many infectious diseases, such as measles, diphtheria, and smallpox, virtually eliminated these diseases, allowing many more people to live longer, healthier lives.

Origins of the Baby Boomers

After World War II, social and economic restraints that were keeping couples from starting families were removed, leading to a "boom" in childbirths. Men who served in the war returned home, married, and started families. Generally, wages were high enough to support a family, so women stayed home and raised children. A period of economic prosperity also contributed to the "baby boom" that lasted from about 1946 until 1964. Between 1940 and 1965 the annual number of births in Canada rose from 253 000 in 1940 to 419 000 in 1965. Over this period of 25 years, the baby boom produced about 1.5 million more births than would otherwise have occurred. By 1965, the boom was fading, as people married at a later age and waited longer to have children.[55]

The decline in female fertility was the main factor that contributed to the end of the baby boom. Women who married after the war ended in 1945 were typically in their 20s, giving them approximately 20 more years of fertility. The introduction of the birth control pill in 1960 also contributed to the slowing birth rate, as it became the most widely used contraceptive method.[56]

GERONTOLOGY is the study of aging and the elderly.

YOUNG OLD is a cohort that consists of people between the ages of 65 and 75.

OLD OLD is a cohort that consists of people over the age of 75.

"SANDWICHED" GENERATION is the generation that takes care of both its children and its elderly parents.

The "Sandwiched" Generation

The baby boomer generation is unique in that it is the first **"sandwiched" generation**—it takes care of both its children and its elderly parents. Most future generations will probably also be sandwiched between their children and their parents because of longer lives and delays in childbearing. This can keep families closer together. The elderly can help their adult children in times of crisis by watching grandchildren, providing temporary housing, giving loans, and offering advice to their adult children.[57] This allows the elderly to stay involved in family life and increases overall life satisfaction.

Gender and Aging: Where Are the Men?

If studies were done about the gender differences between elderly Japanese men and women, the focus would probably concentrate on Japanese women. According to sociologists John Knodel and Mary Beth Ofstedal, concerns about gender inequality have taken too much precedence, and the situation of elderly men is not being considered.[58] The Second World Assembly on Aging produced a report called the "Madrid International Plan of Action" that is almost solely concerned with the situation of aging women. Knodel and Ofstedal were taken aback by the assembly's lack of "willingness to acknowledge that the relationship between gender and

Many baby boomers are finding themselves "sandwiched" between their children and their parents.

nyul/Fotolia

CANADA'S AGING POPULATION—PERCENTAGE OF POPULATION AGED 65 YEARS OR OLDER IN CANADA, 1956–2006

Year	Percentage of Population Aged 65 Years or Older
1956	7.7%
1966	7.7%
1976	8.7%
1986	10.7%
1996	12.2%
2006	13.7%

Source: Adapted from Statistics Canada, "2006 Census: Portrait of the Canadian Population in 2006, by Age and Sex: Provincial/Territorial populations by Age and Sex," July 2007, www.statcan.gc.ca/bsolc/olc-cel/olc-cel?catno=97-551-XWE2006001&lang=eng#olcinfopanel, accessed August 23, 2013.

aging varies across settings and over time."[59] Although it is a noble goal to promote gender equality and empowerment of women, a one-sided view of the situation fails to actually promote gender equality. Knodel and Ofstedal suggest that research should also examine the "experiences of older men and women within the contexts in which they live."[60]

Data from the Philippines, Singapore, Taiwan, Thailand, and Vietnam suggest a relative equality of satisfaction with income for elderly men and women. Vietnam has the greatest disparity, with 52 percent of elderly men satisfied with their income, compared to 40 percent of elderly women. Thailand actually has a higher percentage of elderly women who are satisfied with their income than men, with 74 percent and 68 percent, respectively. Developing countries such as these are home to a large portion of the elderly population and provide useful data about the relative situation of elderly men and women.[61]

The study's authors feel that gender should not be placed above all other markers of disadvantage in old age. A more balanced approach that addresses the disadvantages of both elderly men and women would be better suited to aid current and future generations of the elderly.

CONCERNS ABOUT AGING

Biological Changes

Everyone knows that as you age, certain biological changes take place. Grey hair, wrinkles, and loss of strength and flexibility are all physical signs of aging. As you age, your senses also decline. Your senses of vision, hearing, taste, touch, and smell all become weaker. In fact, in 2006, more than 17 percent of people over the age of 65 reported that their vision was failing, while 11.4 percent reported having trouble hearing.[62] These percentages were higher than those for persons in any other age group.

Many people in our society associate aging with being weaker and less capable of doing normal, everyday activities. It's sentiments like these that can lead to prejudices and discrimination toward the elderly.

Ageism

Steve Richardson has worked as a contractor for Dynamic Solutions since the age of 25. Now that Steve is approaching his 65th birthday, his younger supervisor is pressuring him to retire. The company is offering him good retirement benefits, but he feels that they are attempting to gently push him out the door. However, Steve's work is an essential part of his life, and he has no desire to retire now. Dynamic Solutions views Steve as an outdated employee, who served his purpose when he was younger but is of no use anymore. Although Steve Richardson and Dynamic Solutions don't actually exist, situations like this happen every day in Canada. With an aging population and workforce, the new concern of ageism has come into play. **Ageism** is prejudice and discrimination based solely on age.

AGEISM is prejudice and discrimination based solely on age.

The workplace is the main forum for ageism. Employers seek workers who are energetic and willing to work for a long duration. If an employer feels that someone is too old, the employer may think that the prospective employee is going to be too slow on the job and is more likely to quit because he or she does not really need the job. It is technically illegal to discriminate in hiring on the basis of age, but many elderly people have difficulty finding new employment or find themselves being asked to leave their jobs.

Television and film are major sources of ageism, as entertainment tends to focus on young and attractive people. The elderly are typically shown as senile and frail or are just ignored. Aging movie stars, particularly women, have voiced their discontent at not getting roles. Aging actresses must deal with what is known as "double jeopardy," or the two factors that contribute to the downfall of their career: gender and age.[63]

Generally, in film and television, women have been on relatively equal footing with men, both in employment and compensation. However, the entertainment industry values physical attractiveness first and foremost, and it seems to have little or no place for older, less attractive females. When a society values beauty and youth, the elderly are cast aside. This negative perception of growing old can lead to dissatisfaction in old age.

BIOLOGICAL EFFECTS OF AGING

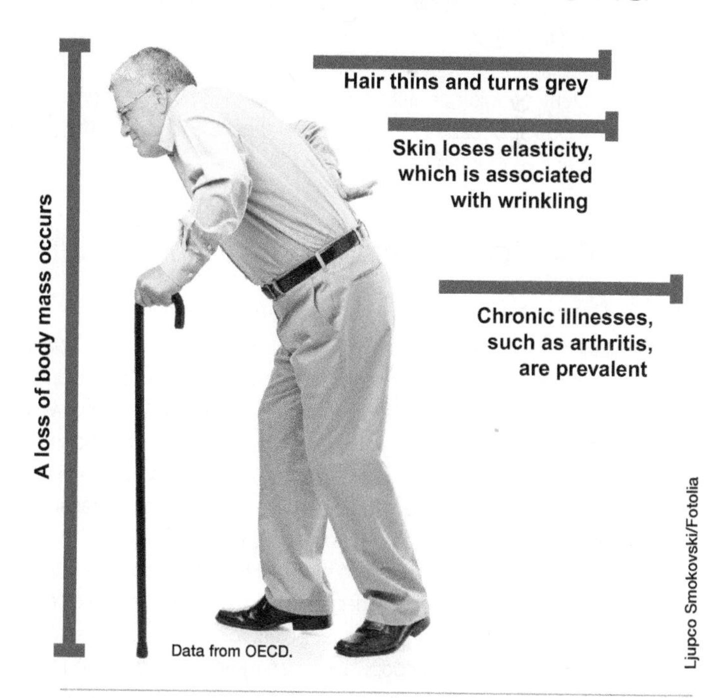
A loss of body mass occurs
Hair thins and turns grey
Skin loses elasticity, which is associated with wrinkling
Chronic illnesses, such as arthritis, are prevalent
Data from OECD.
Ljupco Smokovski/Fotolia

Aging brings along with it certain biological changes. **Grey hair, wrinkles, and liver spots are the inevitable physical markers of the aging process.**

think sociologically: WHAT THEORIES EXIST ABOUT THE AGING PROCESS?

Functionalism—Disengaging from Society

What happens to people's social roles as they reach old age? Many functionalists would suggest that elderly people begin to shed their old social roles and begin to take on new roles in society. Their roles as worker or spouse drop off as they retire or become widowed. Functionalists use the disengagement theory to describe the aging process. The disengagement theory states that reduced interaction between older persons and others is unavoidable, mutual, and acceptable to both the individual and society.[64]

Society disengages people from important positions as they get older so that the social system does not get disrupted. The disengagement theory suggests that the functions of retirement are to make older people less important in society since they are about to die, which, in turn, makes society function better. The older people move out of the way so that the younger population can take their place.

Social distance is provided between death and daily life. Death disrupts many social functions, and retirement decreases the chances that a vital person will be eliminated. Retirement allows for new generations with new ideas to move society forward. The young are promoted, and expensive older workers are let go.

According to Cumming and colleagues, the disengaging process is intrinsic and is desirable for most older people.[65] However, some sociologists disagree. Some sociologists have found that elderly people who take part in activities such as volunteering are "happiest and have the greatest expressed life satisfaction."[66] Symbolic interactionists, whom we will discuss next, often agree with this idea. Other critics of this theory suggest that elderly people don't often vacate their social roles willingly. Instead, elderly people are often forced out of their positions through an exercise of power because employers feel they're too old for the job or are too expensive to keep on.

Symbolic Interactionism—Living an Active Lifestyle

Symbolic interactionists study how factors like environment and relationships with others affect how people experience aging. People develop their sense of "self" through their interactions with others in the social world. This development of self is a lifelong process, so social interactions continue to be important to us as we age. Symbolic interactionists believe that successful aging is a "multifaceted phenomenon that encompasses not only health but also psychological well-being, role integration, and social engagement."[67] In other words, these theorists believe in the activity theory, which states that life satisfaction depends on maintaining an involvement with life by developing new interests, hobbies, roles, and relationships.

One way that the elderly population can remain active is through volunteer work. Sociologists Yunqing Li and Kenneth Ferraro suggest that volunteer work is beneficial for social life and gives people the opportunity to remain socially engaged throughout their entire lives.[68] Volunteering can reduce depression among the elderly population and improve life satisfaction. Why does volunteering have such a positive effect? Like any other activity that involves helping others, volunteering provides the elderly with a sense of meaning and purpose in life. Interacting with others can also help the elderly cope with bereavement due to the loss of a spouse or close friend, and it helps strengthen their relationships with others.

Conflict Theory—Aging and Inequality

Conflict theorists, unlike functionalists and symbolic interactionists, examine how power and economic forces influence aging in society. Those who accept a conflict perspective of aging might consider a number of issues. First, they note that ageism is no different than any other *ism*, like racism and sexism. By placing a negative stigma on the elderly, society segregates them from others.

If you consider retirement, for example, whose benefit does it serve? A few years ago, the college at which I teach had an early retirement buyout. Faculty members were given a bonus to retire early. Why would an organization do this? Because it was significantly cheaper to hire

Rohit Seth/Fotolia

^^^ How might volunteering at a school help the elderly cope with the aging process?

DEPENDENCY RATIO is the ratio of the youth population (0 to 19 years) and senior population (65 or older) to the working-age population (20 to 64 years).

younger faculty at an entry-level salary than to continue to pay some who had been on campus for 25 to 30 years.

One reason for increased conflict could be changes in the **dependency ratio**—the ratio of the youth population (0 to 19 years) and senior population (65 or older) to the working-age population (20 to 64 years). It is expressed as the number of "dependants" for every 100 "workers." As the population ages, the dependency ratio will increase. In 2006, the dependency ratio was 60 dependants per 100 workers, but it is projected to rise to 84 dependants for every 100 workers by 2056, as the proportion of seniors increases.[69]

Conflict theorists suggest that age can play an important role in the formation of social policies. As the number of seniors increases, this group will have more political power. This will probably result in changes to mandatory retirement policies, health care funding, and government pensions.

Feminist Theory—Gender Differences in Aging

Feminist theorists point out that aging impacts men and women differently. For example, while older people generally are not well represented in the media, feminist Betty Friedan found that older women are basically "invisible" in the media. Out of a sample of nearly 300 photographs of faces in the magazine *Vogue*, only one depicted a woman who might be over 60 years old.[70] The message is that older women are not important.

We have seen that women live longer than men, but this is a mixed blessing. A woman who is married will most probably become a widow. Older women are also more likely to experience poverty. Part of the reason is that retired people live off their pensions. Because pensions are related to the individual's lifetime earnings, and because women are more likely to take time off to care for children, or to work part time, their pensions are often quite low. The Old Age Security pension given by the federal government was never designed to be the sole source of income in old age. Even the provincial retirement pensions are often very limited. The result is that many older women live at or below the poverty line.[71]

THINK SOCIOLOGICALLY

AIDS Orphans

UNAIDS estimates that around the world, more than 16 million children have lost one or both parents to AIDS. Around 14.8 million of these children live in sub-Saharan Africa. In some countries, the rate of AIDS orphans is staggering. For example, 16 percent of children in Zimbabwe and 12 percent of children in Botswana are orphaned due to AIDS.[72]

Beyond the incredible emotional tragedy of losing one or both parents, these children also face numerous social challenges. The first is a drop in their standard of living. Because of the loss of a principal income earner, the family's financial situation usually worsens. Children may have to provide financial support to the household by working or begging. They may also have to provide other kinds of care, such as doing more household chores or taking care of younger siblings or the remaining parent, who is often also infected. The additional pressure to provide financial support plus fewer financial resources often means that orphaned children can no longer go to school.

Children whose parents are infected with HIV or who have died of AIDS are often stigmatized by society. In many cases these children are assumed to be HIV positive themselves, whether they are or not. They seldom receive any social support, and they even face open discrimination. The extended family is often the only safety net for most orphaned children.

AIDS is a terrible disease that has wreaked havoc among an entire generation of parents in Africa. It has also created millions of AIDS orphans. These children will grow up with much greater hardship, much less education, and incomprehensible suffering. The long-term social impact on these countries is worrying to many governments and organizations.

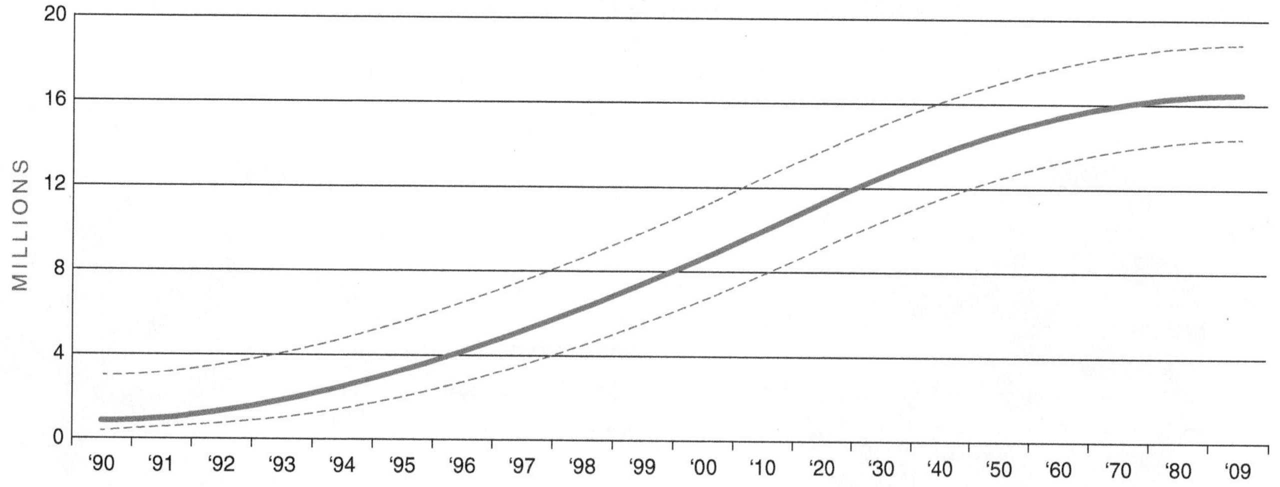

Source: UNAIDS, "Report on the Global AIDS Epidemic—2010," by permission of UNAIDS/ONUSIDA.

WRAP YOUR MIND AROUND THE THEORY

bst2012/Fotolia

Retirement is often a difficult transition for the elderly, as maintaining a sense of self-worth while not working can present a challenge.

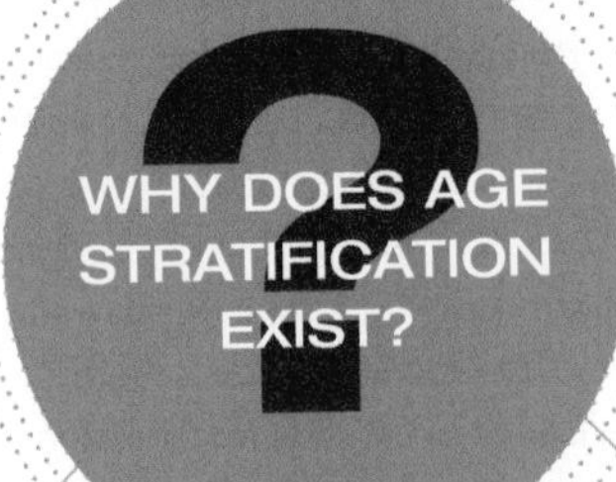
WHY DOES AGE STRATIFICATION EXIST?

FUNCTIONALISM

Functionalists believe that removing the elderly from active participation serves society well. Therefore, retirement helps both society and the elderly person disengage from jobs and other social tasks. Functionalist Elaine Cumming has written about the disengagement theory of aging. Society gradually transfers responsibilities to younger workers, and older workers are phased out of the workplace. In Canada, the federal and provincial governments provide retired workers with pensions to assist them once they have left the workplace.[73]

CONFLICT THEORY

Society is stratified by age, and in Canada, middle-aged people generally have the greatest power and access to social resources. The dependency ratio indicates the number of dependants, both young and old, per working adult. The elderly are often pushed to the side and run a greater risk of living in poverty. This type of ageism reminds one of the ideas of Karl Marx, who states that a capitalist society, with a focus on profit, has no place for less-productive workers. As the elderly become less productive, their importance to society diminishes, so they are removed from positions of importance and are largely ignored.

SYMBOLIC INTERACTIONISM

The symbolic interactionist perspective on aging focuses on the life satisfaction of the elderly. The activity theory states that the elderly are more likely to have a high degree of life satisfaction if they engage in plenty of activities. When the workplace is no longer an option, it is important to replace the time and effort that was focused on work with something else. A study by Soleman Abu-Bader and colleagues found four core components of life satisfaction in the elderly: physical status, emotional health, social support, and locus of control. Their findings indicated that physical health is the most important indicator of overall life satisfaction in the elderly.[74]

FEMINIST THEORY

The feminist perspective points out that men and women experience aging in different ways and face different challenges. Betty Friedan found that older women are virtually invisible in the media. Many women end up alone after their husband dies. Because women often accumulated a lower pension during their working lives, if they worked at all, there is a higher risk that they will end up in poverty.

Grey hair and wrinkles— **symbols of wisdom or weakness?**

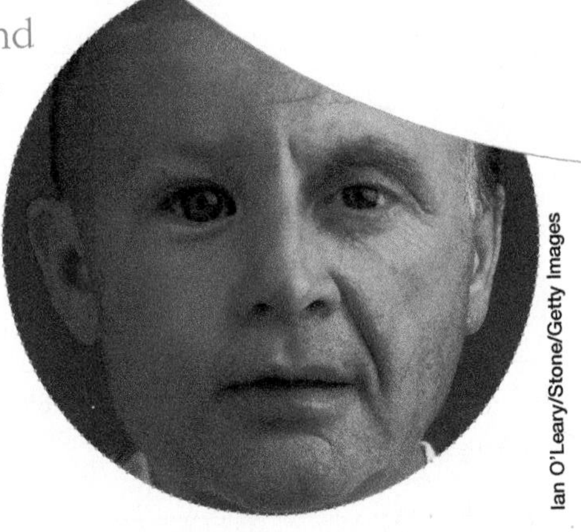

Ian O'Leary/Stone/Getty Images

Maintaining a high level of activity is crucial to satisfaction at all ages but particularly **in the elderly.**

Brooke Fasani Auchincloss/Corbis

discover sociology in action: HOW DO WE TAKE CARE OF RETIRED CANADIANS?

Taking Care of Retired Canadians

Before 1952, when people in Canada retired, they often either lived off what they had saved over a lifetime of working or became dependent on their family or others to provide for them. In Chapter 3, you saw that some of the fundamental values of Canadian culture are compassion and generosity. In 1952, the *Old Age Security Act* was passed. This is the first of the "three pillars" of the Canadian retirement system. The OAS is available to most Canadians after they turn 65 years old. Employment history is not a factor, and the applicant does not even need to be retired. However, this pension is taxable, so if the person has other pensions or continues to work, he or she may pay back some or all of the OAS. However, if an individual has little or no other retirement income, he or she is eligible for the Guaranteed Income Supplement.[75]

The second pillar of the system is the Canada Pension Plan/Quebec Pension Plan (CPP/QPP). In 1966, Parliament passed legislation creating the CPP, a national social insurance plan funded by the contributions of employers, employees, and the self-employed. The CPP operates in all provinces and territories except Quebec, which established its own plan, the QPP. The CPP/QPP was designed to provide workers and their families with a modest pension after retirement. Payments are based on how much an individual contributed over his or her lifetime of working.[76]

The third pillar consists of private pensions and savings. This includes company pensions and Registered Retirement Savings Plans (RRSPs).

The government pension system is a pay-as-you-go system. This means that the present retirees are being paid from future contributions of later generations. We have seen that Canada's population is aging. This means that there will be an increasing number of retirees and, therefore, more people receiving government pensions. As early as the 1990s, people began to worry about the sustainability of the Canadian pension system. It was calculated that if no changes were made, working Canadians in 2030 will need to contribute nearly twice as much as those currently working in order to sustain the system. In 1998, changes were introduced to the CPP which increased contributions modestly. By planning and making changes now, the CPP can remain operational for future generations.[77]

ACTIVITIES

1. Visit a nursing home or retirement centre. Talk with a few residents about aging and listen to their perceptions about how it influences them.
2. Does your college practise ageism? Does it offer discount tuition and other offers to senior citizens who want to enrol?
3. Do you think universal health care is a right or a privilege? If you think health care is a right, then what do you think must be done to provide it to those who need it? If you think it is a privilege, then rationalize why paying for it is acceptable.
4. Pick up a magazine such as *Maclean's* and analyze all the pictures that show people. How many of these pictures show seniors? How many pictures show older women?

CHAPTER

11

HOW DO HEALTH AND AGING AFFECT STRATIFICATION? 203

race, age, social class, and gender affect health; example: people from higher social classes generally have better health

WHAT THEORIES EXIST ABOUT THE AGING PROCESS? 212

functionalism: as people grow older, they reduce their interactions with others—a practice that is unavoidable, mutual, and acceptable to the individual and society
conflict theory: society places a negative stigma on the elderly, which segregates them from others
symbolic interactionism: successful aging encompasses health, psychological well-being, role integration, and social engagement
feminism: men and women experience aging differently, partly because society treats older men and women differently

HOW DO WE TAKE CARE OF RETIRED CANADIANS? 215

first pillar: the Old Age Security pension is given to most Canadians over 65 years old; it is not based on employment earnings, and it is taxable
second pillar: the Canada Pension Plan and Quebec Pension Plan pay a modest pension to working Canadians when they retire; benefits are based on lifetime earnings contributions
third pillar: company pensions and private savings, such as Registered Retirement Savings Plans, are another source of retirement income for Canadians

get the topic: HOW DO HEALTH AND AGING AFFECT STRATIFICATION?

Theories

FUNCTIONALISM 212

- as people age, they shed old social roles and take on new roles
- retirement makes older people less important because they no longer contribute to society
- a new generation moves forward to replace retired workers

CONFLICT THEORY 212

- middle-aged people have the most power
- as the elderly become less productive, their importance in society diminishes
- the elderly are not respected, and ageism occurs

SYMBOLIC INTERACTIONISM 212

- Cooley suggests that people develop the "self" through interaction
- life often improves because retirees develop new activities, hobbies, roles, and relationships
- volunteer work is socially engaging and gives a sense of purpose in life

FEMINIST THEORY 213

- men and women experience aging differently
- older women are almost "invisible" in society
- older women are more likely to be alone and to experience poverty than are older men

Key Terms

Medicare is Canada's government-run health care insurance program that provides health coverage for all Canadians. *203*

health is a state of complete physical, mental, and social well-being and not merely the absence of disease or infirmity. *203*

social epidemiology is the study of the distribution of diseases and health throughout a society's population. *203*

sick role is the expected behaviours and responsibilities appropriate for someone who is ill. *207*

medicalization is the idea that the medical community is the centre of many aspects of our society. *207*

gerontology is the study of aging and the elderly. *210*

young old is a cohort that consists of people between the ages of 65 and 75. *210*

old old is a cohort that consists of people over the age of 75. *210*

"sandwiched" generation is the generation that takes care of both its children and its elderly parents. *210*

ageism is prejudice and discrimination based solely on age. *211*

dependency ratio is the ratio of the youth population (0 to 19 years) and senior population (65 or older) to the working-age population (20 to 64 years). *213*

Sample Test Questions

These multiple-choice questions are similar to those found in the test bank that accompanies this textbook.

1. According to Juha Mikkonen and Dennis Raphael, which of the following is a primary determinant of health?
- **a.** Diet
- **b.** Education
- **c.** Physical activity
- **d.** Medical treatments

2. Which of the following is *not* a reason children are struggling with obesity?
- **a.** Dual-income homes
- **b.** Nutritious school lunches
- **c.** The price of healthy food
- **d.** The popularity of sedentary activities

3. Obesity is most determined by
- **a.** race.
- **b.** gender.
- **c.** social epidemiology.
- **d.** socioeconomic status.

4. The proportion of young and old people to workers in a society is called the
- **a.** working proportion.
- **b.** age pyramid.
- **c.** dependency ratio.
- **d.** disengagement proportion.

5. Which term describes the government pension system in Canada?
- **a.** Pay-as-you-go
- **b.** Pay-when-you-can
- **c.** Take-what-you-need
- **d.** Take-now-pay-later

ANSWERS: 1. b; 2. b; 3. d; 4. c; 5. a

ESSAY

1. How does social class affect health?
2. How can television perpetuate stereotypes about people who are obese?
3. Describe the Canadian health care insurance system.
4. Why has life expectancy increased?
5. What benefits are available to Canadian seniors?

WHERE TO START YOUR RESEARCH PAPER

To learn more about aging around the world, go to http://aarpinternational.org/explore-by-region.

To watch a population pyramid representing Canada's aging population, go to www.statcan.gc.ca/kits-trousses/animat/edu06a_0000-eng.htm.

To learn more about health in Canada, go to the Health Canada website, www.hc-sc.gc.ca/index-eng.php.

To learn more about First Nations and Inuit health, go to www.hc-sc.gc.ca/fniah-spnia/index-eng.php.

To learn more about obesity and its effects on health, go to www.participaction.com and www.obesity.org.

To learn more about baby boomers and their concerns, go to www.babyboomers.com.

Remember to check www.thethinkspot.ca for additional information, downloadable flashcards, and other helpful resources.

DEVIANCE AND CRIME

Martin Cintula/Fotolia

WHAT ARE DEVIANCE AND CRIME?
WHY DO DEVIANCE AND CRIME EXIST?
HOW DO WE DEAL WITH CRIME IN CANADA?

"There are various approaches to understanding youthful offending. These approaches translate, to some extent, into different models of what a youth justice system should look like. Looking at each of these models on its own, in isolation from others, creates something of a caricature of youthful offending. Nevertheless, it is useful as a way of looking at differences.

"In the first place, one can look at offending as a symptom of some kind of underlying problem. This problem could be biological or psychological, or it could be social (e.g., a symptom of inadequacy in child rearing or the impact of poverty). Second, one can see youthful offending as a symptom of an inadequate crime control system (e.g., inadequate numbers of police, inadequate severity of punishments, or inadequate forms of social control in the community). Third, one could look at youthful offending as being a natural consequence of growing up.

"These different 'models' of understanding youthful offending are not simply part of an academic exercise. They suggest quite different approaches for responding to youthful offending. The first model would suggest a focus on the characteristics of individual offenders. If 'offending' is a symptom of a problem, then official responses should focus on the problem, not the symptom. This assumes, of course, that one's goal is 'fixing' the problem. It further assumes that courts, not those responding to youthful offending, both know how to intervene effectively and have adequate available resources.

"If on the other hand, youth crime is seen as the result of an inadequate justice system . . . then the focus of society would be largely on the youth justice system as a 'crime control' system. The underlying justification of a youth justice system would be to stop youth crime. The specific focus would be on the tools available within that system to address this goal.

"Finally, a model that is based on the assumption that youthful offending is, to a large extent, a 'natural' consequence of growing up would have a quite different orientation. Such a system might focus more on responding in a measured way to offending rather than on the traditional utilitarian purposes. If part of what we see as being 'just' in our society is that inappropriate behaviour has consequences, the focus of youth justice would be on ensuring not only that there are consequences, but that these consequences are seen as being appropriate."[1]

How Do Societies Respond *to* Deviance and Crime?

CHAPTER 12

Responding to Youth Crime in Canada by Anthony Doob and Carla Cesaroni reflects the sociological understanding that the youth justice system is just one of many factors affecting youth criminal behaviour.

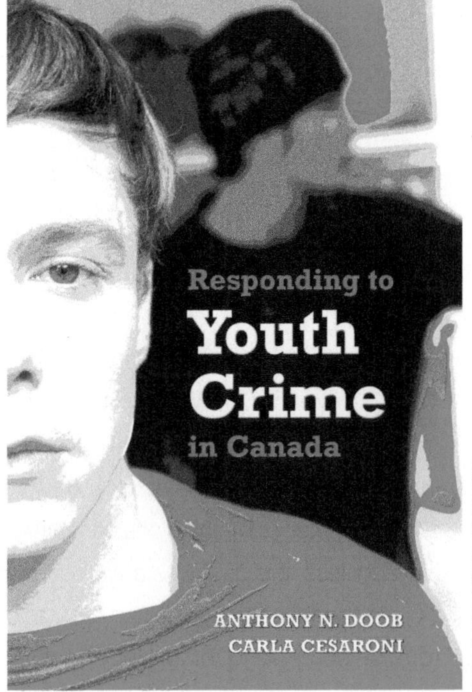

John A. Rizzo/Getty Photo Disc

On September 20, 2011, the Conservative justice minister tabled Bill C-10, also called the *Safe Streets and Communities Act*. This bill proposed several changes to Canada's criminal justice system. Opponents argued that these changes—jail more often, for longer, with more lasting consequences—is a dangerous route that is unsupported by the social science evidence.[2] Do tougher penalties reduce the level of crime? What are the consequences of crime? What can be done about it? In this chapter, we will investigate these and other questions so you can see how sociologists look at these issues.

Deviance

is

the violation of norms that a society agrees upon. **agents of informal control** enforce social norms.

and

- Deviance is linked to time
- Deviance is linked to cultural values
- Deviance is a related to social power
- Deviance is a social construct
- Deviance is a cultural universal

and

NO TRESPASSING

- Retribution
- Incapacitation
- Deterrence
  - General deterrence
  - Specific deterrence
- Restoration
- Rehabilitation

and the goals are

Stigma: a mark of disgrace
- **Discredited stigma:** a stigma that cannot be hidden from others
- **Discreditable stigma:** a stigma that can be concealed from others

Shaming: a deliberate effort to attach a negative meaning to a behaviour
- **Stigmatized shame:** a permanent label given to an offender
- **Reintegrative shaming:** an effort to bring an offender back into the community after punishment

Punishment may involve

get the topic: WHAT ARE DEVIANCE AND CRIME?

Deviance vs. Crime

Deviance is the violation of social norms. For example, people who dye their hair in neon colours would be considered deviant in most parts of our society. Some acts that may be considered socially deviant, like refusing to bathe, for instance, aren't illegal, no matter how much you might wish they were. For something to be considered a **crime**, it has to be a violation of norms that have been written into law. Driving while impaired by alcohol is an example of a crime.

DEVIANCE is the violation of norms that a society agrees upon.
CRIME is the violation of norms that have been written into law.

CRIME TO DEVIANCE

Paolese/Fotolia; middle: Â© Phase4Photography/ShutterStock.com Eugenio Marongiu/Fotolia

WHAT IS DEVIANCE?

If deviance refers to violating socially agreed upon norms, then how do we determine what is and what isn't considered deviant? Sociologists stress the importance of the social context in understanding deviance. For example, wearing a bathing suit at the pool would not be considered deviant, but wearing a bathing suit to your sociology class probably would be. What is deviant to one group may not be considered deviant to another.

There are five specific characteristics that sociologists understand about deviance:

Crime is the violation of norms that have been written into law
Agents of formal control enforce the laws of society

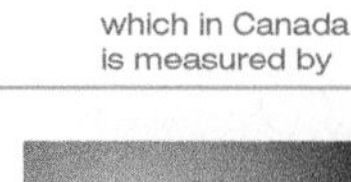

which in Canada is measured by

Uniform Crime Reporting Survey: police statistics of reported crimes
General Social Survey—Victimization measures crime victimization based on a sample of Canadians
Crime rate measures the volume of crime reported to the police
Crime Severity Index measures the seriousness of crime reported to the police

Scott Griessel/Fotolia

Crime trends:

- After peaking in 1991, the crime rate has been decreasing
- The majority of crime in Canada is property crime
- Men have traditionally committed more crime than women
- Aboriginals are more likely to be arrested
- Poor people are more likely to be arrested
- Crime is a young person's game

Laws are created by

Consensus model: laws arise because people see a behaviour they do not like, and they agree to make it illegal
Conflict model: powerful people write laws to protect their own interests while punishing the actions of those they wish to control

1 **Deviance is linked to time.** The definitions of what is considered deviance change over time, so what is considered deviant today may not be deviant tomorrow. One hundred years ago, it was considered deviant for women to wear pants. Today, it's normal for women to dress in pants.

2 **Deviance is linked to cultural values.** How we label an issue determines our moral point of view. Cultural values come from religious, political, economic, or philosophical principles. For example, in Sri Lanka, it is not uncommon for two men to hold hands as they walk down the street. In Canada, this is less common, especially if the two men are heterosexual.

3 **Deviance is a cultural universal.** You can find deviance in every culture on the planet. Regardless of what norms a society establishes, you can always find a small number of nonconformists who will break those rules.

4 **Deviance is a social construct.** Deviance lies not just in the behaviour itself but in the social responses of groups to that behaviour. For example, 30 years ago, it was rare to see a person with a tattoo, and anyone who had one was often suspected of being a criminal. Today it's far more commonplace to see people with tattoos, and their moral character is not suspect. The incredible diversity in what is considered to be deviance suggests that nothing is inherently deviant.

5 **Deviance is a related to social power.** Since deviance is a social construct, it cannot be understood without asking the question "who decides what is deviant?" Often, it is the most powerful groups in society that define what is considered deviant and what the social response will be to various kinds of deviant behaviour.

Crime Statistics

After spending an hour watching a show like *CSI*, you'd think the police are able to solve crimes like they do on TV. Unfortunately, real life isn't as convenient as television. For example, when someone stole a bicycle right out of our garage, I asked the police officer when we might get it back. She said, "Probably never. These kinds of crimes are difficult to solve." She did not even bother filing a report.

UNIFORM CRIME REPORTING (UCR) SURVEY measures the incidence of crime using police statistics of reported crimes gathered from police reports and paperwork.

GENERAL SOCIAL SURVEY (GSS)—VICTIMIZATION measures crime victimization based on a representative sample of nearly 20 000 Canadians over 15 years old.

CRIME RATE measures the volume of crime reported to the police.

By its very nature, crime is difficult to measure. Many crimes go undetected. If someone is speeding down the highway, this is a crime, but if the person is not caught, it is not recorded as a crime. Many crimes are not reported, most often because victims do not think they are important enough to bring to the attention of police. When my bike was stolen, you might say that this was a crime. But since I did not report it, did a crime actually occur?

THE UNIFORM CRIME REPORTING SURVEY AND THE GENERAL SOCIAL SURVEY—VICTIMIZATION

Another aspect of detective work often omitted from television is the paperwork that officers must file. The information in those files is vital to understand crime statistics. Criminologists use two primary sources of data to measure the amount of crime in Canada: the UCR Survey and the GSS—Victimization. Statistics Canada creates the **Uniform Crime Reporting (UCR) Survey** using the official police statistics of reported crimes. Statistics Canada's **General Social Survey (GSS)—Victimization** measures crime victimization by contacting a representative sample of nearly 20 000 Canadians over 15 years old.

UCR surveys contain data only on reported crimes, so when a bicycle is reported as stolen, it becomes a UCR Survey statistic. These data are used to calculate the **crime rate**.[5] In this calculation, all offences

MAKE CONNECTIONS

Crime and Media

Real-world police work is nothing like television crime solving. Most real-world crime involves public disturbances or missing property, but most news reports are about gang shootings or drug busts. The prime-time shows don't exactly help either. Marcus Felson uses the phrase "the dramatic fallacy of crime" to describe how the media, both in news coverage and entertainment shows, paint an unreal picture of the reality of crime.[3]

Most officers never shoot their guns. They spend the majority of their time doing tedious tasks such as "driving around a lot, asking people to quiet down, hearing complaints about barking dogs, filling out paperwork, meeting with other police officers, and waiting to be called up in court."[4]

Most crime is actually rather boring and petty, like a teenager getting drunk and stealing money to buy more alcohol. Since that's not much of a story to broadcast, the media producers prefer something more sensational.

Gina Sanders/Fotolia

>>> **ACTIVITY** Spend two or three nights watching a variety of police shows and local newscasts. Record the types of crimes being described in each type of show. What differences do you see?

<<< **Sociologists who specialize in criminology scientifically study crime, deviance, and social policies that the criminal justice system applies.**

are counted equally—for example, one incident of murder equals one incident of bicycle theft. The crime rate is expressed as number of crimes per 100 000 population.[6] Since 2009, another measure has also been produced by Statistics Canada. The **Crime Severity Index** assigns a weight to each type of crime. More serious crimes are given a higher weight.[7]

Criminologists understand that many crimes go unreported, so they also refer to the GSS—Victimization statistics. Victimization data always indicate more crime than UCR Survey data. In 2004, only about 34 percent of criminal incidents were reported to police.[8] This supports the criminologist's general estimation that more than half the crimes that are committed go unreported.

CRIME SEVERITY INDEX measures the seriousness of crime reported to the police.

CRIME TRENDS

UCR Survey and victimization data are also used to determine crime trends—and the trend that seems most constant is that the crime rates change over time. Since peaking in 1991, the police-reported crime rate, which measures the total volume of crime per 100 000 population, has been decreasing.[9] The majority of crime in Canada is property crime. In 2009, property crimes made up 56 percent of all reported crimes, whereas violent crimes constituted about 18 percent.[10] These trends are in stark contrast to the media's portrayal of crime.

Gender and Crime

Throughout history, men have traditionally committed more crime than women. This demographic characteristic of offenders in Canada has not changed much over time. In 2008, men were considered the accused in 81 percent of cases of violent victimization against women and in 79 percent of cases of violent victimization against men.[11] This is a significant statistic because men make up less than 50 percent of the population. However, several other factors also figure in crime trends.

Ethnicity and Crime

Although the gender differences in crime statistics are fairly easy to distinguish, discussing a link between ethnicity and crime is controversial. The major problem is the long history of racism in Canada. In 2008, aboriginal adults accounted for 22 percent of new prisoners while representing just 3 percent of the Canadian population.[12] Does this disproportionate representation suggest aboriginals commit more crimes, or does the criminal justice system unfairly pursue them?

Some argue that the police's different enforcement practices are responsible for these data. Racial profiling is a controversial police practice of targeting criminals based on their race or ethnicity. David Cole shows that traffic police disproportionately stop members of visible minorities.[13] Jeffrey Reiman suggests that the police seek out the poor for arrest because the poor are easier to catch and easier to convict of crimes.[14] Wealthy people can hire expensive lawyers; poor people must use the public defender system. This increases the odds that official statistics have an inherent ethnic bias because visible minorities disproportionately represent the poor in Canada.

Social Class and Crime

Crime rates are higher in poorer neighbourhoods, but this doesn't necessarily mean people in lower classes commit more crime. Interpreting data on the link between social class and crime is difficult. A number of studies have shown that poorer people are arrested at higher rates,[15] but that doesn't mean everyone who lives in poor neighbourhoods breaks the law or is more likely to break the law.[16]

Reiman believes that social class makes a huge difference in who gets caught and who goes to prison. He argues that laws are applied differently and that dangerous activities performed by the "elite" are not even considered crimes.

For example, doctors who accidentally kill a patient during an unnecessary surgery are not accused of manslaughter. Similarly, Reiman suggests that white-collar crimes often are not reported because people want to avoid a scandal. They also have the power to conceal their illegal activities.

POLICE-REPORTED CRIME RATES, CANADA, 1962 TO 2011

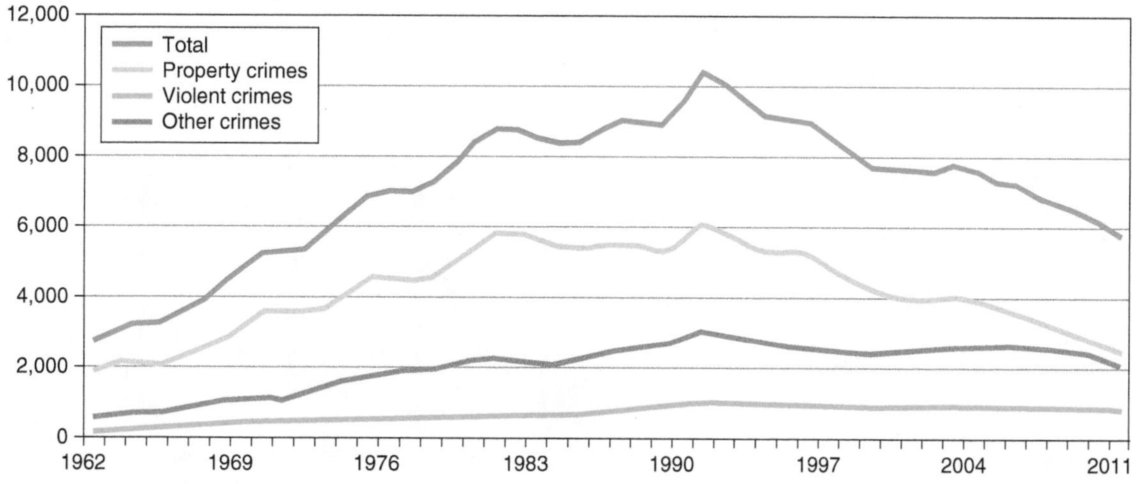

Source: Statistics Canada, Canadian Centre for Justice Statistics, Uniform Crime Reporting Survey. This does not constitute an endorsement by Statistics Canada of this product.

Age and Crime

Essentially, crime is a young person's game. This idea is supported by the relationship between age and crime. It indicates that the majority of arrests peak between the ages of 15 and 25. After that point, they follow a slow but steady decrease throughout life.[17] Arrest data from other cultures and times in history also support this claim.[18]

The link between age and crime is very clear in criminology. Since the early 1970s, declining Canadian fertility rates have resulted in a drop in the proportion of young people aged 15 to 24. A Statistics Canada study found that this demographic shift may be associated with a decline in rates of breaking and entering.[19] Clearly, age matters when discussing crime.

International Comparisons of Crime

To gain a better perspective on crime in Canada, sociologists often make international comparisons. However, making international comparisons

GO GLOBAL

Comparing Crime Rates

Which country has the highest crime rate? The truth is, it is very difficult to answer this question. Remember that the crime rate is defined as the volume of crime reported to the police. If it is not reported, it is not counted. When making cross-country comparisons of crime statistics, you should consider the following methodological difficulties:

- Different countries use different definitions for different types of crime. For example, the definition of *assault* varies from country to country, and this will be reflected in the total number of assault incidents recorded.
- Countries have different levels of reporting and traditions of policing. If there are few police officers, or if they are difficult to contact, a crime is unlikely to be reported. In some societies, the police are mistrusted by the population, and reporting levels are likely to be lower than in cases where the police are regarded as important members of the community.
- Different social norms may influence what people consider to be a crime and what is reported. In some societies it is almost impossible for women to report cases of rape or sexual abuse, while in others women are encouraged to come forward.[20]

The United Nations Office on Drugs and Crime publishes the *Survey on Crime Trends and the Operations of Criminal Justice Systems*. The data from different countries for selected crimes is illustrated in the first chart below. You can see that among these countries, the United States has the highest homicide rate, Canada leads the list for burglaries and rape, and France has the highest rates for assault and car theft.[21]

The actual crime rate may not always reflect people's perception of crime. The United Nations survey also asked people in selected countries about their perception of criminal danger and the effectiveness of police. The responses are summarized in the second chart below. Although Japan had the lowest recorded crime rates of these countries, people in Japan are more afraid to walk after dark, and they have less confidence in the efficiency of police.[22]

These data leave a mixed picture for the international comparison of crime. Living in the United States increases the odds that one might be murdered, yet Americans claim to be the least afraid to walk after dark, and they have the highest confidence in the efficiency of their police officers.

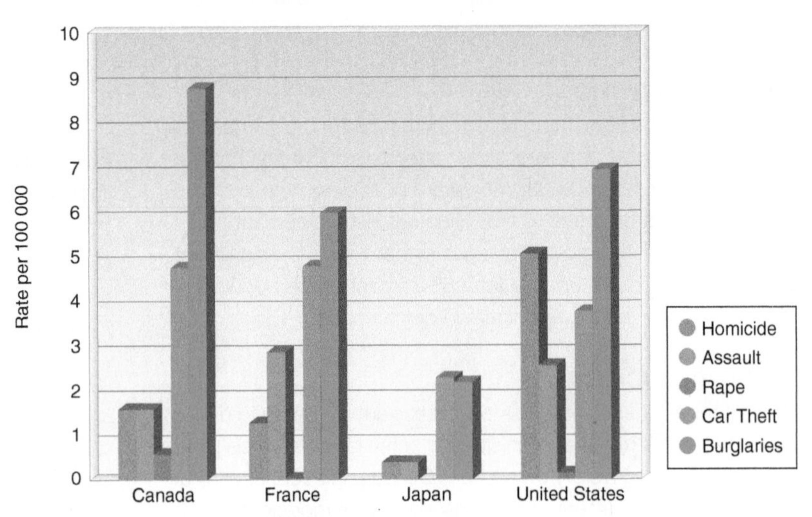

Source: Reprinted by permission of NationMaster.

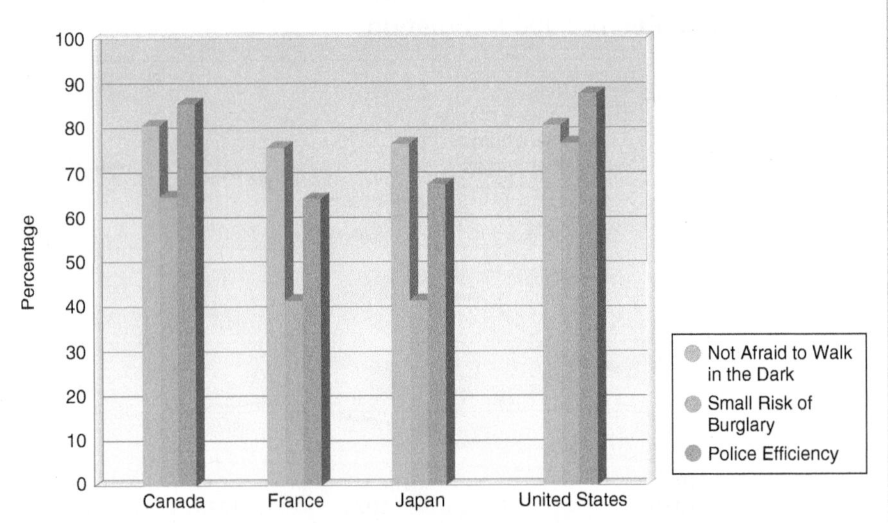

Source: Based on 2011 UNODC Crime and Criminal Justice Statistics (2003–2008).

of crime data creates certain problems for the researcher. Here is a list of potentially complicating factors:

1. Crime numbers may or may not be accurate. Some countries deliberately skew their data to show lower crime rates in order to keep tourism high.
2. Legal definitions of crimes differ among nations. For example, some nations do not recognize marital rape as a crime; others have legalized drugs that are illegal in Canada.
3. Different methods of collecting data can result in differences in reported crimes. Some nations have extraordinarily reliable data collection systems, while others do not.
4. Cultures vary, as do programs to prevent, punish, and curb crime.

Societal Responses to Deviance and Crime

Why are certain things illegal and not others? Laws are created according to two primary models: the consensus model and the conflict model. The **consensus model of law** suggests that laws arise because people see a behaviour they do not like, and they agree to make it illegal. For example, virtually everyone thinks child abuse is wrong. Laws against it arise out of a general agreement about the treatment of children.

The **conflict model of law** proposes that powerful people write laws to protect their own interests while punishing the actions of those they wish to control. For example, laws prohibiting vagrancy, loitering, trespassing, and theft are designed primarily to protect the wealthy from attacks by the poor.

Most of us generally follow the social norms and the laws of our society because we are under the influence of agents of control. **Agents of formal control** are agents who enforce the laws of society, such as the police and the justice system. **Agents of informal control** enforce social norms. This group includes the other agents of socialization, such as your parents, teachers, and friends.

STIGMA

Any convict who's been released from prison will tell you that life on the "outside" is no picnic. That's because people who serve time for a crime and then rejoin society carry with them the label of "ex-con" for the rest of their lives. In other words, we attach a **stigma**, or a mark of disgrace associated with a particular status, quality, or person, to the ex-convict. Sometimes, one's age, religion, sexual orientation, economic status, or race can result in a stigma.

Sociologist Erving Goffman suggests that we all have a positive ideal identity that we hope others will accept. Unfortunately, a stigma points out the differences between our ideal and real selves. There are two types of stigma—discredited stigma and discreditable stigma. A **discredited stigma** is a stigma that cannot be hidden from others, or is no longer hidden from others. A person with a physical handicap has a discredited stigma. A **discreditable stigma** is a stigma that can be concealed from others, such as sexual orientation, sexually transmitted infections, and criminal history.

SHAMING

Shaming is a deliberate effort to attach a negative feeling to a behaviour. John Braithwaite suggests shame can either stigmatize or reintegrate.[23] **Stigmatized shame** is a permanent label given to an offender, which could actually increase the chances of reoffending because the guilty person is forever labelled. In Canada, we stigmatize former inmates when we require them to admit their prior convictions on job applications and housing forms. **Reintegrative shaming** serves to bring the offender back into the community after punishment.

CONSENSUS MODEL OF LAW suggests that laws arise because people see a behaviour they do not like, and they agree to make it illegal.

CONFLICT MODEL OF LAW proposes that powerful people write laws to protect their own interests while punishing the actions of those they wish to control.

AGENTS OF FORMAL CONTROL enforce the laws of society.

AGENTS OF INFORMAL CONTROL enforce social norms.

STIGMA is a mark of disgrace associated with a particular status, quality, or person.

DISCREDITED STIGMA is a stigma that cannot be hidden from others or is no longer hidden from others.

DISCREDITABLE STIGMA is a stigma that can be concealed from others.

SHAMING is a deliberate effort to attach a negative meaning to a behaviour.

STIGMATIZED SHAME is a permanent label given to an offender, which could actually increase the chances of reoffending because the guilty person is forever labelled.

REINTEGRATIVE SHAMING is an effort to bring an offender back into the community after punishment.

RETRIBUTION reflects the belief that someone who commits a crime is responsible for his or her actions and deserves to be punished.

INCAPACITATION prevents a person from committing more crime.

DETERRENCE tries to prevent a person from doing something because of fear of the consequences.

GENERAL DETERRENCE ensures that individuals will not commit a crime because they see the negative consequences applied to others, and they fear experiencing these consequences.

PUNISHMENT

All societies must deal with rule breakers. Historically, punishments were often harsh and included physical torture, exile, forced slavery, or death. Alternative punishments included shaming an offender by placing him in the pillory and stocks in the town square.

In Canada, being sent to prison is the most severe form of punishment. Probation, community service, and fines are other forms of punishment that are often used. The principles underlying the punishment of criminals have changed over time. These changes reflect how criminals are viewed by society, and changes in what people think are the causes of crime and criminal behaviour. There are five goals of punishment:

Retribution reflects the belief that someone who commits a crime is responsible for his or her actions and deserves to be punished. The expression "an eye for an eye" is an example of the retribution goal of punishment.

Incapacitation prevents a person from committing more crime. This usually means sending an offender to prison. Society needs to protect its law-abiding members from criminal behaviour. One way to do this is to incapacitate offenders so that they are unable to commit further crimes. When offenders are sent to prison, being locked up, away from the general public, serves to incapacitate them. They are no longer a threat as long as they are behind bars.

Deterrence tries to prevent a person from doing something because of fear of the consequences. **General deterrence** ensures that individuals will not commit a crime because they see the negative consequences

L. Shat/Fotolia

<<< Who do you think posted this sign? Whom is it meant to keep out?

SPECIFIC DETERRENCE occurs to individuals who have violated the law and have already been punished.

REHABILITATION tries to reform offenders so that they can be returned to society, but will no longer choose to engage in criminal behaviour.

RESTORATION attempts to make the victim, and the community, whole again.

REINTEGRATIVE JUSTICE is based on the principle that offenders can be successfully reintegrated into the wider society.

SENTENCING CIRCLE is a process used by some First Nations communities to the rehabilitate the offender and to heal the community as a whole.

applied to others, and they fear experiencing these consequences. Prison is a general deterrent for many people. **Specific deterrence** occurs to individuals who have violated the law and have already been punished. When we send an offender to prison, we hope he or she will be specifically deterred from committing future offences because of the fear of returning to prison.

Rehabilitation tries to reform offenders so that they can be returned to society, but will no longer choose to engage in criminal behaviour. Prison programs that include counselling or vocational training reflect the rehabilitation goal of punishment.

Restoration attempts to make the victim, and the community, whole again. In Canada, victim impact statements are used to give victims a voice in the criminal justice process. It allows them to participate in the sentencing of an offender by explaining to the court, and the offender, how the crime has affected them.[24]

PRISON AND THE CHARACTERISTICS OF PRISON INMATES

Prison is a last resort in the criminal justice system. The guilty party is locked in a facility for a period of time depending on the crime.

THINK SOCIOLOGICALLY

Reintegrative Justice

Reintegrative justice is based on the principle that offenders can be successfully reintegrated into the wider society to live law-abiding lives in the community following their release. However, it is important to remember that in many cases, the offenders were *not* successfully integrated into their community before they got into trouble with the law. Many were already marginalized in some way and may have lacked the values and behaviours that result in most people obeying the law.

In Canada, reintegrative justice relies on a number of interventions, programs, and services which are designed to help prisoners reenter society following an arrest or incarceration. Recently, more emphasis has been placed on designing comprehensive interventions and a continuity of care to provide consistent assistance to offenders. There is also a growing recognition that preparation for reintegration should begin before the offenders' release.[25]

In Canada, aboriginal justice is based on the concept of restoring peace in communities through compensation, restitution, rehabilitation, reconciliation, and balance. While all Canadians are subject to the *Criminal Code of Canada* and the Canadian legal system, some First Nations communities have adopted a process called *sentencing circles*. A **sentencing circle** is composed of fellow community members, the victim, and often the offender. The circle will make sentencing recommendations, and in many cases the trial judge will accept these recommendations. Through this process, the entire community can be involved and is given the chance to contribute to the rehabilitation of the offender and the healing of the community as a whole.[26]

CRIME SEVERITY INDEX, 2009

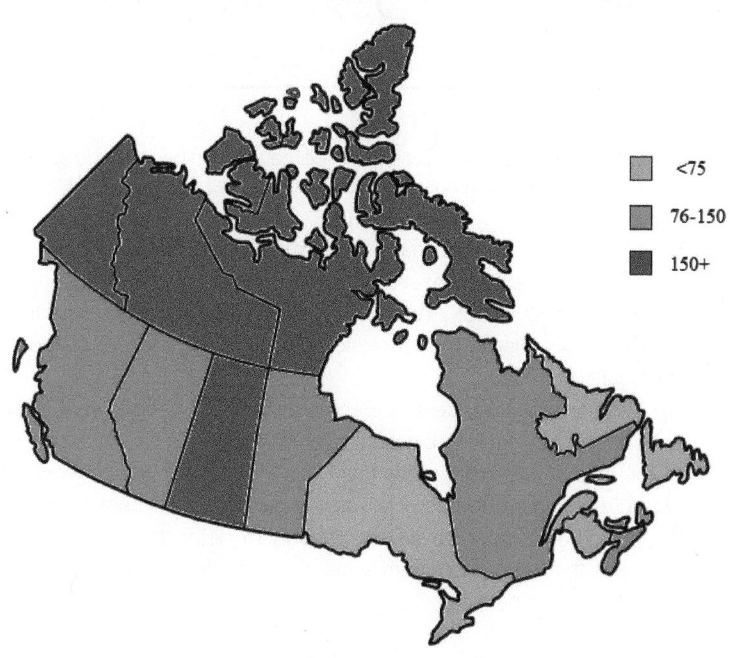

Source: Adapted from Statistics Canada, CANSIM table 252-0052 and Catalogue no. 85-002-X. Last modified: 2010-07-29. www40.statcan.ca/l01/cst01/legal51a-eng.htm. This does not constitute an endorsement by Statistics Canada of this product.

INTERNATIONAL INCARCERATION RATES

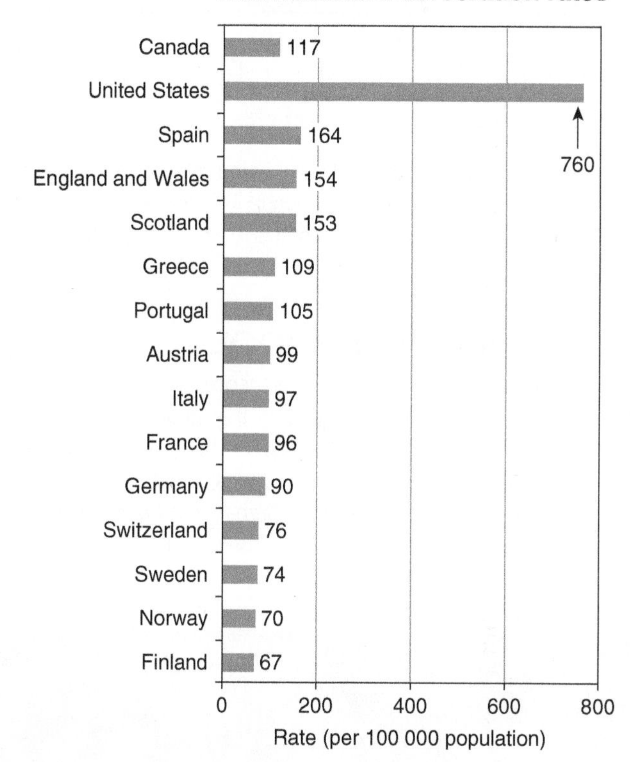

Source: Statistics Canada, "Adult and Youth Correctional Services: Key Indicators," www.statcan.gc.ca/daily-quotidien/091208/dq091208a-eng.htm, accessed October 23, 2010. References to incarceration rates from countries other than Canada are based on data from World Prison Brief, prepared by the International Centre for Prison Studies, King's College London. The rate for Canada is based on data for the fiscal year 2008/2009, and the rate for the United States is based on the calendar year 2008 and excludes youth. The data for other countries are based on the most recent data published by World Prison Brief, and reference years range from between 2008 and 2009. These rates are based on each country's total population and include, with the exception of the United States, the total number of adults and youth in custody. In Canada, a youth is considered to be aged between 12 and 17. The definition of *youth* may vary from one country to another.

RECIDIVISM is the tendency for inmates released from prison to return to prison.

Correctional Service Canada (CSS) is responsible for fulfilling two crucial responsibilities in Canada's criminal justice system: the incarceration of offenders and their safe reintegration into Canadian society.[27]

In 2010/2011, on any given day, more than 38 000 adults and nearly 2000 youth aged 12 to 17 were in custody in Canada. This resulted in an incarceration rate of 140 people in custody for every 100 000 people.[28] However, the rate is much higher for some groups. Aboriginals represent 18 percent of all those in custody. In all the Canadian provinces and territories, the proportion of aboriginal adults in correctional services exceeds their representation in the general population. In 2010/2011, 41 percent of females and 25 percent of males in custody were aboriginal. The overall incarceration rate is highest for adults aged 25 to 34 years old. Females account for only 11 percent of the total population in custody, but this proportion has been increasing in the past 10 years.[29]

Most inmates are eventually released from prison, but what happens to them after prison? Unfortunately, the most likely outcome for inmates released from prison is to return to prison. This is called **recidivism**. If a return to prison is a failure of the prison system, then clearly the system is failing because 37 percent of all inmates will return to prison.[30]

Costs of Incarceration

The actual costs to incarcerate an individual are difficult to determine. Although a dollar amount can be calculated, there are hidden costs associated with the incarcerated—the children left behind in the foster-care system, or families who must use the welfare system to survive. These social costs can't be factored in the prison budget, so the reported cost of incarceration never includes them. Nevertheless, taxpayers are left to pay for all the direct and indirect costs. A Statistics Canada report estimated the average daily cost to be $143.03 per prisoner[31]; this amounts to more than $52 000 per year.

Canadian Incarceration Rates vs. International Incarceration Rates

Canada's incarceration rate has tended to be higher than rates in most western European countries yet lower than that of the United States.[32] The United States has the highest incarceration rate in the world. Policies like the three-strikes law have contributed to the much higher incarceration rate in the United Sates than in similar countries.

In fact, the United States incarcerates at a rate 6 times higher than Canada and 10 times higher than Switzerland. It's important to remember that, just as with crime rates, you should use caution when interpreting international data regarding prison populations. Think about what you already know about international crime and murder rates. What factors do you think contribute to the role of the United States as the world's leader in crime and incarceration?

think sociologically: WHY DO DEVIANCE AND CRIME EXIST?

Historical Roots of Deviance and Crime Theories

The earliest attempts to explain deviance and criminal behaviour arose from two philosophical schools of thought. The classical school argued for a more rational approach to punishment, while positivists looked for why people commit crimes.

THE CLASSICAL SCHOOL

The classical school assumed that all people are self-interested by nature. Classical thinkers also suggested that people are rational and make free-will choices about how to behave. Their primary question was "What keeps us from being criminal?"

Cesare Beccaria's 1764 essay *On Crimes and Punishments* had a great impact on the way the Western world looks at justice and crime.

Scott Griessel/Fotolia

Cesare Lombroso helped perpetuate the idea that some people are "born criminals."

RACIAL PROFILING occurs when police use a person's race as the primary reason to suspect that the individual has broken the law.

Beccaria argued that a legal system must treat everyone equally to protect people against excessive government power. In fact, many ideas contained in our *Charter of Rights and Freedoms* come from Beccaria. He believed that in order to truly deter crime, we needed a fair legal system.[33]

Another classicist, Jeremy Bentham, believed people were inherently *hedonistic,* seeking pleasure over pain. Being a strong supporter of the idea of deterrence, Bentham felt that people would avoid the pleasure of crime only if they feared the pain of punishment. However, the punishment must be severe enough to deter them, but not so severe as to alienate them from society. In other words, the punishment should fit the crime.[34]

RATIONAL CHOICE THEORY

The classical school emphasized that individuals make rational choices based on self-interest. According to rational choice theory, the reason most people do not commit crime is that they fear being punished. So, if the goal of the criminal justice system is to deter crime, classicists believed that the punishments must be swift, certain, and severe enough to deter people's actions. People will consciously and rationally consider the costs and benefits of deviance or crime. If the benefits outweigh the costs, they are more likely to act deviantly. If you are in a convenience store and the clerk is not around, you might be tempted to steal a pack of gum because the chances of getting caught are very low. What the rational choice theory fails to explain is why, given the same context, some people commit crimes while others do not.

THE POSITIVIST SCHOOL

Positivists assumed that people are naturally social beings and are not prone to act criminally unless some biological, psychological, or social factor is involved. To a positivist, the world is orderly and follows natural laws. And since natural law dictates that everything must have a cause, positivists were interested in what factors cause people to commit crime.

Biological Positivism

In the nineteenth century, physician Cesare Lombroso believed that "criminals" could be distinguished by physical characteristics: big ears, protruding jaws, and deep-set eyes.[35] While this idea is clearly preposterous, some scientists still believe there might be a biological element to crime. The search for biological causes for criminality continues to this day. Some test for chemical imbalances in the brain caused by genetic predisposition,[36] low blood sugar,[37] and low levels of serotonin.[38] Others study the hormonal differences between men and women and how they impact criminal behaviour. For example, higher testosterone levels make men more aggressive than women. Could this account for some of the difference between men and women's delinquent behaviours?[39] All these factors are shown to have connections to criminal behaviour, but the statistical links are often weak. The search for a biological cause for deviance and crime is far from complete and often fails to isolate social factors from genetic ones. Of course, this line of thinking can also lead to **racial profiling**, in which police uses a person's race as the primary reason to suspect that the individual has broken the law.

Psychological Positivism

Psychological theories of criminality tend to be positivistic, placing the blame on something abnormal in the individual, such as a low IQ, or a thinking error. The American Psychiatric Association (APA) claims that criminals suffer from an "antisocial" personality disorder that causes them to "fail to conform to social norms with respect to lawful behaviours as indicated by repeatedly performing acts that are grounds for arrest."[40] According to the APA, criminals are impulsive, aggressive, and irritable, and they tend to lie about their behaviours and feel no remorse for their actions.

Sociological Theories

Sociological theories tend to focus on the social context in order to explain deviance and criminality. Some of these theories examine how the social structure contributes to deviance and crime. Other theories look at how social processes and interactions can produce deviant behaviour.

FUNCTIONALISM—FUNCTIONS OF DEVIANCE

Functional theories describe deviance as a response to some social factors, and these theorists look for the causes of deviance. Émile Durkheim noted that deviance exists in all societies because it fulfills one of these three needs:

1. Deviance marks the boundaries of morality. Identifying specific acts and people as deviant helps establish the difference between right and wrong more clearly.
2. Deviance promotes social solidarity. People unify against a common enemy, and deviants are often the common enemy.
3. Deviance can bring about needed change in a social system. Norms and values that may be acceptable at one time may be challenged and redefined as being deviant.[41]

STRAIN THEORY

Robert Merton's strain theory describes how social structures and values cause deviance.[42] Merton suggests that most of us have common goals, including wealth, a home, a career, cars, and a family. Achieving these goals usually involves education, hard work, entrepreneurship, and some luck. However, not everyone has the same opportunities for success. Many in the lower classes have blocked access to these opportunities, so they adapt to their plight in one of five ways:

1 **Conformists** accept society's goals and use socially acceptable means to try to achieve them. They obey rules and work at low-paying jobs with little chance of advancement. One example is a janitor who works three jobs but can't get ahead because of low pay.

2 **Innovators** accept common goals but not the traditional means of reaching them, using socially unacceptable and often illegal means to achieve those goals instead. For example, an innovator might steal goods and sell them at a pawnshop instead of getting a job.

3 **Ritualists** accept the traditional means of achieving the goals but are not as interested in the material goals. Social workers use their advanced degrees to pursue humanitarian efforts rather than monetary benefits.

4 **Retreatists** reject both the means and the goals of society. These people often live in isolation or deal with issues of drug and alcohol abuse, mental illness, or homelessness.

5 **Rebels** use their own means to create new goals, often seeking major societal changes.

Gandhi was a rebel who sought to change society through nonviolent methods.

Few sociologists still accept Merton's theory; however, it clearly draws a connection between social structures and deviance, and it provokes more thinking about the relationships between poverty and crime. The theory is criticized for the assumption of universal goals and its inability to explain violent or white-collar crimes.

>>> Though the acts in which Martin Luther King, Jr., and his followers engaged were considered illegal at the time, **these "deviant" acts helped bring about much-needed change to the racist laws of the United States.**

Library of Congress Prints and Photographs Division[LC-DIG-ppmsca-03128]

PRIMARY DEVIANCE is the initial deviant act itself, which is not followed by some form of labelling.

SECONDARY DEVIANCE refers to the psychological reorientation that occurs when a person is labelled as deviant and assumes that identity.

CONFLICT THEORY—INEQUALITY BETWEEN SOCIAL GROUPS

Conflict theory suggests that deviant behaviour results from social, political, or economic inequalities between social groups. In response to these inequalities, certain groups will act deviantly in order to change their situation, to change the social structure, or to protest against the dominant group. The conflict perspective also focuses on who defines certain acts and groups as deviant.

Social conflict theories usually focus on issues of social class, power, capitalism, and their relation to crime. For instance, Reiman states that "the rich get richer and the poor get prison," meaning if you are part of the upper class, you can get away with criminal acts.[43] Willem Bonger argues that capitalism causes crime by emphasizing selfishness in individuals.[44] Capitalism pits people against each other in a struggle for possessions. It also doesn't help that wealthy people who commit crimes often face more lenient punishment than poor people who commit crimes. Income and wealth inequality lead to abuses of the system, and this structural inequality leads to crime.

Modern conflict theorists continue Bonger's stand that power and wealth inequality leads to crime. Reiman suggests that the inequalities of the justice system are rooted in social class.[45] Although conflict theories focus on the structural reasons for crime, they don't explain why certain individuals commit them.

SYMBOLIC INTERACTIONISM—LEARNING AND LABELLING

Is it how we interact with people that creates deviance and criminality? Criminals engage in social interactions that influence their likelihood of breaking the law. Interaction theories are divided into social process theories and social reaction theories. Social process theories review how criminal behaviours develop, while social reaction theories examine how societal reactions affect criminal behaviour.

DIFFERENTIAL ASSOCIATION THEORY

Edwin Sutherland and Donald Cressey proposed the differential association theory, which emphasizes that deviant behaviour is learned. For instance, a teen might sneak out at night to go hang out with friends. If that teen has a younger sibling, the sibling might learn that it is acceptable to sneak out, and how to do so. Similarly, criminals pass on their attitudes, values, mechanisms, and beliefs about crime to others. People commit crimes because they learn that criminal activity is acceptable and/or normal. Sutherland makes this theory clear with nine propositions listed below. Clearly he is a positivist, asserting that deviance must be learned from others.

Sutherland's Nine Propositions

1. Deviance is learned, not inherited.
2. Deviance is learned through communication.
3. The principal part of learning deviant behaviour occurs within intimate personal groups.
4. The learning includes the techniques of committing the deviant act and the special direction/motives, drives, rationalizations, and attitudes necessary to carry it out.
5. The specific direction of motives and drives is learned from definitions of the legal codes as favourable and unfavourable.
6. A person becomes delinquent because of an excess of definitions favourable to the violation of the law.
7. Differential associations may vary in frequency, duration, priority, and intensity.
8. The process of learning deviant behaviour by association with criminal and noncriminal patterns involves all the same mechanisms that are involved in any other learning.
9. Although deviant behaviour is an expression of general needs and values, it is not explained by those general needs and values.[46]

LABELLING THEORY

Labelling theory states that individuals become deviant when the deviant label is applied to them. They adopt the label and start to exhibit the behaviours, actions, and attitudes associated with the label. This theory helps us to understand how the past behaviours of an individual are reinterpreted in accordance with their label. It is not so much the act itself which is deviant, but how it is interpreted and responded to. Labelling applies a stigma to the individual, which affects how they see themselves and how they are seen by others.

The process of labelling can actually contribute to future deviance or crime. Edwin Lemert proposed two types of deviance: primary and secondary.[47] **Primary deviance** refers to the initial deviant act itself, which is not followed by some form of labelling. If a student cheats on a test and gets caught, the teacher may or may not label that student as a cheater. If the student is reprimanded but not labelled, this is an example of primary deviance. **Secondary deviance** refers to the psychological reorientation that occurs when a person is labelled as deviant and assumes that identity. According to Lemert, secondary deviance often encourages future misdeeds. If the teacher labels the student as a cheater and tells other teachers that this student is a cheater, then the student carries the identity of "cheater" and may start to think that the only way to pass a test is to cheat.

SOCIAL CONTROL THEORIES

Social control theories suggest that people are hedonistic and self-interested. Walter Reckless argued that internal and external factors control behaviour.[48] His containment theory argues that criminals cannot resist the temptations that surround them. Everyone has different levels of internal controls, including the ability to withstand temptations, morality, integrity, self-esteem, fear of punishment, and the desire to be and do good. External forces such as the police, our family, and/or our friends also control us. However, it is the internal control that influences criminality; for example, few people speed in front of a police car.

Travis Hirschi agrees that internal controls predict criminality and suggests that four social bonds—attachment, commitment, involvement, and belief—affect our inner controls.[49] Strong bonds indicate less likelihood toward criminality.

The first bond, attachment, refers to our relationship with others. If a teen hangs out with conformists—friends who do not drink, smoke, or use illegal drugs—he or she is less likely to engage in these behaviours. Commitment refers to our dedication to live a socially acceptable life. By attending school, you are committed to a socially acceptable behaviour. Thus, as we age, we are often more committed to responsible behaviour. Could this explain the age–crime connection? Involvement refers to the level of participation in conventional activities. Teens who are involved in their schools or have extracurricular activities are less likely to be delinquent. This is in part because they have less time for deviance. The final bond, belief,

DmitriMaruta/Shutterstock

According to Sutherland, crime must be taught. Only then will criminal behaviours develop.

refers to a person's conviction of truth. If we believe that living a conventional life is good, then we are unlikely to deviate from that path.

These bonds can act together or independently to influence a person's inner control. For example, the theory would say that cross-dressing occurs because people attach themselves to nonconformists (other cross-dressers). They involve themselves in non-normative behaviours by cross-dressing and believe this is normal and "okay." Involvement in conforming activities may raise the level of attachment to conventional values that could increase a person's belief in those values. Likewise, low levels on these bonds might increase the likelihood that a person will engage in nonconventional activity.

Feminist Theory

Crime is primarily a male activity; females account for only a small proportion of all offenders. As a result, the theories we have seen so far have tended to focus on explaining the causes of male criminal behaviour. From the feminist perspective, the gender differences in crime are largely due to differences in power and control. This is why males are more likely than females to commit crimes, but women are more likely to be the victims.

Feminists also point out that when women commit crimes, they are more likely to commit only certain crimes and to do so for different reasons than men. In 2005, the most frequent offences committed by women in Canada were theft, common assault, bail violations, and fraud.[50]

CHIVALRY HYPOTHESIS suggests that female offenders are treated more leniently by male police officers and judges.

Feminist theorists argue that because of the androcentric bias, women are often treated differently within the criminal justice system. Historically, female criminals have been treated like delinquent children. Their criminal behaviour has been seen to be the result of an illness or a psychological imbalance. This reflects the patriarchal ideology that women need to be protected, and the **chivalry hypothesis** states that female offenders are treated more leniently by male police officers and judges.[51]

The feminist perspective has also brought attention to crimes in which women are often the victims. In 2008 the overall rates of police-reported violent victimization were comparable between men and women, but the nature of their victimization differed. Females were over 10 times more likely than males to be victims of police-reported sexual assault.[52] Women are far more likely than men to be the victims of intimate violence. Finally, women working as police officers, attorneys, and judges often face very different issues than their male counterparts.[53] These are just some of the topics addressed by feminist criminologists.

WRAP YOUR MIND AROUND THE THEORY

These students chose society's traditional means to reach their goals of success.

Monkey Business /Shutterstock

FUNCTIONALISM

For functionalists, deviance is a part of society. Durkheim notes that deviance always exists in society and therefore must serve some function. For Merton, deviance occurs because the pursuit of socially desirable goals is blocked for some people. Therefore, people must adapt. Only one of these modes of adaptation leads to deviance, but all occur because the system blocks some people from the goals to which they aspire.

CONFLICT THEORY

Conflict theory suggests that deviant behaviour results from social, political, or economic inequalities between social groups. In response to these inequalities, certain groups will act deviantly in order to change their situation, to change the social structure, or to protest against the dominant group. Reiman's statement "the rich get richer, the poor get prison" points out that laws are written in the best interest of the wealthy. The wealthy often make the laws that punish poor people who might steal to survive. Meanwhile, illegal acts of the wealthy are often not considered crimes.

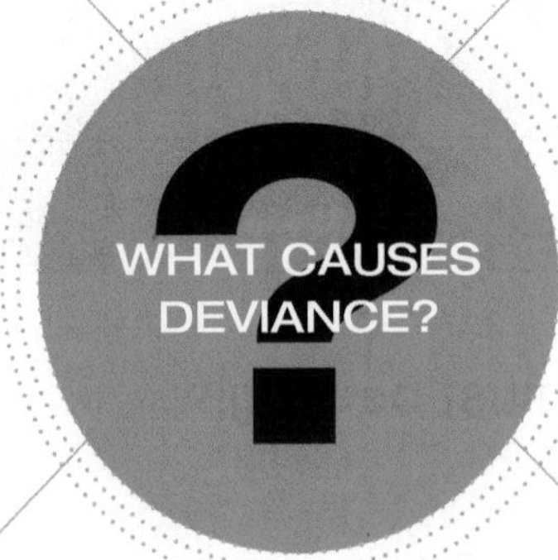

SYMBOLIC INTERACTIONISM

Interactionist theories are divided into social process theories and social reaction theories. Social process theories review how criminal behaviours develop, while social reaction theories examine how societal reactions affect criminal behaviour. The differential association theory emphasizes that deviant behaviour is learned, while labelling theory states that individuals become deviant when the deviant label is applied to them. Containment theory examines the internal and external factors that control behaviour. Travis Hirschi suggests that four social bonds affect our inner controls.

FEMINIST THEORY

Power imbalances in society mean that women are more likely to be the victims of male perpetrators of crime. The reasons women commit crimes are different from those that explain male criminal behaviour. Feminist theorists also draw attention to how female offenders, as well as female police, lawyers, and judges, are treated differently within the criminal justice system.

Russel A. Daniels/ /AP/Corbis

The police enforce laws written by the wealthy. These laws often benefit the wealthy and exploit the poor.

Ken Lax/Science Source/Photo Researchers, Inc

Society and our own social interactions influence our tendencies toward deviance and crime.

discover sociology in action: HOW DO WE DEAL WITH CRIME IN CANADA?

Crime Control: The Criminal Justice System

The Canadian justice system has three parts: *police*, *courts*, and *corrections*. Each of these parts of the system responds to violations of the law, and each reflects the social policies of our country toward crime.

POLICE

Today, there are more than 67 000 police officers across Canada.[54] Police are the ones on the front line against crime. Their role requires police officers to have **discretion**, or the ability to make decisions, which often involves whether or not they will enforce the law. If you've ever received a warning instead of a ticket for speeding through a school zone, you've reaped the benefit of a police officer's discretion.

COURTS

The courts are the second part of the criminal justice system. The basic role of courts in Canada is to help people resolve disputes fairly and with justice. There are four levels of courts in Canada. The provincial and territorial courts handle the majority of cases that come into the system. Second are the provincial/territorial superior courts, which deal with more serious crimes and also hear appeals from provincial/territorial court judgments. At the third level are the provincial/territorial courts of appeal, while the highest level is the Supreme Court of Canada.[55]

Since a crime is considered to be an offence against society as a whole, it is usually the state that starts a criminal trial. The person charged with a crime is called the "accused" and is always presumed innocent until proven guilty. In Canada, there are two types of criminal offences. **Summary conviction offences** are less serious. The accused appears before a provincial court for a trial. The maximum penalty for this type of offence is normally a $5000 fine, six months in prison, or both.

More serious offences are called **indictable offences**. There is often a "preliminary hearing" for indictable offences during which a judge examines the case to decide whether there is enough evidence to proceed with the trial. If the judge decides there is not enough evidence, the case is dismissed. Otherwise, a full criminal trial is ordered. During the trial, the prosecution must prove that the accused is guilty of the charge beyond a reasonable doubt.

DISCRETION is the ability to make decisions.

SUMMARY CONVICTION OFFENCES are less serious offences.

INDICTABLE OFFENCES are more serious offences.

If the accused is found not guilty, he or she is acquitted and is free to go. If the accused is found guilty of the crime, a judge must then decide on an appropriate sentence, which may include a fine, community service, or time in prison.[56]

CORRECTIONAL SERVICES

The correctional system is the third leg of the criminal justice system. It supervises those who are convicted of crimes. Correctional Service Canada is the department responsible for carrying out any sentence imposed by a judge.

The name *Correctional Service* suggests that prisons are supposed to correct the offender and assist in his or her successful reintegration into society. There are six services under the responsibility of Correctional Service Canada:

1. *Custodial remands:* After a person has been arrested and charged with an offence, he or she may be kept in remand (prison) until trial and sentencing. If the trial judge imposes a custodial sentence (a prison term), the time spent in remand is usually deducted from the sentenced time.
2. *Custodial sentences:* At trial, the judge may impose a sentence of custody in prison. In Canada, any custodial sentence longer than two years is served in a federal penitentiary, while sentences of less than two years are served in provincial or territorial facilities.
3. *Conditional sentences:* At the discretion of the trial judge, a conditional sentence may be ordered that allows the offender to serve his or her time in the community under supervision.
4. *Probation:* This may be ordered as the sole condition of the sentence, or it may be required following a term in custody. Probation is a sentence that is served in the community, and the offender is usually required to report to a probation officer.
5. *Conditional release:* This includes temporary leaves for family visits, medical services, or on humanitarian grounds. It also includes day parole or full parole.
6. *Parole boards:* These are administrative tribunals that oversee all issues related to parole. They decide whether a prisoner may be granted parole, and they also can revoke parole if certain conditions are violated.[57]

ACTIVITIES

1. Read stories about prison inmates. Do you see any commonalities in their stories?
2. Research prisons in your province. What are the demographics of the inmates?
3. What types of community service programs are available in your community for inmates to participate in?

CHAPTER

12

WHAT ARE DEVIANCE AND CRIME? 221

deviance: a violation of social norms
crime: a violation of norms that have been written into law

WHY DO DEVIANCE AND CRIME EXIST? 228

positivists: people are not prone to act criminally unless some biological, psychological, or social factor is involved
classicists: people make rational choices to commit crimes based on their self-interests

HOW DO WE DEAL WITH CRIME IN CANADA? 233

through a three-part criminal justice system: police, courts, and corrections

get the topic: WHAT ARE DEVIANCE AND CRIME?

Theories

FUNCTIONALISM 229

- deviance is a response to social factors
- Durkheim's three functions of deviance: it marks the boundaries of morality, it promotes social solidarity, and it brings about needed change
- strain theory: deviance results because the pursuit of socially desirable goals is blocked for some people

SYMBOLIC INTERACTIONISM 230

- differential association theory emphasizes that deviant behaviour is learned
- labelling theory states that individuals become deviant when the deviant label is applied to them
- Containment theory examines the internal and external factors that control behaviour
- Travis Hirschi suggests that four social bonds affect our inner controls

CONFLICT THEORY 230

- deviant behaviour results from social, political, or economic inequalities between social groups
- the wealthy create the laws that punish the poor, while many illegal acts committed by the wealthy are often not considered crimes
- "the rich get rich, the poor get prison"

FEMINIST THEORY 231

- androcentric bias in explaining the causes of criminal behaviour
- chivalry hypothesis means female offenders are treated more leniently
- women experience the justice system differently

Key Terms

deviance is the violation of norms that a society agrees upon. *221*

crime is the violation of norms that have been written into law. *221*

Uniform Crime Reporting (UCR) Survey measures the incidence of crime using police statistics of reported crimes gathered from police reports and paperwork. *222*

General Social Survey (GSS)—Victimization measures crime victimization based on a representative sample of nearly 20 000 Canadians over 15 years old. *222*

crime rate measures the volume of crime reported to the police. *222*

Crime Severity Index measures the seriousness of crime reported to the police. *223*

consensus model of law suggests that laws arise because people see a behaviour they do not like, and they agree to make it illegal. *225*

conflict model of law proposes that powerful people write laws to protect their own interests while punishing the actions of those they wish to control. *225*

agents of formal control enforce the laws of society. *225*

agents of informal control enforce social norms. *225*

stigma is a mark of disgrace associated with a particular status, quality, or person. *225*

discredited stigma is a stigma that cannot be hidden from others or is no longer hidden from others. *225*

discreditable stigma is a stigma that can be concealed from others. *225*

shaming is a deliberate effort to attach a negative meaning to a behaviour. *225*

stigmatized shame is a permanent label given to an offender, which could actually increase the chances of reoffending because the guilty person is forever labelled. *225*

reintegrative shaming is an effort to bring an offender back into the community after punishment. *225*

retribution reflects the belief that someone who commits a crime is responsible for his or her actions and deserves to be punished. *225*

incapacitation prevents a person from committing more crime. *225*

deterrence tries to prevent a person from doing something because of fear of the consequences. *225*

general deterrence ensures that individuals will not commit a crime because they see the negative consequences applied to others, and they fear experiencing these consequences. *225*

specific deterrence occurs to individuals who have violated the law and have already been punished. *226*

rehabilitation tries to reform offenders so that they can be returned to society, but will no longer choose to engage in criminal behaviour. *226*

restoration attempts to make the victim, and the community, whole again. *226*

reintegrative justice is based on the principle that offenders can be successfully reintegrated into the wider society. *226*

sentencing circle is a process used by some First Nations communities to the rehabilitate the offender and to heal the community as a whole. *226*

recidivism is the tendency for inmates released from prison to return to prison. *227*

racial profiling occurs when police use a person's race as the primary reason to suspect that the individual has broken the law. *228*

primary deviance is the initial deviant act itself, which is not followed by some form of labelling. *230*

secondary deviance refers to the psychological reorientation that occurs when a person is labelled as deviant and assumes that identity. *230*

chivalry hypothesis suggests that female offenders are treated more leniently by male police officers and judges. *231*

discretion is the ability to make decisions. *233*

summary conviction offences are less serious offences. *233*

indictable offences are more serious offences. *233*

Sample Test Questions

These multiple-choice questions are similar to those found in the test bank that accompanies this textbook.

1. In Canada, the measure of the incidence of crime using police statistics is called the
- **a.** General Social Survey—Victimization.
- **b.** Crime Severity Index.
- **c.** Uniform Crime Reporting Survey.
- **d.** Consensus Model of Law.

2. According to Jeffrey Reiman, what makes a huge difference in who gets caught and who goes to prison?
- **a.** Age
- **b.** Social class
- **c.** Gender
- **d.** Ethnicity

3. According to Robert Merton, who accepts the common goals but not the traditional means of reaching them?
- **a.** Conformists
- **b.** Retreatists
- **c.** Rebels
- **d.** Innovators

4. What is the last resort in the criminal justice system?
- **a.** Counselling
- **b.** Probation
- **c.** Parole
- **d.** Prison

5. A deviant act that is not followed by some form of labeling is called
- **a.** primary deviance
- **b.** secondary deviance
- **c.** shaming
- **d.** stigmatized shame

ANSWERS: 1. c; 2. b; 3. d; 4. d; 5. a

ESSAY

1. Which groups are most likely to be overrepresented in Canadian prisons?
2. Do poor people commit more crimes than other members of society?
3. Why is it difficult to make international comparisons about crime statistics?
4. Why are only certain things illegal?
5. What are the different sentencing options in the Canadian justice system?

WHERE TO START YOUR RESEARCH PAPER

To learn more about crime in Canada, go to www.justice.gc.ca/eng/index.html.

To learn about the *Youth Criminal Justice Act*, go to www.justice.gc.ca/eng/pi/yj-jj/.

To learn more about Positive Deviance, go to www.positivedeviance.org.

To see statistics about crime in Canada, go to www5.statcan.gc.ca/subject-sujet/subtheme-soustheme.action?pid=2693&id=-2693&lang=eng&more=0.

To read about violence against women, go to www.statcan.gc.ca/pub/85-002-x/2013001/article/11766-eng.pdf.

To learn more about prisons and their administration in Canada, go to www.csc-scc.gc.ca/index-eng.shtml.

To learn more about international police organizations, go to www.interpol.int.

Remember to check www.thethinkspot.ca **for additional information, downloadable flashcards, and other helpful resources.**

THE FAMILY

asife/Fotolia

WHAT IS A FAMILY?
IS THE FAMILY IN DECLINE?
HOW ARE FAMILIES CHANGING?

"Social scientists often get carried away with a definition of terms, discussing fine distinctions between 'statistical families,' 'economic families' and 'extended families.' But the family in our experience is clear. It is the coming together of two adults, usually but not always a man and a woman, usually but not always legally married, to express their mutual love and commitment. If the relationship lasts, children are often produced, and then the family is made of mother, father, and children living together under one roof, developing a long-term economic, social, and emotional unit. Sometimes as the years advance, the family expands to include aging grandparents.

"The big things are commitment, obligation, responsibility. Recognizing that we all must age and that our sexual currency on the love market must decline, physical love is replaced by deeper bases of understanding and support and, often most importantly, the shared love and excitement of raising children. The establishment of the family is an effort to find assured meaning and solace, as well as to express our emotional selves in more fundamental and lasting ways. That was the family. That is the family. And that will be the family in the future. The human species has not yet produced an alternative as fulfilling or as rewarding.

"That fundamental marriage, or common-law, relationship that brings two adults together sets the stage for the bearing and raising of children, for the care and comfort of the old and dying, and for emotional and financial support in our declining years. In the distant past, marriage and the family were the social structure of the species. And today they remain the central social experience of our day-to-day lives.

"The family in this sense is in crisis. It has been in crisis before—when feudalism declined and collapsed; when industrial capitalism emerged; when war, famine, and plague swept a land. But the crisis today, just like previous crises, is specific and needs focussed attention, if only because new embryonic family forms are emerging and urgently appealing for midwives."[1]

How Do Societies Perpetuate Themselves?

CHAPTER 13

In his book *The Canadian Family in Crisis,* John Conway looks at Canadian families in the past, the present, and the future. He examines how changes in the family have different impacts on children, on women, and on men.

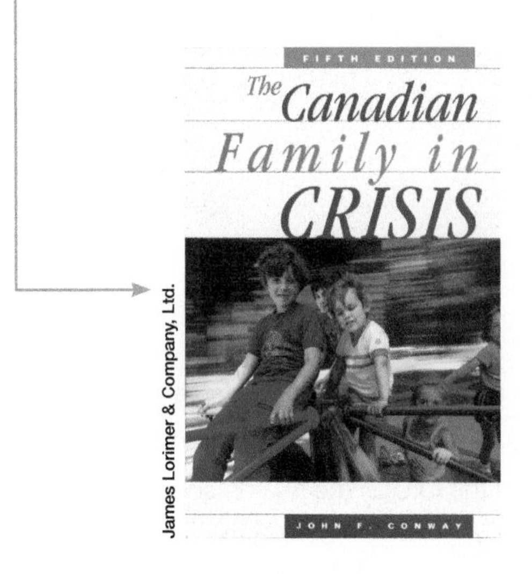

James Lorimer & Company, Ltd.

Here's the story of a lovely lady, who was bringing up three very lovely girls. . . That lovely lady met a man named Brady and soon one of the most beloved sitcoms of all time—*The Brady Bunch*—was born. Families watching the show in the 1970s wanted to be just like them. In fact, the Bradys are still an ideal for many viewers. However, today's family sitcom is more likely to feature a dysfunctional family than a happy, loving family. What happened?

John Conway suggests that most people carry with them a misconception of what the family "ought" to be, which influences their thinking. Each semester, I ask my students to give a definition of *family*. They usually come up with statements like "they are the people who really love you" or "they are the people you can always count on." This exercise usually helps launch us into a discussion that most people never consider. What is a family? Who taught us what a family is? We will address these questions and further investigate families in this chapter.

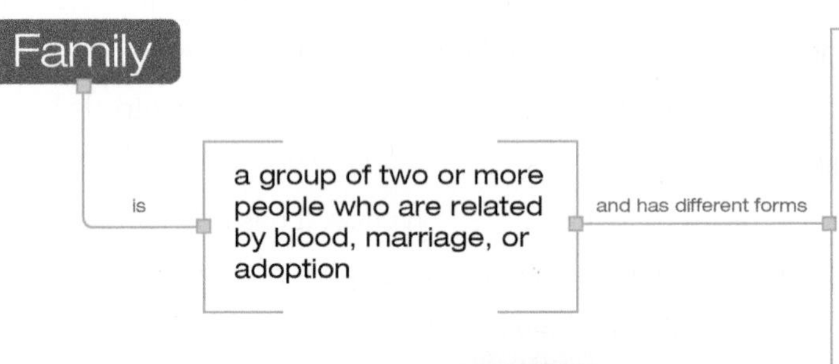

Family

is

a group of two or more people who are related by blood, marriage, or adoption

and has different forms

Nuclear family: a household consisting of a husband, wife, and children
Extended family: a household consisting of a nuclear family plus an additional relative
Family of orientation: the family that you are born into and raised in
Family of procreation: the family that you form through marriage or cohabitation, and in which you raise your children
Stepfamily: a family composed of children and some combination of biological parents

iQoncept/Shutterstock

- Social acceptance
- Ongoing redefinition of family and gender roles
- Ease of filing for a divorce
- Longevity
- Residential mobility of the nuclear family

Sociological reasons for the high divorce rate are

- Relationships
- Child rearing
- Violence
- Divorce

Families face many issues including

get the topic: WHAT IS A FAMILY?

Defining *Family*

The concept of family exists in all societies and comes in all shapes and sizes. But what is a family? The term is difficult to define because the definition changes according to time and place. Keep in mind that what we are defining is the family as a social institution. There are certain people I consider to be my family, but this is a personal definition of my family. As sociologists, we want a definition of family that is broader than this.

There are two ways to approach the definition of family. One strategy is to look at who is included (and who is not included); another strategy is to define the family in terms of what it does. Using the first strategy, we can say that a **family** is a group of two or more people who are related by blood, marriage or other intimate relationship, or adoption. Families are often built on **kinship**, which is a social bond based on common ancestry. This distinguishes a family from other groups of people who live together. Statistics Canada uses the term **household** to refer a person or group of people who occupy the same dwelling.[2] For example, if you share an apartment with one or more roommates, you are a household but not a family.

There are various legal definitions of *family* in Canada. When counting families in Canada, Statistics Canada uses the definition of a **census family**:

FAMILY is a group of two or more people who are related by blood, marriage or other intimate relationship, or adoption.

KINSHIP is a social bond based on common ancestry.

HOUSEHOLD is a person or group of people who occupy the same dwelling.

CENSUS FAMILY is Statistics Canada's definition of a family.

A census family is defined as a married couple and the children, if any, of either or both spouses; a couple living common law and the children, if any, of either or both partners; or, a lone parent of any marital status with at least one child living in the same dwelling and that child or those children. All members of a particular census family live in the same dwelling. A couple may be of opposite or same sex. Children may be children by birth, marriage or adoption regardless of their age or marital status as long as they live in the dwelling and do not have their own spouse or child living in the dwelling. Grandchildren living with their grandparent(s) but with no parents present also constitute a census family.[3]

As you can see, defining a family in this way can be complicated. Yet even legal definitions are not fixed, and they can change as a result of court cases and legislation. For example, in Canada, common-law

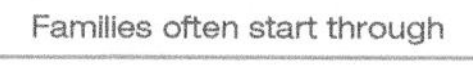

Marriage: a legally and socially recognized union of two or more people

which has different forms:

Monogamy: being married to one person at a time
Polygamy: having more than one spouse at a time

- **Polygyny:** occurs when a man is married to two or more women at the same time
- **Polyandry:** allows a woman to take two or more husbands at the same time

Choosing a mate has different social influences

Propinquity: physical and geographic proximity
Endogamy: the practice of marrying within your social group
Exogamy: the practice of marrying someone from a different social group
Incest taboo: a cultural norm that prohibits marriage between certain relatives
Homogamy: marriage between people with similar backgrounds, such as religion, ethnicity, class, or age

and there are different theories of mate selection

- Stimulus–value–role theory
- Complementary needs hypothesis
- Social exchange theory

>>> When I ask my students to draw their "ideal family," I often get images that look like this—neat, tidy families with a mother, father, and two kids. However, **few families in our society actually look like this.**

yanlev/Fotolia

Bomshtein/Shutterstock

NUCLEAR FAMILY is a household consisting of a husband, a wife, and their children.

EXTENDED FAMILY is a household consisting of a nuclear family plus an additional relative.

FAMILY OF ORIENTATION is the family that you are born into and raised in.

FAMILY OF PROCREATION is the family that you form through marriage or cohabitation and in which you raise your children.

STEPFAMILIES are families composed of children and some combination of biological parents.

spouses have been given many of the same rights and responsibilities as married couples. And in 2005, the federal government passed a law making same-sex marriages legal across Canada.

FAMILY FORMS

Take a look around, and you'll notice that families come in all shapes and sizes. Some families have only one parent in the home, while others have stepparents helping to raise the children. Still others have two parents of the same sex. The drawings my students generally create consist of a husband, a wife, and their children—a group that can also be referred to as a **nuclear family**. This is sometimes called the "standard North American family," or SNAF, and it forms the basis for what many call "traditional family."[4] But other forms of family exist. For various reasons, another relative, like a grandparent or an uncle, may live with a nuclear family, which creates an **extended family**.

Families come in two forms, depending on our perspective: **Family of orientation** is the family that we are born into and raised in; **family of procreation** is the family that we form through marriage or cohabitation and in which we raise our children. We can imagine society as being made up of interlocking sets of nuclear families with individuals being members of both forms; however, this pattern works neatly only if all couples get married or cohabit, have biological children, and never divorce.

OTHER FAMILY FORMS

Remarriage and stepfamilies are also part of the everyday norm. Both of these trends take the traditional idea of a nuclear family and rework it to fit new forms of family. Since the 1950s, traditional roles and rules associated with families have become more varied and complex.[5] For example, I've often heard children say to an adult who is not their biological parent but is living with and providing for them, something like this: "You're not my real mom (or dad), and you can't tell me what to do!" If that's true, what is that person's role in the household? Cohabiters and stepfamilies often experience such questions and stresses over these changing roles in the family.

Some children may grow up in **stepfamilies**, which are families composed of children and some combination of biological parents. In 2011, for the first time, stepfamilies were counted in the census. Of all couple families with children in 2011, 12.6 percent were stepfamilies.[6] Some children grow up in a lone-parent home. In fact, although the percentage of births for married women has decreased in the past 15 years, the percentage of births for unmarried women has increased.[7] These are really two different things. First, some children live in a lone-parent household because their parents are divorced. Other children live in unmarried households due to cohabitation. Either way, social norms are more accepting of unmarried women raising children today than they used to be. In fact, a growing number of children today are expected to live in a lone-parent home at some time.[8] In 2011, 19.3 percent of children under 14 years old lived with a lone parent.[9]

Other changes in the family form include same-sex couples and interracial/interethnic marriages. Compared to the past, stigma surrounding these unions has declined significantly, so that many people no longer keep such unions a secret.[10] What has caused such a change in family forms?

One structural event may help explain what happened. Throughout the 1950s, most children lived with their parents before getting married. During that time, the power of the parents to help select an "acceptable mate" reigned supreme. Now there is an independent life stage as people delay marriage and often live independently from their parents prior to getting married.[11] This geographic split decreases the parents' ability to control the behaviour of their grown children,[12] perhaps leading to greater diversity and partner selection. This, along with changing social norms, seems to allow people to couple in a way that would not have been imaginable 50 or 60 years ago.[13]

Forms of Marriage

Marriage is a legally and socially recognized union of two or more people. Many of you probably grew up under a family system of **monogamy**, which is the practice of being married to one person at a time. However, some societies allow **polygamy**, the practice of having more than one spouse at a time. Polygamy is illegal in Canada, but there is a fundamentalist Mormon community of Bountiful, B.C., where polygamy is practised, in violation of this law. Two leaders of this group—Winston Blackmore and James Oler—were each charged with practising polygamy, but in September 2009 the charges were thrown out. The latest development occurred on November 23, 2011, when the B.C. Supreme Court ruled to uphold Canada's polygamy laws. In his ruling, the judge said that while the law violates the religious freedom of fundamentalist Mormons, the harm against women and children outweighs that concern.[14]

Polygamy itself comes in two forms: polygyny and polyandry. **Polygyny** is more common and consists of a man marrying two or more women. **Polyandry** allows a woman to take two or more husbands. Anthropologists have determined that polyandry is practised to concentrate labour and maintain a comfortable standard of living while limiting animosity. For example, Tibetans practise fraternal polyandry, meaning a woman is married to brothers.[15] All the brothers maintain their land while limiting the number of heirs, which prevents family infighting.[16]

DenisNata/Shutterstock

>>> **I live with my Dad** and his boyfriend Matthew, **Matthew's son Kevin, and our dog Sherlock.**

MARRIAGE is a legally and socially recognized union of two or more people.

MONOGAMY is the practice of being married to one person at a time.

POLYGAMY is the practice of having more than one spouse at a time.

POLYGYNY occurs when a man is married to two or more women at the same time.

POLYANDRY is a form of marriage in which a woman takes two or more husbands at the same time.

COHABITATION (also called living common law) is an intimate relationship in which two people live together without being legally married.

Most of these family types fall under the patriarchal system, which you will recall from Chapter 1 means that men have power over women and children. In contrast, several First Nations groups were originally organized as matriarchal societies.

Trends of the Canadian Family

Ideologies regarding the family are also changing. Years ago, female students were in a race to "get pinned," or engaged, before the end of their last semester of college. As one faculty member put it, "Springtime was for engagement parties." Today, things are different. It's no longer unusual for a woman to graduate from college without having a fiancé.

In 1921, the average age people married was 28 for men and 24.5 for women. By 1971, Canada was in an era that recognized the family as *the* social institution. The average age at first marriage lowered to 25 for men and 22.6 for women. In 2008, the average age at first marriage for men was 31.1 years and for women 29.1 years.[17] These delays in marriage may be due to a number of factors. One of these is an increase in couples who choose to cohabit. **Cohabitation** (also called living common law) is an intimate relationship in which two people live together without being legally married.[18]

It's increasingly common for unmarried, cohabiting couples to have children. Just look at Brad Pitt and Angelina Jolie. This unmarried celebrity couple continues to add to their ever-expanding brood. It has been estimated that 40 percent of all children will spend time in a cohabiting family before their 16th birthdays.[19] Some researchers point out that many cohabitating couples of today resemble families of the past.[20] However, there are other forms of families that have arisen as well.

Sylvie Bouchard/Shutterstock

oil lamp: Lori Martin/Shutterstock

MYTH 1 **The Universal Nuclear Family**
Although common belief is that all families take the form of the traditional nuclear family, the reality is that families vary in organization, membership, life cycle, social networks, and function. What many people consider the "ideal family" only came about with industrialization. When people left the farm, they often didn't take their extended family with them and created smaller family units.

MYTH 2 **The Self-Reliant Traditional Family**
Some people believe that family units carved out their lives on their own and that returning to a more self-reliant family structure would solve many of today's issues. The idealized image of families striking out on their own to settle the west overstates the reality of self-reliance. These families received both government support as well as support from others in the area. Early settlers relied on military protection and government programs designed to move First Nations Peoples off the lands that they were to eventually inhabit. Finally, local families often banded together for childcare, construction projects, and mutual protection and support. In a complex society, no one makes it on his or her own.

MYTH 3 **The Naturalness of Different Responsibilities for Wives and Husbands**
We touched on this subject in the gender chapter, but many people believe that there has always been a clear division between men and women when it comes to childcare and other family roles. Some suggest that if mothers stayed home and "did their jobs" (raising the children), families would function better. The truth is that prior to industrialization, men and women shared almost equally in childcare tasks. Men often worked at home and their children helped them. My mother learned farming techniques from her dad. He taught her to be innovative and never afraid to try new things. So, men did take responsibility for raising their children. Women also worked hard. My grandmother worked with my grandfather and when he died, she remained on the farm, raising the children and working the fields. The notion that family roles were different is not so clear when we look at history.

book: tobkatrina/Shutterstock

MYTH 4 **The Idealized Nuclear Family of the 1950s**
During the 1950s, an image of the family emerged. It was a middle-class family with a stay-at-home mom and a working dad. This image came to be idealized in television shows, and people started buying into this thinking that this is what families should look like. However, there is historical evidence to suggest that for many, this "ideal" family was far from real.

family: Lambert/Getty Images

briefmark: nikolae/Fotolia

The idealized 1950s family did exist but was perpetuated by television. Shows such as *Father Knows Best* and *The Adventures of Ozzie and Harriet* depicted picture-perfect families whose problems were resolved in the span of a half-hour program.

PROPINQUITY is physical and geographic proximity.

Myths about the "Ideal" Family

In the opening excerpt, John Conway discusses how people have idealized the traditional family. He points out that many myths exist about family structure and family life. For example, I thought I lived in a typical home when I was growing up. My mother cooked dinner, and my father mowed the lawn. However, both of my parents worked outside the home, and sometimes my father cooked and sometimes my mother shoveled the driveway. Conway discusses similar myths about families in Canada.

Courtship and Mate Selection

I understand that there are possibly millions of women on the planet with whom I could have a satisfying relationship. Yet I am with someone who is about the same age as me, works at the same college, values family and education, and has a similar ethnic background. Feelings of attraction and affection were part of this decision, but choosing a mate often has to do with finding people who live near you and who share similar values and social traits. **Propinquity**, or physical and geographic proximity, is a major factor for interpersonal attraction. It makes sense that you are attracted to people who live near you.[21]

Finding a mate comes with many unspoken and spoken rules that society, your family, or even you dictate. So, when choosing a mate, what kind of cultural questions arise?

Common Cultural Practices

The process of choosing a mate can be seen as having two forms. In one, the decision is made by the couple, and in the other it is decided by the families of the couple. However, in practice, most relationships lie along a continuum, with completely arranged marriages at one end and completely self-chosen unions at the other. For example, most individuals who choose their partners also consider their parents' feelings about

MAKE CONNECTIONS

Image of the Perfect Family

Stephanie Coontz argues that the image of the perfect family is just that—an image.[22] In fact, the romanticized family portrait of the past often covered up a life of discontent and conformity. Families like the Cleaver family in the 1950s sitcom *Leave It to Beaver* did exist, but only for a tiny blip in history and only for a small portion of the population.

Looking back on it, the 1950s seemed like the golden age of happiness for many North Americans. Divorce rates were down, out-of-wedlock births were low, and marriage was universally esteemed as an institution.[23] Not only was there a housing boom, but the gross national product (the estimated total value of all the goods created in the country) and per-capita income also rose. Even though there is a measure of truth to these points, they don't provide a clear picture of average families. Before people were ever married, they knew exactly what to expect from their lives. After a brief courtship, a couple was married and started a family. They purchased a house, with the husband as breadwinner. His salary was high enough for the wife to stay at home as a homemaker. This routine led some women to believe that life consisted of the four *B*s: booze, bowling, bridge, and boredom.[24]

In fact, "by 1960, almost every major news journal was using the word *trapped* to describe the feelings of the North American housewife."[25] To dull the pain and tedium of making it through the day, some women began drinking and taking tranquillizers.

Men were also dissatisfied with family life and became resentful of women. Publications like *Playboy* encouraged men to take power over areas that women had previously governed. Men were encouraged to have a say in the clothes they wore and the food they ate. *Playboy*'s debut issue contained an article titled "Miss Gold-Digger of 1953," promoting the idea that women were interested in men for material reasons.[26] These negative stereotypes were damaging to both men and women.

Trying to gauge the frequency of events such as violence and incest is difficult because many instances were never reported. These topics were not considered appropriate for conversation. Many women suffered from physical abuse and just dealt with it rather than face the stigma of being a member of a family known to be dysfunctional. In the 1950s, a victim of domestic violence was often viewed "as a masochist who provoked her husband into beating her."[27]

>>> **ACTIVITY** What do current family sitcoms say about the role of the family in our culture? After conducting research, compare this image to reality. Do you see any discrepancies?

Getty Images

>>> In the 1950s sitcom *The Honeymooners*, New York bus driver Ralph Kramden wants to strike it rich, but his wife knows it's not going to happen. **Ralph threatens her by saying, "One of these days, Alice, right in the kisser . . . pow!" Scenes like this trivialized domestic violence in a comedic sketch.**

GO GLOBAL

Networks and Family Change in Japan

Many of the family demographic changes in Canada—increased age at marriage, decreased marital stability, and lower birth rate—have been mirrored by Japan. Traditionally, Japanese family values strongly discouraged these behaviours. However, a survey conducted by Ronald R. Rindfuss and colleagues suggests that Japan might be on the cusp of a major demographic change.[28]

The traditional Japanese family is patriarchal: Men are the authority figures, lineage is traced through the father, and fathers pass wealth on to their sons.[29] Women are left with the bulk of the housework. In 2000, Japanese women spent 29 hours per week on household labour; husbands spent just 3.[30]

However, times are changing. More women are attaining higher levels of education and entering the labour force.[31] As more women enter the full-time workforce, Japan faces an increased need for daycare situations. Some suggest that cohabitation may become more common.[32] In fact, recent studies indicate that 92 percent of Japanese citizens know someone who has engaged in innovative family behaviours.[33] Japan should anticipate more changes in the future.

>>> Some societies feel a strong need to preserve traditional culture. **What motivates societies to cling to traditional values?**

paylessimages/Fotolia

ENDOGAMY is the practice of marrying within your social group.

EXOGAMY is the practice of marrying someone from a different social group.

HOMOGAMY is marriage between people with similar backgrounds, such as religion, ethnicity, class, or age.

their prospective mates. In arranged matches, the couple often will not be forced to marry if either is opposed.

Finding someone to marry can be a daunting prospect, but in Canada the options are relatively open. There are only a few rules: Potential mates cannot already be married, must be of legal age, and must not be closely related. In fact, most cultures have similar restrictions regarding age and other social issues.

Some cultures enforce marrying within the group, which is a practice known as **endogamy**. If, for example, your religion requires you to marry a person of the same faith, your choice of spouse is based on endogamy. For example, a former student of mine often talked about how important it was to her and her family that she marry someone from within the same culture. Although this was not a "rule" to which she had to adhere, the attitudes of her family and friends provided a clear directive that she needed to follow. On the other hand, **exogamy** is the practice of marrying someone from a different group, such as a different religion, race, ethnicity, or other social status. A universal example is the incest taboo, which prohibits sex between certain relatives. Remember that the appropriateness of a spouse is dependent on cultural norms and regulations. Treatment of this issue in different cultures ranges from unspoken disapproval to "illegal" unapproved marriages.

Homogamy

Despite relative freedom in choosing marital partners, many people practise **homogamy**, or marriage between people with the same characteristics. This occurs when people choose a partner with a similar background: religion, ethnicity, class, geographic location, or age. Partners of similar backgrounds are likely to socialize their children the same way, which avoids conflict. Also, coming from similar backgrounds increases the likelihood that the couple will have things in common, which can increase the longevity of the relationship.

Stimulus–Value–Role Theory

Take a look at the stimulus–value–role theory of mate selection shown in the graphic on the following page. This theory, created by sociologist Bernard Murstein, suggests that we select our friends and close partners through a three-stage model.[34] At each stage, we weed out those who do not fit.

Complementary Needs Hypothesis

The complementary needs hypothesis claims that people feel attracted to potential partners who complement them, an assumption that is reflected in the saying "opposites attract." Complementary individuals are assumed to be more attractive because they enhance the likelihood that one's own needs will be satisfied. For example, a person who has a strong, dominant personality may be attracted to someone who is submissive. Young people who lack economic resources may feel attracted to older partners who have acquired economic resources and therefore may be good providers.[35]

Social Exchange Theory

The social exchange theory takes a more practical approach to dating and marriage. The entire courtship process is like a negotiation to find the best deal. Exchange theory essentially states that people seek to maximize rewards and minimize costs. A student of mine told me that he was deeply in love with his girlfriend, but in the end he had to break it off

STIMULUS-VALUE-ROLE THEORY OF MATE SELECTION

Alexander Raths/Fotolia

STIMULUS STAGE

In this stage two people are attracted to each other by some kind of stimulus. This could be something like looks, cool shoes, or a nice car. These are superficial characteristics, which are noticed before two people get to know one another. If a couple stays attracted, they move to the second stage.

micromonkey/Fotolia

VALUE STAGE

In this stage the compatibility of the relationship is tested regarding a variety of mutually held beliefs/ values (religion, politics, familial expectations, attitudes about money). If a couple talks and manages to find common ground in some of these areas, then they may choose to move on to stage three.

Olga Sapegina/Fotolia

ROLE STAGE

After realizing that they share a mutual attraction and a similar set of beliefs, people decide to act out the roles of a couple. This includes dating and sexual behaviour, possibly leading to a long-term relationship.

because she was too jealous. He got tired of the constant phone calls and text messages and her need to always be by his side. In the end, it was just "too much work." Relationships are started and maintained as long as they are rewarding for us. This does not mean it is always "fun" but only that some type of reward—emotional, social, or financial—outweighs the cost. When we cease to benefit from the relationship, we end it.

Issues in the Family

Relationships

One of the biggest worries people have when they start a relationship is whether they are going to be happy. Don't be blinded by movies or novels into thinking you are going to be swept away by your soul mate. In order to be happy, you need to have a solid commitment to one another and understand the variables that make a relationship work.

Research shows that one of the easiest ways to stay satisfied is to spend time together, doing activities both of you enjoy.[36] This means you are engaging in companionship with your partner while also enjoying a leisure activity. However, spending time pursuing activities that only one of you enjoys can create feelings of dissatisfaction over the long term.[37]

"Satisfaction" is difficult to gauge since outside factors such as gender ideologies make satisfaction a social construct. Using data from two-earner, married couples, Daphne Stevens and colleagues studied the relationships between marital satisfaction and labour in marriages. For them, marital work has three components: the level of household labour, the division of the emotional work of the marriage, and how individuals provide status enhancement to each other.[38]

According to Stevens and colleagues, both husbands and wives have increased marital satisfaction when they perceive the division of household labour to be "fair." If one feels overworked, marital satisfaction decreases. Although women usually did more of the housework than men, generally speaking, the more work the husband did around the house, the happier the wife reported she was with her marriage. The same appears to be true for the balance of emotional work. As long as the couple perceived the balance to be at an acceptable level, marital satisfaction increased. With regard to status enhancement, men were happiest in their marriages when they reported that their wives supported their careers. However, women's marital satisfaction was more related to their own ability to improve their status at work than to their husbands' support.[39]

Generally speaking, the more a woman is allowed to work in her career and the less household labour she is required to do, the happier she will be in her marriage. For men, similar findings follow; however, men tended to base their marital satisfaction on their wives' happiness. Interestingly, the study controlled for the number of children, income, and many other variables but showed that marital satisfaction is linked to the couple's comfort with their arrangement.[40]

Rearing

ter 5, we discussed the importance of child-rearing practices ialization. Sociologist Diana Baumrind explored how parental discipline affects children. Although disciplining children is a cultural universal, the manner in which it occurs varies by culture and family style. Baumrind observed that parenting styles have a substantial effect on individual outcomes.[41]

Parents who practise an authoritative style listen to their children's input while consistently enforcing the preset rules. Children reared in such an environment integrate into the world with the most ease because they exhibit high levels of self-esteem and possess the capacities for independence and cooperation with others.

Whereas authoritative parents practise a balanced style of child rearing, permissive and authoritarian parents represent opposite extremes, and neither produces positive outcomes. Permissive parents provide high levels of support but an inconsistent enforcement of rules. This results in a child not understanding boundaries and expectations. The

FOUR PARENTING STYLES

Permissive

Scott Griessel/Fotolia

Authoritarian

dacasdo/Fotolia

Authoritative

Monkey Business/Fotolia

Uninvolved

Monkey Business/Fotolia

FAMILY VIOLENCE refers to a range of abusive behaviours that occur within relationships based on kinship, intimacy, dependency, or trust.[54]

ABUSE refers to any behaviour or situation in which one person takes advantage of a less powerful person.

teenagers on MTV Canada's *My Super Sweet 16* who are showered with lavish gifts and extravagant parties by their affluent parents may be ill equipped to deal with the disappointments and responsibilities that are sure to come later in life.[42]

Conversely, children reared by authoritarian parents experience high levels of social control but low levels of emotional support. Such children understand the rules but have no desire to obey them when their parents are not looking. Often, the most rebellious youths are by-products of very strict households. Baumrind suggests that both permissive and authoritarian styles of parenting produce children with lower self-esteem and less self-assurance.[43]

Finally, uninvolved parents place very few if any demands on their children but also don't respond to them. They are cold and distant and often hostile to a child's need for attention. In extreme cases, this style may take the form of neglect.[44] Because the parents are uncaring, these children are often socially aggressive in order to get the attention they crave but do not get. Uninvolved parenting may be the result of the parent's personality, but it often results from life situations. A family where both parents work long hours, or where a lone parent holds one or more jobs to make ends meet, may find that being involved with the children is difficult. Children with uninvolved parents are most likely to have poor academic performance and weak social skills. They also have the most behavioural problems.[45]

Taking care of a child is expensive. Based on estimates from 2004, the average cost of raising a daughter to age 18 in Canada was $166 549. The amount was slightly higher for boys due to extra costs for food.[46] So, how are children from low-income families affected? Remember that inequality is a vicious cycle. Children from wealthy families remain wealthy, and children from poor families continue to be poor.[47] Sociologist Lisa Strohschein studied the mental health and social behaviour of children from low-income families. She found that "low household income is associated with higher levels of depression and antisocial behaviour; subsequent improvements in household income reduce child mental health problems."[48] However, having children is often seen as a status symbol, and many lower-class families want children because they are a valuable social resource.[49]

WavebreakmediaMicro/Fotolia

<<< Many factors that help make a relationship work—like compromising and spending time together—seem simple. **Why do you think so many marriages end in divorce?**

Family dynamics often shift when children move out of the house. When the last child leaves the house, parents, especially mothers may have a difficult period of adjustment, called "empty nest syndrome." However, many couples report increased marital satisfaction and companionship after their children leave. Sociologist Lillian Rubin says that empty nest syndrome is largely a myth.[50]

A more modern issue is the phenomenon of "extended childhood." Some children wait until a later age to leave home or move back in after college. Tough job markets and high costs of living sometimes make this necessary.[51] However, sociologist Michael Rosenfeld suggests that a certain percentage of adult children have always lived at home.[52]

Violence

At the beginning of this chapter, I told you that many of my students define a family as people who love you and who care for you. We should all feel protected and safe in our family. Yet for many people, it is their own family members who are violent and abusive.

Family violence has probably always existed, although concern about it is relatively recent. The first type of abuse to gain social recognition was child abuse, followed by spousal abuse and now elder abuse. Trying to understand why some people abuse other family members is a complex issue. In Canada, the term **family violence** is used to refer to "a range of abusive behaviours that occur within relationships based on kinship, intimacy, dependency or trust."[53] While we often think of violence as physical, **abuse** is a more general term that refers to any situation in which one person takes advantage of a less powerful person. It also includes neglect, sexual and emotional abuse, and financial exploitation, as well as physical violence.

Family violence has become a social issue, and many groups and organizations have developed strategies for preventing abuse. Victims have become more aware of their rights and of the resources available to them. No one should be subjected to violence within their family, and hopefully with greater understanding of the underlying causes of abuse and social support for survivors, we can eliminate this terrible situation.

Divorce

Frequently, stress stemming from marital troubles causes couples to break up. Divorce is now an accepted and viable option for these couples and is perhaps the single biggest change in the state of marriage in Canada today. In 1901, there were only 3 divorces per 10 000 marriages. That is far less than 1 percent.[55] When asked what the rate is now, students say that 50 percent of marriages end in divorce. They suggest that "everyone knows that." However, is that really true? People get the 50 percent number after comparing the number of marriages and divorces in a given year. Are those getting married really the same people getting divorced? Those getting married are adding more people to the pool of married people, and those getting divorced are subtracting from it. For this reason, sociologists usually do not take this simple calculation seriously.

The table below shows marriage rates and divorce rates for various countries. For example, the Canadian divorce rate of 3.2 in 2005 means

Marriage and Divorce Rates by Country, 1980 to 2005

Country	Marriage Rate*				Divorce Rate**			
	1980	1990	2000	2005	1980	1990	2000	2005
Canada	11.5	10.0	7.5	6.8	3.7	4.2	3.4	3.2
United States	15.9	14.9	12.5	11.2	7.9	7.2	6.2	5.4
Japan	9.8	8.4	9.3	8.4	1.8	1.8	3.1	3.1
Denmark	8.0	9.1	10.8	10.1	4.1	4.0	4.0	4.3
France	9.7	7.7	7.9	7.1	2.4	2.8	3.0	3.5
Germany		8.2	7.6	7.0		2.5	3.5	4.0
Ireland	10.9	8.3	7.6	7.2			1.0	1.2
Italy	8.7	8.2	7.3	6.5	0.3	0.7	1.0	1.2
Netherlands	9.6	9.3	8.2	6.7	2.7	2.8	3.2	2.9
Spain	9.4	8.5	7.9	7.0	0.9		1.4	1.7
Sweden	7.1	7.4	7.0	7.5	3.7	3.5	3.8	3.4
United Kingdom	11.6	10.0	8.0	8.0	4.1	4.1	4.0	3.9

*** The number of marriages per 1000 people in the population aged 15 to 64, per year.**

**** The number of divorces per 1000 people in the population aged 15 to 64, per year.**

▒ = Data not available

Source: U.S. Bureau of Labor Statistics, updated and revised from "Families and Work in Transition in 12 Countries, 1980–2001," *Monthly Labor Review*, September 2003, with unpublished data, www.bls.gov, accessed August 30, 2013; adapted from Statistics Canada, "CANSIM Database Table 101-6501," February 17, 2011.

that in that year, 3.2 Canadians between 15 and 64 years old got a divorce. The United States has the highest divorce rate in this group, but it also has the highest marriage rate. The more marriages you have, the more potential you have for divorces. When a common-law relationship ends, this does not count as a divorce.

If you consider Canada's divorce rate of 3.2 for every 1000 members of the population between 15 and 64 years of age, less than 1 percent of that population experienced a divorce in 2005. Of course, not everyone gets married, but it's clear that married couples' chances of divorce are far lower than the media's commonly reported rate of 50 percent.

Sociological Reasons for the High Divorce Rate

For the first half of the twentieth century, divorce rates in Canada were quite low. Then in 1968 the rate spiked dramatically, and it reached an all-time high in 1987. It has been declining ever since.[56] Why? The short answer is that in each of those two years, there was a change in the law that made it easier to get a divorce. If you use your sociological imagination, you can see that this is good evidence that even a seemingly personal decision, such as getting a divorce, is strongly influenced by the social context. There are other social factors that affect the divorce rate.

1 **Residential mobility of the nuclear family.** Moving around a lot, people don't find the external support for their marriages in the form of family and community. The family becomes isolated from extended family and old friends, and this isolation causes more stress.

2 **Ongoing redefinition of family and gender roles.** Changing gender roles create tension, which can lead to conflict and the dissolution of relationships.

3 **Ease of filing for a divorce.** In 1968, Parliament enacted the federal *Divorce Act*, making it easier for couples to end a marriage. This law was revised in 1985, making it even easier.[57]

4 **Longevity.** People live longer, making it harder to maintain a stable relationship. This increases the chance that you and your spouse will encounter stresses that could lead to your divorce. Generally, as the population ages, the percentage of those who experience divorce increases.

V V V **Getting a divorce in Canada is much easier than getting a divorce in Europe.** Some European countries have up to a six-year waiting period, while most divorces in Canada are finalized in less than three months.[58]

iQoncept/Shutterstock

5 **Social acceptance.** Today, divorce is socially acceptable in Canada. In grade school, I didn't know anyone living in a home of divorce. In my children's school, there are many students with divorced parents. Divorce is much more common today, so the social acceptance may also increase its likelihood.[59]

XiXinXing/Shutterstock

<<< **When children leave home, some parents feel sad, while others feel satisfied.** How did your parents react when you left home for the first time (or how will they react)?

think sociologically: IS THE FAMILY IN DECLINE?

Symbolic Interactionism

Symbolic interactionists investigate how values and definitions of reality influence the way individuals behave. Since it focuses on interactions between individuals, this perspective has often been used as a basis for family therapy. If a therapist can help family members change their interpretations of behaviour (their own and that of others), the quality of their interactions can be improved. Sessions based on better understanding their symbolic interactions may also be used to teach family members different methods of communication. The therapist may facilitate discussion of role expectations within the family unit. Members will have a better understanding of their roles as a result of this type of discussion.

As long as people within a family are able to interact in a productive and supportive manner, the family will survive. In order to determine whether the family is in decline, symbolic interactionists focus on individual families. However, this perspective has been criticized for paying little attention to the impact of the wider society on family relationships, and it generally ignores factors such as laws, economics, or societal values and how these impact individual families.

Feminist Theory

While the feminist movement has made significant gains for women in the public domain, such as paid employment and education, the family still remains a place of unequal division of labour. Marital disagreements sometimes centre on the division of household labour and our two most scarce resources: energy and free time. Historically, men would control these resources, but with changes in the form of family, this is not always true.

Modern times have created many dual-career households. But with both partners working, who's taking care of the house? In *The Second Shift: Working Parents and the Revolution at Home*, Arlie Hochschild argues that working wives end up doing most of the housework. [61] Stevens and colleagues also note the dissatisfaction wives feel when the division of household work is unequal.[62]

In general, the women in *The Second Shift* seem to accept this role as something they cannot change. But some women find difficulties in their "first shift," which frequently doesn't honour their desires to be mothers, employees, and wives. Likewise, some women feel stuck because they realize a divorce will leave them with less income and more work.[63]

Conflict Theory

Friedrich Engels, a colleague of Marx, argued that throughout human history, as the economic system has changed, so has the family. In the pre-industrial age, the family was both a producer and a consumer of goods. As groups began to settle and the mode of production turned to agriculture, the concepts of private property and ownership began to emerge. Laws were created that protected private property, and monogamous marriage developed to solve the problem of the inheritance. With industrialization, work shifted from the home to the factory. It was often the husband/father who would leave the home to work for a wage, and the money earned was used to buy goods and services in the market. The family became a consumption unit of society, and since it was primarily the man who provided the income, this gave him more power over his dependent wife and children.[64]

Conflict theory also suggests that work and family are incompatible due to their different norms and responsibilities. These different norms and responsibilities cause intrusion and spill-over from one domain to the other. For example, an individual spending many hours at work will probably interfere with his or her family life. On the other hand, an individual who has problems at home will often bring them to work.[65]

THINK SOCIOLOGICALLY

Marriage and Men's Lives

Does marriage have special benefits for men? Steven L. Nock, director of the Marriage Matters project, believes so. In *Marriage in Men's Lives*, Nock argues that marriage is a positive force in men's lives, making them less likely to frequent bars and engage in risky behaviours. Men who are married live longer and are healthier overall than men who are not married. Furthermore, they express greater satisfaction in their lives. In a sense, marriage plays an important role for men's happiness, and it also can help them define their masculinity.

Adult males' masculinity is developed and sustained when men enter a marriage characterized by fairly traditional gendered beliefs and practices. In this environment, they are able to fulfill and express their sense of manhood. Nock suggests that this is rooted in a long history in which men play the roles of hunter/gather, protector, and supporter of family. These primitive roles are linked to modern family roles as men now see economic achievement as their obligation and role.[60]

If we are to believe, as Nock argues, that much of men's sense of masculinity comes from the traditional family form, then how is masculinity surviving the changing norms of society? Simply put, am I still a man even if I am economically dependent upon my wife to do housework and cook meals?

Nock suggests a new system in which it is necessary for both partners to feel as though they are contributing equally to the household. However, these new roles are going to be difficult to fill for some men since they had no role models in this form of family. The gender-role stereotype is deeply ingrained in society, so acceptance of new gender roles will take time.

The conflict perspective also focuses on how families compete with other social institutions for scarce resources. For example, companies would prefer that employees not be absent to take care of their elderly parents or to bring their sick child to a doctor's appointment. Conflict theorists might look at how family benefits in the workplace are negotiated between these two groups.

Functionalism

The structural functionalist theory views the family as an institution among other social institutions, such as schools, the workplace, and the health care system. In this view, the family has a number of important functions in society. According to Durkheim, families are functional institutions that increase one's ability to function in society. People must get along with others in their family, and this prepares them for getting along with others in society.[66] Current theorists have identified five basic functions of the family:

1. **Reproduction.** The family is still a legitimate and socially approved relationship in which to have sexual relations and to have children.
2. **Socialization.** Once children are born, the family is still seen as being the primary socializer.
3. **Social placement.** None of us chooses the family we are born into or adopted into, yet our family gives us some of our most significant

EROSION OF THE AMERICAN TV FAMILY

Getty Images

The Adventures of Ozzie and Harriet

1952–1966

The fictitious Nelsons in *Ozzie and Harriet* were based on the adventures of the real-life Nelson family who portrayed themselves. After years of wholesome adventures, the term "Ozzie and Harriet" now refers to the highest standard of American values.

Bettmann/CORBIS

All in the Family

1971–1979

Archie Bunker is famous for not being ashamed of his bigoted opinions of the world. The Bunkers depicted a volatile family that frequently argued or ignored each other.

Paul Drinkwater/NBC/NBCU Photo Bank/Getty Images

Family Ties

1982–1989

A couple of hippies get married and have children who turn out to be conservative. This difference led to discussions on social issues such as teen pregnancy and censorship.

1957–1963

Leave It to Beaver focused on the Cleavers, a typical all-American family handling easily resolved situations stemming from their youngest son, "the Beaver."

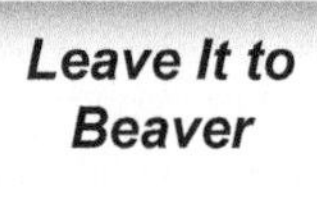

Leave It to Beaver

Everett Collection/Newscom

1974–1979

The Evans family, an African American family of five, provided comedy in a less than cheerful setting. The family faced many trials as it struggled to succeed in a poverty-stricken home in the projects.

Good Times

CBS Photo Archive/Getty Images

1984–1992

Doctor Huxtable, his wife Claire, and their five children are an African American family living in Brooklyn. The show reflects the changing dynamics of family life as the eldest children leave home only to come back once more.

The Cosby Show

KPA Honorar & Belege/United Archives GmbH/Alamy

statuses, such as our social class, our ethnicity, and our religion. You understand that these statuses have a powerful impact on your social experiences.

4. **Economic support.** Although we live in a society characterized as having a "social safety net," the family is often still the primary economic support for non-working members.

5. **Emotional support.** Like many other people, my students recognize that their family is a group like none other in terms of the love, affection, and support that is shared among its members.

When the family performs all these functions well, social stability results. Families may also perform other functions, but these are fundamental. And while other social institutions may share in some of these functions, they can never entirely replace the family.

Yet over time and across cultures, there is change and movement in how these functions are met. The Canadian family is changing in response to changes in the wider social context. Fewer families provide the services that were once seen as their responsibility—caring for the sick, raising children, supporting the elderly. Because of a shortage of services, these functions have not completely disappeared, but more and more, they are shared with people and institutions outside the family. Sick people are sent to hospitals; childcare centres, babysitters, and schools all share the responsibility of raising children; governments provide pensions and family benefits. As the government and other institutions take over many of the functions of the family, some have started to ask "who needs the family?"[67]

COLUMBIA PIC... TELEVISION/Newscom

Married with Children

1987–1997

The Bundys provided a much more cynical view of married life. Even though members were hostile toward one another, the family still contained a sense of solidarity when attacked by an outsider.

KPA/Heritage Images/Glow Images

The Simpsons

1989–present

The Simpsons represent a highly dysfunctional nuclear family. Homer is an incompetent beer lover; Marge, a hardworking homemaker; Bart, a troublesome underachiever; Lisa, a musician/brainiac; and Maggie, a pacifier-loving baby.

Randy Tepper/CBS Photo Archive/Getty Images

King of Queens

1998–2007

Doug and Carrie live in Queens with Carrie's father, Arthur. This family sitcom went against the grain not only because the couple was childless, but also because Carrie was the stronger half of the couple.

1988–1997

The working-class Conner family dealt with the problems of everyday people: money, children, and marriage.

Lynn Goldsmith/Corbis

Roseanne

1996–2005

Ray and Debra live across the street from Ray's parents, who frequently stop by, much to Debra's dismay. *Everybody Loves Raymond* frequently featured the extended family arguing and spending quality time together.

Richard Cartwright/CBS Photo Archive/Getty Images

Everybody Loves Raymond

2009–present

Jay Prichett is re-married to a much younger woman, Gloria. Together they have a baby boy Fulgencio (Joe), and Gloria's 14-year-old son Manny also lives with them. Jay's daughter Claire is married to Phil and they have three children: Haley, Alex, and Luke. Jay's son Mitchell and his partner Cameron have an adopted Vietnamese girl named Lily.

ABC via Getty Images

Modern Family

WRAP YOUR MIND AROUND THE THEORY

bikeriderlondon/Shutterstock

The family **has many traditional functions.** What will happen **if these functions change?**

FUNCTIONALISM

The family is an institution for maintaining social order. The traditional functions of the family include reproduction and socialization of children, social placement, and economic and emotional support for members. Throughout history, people have had these needs and used the family to solve them. The Canadian family is changing in response to changes in the wider social context. Fewer families provide the services that were once seen as their responsibility. As the government and other institutions take over many of the functions of the family, some have started to ask "who needs the family?"

CONFLICT THEORY

Throughout human history, as the economic system has changed, so has the family. In the pre-industrial age, the family was both a producer and a consumer of goods. As the mode of production turned to agriculture, laws were written to protect private property, and monogamous marriage developed to solve the problem of the inheritance. With industrialization, work shifted from the home to the factory. The family became a consumption unit of society, and since it was primarily the man who provided the income, this gave him more power over his dependent wife and children. The conflict perspective also focuses on how families compete with other social institutions for scarce resources.

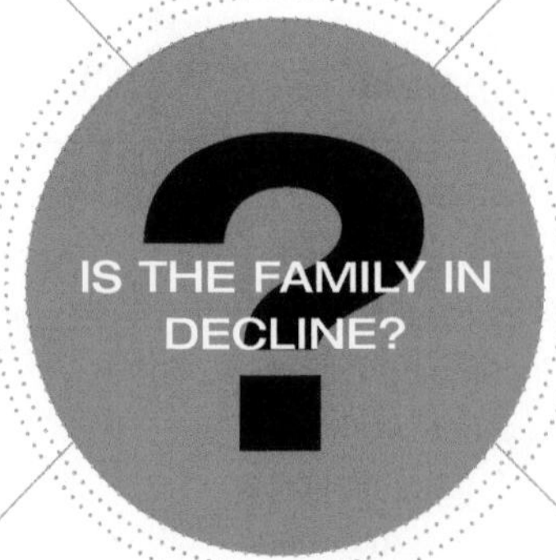

SYMBOLIC INTERACTIONISM

Interactionists look at the family on a micro level, studying the relationships between individual family members. As a result, this perspective has often been used as a basis for family therapy. A therapist can help family members change their interpretations of behaviour and facilitate discussion of role expectations within the family unit. Members will have a better understanding of their roles as a result of this type of discussion. As long as people within a family are able to interact in a productive and supportive manner, the family will survive.

FEMINIST THEORY

The family still remains a place of unequal division of labour. In *The Second Shift*, Hochschild discusses the disparity between men and women in terms of housework and how this leads to conflict between husbands and wives. This argument is about time, energy, and leisure. Wives tend to get stuck with the bulk of the work, leaving many disgruntled. This does not show a breakdown in marriage, but instead, according to Coontz, is a socioeconomic problem. Both parents are forced to work outside the home to survive, unlike many families of the past, and this change creates conflict.

Many **couples fight over** who gets more **free time and leisure.**

stokkete/Fotolia

As **families evolve in order to keep up with social trends,** ideologies associated with the family also need to evolve.

Vibe Images/Fotolia

discover sociology in action: HOW ARE FAMILIES CHANGING?

Same-Sex Marriage in Canada

In 1965, Everett Klippert was being interrogated by police in the Northwest Territories about an arson case. During the interrogation, he admitted that he had had sex with men. Because homosexual acts were illegal under the *Criminal Code*, Klippert was sent to prison indefinitely as a "dangerous sex offender." Two years later, in 1967, Justice Minister Pierre Trudeau proposed a revision of the *Criminal Code* and made his famous statement "There's no place for the state in the bedrooms of the nation." In 1969 the amendments were passed, and homosexuality was decriminalized in Canada. Two years later, Everett Klippert was released.

In 1988, Svend Robinson of the New Democratic Party publicly announced that he was gay, becoming the first member of Parliament to do so. In 1995, an Ontario judge ruled that four lesbians had the right to adopt their partners' children. Ontario became the first province to make it legal for same-sex couples to adopt, and the other provinces soon followed with similar legislation. In May 1999 the Supreme Court of Canada ruled that same-sex couples should have the same social benefits as opposite-sex common-law couples. A year later, Parliament passed a bill that gave same-sex couples the same social and tax benefits as heterosexuals in common-law relationships.

On July 12, 2002, the Ontario Superior Court became the first Canadian court to rule in favour of recognizing same-sex marriages under the law. Later that year, a nation-wide poll found that 45 percent of Canadians would vote Yes if there were a referendum to change the definition of marriage to one that could include same-sex couples. The next year, Prime Minister Jean Chrétien proposed legislation that would make same-sex marriages legal while at the same time permitting religious groups to "sanctify marriage as they see it." In July 2003, British Columbia became the second province to legalize same-sex marriages; a year later, Quebec became the third. Same-sex marriages were now legal in three Canadian provinces, but there was still no national legislation on this issue.

It was bound to happen, and in June 2004, a lesbian couple in Ontario filed for the first same-sex divorce. By 2005, eight provincial courts had passed legislation recognizing same-sex marriages. On July 20, 2005, Bill C-38, a law giving same-sex couples the legal right to marry, received royal assent and became law. Canada was the fourth country in the world to legalize same-sex marriage.[68]

When we discuss this issue in class, some students raise concerns about the sanctity of marriage and the welfare of children involved. However, students who raise concerns over the sanctity of marriage almost never propose eliminating divorce, which is far more common. Also, children raised by gay or lesbian parents have lower rates of child abuse and neglect and better educational attainment compared to their peers in households with heterosexual parents.[69] Regardless of whether a person believes one's sexual orientation is a choice, the question is, really, should government restrict that choice or give benefits to some but not to others? In Canada, we said no.

ACTIVITIES

1. Watch a prime-time sitcom or drama and analyze the depiction of family life on that show. Are the characters married or unmarried? What roles do men and women play in their relationships? Write a paragraph analyzing the show.
2. Interview an elderly family member or acquaintance. Discuss what family life was like when he or she was your age. How did his or her experience differ from your own?

CHAPTER

13

WHAT IS A FAMILY? 239

two or more people who are related by blood, marriage, or adoption

IS THE FAMILY IN DECLINE? 240

functionalism: the family has traditionally filled many social functions
feminist theory: Hochschild says that working women still end up doing most of the housework
conflict theory: as the economic system has changed, so has the family
symbolic interactionism: this perspective focuses on the communication and interactions between members

HOW ARE FAMILIES CHANGING? 253

more interracial marriages and same-sex couples are adopting children

get the topic: WHAT IS A FAMILY?

Theories

SYMBOLIC INTERACTIONISM 249

- expectations of roles help determine the success of the family
- family therapy can help family members communicate more effectively

FEMINIST THEORY 249

- Hochschild's *The Second Shift* says that family is a system in which women are generally stuck doing the majority of the work
- husbands and wives argue about time, energy, and leisure

CONFLICT THEORY 249

- changes in the economic system have an impact on families
- industrialization changed families from producers and consumers to primarily consumers

FUNCTIONALISM 250

- family serves as a way to maintain order
- the family fulfills five social functions

Key Terms

family is a group of two or more people who are related by blood, marriage or other intimate relationship, or adoption. *239*

kinship is a social bond based on common ancestry. *239*

household is a person or group of people who occupy the same dwelling. *239*

census family is Statistics Canada's definition of a family. *239*

nuclear family is a household consisting of a husband, a wife, and their children. *240*

extended family is a household consisting of a nuclear family plus an additional relative. *240*

family of orientation is the family that you are born into and raised in. *240*

family of procreation is the family that you form through marriage or cohabitation and in which you raise your children. *240*

stepfamilies are families composed of children and some combination of biological parents. *240*

marriage is a legally and socially recognized union of two or more people. *241*

monogamy is the practice of being married to one person at a time. *241*

polygamy is the practice of having more than one spouse at a time. *241*

polygyny occurs when a man is married to two or more women at the same time. *241*

polyandry is a form of marriage in which a woman takes two or more husbands at the same time. *241*

cohabitation (also called living common law) is an intimate relationship in which two people live together without being legally married. *241*

propinquity is physical and geographic proximity. *242*

endogamy is the practice of marrying within your social group. *244*

exogamy is the practice of marrying someone from a different social group. *244*

homogamy is marriage between people with similar backgrounds, such as religion, ethnicity, class, or age. *244*

family violence refers to a range of abusive behaviours that occur within relationships based on kinship, intimacy, dependency, or trust. *246*

abuse refers to any behaviour or situation in which one person takes advantage of a less powerful person. *246*

Sample Test Questions

These multiple-choice questions are similar to those found in the test bank that accompanies this textbook.

1. A group of people who occupy the same dwelling is called a
- **a.** nuclear family
- **b.** kinship
- **c.** household
- **d.** extended family

2. Someone who marries within his or her social group is practising
- **a.** polygyny.
- **b.** endogamy.
- **c.** polyandry.
- **d.** exogamy.

3. Women who work a "second shift"
- **a.** come home to hours of housework.
- **b.** must work two jobs to make ends meet.
- **c.** go back and get new jobs when they marry.
- **d.** equally divide responsibilities with their spouses.

4. What happened in Canada on July 20, 2005?
- **a.** The census counted stepfamilies.
- **b.** Same-sex marriage was legalized.
- **c.** Polygamy was legalized.
- **d.** Elder abuse was included in the Criminal Code.

5. Which of the following is one of the listed social reasons for the increased divorce rate in Canada?
- **a.** Infidelity
- **b.** Alcohol and drug abuse
- **c.** Violence
- **d.** Changes in the divorce laws

ANSWERS: 1. c; 2. b; 3. a; 4. b; 5. d

ESSAY

1. Why do so many people consider the 1950s an ideal time for the traditional nuclear family?
2. What are some of the causes of change of the traditional nuclear family?
3. Why do some couples wait to have children?
4. What is the stimulus–value–role theory?
5. What are some of Conway's myths of marriage?

WHERE TO START YOUR RESEARCH PAPER

To find information about Canadian families and the challenges they face in their structural, demographic, economic, cultural, and social diversity, go to www.vifamily.ca.

To learn more about the legalization of same-sex marriage in Canada, legislation, and definitions, go to www.chrc-ccdp.ca/eng/content/submission-standing-committee-justice-and-human-rights-same-sex-marriages.

For the latest statistical information about marriage, common-law unions, and family types, go to www12.statcan.gc.ca/census-recensement/2011/as-sa/98-312-x/98-312-x2011001-eng.pdf.

To learn about marriage and family therapy, go to www.marriageandfamily.ca.

To find more information about the divorce rates in Canada, go to www.divorceincanada.ca.

Remember to check www.thethinkspot.ca for additional information, downloadable flashcards, and other helpful resources.

EDUCATION AND RELIGION

Andres Rodriguez/Fotolia

HOW DO SOCIETIES PASS ON INFORMATION?
HOW DOES EDUCATION AFFECT SOCIETY?
HOW DOES RELIGION AFFECT SOCIETY?
WHAT SOCIAL POLICIES HELP CHILDREN GET A BETTER EDUCATION?

"A majority of Canadians believe that their children will attend a post-secondary educational institution when they finish high school. Further education after high school education is increasingly seen as a vitally important part of a person's life, both for participation and success in the knowledge economy. Human Resources Development Canada has estimated that by 2004 more than 70% of new jobs created will require a college or university education, with nearly half of those new jobs requiring at minimum a Bachelor's degree. . . .

"According to recent reports, Canada has the greatest proportion of citizens with post-secondary education of all the OECD [Organisation for Economic Co-operation and Development] countries. . . . Recognizing the importance of an increasingly educated population, the Canadian Government pledged in 2002 to ensure that '. . . one hundred percent of high school graduates have the opportunity to participate in some form of post-secondary education. . . .' However, questions remain about how accessible post-secondary education really is in Canada. Although participation in post-secondary education has remained strong in the face of rising up-front costs to individual students, it is not clear that particular groups of people are being represented in all aspects of post-secondary education. . . .

"Researchers point to a number of factors, related to socio-economic status or family background, that impact an individual's decision to attend a post-secondary institution. Parental expectations of attendance, attitudes of family and friends, knowledge of costs and funding options, gender, and academic achievement are all related to whether or not individuals are able to choose to further their education after high school."[1]

How Do Societies Pass on Information?

CHAPTER 14

As Andrea Rounce writes—in *Access to Post-secondary Education: Does Class Still Matter?*—despite an official pledge to achieve 100 percent participation in post-secondary education, there are still many social barriers to achieving this goal.

Access to Post-secondary Education: Does Class Still Matter?

By Andrea Rounce

Canadian Centre for Policy Alternatives - Saskatchewan

ISBN: 0-88627-381-1

August 2004

I sometimes ask my students why they are in college. The most common answer is "to get a better job." Upon further questioning, a better job is inevitably one that pays well. Students seem to equate education with higher income, and they are right to do so because this is a social fact that is well established in our society.

After discussing all the benefits of post-secondary education, we end up agreeing that post-secondary education is a good thing. I then ask them, "Well, if getting a college degree is such a great thing, why doesn't everyone get one?"

After a bit of reflection, some will answer "College isn't for everyone." Almost always, they point to individual decisions not to attend.

Perhaps they are right. Some people may decide that high school was difficult enough, and post-secondary education is just not for them. And some of these people go on to find good jobs that pay well. But let's hope that by now, you have enough sociological imagination to appreciate that "decisions" that may seem personal are often made within a social context that has a powerful influence over us. A student whose family and friends don't encourage post-secondary education may more easily "decide" that college is not for him, while another student whose family and friends do encourage it will just as easily "decide" to go to college.

Education

is

the social institution through which society passes on knowledge, skills, and values from one generation to the next

In Canada

- education is the responsibility of each province and territory
- the age for compulsory schooling varies from age 6 to age 16
- almost 98 percent of elementary students go on to the secondary level
- people whose parents have a university degree are much more likely to get a university education
- aboriginal peoples lag behind non-aboriginal Canadian-born people in terms of the percentage with college and university credentials
- recent immigrants far outdo both groups on the university front
- women now earn the majority of university degrees

- **Theism:** the belief in a god or gods
- **Monotheism:** the belief that there is only one God
- **Polytheism:** the belief in multiple gods and demigods
- **Philosophies of life:** focus on a set of ethical, moral, or philosophical principles
- **Totemism:** the practice of honouring a totem or a sacred object
- **Simple supernaturalism:** the belief in a variety of supernatural forces that affect and influence people's lives
- **Animism:** the belief that animate spirits live in natural objects and operate in the world
- **Henotheism:** the worship of one god while recognizing the existence of other deities

some religious organizations are

Cults: new religious movements led by charismatic leaders with few followers
Sects: religious groups that have enough members to sustain themselves and go against society's norms
Church: a large, highly organized group of believers
Theocracy: a government that is controlled by religious leaders
Organization of believers: a group that ensures the prosperity and effectiveness of the religious experience

get the topic: HOW DO SOCIETIES PASS ON INFORMATION?

Education in Society

If you are reading this textbook, chances are that you have already spent many years in school. At times you may have been engaged and excited to learn new things. Other times you may have been bored. In any case, school has had a powerful influence on you. Your experiences in the educational system will largely determine what you do for the rest of your life.

Since the Industrial Revolution, there has been a link between economic advancement and **education**, the social institution through which society passes on knowledge, skills, and values from one generation to the next. Schools are connected to the economy because they train individuals for specific types of work. For example, in order to become a surgeon, students must go through years of schooling and training. However, when they complete school, they have the benefit of a high salary, and the community benefits from their medical knowledge. In order to reach this point, students need to make an extended commitment to their education.

MYTHS OF MODERN EDUCATION

People began going to school to learn the three *R*s—reading, 'riting, and 'rithmetic—right? Actually, the expansion of education systems is a social movement that stems from the ideas of building a nation and building the ideology of a nation's identity. This means that education also serves to ensure that certain "myths" are spread throughout society. These "myths" may or may not be factually true, but they are vital to the success of building a unified nation. Thinking back, do you remember any school activities that supported these myths?

EDUCATION is the social institution through which society passes on knowledge, skills, and values from one generation to the next.

1 **Myth of the individual** The primary unit in society is the individual, not the family, clan, or ethnic group. Therefore, it is up to the individual to improve his or her place in society.

2 **Myth of the nation as a group of individuals** The nation is no longer the property of a king or some group of elites. Individuals make up society and the nation. Therefore, by developing your skills and knowledge, you are bettering yourself and your community.

3 **Myth of progress** Society's goal is to improve the status of both current and future residents. Thus, education for children is one way a nation can support the idea that it is working toward self-improvement.

4 **Myth of socialization and life cycle continuity** Childhood socialization leads to adult character. Therefore, if children are socialized properly, this will lead to good character that ultimately benefits the nation in the long run. Thus, educating children plays a vital role in this endeavour.

5 **Myth of the state as the guardian of the nation** It is the state's job to raise good, loyal, patriotic children, who will then be the next generation of good, loyal, and patriotic adults. In this way, socializing children into the nation becomes the role of the state, not the family.[2]

By looking at these five myths, you can see that state-sponsored schools are an essential part of any strong nation. However, you should note that these myths are not universal. Certain groups see this forced homogenization as detrimental to their way of life. The Africentric

Some issues in education are

- **Grade inflation:** the trend of assigning higher grades for completing the same work
- **Credentialism:** an emphasis on educational degrees in assessing skills and knowledge
- **Home schooling**
- **Teacher expectancy effect:** the impact of a teacher's expectations on a student'sperformance
- **Hidden curriculum:** lessons taught in schools that are unrelated to academic learning

Religion is

a social institution based on a unified system of beliefs and practices related to sacred things

and involves

Some religious beliefs are

Sacred: connected to God or dedicated to a religious purpose
Profane: related or devoted to that which is not sacred
Rituals: established patterns of behaviour closely associated with experience of the sacred
System of beliefs: relates sacred objects to religious rituals and defines and protects the sacred from the profane

EDUCATIONAL ATTAINMENT OF THE POPULATION 15 YEARS AND OLDER, 2012

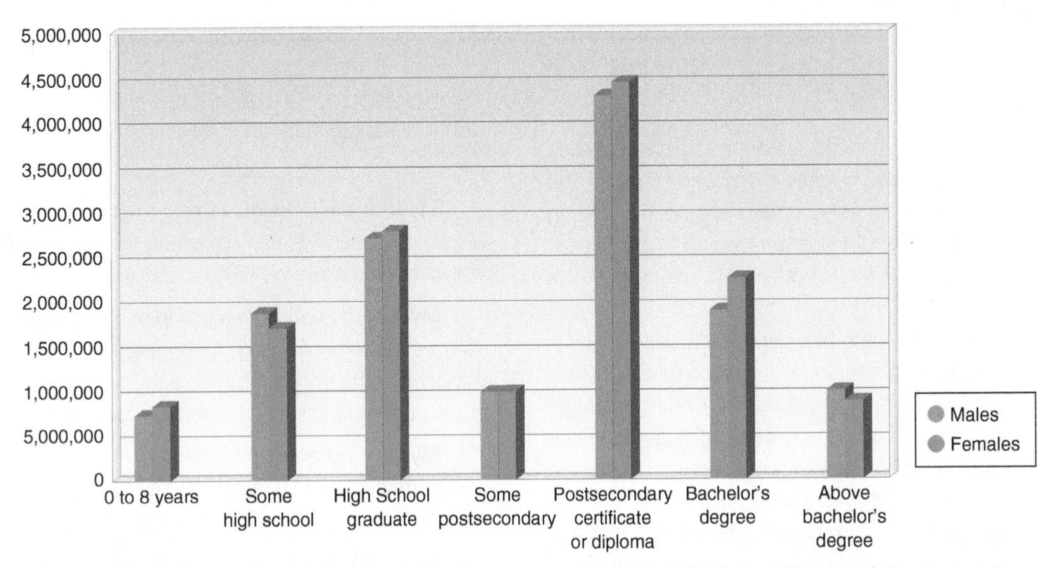

Source: Statistics Canada, "Table 282-0004: Labour Force Survey Estimates (LFS), by Educational Attainment, Sex and Age Group," http://www5.statcan.gc.ca/cansim/a47. This does not constitute an endorsement by Statistics Canada of this product.

Alternative School in Toronto, for example, is working to give students more "culturally relevant resources."[3] (For more on the Africentric Alternative School, see page 275.)

EDUCATION THROUGHOUT THE WORLD

Every nation has some type of educational system; however, not all educational systems are equal. The amount of resources, funding, and worth placed on education varies, which in turn creates inequalities in global education. A country's socioeconomic status has a huge effect on its education system. Systems in developing countries often fail to provide children with basic educational needs and struggle to sustain stable educational institutions. Paraguay, Sri Lanka, and the Philippines are all countries where one in five students goes to a school that has no running water.[4]

Poor education systems often result in low literacy rates, or low percentages of people in the population who can read and write. In Sierra Leone, only 47 percent of men and 24 percent of women over the age of 15 are literate. This falls far below the world literacy rate of 88 percent of men and 79 percent of women.[5] Aside from showing you how poor education systems affect literacy rates, these figures also show you the imbalance of education between men and women. The number of women educated is almost half the number of men educated in Sierra Leone. Similarly, as you can see in the literacy rates map on the next page, in every region of the world, male literacy rates are higher than female literacy rates. In Chapter 10, you learned about gender stratification and how men and women have been treated differently throughout history. Unfortunately, this is still true today.

A country's wealth plays a central role in education, so lack of funding and resources from a nation-state can weaken a system. Governments in sub-Saharan Africa spend only 2.4 percent of the world's public resources on education, yet 15 percent of the school-age population lives there. Conversely, North America and western Europe spend 55.1 percent of all the money spent in the world on education, yet they house only about 8 percent of the world's school-age population.[6]

Total expenditure on education in Canada was $8285 per student in 2007. This is more than the average rate of spending ($7153) in other OECD countries. Exact comparisons between different provinces and territories can't be made easily, but there is significant variation in spending. The lowest rates were in Saskatchewan ($7193) and New Brunswick ($7403), while the highest rates were in Nunavut ($11 666) and Yukon ($18 446). Canada's total public and private spending on education accounted for 6 percent of the GDP in 2007.[7]

As the above figures indicate, colleges and universities receive taxpayer benefits to keep their doors open. I often ask my students, "Who's on welfare in here?" Usually, no one raises a hand. However, attending college or university almost guarantees you are on educational welfare because taxpayers subsidize some part of your education.

No matter what kind of college or university you attend, you'd probably agree that the main goal of attending is to receive a degree. The percentage of Canadians with university degrees rose from 10.9 percent in 1990 to 21.5 percent in 2011.[8] But who exactly is receiving these degrees? Does ethnicity, gender, or socioeconomic status affect educational attainment? You bet it does.

EDUCATION IN CANADA

In Canada, each province and territory is responsible for its own education. Public funding comes from the provincial or territorial governments and through federal transfers and local taxes. The age for compulsory schooling varies from one province to another, but most require attendance in school from age 6 to age 16. In some provinces, compulsory schooling starts at 5 years old, and in others it extends to age 18 or graduation from secondary school. Almost 98 percent of elementary students go on to the secondary level.[9]

REGIONAL LITERACY RATES FOR ADULTS (15+), 2011

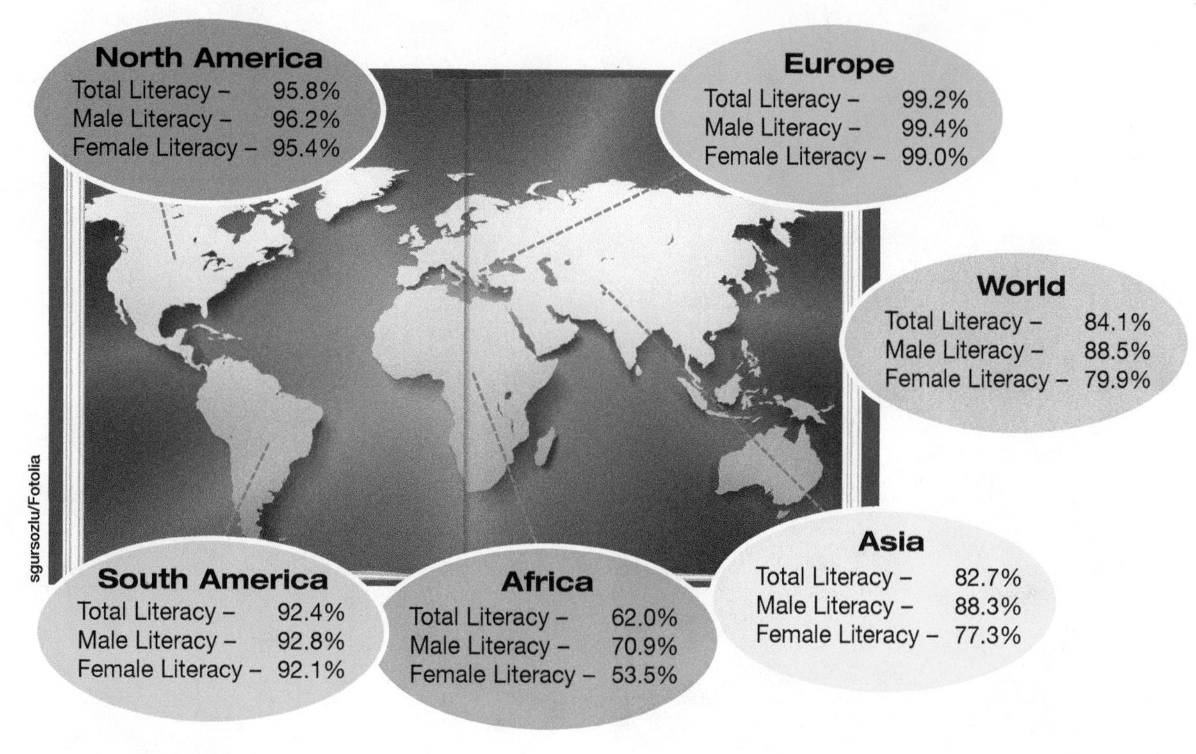

Source: Data from United Nations Educational, Scientific, and Cultural Organization (UNESCO) Institute for Statistics.

"Unfortunately, most Canadians are not aware of the many issues which brought about the need for First Nations Peoples to assert their rightful position in Canadian society. Many are unaware of conditions that aboriginal people experience in Canada—discrimination, exploitation, and violations against basic human rights. Furthermore, all of these infractions are grossly ignored and glossed over by standard Canadian history textbooks." This statement appears on the Assembly of First Nations website.[10]

It's no secret that socioeconomic background is one of the factors that can influence the way a person's education will develop. Aboriginal peoples in Canada today are overcoming an extremely difficult background, and, in the words of one recent study, while many aboriginal people are doing "quite well," the fact is that "on average the aboriginal population suffers from higher unemployment, lower levels of education, below average incomes and many other indicators of limited socioeconomic circumstances." The way to turn this around, the study says, "is through education."[11]

The post-secondary educational figures in Canada show the following: Aboriginal peoples lag behind non-aboriginal Canadian-born people in terms of the percentage with college and university credentials, and recent immigrants far outdo both groups on the university front. Focusing on those aged 25 to 64, the 2006 census revealed that, among aboriginal people, 19 percent had a college diploma and 8 percent a university degree, compared with 22 percent and 20 percent, respectively, of the non-aboriginal Canadian-born population. For recent immigrants, the figures were 51 percent and 11 percent, respectively. (Of immigrants who entered Canada before 2001, 28 percent had a university degree.[12])

Discrepancies at the post-secondary level are a reflection of discrepancies down the line. A 2008 Vancouver newspaper headline read "Study Gives Aboriginal Education a Failing Grade." The study was conducted by Simon Fraser University economist John Richards for the C.D. Howe Institute, and it concluded, in the newspaper's words, that "Aboriginal education is falling further behind schooling for other Canadians, and all levels of government . . . are failing to do much about it."[13] If things don't change, Richards warned, there will be economic losses due to low productivity, as well as an "impact on poverty and racial tension."[14]

People whose parents have a university degree are much more likely to get a university education than people whose parents do not have a degree, although the gap between the two groups has narrowed over time.[15] In 1986, just 12 percent of Canadian-born people aged 25 to 39 whose parents did not complete university had graduated from university; by 2009, this proportion had almost doubled to 23 percent. In comparison, in 1986, 45 percent of people who had at least one parent with a university degree had graduated from a university; by 2009, this proportion had also increased, but at a slower pace, to 56 percent.[16]

The relationship between parents' and children's education levels is due to a number of factors. Better-educated parents tend to also have higher incomes and are therefore better able to afford the costs of education, especially of post-secondary education. However, in Canada, governments and other groups provide financial support for students from lower-income families.

So the ability to pay only partly accounts for the low university participation rate of people from lower-income families. Beliefs and values play an even more important role. What impact might this have on policy decisions?

edbockstock/Fotolia

Because her mother is a graduate, this young girl is more likely to attend university and graduate as well.

GRADE INFLATION is the trend of assigning higher grades than previously assigned to students for completing the same work.

Grade Inflation

In recent years, grade inflation has started to get serious attention in connection with Canadian campuses.[17] **Grade inflation** is the trend of assigning higher grades than previously assigned to students for completing the same work. "Many students now expect high grades for relatively little effort," James Côté and Anton Allahar state in their 2007 Canadian book *Ivory Tower Blues*. "Indeed, grade inflation has become rampant in many institutions throughout Canada and the United States, from high school through university."[18] In one of the first major studies of its kind in Canada, economics professors Paul M. Anglin and Ronald Meng looked at grade patterns over 20 years at seven Ontario universities and concluded that "grade point averages rose in 11 of 12 arts and sciences courses between 1973–74 and 1993–94."[19] (The exception? Sociology.[20]) The study found that a higher percentage of students were getting As and Bs, and fewer were getting Cs, Ds, and Fs.[21]

"It starts in high school," *Ivory Tower Blues* co-author James Côté has said. "Giving higher grades is one way to reward kids fairly easily, boost their self-esteem and stop them from dropping out." Grades, he said, have risen steadily since the 1970s "and have reached a crisis point."[22] Professors face pressure to conform to the trend.[23]

One of my own students recently approached me to discuss her grade. She was very upset because she had received a B in my course. This young woman was visibly distraught, breathing hard, brow furrowed, and as she rapidly began to tell me that she had "never gotten a B" in her life. She felt like a failure. Couldn't she "write an extra paper" or "do some other assignment"?

"Everyone in my high school gets As," she said. "I'm not used to failing." I pointed out that a B was not failing and thought about grade inflation. When a student views a B as failure, what do grades mean? As I said to this student, "If everyone makes an A, then an A means nothing."

Some teachers claim that grade inflation is a result of the pressure that students are under to receive high marks that is then projected onto the instructor. Côté is one of those who believe that standardized testing might help in Canada.[24]

The Cost of Higher Education

Costs can be a factor in determining whether you go to university. Students sometimes base their college choice on factors such as accommodations costs and distance from family or friends, in part to help cut down on their overall expenses. In 2012–2013, undergraduate university tuition cost an average of $5581.[25]

In Canada, the federal government supports post-secondary education only indirectly, through financial transfers to the provinces and funding of university research and student assistance.[26] There are many sources of financing available for students who cannot afford the costs of education up front. The most common source of debt is student loans, and 40 percent of students report this as a source of debt. A 2012 survey of university grads found that the average amount of debt per student (including those without any debt) is $14 453. The median amount of debt is about half that, at $7000.[27]

In some industrialized countries, education at all levels is free. For example, in Sweden, government and institutionally managed schools—primary, secondary, and post-secondary—are free of tuition, courtesy of the Swedish government and taxpayers. This allows all students who meet certain academic standards to attend any school, regardless of their economic status.[28]

Even though college can bring cost concerns, you still decided to go. Why? Sociologists propose a few theories. First, students seek an education as a way to improve their **human capital**, or their combination of skills, knowledge, traits, and personal attributes. Generally, you know that an employer will reward a worker who performs better. Education improves your attractiveness to an employer and perhaps your output for that job. Such skills are important to employers, and you understand that increasing your human capital improves your place in the market for jobs.

Similarly, I know many people who chose to go to college because of the reality of **credentialism**—an emphasis on educational degrees in assessing skills and knowledge. Many jobs today require a post-secondary degree, but this was not always true. When I worked in the cafeterias, many of the managers and directors had finished high school but had no post-secondary education. A climb to a manager or director job with just a high school degree would be almost impossible in today's world. Employers use education as a type of litmus test to determine who is and is not qualified. In North America, the status of holding a degree can be essential for success.[29]

HUMAN CAPITAL is a person's combination of skills, knowledge, traits, and personal attributes.

CREDENTIALISM is an emphasis on educational degrees in assessing skills and knowledge.

Homeschooling

Some parents choose to forgo the offerings of a traditional school education. Around 70 000 students are homeschooled across Canada each year.[30] I have taught some first-year students who were homeschooled. When I ask them why they were homeschooled, I hear a variety of reasons. Some say their parents were concerned about the quality of education at the public school they were assigned, but they couldn't afford a private school. Others cite religious reasons as the primary factor for learning at home. Still others report that a parent was an educator and felt that a caring parent could do a better job of teaching his or her own children than could an overworked stranger. These reports follow the general findings of researchers who study parents who homeschool. Such parents are generally motivated by a desire to be active in their children's learning, and although issues of value and quality are relevant, the strongest motivator of parents who homeschool appears to be a desire to be more deeply involved with their children.[31]

THE FIVE MOST EXPENSIVE CANADIAN AND AMERICAN UNIVERSITIES IN 2008

Most Expensive Canadian Universities		Most Expensive American Universities		
School	Tuition in C$	School	Tuition in $US	Converted to C$
1. Trinity Western University, Langley, BC	17 460	1. Sarah Lawrence College, Bronxville, NY	54 066	57 688
2. Redeemer University College, Ancaster, ON	11 924	2. Georgetown University, Washington, D.C.	50 700	54 097
3. The King's University College, Edmonton, AB	8091	3. George Washington University, Washington, D.C.	50 537	53 923
4. Dalhousie University, Halifax, NS	6990	4. New York University, New York, NY	50 282	53 651
5. Royal Roads University, Victoria, BC	6915	5. Johns Hopkins University, Baltimore, MD	49 778	53 124

Sources: Canadian data: Jason Buckland, "Most Expensive Canadian Universities," *msn.Money*, November 21, 2009, http://money.ca.msn.com/savings-debt/gallery/gallery.aspx?cp-documentid=22656953, accessed October 25, 2010. U.S. data: "Most Expensive Colleges," *CNN Money*, www.fortunesmallbusiness.com/galleries/2009/news/0910/gallery.most_expensive_colleges/index.html, accessed February 16, 2011.

think sociologically: HOW DOES EDUCATION AFFECT SOCIETY?

Symbolic Interactionism: Teacher Expectancy

In Chapter 12, you learned that labelling can create a self-fulfilling prophecy; if someone is labelled as a deviant, she may become one. The same phenomenon has been observed in schools, where it is known as the **teacher expectancy effect**, which is a measure of the impact of a teacher's expectations on a student's performance. If a teacher expects that a student will love the class and do well, the student generally does well. On the other hand, if the teacher labels a student as a trouble-maker or as a poor student, that student is far more likely to not do well. Many studies have found that teachers may indeed influence students' self-perception and that it is that self-perception that influences academic achievement.[32] Other studies have found that teacher expectancies influence not only individual student performance but also the performance of the entire school.[33]

In an article published in 1970, Ray C. Rist reported the results of an observational study of a class of children during their kindergarten, first-, and second-grade years. He described how the kindergarten teacher placed the children in reading groups based on their social class and how these groups persisted throughout the first several years of elementary school. The way in which the teacher behaved toward the different groups became an important influence on the children's achievement.[34]

In another famous study, all the poor children in an elementary school were given a test that supposedly identified the children most likely to show dramatic intellectual growth during the coming year. These students were called "bloomers," and the experimenters gave the names of these children to the teachers. In truth, the test was a traditional IQ test, and the "bloomers" were actually a randomly selected 20 percent of the student population. After retesting the children eight months later, the experimenters found that those predicted to bloom had in fact gained significantly more in total IQ (nearly 4 points) than the control group children. Furthermore, at the end of the study, the teachers rated the experimental children as intellectually more curious, happier, better adjusted, and less in need of approval than their control group peers.[35]

The labels that students are given, even if the labels are positive, such as "smart" or "intelligent," encourage students to live up to what is expected of them. If students are labelled as "slow" or "difficult," they will perform at lower levels than they would were they not given such labels. When I teach statistics, I usually ask my students, "Who is afraid of math?" Many students sheepishly raise their hands. When we discuss why they fear mathematics, students usually say that they "don't get it" and they "hate it." When I ask the math-haters what grade they expect to get in the statistics course, the answer is usually "I just hope I pass." Such a self-fulfilling prophecy forms the core of most research on how educational expectations influence academic outcomes.

Functionalism: Functions of Education

The functionalist perspective focuses on education as a social institution that, like all other institutions, helps society to run smoothly and promotes social stability. Schooling serves several functions in society:

TEACHER EXPECTANCY EFFECT is the impact of a teacher's expectations on a student's performance.

HIDDEN CURRICULUM refers to lessons taught in schools that are unrelated to academic learning.

- *Transmission of knowledge and skills:* You have already seen that this is a manifest function of education. In order to fully participate in twenty-first century Canadian society, people need the academic skills and knowledge that are taught in schools. Reading, writing, math, history, and geography—all of these are formally taught in schools.
- *Research:* Many post-secondary institutions are also the sites of various kinds of research.
- *Social integration:* Look around at the other people in your class. They probably come from different backgrounds. In a diverse country such as Canada, it is likely that your classmates have different ethnicities, religions, and social classes. However, you are all in this same class together. Another function of the educational system is to transmit the predominant social norms and values to a diverse population.
- *Social placement:* Education is a hierarchical system, and aside from any intrinsic benefits, how you perform in school will determine what kinds of jobs you can get. In a class system such as we have in Canada, education is an important factor in social mobility.
- *Latent functions:* These are the less obvious, yet significant, impacts that education has on society. For example, compulsory education also means that we have compulsory childcare, at least for children over 6 years old. This allows more parents to work outside the home. Having a large group of young people spending a lot of time together also promotes the development of a distinct youth culture. With the increasing tendency to stay in school longer, young people are effectively kept out of the full-time labour market until they graduate.

Conflict Theory: The Hidden Curriculum

When I was in high school, we were allowed to choose one of our courses. The choice was between woodworking and home economics. Although the choice was supposed to be open, only the boys chose woodworking, and only the girls chose home economics. Although these were not assigned courses, I certainly learned a not-so-subtle lesson about gender roles.

Schools teach more than just academic subjects. If you think back to elementary school, you'll remember that you learned all kinds of things that are unrelated to academic life, like sharing your pens and pencils and raising your hand if you had a question. Sociologists suggest that the education system plays an important role in society by teaching individuals the values of a community.

Certainly we want to transfer academic knowledge to the next generation, but schools also socialize students in what some call the **hidden curriculum**. The term *hidden curriculum* refers to lessons taught in schools that are unrelated to academic learning. Schools teach children about citizenship when they have mock elections, and they teach us to follow orders, routines, and other seemingly arbitrary regulations. The hidden curriculum also applies to students' socialization of one another. This prepares students for stresses that will occur later in life.

As the name suggests, the hidden curriculum refers to the less-obvious lessons that are taught in schools. From the conflict perspective, these lessons can have a negative impact on some groups of students. One feature of the hidden curriculum is that it creates a subservient workforce that accepts authority. It also promotes an ideology that legitimates inequality, justifies the privileges of some, creates the myth of meritocracy, and attributes poverty to failure to conform and achieve. As described in the example above, the hidden curriculum may also have elements of sexism and racism.

Feminist Theory: Gender and Education

A few years ago, my daughter went to her first day in grade 2 very excited, but she came home feeling down. When I asked why she was so upset, she said it was because she had "a boy for a teacher." I had to explain to her that "boy teachers" could be just as smart and fun as "girl teachers." Two months later, she couldn't wait to catch the bus in the morning to get to his class. Male elementary school teachers don't break any major social taboos today, but 40 years ago, when I was in school, the only men at my school were the gym teacher, the principal, and the janitor.

Historically, men and women have received vastly different educations. In 1872, Mount Allison became the first Canadian university to grant degrees to women.[36] Although women were starting to be offered enrolment in post-secondary studies in North America, they were encouraged to study "feminine" concentrations, such as nursing and teaching. Men, conversely, focused on fields that involved either vocational or intellectual skills. These differences are becoming less pronounced today, but there is still a clear educational divide between men and women nationally.[37]

Even though higher education used to be a primarily masculine pursuit, women now earn the majority of university degrees. For example, Statistics Canada reported that in 2011, 60 percent of all degrees from Canadian universities were awarded to women. Women accounted for 61 percent of the students who received a bachelor's degree, 55 percent of those who received a master's degree, and 44.5 percent of those who received doctorates. The doctorate figure was up from 36.1 percent a decade earlier.[38]

Although this is a major improvement for women in education, the differences in choice of major still reflect traditional gender roles. For example, Statistics Canada's figures for 2011 show that women received about double the number of university qualifications as men in the fields of visual and performing arts and communications technologies, while men far outnumbered women in the fields of architecture, engineering, and related technologies.[39]

If women are earning degrees in greater numbers than men, shouldn't we see the income gap between men and women decrease? Census data show that the income gap between men and women actually becomes wider with higher levels of educational background (as shown in the "Gender Income Gap" figure).

EDUCATION AND RELIGION

Studies have shown that educational attainment and religious practice generally have a positive correlation.[40] In other words, religiously active students are apt to perform well in school and to graduate. For example, the findings of one recent Canadian study suggested that—across all school grades—attending religious services is linked to both lower levels of substance use and higher academic achievement over time.[41]

In an earlier study, Texan Mark Regenerus found that intensely religious students scored better on standardized tests, "even after accounting for other predictors of academic success."[42] He argued that religious involvement gives students "a level of social control and motivation toward education."[43] This trend holds up across all types of neighbourhoods—affluent and poor—and across many different ethnicities. In fact, the more disadvantaged the neighbourhood, the more beneficial a student's church attendance is on educational attainment.[44]

This research points to a possible connection between education and religion. Although certainly not causal, it does show that both of these social institutions perform a similar task—socializing a person into

MAKE CONNECTIONS

Scheduling around the Holidays

In 2007, members of the New York Muslim community called for a change in the school holiday schedule when standardized state tests were scheduled on Id al-Adha, a Muslim holy day. Although students could take excused absences, parents argued that it was unfair that children were off for Christian and Jewish holidays. However, the New York Department of Education refused to add any additional holidays to the school schedule. Many U.S. school districts require that students be in school a certain number of days per school year, so any additional holidays would cause the school year to run longer.[45]

Thoughts of altering the school calendar can get people worked up in Canada, too. There was a stir early in 2010, after the Quebec government moved toward changing the province's school calendar so that schools could stay open on weekends—and, it was initially thought, so that they could substitute their own religious holidays for the standard Christmas, Thanksgiving, and Easter. The Quebec education minister made headlines when she denied that any of the regular statutory holidays would change in the move, which she said was aimed at curbing Quebec's dropout problem.[46]

>>> **ACTIVITY** Create a new school calendar for your province that includes major religious holidays for the top three religions in the province. Remember that most school systems require that students be in school a set number of days and that religious populations vary from province to province. Research the demographics of your province and research the holidays of the three largest religious populations in your area. How difficult is it to create a schedule that meets everyone's religious needs?

THE GENDER INCOME GAP BY LEVEL OF EDUCATION IN 2009

Median Earnings

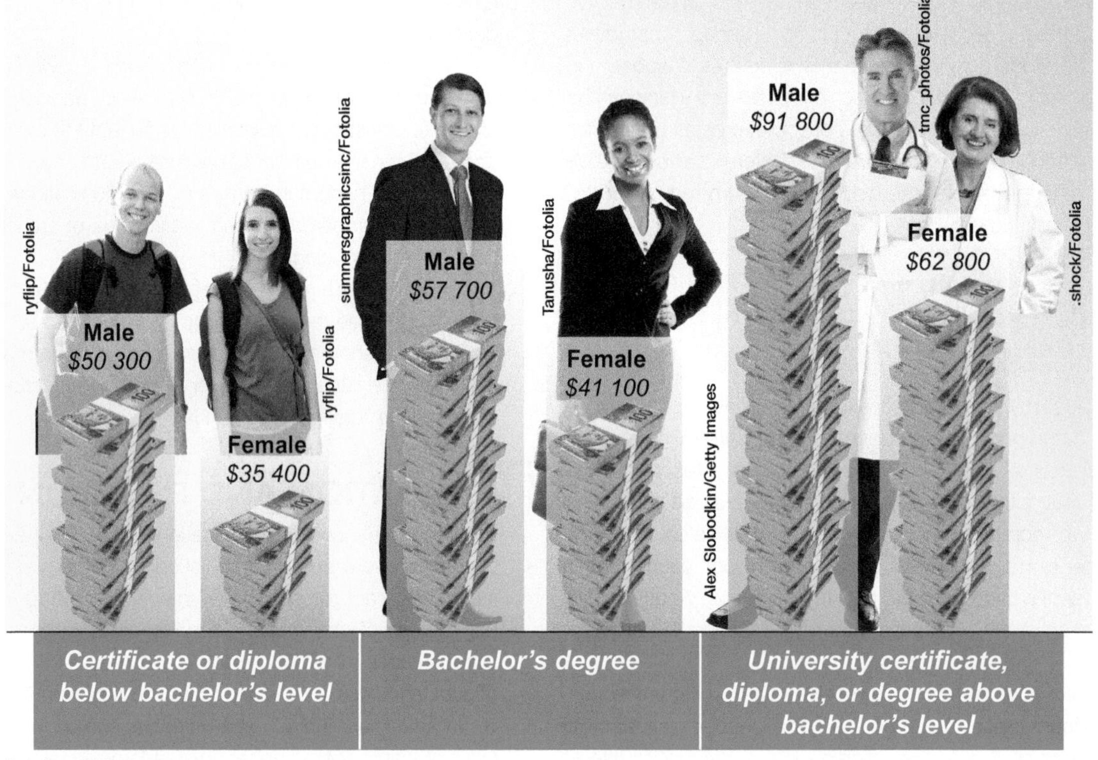

Data from Statistics Canada.

society. Churches do this by socializing us into a value system, and schools do this through their academic mission and their transmission of the hidden curriculum.

Religion in Society

RELIGION is a social institution based on a unified system of beliefs and practices related to sacred things.

THEISM is the belief in a god or gods.

MONOTHEISM is the belief that there is only one God.

POLYTHEISM is the belief in multiple gods and demigods.

PHILOSOPHIES OF LIFE focus on a set of ethical, moral, or philosophical principles.

TOTEMISM is the practice of honouring a totem or a sacred object.

SIMPLE SUPERNATURALISM is the belief in a variety of supernatural forces that affect and influence people's lives.

Sociologists study **religion** in much the same way they study other social institutions. We want to understand how religion is connected to other institutions, how it is practised by various groups, and what impact it has on both society and the lives of individuals. Émile Durkheim defined **religion** as a "unified system of beliefs and practices related to sacred things, that is to say, things set apart and forbidden—beliefs and practices which unite into one single moral community called a Church, all those who adhere to them."[47] Although most societies have some sort of dominant religion, there are many different religions, each of which embraces its own set of beliefs and customs.

TYPES OF RELIGION

The three major religious groups of the West—Christians, Jews, and Muslims—all practise **theism**, the belief in a god or gods. More specifically, these religions practise **monotheism**, meaning they believe that there is only one God.[48]

Not all religions believe that there is one powerful God. Some religions believe in multiple gods or demigods; this belief is called **polytheism**. Instead of having multiple gods be all-powerful, many polytheistic cultures have a single god to represent a specific power or object. For example, in ancient Nordic mythology, Odin was the god of wisdom, and Thor was the warrior god.[49] In some cases, each village in a particular area may have its own god, along with a particular place or a sacred object reserved for worshipping that god.[50]

Some cultures do not have religions per se but have philosophies that help guide people throughout life. **Philosophies of life** focus on a set of ethical, moral, or philosophical principles. Buddhism, Confucianism, and Taoism are all philosophies of life and are dedicated to achieving a kind of moral enlightenment. This enlightenment is attained by following a specific set of rules, such as the teachings of Buddha or the laws of Confucius. The processes of being and becoming are key aspects of these ways of life.[51]

Preliterate societies practised **totemism**—honouring a totem or a sacred object. These totems were symbolic objects that often depicted animals or plants that were important to the community. The totem itself was thought to have divine and mystical powers. In addition to totemism, preliterate societies also practised simple supernaturalism. **Simple supernaturalism** is the belief in a variety of supernatural forces that affect and influence people's lives. Similarly, **animism** is the belief that animate spirits live in natural objects and operate in the world. For example, in Shinto, which is practised in Japan, the natural world is filled with *kami*—spirits that can bring luck or cause mischief.

ANIMISM is the belief that animate spirits live in natural objects and operate in the world.

CULTS are new religious movements led by charismatic leaders with few followers.

SECTS are religious groups that have enough members to sustain themselves and go against society's norms.

CHURCH is a large, highly organized group of believers.

THEOCRACY is a government that is controlled by religious leaders.

SACRED means connected to God or dedicated to a religious purpose.

PROFANE means related or devoted to that which is not sacred.

ORGANIZATION IN RELIGION

Religions go through a series of stages before they become an integrated part of society. Sociologically, all religions begin as cults. **Cults** are new religious movements led by charismatic leaders with few followers. The teachings and practices of the religion are often at odds with the dominant culture and religion, so society is likely to reject the cult. Cults demand intense commitment and involvement by members, and they acquire new members through outside recruitment. Most cults fail because they cannot attract enough followers to sustain themselves.

Once a cult has enough members to sustain itself, it becomes a **sect**. Sects still go against society's norms. Often, members have greater social standing and are usually better integrated into society than members of cults. As a result, they are less likely to be persecuted by the dominant society. As time passes and the sect grows, the members tend to become respectable members of society.[52]

Eventually, sects can evolve into a **church**. The term church does not specifically refer to a building or a denomination of a religion; instead, it is a large, highly organized group of believers. Churches are bureaucratized institutions and may include national and international offices, and leaders must undergo special training to perform established rituals.

If a church becomes highly integrated into the dominant culture, it may join with the state. A **theocracy** is a government that is controlled by religious leaders. For example, Iran has a theocratic government, going so far as placing religious leaders at the pinnacle of executive government decisions.[53]

RELIGIOUS PRACTICES

Durkheim argues that religion and society are so connected that the elementary forms of religion are actually expressions of the importance of the social group. A united group accomplishes more than an individual, and religion became a way that primitive people sought to express and explain this mystery. Concepts of divinity or the supernatural were a means of explanation.[54]

Religions also function to provide cultural norms like values and beliefs that societies hold important. Religions divide the **sacred** (things connected to God or dedicated to a religious purpose) from the **profane** (things related or devoted to that which is not sacred) by labelling certain

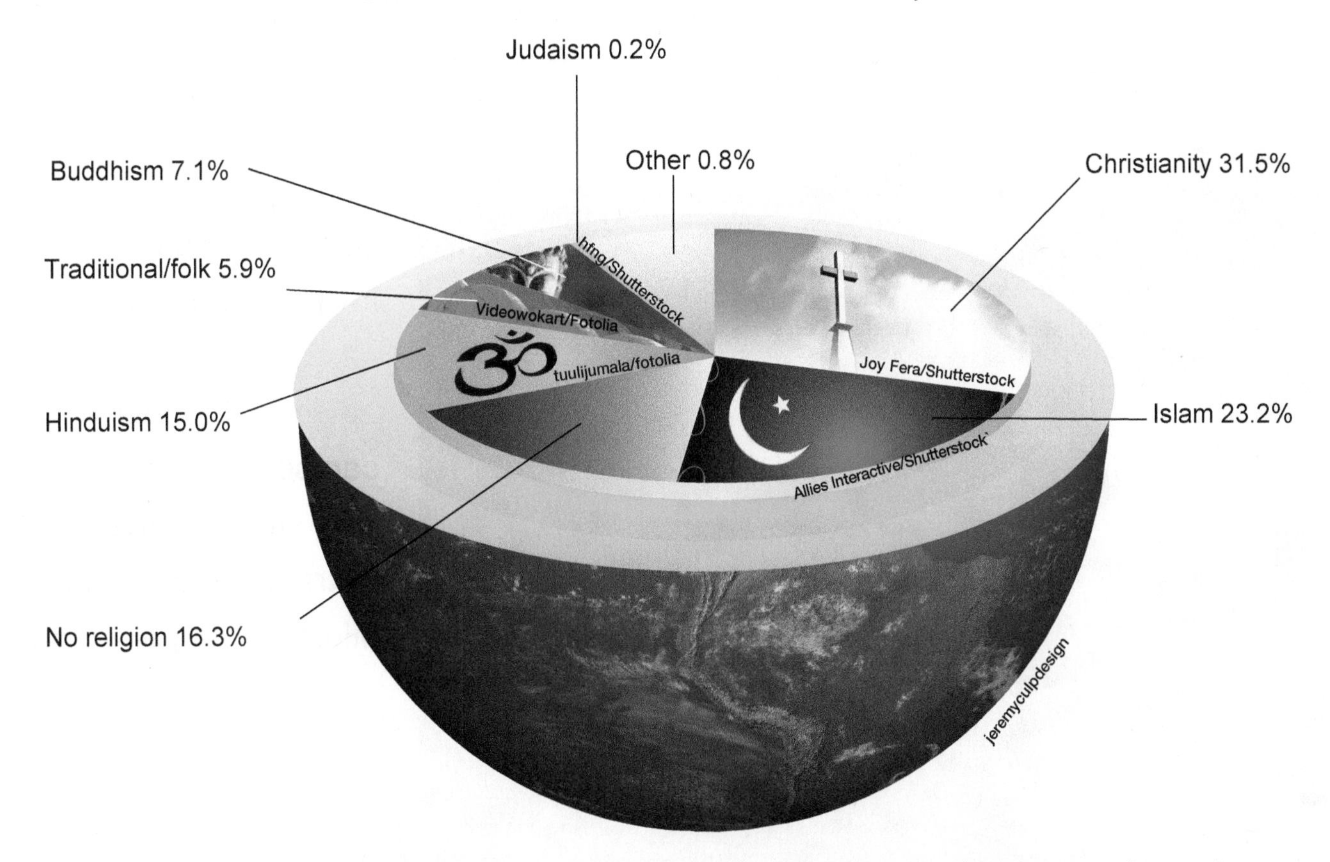

Source: Pew Research Center, "The Global Religious Landscape," *The Pew Forum on Religion & Public Life*, 2012, www.pewforum.org/global-religious-landscape-exec.aspx, accessed August 27, 2013.

THINK SOCIOLOGICALLY

Hinduism in Canada

It should be no surprise that recent immigration patterns influence religious preferences in Canada. The 2001 census—the most recent one dealing with religion—reflected trends toward more immigrants coming from areas outside Europe, especially Asia and the Middle East. One of the religions it showed to have grown "substantially" in Canada is Hinduism.[55] Between 1991 and 2001, the number of people in Canada who identified themselves as Hindu rose by 89 percent, to 297 200—representing about 1 percent of the population. By 2006, this had increased substantially again, to 406 000.[56] Hindus accounted for almost 7 percent of the new immigrants who came to Canada in the 1990s.[57]

Hinduism has existed for thousands of years. It's the world's third largest religion, after Christianity and Islam, and the majority of people in India practise it.[58] Different sources label Hinduism in different ways. But most forms of Hinduism are "henotheistic religions," **Henotheistic** religions "recognize a single deity, and view other Gods and Goddesses as manifestations or aspects of that supreme God."[59]

In 2001, 73 percent of the Hindu population in Canada lived in Ontario.[60] There are more than 50 Hindu temples in the province, mostly around Toronto.[61]

HENOTHEISM is the worship of one god while recognizing the existence of other deities.

RITUALS are established patterns of behaviour closely associated with experience of the sacred.

objects, events, and people as sacred. For example, few people might take offence if I burned this textbook. What if I burned a sacred book like the Bible, the Torah, or the Koran? An object's sacredness is related to the perception of the believer.

Likewise, religious **rituals** develop around these sacred objects, further strengthening the social norm. A ritual is an established pattern of behaviour closely associated with experience of the sacred. Followers come together and contribute to rituals, strengthening the group's common understanding and belief. This in turn helps strengthen the group's bonds and further integrates the individuals into the group. This unity created by religion allows members to integrate by increasing cohesion and functioning as a social control mechanism.

RELIGION AND THE ECONOMY

Karl Marx

Karl Marx didn't view religion as a way to unify people and answer questions. Instead, he viewed religion as the "opium of the people." In other words, Marx believed religion was often used as a tool by the wealthy to mislead the poor about their true social class. He suggested that religion gave people an illusion of happiness but nothing of real, long-lasting value.[62]

Remember that Marx believed that the rich controlled the poor through a variety of means, one of which was ideology. If people believed that something was fair or justified, then they were unlikely to bring about change in the system. Marx thought religions did very little to change the corrupt system of capitalism; instead, they often justified it.

Robert Wallis/Corbis

<<< **Cows are considered sacred beasts in Hindu culture,** and as such are not to be harmed. **In India, you can sometimes see a cow sitting in the middle of traffic, with cars and bikes moving around it.**

>>> This family is performing a ritual for Kwanzaa. **The ritual strengthens the group's common understanding and belief, which in turn strengthens the group's bonds.**

Kwame Zikomo/Purestock/SuperStock

SECULARIZATION is the overall decline in the importance and power of religion in people's lives.

Marx believed the wealthy used their power and influence to ensure that the poor believed their plight was divinely inspired and that some heavenly afterlife would make everything better. Marx suggested that religion helped people feel better by numbing them to their true pain. In short, religion causes people to ignore the real problem—capitalist oppression.[63]

Max Weber

Max Weber agreed with Marx's idea that there is a link between the economy and religion, but he pointed out a connection between Protestant and capitalist values (see Chapter 1). Weber proposed that John Calvin's teachings laid the foundation for capitalism. Therefore, Weber believed capitalism developed in the West primarily because the Calvinist Protestant belief system supported it.[64]

One of Calvin's important philosophical points was the belief in predestination. This teaching suggests that God knows in advance who will and who will not go to Heaven because God is all-knowing. Prosperity is seen as a mark of God's favour because blessings would not be given to the "damned." So hard work and the creation of wealth are positive attributes and signs that you are a "chosen one." While not explicitly stated, notice how this infers that poverty is a sign of God's disfavour. In order to avoid poverty, people have to work hard, save money, and be thrifty. Weber termed this idea the Protestant work ethic.

Furthermore, the Protestant work ethic emphasizes individuality. Protestantism supports the notion of individual salvation, which lays the groundwork for individuals to focus on their own well-being first and the good of others second. Both of these components—prosperity and individuality—laid the foundation for capitalism.[65]

Notice how both Marx and Weber saw a connection between the economy and religion. However, Marx saw religion as a tool to keep the rich wealthy, while Weber saw it as a tool to make people work hard to become prosperous.

CHANGES IN RELIGION

As societies modernized, religions began going through **secularization**, which is an overall decline in the importance and power of religion in

GO GLOBAL

The Golden Rule around the World

Even though many religions hold different beliefs, some ideas are practically universal. An example is the Golden Rule, which states, "Treat others as you want to be treated." You can see that this rule manifests itself in many societies, regardless of the specific belief system.[66]

Buddhism (Udana-Varga 5:18): Hurt no others in ways that you yourself would find hurtful.

Christianity (Matthew 7:12): In everything do to others as you would have them do to you; this is the law and the prophets.

Confucianism (Analects 15:23): Surely it is the maxim of loving-kindness: do not unto others what you would not have done unto you.

Hinduism (Mahabharata 5:1517): This is the sum of duty: do naught unto others, which would cause you pain if done to you.

Islam (Fourth Hadith of an-Nawawi 13): Not one of you is a believer until you wish for others what you wish for yourself.

Judaism (Talmud Shabbat 31a): What is hateful to you, do not to your fellow man, this is the entire law: all the rest is commentary.

> **CIVIL RELIGION** is a binding force that holds society together through political and social issues.

people's lives. Institutional religion weakens as societies become more scientifically advanced.

Secularization theorists generally agree that as society becomes more complex, people become less tied to the "old ways" and more inclined to pursue other avenues.[67] This seems to indicate that secularization is inevitable for society; however, many developing parts of the world show no obvious decline in religious influence.[68]

RELIGION IN CANADA

Canada is one of the world's most religiously diverse countries.[69] In our southern neighbour, the United States, sociologist Robert Bellah and colleagues argue that there is a **civil religion**.[70] A **civil religion** is a binding force that holds society together through political and social issues. Civil religion elevates democracy to sacredness by giving democracy religious undertones. The flag and the cross become equally sacred.

In Canada, though, the parliamentary system—as opposed to the U.S. presidential and congressional system—has not fostered that kind of nationalistic civil religion, *The Canadian Encyclopedia* notes. In fact, "Today, our sacred places may include the Arctic or the Prairie sky as the horizon of our sense of identity."[71]

If we look at the statistics, we see signs of change in Canada's religious makeup in recent years. For example, the percentage of Christians has been dropping at about 0.9 percentage points a year—or almost 10 percent in a decade.[72] However, Canada's biggest single religious group, Catholics, has been growing since it outstripped Protestants in 1971 for the first time since Confederation. In 2001, Catholics made up 43.2 percent of the population, up 4.8 percent in a decade.[73] Just under half of Canada's Catholics lived in Quebec in 2001, making up 83 percent of that province's population (the highest in Canada).[74]

The second biggest religious denomination measured in the 2001 census was "No religion"—16 percent of the population. That group made up less than 1 percent of the population before 1971.[75] Statistics Canada cited immigration as a factor in the blossoming of the "no religion" group, especially because of newcomers from China, Hong Kong, and Taiwan.[76]

However, as suggested when we focused on Hinduism earlier, "The largest gains in religious affiliations occurred among faiths consistent with changing immigration patterns toward more immigrants from regions outside of Europe, in particular Asia and the Middle East."[77] Those identifying themselves as Muslim showed the biggest increase in this group, more than doubling from 1991 to 2001, to represent 2 percent of the country's population and take eighth spot in the ranking of Top 10 religious denominations in the country. A total of 61 percent of all Muslims lived in Ontario.[78]

The number of people identifying themselves as Jewish made up 1.1 percent of Canada's population in 2001, almost unchanged from a decade before. For more than half of them, Ontario was home.[79]

There was a 9 percent decline in two decades in the number of people over age 15 in Canada who attended weekly religious services, Statistics Canada's 2005 General Social Survey showed.

FREQUENCY OF RELIGIOUS ATTENDANCE, 1985–2005

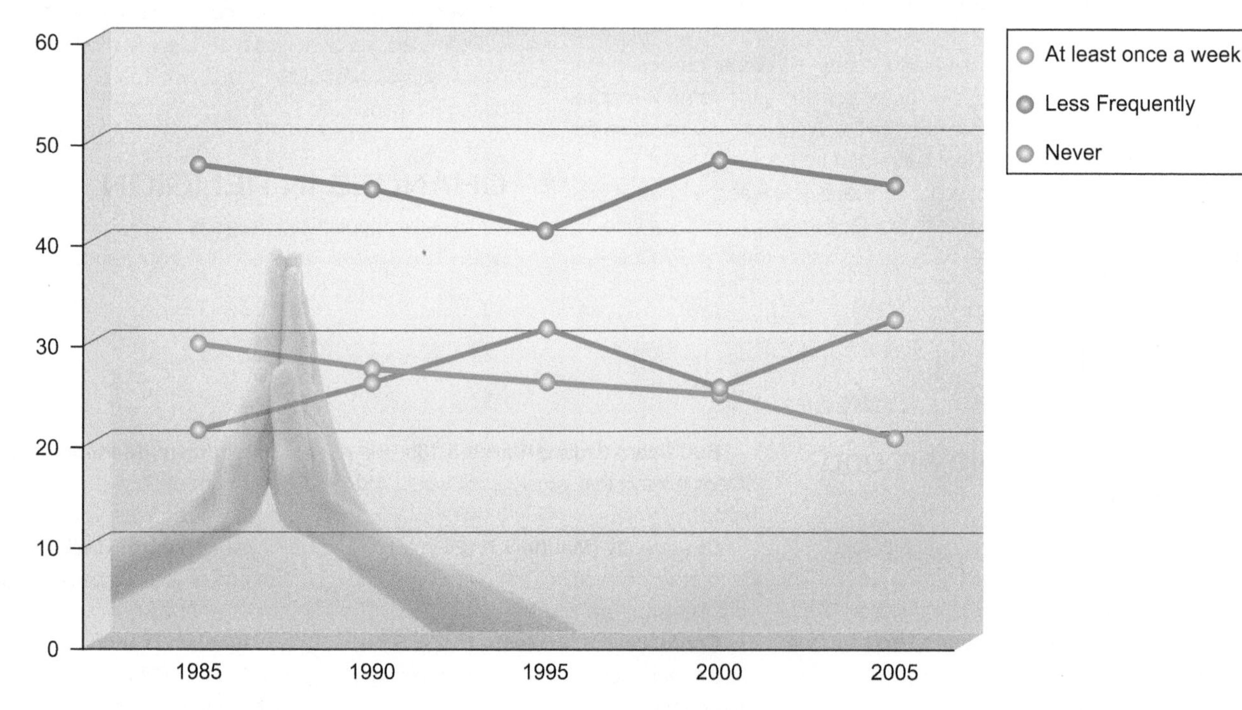

Source: Colin Lindsay, "Canadians Attend Weekly Religious Services Less Than 20 Years Ago," June 2008. Component of Statistics Canada Catalogue no. 89-630-X. www.statcan.gc.ca/pub/89-630-x/2008001/article/10650-eng.pdf.

think sociologically: HOW DOES RELIGION AFFECT SOCIETY?

Symbolic Interactionism: Sacred and Profane

Religious believers feel that everything in the world can be interpreted or defined as either sacred or profane. Almost anything—trees, animals, even bodies of water—can be considered sacred. However, what is sacred to one group may be profane to another. An element can be both sacred and profane for the same religious group. For example, for some Christians, red wine is profane when consumed during an ordinary meal, but the wine is sacred when consecrated by a priest or minister during the ritual of Holy Communion. The setting influences the reverence of an object.

A **system of beliefs** relates sacred objects and actions to religious rituals and defines and protects the sacred from the profane. It labels what is a virtue and what is a sin. These labels provide meaning and morals for specific actions. For example, certain belief systems tell people that sex within marriage is acceptable, but sex outside marriage is sinful. A religion's system of beliefs is maintained by an **organization of believers**, which is a group of people who ensure the prosperity and effectiveness of the religious experience.

An organization of believers is composed of religious leaders and followers who define and guard the sacred. The organization determines possible conflicts with the religion's moral code. For example, there are said to be about 200 000 "Old Order Amish" in Canada and the United States. The Amish community (sometimes known as Amish Mennonites) does not permit its followers to use modern technology. However, some orders show a little leniency toward their members, such as allowing communal telephones and riding in cars when there is an emergency.[80] Without an organization of believers to keep abreast of current developments, a religion becomes extinct.

SYSTEM OF BELIEFS relates sacred objects to religious rituals and defines and protects the sacred from the profane.

ORGANIZATION OF BELIEVERS is a group that ensures the prosperity and effectiveness of the religious experience.

Functionalism: Solidarity Through Worship

Durkheim believed that religion binds the community together through ritual and tradition. Followers gather to celebrate the power of things that are sacred and supernatural. Rituals unite the group as they celebrate and perform the actions together. For example, in the United States Martin Luther King, Jr., was president of the Southern Christian Leadership Conference, an organization that combined religion and politics to promote the 1960s civil rights movement. Thousands of activists joined together to share their faith and beliefs while working toward equality and unity.[81]

Religion also strengthens society's norms and values by including society's values in its own lessons. Religion influences a person's actions in society, often acting as a means of social control. All religions provide rules for adherents to live by, and most suggest that disobedience of these rules leads to negative consequences.

Religion reconciles people to the hardships and inequities of society. It offers the poor and oppressed strong moral codes as a conduit to salvation after death. Religion provides both the reason and the reward to conform to social rules.

However, religion promotes stability, even if the status quo is unfair and unequal. Religion can perpetuate practices like slavery, racism, and sexism. People in power use religion to enforce social hierarchy, maintain social order, and prevent the likelihood of rebellion. Furthermore, technological advancements may go against religious beliefs. When Galileo proposed that Earth orbits the Sun, this conflicted with the geocentric views of the Christian Church at that time. The church forced Galileo to retract his claims and then placed him under house arrest.[82]

Religion can also make it more difficult to resolve political struggles. Think about modern "religious wars." The Jewish/Muslim conflicts in the Middle East and the Protestant/Catholic tensions in Northern Ireland appear to be about religion when, in fact, they are mostly about land—who lives on it and who controls it.

Conflict Theory: Religion and Inequality

Conflict theorists believe that religion legitimizes social inequalities. Think about slavery in the Americas. The practice of owning and abusing another human being was accepted, in part, because some churches condoned it. In the hierarchy of faith, God was at the top of the list, followed by whites. Blacks and other non-whites were viewed as being worth less than whites.[83]

Marx believed that religion promotes capitalism and inequality because churches often support the idea that the wealthy deserve privileges. Weber's ideology that God blesses those who will go to Heaven also indicates that religion and economics are intertwined.

Religion also promotes obedience and legitimizes governments that are not in the best interests of everyone concerned. For example, the imperial family of Japan claims lineage from Amaterasu, Shinto goddess of the Sun. Therefore, to attack the emperor is to attack Amaterasu. Such a system guarantees faithful obedience to political leaders.[84]

Feminist Theory: The Patriarchal Nature of Religion

Many of the world's religions are deeply and formally patriarchal. When discussing religion in class, I might refer to God as "She." Some students become uncomfortable, while others laugh. Eventually, someone will say, "God is a man."

In studying the topic of religion, Johanna Stuckey has described four approaches to religious engagement taken by women. Revisionists accept the basic messages of religions and seek only more gender neutrality. Reformists (or renovationists) expose and refuse to accept any part of the religious tradition that is sexist.

Mark Richards/PhotoEdit

The Promise Keepers is an international organization committed to helping men lead a Christian life. **When people are going through periods of uncertainty, religion can bring them together for support.**

Revolutionaries seek a deeper change to sexist traditions. Rejectionists believe that traditional religions are irremediably sexist, so they seek a new spirituality.[85]

Another feminist writer, Linda Woodhead, also identified four types of reaction to religion in relation to gender. First, religion can serve to reproduce and make legitimate the gender inequality that exists within that religion as well as in the wider society (consolidating). Second, religion can be used to subvert the existing gender order, as in church groups for women in which they actually exercise considerable power and influence (tactical). Third, religion may be used by women for their own personal and spiritual purposes, without challenging the status quo (questing). Finally, religion may become a site in which women openly challenge the gendered distribution of power (counter-cultural).[86]

WRAP YOUR MIND AROUND THE THEORY

On the surface, schools teach academic subjects. The hidden curriculum also teaches individuals the values of the community.

FUNCTIONALISM

The functionalist perspective focuses on education as a social institution that helps society to run smoothly and promotes social stability. Schooling serves several manifest functions in society. It transmits formal knowledge and skills, it is sometimes a site for research, it promotes social integration, and it is a key factor in social placement. Education also has many latent functions, such as providing childcare and keeping young people out of the full-time labour market.

CONFLICT THEORY

From the conflict perspective, schools socialize students through the hidden curriculum. This refers to lessons taught in schools that are unrelated to academic learning, and these can have a negative impact on some groups of students. One feature of the hidden curriculum is that it creates a subservient workforce that accepts authority. It also promotes an ideology that legitimates inequality, justifies the privileges of some, creates the myth of meritocracy, and attributes poverty to failure to conform and achieve.

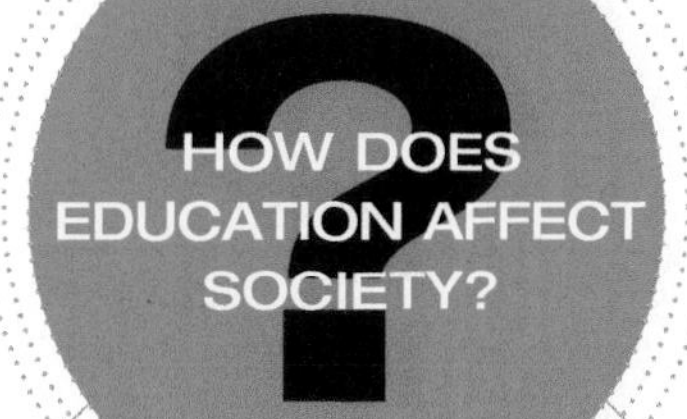

SYMBOLIC INTERACTIONISM

The teacher expectancy effect is a measure of the impact of a teacher's expectations on a student's performance. The labels that students are given, even if the labels are positive, such as "smart" or "intelligent," encourage those students to live up to what is expected of them. If students are labelled as "slow" or "difficult," they will perform at lower levels than they would were they not given such labels.

FEMINIST THEORY

Historically, men and women have received vastly different educations. Although higher education used to be a primarily masculine pursuit, women now earn the majority of university degrees. Nevertheless, the differences in choice of major still reflect traditional gender roles. Despite the fact that women are earning more degrees than men, Census data show that the income gap between men and women actually becomes wider with higher levels of educational background.

In 1872, Mount Allison became the first Canadian university to grant degrees to women. **Now, more women than men are graduating from Canadian universities.**

WRAP YOUR MIND AROUND THE THEORY

Hill Street Studios/Blend Images/Corbis

One of the functions of religion is to bring people together through ritual. This family unites to read from the Koran.

FUNCTIONALISM

Functionalists believe that religion is a social institution that binds members of the community together through participation in rituals that celebrate the supernatural and the sacred. Religion also strengthens society by transmitting norms and values, and this promotes social stability.

CONFLICT THEORY

Conflict theorists see religion as a tool used by powerful groups to make legitimate their authority and to control other groups by using ideology. Marx believed that religion promotes capitalism and inequality because churches often support the idea that the wealthy deserve privileges.

SYMBOLIC INTERACTIONISM

Symbolic interactionists look at the symbolism of religious rituals. The world can be divided into the sacred and the profane, and almost anything can be labelled as sacred. A belief system gives sacred meaning to specific actions and objects.

FEMINIST THEORY

Religion often serves as a tool to further gender inequalities. For centuries, and even now, women have been excluded from leadership in organized religions. Johanna Stuckey has described four approaches to religious engagement taken by women, while Linda Woodhead identified four types of reaction to religion in relation to gender.

AFP/Getty Images

Religion is one way that those in power stay in control. Monarchies can use the power of the people's faith to maintain order and quell any rebellions that could threaten their thrones.

Lawrence Migdale/Lawrence Migdale/Pix

Some religions use totems to portray sacred objects and ideas. In this Tsimshian ceremony, the totems are used as a backdrop for the ritual being performed.

discover sociology in action: WHAT SOCIAL POLICIES HELP CHILDREN GET A BETTER EDUCATION?

"Greg" is a 16-year-old black high school student in Toronto. He is in the "basic" level program and is having problems. This is abbreviated from Lennox V. Farrell's "Greg Is Not His Real Name"[87]:

He is very much for real about his feelings of being in grade ten Basic classes. He is for real about arriving a couple of minutes late each day for class. He hides until the hallway is clear so that other students . . . will not know that he is entering the hated Basic class. He also rushes to leave class before the dismissal bell for the same reason.

And he schemes to get non-Basic texts to display on the outside of the Basic texts. He carries these defensive texts—a shield against the barbs, name-calling, and the possibility that others, especially girls will know the grim truth:

That Greg is Basic!

Greg is sent to the office so often that he will sometimes refuse on other occasions to go there and get something as innocuous as some chalk. If the Principal sees him, no matter what, he will get in trouble, he says.

Later in life, he will also have the same relationship with Police.

His is a life in which every new day is another ambush. And days reach to months, and months to years in which there is an evolution of declining expectations, for him by all others; of him for himself.

He is given options that are constantly being diminished and diminishing. And he does what a normal human being, faced with abnormality would do. He rebels. He becomes obnoxious. He may traffic in illegal drugs. He could use a weapon on another Black youth. For a buck, or less.

In spite of this, he is so much for real that he is among the young Black people who, while being streamed into Basic level programs because authorities judge them unable to "understand" Advanced poetry in school, go on, outside of school to create international art forms like Rap, and Breakdancing!

Despite this, too, he does not think much of his own opinions.

Nobody listens to him, he says.

ACTIVITIES

1. Research details of the Africentric school idea. Do you think the Toronto school is helping struggling students? Do you think the idea could work in any other part of Canada? Do you think it could—or should—be applied to any other groups in society?
2. Have a class debate about the pros and cons of the Africentric Alternative School.

Improving Education with Africentric Schooling

Finding a way to counter high dropout rates for black students in Toronto led to a controversial solution: The city's first Africentric public school opened its doors in September 2009, with 85 students.[88]

Enrolment for the school's second year soared to 160. And along the way, the Africentric Alternative School's 16 grade 3 students "significantly outperformed" the Toronto District School Board and the province as a whole in 2009–2010 EQAO tests, with 69 percent of the grade 3 students at the new school reaching Ontario's Level 3 standard in reading, 80 percent in writing, and 81 percent in math. The respective figures were 60, 70, and 71 percent for the board and 62, 70, and 71 percent for all of Ontario.[89] (Ontario's Education Quality and Accountability Office, or EQAO, is responsible for province-wide assessments.[90])

The school is not just for black students, University of Toronto Professor George Dei explained just before the school first opened. "We're talking about looking at the world through the eyes of African peoples—their experiences, their cultural knowledge and their history." Africentric education regards school as a community endeavour, he said, and instead of treating students as individual learners, "We want them to see themselves as a community of learners with a responsibility to those who are struggling."[91]

Two women—Angela Wilson and Donna Harrow—pushed for the school in order to help black youth succeed. The proposal to create the school was approved 11:9 at a Toronto District School Board meeting in January 2008. School board statistics showed that 40 percent of black youth in the board's schools do not graduate, compared with about 25 percent board-wide. One detractor voiced concern about the decision to "segregate" the education system; another called the school idea "half-baked."[92]

The Africentric Alternative School's principal, Thando Hyman-Aman, stressed from the beginning that children would learn the same curriculum as children in other schools in Ontario. "What makes this school different are the culturally relevant resources that we use," she said.[93]

CHAPTER

14

HOW DO SOCIETIES PASS ON INFORMATION? 259

through education and religion

HOW DOES EDUCATION AFFECT SOCIETY? 264

functionalism: education fulfills important functions for society
conflict theory: the hidden curriculum justifies social inequalities
symbolic interactionism: labelling and teacher expectations can affect students' learning
feminist theory: females and males have different experiences in education

HOW DOES RELIGION AFFECT SOCIETY? 271

functionalism: religion binds people together through ritual and tradition
conflict theory: religion legitimizes social inequalities
symbolic interactionism: everything in the world can be interpreted as profane or sacred and is defined according to a belief system
feminist theory: religion, like all other social institutions, is very patriarchal, but feminists are looking at how women can increase their participation

WHAT SOCIAL POLICIES HELP CHILDREN GET A BETTER EDUCATION? 275

the Africentric Alternative School was opened in Toronto in hopes of reducing the dropout rate of African and Caribbean Canadian students

get the topic: HOW DO SOCIETIES PASS ON INFORMATION?

Theories

FUNCTIONALISM 264

- education is a social institution that helps society to run smoothly and promotes social stability
- schools transmit formal knowledge and skills, they are sometimes sites for research, they promote social integration, and they are a key factor in social placement
- schools have many latent functions, such as providing childcare and keeping young people out of the full-time labour market

SYMBOLIC INTERACTIONISM 264

- the teacher expectancy effect is a measure of the impact of a teacher's expectations on a student's performance
- the labels that students are given encourage them to live up to what is expected of them
- if students are labelled as "slow" or "difficult," they will perform at lower levels than they would were they not given such labels

CONFLICT THEORY 264

- schools socialize students through the hidden curriculum
- one feature of the hidden curriculum is that it creates a subservient workforce that accepts authority
- the hidden curriculum also promotes an ideology that legitimates inequality

FEMINIST THEORY 265

- historically, men and women have received vastly different educations
- women now earn the majority of university degrees
- the income gap between men and women actually becomes wider with higher levels of educational background

Theories

FUNCTIONALISM 271

- religion strengthens norms and values
- it creates social stability that supports governmental authority
- religion acts as a means of social control by influencing a person's actions

SYMBOLIC INTERACTIONISM 271

- everything is either sacred or profane
- a system of beliefs defines the meaning and morals of specific actions
- an organization that supports a belief system ensures continuation and effectiveness of the religious experience

CONFLICT THEORY 271

- religion justifies the inequalities of social classes
- religion was created to benefit the wealthy and condemn the poor
- Marx believed that religion promotes obedience and legitimizes governments that are not in the best interest of everyone

FEMINIST THEORY 271

- religious organizations often reflect the gender inequality of the wider society
- Woodhead described the engagement of women as consolidating, tactical, questing, or counter-cultural
- Stuckey said that women can adopt different strategies to engage with religion: revisionist, reformist, revolutionary, and rejectionist

Key Terms

education is the social institution through which society passes on knowledge, skills, and values from one generation to the next. *259*

grade inflation is the trend of assigning higher grades than previously assigned to students for completing the same work. *262*

human capital is a person's combination of skills, knowledge, traits, and personal attributes. *263*

credentialism is an emphasis on educational degrees in assessing skills and knowledge. *263*

teacher expectancy effect is the impact of a teacher's expectations on a student's performance. *264*

hidden curriculum refers to lessons taught in schools that are unrelated to academic learning. *264*

religion is a social institution based on a unified system of beliefs and practices related to sacred things. *266*

theism is the belief in a god or gods. *266*

monotheism is the belief that there is only one God. *266*

polytheism is the belief in multiple gods and demigods. *266*

philosophies of life focus on a set of ethical, moral, or philosophical principles.

totemism is the practice of honouring a totem or a sacred object. *266*

simple supernaturalism is the belief in a variety of supernatural forces that affect and influence people's lives. *266*

animism is the belief that animate spirits live in natural objects and operate in the world. *267*

cults are new religious movements led by charismatic leaders with few followers. *267*

sects are religious groups that have enough members to sustain themselves and go against society's norms. *267*

church is a large, highly organized group of believers. *267*

theocracy is a government that is controlled by religious leaders. *267*

sacred means connected to God or dedicated to a religious purpose. *267*

profane means related or devoted to that which is not sacred. *267*

henotheism is the worship of one god while recognizing the existence of other deities. *268*

rituals are established patterns of behaviour closely associated with experience of the sacred. *268*

secularization is the overall decline in the importance and power of religion in people's lives. *269*

civil religion is a binding force that holds society together through political and social issues. *270*

system of beliefs relates sacred objects to religious rituals and defines and protects the sacred from the profane. *271*

organization of believers is a group that ensures the prosperity and effectiveness of the religious experience. *271*

Sample Test Questions

These multiple-choice questions are similar to those found in the test bank that accompanies this textbook.

1. Which of the following is *not* a myth associated with education?
- **a.** Society is the primary unit.
- **b.** A nation is merely a group of individuals.
- **c.** Childhood socialization leads to adult character.
- **d.** Learning increases individual and national future progress.

2. Some parents decide to homeschool their children because they are concerned with
- **a.** school size.
- **b.** lack of resources.
- **c.** school segregation.
- **d.** academic instruction.

3. Which of the following statements is true?
- **a.** Improvements in student performance are directly related to religious practice.
- **b.** Religious students from all backgrounds are apt to perform well in school.
- **c.** Intensely religious students do not perform as well as others on standardized tests.
- **d.** Religious practice benefits only poor students.

4. Theocracy is a
- **a.** belief that there is only one God.
- **b.** belief in multiple gods and demigods.
- **c.** worship of a sacred object.
- **d.** a government that is controlled by religious leaders.

5. What is Max Weber's view of religion?
- **a.** Scientific advancement weakens religion.
- **b.** Protestant teachings laid the foundation for capitalism.
- **c.** Religion unites people and answers questions.
- **d.** Elementary forms of religion express the importance of social groups.

ANSWERS: 1. a; 2. d; 3. b; 4. d; 5. b

ESSAY

1. What is the hidden curriculum?
2. How can a person's socioeconomic status affect education?
3. What factors affect educational attainment?
4. How do religions become integrated into society?
5. How can religion be related to capitalism?

WHERE TO START YOUR RESEARCH PAPER

To look at more educational statistics, go to www.unesco.org/en/efareport.

To learn more about grade inflation, go to http://economics.ca/cgi/jab?journal=cpp&view=v26n3/CPPv26n3p361.pdf and www.macleans.ca/article.jsp?content=20070605_153207_13228.

To learn more about homeschooling in Canada, go to www.webring.org/l/rd?ring=homeschooling;id=1;url=http%3A%2F%2Fwww%2Eflora%2Eorg%2Fhomeschool%2Dca%2F.

To learn more about university tuition fees, go to www.aucc.ca/canadian-universities/facts-and-stats/tuition-fees-by-university/.

To learn more about education and religion, go to www.edu.gov.on.ca/eng/document/curricul/religion/religioe.html.

To learn about freedom of religion and religious symbols in public areas such as schools, go to www.parl.gc.ca/content/lop/researchpublications/2011-60-e.htm.

Remember to check www.thethinkspot.ca for additional information, downloadable flashcards, and other helpful resources.

COLLECTIVE BEHAVIOUR AND SOCIAL MOVEMENTS

mario beauregard/Fotolia

WHAT DRIVES SOCIAL CHANGE?
WHAT ARE THE THEORIES BEHIND SOCIAL MOVEMENTS?
HOW DO SOCIAL MOVEMENTS INFLUENCE SOCIETY?

"Rodriguez de Gerada is widely recognized as one of the most skilled and creative founders of culture jamming, the practice of parodying advertisements and hijacking billboards in order to drastically alter their messages. Streets are public spaces, adbusters argue, and since most residents can't afford to counter corporate messages by purchasing their own ads, they should have the right to talk back to images they never asked to see. In recent years, this argument has been bolstered by advertising's mounting aggressiveness in the public domain. . . . Adding even greater urgency to their cause is the belief among many jammers that concentration of media ownership has successfully devalued the right to free speech by severing it from the right to be heard.

"All at once, these forces are coalescing to create a climate of semiotic Robin Hoodism. A growing number of activists believe the time has come for the public to stop asking that some space be left unsponsored, and to begin seizing it back. Culture jamming baldly rejects the idea that marketing—because it buys its way into our public spaces—must be passively accepted as a one-way information flow."[1]

How Do Societies Change?

CHAPTER 15

In *No Logo: Taking Aim at the Brand Bullies,* Naomi Klein describes a number of issues that have been raised by the "anti-globalization movement."

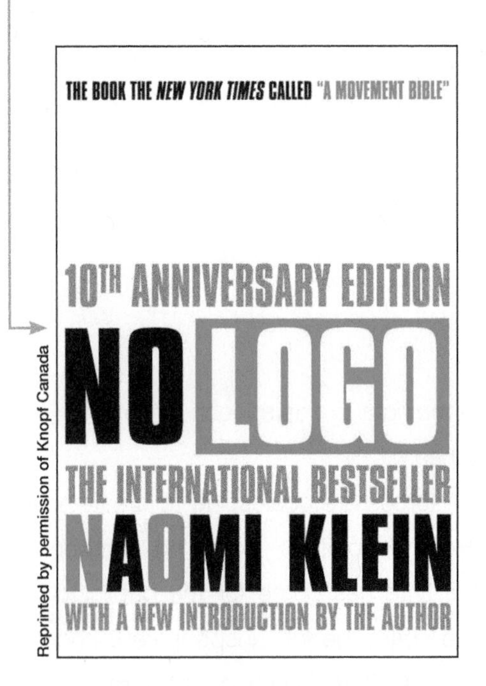

Reprinted by permission of Knopf Canada

Pervasive advertising (including ads in schools), sweatshops, and censorship are just some of the corporate actions that Klein criticizes in *No Logo*. But in addition to condemning the large multinational corporations that seem to rule the world, Klein offers suggestions for how ordinary citizens can reclaim power and a voice. *Culture jamming* is a term used to describe one such strategy.

Jammers such as Rodriguez de Gerada wage a small but persistent war against the ubiquitous corporate logo. They are expressing their social discontent. It is people such as Rodriguez de Gerada who can bring about change in society. Throughout this book, you have seen how society has a powerful impact on you as an individual. In this final chapter, we will look at how individuals can form groups in order to change society. What drives changes, and how do we react to those changes? In this chapter, we review these and other questions as we study social change, collective behaviour, and social movements.

Social Change

is: how culture and social institutions change over time

significant historical changes have been:

- Hunting and gathering societies
- Agricultural societies
- Industrial societies
- Postindustrial societies

Theism: the belief in a god or gods

- Social movements: activities that support or protest social issues, organized by nongovernmental organizations
- Campaigns: organized and ongoing efforts to achieve a specific goal
- Alternative social movements: want to create a change in specific people's thoughts, practices, and beliefs regarding a particular issue
- Redemptive social movements: focus on specific individuals, but the amount of change sought is radical rather than limited
- Reformative social movements: seek to change a society's thoughts and actions but only in a limited way
  - Progressive: favouring or promoting change
  - Regressive: seeking to stop change
- Revolutionary social movements: sometimes called transformative social movements, seek to change the thoughts and actions of all society in a radical fashion

get the topic: WHAT DRIVES SOCIAL CHANGE?

Shifts in Society

> **SOCIAL CHANGE** is how culture and social institutions change over time.

Changes in society are often caused by reactions to events and new opportunities, like the Industrial Revolution. This event brought about great **social change**, which is how culture and social institutions change over time. Recall how the Industrial Revolution brought about changes in social classes. Capitalists became more powerful and wealthy than the old landed aristocracy, while workers struggled to make ends meet.[2]

Around the same time, new ways to think about the world arose, including the science of sociology. Some of these ideas helped form the intellectual basis for creating a new nation, based on common ideals. One merely needs to look at the *Canadian Charter of Rights and Freedoms* to read some of these ideas. Ideas often drive social change. For example, no one recycled in my neighbourhood when I was growing up. Then someone realized that people were wasting too many natural resources and came up with the idea to reuse these materials. Today, recycling is a common practice.

Populations also grew, bringing about demographic changes such as immigration. Immigration and internal migration have changed Canada. Canada is one of the world's three main immigrant-receiving nations.[3] This has shaped the history of Canada. Immigration had helped to push the population up to 3.4 million by 1867.[4] Canada's future Prairie provinces were opened to settlement in the late nineteenth century, and the national population is now spread out across the vast country, with about 90 percent of the population living within 160 kilometres of the Canada–United States border.[5] The country's population has roughly doubled every 40 or so years since 1867, and these days roughly a quarter of a million immigrants enter the country each year.[6]

The population of aboriginal peoples in what is now Canada is estimated to have been roughly 350 000 at the time Europeans first arrived, but it dropped to 137 000 or fewer by 1867 due to disease, starvation, and warfare.[7]

The country's current population was estimated in January 2013 to be 35 056 064.[8] Despite interprovincial migration, more than 13 million people—or about one in three Canadians—currently live in the province of Ontario.[9]

STAGES OF SOCIAL CHANGE

As societies change over time, the complexity of social interaction also changes. With increasing population and technological advancement, societies have become more diverse, which leads to changes in the social structures. American sociologist Gerhard E. Lenski is one of the few theorists who maintain an evolutionary view of society. According to Lenski and colleagues, the evolution of society consists of four main stages—hunting and gathering, agricultural, industrial, and postindustrial.[10]

Resistance to change takes the form of

Futility: the claim that a reform cannot work because the social problem is unsolvable
Perversity: claims that any attempts to fix a problem would actually compound the issues the change was trying to address
Jeopardy: the claim that attempting to solve a problem will only draw attention away from other, more important issues

Social change may involve

and

Collective behaviour: any social interaction in which a group of people engages in behaviour that is not in their normal routine.

- **Crowd:** a large group of influential people who gather for a temporary purpose
- **Mobs:** groups characterized by high levels of emotion that engage in some type of focused action that can be violent or disruptive
- **Riots:** emotional and violent disturbances of the peace by crowds that lack a central focus
- **Fashion:** an object, a style, or a behavior that becomes popular for a period of time
- **Fad:** a temporary fashion or action the public embraces
- **Craze:** a fad that leaves a lasting effect on society
- **Panic:** an extreme fear based on something that might happen
- **Hysteria:** a heightened emotional state that can lead a group to violence
- **Rumours:** stories or statements that lack confirmation or certainty
- **Urban legends:** rumours that are presented as true stories that act as cautionary tales

Hunting and Gathering Societies

Have you ever wondered how you might survive if you were forced to become a hunter-gatherer? Recently, some friends and I took a camping trip into a wilderness area along the Canada–United States border. In such a place, you have only what you bring with you. And if you want to eat, you'd better learn how to fish, patiently, from a lake. I can't say we had much luck living off the land; the one fish I did manage to catch was hardly enough to feed us all. Luckily, the dehydrated food in our backpacks was enough to sustain us.

Of course, the first hunter-gatherers didn't rely on dehydrated food to survive, but they did live off the land and focused most of their efforts on finding food. Archeological evidence supports the idea that *Homo sapiens* lived as hunters and gatherers approximately 50 000 years ago. Beginning in the Neolithic period, hunters and gatherers existed in small groups of approximately 150 people for about 2000 generations. Over this period, their culture and population changed slowly.[11]

In hunting and gathering societies, an individual's status and role were closely linked. Thus, the status of tribal leader was often given to the strongest person or the best hunter. Because there were few roles for people to play in those of societies, Lenski suggests that the division of labour in hunting and gathering societies was very limited.[12] Everyone in the society had to be involved in the production of food for survival.

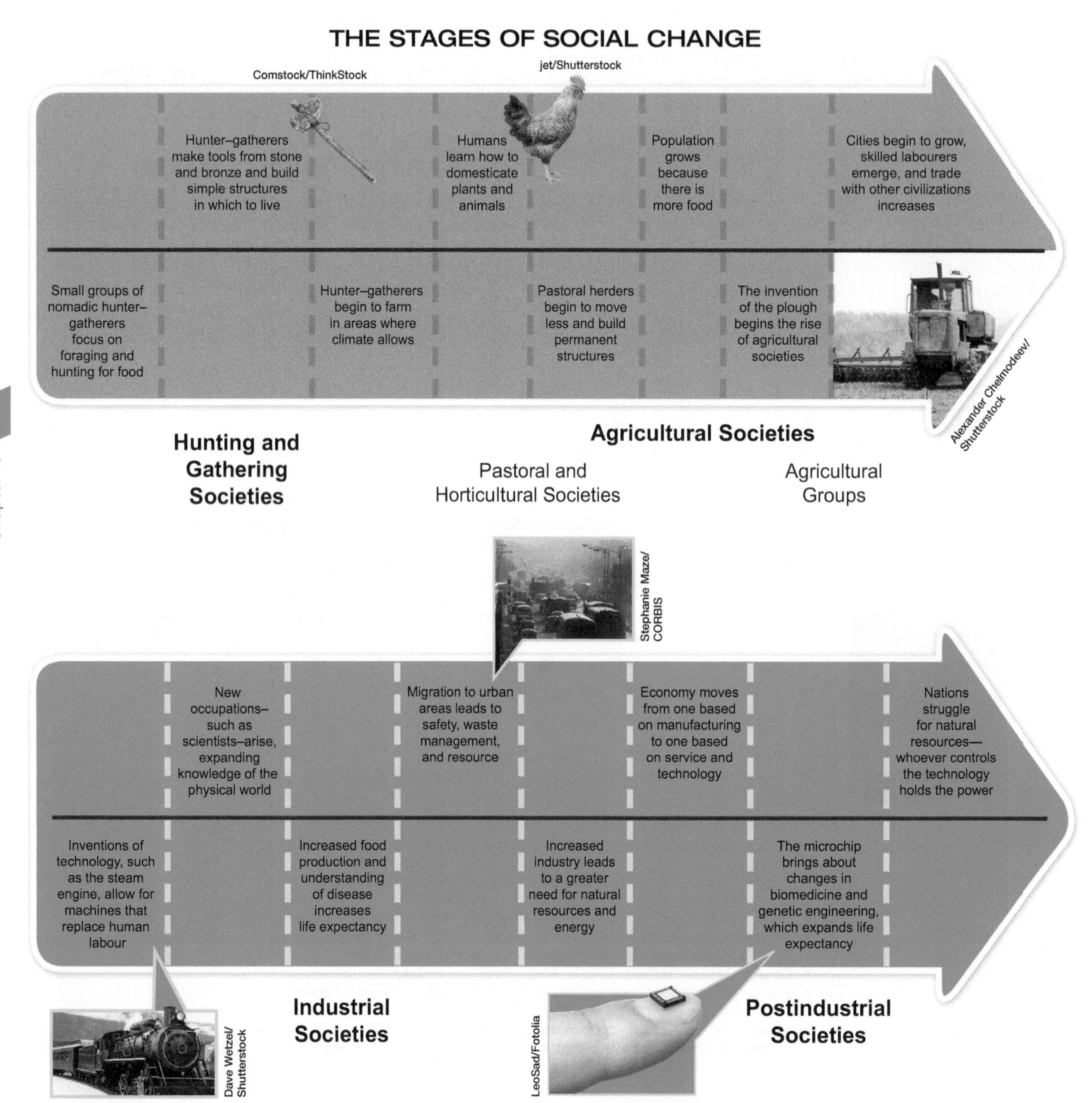
THE STAGES OF SOCIAL CHANGE
Comstock/ThinkStock
jet/Shutterstock
Hunter–gatherers make tools from stone and bronze and build simple structures in which to live
Humans learn how to domesticate plants and animals
Population grows because there is more food
Cities begin to grow, skilled labourers emerge, and trade with other civilizations increases
Small groups of nomadic hunter–gatherers focus on foraging and hunting for food
Hunter–gatherers begin to farm in areas where climate allows
Pastoral herders begin to move less and build permanent structures
The invention of the plough begins the rise of agricultural societies
Alexander Chelmodeev/Shutterstock
Hunting and Gathering Societies
Agricultural Societies
Pastoral and Horticultural Societies
Agricultural Groups
Stephanie Maze/CORBIS
New occupations–such as scientists–arise, expanding knowledge of the physical world
Migration to urban areas leads to safety, waste management, and resource
Economy moves from one based on manufacturing to one based on service and technology
Nations struggle for natural resources—whoever controls the technology holds the power
Inventions of technology, such as the steam engine, allow for machines that replace human labour
Increased food production and understanding of disease increases life expectancy
Increased industry leads to a greater need for natural resources and energy
The microchip brings about changes in biomedicine and genetic engineering, which expands life expectancy
Dave Wetzel/Shutterstock
Industrial Societies
LeoSad/Fotolia
Postindustrial Societies

FUTILITY is the claim that a reform cannot work because the social problem is unsolvable.

PERVERSITY claims that any attempts to fix a problem will actually compound the issues the change was trying to address.

Successful hunters and gatherers adapted to their environment. Geography professor Jared Diamond shows that food supply and available natural resources dictate a great deal about the form of society.[13] People living in areas with abundant food were able to hunt and gather for longer periods than those living in cold climates. Geological differences fostered human innovation. For example, farming and raising animals occurred in areas that supported crop growth and had a suitable climate for animals. This transition ushered in the agricultural stage of society.

Agricultural Societies

Roughly 10 000 years ago, people began to move from hunting and gathering to agrarian-based societies.[14] With this change, society became more complex. Lenski and colleagues divided agricultural societies into two groups: (1) pastoral and horticultural societies and (2) agricultural groups.[15]

Pastoral and horticultural societies appeared when humans learned to domesticate plants and animals. Members of these societies learned to use simple hand tools to till the soil and plant seeds in order to grow grains for food. They figured out that certain grains could be planted in soft ground. Likewise, they developed ways to raise certain types of animals in captivity, such as cows, goats, and chickens, which increased their food supply and allowed them to become less nomadic.[16]

Around 5000 to 7000 years ago, some groups took yet another step in the evolution of society. With the invention of the plough, agricultural societies arose. The simple technology of the animal-drawn plough—a sharp, hard piece of stone, wood, or metal that tills the soil—helped people cultivate lands that had previously been unusable. The dramatic increase in food production promoted the growth of cities.[17] These agrarian city-states were often quite large, with up to 1 million people. Humans lived for approximately 500 generations in agrarian cultures.[18]

Industrial Societies

During the seventeenth and eighteenth centuries, the Western world experienced the Industrial Revolution. Complex machines, such as the steam engine, encouraged the growth of industry. Steam-powered machines made human labour more efficient because the machines could perform a simple task quickly and repeatedly without rest.[19] The steam engine revolutionized the clothing industry, for example, because fabric no longer had to be hand woven. Machines mass-produced fabric, which reduced the cost of labour.

The basic idea of using technology to create goods greatly expanded the surplus of industrial societies. Farming techniques improved through mechanization, and early tractors expanded the farmable land even more. Fewer people were required to produce sufficient food for the population, which allowed for even more specialization of labour. As a result, more new types of jobs were created that ultimately led to new statuses and roles.

Lenski and colleagues suggest that industrial societies actually have less social inequality than agrarian societies.[20] This is largely because the increasing technology and surplus improve the standard of living. Even the poorest people in industrial societies have access to goods and services that are unavailable in agrarian societies.

The industrial society lasted only nine generations in some parts of the world, although it continues in others. The change occurred in some areas as a new form of society began—the postindustrial society.[21]

Postindustrial Societies

The term *postindustrial society* refers to the social change that occurs when people move from an economy based on manufacturing to one based on service and technology. Such societies still require basic food and manufactured goods, but they seek these things from other countries. Before this stage, it's possible for a society to live off its natural resources. Since postindustrial societies can no longer meet their own needs, they must import energy, food, and goods. These societies have become societies vested in a technology that grew exponentially with the invention of the microchip.

Sociologist Daniel Bell suggests three key characteristics of a postindustrial society: (1) a shift from manufacturing to services, (2) the centrality of the new science-based industries, and (3) the rise of new technical elites. These characteristics bring about changes in status and power.[22] The creation of wealth is no longer rooted in controlling land or building factories. Power and wealth are associated with who controls and develops the latest technology. Thus, Bill Gates became one of the richest man in the world by developing computer software.

Postindustrial societies have great surpluses of wealth and goods. Their material culture is the most developed of all societal forms. Consider the fact that even the poorest person in your neighbourhood probably owns a phone or a television. These societies do not provide dramatic changes in where people live or how they are governed, but the advances of technology expand divisions of labour and increase international interdependence.

RESISTANCE TO CHANGE

Whether it happens slowly or quickly, history shows us that social change is inevitable. However, while some people might be pushing for change to occur, there are also some people who wish to resist it. They are happy with the way things are, and they strive to maintain the status quo. Sociologist Albert Hirschman noted that every new idea for constructive change is met with three types of attack by people who want things to stay the way they are.

First, Hirschman says that these protesters will argue **futility**, which claims that the reform cannot work because the social problem is unsolvable. One example of this type of argument can be heard from people who criticize efforts to find cleaner, more efficient alternative energy sources for our motor vehicles. They claim that we're stuck with oil because it's the only thing that really works and that changing to alternative fuels would make transportation unreliable and more costly. People using this and the other forms of attack are often those who benefit from the use of oil and other fossil fuels and desire to maintain the status quo to protect their profits.

Another form of attack that protesters might choose as their argument is **perversity**, which claims that any attempt to fix a problem would actually compound the issues the change was trying to address. This argument is often used in the debate for electric cars. Although plugging in your car might sound like a cleaner solution for the environment, these protesters point out that this electricity must come from somewhere. In many countries, electricity comes from power plants that burn coal, the process of which releases harmful gases and fumes into the air. More electric cars mean that there will be a greater demand for electricity, and more demand for electricity means more coal burning. Their argument is that the additional burning of coal would be worse than the damage we are already doing with oil.

ATTACK STRATEGIES

Rui Vale de Sousa/Fotolia

Robert Hoetink/Fotolia

John Rennison, The Hamilton Spectator

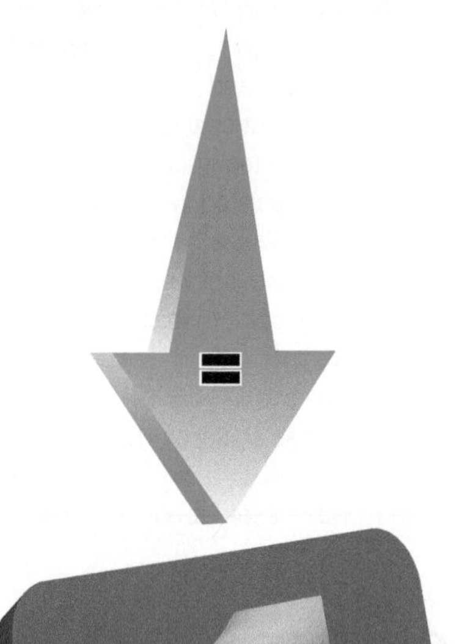

Benny De Grove/Getty Images, Inc. - Image Bank

ThinkStock

Eye Ubiquitous/Alamy

JEOPARDY is the claim that attempting to solve a problem will only draw attention away from other, more important issues.

COLLECTIVE BEHAVIOUR is any social interaction in which a group of people engages in behaviour that is not in their normal routine.

CROWD is a large group of influential people who gather for a temporary purpose.

Yet another way to attack change is the argument of jeopardy. **Jeopardy** claims that attempting to solve the problem will only draw attention away from other, more important issues. People who support the use of oil might say that researching alternative fuels not only is costly, but also is a waste of time. They say that there is plenty of oil and that we do not need to worry about shortages; instead, we need to drill more. Spending money to find new energy sources then draws our attention away from other more important issues such as national security, education, or some other social problem.[23]

Collective Behaviour

People who gather in groups often react and think in the same way when they gather together. **Collective behaviour** is any social interaction in which a group of people engages in behaviour that is not in their normal routine. Depending on the type of collective behaviour, this can be harmful and dangerous.

Crowds

You might not join in the latest fad, craze, or panic, but at some point everyone is part of a large group of influential people, called a crowd. A **crowd** is a large group of people who gather for a temporary purpose. When you attend a football game, you're in a crowd. Members can easily influence each other. For example, when you cheer, others will often join in with you. Other crowds may focus on a cause, like those protesting a political or social issue. Protest crowds can be large or small. For instance, on October 27, 1995, about 100 000 Canadians from across the country

MAKE CONNECTIONS

Internet Petitions

Many people who want society to change sign petitions. Traditionally, this entails someone going around with a piece of paper for others to sign or mark up as a way to show their views on a subject. In recent years, petitions and polls have switched from paper to online. The internet is beneficial because it allows for thousands of replies, as well as links to further information about the topics being addressed.

However, internet petitions are not as effective as people might think. For instance, the distinct handwriting of many participants you find on paper petitions proves that many people signed the petition. However, once a petition is moved to an online format, the individual writing styles become typed text, indistinguishable from one person to the next. Another issue is that the intended audience is often not explicitly mentioned, or the topic itself is too vaguely outlined for readers to understand everything that is being proposed in the petition. There is no guarantee that the petition will reach its intended audience or that the specified recipient actually has the credentials or ability to act upon the petition's results. There's also the fact that signing a petition doesn't actually get anything accomplished. People can sign a petition stating that they want something to be done about global warming, but they themselves do not take the initiative to go out and do something about it with this petition.[24]

Despite these issues, the internet is still a potential way to reach a broader voting population and audience. Online petition companies like www.ipetitions.com, www.thepetitionsite.com, and www.gopetition.com/petition-campaigns/Canada/ have sprung up around the Web, allowing anyone to create a petition. These companies may offer to "make sure" that the petition gets to the person it needs to get to. However, even if the petition doesn't get signed, it may still influence people's opinions. Online petitions can expose people to opinions and causes that they had never thought about before. Even if people don't end up signing a petition, they might be interested in the cause. This may encourage them to go out and do something about the issue themselves, which in effect accomplishes what the petition set out to do in the first place.[25]

>>> **ACTIVITY** Find and read through an online petition. What is the issue the petition is trying to address? Is this an effective petition? Why or why not?

gathered in Montreal for a huge Unity Rally. Held just a few days before a referendum on separatism, the rally appealed to French Canadians to "vote for Canada." Separatism was narrowly defeated in the referendum.[26]

Mobs and Riots

When discontent and tempers run high, violence often follows. Riots and mobs are likely to break out when people assemble in anger, and chaos ensues. **Mobs** are groups characterized by high levels of emotion that engage in some type of focused action that can be violent or disruptive. In June 2010, a peaceful march by about 10 000 protesters against the G-20 political summit in Toronto was followed by violence, riot squad deployment, tear gas, and 412 arrests.[27] Mobs can lead to **hysteria**, a heightened emotional state that can lead a group to violence.

Riots are emotional and violent disturbances of the peace by a crowd. Riots involve high levels of emotion and violence, but unlike mobs, the people taking part in riots have no centralized focus and lash out at anything and everything. Rioters express rage and anger and often spontaneously attack property and people. For example, two fires blazed in the yard of the Edmonton Institution on the evening of Canada Day 2008, after inmates broke into a fenced-off area where wood was kept for sweat-lodge use. By the time a nine-hour standoff was over, 8 inmates had been stabbed and 1 had been shot by a guard. This all apparently started with a clash between rival prison gangs during a recreational period. As many as 40 inmates were involved.[28]

Fashions, Fads, and Crazes

Consumerism, rather than hate, often causes people to go out in droves but to buy things en masse instead of protesting social injustice. In our society, most people have enough disposable income to afford to follow the latest trends and styles. A **fashion** is an object, a style, or a behavior that becomes popular for a period of time. Fashions are often used as markers of social status.

MOBS are groups characterized by high levels of emotion that engage in some type of focused action that can be violent or disruptive.

HYSTERIA is a heightened emotional state that can lead a group to violence.

RIOTS are emotional and violent disturbances of the peace by crowds that lack a central focus.

FASHION is an object, a style, or a behavior that becomes popular for a period of time.

FAD is a temporary fashion or action the public embraces.

While fashions tend to last for a while, a **fad** is a temporary and short-lived fashion or action that the public embraces. Fads can take many forms. One year, my son wanted a Wii gaming system for Christmas, and I was thrown into the midst of an object fad. Finding a Wii was nearly impossible. (Fortunately, Santa was able to get one.)

Fads may also include popular ideas, such as using feng shui to increase the chi, or energy, in one's home. They can also include activities, like in-line skating. Finally, fads can be people. Canadian pop singer Justin Bieber is a human fad who has been taking tween girls by storm.

Sociologist Joel Best suggests that fads such as the hula hoop are one thing, but fads in institutions are another.[29] Institutional fads follow a predetermined cycle: *emerging*, *surging*, and *purging*. At the emerging and surging stages, we embrace institutional change because we are optimistic and believe in progress. Thus, the latest trends take over the way we do business, regardless of their effectiveness.[30] Look at the DARE—Drug Abuse Resistance Education—program, developed in Los Angeles and now used in both Canada and the United States.[31] Police officers teach children about the dangers of drugs, but the results are dubious at best, and some studies actually show that the program makes drug use worse, not better.[32]

The problem with institutional fads is that at the time they are surging, no one really knows if they will work. Usually, the media publicize someone or something as the latest trend in business, education, or medicine. This fad promises to solve a problem or change society. North Americans tend to jump on the bandwagon of the latest institutional fad, so it's only after the fad has proved itself to be a total failure that this changes.

But some fads can actually leave lasting effects on a society. When this occurs, we call it a **craze**. When I was in college, you had to go to video arcades to play games. They were so new that people actually took dates to the arcade. Such a craze has largely ended, but the lasting effect of this video game craze is that many homes have some type of gaming system.

Fear also instigates consumerism. A **panic** is an extreme fear based on something that might happen. You may have heard of the Y2K panic, when many people were convinced that modern life would stop because computers would fail to recognize "00" as 2000. However, when January 1, 2000, came and went without incident, people realized that they'd panicked for nothing.[33] The panic caused by the 9/11 terrorist attacks led the U.S. government to encourage Americans to buy duct tape and plastic to seal doors and windows against a chemical attack. This panic caused a large increase in purchases of these items.[34]

Rumours and Urban Legends

People connect in other ways, too. Sociologists suggest that passing on **rumours**, stories or statements that lack confirmation or certainty, is part of modern culture. A common type of rumour is an urban legend. **Urban legends** are rumours that are presented as true stories and act as cautionary tales. These circulating stories claim to have happened to real people but are actually false. We spread them as if we really saw or heard the event personally to entertain our listeners.[35] One of my favourite rumours is one I call "How long must I wait?"

This legend deals with the supposed rules pertaining to how long students must wait for a professor. When a professor is late, students worry that they might miss something if they leave too soon. The rumour suggests that there's a lateness policy that dictates how long students must wait before they can assume they will not be penalized for leaving class. Wait times vary, depending on the rank of the professor: Graduate assistants get the shortest leeway, while full professors receive the most patience. Truthfully, few colleges have an official faculty lateness policy. Of those that do, academic rank doesn't affect how long you must wait. To be safe, check your student handbook or ask your professor what policy he or she has about this matter.

THEORIES OF COLLECTIVE BEHAVIOUR

Contagion Theory

One of the first people to try to develop a theory of collective behaviour was the French sociologist Gustave Le Bon.[36] His theory begins with the observation that when people are in a crowd, they sometimes behave differently than they would if they were alone. Why is this? Le Bon suggested that three factors that are present in a crowd influence the individual's behaviour. First of all, being part of a large group gives one a sense of anonymity, and this can make the individual feel less responsible and more invincible. This can then create the second factor, suggestibility, where individuals are more open to ideas and behaviours that they might not normally consider or engage in. Both of these factors can then produce the third factor, contagion, which refers to the spread of ideas and behaviours throughout the crowd, much like a contagious disease can spread through a population.

CRAZE occurs when a fad leaves a lasting effect on society.

PANIC is an extreme fear based on something that might happen.

RUMOURS are stories or statements that lack confirmation or certainty.

URBAN LEGENDS are rumours that are presented as true stories that act as cautionary tales.

SOCIAL MOVEMENTS are activities that support or protest social issues, and they are usually organized by nongovernmental organizations.

CAMPAIGNS are organized and ongoing efforts to achieve a specific goal.

Convergence Theory

Convergence theory suggests that collective behaviour may be more attractive to some individuals than to others. These people are more likely to join crowds. In other words, like-minded people will converge, or get together, to engage in collective behaviour. People who are more likely to react strongly in any social situation are also more likely to join a mob or a riot.

Emergent Norms Theory

According to Ralph Turner and Lewis Killian, crowds develop their own definition of a situation and establish new norms of behaviour that reflect this definition.[37] For example, people in a crowd will start to get upset about something (such as not getting in when a concert is cancelled); they then interpret this as an unusual situation, so the old norms no longer apply; new norms (such as throwing things or breaking windows) emerge in the crowd, and a riot starts. In short, people in crowds make their own rules as they act.

Social Movements

Social movements are activities that support or protest social issues, and they are usually organized by nongovernmental groups or organizations. In other words, social movements allow regular folk to participate in the political process, diffusing ideas and beliefs. Many social movements want to bring about social change, while others seek to maintain the status quo. According to sociologist Charles Tilly, three elements exist in all social movements.[38]

The first element in a social movement is the promotional campaign. **Campaigns** are organized and ongoing efforts to achieve a specific goal. For instance, when it's time for elections, politicians have campaigns geared to the voters. They make claims of what they will do if they are elected to office and try to convince the voter that they would be the best candidate for the position.

STAGES OF SOCIAL MOVEMENTS

All social movements go through a set of predictable stages of development. In the first stage, emergence, people become aware of a problem and begin to notice that others feel the same way. Fifty years ago, few Canadians were concerned about the environment. But after a few people began to take notice in the 1960s, they took the first steps for any social movement—making people aware of the problem. The 1971 actions of Don't Make a Wave (see the Think Sociologically feature on Greenpeace on the next page) are a good example.

In the next stage, social movements seek to define their goals and design a plan to get their goals met. This state is known as coalescence.

Christopher J. Morris/CORBIS

The 1995 Unity Rally drew 100 000 people to the streets in Montreal in a successful bid to defeat a referendum on separatism.

REPERTOIRES are actions used to promote interest and involvement within a movement.

WUNC refers to the members of a movement who want to show the public the worthiness, unity, numbers, and commitment of their movement.

In this stage, groups reach out to other groups and individuals to gain membership. The movement then grows and increases the public awareness of the problem. In Canada, environmental organizations such as Greenpeace were born out of the first major wave of environmentalism and continued growing. By the late 1980s, interest in the environment had surged throughout North America.[46]

The environmental movement has become a political force internationally, and it has moved into bureaucratization. The myriad social movements dedicated to the environment show that this concern will not go away. Organizations like Greenpeace International now strive to achieve what Don't Make a Wave dreamed was possible in Vancouver in 1971.

When an organization completes its goal or is seen as irrelevant, it falls into the final stage, decline. If and when the day comes that we have clean energy and recycling becomes the norm, the clean air movement may decline because it will have achieved some of its goals.[47]

TYPES OF SOCIAL MOVEMENTS

Although all social movements are essentially sustained campaigns that support a goal, there is no standard type of social movement. They have different methods of approaching their goals and identifying potential followers. David F. Aberle developed an early typology of social movements in 1966.[48] He categorized movements based on two dimensions:

GO GLOBAL

Rescuing Rainforests

Sociologists are interested in studying and understanding the effects that humans have on the environment. Deforestation, pollution, and poaching are just three ways that humans have negatively impacted the environment.[39] It's no surprise, then, that conservation movements are gaining popularity around the world.

One conservation movement is rainforest conservation. Rainforests clean the air, provide food and raw materials, and are home to half of the world's population of plants and animals.[40] To maintain and protect these vital areas, organizations like the World Wildlife Foundation (WWF) and the Rainforest Alliance work alongside individuals, governments, and other organizations. Members can help by donating money to the conservation projects or by volunteering in local and national conservation efforts.[41] The WWF also focuses on helping the people who live in the area surrounding the rainforests. These people rely on the forest for their livelihood, so they work with organizations to safely harvest items from the forest while protecting its valuable natural resources.[42]

Activist groups like the Rainforest Action Network (RAN) employ different methods to get their point across. In 1987, RAN's successful boycott against Burger King stopped the fast-food chain's practice of buying cheap beef from areas that were once rainforests.[43] The group calls for nonviolent protests to make the public aware of important issues.

Another element used is repertoire. **Repertoires** are actions used to promote interest and involvement within a movement. For example, several hundred people marched on Parliament Hill in Ottawa in March 2009 as part of international lobbying to mark the fiftieth anniversary of the Raise the Tibet Flag Campaign, which aims to "generate awareness and solidarity amongst Tibetans and Tibet supporters alike" for the recognition of Tibet as an occupied country and the recognition of the Tibetan government in exile as the sole legitimate government of Tibetans. Other Canadian demonstrations included gatherings at the Chinese Consulates in Vancouver and Toronto.[44]

Finally, some members of a movement want to show the public the worthiness, unity, numbers, and commitments of their movement (**WUNC**). They're the people who organize the events, participate in the activities, and do what they can to get the word out about their organization. Remember that people committed to a cause do not constitute a movement. Movements need WUNC members to help lead and keep it focused.

Tilly suggests that before the eighteenth century, there was no such thing as a true "social movement." It's true that there were violent revolutions and rebellions demanding changes in society before this period; however, these movements were not social movements because they didn't bring about organizations. It was not until the 1800s that movements arose over issues such as unionism in response to capitalism, women's suffrage, and many other issues.[45]

ALTERNATIVE SOCIAL MOVEMENTS want to create a change in specific people's thoughts, practices, and beliefs regarding a particular issue.

REDEMPTIVE SOCIAL MOVEMENTS focus on specific individuals, but they seek radical, rather than limited, change.

the orientation of change (society as a whole or individuals) and the amount of change sought (limited or radical). This classification created four categories of social movement: alternative, redemptive, reformative, and revolutionary.[49] Each category seeks a different combination of target audience and level of change.

Alternative Social Movements

Alternative social movements want to create a change in specific people's thoughts, practices, and beliefs regarding a specific issue. Their goal is to encourage a small, defined change in the way a particular group of people think and act in order to solve a problem. Mothers Against Drunk Driving (MADD) Canada is an alternative social movement organization whose mission is "To stop impaired driving and to support victims of this violent crime."[50]

MADD Canada was formed in 1990. Using a method developed by James Fell, the organization calculates that the number of lives saved due to reduction in alcohol-related fatal crashes in Canada rose from 221 in 1982 to 1151 in 2007, for a 1982–2007 total of 32 883 lives. "The figures provide us with an important perspective on the progress that has been made since the founding of MADD Canada and its predecessor organizations," one MADD research document states.[51] In an April 2008 news release, the organization noted that Transport Canada had reported a total of 39 487 alcohol-related fatalities on Canadian roads since 1982. "Had there been no effort to reduce impaired driving deaths, MADD Canada estimates the number could have been 70 000 in alcohol-related fatalities."[52]

Redemptive Social Movements

Redemptive social movements also focus on specific individuals, but the amount of change sought is radical rather than limited. Religious movements, such as those involving evangelical Christians, are typically categorized as redemptive because they encourage a specific group of nonbelievers to make a dramatic lifestyle change by converting to or adopting a new religion. Christian missionaries have held a quiet presence in traditionally Islamic states in the Middle East for centuries. However, this missionary movement has surged in recent years. According to the Center for the Study of Global Christianity at Gordon-Conwell Theological Seminary in South Hamilton, Massachusetts, the number of missionaries to Islamic countries increased from about 15 000 in 1982 to more than

<<< **Parliament Hill was one of several Canadian demonstration sites during the international 50th anniversary of the Raise the Tibet Flag Campaign, held in March 2008.** Participants want freedom for Tibet, which has been under China's rule since 1959.

AP Photo/The Canadian Press,Sean Kilpatrick

THINK SOCIOLOGICALLY

Greenpeace

It started with a small group of activists sailing out of Vancouver in a leaky fishing boat in 1971, to "bear witness" to U.S. nuclear testing in the northerly Aleutian Islands. Four decades later, the international organization that grew out of that first step is known as "the world's leading environmental watchdog" and has more than 2.9 million members.[53]

Greenpeace describes itself as "an independent, non-profit, global campaigning organization that uses non-violent, creative confrontation to expose global environmental problems and their causes." The organization's goal is "to ensure the ability of Earth to nurture life in all its diversity."[54]

Among its substantial successes, Greenpeace Canada lists the 1982 European Council ban on the import of seal pup skins after Greenpeace actions in Canada and the resulting public outcry, and the 2006 provincial government announcement of an agreement that should ensure the protection of the Great Bear Rainforest in British Columbia.

On the international front, Greenpeace organizations had started in a number of countries before Greenpeace International was formed in 1979. Today the international organization is based in Amsterdam. A Greenpeace list highlighting close to 100 international successes includes such events as the shelving in 2009—after a 3-year Greenpeace campaign—of plans to build what would have been the first new coal power plant in the United Kingdom in 20 years, and Iceland's stepping back in 2004 from plans to kill 500 minke, sei, and fin whales over 2 years, announcing instead a quota of just 25 minkes for the year. Greenpeace Web activists "fuelled domestic opposition" by getting 50 000 pledges from around the world to visit Iceland if the government would stop whaling.

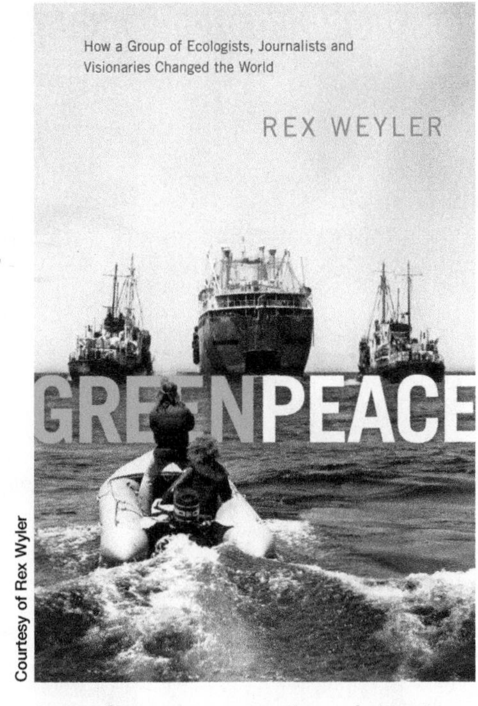

How a Group of Ecologists, Journalists and Visionaries Changed the World
REX WEYLER
GREENPEACE

Courtesy of Rex Wyler

<<< The photo on the cover of Greenpeace co-founder Rex Weyler's book *Greenpeace* shows **underdog activists at work on the high seas.**

And the very first leaky boat trip from Vancouver in 1971? That forerunner to Greenpeace was called Don't Make a Wave, and it comprised Vancouver environmentalists who wanted to stop the second planned U.S. nuclear test on the tiny island of Amchitka, in the Aleutians. Thousands of protesters had gathered on the Canada–United States border before the first test because they feared the blast would cause an earthquake, but the initial test went ahead anyway. Greenpeace never made it to the actual test zone—despite two attempts—but it managed to stir up public concern about the second test. Five months after Don't Make a Wave sailed out from Vancouver, the United States announced it was stopping Aleutian Island nuclear testing. Today, the island is a bird sanctuary.

Incidentally, the nonviolent protest style Greenpeace uses to "bear witness" is based on a Quaker tradition of silent protest.[55]

REFORMATIVE SOCIAL MOVEMENTS seek to change a society's thoughts and actions but only in a limited way.

PROGRESSIVE means favouring or promoting change.

REGRESSIVE means seeking to stop change.

REVOLUTIONARY SOCIAL MOVEMENTS, sometimes called transformative social movements, seek to change the thoughts and actions of all society in radical fashion.

27 000 in 2001.[56] The 9/11 attacks pushed the movement even further. Some Christian missionaries enter Islamic countries with the sole intention of providing aid to the region's struggling communities; however, evangelical missionaries proceed with the primary goal of converting Muslims to Christianity. This practice is controversial in both Muslim and Christian communities.

Reformative Social Movements

Not all social movements are targeted to specific individuals or groups. Some social movements attempt to tether all of society to their mission. **Reformative social movements** seek to change a society's thoughts and actions, but only in a limited way. This type of movement can be **progressive**, favouring or promoting change, or **regressive**, seeking to stop change. Progressive reformative social movements ask society to accept something new into the social order. For example, environmental groups ask society to participate in or support conservation efforts like recycling programs, clean air legislation, or alternative fuel funding. This movement has grown by leaps and bounds, as conservation has become a growing global concern.

Revolutionary Social Movements

The most ambitious type of social movement is the **revolutionary social movement**, sometimes called the *transformative social movement*. This type of movement seeks to change the thoughts and actions of all society in radical fashion. Social movement groups that are considered revolutionary aim to completely restructure society. While the anti-globalization movement espoused by Naomi Klein covers a broad spectrum, some elements of that movement would certainly be considered revolutionary. When a revolutionary social movement organization attempts to fulfill its missions, it is called a revolution.

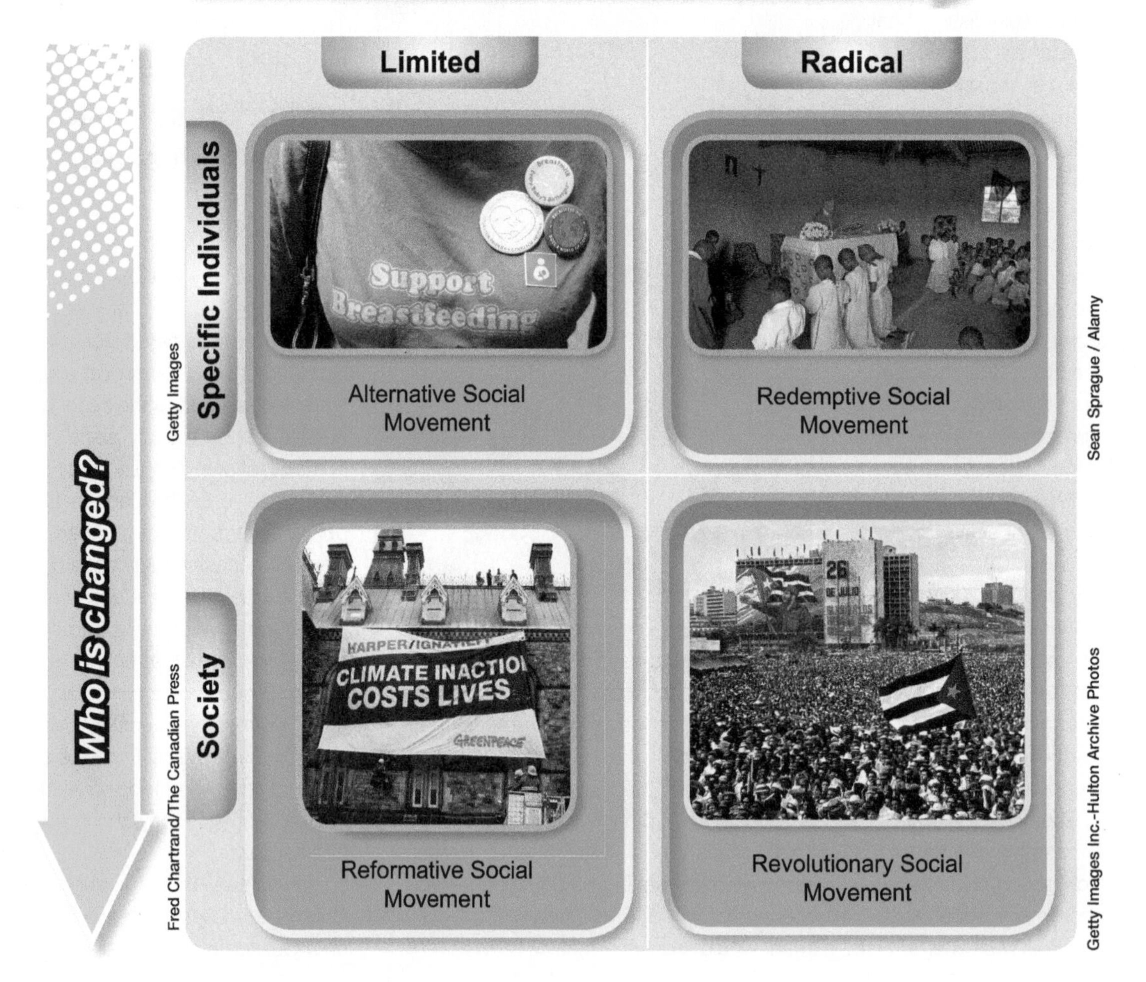

On July 26, 1953, Fidel Castro organized rebel forces and launched an attack on the Moncada military barracks in Santiago de Cuba. The revolution was an attempt to spark an uprising against Fulgencio Batista's regime. After the attack failed to dismantle the existing government, Castro moved his efforts to Mexico, where he organized Cuban exiles into a revolutionary group called the 26th of July Movement. After gaining the support of numerous Cuban citizens through the distribution of political propaganda, the movement's guerrilla forces defeated the existing Cuban government and enlisted Castro as president in 1960. The movement asked all citizens on the island of Cuba to change their ideology and support a government that would reinstate full civil and political liberties and assume moderate reforms. Unfortunately, the initial goals of the movement were never realized, as Castro changed his policies once he was in power.[57]

<<< Idle No More is a grassroots reformative social movement **whose issues are the sovereignty, rights, and respect for the treaties of First Nations people. The movement's goals include** stopping environmental damage and reducing social inequality.

think sociologically: WHAT ARE THE THEORIES BEHIND SOCIAL MOVEMENTS?

Conflict Theory: Deprivation

Conflict theorists believe that social movements are inevitable events in a social world that has inequality. This can arise because of social inequalities or because of perceived inequalities. As Marx suggested, inequality makes social change not only necessary but likely. Why? Because people eventually notice their plight and decide to do something about it. Many social movements are reactions to relative deprivation. **Relative deprivation** refers to the gaps between what people have and what they expect. For example, say that you have a cheap car, but you believe that you should have an expensive car, like your friend's. You feel deprived when you see his car and you think it is better than your own. You forget to consider the people who drive cars that are not as nice as your car or the people who don't have cars at all. You focus on the envy you feel when you see people with things that are "better" than yours.[58]

James Chowning Davies applies this theory to social movements by explaining that when people's expectations are met, they are unlikely to organize and work to make changes.[59] They are satisfied with what they have and are unlikely to complain. So, it's only natural to assume that people will be unhappy and more willing to protest when their expectations are not being met. Collective violence will most likely occur after a period of rising expectations, and a steep decline and reversal of the people's fortunes follows increased gratification.

Ted Gurr suggests that deprivation creates discontent, which leads to civil strife. If social institutions can absorb some of the stress or channel it into something other than violence, revolution is unlikely. Nonviolent strife consists of turmoil such as riots and demonstrations. Violent strife consists of revolution and terrorism.[60]

Social movements are in competition with each other for resources. Resource mobilization theory suggests that organizations that are best able to gain access to money, media, and larger audiences are more likely to succeed. The nature of the scarcity of resources causes movements to compete for those resources. The ones that compete most effectively are the ones that are going to survive.[61]

Functionalism: Value-Added Theory

Neil Smelser's value-added theory of collective behaviour identifies six factors, each of which is a necessary but not sufficient determinant of collective activity.[62] These six factors are also ordered in a value-added arrangement, such that each successive factor will increasingly determine the nature and likelihood of an episode of collective behavior. The following are Smelser's determinants of collective behaviour:

1. *Structural conduciveness:* The existing social and political conditions influence both the possibility and type of collective behaviours that may occur.
2. *Structural strain:* Unless there is something that prompts people to engage in collective behaviour, such activity is not warranted. A real or perceived strain may incite collective behaviour as a response to that strain.
3. *Growth and spread of a generalized belief:* Underlying any social activity is an ideology which justifies that activity and makes it meaningful to the actors. In the case of collective behaviour, a generalized belief identifies and defines the source of strain, attributes characteristics to this source, and specifies responses that are possible and appropriate.
4. *Precipitating factors:* A precipitating event will often bring into sharper focus a condition of strain. It is also the spark that ignites further response.
5. *Mobilization for action:* This involves assembling participants and directing their behaviour.
6. *Social control:* The last factor that affects collective behaviour is the response of agents of social control to the episode. This response may be to minimize the strain and therefore avoid a more serious response. Alternatively, the authorities may only react after the collective behaviour has materialized, which may provoke further discontent.

RELATIVE DEPRIVATION points to the gaps between what people have and what they expect.

FRAME ALIGNMENT PROCESS occurs when social movement organizations link their goals to the goals of other organizations.

Symbolic Interactionism: Framing Processes

In social movement studies, the idea of frames in social movements has its roots in the work of Erving Goffman.[63] Frames provide an individual an opportunity to identify, understand, and label events as they occur in the social world. Frames are templates that organize how we behave publicly. They do not completely limit our understanding of social events, like a picture frame limits the edges of a photo; instead, they provide the building blocks by which we understand the world. Frames exist before us, and we become part of them through social processes that teach us how to dress, communicate, and interact within them.[64] For example, if you're on an elevator, you probably do not speak to strangers. At a sporting event, you might hug a stranger if you're caught up in the moment. The frames of the events provide the parameters for understanding that interaction.

Successful social movements use frames to further their cause. If a movement hopes to bring about a change, it must frame its argument successfully. There are three core tasks in framing:

1 **Diagnostic framing** This type of framing creates a frame that states the problem clearly. Is this really a problem? Why? For example, the movement to move the economy away from petroleum relies on accurately and effectively pointing to the problems associated with continued dependence on oil.[65]

2 **Prognostic framing** This type of framing provides the solution to the diagnostic framing problem. Currently, there are a host of social movements competing to be the solution to the problem. Is natural gas the best alternative, or are there better choices, such as hydroelectric, solar, wind, nuclear energy, or bio-fuels? Each group competes against others and provides a prognosis of how its solution will be the best one.[66]

3 **Motivational framing** This type of framing calls people to take action. It makes an argument that people need to do more than merely talk about a problem; they must also take action. When groups urge you to buy a hybrid car or put up a windmill, they are using the motivational frame.[67]

Of course, in an environment such as this, where energy concerns continue to take centre stage in the national debate, it is not surprising that some groups are coming together to provide answers. This **frame alignment process** occurs when social movement organizations link

FRAME BRIDGING occurs when two or more groups that may be somewhat opposed to each other join forces.

AMPLIFICATION occurs when ideas become elaborated and sometimes exaggerated.

EXTENSION refers to the way social movement organizations seek to align their interests with those of other groups that are related, sometimes furthering ideas that were not originally in their frame.

TRANSFORMATION changes the old meanings and understandings of the problem and creates new and innovative ones.

their goals to the goals of other organizations. Four processes occur when organizations are involved in the frame alignment process: bridging, amplification, extension, and transformation.[68]

Frame bridging occurs when two or more groups that may be somewhat opposed to each other join forces. Within the public debate over the oil-based economy, solar and natural gas power proponents have bridged, suggesting that both sources of energy are renewable and clean, and they should work together to change the country's collective understanding about how to power their homes and cars.[69]

Amplification occurs when ideas become elaborated and sometimes exaggerated. Groups seek to engage people by illuminating the social issue. The closer this issue is to an already existing value or cultural belief, the more likely amplification is to work.[70] For example, in the 1980s, I was a member of a group that proposed using wind power for electricity generation. However, we had little success because the price of oil was still low, and energy seemed plentiful. As times change, North Americans are warming up to the idea of wind power if it means they can continue to have air conditioning they can afford.

Extension of the frame alignment refers to the way in which social movement organizations seek to align their interests with those of other groups that are related, sometimes furthering ideas that were not originally in their frame. For example, the solar movement is often connected in the public discourse to the use of biological fuels. Finally, frames can experience transformation when they become aligned.[71]

Transformation changes the old meanings and understandings of the problem and creates new and innovative ones. To push our example further, the energy independence frame is transforming into an organization that once sought to foster only renewable and clean energy, but now often includes a discussion of coal and nuclear power as well.[72]

Feminist Theory: An On-Going Social Movement

Feminism itself is the product of a social movement. For feminist theorists, the fundamental inequality in most societies that needs to be redressed is gender inequality. As we have seen in earlier chapters, the feminist movement in Canada has achieved many significant changes in Canadian society. Because of women like Nellie McClung, Dorothy Smith, and Margaret Eichler, Canadian women are able to vote, hold political office, and go to school and work alongside men. In Canada, equality of the sexes is a fundamental principle in the *Canadian Charter of Rights and Freedoms*.

The history of the feminist movement in Canada goes back to the nineteenth century and can be divided into three "waves."

FIRST-WAVE FEMINISM

The first wave of feminism, which began in the late nineteenth and early twentieth centuries, revolved around the women's suffrage movement. One of the leading figures of this movement was Nellie McClung. In 1914, McClung and other Canadian suffragettes held a "mock parliament" in Winnipeg. This was a satirical parody on the dangers of giving men the right to vote, and it drew attention to the cause of women's suffrage. The strategy worked; in 1916, Manitoba became the first Canadian province to grant women the right to vote, although only in provincial elections. Other provinces soon followed with similar laws, except Quebec, where women were not allowed to vote until 1940. In 1918, *An Act to Confer the Electoral Franchise upon Women* allowed Canadian women to vote in federal elections. However, women were still not allowed to hold a seat in the Canadian Senate. The *British North America Act*, Canada's constitution at that time, stated that one must be a "person" in order to serve in the Senate, but the term *person* did not include women, only men. In 1927, Nellie McClung, Emily Murphy, Irene Parlby, Louise McKinney, and Henrietta Edwards submitted to the British Privy Council, the highest

THE HISTORY OF FEMINISM

Second-Wave Feminism

Hulton Archive/ Getty Images

1914
Nellie McClung and other suffragettes hold "mock parliament" parodying dangers of giving men the right to vote

1916
Manitoba becomes the first province to grant women the right to vote; all but Quebec soon follow

1918
Canadian women are allowed to vote in federal elections

1929
Canadian women ruled to be persons, two years after McClung et al. launched the Persons Case

1940
Women in Quebec are allowed to vote

1960s
The Women's Liberation movement begins

1963
Betty Friedan publishes *The Feminine Mystique*, which helps further ignite the Women's Lib movement

1960s and 1970s
Women begin to go to college and pursue careers in significant numbers

C.Jessop/National Archives of Canada/Canadian Press Images

First-Wave Feminism

CP PHOTO/ Files-Calgary Herald/CP

constitutional court for Canada, what would famously become known as the "Persons Case." In October 1929, the Council's Judicial Committee ruled that Canadian women are, in fact, persons and can be appointed to the Senate.[73]

SECOND-WAVE FEMINISM

The second wave of feminism occurred during the women's liberation movement that began in the 1960s. Whereas first-wave feminism protested legal inequality, second-wave feminism also sought equality in the workplace, equality in education, and social independence from men.

In 1963, Betty Friedan published a book called *The Feminine Mystique*, which brought attention to the idea that a woman should seek personal fulfillment outside her home and family. The book attacked a social system in which women were treated as nothing more than homemakers and childbearers.[74] Friedan is said to have ignited the women's lib movement with this book, although she has also been criticized for focusing exclusively on the plight of white middle- and upper-class women.[75]

In addition to equal rights in education and the workplace, second-wavers demanded reproductive rights and protection from domestic and sexual violence. These demands caused a great deal of controversy, as many conservatives felt that contraceptives and abortion go against traditional morals.

In Canada, the *Royal Commission on the Status of Women* was established in 1967. In 1970, the Commission published a comprehensive report called the "Report of the Royal Commission on the Status of Women in Canada." The report made 167 recommendations that would address and correct many issues of women's inequality in Canadian society. In 1972, the National Action Committee on the Status of Women (NAC) was formed as an umbrella organization of women's organizations throughout Canada.[76]

THIRD-WAVE FEMINISM

Beginning in the early 1990s, the third wave of feminism branched out to include multiple racial and socioeconomic groups. Gloria Anzaldua, (née Gloria Jean Watkins), bell hooks, Maxine Hong Kingston, and Audre Lorde are feminist leaders associated with the third wave in North America. Author and social activist bell hooks, for example, has connected topics like race, capitalism, and gender within her works. She emphasizes the fact that all three topics are interconnected and that they need to be addressed at the same time.[77]

>>> For years activists have written and spoken about the state of the environment. In 2006, Al Gore's ***An Inconvenient Truth*** gave a huge boost to environmental awareness.

© Paramount Classics/Photofest

Whereas the second wave of feminism pushed for changes to legislation, the third wave is about changing social attitudes. Despite many improvements in the past 50 years, there still remain significant inequalities between men and women in Canada. The wage gap between men and women has narrowed only slightly since 1960. Women still hold fewer seats in the federal Parliament. The top boardrooms in the country are still dominated by men. It is clear that the goal of complete equality has not yet been achieved.

The discrepancy is especially pronounced for certain groups of women. Increasing attention is being paid to the situation of immigrant women and aboriginal women, two groups of Canadians who continue to experience significant discrimination and inequality in Canadian society.[78]

The struggle for gender equality has been won on many fronts. It has resulted in changes to many laws. But gender equality is more than just a legal issue. True gender equality will be achieved when there is a fundamental change in society—in the ideology that guides our behaviour. Feminist theory has been included as a sociological perspective in this book because it draws attention to issues that concern women and because it offers yet another way of looking at our social world.

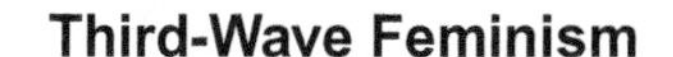

Third-Wave Feminism

Lindsay Brice/Michael Ochs Archives/Getty Images

Royal Commission on Status of Women is established **1967**

Early 1990s The third wave of feminism begins to address the failures of the second wave

Feminist leaders Gloria Anzaldua, bell hooks, Maxine Kingston, and Audre Lorde promote the feminist cause **Early 1990s**

Early 1990s Bands like Bratmobile, Bikini Kill, and Huggy Bear communicate the message of third-wave feminism

Groups such as Take Back the Night and Dress for Success emerge **1900s**

Globe and Mail/ Denis Robinson

WRAP YOUR MIND AROUND THE THEORY

These protesters are part of the **Idle No More reformative social movement,** which aims to stop environmental damage and reduce social inequality.

FUNCTIONALISM

Neil Smelser's value-added theory of collective behaviour identifies six factors, each of which is a necessary but not sufficient determinant of collective activity. These six factors are also ordered in a value-added arrangement, such that each successive factor will increasingly determine the nature and likelihood of an episode of collective behavior. The six factors are structural conduciveness, structural strain, growth and spread of a generalized belief, precipitating factors, mobilization for action, and social control.

CONFLICT THEORY

Conflict theorists believe that social movements arise because of social inequalities or because of a perceived inequality. People eventually notice their plight and decide to do something about it. Many social movements are reactions to relative deprivation, which refers to the gaps between what people have and what they expect. When people's expectations are met, they are unlikely to organize and work to make changes. They are satisfied with what they have and are unlikely to complain. People will be unhappy and more willing to protest when their expectations are not being met.

SYMBOLIC INTERACTIONISM

Frames are templates that organize how we behave publicly, and they provide the building blocks by which we understand the world. Successful social movements use frames to further their cause. If a movement hopes to bring about a change, it must frame its argument successfully. There are three core tasks in framing: diagnostic framing, prognostic framing, and motivational framing. The frame alignment process occurs when social movements link their goals to the goals of other organizations. Four processes occur when organizations are involved in the frame alignment process: bridging, amplification, extension, and transformation.

FEMINIST THEORY

Feminism itself is the product of a social movement. For feminist theorists, the fundamental inequality in most societies that needs to be redressed is gender inequality. The history of the feminist movement in Canada goes back to the nineteenth century and can be divided into three "waves." The first wave, which began in the late nineteenth and early twentieth centuries, revolved around the women's suffrage movement. The second wave occurred during the women's liberation movement that began in the 1960s. Beginning in the early 1990s, the third wave of feminism branched out to include multiple racial and socioeconomic groups. The struggle for gender equality has been won on many fronts and has resulted in changes to many discriminatory laws. However, true gender equality will be achieved when there is a fundamental change in society—in the ideology that guides our behaviour.

Greg Locke Photo

Workers will often strike if their expectations are not met. Thousands went on strike in 1986 when the Newfoundland Association of Public Employees (NAPE) was caught up in a battle with the province over legislation limiting the right to strike.[79]

discover sociology in action: HOW DO SOCIAL MOVEMENTS INFLUENCE SOCIETY?

Social Policy: Government Cash for Clunkers

Blessed Unrest author Paul Hawken discusses how people and organizations are working without a formal system of leadership to oversee their actions.[80] Together, these people and organizations make up groups that focus on human rights, the environment, and other issues dedicated to improving people's lives. They make up a loose configuration of groups dedicated to change. These independent movements have a strong force behind them, despite their unconventional structure. So, what would happen if government decided to take part, too?

One way the government is joining in is by providing incentives to help put more fuel-efficient cars on the roads. In British Columbia, for instance, the Scrap-It program allows car owners to trade in their old vehicles for cash. A car owner can save or receive up to $550 when trading in an old clunker for a new, efficient car. Those who want to replace the old clunker with a bicycle instead can receive $500 toward its purchase. Additional incentives include car-sharing and transit passes.[81]

On the national level, the federal government was set to begin regulating fuel consumption of vehicles in 2011. Fuel consumption standards have existed in Canada for several decades, but until recently, they were only voluntary for vehicle manufacturers. In 2008 federal Transport Minister Lawrence Cannon announced, "Our government recognizes that the transportation sector is one of the largest sources of greenhouse gas [GHG] and air pollutant emissions in Canada, accounting for 25 per cent of all Canada's GHG emissions. That's why we are taking action now to make sure that, into the future, we have the most environmentally responsible cars and trucks on Canadian roads." The new regulated standards, which began with 2011 models, aim to match, and possibly exceed, the U.S. fuel consumption target of 6.7 litres of gas per 100 kilometres by 2020. (In 2006, the average fuel consumption for new vehicles in Canada was 8.6 L/100 km.)[82]

More fuel-efficient cars are already in production, and companies like Nissan and Ford have introduced electric vehicles such as the Leaf and the Focus Electric.[83] In January 2010, General Motors did its last run of the H3 and H3T, the only remaining Hummers that were still being produced. The Hummer, an SUV, was "the perfect target for the green movement."[84] It's predicted that in the future, people will drive smaller, more efficient vehicles and use less gas.[85]

As you fill your car with expensive gas, think how glad you would be to have increased fuel efficiency. Of course, what will happen to those large SUVs and gas-guzzling pickups? Who will be able to afford these new, more efficient cars? Are there sources of energy that we could use other than gasoline? These and other questions remain to be answered, but the policy of rewarding moves to more fuel-efficient cars is one way governments are trying to help reduce fuel consumption and GHG emissions.

ACTIVITIES

1. Think about some of the social policies in Canada. Choose three and look for information about when they came into effect and what spurred the movement.
2. Use the internet to find out about popular fads in Canada beginning with the 1900s and continuing today. Create a time line or graphic showing what the latest fads have been from each decade.
3. Research an environmental group that is located in your community or province. Find out what the group's mission statement is and what steps it has taken to improve the environment. Design an advertisement for the group that might inspire others to join.

CHAPTER

15

WHAT DRIVES SOCIAL CHANGE? 281

reactions to events and new opportunities

WHAT ARE THE THEORIES BEHIND SOCIAL MOVEMENTS? 291

functionalism: social movements challenge the equilibrium of society and give people a way to relieve their frustrations and emotions about a particular subject
conflict theory: social inequality creates discontent among some, which can lead to social movements
symbolic interactionism: social movements use frames to define and further their cause
feminist theory: feminism is itself an example of a social movement

HOW DO SOCIAL MOVEMENTS INFLUENCE SOCIETY? 295

social movements: provide an ever-changing sociological landscape; encourage the development of new theory and the application of existing theory

get the topic: WHAT DRIVES SOCIAL CHANGE?

Theories

CONFLICT THEORY 291

- people concentrate on the things that they do not have, and inequality causes discontent
- relative deprivation refers to the gaps between what people have and what they expect

FUNCTIONALISM 291

- smelser's value-added theory looks at how structural factors influence the possibility and kinds of collective behaviour
- each factor is a necessary but not sufficient determinant of collective behaviour

SYMBOLIC INTERACTIONISM 291

- successful social movements use frames to further their cause
- the frame alignment process occurs when social movements link their goals to the goals of other organizations

FEMINIST THEORY 292

- for feminist theorists, the fundamental inequality in most societies that needs to be redressed is gender inequality
- true gender equality will exist when there has been a fundamental change in the ideology that guides our behaviour

Key Terms

social change is how culture and social institutions change over time. *281*

futility is the claim that a reform cannot work because the social problem is unsolvable. *283*

perversity claims that any attempts to fix a problem will actually compound the issues the change was trying to address. *283*

jeopardy is the claim that attempting to solve a problem will only draw attention away from other, more important issues. *284*

collective behaviour is any social interaction in which a group of people engages in behaviour that is not in their normal routine. *284*

crowd is a large group of influential people who gather for a temporary purpose. *284*

mobs are groups characterized by high levels of emotion that engage in some type of focused action that can be violent or disruptive. *285*

hysteria is a heightened emotional state that can lead a group to violence. *285*

riots are emotional and violent disturbances of the peace by crowds that lack a central focus. *285*

fashion is an object, a style, or a behavior that becomes popular for a period of time. *285*

fad is a temporary fashion or action the public embraces. *285*

craze occurs when a fad leaves a lasting effect on society. *286*

panic is an extreme fear based on something that might happen. *286*

rumours are stories or statements that lack confirmation or certainty. *286*

urban legends are rumours that are presented as true stories that act as cautionary tales. *286*

social movements are activities that support or protest social issues, and they are usually organized by nongovernmental organizations. *286*

campaigns are organized and ongoing efforts to achieve a specific goal. *286*

repertoires are actions used to promote interest and involvement within a movement. *287*

WUNC refers to the members of a movement who want to show the public the worthiness, unity, numbers, and commitment of their movement. *287*

alternative social movements want to create a change in specific people's thoughts, practices, and beliefs regarding a particular issue. *288*

redemptive social movements focus on specific individuals, but they seek radical, rather than limited, change. *288*

reformative social movements seek to change a society's thoughts and actions but only in a limited way. *289*

progressive means favouring or promoting change. *289*

regressive means seeking to stop change. *289*

revolutionary social movements, sometimes called transformative social movements, seek to change the thoughts and actions of all society in radical fashion. *289*

relative deprivation points to the gaps between what people have and what they expect. *291*

frame alignment process occurs when social movement organizations link their goals to the goals of other organizations. *291*

frame bridging occurs when two or more groups that may be somewhat opposed to each other join forces. *292*

amplification occurs when ideas become elaborated and sometimes exaggerated. *292*

extension refers to the way social movement organizations seek to align their interests with those of other groups that are related, sometimes furthering ideas that were not originally in their frame. *292*

transformation changes the old meanings and understandings of the problem and creates new and innovative ones. *292*

Sample Test Questions

These multiple-choice questions are similar to those found in the test bank that accompanies this textbook.

1. Which of the following statements about mobs is *false*?
- **a.** They are violent and disruptive.
- **b.** They have high levels of emotions.
- **c.** They have no central focus or intent.
- **d.** They are one form of collective behaviour.

2. Social protesters who argue perversity claim that
- **a.** there is no solution to the problem.
- **b.** any change will only make the problem worse.
- **c.** the so-called problem is not really a problem at all.
- **d.** focusing on the problem means ignoring more important things.

3. Which term describes the process of social movement organizations linking their goals to the goals of other organizations?
- **a.** Frame bridging
- **b.** Frame alignment
- **c.** Structural conduciveness
- **d.** Relative deprivation

4. Which of the following is an example of a craze?
- **a.** People redecorating their home using feng shui techniques
- **b.** People going on a date at a video arcade
- **c.** People attending a DARE presentation
- **d.** People waiting in line to buy a Wii

5. Which type of social movement seeks to create limited change for the entire society?
- **a.** An alternative social movement
- **b.** A redemptive social movement
- **c.** A reform social movement
- **d.** A revolutionary social movement

ANSWERS: 1. c; 2. b; 3. b; 4. b; 5. d

ESSAY

1. Discuss the four types of social movements and the features of each one.
2. What are the stages of social change?
3. What is relative deprivation?
4. How do sociologists from the four sociological paradigms view social movements?
5. How does the culture jamming movement that Naomi Klein discusses differ from other social movements?

WHERE TO START YOUR RESEARCH PAPER

For examples of social movements and groups in Canada, go to:

Greenpeace: www.greenpeace.org/canada.

Gwen Jacobs (Ontario law for women to be topless): www.fcn.ca/Gwen.html.

David Suzuki Foundation: www.davidsuzuki.org.

October Crisis in Quebec, 1970: www.historyofrights.com/events/flq.html.

Aboriginal rights in B.C.: www.bctreaty.net/files/about_us.php.

Universal health care in Canada: www.cupe1975.ca/bursary/burs5.html.

Remember to check www.thethinkspot.ca for additional information, downloadable flashcards, and other helpful resources.

GLOSSARY

Parenthetical numbers refer to the pages on which the term is introduced.

aboriginal is a person who is Indian, Inuit, or Métis. (169)
absolute poverty is poverty so severe that one lacks resources to survive. (119)
abuse refers to any behaviour or situation in which one person takes advantage of a less powerful person. (246)
achieved status is a type of position that you earn or do something to attain. (90)
affirmative action is a social policy designed to help minority groups gain opportunities through employment and education. (181)
age-specific death rate is the number of deaths in a particular age group during a given year. (152)
ageism is prejudice and discrimination based solely on age. (211)
agents of formal control enforce the laws of society. (225)
agents of informal control enforce social norms. (225)
agents of socialization are the people, groups, and institutions that shape our self-concept, beliefs, and behaviour. (76)
alternative social movements want to create a change in specific people's thoughts, practices, and beliefs regarding a particular issue. (288)
amplification occurs when ideas become elaborated and sometimes exaggerated. (292)
androcentric bias is a focus on men that influences sociology in terms of how social research is done and which issues and topics are studied. (19)
animism is the belief that animate spirits live in natural objects and operate in the world. (267)
anthropocentric bias is the belief that humans are the most significant species in nature. (159)
ascribed status is a position in society that is given or assigned. (90)
asexual describes people who are not sexually attracted to people of either sex. (188)
assimilation is the process by which minority groups adopt the patterns of the dominant culture. (175)
assimilationist minorities are groups that seek to shed their old ways and integrate themselves into mainstream society. (176)
autocratic leaders are leaders who determine the group policies and assign tasks. (97)

backstage is the demeanour that incorporates our true feelings and beliefs. (71)
bias is the likelihood that a nonrepresentative sample may lead to inaccurate results. (35)
bisexual describes people who are sexually attracted to people of either sex. (188)
bounded relationships are relationships that exist only under specific conditions. (94)
bourgeoisie refers to members of the capitalist class who own the means of production. (12)
bureaucracy is a formal organization that is organized into a hierarchy of smaller departments. (102)
bureaucrats are managers of business and government agencies. (117)

campaigns are organized and ongoing efforts to achieve a specific goal. (286)
case studies are investigations of one person or event in detail. (38)
caste system is a system in which a person's position may be a position of power and privilege or of disadvantage; his or her place is permanently fixed. (115)
causal relationship is a relationship in which one condition or variable leads to a certain consequence. (33)
census family is Statistics Canada's definition of a family. (239)
central tendency is the middle of the distribution of a variable. (40)
chattel slavery is a form of slavery in which a slave is considered property. (114)
chivalry hypothesis suggests that female offenders are treated more leniently by male police officers and judges. (231)
church is a large, highly organized group of believers. (267)
citizen media refers to content produced, collected, and shared by private citizens. (78)
civil religion is a binding force that holds society together through political and social issues. (270)
class consciousness is an understanding of one's position in the class system. (12)
class system is a form of stratification that allows social mobility. (115)
coercive organization is an organization that people are forced to join. (101)
cognitive development is a person's ability to think and reason. (72)
cohabitation (also called living common law) is an intimate relationship in which two people live together without being legally married. (241)
cohort is a specific group of people used in a study. (33)
collective behaviour is any social interaction in which a group of people engages in behaviour that is not in their normal routine. (284)
colour-blind racism is the idea that racism still exists in society in more subtle ways. (178)
comparative studies use data from different sources in order to compare them against each other. (33)
concepts are abstract ideas that refer to objects, ideas, or behaviours. (32)
concrete operational stage is the stage (ages 7 through 12 years) at which children can think about objects in the world in more than one way and start to understand causal connections in their surroundings. (74)
conflict model of law proposes that powerful people write laws to protect their own interests while punishing the actions of those they wish to control. (225)
conflict theory is a theoretical perspective that views society as various groups that are in a constant struggle over scarce resources. (9)
conformity is the degree to which we will alter our behaviour, attitudes, and points of view to fit into our perceived expectation of what is appropriate. (98)
consensus model of law suggests that laws arise because people see a behaviour they do not like, and they agree to make it illegal. (225)
conspicuous consumption is the purchase of goods or services for the specific purpose of displaying one's wealth. (124)
content analysis is a type of research in which the sociologist looks for common words or themes in newspapers, books, or structured interviews. (38)
contract slavery is a form of slavery in which a person signs a work contract, receives food and shelter from an employer, but is threatened when he or she tries to leave the contract. (115)
control variables are variables that are kept constant to accurately test the impact of an independent variable. (32)
convenience sample is a nonrandom sample of people conveniently or easily available to the researcher. (35)
conventional level is the second stage of moral development that arises before puberty and uses the lens of norms and rules to determine what is right and wrong. (75)
correlation is an indication that when one factor changes, so does another. (33)
counterculture is a group with values and norms that are in opposition to the dominant culture's values and norms. (58)
craftspeople are skilled labourers such as plumbers or carpenters. (117)
craze occurs when a fad leaves a lasting effect on society. (286)
credentialism is an emphasis on educational degrees in assessing skills and knowledge. (263)
crime is the violation of norms that have been written into law. (221)
crime rate measures the volume of crime reported to the police. (222)
Crime Severity Index measures the seriousness of crime reported to the police. (223)
cross-sectional studies look at an event at a single point in time. (33)

crowd is a large group of influential people who gather for a temporary purpose. (284)

crude birth rate is the number of births for every 1000 people each year. (152)

crude death rate is the number of deaths for every 1000 people each year. (152)

cults are new religious movements led by charismatic leaders with few followers. (267)

cultural imperialism refers to a global situation in which powerful culture industries located almost exclusively in the West, in particular in the United States, dominate other local, national, and regional cultures. (59)

cultural lag occurs when social and cultural changes occur at a slower pace than technological changes. (59)

cultural relativism means making a deliberate effort to appreciate a group's ways of life without prejudice. (58)

cultural transmission is culture passing from one generation to the next. (50)

cultural universals are elements that are common to all human cultures worldwide. (57)

culture is the symbols, values, norms, and material objects that societies create. (50)

culture shock occurs when a person encounters a culture foreign to his or her own and has an emotional response to the differences between the cultures. (59)

cycle of poverty refers to the vicious circle in which poor children are likely to remain poor as adults. (140)

debt bondage is a form of slavery in which someone borrows money in order to repay a different debt and works to pay off the new debt. (114)

debunking is the practice of looking beyond the surface or obvious explanation and seeking out deeper explanations. (7)

deep ecology is a perspective based on the belief that we are just one species among many, that our role and our activities are no more important than any other species', and that our primary concern should be ecological viability and preservation rather than economic growth. (159)

democratic leaders are leaders who strive to set group policy by discussion and agreement. (97)

demographic transition theory suggests that people control their own fertility as they move from agrarian to industrial societies. (156)

demography is the study of population size and composition. (151)

dependency ratio is the ratio of the youth population (0 to 19 years) and senior population (65 or older) to the working-age population (20 to 64 years). (213)

dependent variables are the response to the manipulated variable. (32)

deterrence tries to prevent a person from doing something because of fear of the consequences. (225)

deviance is the violation of norms that a society agrees upon. (221)

diffusion occurs when an item or a method of doing things is transmitted from one culture to another. (59)

discovery occurs when we better understand or observe something that already exists. (59)

discreditable stigma is a stigma that can be concealed from others. (225)

discredited stigma is a stigma that cannot be hidden from others or is no longer hidden from others. (225)

discrimination is the unfair treatment of people based on their social category membership rather than on merit. (172)

dominant culture is usually but not always practised by the majority and controls of many of the social institutions (57)

dominant group is the group that has the greatest power but not necessarily the greatest numbers. (171)

double consciousness is the sense that a person must keep a foot in two worlds, one in the majority group's world and one in the minority group's world. (179)

doubling time refers to the number of years it takes for a population to double. (155)

dramaturgy is a theory of interaction in which all social life is like acting. (17)

dyad is a group consisting of only two people. (96)

ecofeminist theory is a merging of ecological and feminist thought that focuses on the common experiences of women and nature. (159)

education is the social institution through which society passes on knowledge, skills, and values from one generation to the next. (259)

emigration is the movement of people out of an area. (154)

endogamy is the practice of marrying within your social group. (244)

entrepreneurs are the business class, as identified by Weber. (117)

environmental sociology is concerned with the reciprocal relationship between societies and their environments. (158)

ethics is a system of values or principles that guide one's behaviour. (41)

ethnic cleansing refers to persecution through imprisonment, expulsion, or murder of members of an ethnic minority by a majority to achieve ethnic homogeneity in majority-controlled territory. (174)

ethnic enclaves are neighbourhoods where people from similar cultures live together and assert cultural distinction from the dominant group. (177)

ethnicity is the classification of people based on a common cultural, linguistic, or ancestral heritage. (169)

ethnocentrism occurs when a person uses his or her own culture to judge another culture. (58)

ethnography is a research method that aims to understand the social perspective and cultural values of a particular group by participating in or getting to know their activities in detail. (38)

exchange mobility is a concept which suggests that, within a country, each social class contains a relatively fixed number of people. (140)

exogamy is the practice of marrying someone from a different social group. (244)

experiment is a method in which researchers control variables in order to test causes and effects. (36)

expressive role is focused on the socialization of children and meeting the family's emotional needs. (192)

expulsion or confinement occurs when the dominant group expels or forcibly confines a minority group. (173)

extended family is a household consisting of a nuclear family plus an additional relative. (240)

extension refers to the way social movement organizations seek to align their interests with those of other groups that are related, sometimes furthering ideas that were not originally in their frame. (292)

face-saving work is a reaction to embarrassment in the form of either humour, anger, or retreat. (71)

fad is a temporary fashion or action the public embraces. (285)

false consciousness is a person's lack of understanding of his or her position in society. (12)

family is a group of two or more people who are related by blood, marriage or other intimate relationship, or adoption. (239)

family of orientation is the family that you are born into and raised in. (240)

family of procreation is the family that you form through marriage or cohabitation and in which you raise your children. (240)

family violence refers to a range of abusive behaviours that occur within relationships based on kinship, intimacy, dependency, or trust. (246)

fashion is an object, a style, or a behavior that becomes popular for a period of time. (285)

feminist theory is a theoretical perspective that focuses on gender inequalities which are built into the social structure. (9)

feminization of poverty refers to the fact that, around the world, women experience poverty at far higher rates than men. (142)

field research is research conducted in a natural setting. (37)

folkways are informal types of norms that are not strictly enforced. (55)

formal operational stage is the stage (ages 12 years and above) at which people become able to comprehend abstract thought. (74)

formal organizations are groups created for a certain purpose and built for maximum efficiency. (100)

formal rationality is the reasonable actions that organizations and bureaucracies take to achieve goals in the most effective way. (102)

formal structures are the explicit rules, goals, and guidelines of an organization. (101)

frame alignment process occurs when social movement organizations link their goals to the goals of other organizations. (291)

frame bridging occurs when two or more groups that may be somewhat opposed to each other join forces. (292)

front stage is what the audience sees, or the part of ourselves that we present to others. (71)
functionalism is a theoretical perspective that sees society as a system of interrelated parts. (9)
functions are social factors that affect people in a society. (10)
futility is the claim that a reform cannot work because the social problem is unsolvable. (283)

game stage is Mead's third stage of development, which never truly ends, and is the stage in which we begin to understand that others have expectations and demands placed upon them. (71)
Gemeinschaft refers to community connections involving personal relationships based on friendship and kinship ties, such as family. (93)
gender is defined as the social, cultural, and psychological traits and behaviours connected with being masculine or feminine. (187)
gender identity is our perception of ourselves as male or female. (187)
gender roles are society's expectations of how males and females should think and act. (189)
gender socialization teaches us about the attitudes and behaviours that a society defines as appropriate for each sex. (80)
general deterrence ensures that individuals will not commit a crime because they see the negative consequences applied to others, and they fear experiencing these consequences. (225)
General Social Survey (GSS)—Victimization measures crime victimization based on a representative sample of nearly 20 000 Canadians over 15 years old. (222)
generalization is the extent that what is learned from a sample can be applied to the population from which the sample is taken. (34)
generalized other is a sense of the norms, beliefs, and expectations specific to our culture. (71)
generational replacement level is the fertility rate (2.1 children per woman) that must be maintained to replace the population in the absence of migration. (152)
genocide is the attempt to destroy or exterminate a people based on their race or ethnicity. (173)
gerontology is the study of aging and the elderly. (210)
Gesellschaft refers to social connections that are more formal and impersonal. (93)
gestures are symbols we make using our bodies, such as facial expressions, hand movements, eye contact, and other types of body language. (52)
Gini index is a measure of income inequality. (118)
glass ceiling is an invisible barrier preventing women from reaching executive-level positions in the workplace. (191)
global stratification refers to the ranking of countries that highlights social and economic inequality throughout the world. (118)
global village refers to the "shrinking" of the world through immediate electronic communications. (59)
globalization is a complex process by which the world and its international economy are becoming more and more intertwined. (123)
grade inflation is the trend of assigning higher grades than previously assigned to students for completing the same work. (262)
gross national income is a measure of the value of goods and services produced by a country. (118)
groupthink is the term for group decisions that are made without objective thought. (98)

Hawthorne effect occurs when people behave differently because they know they are being studied. (37)
health is a state of complete physical, mental, and social well-being and not merely the absence of disease or infirmity. (203)
hedonism is seeking pleasure over pain. (75)
henotheism is the worship of one god while recognizing the existence of other deities. (268)
heterosexual describes people who are sexually attracted to people of the opposite sex. (188)
hidden curriculum refers to lessons taught in schools that are unrelated to academic learning. (264)
homogamy is marriage between people with similar backgrounds, such as religion, ethnicity, class, or age. (244)
homophobia is a negative attitude toward homosexuals and homosexuality. (189)
homosexual describes people who are sexually attracted to people of the same sex. (188)
horizontal mobility refers to moving within the same status category. (140)
household is a person or group of people who occupy the same dwelling. (239)
human capital is a person's combination of skills, knowledge, traits, and personal attributes. (263)
human development index (HDI) is a new way of ranking countries by combining indicators of life expectancy, educational attainment, and income. (118)
human ecology recognizes that the natural environment performs many services for human beings. (158)
hypothesis is a statement about how variables relate. (32)
hysteria is a heightened emotional state that can lead a group to violence. (285)

I self is the subjective part of the self. (71)
ideology is a set of cultural beliefs that justifies various social arrangements, including inequality. (113)
imitation stage is Mead's first stage of development, which is the period from birth to about age 2, when children merely copy the behaviours of those around them. (71)
immigration is the movement of people into an area. (153)
impression management is management of the impression that a performer makes on others. (71)
incapacitation prevents a person from committing more crime. (225)
incest taboo is a cultural universal which prohibits sex between closely related individuals. (188)
income is the money received for work or through investments. (133)
independent variables are variables that are deliberately manipulated in an experiment. (32)
indictable offences are more serious offences. (233)
indigenous superordination is the subordination of an immigrant group to a dominant group. (174)
infant mortality rate is the number of deaths of children less than 1 year of age per 1000 live births in the same year. (152)
informal structures are friendships, allegiances, and loyalties among members of an organization. (101)
in-group is a group to which we feel an affinity or a closeness. (95)
in-group bias is the feeling that a person's in-group is superior to others. (95)
institutional discrimination maintains the advantage for the dominant group, while providing the appearance of fairness to all. (179)
instrumental role is focused on working to provide for the family in a financial way. (192)
intergenerational mobility refers to the change that family members make from one social class to the next through generations. (140)
intersectionality is a term used to describe the fact that women experience oppression based on a number of minority statuses. (179)
intersexed refers to a person whose body has both male and female characteristics. (187)
intimate distance is distance reserved for those with whom we are very close. (105)
intragenerational mobility occurs when an individual changes social standing, especially in the workforce. (140)
invention occurs when something is deliberately changed or made to produce something new. (59)
iron cage is a concept introduced by Max Weber that refers to the way in which bureaucracies make workers feel trapped and turn them into little more than robots accomplishing tasks. (102)

jeopardy is the claim that attempting to solve a problem will only draw attention away from other, more important issues. (284)

kinship is a social bond based on common ancestry. (239)

laissez-faire leaders are leaders who lead by absence and may in fact not want to be leaders at all. (97)
language is a system of spoken and/or written symbols used to convey meaning and to communicate. (52)
latent functions are factors that lead to unforeseen or unexpected consequences. (10)
laws are formal norms that are enforced through social institutions. (55)
leadership style is a behavioural mode that leaders use to influence group members. (97)

life expectancy is the average number of years a person is expected to live. (152)
literature review is a study of relevant academic articles and information. (31)
longitudinal studies include data from observations over time using a cohort. (33)
looking-glass self is the theory that the self develops through a process of reflection, like a reflection in a mirror. (71)
lower class is a social class living in poverty. (138)

macro is a large-scale perspective. (7)
Malthusian theorem is a population projection which suggests that the population will exceed the available food supply because populations grow at geometric rates, whereas food supplies grow at arithmetic rates. (155)
manifest functions are factors that lead to an expected consequence or outcome. (10)
marginal poverty is a state of poverty that occurs when a person lacks stable employment. (134)
marriage is a legally and socially recognized union of two or more people. (241)
mass media are forms of communication such as television, newspapers, radio, and magazines that are designed to reach a large audience. (77)
master status is the most important status. (90)
material culture consists of the physical items that we use. (51)
me self is the objective part of the self. (71)
mean is an average. (40)
mechanical solidarity refers to the type of community bonding usually found in traditional societies, in which people share beliefs and values and perform common activities. (93)
median refers to the midpoint in a distribution of numbers. (40)
medicalization is the idea that the medical community is the centre of many aspects of our society. (207)
Medicare is Canada's government-run health care insurance program that provides health coverage for all Canadians. (203)
meritocracy argument states that those who get ahead do so based on their own merit. (141)
micro is a small-scale perspective. (7)
middle class is a social class that consists of those who have moderate incomes. (138)
migrant superordination is the conquest of a native population by a more powerful group. (174)
migration is the movement of people from one area to another. (153)
militant minorities are groups that seek to overthrow the existing system because they see it as unjust. (177)
minority group is any group that holds less power than the majority group. (171)
mobs are groups characterized by high levels of emotion that engage in some type of focused action that can be violent or disruptive. (285)
mode refers to the most common value in a distribution. (40)
monogamy is the practice of being married to one person at a time. (241)
monotheism is the belief that there is only one God. (266)
morality of care is morality decided by a standard of how best to help those who are in need. (76)
morality of justice is morality based on the rule of law. (76)
mores are norms that represent a community's most important values. (55)
multiculturalism is a concept that supports the inherent value of different cultures within society. (175)

nature theory states that the genes we get from our parents are the primary cause of human behaviour. (69)
negative correlation describes two variables that move in opposite directions. (33)
neocolonialism is a process in which powerful nations use loans and economic power to maintain control over poor nations. (123)
nonmaterial culture consists of the nonphysical products of society, such as values and beliefs. (51)
normative organization is an organization that exists to achieve a worthwhile goal. (101)
norms are culturally defined rules for appropriate social behavior. (54)
nuclear family is a household consisting of a husband, a wife, and their children. (240)
nurture theory states that our environment is the primary influence on the way we think, feel, and behave. (69)

objectivity is the ability to conduct research without allowing personal biases or prejudices to influence findings. (31)
old old is a cohort that consists of people over the age of 75. (210)
operationalizing is turning abstract ideas into something measurable. (32)
organic solidarity occurs when people live in a society with a diverse division of labour. (93)
organization of believers is a group that ensures the prosperity and effectiveness of the religious experience. (271)
organizations are formal groups that exist to achieve desired goals. (100)
out-group is a group from which we are disconnected. (95)

panic is an extreme fear based on something that might happen. (286)
parameter is a number that describes a population. (34)
participant observation is a type of field research in which the researcher poses as a person who is normally in the environment. (37)
patriarchal refers to a social system that benefits men. (9)
peers are people who are similar in age and who share many common interests. (77)
personal distance is distance that ranges from 45 centimetres to 1.2 metres; this distance is for normal conversations. (102)
personal space is the invisible bubble that each of us has around us that insulates us from others. (105)
perversity claims that any attempts to fix a problem will actually compound the issues the change was trying to address. (283)
petite bourgeoisie are small-business owners in Weber's class system. (12)
petite bourgeoisie refers to the class of people who have their own businesses but do not employ others. (117)
philosophies of life focus on a set of ethical, moral, or philosophical principles. (266)
play stage is Mead's second stage of development, which occurs around the ages of 2–4 years, during which children play roles and begin to take on the characteristics of important people in their world. (71)
pluralistic minorities are groups that enter into an area voluntarily but seek to maintain their own culture while also integrating into the dominant group. (175)
polyandry is a form of marriage in which a woman takes two or more husbands at the same time. (241)
polygamy is the practice of having more than one spouse at a time. (241)
polygyny occurs when a man is married to two or more women at the same time. (241)
polytheism is the belief in multiple gods and demigods. (266)
population is the entire group of people you wish to describe. (34)
positive correlation describes two variables that move in the same direction. (33)
postconventional level is the third stage of moral development that refers to a morality based on abstract principles. (75)
power is the ability to carry out your will and impose it on others. (136)
power elite is a small group of people who hold immense power. (136)
preconventional level is the first stage of moral development that lasts through the elementary school years; at this level, children make their moral judgments within a framework of hedonistic principles. (75)
prejudice refers to negative attitudes about an entire social category of people. (172)
preoperational stage is the stage (ages 2 through 7 years) at which the ability to speak grows rapidly. (74)
prestige is the level of esteem associated with one's status and social standing. (136)
primary deviance is the initial deviant act itself, which is not followed by some form of labelling. (230)
primary groups are groups that are small, intimate, and enduring. (94)
primary socialization is socialization that occurs during childhood. (69)
profane means related or devoted to that which is not sacred. (267)
progressive means favouring or promoting change. (289)
proletariat refers to members of the working class who sell their labour for wages. (12)
propinquity is physical and geographic proximity. (242)
psychosocial crisis is a crisis occurring during each of Erikson's stages that will be resolved either positively or negatively, and each outcome will have an effect on our ability to deal with the next one. (72)

public distance is the zone of interaction that is used in highly formal settings; this distance includes everything greater than 3.6 metres. (105)
push-pull, or neo-classical, migration theory suggests that migration depends on the supply and demand for labor, both in the sending area and the receiving are. (154)

qualitative data include words, pictures, photos, or any other type of information that comes to the researcher in a non-numeric form. (33)
quantitative data refer to data based on numbers. (33)
quintile is one of five groups of households, ranked by income. (133)

race is the socially defined classification of people based on certain physical characteristics. (169)
racial profiling occurs when police use a person's race as the primary reason to suspect that the individual has broken the law. (228)
racism refers to an ideology that maintains that one racial group is inherently superior to another. (172)
random sample is a sample chosen so that each member of the population has the same chance of being selected. (35)
rate of natural increase (RNI) is the crude birth rate minus the crude death rate of a population. (154)
re-appropriation is the process by which a group reclaims—re-appropriates—terms or objects that were previously used in a negative way toward that group. (60)
recidivism is the tendency for inmates released from prison to return to prison. (227)
redemptive social movements focus on specific individuals, but they seek radical, rather than limited, change. (288)
reference group is the group that you use to evaluate yourself. (96)
reformative social movements seek to change a society's thoughts and actions but only in a limited way. (289)
regressive means seeking to stop change. (289)
rehabilitation tries to reform offenders so that they can be returned to society, but will no longer choose to engage in criminal behaviour. (226)
reintegrative justice is based on the principle that offenders can be successfully reintegrated into the wider society. (226)
reintegrative shaming is an effort to bring an offender back into the community after punishment. (225)
relative deprivation points to the gaps between what people have and what they expect. (291)
relative poverty is based on comparing ourselves to those around us. (119)
reliable means you get consistent results each time you measure. (32)
religion is a social institution based on a unified system of beliefs and practices related to sacred things. (266)
rentiers are the wealthy members of a society, as identified by Weber. (117)
repertoires are actions used to promote interest and involvement within a movement. (287)
representative sample is a sample in which the relevant characteristics of the sample are the same as the characteristics of the population. (34)
research design refers to the process used to collect data. (33)
research methods are the scientific procedures that sociologists use to conduct research and collect data about a particular topic. (31)
residual poverty is chronic and multigenerational poverty. (134)
resocialization is the process of learning new norms, values, attitudes, and behaviours and abandoning old ones. (78)
resource management focuses on negotiating and regulating the extraction of resources and the disposal of hazardous waste. (159)
restoration attempts to make the victim, and the community, whole again. (226)
retribution reflects the belief that someone who commits a crime is responsible for his or her actions and deserves to be punished. (225)
revolutionary social movements sometimes called transformative social movements, seek to change the thoughts and actions of all society in radical fashion. (289)
riots are emotional and violent disturbances of the peace by crowds that lack a central focus. (285)
rituals are established patterns of behaviour closely associated with experience of the sacred. (268)
role is the behaviour associated with a specific status. (91)
role conflict is a phenomenon that occurs when one is forced to choose between the competing demands of multiple roles. (92)
role expectations are the socially defined behaviours appropriate for a particular status. (91)
role performance refers to how a person actually plays a role. (92)
role strain occurs when the demands and expectations of one role are impossible for us to satisfy. (92)
rumours are stories or statements that lack confirmation or certainty. (286)

sacred means connected to God or dedicated to a religious purpose. (267)
sample is a subset of a population. (34)
sanction is a reward for following a norm or a punishment for violating it. (54)
"sandwiched" generation is the generation that takes care of both its children and its elderly parents. (210)
secessionist minorities are groups that voluntarily separate themselves from the dominant group and view the dominant group with disdain, believing that it will corrupt the group's belief system. (176)
secondary data analysis is the process of using and analyzing data that others have collected. (38)
secondary deviance refers to the psychological reorientation that occurs when a person is labelled as deviant and assumes that identity. (230)
secondary groups are groups that are formal, superficial, and temporary. (94)
secondary socialization is socialization that continues throughout our lives. (69)
sects are religious groups that have enough members to sustain themselves and go against society's norms. (267)
secularization is the overall decline in the importance and power of religion in people's lives. (269)
segregation is forced separation because of factors such as race, gender, or ethnicity. (174)
self refers to a person's identity and what makes that person different from others. (17)
semi-skilled manual workers are workers who have some training and may work in factories. (117)
sensorimotor stage is the stage (birth to 2 years) at which infants learn to experience and think about the world through their senses and motor skills. (72)
sentencing circle is a process used by some First Nations communities to the rehabilitate the offender and to heal the community as a whole. (226)
sex refers to the biological characteristics that distinguish males and females. (187)
sexism is the belief that one sex is superior to the other. (188)
sexual orientation is a reflection of a person's preference for sexual partners. (188)
sexuality refers to a particular kind of social interaction in which we express ourselves as sexual beings. (188)
shaming is a deliberate effort to attach a negative meaning to a behaviour. (225)
sick role is the expected behaviours and responsibilities appropriate for someone who is ill. (207)
significant others are the people we consider to be important and who we want to impress. (71)
simple supernaturalism is the belief in a variety of supernatural forces that affect and influence people's lives. (266)
slavery is a stratification system in which one person has complete control over another. (113)
social capital is a sociological concept that refers to the individual and collective resources available to a person. (99)
social change is how culture and social institutions change over time. (281)
social class refers to a group of people with similar access to power, wealth, and prestige. (89)
social Darwinism is a notion which suggests that strong societies survive and weak ones become extinct. (10)
social distance is distance that ranges from about 1.2 metres to 3.6 metres and is usually reserved for formal settings. (105)
social dynamics are changes in the structural elements of society. (10)
social epidemiology is the study of the distribution of diseases and health throughout a society's population. (203)
social group is any number of people with similar norms, values, and behaviours who frequently interact with one another. (94)
social institutions are structures that provide for patterned relationships and that are organized around a central activity or social need. (92)

social interaction refers to all the ways people behave and communicate in social situations (94)
social laws are statements of fact that are unchanging under given conditions and can be used as ground rules for any kind of society. (10)
social media are forms of electronic communication such as blogs, forums, podcasts, and sites for social networking through which users create and share information, ideas, personal messages, and other content. (77)
social mobility is the ability to change social classes. (140)
social movements are activities that support or protest social issues, and they are usually organized by nongovernmental organizations. (286)
social network is the web of ties you have with others. (99)
social policies are deliberate strategies designed to correct recognized social problems. (82)
social statics are the existing structural elements of society. (10)
social status refers to socially defined positions that are characterized by certain expectations, rights, and duties. (90)
social stratification refers to the ranking of people and the rewards they receive, based on social factors, often including wealth, power, and/or prestige. (112)
social stratification systems are systems societies use to rank different groups. (113)
social structures are patterns of relationships that endure from one generation to the next. (89)
socialization is the lifelong process by which the norms, values, and other aspects of a culture are learned and internalized by group members and provides the individual with the skills necessary for participating in society. (68)
society refers to a group of people who live in a defined territory and who share social structures and who interact with each other. (5)
socioeconomic status is a measure of an individual's or family's position within the social structure. (77)
sociological imagination is the ability to understand how social forces influence the lives of individuals. (7)
sociology is a science guided by the understanding that our lives are affected not only by our individual characteristics but by powerful social forces and our place in the social world. (5)
specific deterrence occurs to individuals who have violated the law and have already been punished. (226)
spurious correlation occurs when two variables appear to be related but both may have an underlying cause. (33)
statistic is a number that describes a sample. (34)
status set is all the statuses we occupy. (90)
status symbols are material signs that represent a specific status. (91)
stepfamilies are families composed of children and some combination of biological parents. (240)
stereotypes are simplified perceptions people have of an entire group, usually based on a false assumption. (172)
stigma is a mark of disgrace associated with a particular status, quality, or person. (225)
stigmatized shame is a permanent label given to an offender, which could actually increase the chances of reoffending because the guilty person is forever labelled. (225)
structural mobility occurs when social changes affect large numbers of people. (140)
subculture is a subset of the dominant culture that has distinct values, beliefs, and norms. (57)
summary conviction offences are less serious offences. (233)
survey is an investigation of the opinions or behaviours of a group of people by asking them questions. (35)
sustainable development is based on the premise that economic development and environmental protection are compatible goals. (159)
symbolic interactionism is a theoretical perspective that focuses on how people interact with others in their everyday lives. (9)
symbols are things that represent, suggest, or stand for something else. (51)
system of beliefs relates sacred objects to religious rituals and defines and protects the sacred from the profane. (271)

teacher expectancy effect is the impact of a teacher's expectations on a student's performance. (264)
dominant culture is usually but not always practised by the majority and controls many of the social institutions. (57)
The Sapir-Whorf hypothesis is a hypothesis that the structure of a language determines a native speaker's perception and categorization of experience. (52)
theism is the belief in a god or gods. (266)
theocracy is a government that is controlled by religious leaders. (267)
Thomas theorem states that situations that are defined as real are real in their consequences. (15)
total fertility rate refers to the number of children that a woman would have over the course of her reproductive life. (151)
total institutions are places in which the most effective forms of resocialization can occur because they isolate people from outside influences so they can be reformed and controlled. (78)
totemism is the practice of honouring a totem or a sacred object. (266)
transformation changes the old meanings and understandings of the problem and creates new and innovative ones. (292)
transgender individuals have a biological sex but possess a gender identity other than that typically assigned to their sex. (187)
transitional poverty is a temporary state of poverty that occurs when someone loses a job for a short time. (134)
transsexual refers to people who born as one identifiable sex and have undergone surgical modifications and hormonal interventions to become the other sex. (187)
triad is a group consisting of three people. (96)
triangulation is the process of using multiple approaches to study a phenomenon. (38)

underclass includes the homeless and people living in substandard housing. (139)
Uniform Crime Reporting (UCR) Survey measures the incidence of crime using police statistics of reported crimes gathered from police reports and paperwork. (222)
unskilled workers are the lowest class, consisting of people who frequently perform manual labour jobs that are often unpleasant and sometimes dangerous. (117)
upper middle class is a social class that consists of high-income members of society who are often well educated but do not belong to the elite membership of the super wealthy. (137)
upper, or elite, class is a social class that is very small in number and holds significant wealth. (137)
urban legends are rumours that are presented as true stories that act as cautionary tales. (286)
utilitarian organization is an organization in which people receive wages in exchange for work. (101)

validity means that you're actually measuring what you set out to measure. (32)
values are a part of a society's nonmaterial culture that represent cultural standards by which we determine what is good or bad, right or wrong. (52)
variable is a characteristic or trait that can be measured. (32)
verstehen means understanding the meaning of action from the actor's point of view. (31)
vertical mobility refers to moving from one social status to another. (140)
visible minority is a person, other than an aboriginal, who is non-Caucasian in race or non-white in colour. (169)
voluntary association is the act of joining an organization that offers no pay and that expands social networks through interaction. (100)
voluntary migration refers to the willing movement of people from one society to another. (173)

wealth is all of your material possessions. (133)
working class is a social class generally made up of people with high school diplomas and lower levels of education. (138)
WUNC refers to the members of a movement who want to show the public the worthiness, unity, numbers, and commitment of their movement. (287)

xenocentrism is perceiving other groups or societies as superior to your own. (58)
xenophobia refers to fear and hostility toward people who are from other countries or cultures. (58)

young old is a cohort that consists of people between the ages of 65 and 75. (210)

ENDNOTES

CHAPTER 1

1. Margot Young, Susan Boyd, Gwen Brodsky, and Shelagh Day (eds.), *Poverty: Rights, Social Citizenship, and Legal Activism* (Vancouver: UBC Press, 2007).
2. C. Wright Mills, *The Sociological Imagination* (New York: Oxford, 1959).
3. Ibid.
4. Peter L. Berger, *Invitation to Sociology: A Humanistic Perspective* (Garden City, NY: Anchor, 1963).
5. Jean Stockard and Robert M. O'Brien, "Cohort Effects on Suicide Rates: International Variations," *American Sociological Review*, 2002. 67(6): 854–872.
6. Ibid.
7. Émile Durkheim, *Suicide*, George Simpson (ed.), John A. Spaulding and George Simpson (trans.) (New York: The Free Press, 1897/1966).
8. Stéphanie Langlois and Peter Morrison, "Suicide Deaths and Suicide Attempts," *Health Reports*, 2002. 13: 9–22. www.statcan.gc.ca/studies-etudes/82-003/archive/2002/6060-eng.pdf, accessed August 28, 2008.
9. Kenneth Thompson, *Auguste Comte: The Foundation of Sociology* (New York: Halsted Press, 1975).
10. Jonathan Turner, Leonard Beeghily, and Charles H. Powers, *The Emergence of Sociological Theory* (Albany, NY: Wadsworth Publishing Company, 1998).
11. Talcott Parsons, *The Social System* (Glencoe, IL: The Free Press, 1951).
12. Ibid.
13. Robert K. Merton, *Social Theory and Social Structure* (Glencoe, IL: The Free Press, 1957).
14. Ibid.
15. Karl Marx, *Selected Writings in Sociology & Social Philosophy*, T. B. Bottomore and Maximilien Rubel (eds.), T. B. Bottomore (trans.) (New York: McGraw-Hill, 1964); Karl Marx, "Economic and Philosophic Manuscripts of 1844," pp. 37–42 in *Readings in Social Theory: The Classical Tradition to Post-Modernism*, 4th ed. James Farganis (ed.) (New York: McGraw-Hill, 1844/2004); Karl Marx, *Capital: A Critique of Political Economy, Vol. 1* (New York: International Publishers, 1867/1967); Karl Marx and Friedrich Engels, "Manifesto of this Communist Party" pp. 26–36 in *Readings in Social Theory: The Classical Tradition to Post-Modernism*, 4th ed. James Farganis (ed.) (New York: McGraw-Hill, 1845/2004); Karl Marx and Friedrich Engels, "The German Ideology," pp. 43–46 in *Readings in Social Theory: The Classical Tradition to Post-Modernism*, 4th ed. James Farganis (ed.) (New York: McGraw-Hill, 1974/2004).
16. "W.E.B. Du Bois," NAACP, www.naacp.org/about/history/dubois/, accessed October 21, 2008.
17. W.E.B. Du Bois (William Edward Burghardt), "The Philadelphia Negro: A Social Study," pp. 167–170 in *Readings in Social Theory: The Classical Tradition to Post-Modernism*, 4th ed. James Farganis (ed.) (New York: McGraw-Hill, 1899/2004).
18. Tukufu Zuberi, "Being Here and Being There: Fieldwork Encounters and Ethnographic Discoveries: W.E.B. Du Bois's Sociology: *The Philadelphia Negro* and Social Science," *The Annals of the American Academy of Political and Social Science*, 2004. 595: 146–156.
19. Joseph P. DeMarco, *The Social Thought of W.E.B. Du Bois* (Lanham, MD: University Press of American Inc., 1983).
20. Ralf Dahrendorf, *Class and Class Conflict in Industrial Society* (London: Lowe & Brydone (Printers) Ltd., 1959).
21. John Bellamy Foster, "The End of Rational Capitalism," *Monthly Review*, March 2005, http://findarticles.com/p/articles/mi_m1132/is_10_56/ai_n16126168/pg_1?tag5artBody;col1, accessed September 11, 2008.
22. W. I. Thomas and D. S. Thomas, *The Child in America: Behavior Problems and Programs* (New York: Knopf, 1928).
23. George H. Mead, *Mind, Self, and Society: From the Standpoint of a Social Behaviorist* (Chicago: University of Chicago Press, 1934/1962).
24. Herbert Blumer, "Society as Symbolic Interaction," in Arnold M. Rose, *Human Behavior and Social Process: An Interactionist Approach* (Boston: Houghton-Mifflin, reprinted in 1969).
25. Erving Goffman, *The Presentation of Self in Everyday Life* (Edinburgh: University of Edinburgh, Social Sciences Research Centre, 1958).
26. Suzanne Speak and Graham Tipple, "Perceptions, Persecution, and Pity: The Limitations of Interventions for Homelessness," *International Journal of Urban and Regional Research*, 2006. 30(1): 172–188.
27. Goffman, *The Presentation of Self in Everyday Life*.
28. Howard S. Becker, *Outsiders: Studies in the Sociology of Deviance* (New York: The Free Press, 1963).
29. Catalyst, *Women CEOs and Heads of the Financial Post 500*. www.catalyst.org/publication/271/women-ceos-and-heads-of-the-financial-post-500, accessed September 2, 2010.
30. Susan Hoecker-Drysdale, *Harriet Martineau: First Woman Sociologist* (New York: St. Martin's Press, 1992).
31. Ibid.
32. Allen F. Davis, *American Heroine: The Life and Legend of Jane Addams* (New York: Oxford University Press, 1973).
33. Mary Jo Deegan, *Jane Addams and the Men of the Chicago School, 1892–1918* (New Brunswick, NJ: Transaction Books, 1988).
34. Dorothy Smith, *The Conceptual Practices of Power: A Feminist Sociology of Knowledge* (Toronto: University of Toronto Press, 1990).
35. Ibid.
36. Jonathan Turner, Leonard Beeghily, and Charles H. Powers, *The Emergence of Sociological Theory* (Albany, NY: Wadsworth Publishing Company, 1998).
37. Max Weber, *The Protestant Ethic and the Spirit of Capitalism*. (London: Allen and Unwin, 1930)

CHAPTER 2

1. From Eileen Barker, "The Scientific Study of Religion? You Must Be Joking!" *Journal for the Scientific Study of Religion*, 1995. 34: 287–310.
2. Ibid., p. 7.
3. "Cult Killer Denied Parole," *CBC News*, July 11, 2002, www.cbc.ca/canada/new-brunswick/story/2002/07/11/sv_parol071102.html, accessed September 27, 2010; "Quebec Cult Leader Theriault Denied Parole," *CTV News*, July 11, 2002, www.ctv.ca/CTVNews/CTVNewsAt11/20020711/theriault_cult_parole_020711/, accessed September 27, 2010.
4. Lorne L. Dawson, "The Study of New Religious Movements," *Cults and New Religious Movements*, p. 5.
5. Max Weber, "Class, Status, Party," in *Readings in Social Theory: The Classical Tradition to Post-Modernism*, 4th ed. James Farganis (ed.) (New York: McGraw-Hill, 1978/2004).
6. Earl Babbie, *The Practice of Social Research*, 8th ed. (Belmont, CA: Wadsworth Publishing Company, 1998).
7. Statistics Canada and Council of Ministers of Education, Canada. 2007. *Education Indicators in Canada: Report of the Pan-Canadian Education Indicators Program*. Catalogue no. 81-582-XIE. Ottawa. Updated June 16, 2008.
8. Timothy A. Judge and Daniel M. Cable, "The Effect of Physical Height on Workplace Success and Income: Preliminary Test of a Theoretical Model," *Journal of Applied Psychology*, 2004. 89(3): 428–441.
9. Steven Stack and Jim Gundlach, "The Effect of Country Music on Suicide," *Social Forces*, 1992. 72: 211–218.
10. Steven Stack, Jim Gundlach, and Jimmie L. Reeves, "The Heavy Metal Subculture and Suicide," *Suicide and Life-Threatening Behavior*, 1994. 24(1): 15–23.
11. David Lester and John F. Gunn, "National Anthems and Suicide Rates," *Psychological Reports*, 2011. 108: 43–44.
12. United Nations Office on Drugs and Crime, graph on "Seizures of Cannabis Herb in kg and %—by Region—in 2008," on p. 1 of "Global and Regional Seizure Totals," part of the *World Drug Report 2010* package at www.unodc.org/unodc/en/data-and-analysis/WDR-2010.html, accessed September 24, 2010.
13. *World Drug Report 2010*, main document, pp. 8–9, www.unodc.org/unodc/en/data-and-analysis/WDR-2010.html, accessed September 24, 2010.
14. Drug Policy Alliance, "Drug Policy around the World," www.drugpolicy.org/global/drugpolicyby/westerneurop/thenetherlan/, accessed May 21, 2008.
15. Ibid.
16. "Should He Be Extradited? Arrest of 'Prince of Pot' Seeds a Political Uproar: Marijuana Party Leader Wanted by U.S. Authorities," by Tracey Tyler, from *The Toronto Star*, August 8, 2005, reproduced at http://osgoode.yorku.ca/media2.nsf/releases/732A9DD2CE3A28DC8525705700567AD8, accessed September 27, 2010.
17. "Pot Activist Marc Emery Gets 5 Years in U.S. Jail," by CTV.ca News Staff, September 10, 2010, www.ctv.ca/CTVNews/TopStories/20100910/marc-emery-sentenced-100910/, accessed September 27, 2010.

18. "An Open Letter to Rob Nicholson, Canada's Minister of Justice," by Karen Selick, from longer version of article that ran in *National Post* on January 2, 2008, www.karenselick.com/NP080102.html, accessed September 27, 2010.
19. "WeBeHigh.com: A Traveler's Guide to Getting High," www.webehigh.com/city/detail.php?CITYID=2024, accessed September 27, 2010.
20. Chris Clarke, "Canada Bans Pot but Taxes Seeds," *Capital News Online*, January 28, 2005, http://carleton.ca/Capital_News/28012005/n6.shtml, accessed September 24, 2010.
21. Statistics Canada, "Police-Reported Crime for Selected Offences, Canada," table, *The Daily*, July 20, 2010, www.statcan.gc.ca/daily-quotidien/100720/t100720a1-eng.htm, accessed September 12, 2010.
22. Fritz J. Roethlisberger and William J. Dickson, *Management and the Worker* (Cambridge, MA: Harvard University Press, 1939).
23. Stanley Milgram, *Obedience to Authority: An Experimental View* (New York: Harper & Row, 1974).
24. Petticrew et al., *Covert Observation in Practice: Lessons from the Evaluation of the Prohibition of Smoking in Public Places in Scotland.* BioMed Central Ltd., 2007, www.biomedcentral.com/1471-2458/7/204, accessed September 27, 2010.
25. Anthony R. Ward, "Isabelle," *Feral Children*, www.feralchildren.com/en/showchild.php?ch5isabelle, accessed August 26, 2008.
26. Robert Yin, *Applications of Case Study Research*, 2nd ed. (Thousand Oaks, CA: Sage Publishing, 2003).
27. Morris Freilich, "Scientific Possibilities in Iroquoian Studies: An Example of Mohawks Past and Present," *Anthropologica*, 1963. 5(2): 180–181. www.jstor.org/stable/25604582, accessed September 14, 2010.
28. H. Russell Bernard, *Social Research Methods: Qualitative and Quantitative Approaches* (Thousand Oaks, CA: Sage Publications, 2000), p. 357. http://books.google.ca/books, accessed September 10, 2010.
29. Morris Freilich, "Scientific Possibilities in Iroquoian Studies," pp. 182–183.
30. Norman K. Denzin, *The Research Act in Sociology* (Chicago: Aldine Publishing Company, 1970).
31. Canadian Institutes of Health Research, the Natural Sciences and Engineering Research Council of Canada, and the Social Sciences and Humanities Research Council of Canada, *Tri-Council Policy Statement [TCPS]: Ethical Conduct for Research Involving Humans*, 2nd ed., December 2009, http://pre.ethics.gc.ca/pdf/eng/Revised%20Draft%202nd%20Ed%20PDFs/Revised%20Draft%202nd%20Edition%20TCPS_EN.pdf, accessed September 14, 2010.
32. Ibid.; points that follow are abbreviated from pp. 4–7.
33. Abbreviated from "Statement of Professional Ethics," Canadian Sociological Association, approved June 1994, revised August 2010, pp. 4–9, www.csa-scs.ca/code-of-ethics, accessed September 14, 2010.
34. *TCPS*, p. 1.
35. "Statement of Professional Ethics," p. 3.
36. Factcheck.org, "Misstatement of the Union: The President Burnishes the State of the Union through Selective Facts and Strategic Omissions," http://factcheck.org/article376.html#, accessed August 26, 2008.

CHAPTER 3

1. Thomas Homer-Dixon, "A Canadian Is . . . " in Irvin Studin (ed.), *What Is a Canadian? Forty-Three Thought-Provoking Responses* (Toronto: McClelland & Stewart Ltd., 2006). Reprinted with permission.
2. Central Intelligence Agency, "Rank Order—Electricity—Consumption," *The World Factbook*, www.cia.gov/library/publications/the-worldfactbook/rankorder/2042rank.html, accessed March 30, 2006; Central Intelligence Agency, "Rank Order—Oil—Consumption," *The World Factbook*, www.cia.gov/library/publications/the-world-fact-book/rankorder/2174rank.html, accessed March 30, 2006; Central Intelligence Agency, "Rank Order—Population," *The World Factbook*, www.cia.gov/library/publications/the-world-factbook/rankorder/2174rank.html, accessed March 30, 2006.
3. "Crucifix Has Deep Constitutional Roots in Quebec," *Montreal Gazette*, May 26, 2008.
4. Jan Kavan, "International Mother Language Day: Address to the Fifty-seventh Session of the United Nations General Assembly," Office of the President of the General Assembly, www.un.org/ga/president/57/pages/speeches/statement210203-MotherTongue.htm, accessed September 18, 2008.
5. Noam Chomsky, *Reflections on Language* (New York: Pantheon Books, 1975).
6. Marie Coppola and Elissa L. Newport, "Grammatical Subjects in Home Sign: Abstract Linguistic Structure in Adult Primary Gesture Systems without Linguistic Input," *Proceedings of the National Academy of Sciences of the United States*, 2005. 103(52): 19249–19253.
7. Benjamin L. Whorf, *Language, Thought, and Reality* (New York: Wiley, 1956).
8. Richard Monastersky, "Speak before You Think," *Chronicle of Higher Education*, 00095982, 2002. 48(29): A17–A19.
9. Elections Canada, www.elections.ca/content.aspx?section=ele&dir=turn&document=index&lang=e, accessed August 15, 2013.
10. Spicer Commission, "1991 Citizen's Forum on Canadian Unity," www.uni.ca/initiatives/spicer.html, accessed September 3, 2010.
11. Seymour Martin Lipset, *Continental Divide: The Values and Institutions of the United States and Canada* (New York: Routledge, Chapman and Hall, Inc., 1990).
12. George P. Murdock, "The Common Denominator of Culture," in *The Science of Man in the World Crisis*, Ralph Linton (ed.) (New York: Columbia University Press, 1945).
13. Peijia Zha, Jeffrey J. Walczyk, Diana A. Griffith-Ross, Jerome J. Tobacyk, and Daniel F. Walczyk, "The Impact of Culture and Individualism–Collectivism on the Creative Potential and Achievement of American and Chinese Adults," *Creativity Research Journal*, 2006. 18(3): 355–366.
14. Chuansheng Chen, Shin-ying Lee, and Harold W. Stevenson, "Response Style and Cross-cultural Comparisons of Rating Scales among East Asian and North American Students," *Psychological Science*, 1995. 6(3): 170–175.
15. Ibid.
16. Theodore T. Roszak, *The Making of a Counter Culture: Reflections on the Technocratic Society and Its Youthful Opposition* (Garden City, NY: Anchor Books, 1969).
17. Keith A. Roberts, "Toward a Generic Concept of Counter-culture," *Sociological Focus*, 1978. 11(2): 111–126.
18. Elizabeth Cashdan, "Ethnocentrism and Xenophobia: A Cross-cultural Study," *Current Anthropology*, 2001. 42(5): 760–765.
19. Robert B. Edgerton, *Sick Societies: Challenging the Myth of Primitive Harmony* (New York: The Free Press, 1992).
20. Corey Rayburn, "After Napster", *Virginia Journal of Law and Technology*, 2001, 6(16). http://www.vjolt.net/vol6/issue3/v6i3-a16-Rayburn.html, accessed January 2, 2014.
21. Marshall McLuhan, *The Gutenberg Galaxy: The Making of Typographic Man* (Toronto: University of Toronto Press, 1962).
22. William F. Ogburn, "Cultural Lag as Theory," *Sociology & Social Research*, 1957. 41(3): 167–174.
23. Daniel M. Kammen, "Cookstoves for the Developing World," *Scientific American*, 1995. 273(1): 72–76.
24. Adam M. Croom, "Slurs," *Language Sciences*, 2011. 33(3): 343–358.
25. Canadian Radio-television and Telecommunications Commission, "About the CRTC," www.crtc.gc.ca/eng/backgrnd/brochures/b29903.htm, accessed October 5, 2010.
26. "Residential Schools Event Needs Volunteers," *CBC News*, June 8, 2010, www.cbc.ca/news/canada/manitoba/story/2010/06/08/mb-trc-national-event-volunteers-reconciliation-winnipeg.html, accessed August 15, 2013.
27. "Residential Schools: A History of Residential Schools in Canada," *CBC News*, June 14, 2010, www.cbc.ca/news/canada/story/2008/05/16/f-faqs-residential-schools.html, accessed August 15, 2013.
28. Nancy Théberge, *Higher Goals: Women's Ice Hockey and the Politics of Gender* (Albany, NY: State University of New York Press, 2000).
29. Philip Resnick, "Quebecers Signal a Return to the Two Solitudes," *The Vancouver Sun*, May 13, 2010; Benoit Aubin, "Bill 101: A Gift We Never Expected," *Maclean's*, 2007. 120(31/32), 18–20.

CHAPTER 4

1. Gwynne Dyer, *War: The New Edition* (Toronto: Vintage Canada, 2005).
2. Talcott Parsons, *The Social System* (New York: The Free Press, 1951).
3. Talcott Parsons and Robert Bales, *Socialization and the Interaction Process* (New York: The Free Press, 1955).
4. Orville G. Brim, Jr., "Socialization through the Life Cycle," in Orville Brim and Stanton Wheeler (eds.), *Socialization after Childhood: Two Essays* (New York: Wiley, 1966).
5. Theodore E. Long and Jeffrey K. Hadden, "Reconception of Socialization," *Sociological Theory*, 1985. 3(1): 39–49.
6. Brim, "Socialization through the Life Cycle."
7. Richard Dawkins, *The Selfish Gene* (Oxford: Oxford University Press, 1989).
8. Edward O. Wilson, *Sociobiology: The New Synthesis* (Cambridge, MA: Harvard University Press, 1975).
9. W. L. Reese, *Dictionary of Philosophy and Religion: Eastern and Western Thought* (Atlantic Highlands, NJ: Humanities Press Inc., 1987).
10. Paul R. Ehrlich, *Human Natures: Genes, Cultures, and the Human Prospect* (Washington, DC: Island Press, 2000).
11. Harry F. Harlow and Margaret Harlow, "Social Deprivation in Monkeys," *Scientific American*, 1962. November: 137–146.
12. Charles H. Cooley, *Human Nature and the Social Order* (New York: Schocken Books, 1902, 1964).

13. King-To Yeung and John L. Martin, "The Looking Glass Self: An Empirical Test and Elaboration," *Social Forces*, 2003. 81(3): 843–879.
14. Ibid.
15. George Herbert Mead, *Mind, Self, and Society*, Charles W. Morris (ed.) (Chicago: University of Chicago Press, 1934, 1962).
16. Ibid.
17. Ibid.
18. Erving Goffman, *The Presentation of Self in Everyday Life* (Garden City, NY: Doubleday Anchor Books, 1959).
19. Erik Erikson, *Childhood and Society* (New York: Norton Press, 1963).
20. "Nude Photos of Judge Contained in Complaint," *CBC News*, August 31, 2010, www.cbc.ca/canada/manitoba/story/2010/08/31/judge-manitoba-douglas.html, accessed October 4, 2010; *Winnipeg Free Press*, "Judge Embroiled in Sex Scandal Removes Self from Bench," August 31, 2019, accessed October 4, 2010.
21. Public Broadcasting Service, "Secret of the Wild Child," *Nova*, aired March 4, 1997. www.pbs.org/wgbh/nova/transcripts/2112gchild.html, accessed October 3, 2010.
22. Jean Piaget and Barbel Inhelder, *The Psychology of the Child* (New York: Basic Books, 1969, 2000).
23. Sandy J. Wayne and Robert C. Liden, "Effects of Impression Management on Performance Ratings: A Longitudinal Study," *The Academy of Management Journal*, 1995. 38(1): 232–260.
24. Ibid.
25. Ibid.
26. Ibid.
27. Ibid.
28. Lawrence Kohlberg, *The Psychology of Moral Development: The Nature and Validity of Moral Stages* (New York: Harper & Row, 1981).
29. Ibid.
30. Ibid.
31. Ibid.
32. "Jim Crow" entry, *Canadian Oxford Dictionary*, 2nd ed., Katherine Barber (ed.) (Toronto: Oxford University Press, 2004).
33. Charles Helwig and Urszula Jasiobedzka, "The Relation between Law and Morality: Children's Reasoning about Socially Beneficial and Unjust Laws," *Child Development*, 2001. 72: 1382–1394.
34. Anne Colby and William Damon, *Some Do Care: Contemporary Lives of Moral Commitment* (New York: The Free Press, 1992).
35. Carol Gilligan, *In a Different Voice: Psychological Theory and Women's Development* (Cambridge, MA: Harvard University Press, 1982).
36. Ibid.
37. Elliott Turiel, "The Development of Morality," in W. Damon (ed.), *Handbook of Child Psychology*, 5th ed., vol. 3, 863–932 (New York: Wiley, 1998).
38. Eva A. Skoe and Alethia Gooden, "Ethics of Care and Real-Life Moral Dilemma Content in Male and Female Early Adolescents," *Journal of Early Adolescence*, 1993. 13(2): 154–167.
39. Ruth K. Chao, "Beyond Parental Control and Authoritarian Parenting Style: Understanding Chinese Parenting through the Cultural Notion of Training," *Child Development*, 1994. 65(4): 1111–1119.
40. Ibid.
41. Min Zhou, *Chinatown: The Socioeconomic Potential of an Urban Enclave* (Philadelphia, PA: Temple University Press, 1992).
42. Min Zhou and Carl L. Bankston, III, "Social Capital and the Adaptation of the Second Generation: The Case of Vietnamese Youth in New Orleans," pp. 197–220 in *The New Second Generation*, Alejandro Portes (ed.) (New York: Russell Sage Foundation 1996).
43. "Canada," *NewMedia TrendWatch*, 2013, www.newmediatrendwatch.com/markets-by-country/11-long-haul/45-canada, accessed August 15, 2013.
44. Vikas Sharm, Mehar Singh, and Amit Kumar Pahwa, "The Revolution in Digitized ICTs and Emergence of Social Networking Sites Transformed Traditional Media to New Mass Media: A Rise of New Age Media," *Indian Streams Research Journal*, 2012. 2(4): 1–4.
45. Sean Gelles, "Social Media Is Mass Media," March 14, 2013, www.econtentmag.com/Articles/Column/Social-Pulse/-Social-Media-is-Mass-Media-88315.htm, accessed August 15, 2013.
46. Erving Goffman, *Asylums: Essays on the Social Situation of Mental Patients and Other Inmates* (Chicago: Aldine, 1961).
47. Alvin Powell, "Former Canadian Leader Campbell Addresses Gender Bias: Discusses 'If She Knew Then What She Knows Now' with Harvard Women's Group," *Harvard University Gazette*, 2007, www.news.harvard.edu/gazette/2003/02.27/03-campbell.html, accessed October 5, 2010.
48. Ibid.
49. Kirstie Farrar, Dale Kunkel, Erica Biely, Keren Eyal, Rena Fandrich, and Edward Donnerstein, "Sexual Messages during Primetime Programming," *Sexuality & Culture*, 2003. 7(3): 7–38.
50. Harold Garfinkel, "Conditions of Successful Degradation Ceremonies," *American Journal of Sociology*, 1956. 61(2): 420–424.
51. Howard S. Becker, "The Politics of Presentation: Goffman and Total Institutions," *Symbolic Interaction*, 2003. 26(4): 659–669.
52. "Public Postsecondary Enrolments and Graduates, 2010/2011," *Statistics Canada*, January 23, 2013, www.statcan.gc.ca/daily-quotidien/130123/dq130123a-eng.pdf, accessed August 15, 2013.
53. "Impact," *The Charter of Rights and Freedoms*, http://charterofrights.ca/en/02_00_01, accessed October 3, 2010.
54. David Hutton, "'Just Society' Has Evolved, Justin Trudeau Says," *The Vancouver Sun*, www.vancouversun.com/news/Just+society+evolved+Justin+Trudeau+says/3599384/story.html#ixzz11JedbBv7, accessed October 3, 2010.
55. "History," *The Charter of Rights and Freedoms*, http://charterofrights.ca/en/26_00_01, accessed October 3, 2010.
56. "Impact," *The Charter of Rights and Freedoms*.
57. Canadian Human Rights Commission, "The *Canadian Charter of Rights and Freedoms*," www.chrc-ccdp.ca/en/timePortals/milestones/113mile.asp, accessed October 3, 2010.

CHAPTER 5

1. Francis Adu-Febiri and Everett Ofori, *Succeeding from the Margins of Canadian Society: A Strategic Resource for New Immigrants, Refugees and International Students* (British Columbia: CCB Publishing, 2009). Reprinted with permission of CCB Publishing.
2. Statistics Canada, "Table 202-0405: Upper Income Limits and Income Shares of Total Income Quintiles, by Economic Family Type, 2008 Constant Dollars, Annual," *CANSIM* (database), http://estat.statcan.gc.ca/cgi-win/cnsmcgi.exe?Lang=E&EST-Fi=EStat/English/CII_1-eng.htm, accessed September 20, 2010.
3. Lindsay McLaren, Jenny Godley, and Ian A. S. MacNairn, "Social Class, Gender, and Time Use: Implications for the Social Determinants of Body Weight?" November, 2009, www.statcan.gc.ca/pub/82-003-x/2009004/article/11020-eng.pdf, accessed August 16, 2013.
4. Yanjie Bian, "Chinese Social Stratification and Social Mobility," *Annual Review of Sociology*, 2002. 28: 91–116.
5. James FitzGerald, *Old Boys: The Powerful Legacy of Upper Canada College* (Toronto: Macfarlane, Walter & Ross, 1994), http://jamesfitzgerald.info/Excerpts.html, accessed September 29, 2010.
6. Ibid.
7. Ibid.
8. Robert K. Merton, "The Role-Set: Problems in Sociological Theory," *British Journal of Sociology*, 1957. 8: 106–120; Robert K. Merton, *Social Theory and Social Structure*, revised and enlarged ed. (New York: The Free Press, 1968).
9. Jonathan Turner (1997) quoted in Seumas Miller, "Social Institutions," *The Stanford Encyclopedia of Philosophy*, Fall 2012, http://plato.stanford.edu/archives/fall2012/entries/social-institutions/, accessed August 16, 2013.
10. Stephanie Coontz, *Marriage, a History: How Love Conquered Marriage* (New York: Penguin Publishing, 2005).
11. Library and Archives Canada, www.collectionscanada.gc.ca/sos/002028-5100-e.html, accessed September 19, 2010; The Weather Doctor, www.islandnet.com/~see/weather/almanac/arc2008/alm08jan.htm, accessed September 19, 2010.
12. Émile Durkheim, *The Division of Labor in Society*, with introduction by Lewis A. Coser, W. D. Halls (trans.) (New York: The Free Press, 1893/1997).
13. Ibid.
14. Ibid.
15. Ferdinand Tönnies, *Community and Society (Gemeinschaft und Gesellschaft)*. Charles P. Loomis (trans., ed.) (East Lansing, MI: Michigan State University Press, 1887).
16. Steven Brint, "*Gemeinschaft* Revisited: A Critique and Reconstruction of the Community Concept," *Sociological Theory*, 2001. 19(1): 1–23.
17. Charles H. Cooley, *Human Nature and Social Order*, revised ed. (New York: Scribner and Sons, 1922).
18. Ibid.
19. Henry Tajfel, "Social Categorization, Social Identity, and Social Comparison," pp. 61–76, in *Differentiation between Social Groups: Studies in Social Psychology of Intergroup Relations*, Henry Tajfel (ed.) (London: Academic Press, 1978); Robert K. Merton, *Social Theory and Social Structure* (New York: The Free Press, 1968).
20. Merton, *Social Theory and Social Structure*.

21. Daan Scheepers, Russell Spears, Bertjan Doosje, and Antony S. R. Manstead, "Diversity in In-group Bias: Structural Factors, Situational Features, and Social Functions," *Journal of Personality and Social Psychology*, 2006. 90(6): 944–960.
22. B. Ann Bettencourt, Kelly Charlton, and Nancy Dorr, "Status Differences and In-group Bias: A Meta-analytic Examination of the Effects of Status Stability, Status Legitimacy, and Group Permeability," *Psychological Bulletin*, 2001. 127(4): 520–542.
23. Henry Tajfel and John Turner, "The Social Identity Theory of Intergroup Behavior," pp. 7–24, in S. Worschel and W. G. Austin (eds.), *Psychology and Intergroup Relations* (Chicago: Nelson-Hall, 1986).
24. Courtney D. Von Hippel, "When People Would Rather Switch Than Fight: Out-group Favoritism among Temporary Employees," *Group Processes and Intergroup Relations*, 2006. 9(4): 533–546.
25. Ibid.
26. Ibid.
27. Charles H. Cooley, *Human Nature and the Social Order*.
28. Georg Simmel, *The Sociology of Georg Simmel*, Kurt Wolfe (ed.) (New York: The Free Press, 1902/1950).
29. Ibid.
30. Ron Adams, "Hikikomori/Otaku Japan's Latest Out-Group," http://eclip5e.visualassault.org/assets/Hikikomori_Japans_Latest_Outcasts.pdf, accessed June 11, 2008.
31. Ibid.
32. Ibid.
33. Ibid.
34. Martin O'Malley, "One of Our Best and Brightest," *CBC News*, www.canadahistory.com/sections/Politics/pm/pierretrudeau.htm, accessed October 13, 2010.
35. Ibid.; "The October Crisis," *Historica*, www.histori.ca/peace/page.do?pageID=342, accessed October 13, 2010.
36. "Pierre Elliott Trudeau: Philosopher and Prime Minister," *CBC Digital Archives*, http://archives.cbc.ca/politics/prime_ministers/topics/2192/, accessed October 13, 2010.
37. Henry Hamburger, Melvin Guyer, and John Fox, "Group Size and Composition," *The Journal of Conflict Resolution*, 1975. 19(3): 503–531.
38. James Tucker and S. Thomas Friedman, "Population Density and Group Size," *American Journal of Sociology*, 1972. 77(4): 742–749.
39. Kurt Lewin, Ronald Lippit, and Ralph K. White, "Patterns of Aggressive Behavior in Experimentally Created Social Climates," *Journal of Social Psychology*, 1939. 10: 271–299.
40. Ibid.
41. Ibid.
42. Ibid.
43. John C. Maxwell, *Leadership 101: What Every Leader Needs to Know* (Nashville, TN: Thomas Nelson Publishers, 2002).
44. Solomon Asch, *Social Psychology* (Englewood Cliffs, NJ: Prentice Hall, 1952).
45. Irving L. Janis, *Victims of Groupthink: A Psychological Study of Foreign-Policy Decisions and Fiascoes* (Boston: Houghton Mifflin, 1972); Irving L. Janis, *Groupthink: Psychological Studies of Policy Decisions and Fiascoes* (Boston: Houghton Mifflin, 1983).
46. Janis, *Groupthink*.
47. James S. Coleman, "Social Capital in the Creation of Human Capital," *American Journal of Sociology*, 1988. 94(S): 95–120.
48. Coleman, "Social Capital in the Creation of Human Capital"; Pierre Bourdieu, "The Forms of Capital," *Handbook of Theory and Research for the Sociology of Education*, John G. Richardson (ed.) (New York: Greenwood, 1986).
49. L. Li Xue, *Social Capital and Employment Entry of Recent Immigrants to Canada: Evidence from the Longitudinal Survey of Immigrants to Canada (LSIC) Wave 1 and Wave 2*, 2007, http://ceris.metropolis.net/9thMetropolisConference/WorkshopPresentations/B1_Xue.pdf, accessed October 12, 2010.
50. Mark S. Granovetter, "The Strength of Weak Ties," *American Journal of Sociology*, 1973. 78(6): 1360–1380.
51. Robert D. Putnam, "Bowling Alone: America's Declining Social Capital," *Journal of Democracy*, 1995. 6(1): 65–78.
52. Jennifer Barber, Lisa D. Pearce, Indra Chaudhury, and Susan Gurung, "Voluntary Associations and Fertility Limitation," *Social Forces*, 2002. 80(4): 1369–1401.
53. Amitai Etzioni, *A Comparative Analysis of Complex Organizations: On Power, Involvement, and Their Correlates* (New York: The Free Press, 1975).
54. Ibid.
55. Ibid.
56. Ibid.
57. Amitai Etzioni and Edward W. Lehman, *A Sociological Reader on Complex Organizations*, 3rd ed. (New York: Holt, Rinehart and Winston, 1980).
58. Max Weber, "Max Weber Bureaucracy," pp. 99–108, in *Readings in Social Theory: The Classical Tradition to Post-Modernism*, 4th ed., James Farganis (ed.) (New York: McGraw-Hill, 1978/2004); Max Weber, *Max Weber: Essays in Sociology*, Hans H. Gerth and C. Wright Mills (trans., ed.) (New York: Oxford University Press, 1946).
59. Ibid.
60. Émile Durkheim, *Rules of Sociological Method*, George E. G. Catlin (ed.), Sarah A. Solovay and John H. Mueller (trans.) (New York: The Free Press of Glenco, 1895).
61. Jared Diamond, *Collapse: How Societies Choose to Fail or Succeed* (New York: Viking Penguin Press, 2005).
62. Jared Diamond, *Guns, Germs, and Steel: The Fates of Human Societies* (New York: W.W. Norton and Company, 1999).
63. Durkheim, *Rules of Sociological Method*; D. F. Aberle, A. K. Cohen, A. K. Davis, M. J. Levy Jr., and F. X. Sutton, "The Functional Prerequisites of a Society," *Ethics*, 1950. 60(2): 100–111; Raymond W. Mack and Calvin P. Bradford, *Transforming America: Patterns of Social Change*, 2nd ed. (New York: Random House, 1979); Diamond, *Guns, Germs, and Steel*; Diamond, *Collapse*.
64. "Critique of Hegel's *Philosophy of Right Karl Marx, 1843*," www.marxists.org/archive/marx/works/1843/critiquehpr/ch03.htm#027, accessed August 28, 2008.
65. Richard D. Rosenberg and Eliezer Rosenstein, "Participation and Productivity: An Empirical Study," *Industrial and Labor Relations Review*, 1980, 33(3): 355–367; Henry Levin, "Worker Democracy and Worker Productivity," *Social Justice Research*, 2006. 19(1): 109–121.
66. Tove H. Hammer, Steven C. Curral, and Robert N. Stern, "Worker Representation on Boards of Directors: A Study of Competing Roles," *Industrial and Labor Relations Review*, 1991. 44(4): 661–680.
67. Statistics Canada, "Average Hourly Wages of Employees by Selected Characteristics and Profession, Unadjusted Data, by Province (monthly)," www40.statcan.ca/l01/cst01/labr69a-eng.htm, accessed October 4, 2010.
68. HRSDC, "Gender Composition and Wages: Why Is Canada Different from the United States?" 2006, www.hrsdc.gc.ca/eng/cs/sp/hrsd/prc/publications/research/2000-000181/page04.shtml, accessed September 30, 2010.
69. Marie Drolet, "New Evidence on Gender Pay Differentials: Does Measurement Matter?" *Canadian Public Policy*, March 2002. 28(1), 1–16. www.jstor.org/stable/3552156, accessed October 4, 2010.
70. Edward T. Hall, *The Hidden Dimension* (New York: Anchor Books, 1966, 1982). Hall's study was conducted in the United States. However, Canada and the U.S. are both "low-context" cultures where such features as personal space are alike.
71. Ibid.
72. Cleveland Gordon, Barry Forer, Douglas Hyatt, Christa Japel, and Michael Krashinsky. "New Evidence about Child Care in Canada: Use Patterns, Affordability and Quality," *IRPP Choices*, 2008. 14(12), p. 8.
73. Lynn Robson, "A Snap Shot of Child Care," *CBC News*, February 9, 2005. www.cbc.ca/news/background/daycare/canada_snapshot.html, accessed September 19, 2010.
74. *New Evidence about Child Care in Canada*.
75. Ibid.
76. Cleveland Gordon, Barry Forer, Douglas Hyatt, Christa Japel, and Michael Krashinsky. "New Evidence about Child Care in Canada: Use Patterns, Affordability and Quality," *IRPP Choices*, 2008. 14(12), p. 8.
77. "Budget 2010 Proposes Changes to Universal Child Care Benefit," *Government of Canada*, www.universalchildcare.ca/eng/messages/2010/100603.shtml, accessed September 19, 2010.
78. "Daycare: The Debate over Space," *CBC News*, February 11, 2009, www.cbc.ca/consumer/story/2009/02/06/f-daycare.html, accessed September 19, 2010.

CHAPTER 6

1. Stephen Lewis, *Race against Time* (Toronto: House of Anansi Press, 2005). Reprinted by permission of House of Anansi Press.
2. Kevin Bales, *Disposable People: New Slavery in the Global Economy* (Berkeley, CA: University of California Press, 1999).
3. Central Intelligence Agency, "Country Comparison: Population," *The World Factbook*, www.cia.gov/library/publications/the-world-factbook/rankorder/2119rank.html, accessed September 4, 2013.
4. Bales, *Disposable People*.
5. Michael Overall, "Workers Allege Abuses," *Tulsa World*, February 1, 2002, p. 1; Michael Overall, "Workers Free to Leave, Pickle Testifies," *Tulsa World*, September 11, 2003, p. A1; Michael Overall, "Verdict:

Guilty: Judgment Exceeds $1 Million," *Tulsa World*, May 25, 2006, p. A1.
6. John Henry Hutton, *Caste in India, Its Nature, Function and Origin*, 4th ed. (Oxford: Oxford University Press, 1963).
7. David K. Shipler, *The Working Poor: Invisible in America* (New York: Vintage Books, 2005).
8. Robin W. Winks, "Slavery," *The Canadian Encyclopedia*, www.thecanadianencyclopedia.com, accessed October 17, 2010.
9. "Sex Slaves Staffed Brothels, Police Say," *CBC News*, October 13, 2010, www.cbc.ca/canada/british-columbia/story/2010/10/13/bc-metro-vancouver-brothels-sex-slaves.html, accessed October 17, 2010.
10. Winks, "Slavery."
11. "Black History in Canada," *Owen Sound's Black History* website, www.osblackhistory.com/history.php, accessed October 17, 2010.
12. Winks, "Slavery"; Linda L. Lindsay, Stephen Beach, and Bruce Ravelli, *Core Concepts in Sociology*, 2nd Canadian in-class ed. (Toronto: Pearson Education Canada, 2009); "Black History in Canada."
13. Hutton, *Caste in India*; Narendra Jadhav, *Untouchables: My Family's Triumphant Journey Out of the Caste System in Modern India* (New York: Scribner, 2007).
14. Karl Marx, "Economic and Philosophic Manuscripts of 1844," pp. 37–42, in *Readings in Social Theory: The Classical Tradition to Post-Modernism*, 4th ed., by James Farganis (ed.) (New York: McGraw-Hill, 1844/2004); Karl Marx, *Capital: A Critique of Political Economy*, Vol. 1. (New York: International Publishers, 1867/1967); Karl Marx and Friedrich Engels, "Manifesto of This Communist Party," pp. 26–36, in *Readings in Social Theory: The Classical Tradition to Post-Modernism*, 4th ed., James Farganis (ed.) (New York: McGraw-Hill, 1845/2004).
15. Ibid.
16. Ibid.
17. Max Weber, *Economy and Society: An Outline of Interpretive Sociology*, Guether Rothe and Claus Wittich (eds.) (Berkeley: University of California Press, 1978); Max Weber, "Class, Status, Party," pp. 116–126, in *Readings in Social Theory: The Classical Tradition to Post-Modernism*, 4th ed., James Farganis (ed.) (New York: McGraw-Hill, 1978/2004).
18. Marx, "Economic and Philosophic Manuscripts of 1844"; Marx, *Capital*; Marx and Engels, "Manifesto of This Communist Party."
19. World Bank Group, "Poverty," 2011, http://go.worldbank.org/VL7N3V6F20, accessed August 16, 2013.
20. World Bank Group, "How We Classify Countries," 2013, http://data.worldbank.org/about/country-classifications, accessed August 16, 2013.
21. Conference Board of Canada, "World Income Inequality," 2013, www.conferenceboard.ca/hcp/hot-topics/worldinequality.aspx, accessed August 16, 2013.
22. UNDP, "Human Development Report," 2013, http://hdr.undp.org/en/humandev/, accessed August 16, 2013.
23. Ibid.
24. The Praxis Ethiopia Foundation, "The 7 Facts You Need to Know about Extreme Poverty," www.praxisethiopia.org/ep/extreme_poverty.htm, accessed October 15, 2010.
25. Conference Board of Canada, "World Income Inequality."
26. United Nations, "The Millennium Development Goals Report: Statistical Annex 2006," http://unstats.un.org/unsd/mdg/Default.aspx, accessed April 23, 2007.
27. World Health Organization, UNICEF, UNFPA and The World Bank, *Trends in Maternal Mortality: 1990 to 2008*, 2010, pp. 1, 42, www.who.int/reproductivehealth/publications/monitoring/9789241500265/en/, accessed September 5, 2013.
28. Ibid, p. 42 (Appendix 12). (Note: WHO defines maternal death as "The death of a woman while pregnant or within 42 days of termination of pregnancy, irrespective of the duration and site of the pregnancy, from any cause related to or aggravated by the pregnancy or its management but not from accidental or incidental causes," p. 4.)
29. Timothy M. Smeeding and Lee Rainwater, "Comparing Living Standards across Nations: Real Incomes at the Top, the Bottom, and the Middle," *Social Policy Research Centre*, December 2002, http://apps.olin.wustl.edu/macarthur/papers/smeeding-livingstandards.pdf, accessed September 5, 2013.
30. Mercer LLC, "Quality of Living Worldwide City Rankings 2010—Mercer Survey," May 26, 2010, www.mercer.com/press-releases/quality-of-living-report-2010, accessed October 8, 2010.
31. Ibid.
32. "Country Comparison: Life Expectancy at Birth," *CIA Factbook*, www.cia.gov/library/publications/the-world-factbook/rankorder/2102rank.html, accessed October 15, 2010.
33. Daniel J. Slottje, Gerald W. Scully, Joseph Gerald Hirschberg, and Kath Hayes "Measuring the Quality of Life across Countries," *Review of Economics and Statistics*, 1991. 73(4): 684–693.
34. Kai Müller, "The World Economic and Social Development Ranking List," *Global Policy Forum*, March 18, 2000, www.globalpolicy.org/nations/kaiswork.htm.
35. Daniel J. Slottje, 1991 table reproduced in Myles I. Friedman, *Improving the Quality of Life: A Holistic Scientific Strategy* (Westport, CT: Praeger Publishers, 1997).
36. Li Lian Ong and Jason D. Mitchell, "Professors and Hamburgers: An International Comparison of Real Academic Salaries," *Applied Economics*, 2000. 32: 869–876.
37. Walter W. Rostow, *The Stages of Economic Growth* (London: Cambridge University Press, 1962).
38. Jared Diamond, *Guns, Germs, and Steel: The Fates of Human Societies* (New York: W.W. Norton & Company, 1997).
39. Ibid.
40. Ibid.
41. Ibid.
42. Jacques Diouf, "Food Security and the Challenge of the MDGs," *UN Chronicle*, No. 4, 2007.
43. Ibid.
44. Diamond, *Guns, Germs, and Steel.*
45. Immanuel Wallerstein, *The Modern World System: Capitalist Agriculture and the Origins of the European World-Economy in the Sixteenth Century* (New York: Academic Press, 1974); Immanuel Wallerstein, *The Capitalist World-Economy* (New York: Cambridge University Press, 1979).
46. Central Intelligence Agency, "Nigeria," *The World Factbook*, www.cia.gov/library/publications/the-world-factbook/print/ni.html, accessed July 24, 2008; Central Intelligence Agency, "Iraq," *The World Factbook*, www.cia.gov/library/publications/the-world-factbook/print/iz.html, accessed July 24, 2008.
47. Richard H. Robbins, *Talking Points on Global Issues: A Reader* (Boston: Allyn & Bacon, 2004); Richard H. Robbins, *Global Problems and the Culture of Capitalism* (Boston: Allyn & Bacon, 1999).
48. Michael Harrington, *The Vast Majority: The Journey to the World's Poor* (New York: Simon & Schuster, 1977).
49. Margaret Hanson and James J. Hentz, "Neocolonialism and Neoliberalism in South Africa and Zambia," *Political Science Quarterly*, 1999. 114(3): 479–502.
50. Leslie Sklair, "The Transnational Capitalist Class and Global Politics: Deconstructing the Corporate State Connection," *International Political Science Review*, 2002. 23(2): 159–174.
51. Günseli Berik, Yan van der Meulen Rodgers, and Joseph E. Zveglich, "International Trade and Gender Wage Discrimination, Evidence from East Asia," *Review of Development Economics*, 2004. 8(2): 237–254.
52. A. Aboubakr Badawi, "The Social Dimension of Globalization and Health," *Perspectives on Global Development and Technology*, 2004. 3(1–2): 73–90.
53. Bales, *Disposable People*.
54. Jonathan Crush, "The Global Raiders: Nationalism, Globalization and the South African Brain Drain," *Journal of International Affairs*, 2002. 56(1): 147–173.
55. Max Weber, *The Protestant Ethic and the Spirit of Capitalism* (London: Allen and Unwin, 1930).
56. Thorstein Veblen, *The Theory of the Leisure Class: An Economic Study in the Evolution of Institutions* (Middlesex: The Echo Library, 2007).
57. Public Health Agency of Canada, *Maternal Mortality in Canada*, www.phac-aspc.gc.ca/rhs-ssg/maternal-maternelle/mortality-mortalite/index-eng.php#tbl1, Accessed August 24, 2013.
58. UNFPA, "Gender Equality Fact Sheet," www.unfpa.org/swp/2005/presskit/factsheets/facts_gender.htm, accessed October 18, 2010; M. Buvinic, "Women in Poverty: A New Global Underclass," *Foreign Policy*, 1997. 108, retrieved from Ebsco database.
59. McDonalds.ca, "McDonald's Worldwide," 2013, www.mcdonalds.ca/ca/en/our_story/mcdonalds_worldwide.html, accessed August 16, 2013.
60. USAID, "New Frontiers in U.S. Foreign Aid," www.usaid.gov/policy/, accessed July 9, 2007.
61. "Canadian Foreign Aid," *Maps of the World* website, http://finance.mapsofworld.com/aid/foreign/canadian.html, accessed October 18, 2010.
62. Anup Shah, "Foreign Aid for Development Assistance," *Global Issues*, updated April 25, 2010. www.globalissues.org/article/35/foreign-aid-development-assistance, accessed October 18, 2010.
63. Ibid. (using OECD figures).
64. "Development Aid Rose in 2009 and Most Donors Will Meet 2010 Aid Targets," *OECD*, April 14, 2010, www.oecd.org/investment/stats/devel-

opmentaidrosein2009andmostdonorswillmeet2010aidtargets.htm, accessed September 4, 2013.

CHAPTER 7

1. John Porter, *The Vertical Mosaic: An Analysis of Social Class and Power in Canada*, (Toronto: University of Toronto Press, 1965). Reprinted with permission of the publisher.
2. Statistics Canada, "Income of Canadians, 2010," www.statcan.gc.ca/daily-quotidien/120618/dq120618b-eng.htm, accessed August 18, 2013.
3. Statistics Canada, Table 202-0701, "Market, Total and After-tax Income, by Economic Family Type and Income Quintiles, 2010 Constant Dollars," www5.statcan.gc.ca/cansim/pick-choisir?lang=eng&p2=33&id=, accessed September 4, 2013.
4. Statistics Canada, "Income of Canadians, 2010."
5. Armine Yalnizyan, "The Rise of Canada's Richest 1%," *Canadian Centre for Policy Alternatives*, December 2010, www.policyalternatives.ca/sites/default/files/uploads/publications/National%20Office/2010/12/Richest%201%20Percent.pdf, accessed August 18, 2013.
6. Conference Board of Canada, "Income Inequality," www.conferenceboard.ca/hcp/details/society/income-inequality.aspx, accessed August 18, 2013.
7. Statistics Canada, "The Wealth of Canadians: An Overview of the Results of the Income Statistics Division," http://dsp-psd.pwgsc.gc.ca/Collection/Statcan/13F0026M/13F0026MIE2006001.pdf, accessed September 23, 2010.
8. Statistics Canada, Table 4, "Market Basket Measure Thresholds for Reference Family of Two Adults and Two Children, by MBM Region," June 18, 2012, www.statcan.gc.ca/pub/75f0002m/2012002/tbl/tbl04-eng.htm, accessed May 14, 2013.
9. Human Resources and Skills Development Canada, "Indicators of Well-Being in Canada," www4.hrsdc.gc.ca/h.4m.2@-eng.jsp, accessed September 24, 2010.
10. Human Resources and Skills Development Canada, "Low Income in Canada: 2000–2006 Using the Market Basket Measure," www.hrsdc.gc.ca/eng/publications_resources/research/categories/inclusion/2008/sp-864-10-2008/page00.shtml, accessed September 23, 2010; Statistics Canada, "Low Income Lines: 2008–2009," www.statcan.gc.ca/pub/75f0002m/75f0002m2010005-eng.htm, accessed September 22, 2010.
11. C. Wright Mills, *The Power Elite* (New York: Oxford University Press, 1956).
12. Wallace Clement, "Elites," *The Canadian Encyclopedia*, www.thecanadianencyclopedia.com/index.cfm?PgNm=TCE&Params=A1ARTA0002573, accessed September 20, 2010.
13. Michael D. Martinez, "Voters and Nonvoters in Canadian Federal Elections," www.clas.ufl.edu/users/martinez/cpsa08/martinez_cpsa08.pdf, accessed September 22, 2010.
14. Monica Boyd, "A Socioeconomic Scale for Canada: Measuring Occupational Status from the Census," *Canadian Review of Sociology*, 2008. 45: 51–91.
15. Lee Rainwater and William Yancey, *The Moynihan Report and the Politics of Controversy* (Cambridge, MA: The MIT Press, 1968).
16. Feeding America, "Hunger and Poverty Statistics," http://feedingamerica.org/faces-of-hunger/hunger-101/hunger-and-poverty-statistics.aspx, accessed January 20, 2011.
17. Ibid.
18. ChildStats.gov, "America's Children in Brief: Key National Indicators of Well-Being, 2008," www.childstats.gov/americaschildren/econ_fig.asp, accessed July 21, 2008.
19. Ibid.
20. Sean Alfano, "Senators Are in the Money, 54 Are Millionaires, According to Financial Disclosure Records," *New York Daily News*, October 28, 2010, www.nydailynews.com/news/politics/2010/10/28/2010-10-22_senators_are_in_the_money_54_are_millionaires_according_to_financial_disclosure_.html, accessed January 20, 2011.
21. Ibid.
22. John Goyder, "The Dynamics of Occupational Prestige: 1975–2000," *Canadian Review of Sociology & Anthropology*, 2005. 42: 1–23.
23. Monica Boyd, "A Socioeconomic Scale for Canada: Measuring Occupational Status from the Census," *Canadian Review of Sociology*, 45: 51–91.
24. Porter, *The Vertical Mosaic: An Analysis of Social Class and Power in Canada*, (Toronto: University of Toronto Press, 1965).
25. Harold R. Kerbo, *Social Stratification and Inequality: Class Conflict in Historical, Comparative and Global Perspective*, 6th ed. (New York: McGraw-Hill, 2006).
26. Ashbury College, "An International Education in the Heart of the Nation's Capital," www.ashbury.on.ca/Page.aspx?pid=594, accessed September 19, 2010.
27. Dennis Gilbert, *The American Class Structure in an Age of Growing Inequality*, 6th ed. (Belmont, CA: Wadsworth, 2003).
28. Catherine E. Ross, John R. Reynolds, and Karlyn J. Geis, "The Contingent Meaning of Neighborhood Stability." *American Sociological Review*, 2000. 65: 581-597.
29. Catherine S. Ford, "Concentrated Poverty in Urban Canada: Health Issues for Consideration," www.fp.ucalgary.ca/chaps/Ford.pdf, accessed September 19, 2010.
30. Jeanne Brooks-Gunn, Greg Duncan, Pamela Klebanove, and Naomi Sealand, "Do Neighborhoods Influence Child and Adolescent Development?" *American Journal of Sociology*, 1993. 99: 353–395.
31. Gary Solon, "Intergenerational Income Mobility in the United States," *The American Economic Review*, 1992. 82: 393–408;
32. Kingsley Davis and Wilbert E. Moore, "Some Principles of Stratification," *American Sociological Review*, 1944. 10: 242–249.
33. Statistics Canada, "Average Weekly Earnings (Including Overtime), Educational and Related Services, by Province and Territory," March 27, 2013, www.statcan.gc.ca/tables-tableaux/sum-som/l01/cst01/educ05-eng.htm, accessed August 18, 2013.
34. Statistics Canada, "Average Annual Employment Income in Constant 2005 Dollars, Canada," www.statcan.gc.ca/pub/85-002-x/2008010/article/10730/tbl/tbl04-eng.htm, accessed September 20, 2010.
35. Sports City, "NHL Salaries: 2012–13 Top 20 Salaries for Centers," November 14, 2012, www.sportscity.com/nhl-salaries-2012-13-top-20-salaries-for-centers/2012/11/14/, accessed August 18, 2013.
36. Melvin Tumin, "On Inequality," *American Sociological Review*, 1963. 28: 19–26.
37. Edward G. Grabb and Ronald D. Lambert, "The Subjective Meanings of Social Class among Canadians," *The Canadian Journal of Sociology*, 1982. 7: 297–307.
38. Statistics Canada, "Table 202-0101: Distribution of Earnings, by Sex, 2010 Constant Dollars," www5.statcan.gc.ca/cansim/pick-choisir?lang=eng&p2=33&id=2020101, accessed September 4, 2013.
39. "Quebec Doctors Lagging in Fee-for-Service Payments," *CTV News*, December 21, 2006, www.ctv.ca/CTVNews/Health/20061221/quebec_doctors_061221/, accessed September 20, 2010.
40. Grabb and Lambert, "The Subjective Meanings of Social Class."
41. Senate of Canada, "In from the Margins: A Call to Action on Poverty, Housing and Homelessness," www.parl.gc.ca/40/2/parlbus/commbus/senate/com-e/citi-e/rep-e/rep02dec09-e.pdf, accessed September 20, 2010.
42. "Minimum Wage Laws—The State of Pay in Canada," *CBC News*, January 23, 2009, www.cbc.ca/money/story/2009/01/23/f-money-minimum-wage.html, accessed August 18, 2013.
43. Ibid.

CHAPTER 8

1. Melody Hessing, Michael Howlett, and Tracy Summerville, *Canadian Natural Resource and Environmental Policy: Political Economy and Public Policy*, 2nd ed. (Vancouver: UBC Press. 2005). Reprinted by permission of UBC Press.
2. Central Intelligence Agency, "Country Comparison: Population," *The World Factbook*, www.cia.gov/library/publications/the-world-factbook/rankorder/2119rank.html, accessed September 4, 2013.
3. Statistics Canada, "Population Estimate (May 24, 2013)," www.statcan.gc.ca/start-debut-eng.html, accessed August 18, 2013.
4. Statistics Canada, "Births, 2009," www.statcan.gc.ca/pub/84f0210x/84f0210x2009000-eng.pdf, accessed August 18, 2013.
5. Statistics Canada, "Deaths, 2009," www.statcan.gc.ca/daily-quotidien/120531/dq120531e-eng.pdf, accessed August 18, 2013.
6. Statistics Canada, "Infant Mortality Rates by Province and Territory (Both Sexes)," www.statcan.gc.ca/tables-tableaux/sum-som/l01/cst01/health21a-eng.htm, accessed August 18, 2013.
7. Statistics Canada, "Deaths, 2009."
8. Eric Neumayer, "HIV/AIDS and Cross-National Convergence in Life Expectancy," *Population and Development Review*, 2004. 30(4): 727–742.
9. Central Intelligence Agency, "Country Comparison: Life Expectancy at Birth," *The World Factbook*, www.cia.gov/library/publications/the-world-factbook/rankorder/2102rank.html?countryName=Canada&countryCode=ca®ionCode=noa&rank=12#ca, accessed August 18, 2013.
10. Eric Neumayer, "HIV/AIDS and Cross-National Convergence in Life Expectancy."
11. Statistics Canada, "Age Pyramid of Population of Canada, July 1, 1901–2001," www12.statcan.gc.ca/english/census01/products/analytic/Multimedia.cfm?M=1, accessed August 18, 2013.
12. A. Milan, "Migration: International, 2009," www.statcan.gc.ca/pub/91-209-x/2011001/article/11526-eng.pdf, accessed August 18, 2013.

13. John R. Bermingham, "Exponential Population Growth and Doubling Times: Are They Dead or Merely Quiescent?" *Population and Environment*, 2003. 24(4): 313–327.
14. Kingsley Davis, "The World Demographic Transition," *The Annals of the American Academy of Political and Social Science*, 1945. 237: 1–11; Edward M. Crenshaw, Matthew Christenson, and Doyle Ray Oakey, "Demographic Transition in Ecological Focus," *American Sociological Review*, 2000. 65(3): 371–391.
15. Naohiro Ogawa and Robert D. Retherford, "The Resumption of Fertility Decline in Japan: 1973–92," *Population and Development Review*, 1993. 19(4): 703–741.
16. Robert D. Retherford, Naohiro Ogawa, and Satomi Sakamoto, "Values and Fertility Change in Japan," *Population Studies*, 1996. 50(1): 5–25.
17. Cynthia G. Wagner, "Promoting Parenthood in Japan," *Futurist*, 2007. 41(3): 9–13.
18. Hayashi Yuka and Sebastian Moffett, "Cautiously, an Aging Japan Warms to Foreign Workers," *Wall Street Journal*, May 25, 2007. 249(122): A1–A12.
19. Paul Ehrlich, *The Population Bomb* (Cutchogue, NY: Buccaneer Books, 1968).
20. Donella H. Meadows, Dennis L. Meadows, Jorgen Randers, and William W. Behrens III, *The Limits to Growth* (New York, NY: Universe Books, 1972).
21. Kingsley Davis, "The World Demographic Transition"; Sarah F. Harbison and Warren C. Robinson, "Policy Implications of the Next World Demographic Transition," *Studies in Family Planning*, 2002. 33(1): 37–48.
22. Dudley Kirk, "Demographic Transition Theory," *Population Studies*, 1996. 50(3): 361–387.
23. Kingsley Davis, "The World Demographic Transition."
24. Edward M. Crenshaw, Matthew Christenson, and Doyle Ray Oakey, "Demographic Transition in Ecological Focus"; Richard A. Easterlin, "The Worldwide Standard of Living since 1800," *The Journal of Economic Perspectives*, 2000. 14(1): 7–26; Julian L. Simon, *Population Matters: People, Resources, Environment, and Immigration* (New Brunswick, NJ: Transactions Press, 1990); Julian L. Simon, *Theory of Population and Economic Growth* (New York: Basil Blackwell, 1986); Julian L. Simon, "One Aggregate Empirical Studies Relating to Population Variables to Economic Development," *Population and Development Review*, 1989. 15(2): 323–332.
25. Dudley Kirk, "Demographic Transition Theory."
26. Ibid.
27. Ibid.
28. U.S. Census Bureau, "International Data Base," www.census.gov/ipc/www/idb/, accessed September 19, 2008.
29. Canadian Sociological Association, "Environmental Sociology," www.csa-scs.ca/files/webapps/csapress/environment/?page_id=109, accessed August 18, 2013.
30. Riley E. Dunlap and Brent K. Marshall, "Environmental Sociology," pp. 329–340, in Clifton D. Bryant and Dennis L. Peck (eds.) *21st Century Sociology: A Reference Handbook* (Thousand Oaks, CA: SAGE Publications, 2007), www.sagepub.com/leonguerrero3e/study/chapters/handbook_articles/Handbook%2015.1.pdf, accessed August 18, 2013.
31. Daniel G. Bates and Judith Tucker (eds.), *Human Ecology: Contemporary Research and Practice* (New York: Springer Science and Business Media, 2010).
32. Hessing, Howlett, and Summerville, *Canadian Natural Resource and Environmental Policy*.
33. Dunlap and Marshall, "Environmental Sociology."
34. Ibid.
35. Dunlap and Marshall, "Environmental Sociology."
36. Hessing, Howlett, and Summerville, *Canadian Natural Resource and Environmental Policy*.
37. Leila R. Brammer, "Ecofeminism, the Environment, and Social Movements," paper presented at the National Communication Association Convention, New York, 1998, http://homepages.gac.edu/~lbrammer/Ecofeminism.html, accessed August 18, 2013.
38. Ibid.
39. Hessing, Howlett, and Summerville, *Canadian Natural Resource and Environmental Policy*.
40. Richard York, Eugene A. Rosa, and Thomas Deitz, "Bridging Environmental Science with Environmental Policy: Plasticity of Population, Affluence, and Technology," *Social Science Quarterly*, 2002. 83(1): 18–34; Richard York, Eugene A. Rosa, and Thomas Deitz, "Footprints on the Earth: The Environmental Consequences of Modernity," *American Sociological Review*, 2003. 68(2): 279–300.
41. Andrew K. Jorgenson and Thomas J. Burns, "The Political-Economic Causes of Change in the Ecological Footprints of Nations, 1991–2001: A Quantitative Investigation," *Social Science Research*, 2007. 36: 834–853.
42. Intergovernmental Panel on Climate Change, "Climate Change 2007: Synthesis Report," November 17, 2007, www.ipcc.ch/pdf/assessment-report/ar4/syr/ar4_syr.pdf, accessed September 4, 2013.
43. Linda Catoe, "Endangered Island Nations Call for Global Action on Climate Change," *The Guilfordian*, April 6, 2012. www.guilfordian.com/worldnation/2012/04/06/endangered-island-nations-call-for-global-action-on-climate-change/, accessed August 18, 2013.
44. Paul Hawken, *The Ecology of Commerce* (New York: Harper-Collins, 1994).
45. James Lee and Feng Wang, *One Quarter of Humanity: Malthusian Mythology and Chinese Realities, 1700–2000* (Cambridge, MA: Harvard University Press, 1999); Rachel Murphy, "Fertility and Distorted Sex Ratios in a Rural Chinese County: Culture, State, and Policy," *Population and Development Review*, 2003. 29(4): 595–626; Nancy E. Riley, "China's Population: New Trends and Challenges," *Population Bulletin*, 2004. 59(2): 3–36.
46. "Report: China's One-Child Policy Has Prevented 400 Million Births," *The International Herald Tribune*, November 9, 2006, www.iht.com/articles/ap/2006/11/09/asia/AS_GEN_China_One_Child_Policy.php.
47. Rachel Murphy, "Fertility and Distorted Sex Ratios in a Rural Chinese County: Culture, State, and Policy," *Population and Development Review*, 2003. 29(4): 595–626; Nancy E. Riley, "China's Population: New Trends and Challenges," *Population Bulletin*, 2004. 59(2): 3–36.
48. James Lee and Feng Wang, *One Quarter of Humanity*.
49. Ibid.

CHAPTER 9

1. Leo Driedger and Shiva S. Halli, "The Race Challenge 2000," pp. 1-3 in *Race and Racism: Canada's Challenge*, Leo Driedger and Shiva S. Halli (eds.) (Montreal: McGill-Queen's University Press, 2000).
2. American Anthropological Association, "American Anthropological Association Statement on 'Race,'" May 17, 1998, www.aaanet.org/stmts/racepp.htm, accessed August 23, 2013.
3. Statistics Canada, "Census Variables," www12.statcan.ca/census-recensement/2006/ref/dict/overview-apercu/pop5-eng.cfm, accessed September 29, 2010.
4. Ibid.
5. Ibid
6. Statistics Canada, "Profile for Canada, Provinces and Territories," www12.statcan.gc.ca/census-recensement/2006/dp-pd/prof/sac/Av-eng.cfm?LANG=E&APATH=3&DETAIL=1&DIM=2&FL=A&FREE=1&GC=0&GID=0&GK=0&GRP=1&PID=98628&PRID=0&PTYPE=89103&S=0&SHOWALL=No&SUB=0&Temporal=2006&THEME=81&VID=17646&VNAMEE=&VNAMEF=, accessed 2009.
7. Statistics Canada, "Canada Year Book 2011 – Aboriginal Peoples." www.statcan.gc.ca/pub/11-402-x/2011000/chap/ap-pa/ap-pa-eng.htm, accessed 2011.
8. Canadian Index of Well-Being, "Fact Sheet—How Are Canadians Really Doing? A Closer Look at Select Groups," www.ciw.ca/en/Media/09-12-16/df39996f-52af-4c21-a004-823133c15744.aspx, accessed October 9, 2010.
9. Feng Hou and Simon Coulombe, "Earnings Gaps for Canadian-Born Visible Minorities in the Public and Private Sectors," *Canadian Public Policy*, 2010. 36(1): 29–43.
10. Louis Wirth, "The Problem of Minority Groups," in *The Science of Man in the World Crisis*, Ralph Linton (ed.) (New York: Columbia University Press, 1945).
11. "Apartheid: Africana: The Encyclopedia of the African and African American Experience," Kwame Anthony Appiah and Henry Louis Gates, Jr., (eds.) in *Featured Selections*, www.africanaencyclopedia.com/apartheid/apartheid.html, accessed August 12, 2008.
12. CBC, "Reluctant Hero: The Donald Marshall Story," www.cbc.ca/lifeandtimes/marshall.html, Accessed October 9, 2010; Edward Butts, "Marshall, Donald, Jr.," *The Canadian Encyclopedia*, www.canadianencyclopedia.ca/index.cfm?PgNm=TCE&Params=A1ARTA0005123, accessed October 9, 2010.
13. Statistics Canada, "2011 National Household Survey: Immigration, Place of Birth, Citizenship, Ethnic Origin, Visible Minorities, Language and Religion," May 8, 2013, www.statcan.gc.ca/daily-quotidien/130508/dq130508b-eng.htm, accessed August 23, 2013.
14. Kathryn Blee, *Inside Organized Racism: Women in the Hate Movement* (Berkeley, CA: University of California Press, 2002).
15. Mark E. Hill, "Skin Color and Perception of Attractiveness among African Americans: Does Gender Make a Difference?" *Social Science Quarterly*, 2002. 65(1): 77–91.
16. Jared Diamond, *Guns, Germs, and Steel: The Fates of Human Societies* (New York: W.W. Norton and Company, 1999).
17. Chinese Canadian National Council, "History: The Chinese Head Tax and Exclusion Act," www.ccnc.ca/redress/history.html, accessed October 7, 2010.
18. Human Rights Watch, "Children Targeted in the Genocide," http://hrw.org/reports/2003/rwanda0403/rwanda0403-03.htm, accessed September 10, 2008.

19. Library and Archives Canada, "The Anti-Slavery Movement in Canada," www.collectionscanada.gc.ca/anti-slavery/index-e.html, accessed October 5, 2010.
20. Public Broadcasting Service, "Srebrenica: A Cry from the Grave," www.pbs.org/wnet/cryfromthegrave/massacre/massacre.html, accessed August 12, 2008.
21. Marcus Cox, "The Right to Return Home: International Intervention and Ethnic Cleansing in Bosnia and Herzegovina," *The International and Comparative Law Quarterly*, 1998. 47(3): 599–631.
22. Chris Stephen, "Court Wants Exemplary Karadzic Trial," *BBC News*, July 24, 2008, http://news.bbc.co.uk/2/hi/europe/7522908.stm, accessed August 12, 2008.
23. Stopracism.ca, "Groups and Individual Cases," www.stopracism.ca/content/groups-and-individual-cases, accessed October 8, 2010.
24. Ralph T. Pastore, "The Beothuks," www.heritage.nf.ca/aboriginal/beothuk.html, accessed October 3, 2010.
25. Harald Bauder and Bob Sharpe, "Residential Segregation of Visible Minorities in Canada's Gateway Cities," *Canadian Geographer*, 2002. 46(3): 204–222.
26. "Speaking out: Quebec's Debate over Language Laws," *CBC News*, www.cbc.ca/canada/story/2009/10/22/f-quebec-language-laws-bill-101.html, accessed October 7, 2010.
27. Eric Fong and Milena Gulia, "Differences in Neighborhood Qualities among Racial and Ethnic Groups in Canada," *Sociological Inquiry*, 1999. 69(4): 575–598.
28. Efie Gavaki, "Greek Immigration to Quebec: The Process and the Settlement," http://thesis.haverford.edu/dspace/bitstream/handle/10066/5554/Gavaki_17_1.pdf, accessed February 12, 2011.
29. Elections Canada, "Elections," www.elections.ca/content.aspx?section=ele&dir=turn&document=index&lang=e, accessed August 23, 2013.
30. Gerhard P. Bassler, "Germans," *The Canadian Encyclopedia*, www.thecanadianencyclopedia.com/index.cfm?PgNm=TCE&Params=A1ARTA0003238, accessed October 8, 2010.
31. Harry Loewen, "Mennonites," *Multicultural Canada*, www.multicultural-canada.ca/Encyclopedia/A-Z/m6, accessed October 8, 2010.
32. "Separation Anxiety: The 1995 Quebec Referendum," *CBC News*, http://archives.c.ca/politics/federal_politics/topics/1891/, accessed October 8, 2010.
33. "Castro, Fidel," *Encyclopœdia Britannica, 2008*, http://search.eb.com/eb/article-9020736, accessed September 30, 2008.
34. "Gandhi, Mohandas Karamchand," *Encyclopœdia Britannica, 2008*, http://search.eb.com/eb/article-22639, accessed September 30, 2008.
35. Ashley W. Doane, Jr., "Dominant Group Ethnic Identity in the United States: The Role of 'Hidden' Ethnicity in Intergroup Relations," *The Sociological Quarterly*, 1997. 38(3): 375–397.
36. Edna Bonacich, "A Theory of Ethnic Antagonism: The Split Labor Market". *American Sociological Review*, 1972, *37*(5), 547–559.
37. "RBC Replaces Canadian Staff with Foreign Workers," *CBC News*, April 6, 2013, www.cbc.ca/news/canada/british-columbia/story/2013/04/05/bc-rbc-foreign-workers.html, accessed August 23, 2013.
38. Jonathan Kozol, *Savage Inequalities: Children in America's Schools* (New York: Crown Publishers, 1991); Mary C. Waters and Karl Eschbach, "Immigration and Ethnic and Racial Inequality in the United States," *Annual Review of Sociology*, 1995. 21: 419–446; Grace Kao and Jennifer S. Thompson, "Racial and Ethnic Stratification in Educational Achievement and Attainment," *Annual Review of Sociology*, 2003. 29: 417–443; Rory McVeigh, "Structured Ignorance and Organized Racism in the United States," *Social Forces*, 2004. 82(3): 895–936.
39. Eduardo Bonilla-Silva, "The Linguistics of Color Blind Racism: How to Talk Nasty about Blacks without Sounding 'Racist,'" *Critical Sociology*, 2002. 28(1–2): 41–64.
40. Ibid.
41. Constance Backhouse, *Colour-Coded: A Legal History of Racism in Canada, 1900–1950* (Toronto: Osgoode Society for Canadian Legal History, 1999).
42. W.E.B. Du Bois, *The Souls of Black Folk* (New York: Penguin, 1903/1996).
43. Patricia Hill Collins, *Black Feminist Thought* (New York: Routledge, 1990); Darlene Clark Hine, "In the Kingdom of Culture: Black Women and the Intersection of Race, Gender, and Class," in *Lure and Loathing: Essays on Race, Identity and the Ambivalence of Assimilation*, Gerald Early (ed.) (New York: Penguin Press, 1993).
44. Ibid.
45. Supreme Court of Canada, SCC Case Information, May 22, 2009, www.scc-csc.gc.ca/case-dossier/cms-sgd/sum-som-eng.aspx?cas=33651, accessed January 23, 2011.
46. Barbara Bagilhole, *Understanding Equal Opportunities and Diversity: The Social Differentiations and Intersections of Inequality* (Bristol, UK: The Policy Press, 2009).
47. William J. Wilson, *The Declining Significance of Race: Blacks and Changing American Institutions*, 2nd ed. (Chicago: University of Chicago Press, 1980).
48. Eduardo Ramirez, "Revision of Minority Advantage," http://imprint.uwaterloo.ca/2010/jul/30/cover/revision-minority-advantage/, accessed October 9, 2010; Nick Aveling, "Tories to Review Affirmative-Action Hiring Practices," *Vancouver Sun*, July 23, 2010.

CHAPTER 10

1. Margrit Eichler, *The Double Standard: A Feminist Critique of Feminist Social Sciences* (London: Croom Helm Ltd., 1980).
2. Arlie Russell Hochschild and Anne Machung, *The Second Shift: Working Parents and the Revolution at Home* (New York: Penguin Books, 1989/2003).
3. "Men Doing More Housework, StatsCan Says," *CBC News*, March 4, 2008, www.cbc.ca/consumer/story/2008/03/04/housework-men.html, accessed October 19, 2010.
4. Britta N. Torgrimson and Christopher T. Minson, "Sex and Gender: What Is the Difference?" *Journal of Applied Physiology*, 2005. 99(3): 785–787.
5. Ivy Kennelly, Sabine N. Merz, and Judith Lorber, "What Is Gender?" *American Sociological Review*, 2001. 66(4): 598–605.
6. "Baby Raised Without 'Gender' Sets off Debate," *CTV News*, May 26, 2011, www.ctvnews.ca/baby-raised-without-gender-sets-off-debate-1.649286, accessed August 23, 2013.
7. Candace West and Don H. Zimmerman, "Doing Gender," *Gender and Society*, 1987. 1(2): 125–151.
8. Torgrimson and Minson, "Sex and Gender: What is the Difference?"
9. Michael A. Messner, "Barbie Girls versus Sea Monsters: Children Constructing Gender," *Gender and Society*, 2000. 14(6): 765–784.
10. Ibid.
11. Stephanie Coontz, *Marriage, a History: From Obedience to Intimacy, or How Love Conquered Marriage* (New York: Viking, 2005).
12. Government of Canada, "Justice Laws Website," http://laws-lois.justice.gc.ca/eng/acts/C-46/section-155.html, accessed August 23, 2013.
13. Alfred C. Kinsey, Wardell R. Pomeroy, and Clyde E. Martin, *Sexual Behavior in the Human Male* (Philadelphia, PA: W.B. Saunders, 1948).
14. Canadian Heritage, "Sexual Orientation and Human Rights," www.pch.gc.ca/pgm/pdp-hrp/canada/sxrnt-eng.cfm, accessed August 23, 2013.
15. Manhattan Toy Online Store, http://store.manhattantoy.com, accessed July 28, 2008.
16. Nerf, www.hasbro.com/nerf, accessed July 28, 2008.
17. Sharyn Graham Davis, *Challenging Gender Norms: Five Genders among the Bugis in Indonesia* (Belmont, CA: Thomson Wadsworth, 2007).
18. Ibid.
19. Statistics Canada, "Table 202-0101: Distribution of Earnings, by Sex, 2010 Constant Dollars, Annual, CANSIM (Database)," www5.statcan.gc.ca/cansim/a26, accessed August 23, 2013.
20. Statistics Canada, "Labour Force Survey, 2009," www40.statcan.gc.ca/l01/cst01/labor05-eng.htm, accessed October 21, 2010.
21. Families Count: "Profiling Canada's Families, 2010," www.vifamily.ca/media/webfm-uploads/Publications/FamiliesCount/Families_Count.pdf, accessed October 21, 2010.
22. Brian L. Rich, "On Inequality," *Sociological Perspectives: Papers from the 56th Annual Meeting*, Autumn 1995. 38(3): 357–380.
23. Miriam David, "Choice, Diversity and Equity in Secondary Schooling," *Oxford Review of Education*, 1997. 23(1): 77–87.
24. Geert Hofstede, "A Case for Comparing Apples with Oranges," *International Journal of Comparative Sociology*, 1998. 39(1): 16–31.
25. Kwintessential, "Masculinity," www.kwintessential.co.uk/intercultural/masculinity.html, accessed August 23, 2013.
26. The Hofstede Centre, "Canada," http://geert-hofstede.com/canada.html, accessed August 23, 2013.
27. "Women CEOs and Heads of the Financial Post 500," Catalyst.org, www.catalyst.org/publication/271/women-ceos-and-heads-of-the-financial-post-500, accessed October 21, 2010.
28. Margaret Mead, *Sex and Temperament* (New York, Harper Perennial, 1935).
29. Ibid.
30. Derek Freeman, *Margaret Mead and Samoa: The Making and Unmaking of an Anthropological Myth* (Cambridge, MA: Harvard University Press, 1983).
31. G. P. Murdock, "Comparative Data on the Division of Labor by Sex," *Social Forces*, 1937. 15: 551–553.
32. Hochschild and Machung, *The Second Shift: Working Parents and the Revolution at Home.*

33. Shelley J. Correll, "Gender and the Career Choice Process: The Role of Biased Self-Assessments," *The American Journal of Sociology*, 2001. 106(6): 1691–1730.
34. Talcott Parsons and Robert F. Bales, *Family Socialization and Interaction Processes* (London: Routledge and Kegan Paul Ltd., 1956).
35. "Women in National Parliaments: Situation as of 30 September 2010," *Inter-Parliamentary Union*, www.ipu.org/wmn-e/classif.htm, accessed October 22, 2010.
36. "Prime Minister Golda Meir," *The President and Prime Minister Memorial Council*, www.pmo.gov.il/PMOEng/Government/Memorial/PrimeMinisters/Golda.htm, accessed August 15, 2008; "Benazir Bhutto," Benazirbhutto.org, www.benazirbhutto.org/mbb-profile.html, accessed August 15, 2008; "Benazir Bhutto," *Encyclopædia Britannica Online*, http://search.eb.com/eb/article-9079076, accessed August 27, 2008.
37. Hendrik Hertzberg, "Exhillaration," *The New Yorker*, June 23, 2008, http://www.newyorker.com/talk/comment/2008/06/23/080623taco_talk_hertzberg, accessed August 26, 2008.
38. Susan Carroll, "Women Voters and the Gender Gap," www.apsanet.org/content_5270.cfm, accessed August 18, 2008.
39. Christine Williams, "The Glass Escalator: Hidden Advantages for Men in the 'Female' Professions," *Men's Lives*, 2007, http://jan.ucc.nau.edu/hdh9/ereserves/Williams_-_The_glass_escalator_PDF-1.pdf, accessed August 15, 2008.
40. "Former Governors General," *The Governor General of Canada*, www.gg.ca/document.aspx? id=55, accessed October 22, 2010.
41. Hugh Segal, quoted in *Debates of the Senate (Hansard)*, 2nd Session, 39th Parliament, Vol. 144, Issue 23, Dec. 12, 2007, www.patcarney.ca/pdf/RetirementTributesDecember12,2007.pdf, accessed October 22, 2010.
42. Ibid.
43. "Hon. Pat Carney, P.C.: Official Biography," www.patcarney.ca/officialbio.html, accessed October 22, 2010.
44. Andrea Dworkin, *Woman Hating* (Boston: Dutton, 1974).
45. Department of National Defence figures, cited in "Women in the Military," *CBC News*, May 30, 2006, www.cbc.ca/news/background/cdnmilitary/women-cdnmilitary.html, accessed October 22, 2010.
46. Janet Saltzman Chafetz, "Feminist Theory and Sociology: Underutilized Contributions for Mainstream Theory," *Annual Review of Sociology*, 1997. 23: 97–120.
47. "Rule of Thumb," *The Phrase Finder*, www.phrases.org.uk/meanings/rule-of-thumb.html, accessed August 28, 2008.
48. Talcott Parsons, "Age and Sex in the Social Structure of the United States," *American Sociological Review*, 1942. 7(5): 604–616.
49. Ibid.
50. Ibid.
51. Ibid.
52. Janet Saltzman Chafetz, "Feminist Theory and Sociology: Underutilized Contributions for Mainstream Theory," *Annual Review of Sociology*, 1997. 23: 97–120.
53. Ibid.
54. Friedrich Engels, *The Origin of the Family, Private Property and the State* (Resistance Books, 1884).
55. Chafetz, "Feminist Theory and Sociology."
56. West and Zimmerman, "Doing Gender."
57. Chafetz, "Feminist Theory and Sociology."
58. Deborah Tannen, *You Just Don't Understand: Women and Men in Conversation* (New York: HarperCollins Publishers, 2007).
59. Chafetz, "Feminist Theory and Sociology."
60. Ibid.
61. Gloria Gonzalez-Lopez, "Beyond Machos and Machoism: Mexican Immigrant Men, Sexuality, and Intimacy," *Men's Lives*, July 11, 2003, www.allacademic.com/meta/p_mla_apa_research_citation/1/0/9/1/5/pages109159/p109159-1.php, accessed January 2, 2014.
62. Chafetz, "Feminist Theory and Sociology."
63. Samuel Perreault and Shannon Brennan, "Criminal Victimization in Canada, 2009," Statistics Canada, September 2010, www.statcan.gc.ca/pub/85-002-x/2010002/article/11340-eng.pdf, accessed August 23, 2013.
64. Ibid.
65. U.S. Department of Justice, "About Domestic Violence," www.ovw.usdoj.gov/domviolence.htm, accessed August 15, 2008.
66. Frank J. Porporino, "Differences in Response to Long-Term Imprisonment: Implications for the Management of Long-Term Offenders," Correctional Service Canada, November 25, 2008, www.csc-scc.gc.ca/text/rsrch/reports/r10/r10e-eng.shtml, accessed October 22, 2010.
67. "Canada Takes Action to Strengthen the National Sex Offender Registry and the National DNA Data Bank," *Public Safety Canada*, March 17, 2010, www.publicsafety.gc.ca/media/nr/2010/nr20100317-1-eng.aspx, accessed October 22, 2010.
68. Ibid.
69. "Williams's Murder Victims Pleaded for Their Lives," *CBC News*, October 19, 2010, www.cbc.ca/canada/story/2010/10/19/russell-williams-day-2.html, accessed October 22, 2010.
70. Perreault and Brennan, "Criminal Victimization in Canada, 2009."
71. "Cost of Intimate Partner Violence against Women in the United States," *Centers for Disease Control and Prevention*, www.cdc.gov/ncipc/pubres/ipv_cost/01_executive.htm, accessed September 17, 2008.

CHAPTER 11

1. Terrence J. Montague, *Patients First: Closing the Health Care Gap in Canada* (Toronto: Canadian Copyright Licensing Agency, 2004). Reprinted with permission of John Wiley & Sons.
2. Canadian Museum of Civilization, "Making Medicare: The History of Health Care in Canada, 1914–2007," www.civilisations.ca/cmc/exhibitions/hist/medicare/medic00e.shtml, accessed October 12, 2010.
3. Kevin Kinsella and Victoria A. Velkoff, U.S. Census Bureau, Series P95/01-1, *An Aging World: 2001* (Washington, DC: U.S. Government Printing Office, 2001).
4. World Health Organization, "WHO Definition of Health," www.who.int/about/definition/en/print.html, accessed September 4, 2013.
5. Juha Mikkonen and Dennis Raphael, *Social Determinants of Health: The Canadian Facts* (Toronto: York University School of Health Policy and Management, 2010).
6. Public Health Agency of Canada 2010, "Toward a Healthy Future: Second Report on the Health of Canadians." Reproduced with permission from the Minister of Health, 2013.
7. Public Health Agency of Canada, "What Makes Canadians Healthy or Unhealthy?" January 15, 2013, www.phac-aspc.gc.ca/ph-sp/determinants/determinants-eng.php, accessed August 23, 2013.
8. Statistics Canada, "Study: Income and Psychological Distress," www.statcan.gc.ca/daily-quotidien/090121/dq090121b-eng.htm, accessed August 23, 2013.
9. Public Health Agency of Canada, "What Makes Canadians Healthy or Unhealthy?"
10. Canadian Medical Association, "12th Annual National Report Card on Health Care," August 2012, www.cma.ca/multimedia/CMA/Content_Images/Inside_cma/Media_Release/2012/reportcard/CMA-2012National-Report-Card_en.pdf, accessed August 23, 2013.
11. Public Health Agency of Canada, "What Makes Canadians Healthy or Unhealthy?"
12. Human Resources and Skills Development Canada, "Health: Self-rated Health," 2013. www4.hrsdc.gc.ca/.3ndic.1t.4r@-eng.jsp?iid=10, accessed September 4, 2013.
13. John Knodel and Mary Beth Ofstedal, "Gender and Aging in the Developing World: Where Are the Men?" *Population and Development Review*, 2003. 29: 677–698.
14. Index Mundi, "Canada Life Expectancy at Birth," www.indexmundi.com/canada/life_expectancy_at_birth.html, accessed October 12, 2010.
15. Knodel and Ofstedal, "Gender and Aging in the Developing World."
16. "Women Visit Doctors More Than Men," CNN.com, http://transcripts.cnn.com/TRANSCRIPTS/0606/17/hcsg.01.html, accessed August 28, 2008.
17. Clarian Health, "Healthy Living for Men," *The Commonwealth Fund News Release*, www.clarian.org/portal/patients/healthyliving?paf_gear_id5200001&paf_dm5full&paf_gm5content&task_name5articleDetail&articleId59764§ionId59, accessed August 28, 2008.
18. Gina Kolata, "Ideas & Trends: In Medical Research Equal Opportunity Doesn't Always Apply," *New York Times*, March 14, 1991.
19. Terrence D. Hill, Catherine E. Ross, and Ronald J. Angel, "Neighborhood Disorder, Psychophysiological Distress, and Health," *Journal of Health and Social Behavior*, 2005. 46: 170–186.
20. Ibid.
21. Robert E. Bullard, *Confronting Environmental Racism: Voices from the Grass Roots* (Boston: MA: South End Press, 1993); Robert E. Bullard, "Anatomy of Environmental Racism and the Environmental Justice Movement," in *The Environment and Society Reader*, R. Scott Free (ed.) (Needham Heights, MA: Allyn & Bacon, 2001).
22. Natan Keyfitz, "Population Growth, Development, and the Environment," *Population Studies*, 1996. 50: 335–359; Beverly H. Wright, "Endangered Communities: The Struggle for Environmental Justice in Louisiana's Chemical Corridor," *Journal of Public Management and Social Policy*, 1998. 4: 181–191.
23. Moira Welsh, "Poorest Areas Also Most Polluted, Report Shows," *The Toronto Star*, November 27, 2008.

24. Assembly of First Nations, "Fact Sheet," www.afn.ca/article.asp?id=764, accessed October 12, 2010.
25. Ibid.
26. Centre for Social Justice, "Aboriginal Issues," www.socialjustice.org/index.php?page=aboriginal-issues, accessed October 12, 2010.
27. Talcott Parsons, "The Sick Role and the Role of Physicians Reconsidered," *Milbank Medical Fund Quarterly Health and Society*, 1975. 53: 257–278.
28. Ivan Illich, *Medical Nemesis* (New York: Pantheon Books, 1975); Peter Conrad and Joseph Schneider, *Deviance and Medicalization: From Badness to Sickness* (Philadelphia, PA: Temple University Press, 1992).
29. Thomas Szasz, *The Myth of Mental Illness: Foundations of a Theory of Personal Conduct* (New York: Harper & Row, 1974).
30. Ibid.
31. Paula Caplan, *They Say You're Crazy: How the World's Most Powerful Psychiatrists Decide Who Is Normal* (New York: Perseus Books Group, 1995).
32. Ibid.
33. Rob Merrifield, "Healthy Weights for Healthy Kids: Report of the Standing Committee on Health," www.ccfn.ca/pdfs/healthyweightsforhealthykids.pdf, accessed October 12, 2010.
34. Pamela M. Anderson and Kristin F. Butcher, "Childhood Obesity: Trends and Potential Causes," *The Future of Children*, 2006. 16: 19–45.
35. Centre for Science in the Public Interest (Canada), "A National Nutritious School Meal Program for Canadian Children," http://cspinet.org/canada/pdf/child-nutrition-backgrounder-jan2009-budget.pdf, accessed October 12, 2010.
36. Ibid.
37. Ibid.
38. Deborah Carr and Michael A. Friedman, "Is Obesity Stigmatizing? Body Weight, Perceived Discrimination, and Psychological Well-Being in the United States," *Journal of Health and Social Behavior*, 2005. 46: 244–259.
39. Ibid.
40. Arielle Concilio, Sydney Lake, and Gabrielle Milner, "Lack of Resources and Outdoor Space Lead to High Rate of Obesity in Bronx," *New York Daily News*, August 19, 2008.
41. Ibid.
42. Jason D. Boardman, Jarron M. Saint Onge, Richard G. Rogers, and Justin T. Denney, "Differentials in Obesity: The Impact of Place," *Journal of Health and Social Behavior*, 2005. 46: 229–243.
43. Rob Merrifield, "Healthy Weights for Healthy Kids."
44. Public Health Agency of Canada, "Obesity in Canada," www.phac-aspc.gc.ca/hp-ps/hl-mvs/oic-oac/assets/pdf/oic-oac-eng.pdf, accessed August 29, 2013.
45. Health Canada, "Health Care System," www.hc-sc.gc.ca/hcs-sss/index-eng.php, accessed October 12, 2010.
46. Odette Madore, "The Canada Health Act: Overview and Options," www2.parl.gc.ca/content/lop/researchpublications/944-e.htm, accessed October 12, 2010.
47. Ibid.
48. Ronald M. Davis, "Resolutions for a Healthy New Year," *American Medical Association*, January 3, 2008, www.ama-assn.org/ama/pub/category/18240.html, accessed January 2, 2014.
49. Kaiser Family Foundation, "Summary of Coverage Provisions in the Patient Protection and Affordable Care Act," http://kff.org/health-costs/issue-brief/summary-of-coverage-provisions-in-the-patient/, accessed August 29, 2013.
50. World Health Organization, *The World Health Report 2000—Health Systems: Improving Performance* (Geneva: WHO, 2000).
51. Ibid.
52. Statistics Canada, "Canada's Population Estimates: Age and Sex, July 1, 2012," www.statcan.gc.ca/daily-quotidien/120927/dq120927b-eng.htm, accessed August 23, 2013.
53. Statistics Canada, "Population Projections: Canada, the Provinces and Territories," www.statcan.gc.ca/daily-quotidien/100526/dq100526b-eng.htm, accessed October 15, 2010.
54. Statistics Canada, "Population and Demography," www41.statcan.gc.ca/2009/3867/cybac3867_000-eng.htm, accessed October 15, 2010.
55. Jacques Henripin, "Baby Boom," *Canadian Encyclopedia*, http://thecanadianencyclopedia.com/index.cfm?PgNm=TCE&Params=A1ARTA0000437, accessed October 15, 2010.
56. Charles F. Westoff and Elise F. Jones, "The End of 'Catholic' Fertility," *Demography*, 1979. 16(2): 209–217.
57. Berit Ingersoll-Dayton, Margaret B. Neal, and Leslie B. Hammer, "Aging Parents Helping Adult Children: The Experience of the Sandwiched Generation," *Family Relations*, 2001. 50: 262–271.
58. Knodel and Ofstedal, "Gender and Aging in the Developing World."
59. Ibid.
60. Ibid.
61. Ibid.
62. National Center for Health Statistics, *Health, United States, 2007 with Chartbook on Trends in the Health of Americans* (Hyattsville, MD: Author, 2007).
63. Anne E. Lincoln and Michael Patrick Allen, "Double Jeopardy in Hollywood: Age and Gender in the Careers of Film Actors, 1926–1999," *Sociological Forum*, 2004. 19: 611–631.
64. Elaine Cumming, Lois R. Dean, David S. Newell, and Isabel McCaffrey, "Disengagement—A Tentative Theory of Aging," *Sociometry*, 1960. 23: 23–35.
65. Ibid.
66. Jaber F. Gubrium and James A. Holstein (eds.), *Aging and Everyday Life* (Malden, MA: Blackwell Publishers Ltd, 2000).
67. Robert Crosnoe and Glen H. Elder, Jr., "Successful Adaptation in the Later Years: A Life Course Approach to Aging," *Social Psychology Quarterly*, 2002. 65: 309–328.
68. Yunqing Li and Kenneth F. Ferraro, "Volunteering and Depression in Later Life: Social Benefit or Selection Processes?" *Journal of Health and Social Behavior*, 2005. 46: 68–84.
69. Statistics Canada, "Dependency Ratio," www.statcan.gc.ca/pub/82-229-x/2009001/demo/dep-eng.htm, accessed October 15, 2010.
70. Betty Friedan, *The Fountain of Age* (New York: Simon & Schuster, 1993).
71. Statistics Canada, "Women in Canada: A Gender-based Statistical Report," www.statcan.gc.ca/pub/89-503-x/89-503-x2005001-eng.htm, accessed October 15, 2010.
72. UNAIDS, "Report on the Global AIDS Epidemic—2010," www.unaids.org/en/media/unaids/contentassets/documents/unaidspublication/2010/20101123_globalreport_en.pdf, accessed January 11, 2011.
73. Service Canada, "Overview of the Old Age Security Program," www.servicecanada.gc.ca/eng/isp/oas/oasoverview.shtml, accessed October 15, 2010.
74. Soleman H. Abu-Bader, Anissa Rogers, and Amanda S. Barusch, "Predictors of Life Satisfaction in Frail Elderly," *Journal of Gerontological Social Work*, 2002. 38: 3–17.
75. Service Canada, "Overview of the Old Age Security Program," www.servicecanada.gc.ca/eng/isp/oas/oasoverview.shtml, accessed October 15, 2010.
76. Human Resources and Skills Development Canada, "Canada Pension Plan and Old Age Security," www.hrsdc.gc.ca/eng/oas-cpp/index.shtml, accessed October 15, 2010.
77. Human Resources and Skills Development Canada, "Making the Canada Pension Plan Secure," www.rhdcc-hrsdc.gc.ca/eng/oas-cpp/cpp_disability/future/5thpg3.shtml, accessed October 15, 2010.

CHAPTER 12

1. Anthony N. Doob and Carla Cesaroni, *Responding to Youth Crime in Canada* (Toronto: University of Toronto Press, 2004).
2. Canadian Civil Liberties Association, "Omnibus Crime Bill C-10," http://ccla.org/omnibus-crime-bill-c-10/, accessed August 24, 2013.
3. Marcus Felson, *Crime & Everyday Life* (Thousand Oaks, CA: Pine Forge Press, 1998).
4. Ibid.
5. Mia Dauvergne and John Turner, "Police-Reported Crime Statistics in Canada, 2009," www.statcan.gc.ca/pub/85-002-x/2010002/article/11292-eng.htm, accessed October 23, 2010.
6. Ibid.
7. Ibid.
8. Maire Gannon and Karen Mihorean, "Criminal Victimization in Canada, 2004," www.statcan.gc.ca/pub/85-002-x/85-002-x2005007-eng.pdf, accessed October 23, 2010.
9. Shannon Brennan, "Police-Reported Crime Statistics in Canada, 2011," www.statcan.gc.ca/pub/85-002-x/2012001/article/11692-eng.pdf, accessed August 24, 2013.
10. Roxan Vaillancourt, "Gender Differences in Police-Reported Violent Crime in Canada, 2008," www.statcan.gc.ca/pub/85f0033m/85f0033m2010024-eng.htm, accessed October 23, 2010.
11. Ibid.
12. Statistics Canada, "Study: Exploring Crime Patterns in Canada," *The Daily*, www.statcan.gc.ca/daily-quotidien/050629/dq050629b-eng.htm, accessed October 23, 2010.
13. David Cole, *No Equal Justice: Race and Class in the American Criminal Justice System* (New York: New Press, 1999).
14. Jeffrey Reiman, *The Rich Get Richer and the Poor Get Prison* (New York: Allyn & Bacon, 2008).
15. John Braithwaite, "The Myth of Social Class and Criminality Reconsidered," *American Sociological Review*, 1981. 46: 36–57; Margaret Farnsworth, *Social*

Background and the Early Onset of Delinquency: Exploring the Utility of Various Indicators of Social Class Background (Albany, NY: Hindelang Criminal Justice Research Center, 1990).

16. Elijah Anderson, "Ideologically Driven Critique," *American Journal of Sociology*, 2002. 197(6): 1533–1550.
17. Valerie Pottie Bunge, Holly Johnson, and Thierno A. Baldé, "Exploring Crime Patterns in Canada," www.statcan.gc.ca/pub/85-561-m/85-561-m2005005-eng.pdf, accessed October 23, 2010.
18. Michael Gottfredson and Travis Hirschi, *A General Theory of Crime* (Stanford, CA: Stanford University Press, 1990).
19. Statistics Canada, "Study: Exploring Crime Patterns in Canada," *The Daily*, www.statcan.gc.ca/daily-quotidien/050629/dq050629b-eng.htm, accessed October 23, 2010.
20. UNODC, "Compiling and Comparing International Crime Statistics," www.unodc.org/unodc/en/data-and-analysis/Compiling-and-comparing-International-Crime-Statistics.html, accessed July 5, 2011.
21. UNODC, "Crime and Criminal Justice Statistics," www.unodc.org/unodc/en/data-and-analysis/crimedata.html, accessed July 5, 2011.
22. NationMaster, "Crime Statistics," www.nationmaster.com/index.php, accessed July 5, 2011.
23. John Braithwaite, *Crime, Shame, and Reintegration* (New York: Cambridge University Press, 1989).
24. Frank Schmalleger, David MacAlister, Paul F. McKenna, and John Winterdyk, *Canadian Criminal Justice Today: An Introductory Text for the Twenty-First Century* (Toronto: Prentice Hall Canada Inc., 2000); Canadian Resource Centre for Victims of Crime, "Victim Impact Statements," www.crcvc.ca/docs/VictimImpactStatements.pdf, accessed October 24, 2010.
25. Curt T. Griffiths, Yvon Dandurand, and Danielle Murdoch, "The Social Reintegration of Offenders and Crime Prevention," 2007, http://curt-griffiths.com/pdfs/Social%20reintegration.pdf, accessed September 4, 2013.
26. Melanie Spiteri, "Sentencing Circles for Aboriginal Offenders in Canada: Furthering the Idea of Aboriginal Justice within a Western Justice Framework," www.sfu.ca/crj/fulltext/spiteri.pdf, accessed October 24, 2010.
27. Parliament of Canada, "House of Commons Standing Committee on Public Accounts Fourth Report," www.parl.gc.ca/HousePublications/Publication.aspx?DocId=1031645&Mode=1&Language=E, accessed August 24, 2013.
28. Statistics Canada, "Adult Correctional Services, 2010/2011," www.statcan.gc.ca/daily-quotidien/121011/dq121011c-eng.pdf, accessed August 24, 2013.
29. Mia Dauvergne, "Adult Correctional Statistics in Canada, 2010/2011". 2012. www.statcan.gc.ca/pub/85-002-x/2012001/article/11715-eng.pdf, accessed August 24, 2013.
30. Correctional Services Canada, "FORUM on Corrections Research," www.csc-scc.gc.ca/text/pblct/forum/e053/e053h-eng.shtml, accessed October 24, 2010.
31. Laura Landry and Maire Sinha, "Adult Correctional Services in Canada, 2005/2006," www.statcan.gc.ca/pub/85-002-x/85-002-x2008006-eng.pdf, accessed October 24, 2010.
32. Statistics Canada, "Adult and Youth Correctional Services: Key Indicators," www.statcan.gc.ca/daily-quotidien/091208/dq091208a-eng.htm, accessed October 23, 2010.
33. Cesare Beccaria, *Essays on Crimes and Punishments*, Henry Paolucci (trans.) (Indianapolis, IN: Bobbs-Merrill, 1764/1963).
34. Jeremy Bentham, *An Introduction to the Principles of Morals and Legislation*, J. H. Burns and H. L. A. Hart (eds.) (London: Athlone Publishing, 1789/1970).
35. Cesare Lombroso, "Introduction," in *Criminal Man According to the Classification of Cesare Lombroso* Gena Lombroso-Ferrero (Montclair, NJ: Patterson Smith, 1911/1972).
36. Alan Booth and D. Wayne Osgood, "The Influence of Testosterone on Deviance in Adulthood: Assessing and Explaining the Relationship," *Criminology*, 1993. 31: 93–117; J. R. Sanchez-Martin, E. Fano, L. Ahedo, J. Cardas, P. F. Brain, and A. Azpiroz, "Relating Testosterone Levels and Free Play Social Behavior in Male and Female Preschool Children," *Psychoneuroendocrinology*, November 25, 2000, 773–783.
37. James J. Hudziak and Lawrence P. Rudiger, "A Twin Study of In attentive, Aggressive and Anxious/Depressed Behaviors," *Journal of American Academy of Child and Adolescent Psychiatry*, 2000. 39: 469–476.
38. William Duffy, *Sugar Blues* (Pandor, PA: Childton Book Co., 1975).
39. Abdulla Badawy, "Alcohol and Violence and the Other Possible Role of Serotonin," *Criminal Behaviour and Mental Health*, 2003. 12: 31–45.
40. DSM, *Diagnostic and Statistical Manual of Mental Disorders*, 4th ed. (Washington, DC: American Psychiatric Association, 1994).
39. Travis Hirschi and Michael J Hindelang, "Intelligence and Delinquency: A Revisionist Review," *American Sociological Review*, 1977. 42: 57–87.
40. Stanton E. Samenow, *Inside the Criminal Mind*, revised and updated edition (New York: Crown Publishers, 2004).
41. Émile Durkheim, *The Rules of Sociological Method*, 8th ed., George E. G. Catlin (ed.), Sarah A. Solovay and John H. Mueller (trans.) (New York: The Free Press, 1895/1964).
42. Robert K. Merton, "Social Structure and Anomie," *American Sociological Review*, 1938. 3: 672–682.
43. Jeffrey Reiman, *The Rich Get Richer and the Poor Get Prison: Ideology, Class and Criminal Justice* (Needham Heights, MA: Pearson Education, 1998).
44. Willem A. Bonger, *Criminality and Economic Conditions* (Bloomington, IN: Indiana University Press, 1969).
45. Reiman, *The Rich Get Richer and the Poor Get Prison*.
46. Edwin Sutherland and Donald Cressey, *Principles of Criminology*, 11th ed. (General Hall/Altamira Press), 1992, by permission of Rowman & Littlefield.
47. Edwin M. Lemert, *Social Pathology* (New York: McGraw-Hill, 1951); Edwin M. Lemert, *Human Deviance, Social Problems and Social Control* (Englewood Cliffs, NJ: Prentice Hall, 1967).
48. Walter C. Reckless, *The Crime Problem* (New York: Appleton-Century-Crofts, 1955).
49. Travis Hirschi, *Causes of Delinquency* (Berkeley, CA: University of California Press, 1969).
50. Statistics Canada, "Study: Female Offenders," www.statcan.gc.ca/daily-quotidien/080124/dq080124a-eng.htm, accessed October 24, 2010.
51. Sally S. Simpson and Denise C. Herz, "Gender, Crime, and Criminal Justice," *Handbook of the Sociology of Gender*, Janet Saltzman Chafetz (ed.) (New York: Kluwer Academic/Plenum Publishers, 1999).
52. Laura Landry and Maire Sinha, "Adult Correctional Services in Canada, 2005/2006," www.statcan.gc.ca/pub/85-002-x/85-002-x2008006-eng.pdf, accessed October 24, 2010.
53. Susan F. Sharp, "Editorial," *Feminist Criminology*, 2006. 1(1): 3–5.
54. Statistics Canada, "Police Officers, by Province and Territory," www40.statcan.gc.ca/l01/cst01/legal05a-eng.htm, accessed October 24, 2010.
55. Justice Canada, "Canada's Court System," www.justice.gc.ca/eng/dept-min/pub/ccs-ajc/page2.html, accessed October 24, 2010.
56. Justice Canada, "Canada's System of Justice," www.justice.gc.ca/eng/dept-min/pub/just/08.html, accessed October 24, 2010.
57. Statistics Canada, "Adult Correctional Services in Canada," www.statcan.gc.ca/pub/85-002-x/85-002-x2006005-eng.pdf, accessed October 24, 2010.

CHAPTER 13

1. John Frederick Conway, *The Canadian Family in Crisis* (Toronto: James Lorimer & Company Ltd., 2003).
2. Statistics Canada, "Size of Household," www.statcan.gc.ca/concepts/definitions/hsize-tmenage-eng.htm, accessed August 24, 2013.
3. Statistics Canada, "Family Structure of Census Family," www.statcan.gc.ca/concepts/definitions/cffamstr-strfamfr-eng.htm, accessed August 24, 2013. This does not constitute an endorsement by Statistics Canada of this product.
4. Dorothy E. Smith, "The Standard North American Family: SNAF as an Ideological Code," *Journal of Family Issues*, 1993. 14: 50–65.
5. Andrew J. Cherlin and Frank F. Furstenberg, Jr., "Stepfamilies in the United States: A Reconsideration," *Annual Review of Sociology*, 1994. 20: 359–381.
6. Statistics Canada, "Portrait of Families and Living Arrangements in Canada," www12.statcan.ca/census-recensement/2011/as-sa/98-312-x/98-312-x2011001-eng.cfm, accessed August 24, 2013.
7. Statistics Canada, "Table 102-4506—Live Births, by Marital Status of Mother, Canada, Provinces and Territories, Annual, CANSIM (database)," http://cansim2.statcan.gc.ca/cgi-win/cnsmcgi.exe?Lang=E&CNSM-Fi=CII/CII_1-eng.htm, accessed October 27, 2010.
8. Anne-Marie Ambert, "One Parent Families: Characteristics, Causes, Consequences, and Issues," www.vifamily.ca/media/node/396/attachments/oneparent_families.pdf, accessed October 27, 2010.
9. Statistics Canada, "Portrait of Families and Living Arrangements in Canada."
10. Michael J. Rosenfeld and Byung-Soo Kim, "The Independence of Young Adults and the Rise of Interracial and Same-Sex Unions," *American Sociological Review*, 2005. 70: 541–562.
11. Ibid.
12. David Popenoe, "American Family Decline, 1960–1990: A Review and Appraisal," *Journal of Marriage and the Family*, 1993. 55: 527–542.
13. Rosenfeld and Kim, "The Independence of Young Adults."
14. National Post, "B.C. Supreme Court Rules Polygamy Ban Is Constitutional, but Flawed," http://news.nationalpost.com/2011/11/23/b-c-supreme-court-rules-polygamy-law-is-constitutional/, accessed August 30, 2012.
15. Melvyn C. Goldstein, "Pahair and Tibetan Polyandry Revisited," The Center for Research on Tibet, www.case.edu/affil/tibet/tibetanSociety/marriage.htm, accessed July 28, 2008.
16. Ibid.

17. Human Resources and Skills Development Canada, "Family Life—Marriage," www4.hrsdc.gc.ca/.3ndic.1t.4r@-eng.jsp?iid=78, accessed August 24, 2013.
18. Statistics Canada, "Common Law Status of Person 15 Years or Over," www.statcan.gc.ca/concepts/definitions/marital3-matrimonial3-eng.htm, accessed August 24, 2013.
19. Urban Institute, "Introduction," www.urban.org/publications/310962.html, accessed July 20, 2008.
20. Larry L. Bumpass, James A. Sweet, and Andrew Cherlin, "The Role of Cohabitation in Declining Rates of Marriage," *Journal of Marriage and the Family*, 1991. 53: 913–927.
21. Maurice R. Davie and Ruby Jo Reeves, "Propinquity of Residence Before Marriage," *The American Journal of Sociology*, 1939. 44: 510–517; Joseph R. Marches and Gus Turbeville, "The Effect of Residential Propinquity on Marriage Selection," *The American Journal of Sociology*, May 1953. 58: 592–595; James H. S. Bossard, "Residential Propinquity as a Factor in Marriage Selection," *The American Journal of Sociology*, 1932. 38: 219–224.
22. Stephanie Coontz, *The Way We Never Were: American Families and the Nostalgia Trap* (New York: Basic Books, 2000).
23. Ibid.
24. Ibid.
25. Ibid.
26. Ibid.
27. Ibid.
28. Ronald R. Rindfuss, Minja Kim-Choe, and Larry L. Bumpass, "Social Networks and Family Change in Japan," *American Sociological Review*, 2004. 69: 838–861.
29. Ibid.
30. Noriko O. Tsuya, "Gender, Employment, and Housework in Japan," Paper presented at the annual meeting of the Population Association of America, Boston, MA, April 1–3, 2004.
31. Minja Kim-Choe, Larry L. Bumpass, and Noriko O. Tsuya, "Employment," from *Marriage, Work, and Family Life in Comparative Perspective: Japan, South Korea, and the United States*, Noriko O. Tsuya and Larry L. Bumpass (eds.) (Honolulu, HI: University of Hawaii Press, 2004), 95–113.
32. Rindfuss, Kim-Choe, and Bumpass, "Social Networks and Family Change in Japan."
33. Ibid.
34. Bernard I. Murstein, "Stimulus, Value, Role: A Theory of Marital Choice," *Journal of Marriage and Family*, 1970. 32(3): 465–481.
35. Robert F. Winch, Thomas Ktsanes, and Virginia Ktsanes, "The Theory of Complementary Needs in Mate-Selection: An Analytic and Descriptive Study," *American Sociological Review*, 1954. 19(3): 241–249.
36. Duane W. Crawford, Renate M. Houts, Ted L. Huston, and Laura J. George, "Compatibility, Leisure, and Satisfaction in Marital Relationships," *Journal of Marriage and the Family*, 2002. 64(2): 433–449.
37. Ibid.
38. Daphne Stevens, Gary Kiger, and Pamela Riley, "Working Hard and Hardly Working: Domestic Labor and Marital Satisfaction among Dual-Earner Couples," *Journal of Marriage and Family*, 2002. 63: 514–526.
39. Ibid.
40. Ibid.
41. Diana Baumrind, "Current Patterns of Parental Authority," *Developmental Psychology Monographs*, 1971. 4(1, pt. 2):103; Diana Baumrind, "Parental Disciplinary Patterns and Social Competence in Children," *Youth and Society*, 1978. 9: 239–276; Diana Baumrind, "The Discipline Controversy Revisited," *Family Relations*, 1996. 5(4): 405–415.
42. The show was included in the 2010 program schedule at MTV.ca. Note that the Media Awareness Network carries a 1998 reference to MTV being the most watched network for girls aged 11 to 19 in Canada. (See "1998: Girls and TV [Canada]" section, using figures from Saatchi and Saatchi, "SmartGirl Internette and Teenage Research Unlimited," cited in *KidScreen*, August 1998, www.media-awareness.ca/english/resources/research_documents/statistics/television/tv_viewing_habits.cfm, accessed October 3, 2010.)
43. Ibid.
44. Leslie G. Simons and Rand D. Conger, "Linking Mother–Father Differences in Parenting to a Typology of Family Parenting Styles and Adolescent Outcomes". *Journal of Family Issues*, 2007 *28*, 212–241.
45. Changkuan Xu, "Direct and Indirect Effects of Parenting Style with Child Temperament, Parent–Child Relationship, and Family Functioning on Child Social Competence in the Chinese Culture: Testing the Latent Models" (Doctoral dissertation, University of North Texas), 2007, http://digital.library.unt.edu/permalink/meta-dc-3592:1, accessed August 24, 2013.
46. Canadian Council on Social Development, "Families: A Canadian Profile," www.ccsd.ca/factsheets/family/, accessed October 27, 2010.
47. Sara McLanahan and Christine Percheski, "Family Structure and the Reproduction of Inequalities," *The Annual Review of Sociology*, 2008. 34: 12.1–12.19.
48. Lisa Strohschein, "Household Income Histories and Child Mental Health Trajectories," *Journal of Health and Social Behavior*, 2005. 46: 359–375.
49. Robert Schoen, Young J. Kim, Constance A. Nathanson, Jason Fields, and Nan Marie Astone, "Why Do Americans Want Children?" *Population and Development Review*, June 1997. 23: 333–358.
50. Lillian B. Rubin, "Women of a Certain Age: The Midlife Search for Self," *Contemporary Sociology*, May 1981. 10: 460–462.
51. Arlene Saluter and Terry Lugaila, "Marital Status and Living Arrangements: March 1996," *Current Population Reports: Population Characteristics*, www.census.gov/prod/3/98pubs/p20-496.pdf, accessed August 21, 2008.
52. Michael J. Rosenfeld, *The Age of Independence: Interracial Unions, Same Sex Unions and the Changing American Family* (Cambridge, MA: Harvard University Press, 2007).
53. Maire Sinha, "Family Violence in Canada: A Statistical Profile, 2010," www.statcan.gc.ca/pub/85-002-x/2012001/article/11643-eng.pdf, accessed April 15, 2013.
54. Ibid.
55. Anne Milan, "One Hundred Years of Families," *Canadian Social Trends*, www.statcan.gc.ca/pub/11-008-x/1999004/article/4909-eng.pdf, accessed October 27, 2010.
56. Ibid.
57. Mary Bess Kelly, "The Processing of Divorce Cases through Civil Court in Seven Provinces and Territories," *Juristat*, www.statcan.gc.ca/pub/85-002-x/2010001/article/11158-eng.htm, accessed October 27, 2010.
58. Kelly, "The Processing of Divorce Cases through Civil Court in Seven Provinces and Territories."
59. Stephanie Coontz, *Marriage, A History: How Love Conquered Marriage* (New York: Penguin, 2006).
60. Steven L. Nock, *Marriage in Men's Lives* (New York: Oxford University Press, 1998).
61. Arlie Russell Hochschild with Anne Machung, *The Second Shift: Working Parents and the Revolution at Home* (New York: Penguin Books, 1989/2003).
62. Stevens, Kiger, and Riley, "Working Hard and Hardly Working: Domestic Labor and Marital Satisfaction among Dual-Earner Couples."
63. Kristin Byron, "A Meta-Analytic Review of Work–Family Conflict and Its Antecedents," *Journal of Vocational Behavior*, 2005. 67: 169–198.
64. Friedrich Engels, *The Origin of the Family, Private Property and the State* (Chippendale, NSW: Resistance Books, 2004), http://readingfromtheleft.com/PDF/EngelsOrigin.pdf, accessed June 3, 2012.
65. Stevens, Kiger, and Riley, "Working Hard and Hardly Working."
66. Herbert Bynder, "Émile Durkheim and the Sociology of the Family," *Journal of Marriage and Family*, 1969. 31: 527–533.
67. Canada Free Press, "Who Needs the Family?" www.canadafreepress.com/index.php/article/53237?utm_source=CFP+Mailout&utm_campaign=66d5e43c2a-Call_to_Champions&utm_medium=email, accessed May 30, 2013.
68. "Same-Sex Rights: Canada Timeline," *CBC News*, March 1, 2007, www.cbc.ca/news/background/samesexrights/timeline_canada.html, accessed October 27, 2010.
69. William Meezan and Jonathan Rauch, "The Future of Children," *Marriage and Child Wellbeing*, 2005. 15: 97–115.

CHAPTER 14

1. Andrea Rounce, *Access to Post-secondary Education: Does Class Still Matter?* (Canadian Centre for Policy Alternatives, 2004). Reprinted with permission.
2. Francisco O. Ramirez and John Boli, "The Political Construction of Mass Schooling: European Origins and Worldwide Institutionalization," *Sociology of Education*, 1987. 60: 2–17.
3. "Toronto's 1st Africentric School Set to Open," *CBC News*, September 4, 2009, www.cbc.ca/canada/toronto/story/2009/09/04/africentric-school.html, accessed October 28, 2010.
4. "Underprivileged Children Also Disadvantaged in the Classroom," *UNESCO Institute for Statistics*, May 29, 2005, http://en.unesco.org/themes/education-21st-century, accessed September 4, 2013.
5. "Literacy Rates," *UNESCO Institute for Statistics*, http://stats.uis.unesco.org/unesco/TableViewer/document.aspx?ReportId5121&IF_Language5eng&BR_Country56940, accessed August 12, 2008; Central Intelligence Agency, "Sierra Leone," *The World Fact Book*, www.cia.gov/library/publications/the-worldfactbook/print/sl.html, accessed July 17, 2008.
6. Statistics Canada, *Education Indicators in Canada: Report of the Pan-Canadian Education Indicators Program 2007*, Catalogue 81-582-X, pp. 29–31.

7. Statistics Canada, "Education Indicators in Canada: An International Perspective," 2011, www.cmec.ca/Publications/Lists/Publications/Attachments/271/education-indicators-canada-international-perspective-2011.pdf, accessed August 24, 2013.
8. Human Resources and Skills Development Canada, "Learning—Educational Attainment," 2013, www4.hrsdc.gc.ca/.3ndic.1t.4r@-eng.jsp?iid=29, accessed September 4, 2013.
9. Council of Ministers of Education, Canada, "Education in Canada: An Overview," www.cmec.ca/299/Education-in-Canada-An-Overview/index.html, accessed August 24, 2013.
10. "Assembly of First Nations—The Story," *Assembly of First Nations*, www.afn.ca/article.asp?id=59, accessed October 25, 2010.
11. Michael Mendelson, *Aboriginal Peoples and Postsecondary Education in Canada* (Ottawa: Caledon Institute of Social Policy, 2006).
12. Statistics Canada, 2006 Census, analysis series, 97-560-XIE2006001. www12.statcan.ca/census-recensement/2006/as-sa/97-560/index-eng.cfm?CFID=96864&CFTOKEN=86496165, accessed September 4, 2013.
13. "Study Gives Aboriginal Education a Failing Grade," *Vancouver Sun*, October 29, 2008, www.canada.com/vancouversun/news/westcoastnews/story.html?id=6fafa6b0-7366-4d77-bc1a-66a151a4e194, accessed October 25, 2010.
14. Ibid., quoting John Richards's report.
15. Martin Turcotte, "Intergenerational Education Mobility: University Completion in Relation to Parents' Education Level," 2011, www.statcan.gc.ca/pub/11-008-x/2011002/article/11536-eng.pdf, accessed August 24, 2013.
16. Ibid.
17. Paul M. Anglin and Ronald Meng, "Evidence on Grades and Grade Inflation at Ontario's Universities," *Canadian Public Policy*, 2000. 26(3): 361.
18. James E. Côté and Anton L. Allahar, *Ivory Tower Blues: A University System in Crisis* (Toronto: University of Toronto Press, 2007).
19. Daniel Girard, "Prof Says Pressure Is on to Accept 'Grade Inflation,'" *Toronto Star*, June 11, 2007, www.thestar.com/article/223884, accessed October 23, 2010.
20. Anglin and Meng, "Evidence on Grades and Grade Inflation."
21. Girard, "Prof Says Pressure Is On to Accept 'Grade Inflation.'"
22. Quoted in Michael Woods, "Making the Grade," Queen's University's *The Journal*, September 19, 2008, www.queensjournal.ca/story/2008-09-19/features/making-the-grade/, accessed October 23, 2010.
23. Girard, "Prof Says Pressure Is On to Accept 'Grade Inflation.'"
24. Quoted in Woods, "Making the Grade."
25. Statistics Canada, "Undergraduate Tuition Fees for Full Time Canadian Students, by Discipline, by Province," 2012, www.statcan.gc.ca/tables-tableaux/sum-som/l01/cst01/educ50a-eng.htm, accessed August 24, 2013.
26. "Higher Education Finance and Cost-Sharing in Canada" (updated April 9, 2010), p. 1, part of The International Comparative Higher Education and Finance Project, operated through the State University of New York at Buffalo, http://gse.buffalo.edu/org/inthigheredfinance/project_profiles.html, accessed October 24, 2010.
27. Canadian University Survey Consortium, "Canadian University Survey Consortium 2012 Survey of Graduating Undergraduate Students," 2012, www.sfu.ca/content/dam/sfu/irp/surveys/cusc/cusc2012reportSFU.pdf, accessed August 24, 2013.
28. "Higher Education," *Estia*, www.estia.educ.goteborg.se/svestia/edu/edu_sys5.html, accessed September 2, 2008.
29. Randall Collins, *The Credential Society* (New York: Academic Press, 1979); Randall Collins, "Functional and Conflict Theories of Educational Stratification," *American Sociological Review*, 1971. 36: 1002–1019.
30. Deani Van Pelt, *Home Education in Canada: A Summary of the Pan-Canadian Study on Home Education 2003*, Canadian Centre for Home Education and Home School Legal Defence Association, p. 1, www.hslda.ca/cche_research/SummaryFinal.pdf, accessed October 26, 2010.
31. Crista L. Green and Kathleen Hoover-Dempsey, "Why Do Parents Homeschool?" *Education & Urban Society*, 2007. 39(2): 264–285.
32. Hussain Al-Fadhili and Madhu Singh, "Teachers' Expectancy and Efficacy as Correlates of School Achievement in Delta, Mississippi," *Journal of Personnel Evaluation in Education*, 2006. 19(1–2): 51–67.
33. Margaret R. Kuklinksy and Rhona S. Weinstein, "Classroom and Developmental Differences in a Path Model of Teacher Expectancy Effects," *Child Development*, 2001. 72(5): 1554–1579.
34. Ray C. Rist, "HER Classic: Student Social Class and Teacher Expectations: The Self-Fulfilling Prophecy in Ghetto Education," *Harvard Educational Review*, 2000. 70(3), 257–301.
35. Stephen W. Raudenbush, "Magnitude of Teacher Expectancy Effects on Pupil IQ as a Function of the Credibility of Expectancy Induction: A Synthesis of Findings from 18 Experiments," *Journal of Educational Psychology*, 1984. 76(1): 85–97.
36. Marie Hammond Callaghan, "We Were Here: Exploratory Essays on Women's History at Mount Allison University," 2006, www.mta.ca/wewerehere/06/intro.html, accessed October 20, 2010.
37. "Colleges for Women," *National Women's History Museum*, www.nmwh.org/exhibits/education/1800s_6.htm, accessed August 18, 2008.
38. Statistics Canada, "Table 477-0020: Public Postsecondary Graduates, by Pan-Canadian Standard Classification of Education (PCSCE), Classification of Instructional Programs, Primary Grouping (CIP_PG), Sex and Immigration Status, Annual (Number), CANSIM (Database)," 2013, www5.statcan.gc.ca/cansim/pick-choisir?lang=eng&p2=33&id=4770020, accessed September 4, 2013.
39. Ibid.
40. Mark D. Regenerus, "Religion and Positive Adolescent Outcomes: A Review of Research and Theory," *Review of Religious Research*, 2003. 44(4): 394–413.
41. Marie Good and Teena Willoughby, "Evaluating the Direction of Effects in the Relationship between Religious versus Non-Religious Activities, Academic Success, and Substance Use," *Journal of Youth and Adolescence*, August 14, 2010, www.springerlink.com, accessed September 29, 2010.
42. Regenerus, "Religion and Positive Adolescent Outcomes."
43. Ibid.
44. Min Zhou and Carl L. Bankston, III, "Social Capital and the Adaptation of the Second Generation: The Case of Vietnamese Youth in New Orleans," pp. 197–220, in *The New Second Generation*, Alejandro Portes (ed.) (New York: Russell Sage Foundation, 1996).
45. "Selected Characteristics of Public School Teachers: Selected Years, Spring 1961 through Spring 2001," *Digest of Educational Statistics*, http://nces.ed.gov/programs/digest/d05/tables/dt05_068.asp, accessed July 9, 2008; "Secondary Education: Teacher's Characteristics," *Institute of Educational Sciences*, http://nces.ed.gov/surveys/international/intlindicators/index.asp?SectionNumber53&SubSectionNumber56&IndicatorNumber584, accessed July 9, 2008; "2008 Federal Holidays," *National Archives News*, www.archives.gov/news/federal-holidays.html, accessed July 9, 2008; Emily Brady, "For Muslim Students, a Drive to Deem Holy Days as Holidays," *The New York Times*, April 29, 2007, www.nytimes.com/2007/04/29/nyregion/thecity/29holi.html, accessed August 24, 2013.
46. "Schools Won't Lose Stat Holidays: Minister," *CBC News*, March 24, 2010, www.cbc.ca/canada/montreal/story/2010/03/24/mtl-courchesne-holidays.html, accessed October 26, 2010.
47. Émile Durkheim, *Elementary Forms of the Religious Life*, Karen Fields (trans.) (New York: The Free Press, 1912/1995).
48. Ibid.
49. Huston Smith, *The World's Religions: Our Great Wisdom Traditions* (New York: HarperCollins, 1958/1991).
50. Ibid.
51. Durkheim, *Elementary Forms of the Religious Life*; Smith, *The World's Religions*.
52. Benton Johnson, "On Church and Sect," *American Sociological Review*, 1963. 28: 539–549.
53. Hoa Omid, "Theocracy or Democracy? The Critics of 'Westoxification' and the Politics of Fundamentalism in Iran," *Third World Quarterly*, 1992. 13(4): 675–690.
54. Durkheim, *Elementary Forms of the Religious Life*.
55. "Religion Data from the 2001 Canadian Census," www.religioustolerance.org/can_rel0.htm, accessed October 27, 2010; Statistics Canada, *2001 Census: Analysis Series, Religions in Canada*, catalogue no. 96F0030XIE2001015, p. 5. www12.statcan.gc.ca/access_acces/archive.action-eng.cfm?/english/census01/products/analytic/companion/rel/pdf/96F0030XIE2001015.pdf, accessed September 4, 2013.
56. Statistics Canada, "Population by Religious Denomination and Projection Scenario, Canada, 2006 and 2031," 2010, www.statcan.gc.ca/pub/91-551-x/2010001/tbl/tbl005-eng.htm, accessed August 24, 2013.
57. Statistics Canada, *2001 Census: Analysis Series, Religions in Canada*.
58. *Religions in Canada*, 2nd ed. (Ottawa: Directorate of Human Rights and Diversity, 2008).
59. "Hinduism: The World's Third Largest Religion," www.religioustolerance.org/hinduism.htm, accessed October 27, 2010.
60. Statistics Canada, *2001 Census: Analysis Series, Religions in Canada*.
61. David J. Goa and Harold G. Coward, "Hinduism," *The Canadian Encyclopedia*, www.thecanadianencyclopedia.com, accessed October 27, 2010.
62. Karl Marx, *Karl Marx: Selected Writings*, 2nd ed., David McLellan (ed.) (Oxford: Oxford University Press, 1844/2000).
63. Ibid.
64. Max Weber, *The Protestant Ethic and a Spirit of Capitalism: And Other Writings*, Peter Caehr and Gordon C. Wells (trans.) (New York: Penguin Books, 2002).

65. Ibid.
66. "A Humanist Discussion of . . . The Golden Rule," *British Humanist Association*, February 2006, www.humanism.org.uk/site/cms/contentView-Article.asp? article51222.
67. Peter Berger, *The Sacred Canopy: Elements of the Sociology of Religion* (Garden City, NY: Doubleday, 1969).
68. Peter Berger, "The Desecularization of the World, a Global Overview," in *The Desecularization of the World: Resurgent Religion and World Politics*, Peter Berger (ed.) (Grand Rapids, MI: Eerdmans, 1999), pp. 1–18.
69. "Information about Religion in Canada," *ReligiousTolerance.org*, www.religioustolerance.org/can_rel.htm, accessed October 27, 2010.
70. Robert Bellah, Richard Madsen, William M. Sullivan, Ann Swidler, and Steve Tipton, *Habits of the Heart: Individualism and Commitment in American Life* (Berkeley, CA: University of California Press, 1996).
71. Harold Coward and Roland Chagnon, "Religion," *The Canadian Encyclopedia*, www.thecanadianencyclopedia.com/articles/religion, accessed September 4, 2013.
72. "Information about Religion in Canada," ReligiousTolerance.org.
73. Statistics Canada, *2001 Census: Analysis Series, Religions in Canada*.
74. Ibid.
75. Ibid.
76. Ibid.
77. Ibid.
78. Ibid.
79. Ibid.
80. "The Amish," *ReligionFacts*, www.religionfacts.com/christianity/denominations/amish.htm, accessed October 27, 2010; "The Amish," *Encyclopedia Britannica*, http://search.eb.com/eb/article-233461, accessed July 11, 2008.
81. "Martin Luther King, Jr.: Biography," *The Nobel Foundation*, http://nobelprize.org/nobel_prizes/peace/laureates/1964/king-bio.html, accessed September 3, 2008.
82. Megan Wilde, "Galileo and the Inquisition," *The Galileo Project*, http://galileo.rice.edu/bio/narrative_7.html, accessed September 2, 2008.
83. Shirley Ann Rainey, "Great Chain of Being," *Encyclopedia of Race and Racism* (New York: MacMillan, 2007).
84. "Amaterasu," *Encyclopedia Britannica*, http://search.eb.com/eb/article-9006019, accessed September 2, 2008; "Religion & Ethics: Shinto—The Imperial Family," BBC.com, www.bbc.co.uk/religion/religions/shinto/texts/stories_5.shtml, accessed September 2, 2008.
85. Johanna Stuckey, *Women's Spirituality: Contemporary Feminist Approaches to Judaism, Christianity, Islam and Goddess Worship* (Toronto: Inanna Publications and Education, 2010).
86. Linda Woodhead, "Gender Differences in Religious Practice and Significance," pp. 550–570, in J. Beckford and N. J. Demerath III (eds.), *The Sage Handbook of the Sociology of Religion* (Los Angeles: Sage, 2007).
87. Abbreviated extract from Lennox V. Farrell, "Greg Is Not His Real Name," 1998, *TimBookTu: Stories, Poetry & Essays with an African-American Flavor*, www.timbooktu.com/lennox/ythprobl.htm, accessed October 23, 2010.
88. "Toronto's 1st Africentric School Set to Open," *CBC News*.
89. Moira MacDonald, "Africentric School Shines: MacDonald," *Toronto Sun*, September 25, 2010, www.torontosun.com/comment/columnists/moira_macdonald/2010/09/24/15469271.html, accessed October 28, 2010.
90. Information from report abbreviated as "Elementary School Report" under 2009–2010 EQAO Provincial Reports, at www.eqao.com/pdf_e/11/EQAO_ProvincialReport_Elementary2011.pdf, accessed September 4, 2013.
91. Quoted in Scott Anderson, "Afrocentric Schools," *University of Toronto Magazine*, Autumn 2009, www.magazine.utoronto.ca/leading-edge/afrocentric-schools/, accessed October 28, 2010.
92. Natalie Alcoba, "Toronto Trustees Vote in Favour of Afrocentric School," *National Post*, January 29, 2008, www.nationalpost.com/news/story.html?id=272389, accessed October 28, 2010.
93. "Toronto's 1st Africentric School Set to Open," *CBC News*.

CHAPTER 15

1. Naomi Klein, *No Logo: Taking Aim at the Brand Bullies* (Toronto: Vintage Canada, 2000).
2. Pat Hudson, *The Industrial Revolution: Reading History* (New York: Hodder Arnold, 1992).
3. Warren E. Kalbach, "Population," *The Canadian Encyclopedia*, www.thecanadianencyclopedia.com/articles/population, accessed September 4, 2013.
4. Kalbach, "Population."
5. Harold Troper, "Immigration," *The Canadian Encyclopedia*, www.thecanadianencyclopedia.com/articles/immigration, accessed September 4, 2013; "Canada," WorldRover.com, citing CIA statistics, www.worldrover.com/vital/canada.html, accessed October 30, 2010.
6. Irvin Studin, "Canada—Population 100 Million," *Global Brief*, June 14, 2010, http://globalbrief.ca/blog/2010/06/14/canada-%E2%80%93-population-100-million/, accessed October 30, 2010.
7. Frank Trovato, "Aboriginal People, Demography," *The Canadian Encyclopedia*, www.thecanadianencyclopedia.com/articles/native-people-demography, accessed September 4, 2013.
8. Statistics Canada, "Main Page,"2013, www.statcan.gc.ca/start-debut-eng.html, accessed August 24, 2013.
9. "People and Culture—Population Densities," *Government of Ontario*, www.ontario.ca/en/about_ontario/EC001035, accessed October 30, 2010.
10. Gerhard Lenski, Jean Lenski, and Patrick Nolan, *Human Societies* (New York: McGraw-Hill, 1990).
11. Douglas S. Massey, "A Brief History of Human Society: The Origin and Role of Emotion in Social Life: 2001 Presidential Address," *American Sociological Review*, 2002. 67(1): 1–29.
12. Gerhard E. Lenski, *Power and Privilege: A Theory of Social Stratification* (Chapel Hill, NC: University of North Carolina Press, 1966).
14. Jared Diamond, *Collapse: How Societies Choose to Fail or Succeed* (New York: Viking Penguin Press, 2005).
15. Lenski, Lenski, and Nolan, *Human Societies*.
16. Ibid.
17. Ibid.
18. Massey, "A Brief History of Human Society."
19. Lenski, Lenski, and Nolan, *Human Societies*.
20. Ibid.
21. Massey, "A Brief History of Human Society."
22. Daniel Bell, *The Coming of Post-Industrial Society: A Venture in Social Forecasting* (New York: Basic Books, 1973, 1999).
23. Albert Hirschman, *The Rhetoric of Reaction: Perversity, Futility, Jeopardy* (Cambridge, MA: Harvard University Press, 1991).
24. "Internet Petitions," Snopes.com, www.snopes.com/inboxer/petition/internet.asp, accessed September 11, 2008.
25. Ibid.
26. "1995 Referendum," *Canada History, Part of The History Project*, www.canadahistory.com/sections/eras/moderncanada/1995_referendum.htm, accessed August 24, 2013.
27. "G20 Protest Violence Prompts over 400 Arrests," *CBC News*, June 27, 2010, www.cbc.ca/canada/story/2010/06/26/g20-saturday-protests.html, accessed October 30, 2010.
28. "Violent Riot Ends in Shooting at Edmonton Prison," *Edmonton Journal*, July 2, 2008, at www.canada.com/globaltv/national/story.html?id=025998f4-9969-4b7f-806e-7ddbcbaa0ea3, accessed October 30, 2010.
29. Joel Best, *Flavor of the Month: Why Smart People Fall for Fads* (Berkeley, CA: University of California Press, 2006).
30. Ibid.
31. "Drug Abuse Resistance Education, Saint John, NB," www.daresj.com/dare_in_canada.php, accessed October 30, 2010.
32. Best, *Flavor of the Month*.
33. "FEMA for Kids: Y2K for Kids," *Federal Emergency Management Agency*, www.fema.gov/kids/y2k.htm, accessed September 11, 2008; "Are You Ready?" *The White House*, February 3, 2003, www.whitehouse.gov/news/releases/2003/02/20030207-10.html, accessed September 4, 2013; Jeanne Meserve, "Duct Tape Sales Rise Amid Terror Fears," CNN.com, February 11, 2003, www.cnn.com/2003/US/02/11/emergency.supplies/, accessed August 24, 2013.
34. Meserve, "Duct Tape Sales Rise."
35. Bernard Guerin and Yoshihiko Miyazaki, "Analyzing Rumors, Gossip, and Urban Legends through Their Conversational Properties," *Psychological Record*, Winter 2006. 56(1): 23.
36. Gustave Le Bon, *The Crowd: A Study of the Popular Mind* (Kitchener: Batoche Books. 1896/2009).
37. Ralph H. Turner and Lewis M. Killian, *Collective Behavior* (Englewood Cliffs, NJ: Prentice Hall, 1972).
38. Charles Tilly, *Social Movements, 1768–2004* (Boulder, CO: Paradigm Publishers, 2004).
39. Rhett Butler, "Rainforests Face Array of Emerging Threats," *Mongabay.com*, June 15, 2008, http://news.mongabay.com/2008/0614-laurance.html, accessed August 24, 2013.
40. Rainforest Alliance, "Research & Resources: Tropical Forests in Our Daily Lives," www.rainforest-alliance.org/resources.cfm?id5daily_lives, accessed September 11, 2008; J. Louise Mastrantonio and John K. Francis, "A Student Guide to Tropical Forest Conservation," October 1997, www.srs.fs.usda.gov/pubs/2792, accessed September 4, 2013.

41. "World Wildlife Fund," http://wwf.worldwildlife.org/site/PageServer?pagename5can_home&JServSessionIdr01256kimssfum2.app13a, accessed September 11. 2008; "The Nature Conservancy 2008," www.nature.org/?src5logo, accessed September 11, 2008.
42. "WWF Amazon Project 2008," www.worldwildlife.org/what/wherewework/amazon/item1376.html, accessed September 11, 2008.
43. Rainforest Action Network, "Our Mission and History," http://ran.org/who_we_are/our_mission_history/, accessed September 11, 2008.
44. "International Tibet Support Network," www.tibetnetwork.org, accessed October 30, 2010.
45. Tilly, *Social Movements*.
46. George Hoberg, "Governing the Environment," pp. 343–345, in Keith G. Banting, George Hoberg, and Richard Simeon (eds.), *Degrees of Freedom: Canada and the United States in a Changing World* (McGill-Queen's University Press, 1997).
47. Charles Tilly, *From Mobilization to Revolution* (Reading MA: Addison-Wesley, 1978).
48. David F. Aberle, *The Peyote Religion among the Navaho* (Norman, OK: University of Oklahoma Press, 1966).
49. Frances A. DellaCava, Norma Kolko Phillips, and Madeline H. Engel, "Adoption in the U.S.: The Emergence of a Social Movement," *Journal of Sociology and Social Welfare*, December 2004, www.thefreelibrary.com/Adoption+in+the+U.S.%3A+the+emergence+of+a+social+movement.a0126791650, accessed September 4, 2013.
50. "2009/2010 Annual Report," *MADD, Mothers Against Drunk Driving Canada*, p. 1, www.madd.ca/english/about/annualreports.html, accessed October 30, 2010.
51. "Lives Saved," *MADD Canada*, www.madd.ca/english/research/lives_saved.pdf, accessed October 30, 2010.
52. "Over 30,000 Lives Saved Fighting Impaired Driving Since 1982," *MADD Canada*, April 24, 2008, www.madd.ca/english/news/pr/p20080424.htm, accessed October 30, 2010.
53. "History," *Greenpeace Canada*, www.greenpeace.org/canada/en/About-us/History/, accessed August 24, 2013; "Greenpeace: Always Bearing Witness," *CBC Digital Archives*, http://archives.cbc.ca/environment/environmental_protection/topics/867/, accessed October 30, 2010.
54. Information taken from Greenpeace Canada and Greenpeace International websites, www.greenpeace.org/canada/en/, accessed October 30, 2010; www.greenpeace.org/international/, accessed October 30, 2010; "The Birth of Greenpeace," *CBC Digital Archives*, http://archives.cbc.ca/environment/environmental_protection/clips/5000/, accessed October 30, 2010.
55. Ibid.
56. Danuta Otfinowski, "Should Christians Convert Muslims?" *Time*, June 22, 2003, www.time.com/time/magazine/article/0,9171, 1101030630-460157,00.html?CNN5yes, accessed October 30, 2010.
57. "Fidel Castro," *Encyclopedia Britannica Online*, www.britannica.com/EBchecked/topic/98822/Fidel-Castro, accessed September 11, 2008.
58. Denton E. Morrison, "Some Notes toward Theory on Relative Deprivation, Social Movements and Social Change," *American Behavioral Scientists*, 1971. 14(5): 675–690; David A. Locher, *Collective Behavior* (Upper Saddle River, NJ: Prentice Hall, 2002).
59. James Chowning Davies, "The J-Curve and Power Struggle Theories of Collective Violence," *American Sociological Review*, 1974. 39(4): 607–610; James Chowning Davies, *When Men Revolt and Why: A Reader in Political Violence and Revolution* (New York: The Free Press, 1970).
60. Ted Robert Gurr, *Why Men Rebel* (Princeton, NJ: Princeton University Press, 1970).
61. Locher, *Collective Behavior*.
62. Neil J. Smelser, *Theory of Collective Behavior* (New York: The Free Press, 1962).
63. Erving Goffman, *Frame Analysis: An Essay on the Organization of Experience* (Cambridge, MA: Harvard University Press, 1974).
64. David A. Snow, E. Burke Rochford, Jr., Steven K. Worden, and Robert D. Benford, "Frame Alignment Processes, Micromobilization, and Movement Participation," *American Sociological Review*, 1986. 51: 464–481.
65. Robert D. Benford and David A. Snow, "Framing Processes and Social Movements: An Overview and Assessment," *Annual Review of Sociology*, 2000. 26: 611–639.
66. Ibid.
67. Ibid.
68. Snow, Rochford, Worden, and Benford, "Frame Alignment Processes."
69. Ibid.
70. Ibid.
71. Ibid.
72. Ibid.
73. Information in this section from Joanne Goodrich (ed.), *Famous Women in Canada*, The Centre for Canadian Studies at Mount Allison University, 2001, "Introduction" and "Nellie McClung," www.mta.ca/about_canada/study_guide/famous_women/index.html, accessed October 21, 2010; "Women's Right to Vote in Canada," *Parliament of Canada* compilation, rev. 2007, www2.parl.gc.ca/parlinfo/compilations/provinceterritory/ProvincialWomenRightToVote.aspx, accessed October 21, 2010.
74. Betty Friedan, *The Feminine Mystique* (New York: W.W. Norton and Company, 1963).
75. Barbara Epstein, "Feminist Consciousness after the Women's Movement," *Monthly Review*, 2002. 54(4).
76. Information in this section from Dawn Elizabeth Monroe, "Famous Canadian Women's Historical Timeline," 2009, www.famouscanadianwomen.com/timeline/timeline1910-1919.htm, accessed October 22, 2010; Dominique Clément, "The Royal Commission on the Status of Women," *Canada's Rights Movement: A History*, www.historyofrights.com/events/rcsw.html, accessed October 22, 2010; Royal Commission on the Status of Women in Canada, *Report of the Royal Commission on the Status of Women in Canada* (Ottawa: Information Canada, 1970).
77. "Bell Hooks," *Contemporary Educational Thought*, University of Miami, www.education.miami.edu/ep/contemporaryed/Bell_Hooks/bell_hooks.html, accessed August 15, 2008.
78. Tobi Cohen, "Second Wave of Feminism Revisited at Rideau Hall," *Postmedia News*, September 9, 2010, www.canada.com/news/Second+wave+feminism+revisited+Rideau+Hall/3501518/story.html, accessed October 22, 2010.
79. Sean Thomas Cadigan, *Newfoundland and Labrador: A History* (Toronto: University of Toronto Press, Scholarly Publishing Division, 2009).
80. Paul Hawken, *Blessed Unrest: How the Largest Social Movement in History Is Restoring Grace, Justice, and Beauty to the World* (New York: Viking Penguin, 2007).
81. "BC SCRAP-IT Program," www.scrapit.ca/p4incentivechoices.htm, accessed October 29, 2010.
82. "Canada's First Motor Vehicle Fuel Consumption Regulations: Consultations Begin," *Transport Canada*, January 17, 2008, www.tc.gc.ca/eng/mediaroom/releases-nat-2008-08-h006e-4909.htm, accessed October 29, 2010.
83. "Electric Vehicles Available in Canada," *Canadian Automobile Association*, http://electricvehicles.caa.ca/electric-vehicles-available-in-canada/, accessed August 30, 2013.
84. "GM Says Hasta la Vista to Hummer," *MSN Money*, January 1, 2010, http://articles.moneycentral.msn.com/SavingandDebt/SaveonaCar/gm-halts-hummer-production.aspx, accessed November 1, 2010.
85. Hawken, *Blessed Unrest*.

INDEX

N

O

P

T

U

V

W

X

Y

Z

THINK

SOCIOLOGY Study Card

The scientific study of society and human behaviour.

PEARSON

The Sociological Perspective

What Is Sociology?

Discovering Sociology

- sociology is a science guided by the understanding that our lives are affected not only by our individual characteristics but by powerful social forces and our place in the social world.
- society refers to a group of people who live in a defined territory and who share social structures and who interact with each other.

Thinking Sociologically

- individual behaviour must be examined and understood in its social context.
- people tend to behave in predictable ways.
- people are products of their time and place in history and society.
- people construct their own society and social reality.
- social behaviour is complex and has multiple causes and effects.
- debunking is the practice of looking beyond the surface or obvious explanation and seeking out deeper explanations.
- sociological imagination is the ability to understand how social forces influence the lives of individuals.
- *Verstehen* means understanding the meaning of action from the actor's point of view.

Sociological Theory

- micro is a small-scale perspective.
- macro is a large-scale perspective.

Functionalism is a theo retical perspective that defines society as a system of interrelated parts.

- focuses on society as a system of connected parts working together to keep society intact.
- it is important to consider the manifest and latent functions of any issue or institution.
- society is fairly stable.

Conflict theory is a theoretical perspective that views society as an unequal system that brings about conflict and change.

- focuses on social classes and groups and the differences in wealth, power, and prestige.
- powerful groups control society's wealth and resources and exploit the weaker groups.
- groups that have power are likely to create advantages for themselves.

Symbolic interactionism is a theoretical perspective that focuses on how people interact with others in their everyday lives.

- focuses on the way people interact with each other to create the social world.
- communication is central to all human interactions and is possible because of symbols.
- disputes arise when people do not share the same definitions of symbols.

Feminist theory is a theoretical perspective that focuses on gender inequalities that are built into the social structure.

- focuses on gender inequality in society.
- social structures are patriarchal, meaning that they benefit men more than women.
- traditional sociology has ignored issues that are important to women.

Sociological Research

- sociological research examines empirical data gathered from the social world through social research methods.

Two types of data are collected:

- quantitative—numerical data
- qualitative—nonnumeric data

Steps in the Research Process

- decide on a topic.
- review the literature.
- develop a hypothesis.
- select a research design and collect data.
- analyze results.
- share and publish results.

Types of Studies

- comparative studies use data from different sources in order to compare them.
- cross-sectional studies look at an event at a single point in time.
- longitudinal studies include data from observations over time using a cohort.

Research Methods

- survey is an investigation of the opinions or behaviours of a group of people by asking them questions.
- experiment is a method in which researchers control variables in order to test causes and effects.
- field research is research conducted in a natural setting.
- participant observation is a type of field research in which the researcher poses as a person who is normally in the environment.
- case study is an investigation of one person or event in detail.
- ethnography is a research method that aims to understand the social perspective and cultural values of a particular group by participating in or getting to know their activities in detail.
- secondary data analysis is the process of using and analyzing data that others have collected.
- content analysis is a type of research in which the sociologist looks for common words or themes in newspapers, books, or structured interviews.
- triangulation is the process of using multiple approaches to study a phenomenon.

Individuals and Society

Culture

- culture is the symbols, values, norms, and material objects that societies create.
- cultural transmission is culture passing from one generation to the next.
- material culture consists of the physical items that we use.
- nonmaterial culture consists of the nonphysical products of society, such as values and beliefs.

Components of Culture

- symbols are things that represent, suggest, or stand for something else.
- language is a system of spoken and/or written symbols used to convey meaning and to communicate.
- values are a part of a society's nonmaterial culture that represent cultural standards by which we determine what is good and bad, right and wrong.
- norms are culturally defined rules for appropriate social behavior.

Studying Culture

- ethnocentrism occurs when a person uses his or her own culture to judge another culture.
- cultural relativism means making a deliberate effort to appreciate a group's ways of life without prejudice.

Socialization

- socialization is the lifelong process by which the norms, values, and other aspects of a culture are learned and internalized by group members and provides the individual with the skills necessary for participating in society.
- primary socialization is socialization that occurs during childhood.

continued next page

Social Institutions

Health and Medicine

- **health** is a state of complete physical, mental, and social well-being and not merely the absence of disease or infirmity.
- **social epidemiology** is the study of the distribution of diseases and health throughout a society's population.
- **sick role** is the expected behaviours and responsibilities appropriate for someone who is ill.
- **medicalization** is the idea that the medical community is the centre of many aspects of our society.

The Canadian Health Care System

Medicare: a system of interlocking health insurance plans.

- **Public administration:** each province administers a health insurance plan.
- **Comprehensiveness:** all services that are "medically necessary" are covered.
- **Universality:** all residents are covered.
- **Portability:** citizens are insured even if they are temporarily absent from their province of residence or from Canada.
- **Accessibility:** everyone must have reasonable and uniform access.

Family

Types of Families

- **family** is a group of two or more people who are related by blood, marriage, or adoption.
- **kinship** is a social bond based on common ancestry.
- **household** is a person or group of people who occupy the same dwelling.
- **census family** is Statistics Canada's definition of a family.
- **nuclear family** is a household consisting of a husband, wife, and children.
- **extended family** is a household consisting of a nuclear family plus an additional relative.
- **family of orientation** is the family that you are born into and raised in.
- **family of procreation** is the family that you form through marriage or cohabitation, and in which you raise your children.
- **stepfamily** is a family composed of children and some combination of biological parents.

Forms of Marriage

- **marriage** is a legally and socially recognized union of two or more people.
- **monogamy** is the practice of being married to one person at a time.
- **polygamy** is the practice of having more than one spouse at a time.
- **polygyny** occurs when a man is married to two or more women at the same time.
- **polyandry** allows a woman to take two or more husbands at the same time.
- **Same-sex marriage:** marriage between partners of the same sex.

Mate Selection

- **propinquity** is physical and geographic proximity.
- **endogamy** is the practice of marrying within one's social group.
- **exogamy** is the practice of marrying someone from a different social group.
- **incest taboo** is a cultural norm that prohibits marriage between certain relatives.
- **homogamy** is marriage between people with similar backgrounds, such as religion, ethnicity, class, or age.
- **cohabitation:** a couple living together without legal marriage.

Education

- **education** is the social institution through which society passes on knowledge, skills, and values from one generation to the next.

Issues in Education

- **grade inflation** is the trend of assigning higher grades than previously assigned to students for completing the same work.
- **human capital** is a person's combination of skills, knowledge, traits, and personal attributes.
- **credentialism** is an emphasis on educational degrees in assessing skills and knowledge.
- **teacher expectancy effect** is the impact of a teacher's expectations on a student's performance.
- **hidden curriculum** refers to lessons taught in schools that are unrelated to academic learning.

Religion

- **religion** is a social institution based on a unified system of beliefs and practices related to sacred things.
- **sacred** means connected to God or dedicated to a religious purpose.
- **profane** means related or devoted to that which is not sacred.
- **rituals** are established patterns of behaviour closely associated with experience of the sacred.
- **system of beliefs** relates sacred objects to religious rituals and defines and protects the sacred from the profane.

Types of Belief Systems

- **theism** is the belief in a god or gods.
- **monotheism** is the belief that there is only one God.
- **polytheism** is the belief in multiple gods and demigods.
- **philosophy of life** focuses on a set of ethical, moral, or philosophical principles.
- **totemism** is the practice of honouring a totem or another sacred object.
- **simple supernaturalism** is the belief in a variety of supernatural forces that affect and influence people's lives.
- **animism** is a belief which recognizes that animate spirits live in natural objects and operate in the world.
- **henotheism** is the worship of one god while recognizing the existence of other deities.

Religious Organizations

- **cults** are new religious movements led by charismatic leaders with few followers.
- **sects** are religious groups that have enough members to sustain themselves and go against society's norms.
- **church** is a large, highly organized group of believers.
- **theocracy** is a government that is controlled by religious leaders.
- **organization of believers** is a group that ensures the prosperity and effectiveness of the religious experience.

Social Change

- **Social change** is how culture and social institutions change over time.
- **collective behaviour** is any social interaction in which a group of people engages in behaviour that is not in their normal routine.

Types of Collective Behaviour

- **crowd** is a large group of influential people who gather for a temporary purpose.
- **mobs** are groups characterized by high levels of emotion that engage in some type of focused action that can be violent or disruptive.
- **riots** are emotional and violent disturbances of the peace by crowds that lack a central focus.
- **fashion** is an object, a style, or a behavior that becomes popular for a period of time.
- **fad** is a temporary fashion or action the public embraces.
- **craze** is a fad that leaves a lasting effect on society.
- **panic** is an extreme fear based on something that might happen.
- **hysteria** is a heightened emotional state that can lead a group to violence.
- **rumours** are stories or statements that lack confirmation or certainty.
- **urban legends** are rumours that are presented as true stories that act as cautionary tales.

Types of Social Movements

- **social movements** are activities that support or protest social issues and are organized by non-governmental organizations.
- **campaigns** are organized and ongoing efforts to achieve a specific goal.
- **alternative social movements** want to create a change in specific people's thoughts, practices, and beliefs regarding a particular issue.
- **redemptive social movements** focus on specific individuals, but the amount of change sought is radical rather than limited.
- **reformative social movements** seek to change a society's thoughts and actions but only in a limited way.
- **revolutionary social movements**, sometimes called transformative social movements, seek to change the thoughts and actions of all society in a radical fashion.

PEARSON

www.thethinkspot.ca

- **rehabilitation** tries to reform offenders so that they can be returned to society.
- **restoration** attempts to make the victim, and the community, whole again.

Social Stratification

- **social stratification** refers to the ranking of people and the rewards they receive based on social factors, often including wealth, power, and/or prestige.
- **global stratification** refers to the ranking of countries which highlights social and economic inequality throughout the world.
- **ideology** is a set of cultural beliefs that justifies various social arrangements, including inequality.

Social Stratification Systems

- **social stratification systems** are how societies rank different groups.
- **slavery** is a stratification system in which one person has complete control over another.
- **caste systems** are systems in which a person's position may be a position of power and privilege or of disadvantage, but in either case his or her place is permanently fixed.
- **class systems** represent a form of stratification that allows social mobility.

Poverty

- **marginal poverty** is a state of poverty that occurs when a person lacks stable employment.
- **residual poverty** is chronic and multigenerational poverty.
- **absolute poverty** is poverty so severe that one lacks resources to survive.
- **relative poverty** is based on comparing ourselves to those around us.
- **transitional poverty** is a temporary state of poverty that occurs when someone loses a job for a short time.
- **cycle of poverty** refers to the vicious circle where poor children are more likely to be poor as adults.
- **feminization of poverty** refers to the fact that around the world, women experience poverty at far higher rates than men.

Social Classes in Canada

- **upper or elite class** is a social class that is very small in number and holds significant wealth.
- **upper middle class** is a social class that consists of high-income members of society who are often well educated but do not belong to the elite membership of the super wealthy.
- **middle class** is a social class that consists of those who have moderate incomes.
- **working class** is a social class generally made up of people with high school diplomas and lower levels of education.
- **lower class** is a social class living in poverty.
- **underclass** includes homeless people and people living in substandard housing.

Social mobility: the ability to change social classes.

- **horizontal mobility** refers to moving within the same status category.
- **vertical mobility** refers to moving from one social status to another.
- **intragenerational mobility** occurs when an individual changes social standing, especially in the workforce.
- **intergenerational mobility** refers to the change that family members make from one social class to the next through generations.
- **structural mobility** occurs when social changes affect large numbers of people.
- **exchange mobility** is a concept suggesting that, within a country, each social class contains a relatively fixed number of people.

Race and Ethnicity

- **race** is the socially defined classification of people based on certain physical characteristics.
- **ethnicity** is the classification of people based on a common cultural, linguistic, or ancestral heritage.
- **visible minority** is a person, other than an aboriginal, who is non-Caucasian in race or non-white in colour.
- **aboriginal** is a person who is Indian, Inuit, or Métis.

Dominant-Minority Relations

- **voluntary migration** refers to the willing movement of people from one society to another.
- **expulsion or confinement** occurs when the dominant group expels or forcibly confines a minority group.
- **genocide** is the attempt to destroy or exterminate a people based on their race or ethnicity.
- **ethnic cleansing** refers to persecution through imprisonment, expulsion, or murder of members of an ethnic minority by a majority to achieve ethnic homogeneity in majority-controlled territory.
- **multiculturalism** is a concept that supports the inherent value of different cultures within society.
- **assimilation** is the process by which minority groups adopt the patterns of the dominant culture.
- **segregation** is forced separation because of factors such as race, gender, or ethnicity.
- **migrant superordination** is the conquest of a native population by a more powerful group.
- **indigenous superordination** is the subordination of an immigrant group to a dominant group.

Racial and Ethnic Stratification

- **racism** refers to an ideology that maintains that one racial group is inherently superior to another.
- **prejudice** refers to negative attitudes about an entire social category of people.
- **stereotypes** are simplified perceptions people have of an entire group, usually based on a false assumption.
- **discrimination** is the unfair treatment of people based on their social category membership rather than on merit.
- **institutional discrimination** maintains the advantage for the dominant group while providing the appearance of fairness to all.
- **intersectionality** is a term used to describe the fact that women experience oppression based on a number of minority statuses.

Gender and Sexuality

Sex and Gender

- **sex** refers to the biological characteristics distinguishing males and females.
- **intersexed** refers to a person whose body has both male and female characteristics.
- **transsexual** refers to people who feel like they are one sex even though biologically they are identified as the other.
- **gender** is defined as the social, cultural, and psychological traits and behaviours connected with being masculine or feminine.
- **transgender individuals** have a biological sex but possess a gender identity other than that typically assigned to their sex.

Gender Socialization

- **gender identity** is our perception of ourselves as masculine or feminine.
- **gender roles** are society's expectations of how males and females should think and act.

Sexuality

- **sexuality** refers to a particular kind of social interaction in which we express ourselves as sexual beings.
- **sexual orientation** is a reflection of a person's preference for sexual partners.
- **heterosexual** describes people who are sexually attracted to people of the opposite sex.
- **homosexual** describes people who are sexually attracted to people of the same sex.
- **bisexual** describes people who are sexually attracted to people of either sex.
- **asexual** describes people who are not sexually attracted to people of either sex.

Sexual Stratification

- **sexism** is the belief that one sex is superior to the other.
- **homophobia** is a negative attitude toward homosexuals and homosexuality.

Age

- **gerontology** is the study of aging and the elderly.

Age Stratification

- **ageism** is prejudice and discrimination based solely on age.
- **dependency ratio** is the ratio of the youth population (0 to 19 years) and senior population (65 or older) to the working-age population (20 to 64 years).

continued next page

- **secondary socialization** is socialization that continues throughout our lives.
- **resocialization** is the process of learning new norms, values, attitudes, and behaviours and abandoning old ones.
- **gender socialization** teaches us about the attitudes and behaviours that a society defines as appropriate for each sex.

Agents of socialization are people, groups, and institutions that shape our self-concept, beliefs, and behaviour. They include the following:

- family
- school
- peers
- media

Theories of Development

Cooley: Coined the term **looking-glass self** to describe the process by which a sense of self is developed.
Mead: explored the manner in which children and adults explore, come to understand, and eventually take on (as adults) various roles in society.
Goffman: developed a theory of interaction called **dramaturgy**, which suggests that life is like acting.
Erikson: proposed that humans develop a personality in eight psychosocial, or psychological and social, stages.
Piaget: explored the process through which humans gain the ability to reason logically.
Kohlberg: suggested that moral reasoning occurs on three specific levels.
Gilligan: concluded that moral decisions arise from two different principles: the morality of justice and the morality of care.

Social Structures and Interaction

Social Structures

- **social structures** are patterns of relationships that endure from one generation to the next.
- **social class** refers to a group of people with similar access to power, wealth, and prestige.
- **social institutions** are structures that provide for patterned relationships and that are organized around a central activity or social need.

Statuses and Roles

- **social status** refers to socially defined positions that are characterized by certain expectations, rights, and duties.
- **achieved status** is a type of position that you earn or do something to attain.
- **ascribed status** is a position in society that is given or assigned.
- **status symbols** are material signs that represent a specific status.
- **role** is the behaviour associated with a specific status.
- **role expectations** are the socially defined behaviours appropriate for a particular status.
- **role performance** refers to how a person actually plays a role.
- **role conflict** is a phenomenon that occurs when one is forced to choose between the competing demands of multiple roles.
- **role strain** occurs when the demands and expectations of one role are impossible for us to satisfy.

Solidarity

- **mechanical solidarity** refers to the type of community bonding usually found in traditional societies in which people share beliefs and values and perform common activities.
- **organic solidarity** occurs when people live in a society that has a diverse division of labour.
- ***Gemeinschaft*** refers to community connections involving personal relationships based on friendship and kinship ties, such as family.
- ***Gesellschaft*** refers to social connections that are formal and impersonal.

Groups and Interaction

- **social groups** are any number of people with similar norms, values, and behaviours who frequently interact with one another.
- **primary groups** are groups that are small, intimate, and enduring.
- **secondary groups** are groups that are formal, superficial, and temporary.
- **conformity** is the degree to which we alter our behaviour, attitudes, and points of view to fit into our perceived expectation of what is appropriate.
- **groupthink** is the term for group decisions that are made without objective thought.
- **social capital** is a sociological concept that refers to the individual and collective resources available to a person.
- **social network** is the web of ties you have with others.

Deviance and Crime

- **deviance** is the violation of norms that a society agrees upon.
- **crime** is the violation of norms that have been written into law.
- **laws** are formal norms which are enforced through social institutions.

Social Control

- **stigma** is a mark of disgrace associated with a particular status, quality, or person.
- **discredited stigma** is a stigma that cannot be hidden from others or is no longer hidden from others.
- **discreditable stigma** is a stigma that can be concealed from others.
- **shaming** is a deliberate effort to attach a negative meaning to a behaviour.
- **stigmatized shame** is a permanent label given to an offender, which could actually increase the chances of reoffending because the guilty person is forever labelled.
- **reintegrative shaming** is an effort to bring an offender back into the community after punishment.
- **recidivism** is the tendency for inmates released from prison to return to prison.
- **reintegrative justice** is based on the principle that offenders can be successfully reintegrated into the wider society.
- **sentencing circle** is a process used by some First Nations communities to rehabilitate an offender and to heal the community as a whole.
- **racial profiling** occurs when police use a person's race as the primary reason to suspect that the individual has broken the law.
- **primary deviance** is an initial deviant act that is not followed by some form of labelling.
- **secondary deviance** refers to the psychological reorientation that occurs when a person is labelled as deviant and assumes that identity.
- **chivalry hypothesis** suggests that female offenders are treated more leniently than males by male police officers and judges.

Theories of Deviance

- **rational choice theory:** individuals make rational choices based on self-interest.
- **biological positivism:** criminals have certain physical characteristics; there are genetic and biological causes of criminal behaviour.
- **psychological positivism:** something abnormal in the individual, such as a low IQ, or a thinking error.
- **functions of deviance:**
  - deviance marks the boundaries of morality.
  - deviance promotes social solidarity.
  - deviance can bring about needed change in a social system.
- **strain theory:** many in the lower classes have blocked access to opportunities, so they adapt to their plight
- **social conflict theory:** deviant behaviour results from social, political, or economic inequalities between social groups.
- **differential association theory:** emphasizes that deviant behaviour is learned.
- **labelling theory:** individuals become deviant when the deviant label is applied to them.
- **social control theories:** everyone has different levels of internal controls; external forces such as the police, our family, and/or our friends also control us.
- **feminist theory:** gender differences in crime are largely due to differences in power and control between men and women.

Goals of Punishment

- **retribution** says that someone who commits a crime deserves to be punished.
- **incapacitation** usually means sending an offender to prison.
- **deterrence** tries to prevent a person from doing something because of fear of the consequences.
  - **general deterrence** ensures that individuals will not commit a crime because they see the negative consequences applied to others.
  - **specific deterrence** occurs to individuals who have violated the law and have already been punished.

continued next page